World War II begins
1939

World War II
ends
1945

World War I ends
1918

Royal Canadian
Navy created
1910

WITHDRAWN

1940	1930	1920	1910	1900

Royal Canadian Air
Force created
1924

Canadians take
Vimy Ridge
1917

WWI begins
1914

Dieppe
raid
1942

THE OXFORD COMPANION TO
CANADIAN
MILITARY HISTORY

THE OXFORD COMPANION TO
CANADIAN
MILITARY HISTORY

J.L. Granatstein and Dean F. Oliver

OXFORD
UNIVERSITY PRESS

8 Sampson Mews, Suite 204,
Don Mills, Ontario M3C 0H5
www.oupcanada.com

Oxford University Press is a department of the University of Oxford.
It furthers the University's objective of excellence in research, scholarship,
and education by publishing worldwide in

Oxford   New York

Auckland   Cape Town   Dar es Salaam   Hong Kong   Karachi
Kuala Lumpur   Madrid   Melbourne   Mexico City   Nairobi
New Delhi   Shanghai   Taipei   Toronto

With offices in

Argentina   Austria   Brazil   Chile   Czech Republic   France   Greece
Guatemala   Hungary   Italy   Japan   Poland   Portugal   Singapore
South Korea   Switzerland   Thailand   Turkey   Ukraine   Vietnam

Oxford is a trade mark of Oxford University Press
in the UK and in certain other countries

Published in Canada
by Oxford University Press

Library and Archives Canada Cataloguing in Publication

Granatstein, J. L., 1939–
The Oxford companion to Canadian military history
/ J. L. Granatstein, Dean Oliver.
Includes bibliographical references.
ISBN 978-0-19-543088-2
1. Canada—History, Military. I. Oliver, Dean Frederick, 1965–
II. Title.
FC226.G733 2010 355.00971 C2010-902058-8

1 2 3 4 — 13 12 11 10

Front cover
Photographs taken during the Battle of Vimy Ridge: Some of the Byng Boys
returning from action after defeating the Bavarians at Vimy Ridge
CWM 19920085-292, George Metcalf Archival Collection
Canadian War Museum

Front flap
His Majesty's Pigeon Service—Despatch rider with pigeons leaving for the
trenches
CWM 19930013-435, George Metcalf Archival Collection
Canadian War Museum

Back cover
Allan Harding MacKay, *Coalition Soldiers, Kandahar Air Base, July 2003*
CWM 20040060-001, Beaverbrook Collection of War Art
Canadian War Museum

The Dieppe operation, 19 August 1942
CWM 19980056-218, George Metcalf Archival Collection
Canadian War Museum
National Defence/Reproduced with the permission of the Minister of Public
Works and Government Services, 2010

Yousuf Karsh, Studio portrait of Lt.Crd. Nancy Pyper in uniform
CWM 19860074-001, George Metcalf Archival Collection
© Yousuf Karsh

Contents

WAR MAP of
Europe

Compiled, Drawn and Published by

Lloydhirst Maps
371 Bay Street   TORONTO-CANADA

List of Maps

Preface

Notwithstanding a past full of conflict, present-day Canadians sometimes seem to believe that Canada has never fought a war. To many, even the war in Afghanistan seems a peacekeeping mission gone astray. And when fighting erupts and people die, the cries of foul arise: this is not what Canadians do, or have done, they say, so we must cease in order to preserve honour and retreat in order to restore hope.

The popular wisdom on Canada-as-peacekeeper is a storied gripe, laughably imprecise and brown with age. The truth is that we are a country made by war and composed in some important measure of warriors. The rise and fall of the First Nations' empires, the course of European encroachment, the settlement of continental fates, the consolidation of political control in the vast west and north: arrows, muskets, drums, and cannons impelled them all and determined most. New France was an armed camp; British North America was an imperial frontier. A steadfast ally and skilled combatant in history's first total war, we were a nation-in-arms against Fascism, a crusader against Communism, an armed intervener in dozens of struggles, from Congo to Kandahar, Cyprus to Somalia. We have not been uniformly just, or effective, and rarely selfless. We violated liberties and suppressed freedoms; we have massacred, violated, incinerated, and pillaged. We have also saved and liberated, defended and upheld, protected and preserved. We have fought good wars for the right reasons, with the right allies, though not always upholding at home the same principles for which we waged war abroad. Few countries can claim as much. It is a vexed, complex, exhilarating tale, filled with heroes, dotted with incompetence, laden with debate. Bumper stickers pronounce our support for far-off soldiers, for peace, for veterans, for disarmament: the military past subsumes them all, exposing glibness as propaganda, zealotry as ignorance. To misunderstand the past is almost as bad as to forget it entirely. Canadian history, education, and civil discourse have witnessed plenty of both.

This book reminds Canadians that war has shaped their nation's past and present. It will undoubtedly contour its future. Canadians will always have interests to be advanced and protected, allies to assist, enemies to be forestalled. Sometimes this will require military force. Canadians will kill others in these pursuits and be killed in them as well. History offers no clearer insight. Organized human violence—war—has had its way with us, and us with it. Canadians are different as a result. Canada is too. The Conquest, conscription, Vimy, Normandy, Lundy's Lane, Riel, the internment of enemy aliens, 9/11, and, yes, peacekeeping: they are the sources of abiding hate, fear, hubris, joy, memory, affection, puzzlement. They affirm and inform identity and sense of mission or possibility; they encumber with the weight of past injustices or the lingering sting of unwarranted slights. Military history is not a restorative or a call to politicize the act of remembrance, but a source of understanding, of critical inquiry. It is a sometimes ignored, often misrepresented, strand of our historical DNA. We want to make it a little less of both.

Our intention here was not to cover every topic, something wholly impossible in any case, or to echo the work of others, but instead to treat—as we understood them—the key events, issues, ideas, and individuals that have populated Canada's military past. We did not, for example, feel it necessary to include an entry for every prime minister or minister of national defence, but only those whose tenure included significant military events—Mackenzie King, in other words, but not Mackenzie Bowell. Nor did we want to discuss every general officer, each skirmish at home or abroad, every piece of equipment, or each of the countless statutes that touched on military matters. Only the most important made it into these pages. On the other hand, we did believe it essential to consider such subjects as the home front during the two world wars, popular wartime music, colourful military language, and the changing nature of how we understand battle casualties. Our selections will displease and disappoint in many cases. The authors accept full responsibility for their inclusions and exclusions.

As this explanation suggests, this Oxford Companion has been written by two authors and not by an editorial team with platoons of contributors. It is also the product of an extraordinary co-operative effort between the Canadian Museum of Civilization Corporation, of which the Canadian War Museum forms part, and Oxford University Press. This partnership could have resulted in untold numbers of difficulties but, happily, they have not arisen. The War Museum's extraordinary holdings of war art, photographs, and maps are featured in this volume, one of the great benefits of this collaboration.

J.L.G., D.F.O.

Acknowledgements

The authors have benefitted greatly from the knowledge, advice, and warnings of many friends and colleagues. We are most grateful to Dr Roger Sarty, General (Ret'd) Paul Manson, Major J.R. Milne, Dr Norman Hillmer, Dr David Bercuson, Dr William Kaplan, Dr Lieutenant-Colonel (Ret'd) Douglas Delaney, Colonel (Ret'd) Gary Rice, Patricia Grimshaw, Teresa Iacobelli, and Alex Comber. We thank Dr Serge Bernier of the Directorate of History and Heritage at National Defence Headquarters, Ottawa, for permission to make use of the splendid maps produced in his directorate.

The staff of the Canadian War Museum (CWM) provided exemplary assistance at every stage of this project. We are especially grateful for the assistance of the staff of the Military History Research Centre; manager Jane Naisbitt, collections managers Carol Reid and Maggie Arbour-Doucette, librarians Lara Andrews and Emily Porter, image reproduction officer Susan Ross, and cataloguer Dennis Fletcher answered our stupid questions, found reams of material, and, in general, offered their usual superb service. Historians Dr Andrew Burtch, Dr Tim Cook, Dr Peter MacLeod, Dr Jeff Noakes, Dr Amber Lloydlangston, and Dr Laura Brandon were a regular sounding board for ideas and inclusions/exclusions, proofread several entries, and assisted in myriad ways, not least by maintaining the country's finest research unit whose insights and expertise the authors soaked up, from Casualties to Kiska and from Amherst to the Yukon Field Force.

The Board of Trustees of the Canadian Museum of Civilization Corporation (CMCC), of which Jack Granatstein has been a member since 2006, approved this project, as required under the terms of the Financial Administration Act. The President and CEO of the CMCC, Dr Victor Rabinovitch, and the Director-General of the CWM, Mark O'Neill, supported this book from its outset, seeing mutual advantage in a relationship between Canada's most successful museum corporation and the Oxford brand. They rendered with enthusiasm every form of assistance for which we asked. As an employee of the Corporation, Dean Oliver wrote and edited on his own time, to avoid conflicts of interest, real and perceived. The authors are grateful to the Trustees and officers of the Corporation.

At Oxford University Press in Toronto, we have received exemplary assistance from Dr Jennie Rubio, our very able editor, and her team: Katie Scott, Meg Patterson, and Rachel Geertsema, as well as copy editor Maria Jelinek. We are grateful to them all.

J.L.G., D.F.O.

Timeline

1609–1701	French-Iroquois Wars		1871	Canada creates first permanent artillery units
1629	Quebec falls to British		1876	Royal Military College established
1632	Quebec and Acadia returned to French control		1883	First permanent infantry and cavalry units
1711	British fail to take Quebec		1884	Voyageurs dispatched on Nile Expedition
1713	France loses Acadia after War of Spanish Succession		1884–1885	Northwest Rebellion
1720–1745	France builds Louisbourg fortress		1898	Yukon Field Force dispatched
1749	Britain builds naval base at Halifax		1899	South African War begins; Canada dispatches Royal Canadian Regiment
1756	Seven Years' War begins		1900	Battle of Paardeberg
1759	Quebec taken by British		1910	Naval Service Act creates RCN
1763	France cedes New France to Britain		1912	Naval Aid Bill
1775	Americans attack Quebec		1914	World War I begins; Canada at war from 4 August
1812	United States declares war on Britain		1914	First Contingent assembles at Valcartier
1812	British troops capture Michilimackinac		1915	Battle of Ypres
1812	Fort Detroit surrenders to British		1915	Canadian Corps formed
1812	Battle of Queenston Heights		1916	Battle of the Somme
1813	York burned by US troops		1917	Battle of Vimy Ridge
1813	Battle of Stoney Creek		1917	Arthur Currie takes command of Canadian Corps
1813	Battle of Moraviantown		1917	Conscription Crisis
1813	Battle of Chateauguay		1917	Halifax explosion
1813	Battle of Crysler's Farm		1918	The Hundred Days
1814	Battle of Lundy's Lane		1918	Armistice, 11 November
1814	Treaty of Ghent ends War of 1812		1918	Canadians dispatched to Russia
1832–1836	Construction of Rideau Canal and Fort Henry		1919	Repatriation of Canadian Corps
1837	Rebellion in Lower Canada		1924	Creation of RCAF
1837	Rebellion in Upper Canada		1939	World War II begins; Canada declares war 10 September
1855	Militia Act passed in the Canadas		1939	1st Canadian Division dispatched to Britain
1866	Fenian raid, Battle of Ridgeway			
1868	First Militia Act of the Dominion of Canada			
1870	Red River Rebellion			
1870	Last Fenian raid, Quebec-Vermont border			

1939	British Commonwealth Air Training Plan agreed	1956	Canadian peacekeepers to Suez
1940–1945	Battle of the Atlantic	1957	NORAD signed
1940	Ogdensburg Agreement	1959	Avro Arrow scrapped
1941	Fall of Hong Kong to Japanese	1960	Canadian peacekeepers to Congo
1942	Conscription plebiscite	1962–1963	Nuclear Crisis
1942	Dieppe raid	1964	Peacekeepers to Cyprus
1943	Creation of No. 6 Bomber Group, RCAF	1964–1968	Integration and Unification of Canadian Forces
1943	Creation of First Canadian Army	1970	October Crisis
1943	Invasion of Sicily	1990	Oka crisis
1943	Invasion of Italy	1990	Gulf War
1943	Battle of Ortona	1992	Canadians dispatched to former Yugoslavia
1944	Hitler Line battles	1992	Canadians to Somalia
1944	D-Day invasion	1993	Canadian NATO contingent withdrawn
1944	Closing of Falaise Gap	2001	al Qaeda attacks, 11 September
1944	Gothic Line broken by I Canadian Corps	2002	Canadians dispatched to Afghanistan
1944	Battle of the Scheldt	2006	Canadians take up combat role in Kandahar
1945	Liberation of the Netherlands		
1945	Germany, Japan surrender		
1950	Korean War begins		
1951	Canadians dispatched to Europe for NATO service		

Abbott, Douglas Charles (1899–1987). Abbott was a World War I soldier and later an attorney who entered Parliament in 1940 as a Liberal from Montreal. He became minister of national defence for naval services in April 1945 and minister of national defence in August, a position he held until December 1946. His principal task was to oversee the military's transition from its unprecedented size and complexity during World War II to the far more limited functions envisaged for the postwar era, a challenge he negotiated skilfully and without major incident. As minister of finance in the postwar governments of Mackenzie King and Louis St Laurent, he played a key role in the development of Canada's early Cold War security architecture.

ABC-1. American and British military staffs met for secret conversations in the United States from 29 January to 27 March 1941, to plan for the future. ABC-1, the main agreement reached, specified that in the event of a two-theatre war against Germany and Japan, the two great democracies would work to defeat Germany first. Given that the United States was still neutral, the conversations and the results were remarkable. For Canada, hitherto Britain's most important ally and a defence partner since the August 1940 Ogdensburg Agreement established the Permanent Joint Board on Defence with the United States, to be kept out of these discussions rankled and led to pressure for a Canadian military mission to be sent to Washington. SEE ALSO: CANADA–UNITED STATES DEFENCE RELATIONS.

ABC-22. Officials of the Permanent Joint Board on Defence developed a "Joint Canadian–United States Basic Defense Plan No. 2," or ABC-22, through the spring and summer of 1941, as a follow-up to the earlier ABC-1 conversations. ABC-22 envisaged US–Canadian co-operation in the defence of the North American continent (less Greenland) in the context of an offensive campaign against the Axis Powers, including the protection of sea lines of communication in the Atlantic and Pacific oceans. American military planners sought to secure strategic control over Canadian forces, but the Canadian government and the military chiefs successfully resisted, pledging only "mutual co-operation." US President Roosevelt approved the plan on 29 August; the War Cabinet of Prime Minister Mackenzie King accepted it on 15 October 1941. SEE ALSO: CANADA–UNITED STATES DEFENCE RELATIONS.

Abercromby, James (1706–1781). Abercromby was age 11 when he entered the British army as an ensign, and went on to become a career soldier and sometime Member of Parliament. He came to North America in 1756 as deputy to the Earl of Loudoun, the commander-in-chief, whom he replaced the following year. General Abercromby led one of three major assaults on French Canada in 1758, bringing 15,000 troops, including 6,000 British regulars, along Lake George to Fort Carillon (Ticonderoga, NY). Without artillery support, he attacked the hastily erected field fortifications of the Marquis de Montcalm's much smaller French force on 8 July and was repulsed with nearly 2,000 casualties. Abercromby's subsequent retreat in the face of a still numerically inferior enemy led to his recall in September and replacement by Jeffrey Amherst who had captured Louisbourg in July. He did not see active service again. SEE ALSO: SEVEN YEARS' WAR.

ACE Mobile Force (AMF). The Allied Command Europe (ACE) Mobile Force was a small, rapid-reaction contingent of air and ground forces from several members of the North Atlantic Treaty Organization (NATO). It was created in 1960, with headquarters near Heidelberg, West Germany, and disbanded in 2002. Force elements exercised regularly, but were first used in early 1991 during the first Gulf War to monitor the Turkey/Iraq border. In 1999, AMF units went to Albania to help administer aid and humanitarian assistance to refugees who had fled fighting between Serbian security forces and ethnic Albanians in neighbouring Kosovo. Canada committed one army battalion to the AMF for many years and commanded the brigade-sized ground force several times. SEE ALSO: NORTH ATLANTIC TREATY ORGANIZATION.

Acting Sub-Militia Council for Overseas Canadians. Minister of Militia and Defence Sir Sam Hughes created the Council in September 1916 as an advisory body on matters pertaining to the Canadian Expeditionary Force, Canada's overseas army in World War I. Hughes chose a close associate, John Wallace Carson, as president, and his son-in-law as a member, and organized the Council to report directly to himself in Ottawa. The move defied Prime Minister Sir Robert Borden, who had already been considering the replacement of the volatile Hughes. It also risked opening the overseas forces to greater interference and manipulation by the erratic militia minister, something the prime minister had been labouring strenuously to prevent. Two months later, Hughes's furious and impertinent reaction to Borden's establishment of the Overseas Military Forces of Canada, a ministry reporting to the Cabinet instead, precipitated his firing. SEE ALSO: HUGHES; WORLD WAR I.

Active Militia. In the mid-nineteenth century, declining tension between Great Britain and the United States, London's growing awareness of the indefensibility of its North American possessions, and British involvement in the Crimean War (1854–1856)

against Russia led to the creation of an Active Militia in the Province of Canada.

After years of military decline, legislation in 1846 had re-established the structure for a large Sedentary Militia. On paper, this consisted of every one of the Province's roughly 500,000 able-bodied males, but no regular force or Active Militia of centrally paid, trained, and armed soldiers. Financial support for the Sedentary Militia proved limited, and few Canadians participated in the sometimes farcical militia musters. In theory, the force could be called upon to provide 30,000 soldiers for active duty in an emergency, but in practice, Canadian security continued to rely on the Royal Navy and a small but dwindling garrison of British army regulars.

The outbreak of the Crimean War in 1854 prompted a patriotic outburst in support of the Empire and further efforts at military reform. A commission to assess the Province's defences advised the creation of a 5,000-strong Active Militia, a recommendation embodied in the Militia Act of 1855. Unlike the largely notional Sedentary force, the Active Militia was to be armed, clothed, equipped, and paid for up to 10 days of training each year, or 20 days for the artillery. Early recruiting efforts met success and, by 1856, the enrolment target had been raised to 10,000. But militia enthusiasm proved short-lived. The end of the Crimean War overseas, coupled with economic pressure and political disinterest at home, curtailed public support and saw many newly created units collapse.

After Confederation in 1867, several Militia Acts—the first in 1868—sought to expand and strengthen the Active Militia. After the establishment of a regular (or permanent) force from the 1880s, the militia was usually called the Non-Permanent Active Militia. However, scarce funds, limited training, and lack of equipment hindered effectiveness and recruitment. Nevertheless, the small size of Canada's poorly funded Permanent Force (sometimes called a "Permanent Active Militia") left to part-time soldiers the bulk of local defence duties. Militia units became and remained powerful centres of political patronage, local pride, and historical commemoration well into the twentieth century.

Admirals, World War II. The Royal Canadian Navy (RCN), the smallest of Canada's three prewar armed services, sailed mainly in small flotillas in home waters or with its ships mixed into Royal Navy squadrons under British command. The small size and limited capacity of the prewar fleet reduced dramatically the pool from which to draw qualified wartime leaders. These weaknesses were accentuated by Ottawa's reluctance to appoint more experienced Royal Navy officers to senior Canadian billets, and by incessant squabbling among the RCN's tiny but fiercely competitive leadership cadre.

In Ottawa, the chief of the naval staff (CNS) was Percy Nelles from 1934 until the minister of national defence for naval services, Angus L. Macdonald, forced his ouster in January 1944. The second cadet in Canada's navy in 1908, two years before the navy's official creation, the administratively capable Nelles ran the RCN's huge expansion during most of World War II. The Navy's difficulties in fighting U-boats, its slowness in modernizing ships, and tensions among regular RCN officers and between them and wartime RCN Volunteer Reserve officers made Nelles politically vulnerable; with public scandal threatening, the minister neatly dodged potential accountability by shipping Nelles overseas, nominally promoting him to head of Canadian naval operations for the impending invasion of northwest Europe.

Nelles's replacement as CNS, then-vice-chief of the naval staff, George C. Jones, had joined the navy in 1911, serving in British ships until 1919. Nicknamed "Jetty," possibly from widespread—and inaccurate—doubt in his willingness to go to sea and his record as a ship handler, Jones was an ambitious, politically savvy careerist little liked by most sailors. He was a highly capable staff officer, however, a lifelong workaholic, and capable of inspiring fierce loyalty in selected subordinates. Jones parlayed his friendship with Macdonald, a fellow Haligonian (native of Halifax) into a better civil-military relationship and political approval of a powerful,

balanced late-war naval program. Jones died in February 1946, at age 50, of a heart attack brought on by hypertension, the only CNS to have died in office in Canadian naval history.

The wartime navy's most important operational commander was Leonard Murray. Murray had charge of the Newfoundland Escort Force and then of Canadian North-west Atlantic Command. He was very successful in the latter job, as rear-admiral, but the Halifax riots on VE Day, which saw drunken naval and military personnel trashing a portion of the navy's principal port city, ended his career. Admiral Jones, with whom Murray had skirmished continually over the years, took over his duties on 12 May 1945; Murray, denied a command position to conclude gracefully his naval service and held responsible for the public relations catastrophe of the riot, was immediately retired, leaving Jones as both the navy's chief of staff and its most senior operational commander.

On the West Coast, the most important commanding officer was Rear-Admiral Victor Brodeur, a francophone whose father, as minister of marine and fisheries in the Laurier government, had played a large role in creating the navy. Brodeur had joined as a cadet in 1909. He was a staunch Canadian nationalist who, in senior positions, worked effectively with other senior officers, including Percy Nelles, who were more imperial, or pro-British, in outlook. In Britain, the RCN had no senior officer until Nelles's removal as CNS led to his appointment as senior Canadian flag officer overseas. This was effectively a title without much of a role. (A list of the RCN's other key staff officers can be found as Appendix 1 to W.A.B. Douglas et al., *A Blue Water Navy* [2007]). SEE ALSO: ROYAL CANADIAN NAVY.

READING: Michael Whitby et al., eds., *The Admirals: Canada's Senior Naval Leadership in the Twentieth Century* (Toronto, 2006); Richard O. Mayne, *Betrayed: Scandal, Politics, and Canadian Naval Leadership* (Vancouver, 2006).

Afghanistan War (2001–present). Afghanistan is the longest war in Canadian military history. With approximately two rotations of its army battle group per year since 2002, plus regular rotations of air, naval, and support personnel, it has seen more Canadian service personnel than any war since 1945, exceeding by at least one-third the number who served in Korea—in a brigade-sized army deployment plus warships and transport aircraft—between 1950 and 1953. The announcement in early 2008, confirmed in March 2010, by the Conservative government of Stephen Harper that Canada would in 2011 withdraw its troops from the volatile southern region around Kandahar will also make it the first time that Canada has withdrawn voluntarily from ongoing wartime commitments before the war has actually ended.

Canadian air, sea, and land forces deployed to Afghanistan, the waters of the Indian Ocean, and nearby territories as part of a major international mission sparked by a series of devastating terrorist attacks on the United States on 11 September 2001. Known collectively as 9/11, the attacks by members of the transnational terrorist network al Qaeda left some 3,000 civilians (including 24 Canadians) dead at three sites on America's eastern seaboard, including New York City and Washington, DC. The following day, 12 September, both the North Atlantic Treaty Organization (NATO) and the United Nations (UN) took steps to condemn and respond to the strikes. In NATO's case, this took the form of invoking the principle of Article V of the North Atlantic Treaty, the self-defence mechanism of the alliance's founding charter. Two weeks later, NATO formally invoked the article, pledging alliance support to what would become a US-led military campaign against terrorist bases in Afghanistan and the fundamentalist Muslim government of that country, the Taliban movement, from which the terrorists had drawn support. By early October, with firm United Nations backing to operate militarily against the terrorist establishments responsible for 9/11, Canada had pledged substantial forces to what the United States called Operation Enduring Freedom and Canada labelled Operation Apollo.

In making its initial commitment, the government of Prime Minister Jean Chrétien appeared more bellicose than many observers had predicted, especially in light of widespread complaints that Ottawa's initial official response to the terrorist attacks had been lukewarm and somewhat tardy. Canada would send several warships, air personnel, support staff, special operations forces, and—in early 2002—an army battle group for service on the ground with US forces. The mission would alter substantially in the coming months, as US troops operating with an anti-Taliban movement called the Northern Alliance quickly swept the Taliban from power and routed al Qaeda from its state-supported training camps. Thereafter, a long and complex counter-insurgency struggle slowly developed. International forces, including those from Canada, would bolster a new and democratically elected Afghan government in the areas of security, development, and democratic reforms, while also prosecuting intensive military operations against the ousted Taliban, terrorists, and other anti-government forces.

Canada's initial naval commitment peaked at six warships and some 1,500 personnel in early 2002, a complete naval task group that played a central role in coalition naval operations in and around the Arabian Sea well into 2003. Naval interdiction at this scale was a massive, draining commitment for a force of barely 8,000 sea-going personnel, but it soon faded in public perceptions against the activities of troops ashore, who undertook seemingly interminable security patrols against largely invisible enemies. The speed and competence of the military's Afghan deployment was far better than Canadians could reasonably have expected from a military that had long struggled for additional resources, but the strain on people and equipment would mount inexorably as an army organized for major interstate war adapted itself, under trying battlefield conditions, to the guerrilla operations and security missions of Afghanistan. While the appropriateness of Canadian camouflage uniforms and an unfortunate friendly fire incident in early 2002 at Tarnak Farm drew exaggerated attention to minor or non-existent problems, the campaign also exposed more serious structural or technical challenges, including training capacity, helicopter support, sea and air transport, and the protection of personnel from mines and improvised explosives. Moreover, the capacity to project power over great distances for extended periods became an immediate subject of debate over long-term weapons and equipment acquisitions, as well as the social costs on Canadian military families of repeated military deployments overseas. Most infantry battalions, for example, were deployed to Afghanistan once every second year or so after 2002, each time for approximately six months. Not including time spent in training before any mission—which often included extended stays at training facilities in the United States and specialist instruction at bases elsewhere in Canada—it was common for Canadian soldiers to have been absent from home for 18 to 24 months during the first eight years of war, or up to 25 percent of the time.

The focus of Canadian operations changed several times after early 2002, when a battalion of the Princess Patricia's Canadian Light Infantry, reconnaissance troops from Lord Strathcona's Horse (Royal Canadians), and some special forces joined American troops in extensive combat operations against residual Taliban troops and suspected al Qaeda bases and hideouts. From mid-2003, Canada would play a leading role in NATO's International Security Assistance Force (ISAF), at first in Kabul, Afghanistan's capital city, and later in and around Kandahar farther south. While the Kabul mission for much of 2004 focused on preparing for the Afghan national election in October, with ISAF commanded through most of the year by Canadian Lieutenant-General Rick Hillier, a future chief of the defence staff (CDS), from early 2006 its focus in Kandahar was on security and development support in a more volatile region closer

▲ Canadian soldiers, members of a Provincial Reconstruction Team, patrol Kandahar in April 2008, on continuous alert against suicide bombers, explosives, and other threats.

to Taliban strongholds and supply lines from Pakistan's western frontier. In addition to Kandahar and Kabul, Canadian personnel operated from a support base in the Persian Gulf, from Canadian and coalition warships in the Arabian Sea, and from airfields in several surrounding countries.

From the main coalition base in Kandahar and a series of more exposed positions in the rugged surrounding countryside, Canadian forces were the principal ISAF field force in the region from early 2006. Supported by a wide array of coalition firepower, including aircraft and remotely piloted vehicles, Afghan military personnel, and, from August 2008, American infantry battalions, Canadian troops fought a long and bloody five-year campaign against Taliban insurgents. Most of the 150 Canadian soldiers killed (as of June 2010) and 529 wounded in action (to the end of February 2010) during the war were lost in combat, bombings, or enemy suicide attacks in the south, an area that has seen the largest and most complex all-arms offensive operations by Canadian troops since World War II. In early 2010, the size and complexity of the Kandahar mission was indicated by its organizational structure, which included command and headquarters staff, an air force contingent, helicopters and unmanned aerial vehicles (drones), intelligence and communications troops, special forces, mentor and liaison teams working with Afghan military and paramilitary units, an infantry battalion, a tank squadron, armoured reconnaissance troops, military police, an artillery battery, an engineer squadron, medical personnel, and substantial numbers of American infantry. It also included a Provincial Reconstruction Team, or PRT, based at Camp Nathan Smith, designed to assist the Afghan government in development and civil society projects, and consisting of diplomats, development specialists, police and corrections officers, and military personnel working on a range of projects, including irrigation, education, and policing. Called since July 2003 Operation Athena, the Kandahar mission was the principal component of Canada's Joint Task Force Afghanistan, a command that included much smaller liaison staffs supporting American, United Nations, and Afghan national efforts, and, sometimes controversially, offering strategic advice to the government in Kabul.

The Afghanistan war generally and the Kandahar mission in particular were the subject of intense domestic political debate in Canada. Even in the immediate aftermath of al Qaeda's terrorist attack on the United States, Canadian opinion polls expressed the widespread fear that American foreign policy in the Middle East had somehow provoked the disaster. This ambiguity in Canadian attitudes was reflected in Ottawa's initially muted response to 9/11 but did not prevent an outpouring of public sympathy for the United States and solid margins in support of a joint international military response. In 2003, with Washington pressing its allies for contributions to a new war in Iraq against what senior American officials assured the world was the clear evidence of an Iraqi program to build weapons of mass destruction (WMDS) in defiance of United Nations edicts, Canada chose to continue its Afghanistan obligations while rejecting American overtures on Iraq. Solid opposition to Washington's Iraq policy was most evident in Quebec, where all provincial political parties opposed Canadian involvement, but doubt and disappointment over American leadership in the War on Terror were increasingly widely shared. They grew exponentially after American forces failed to find any evidence of Iraqi WMDS, and as Canadian combat casualties mounted in Afghanistan during the fourth year of fighting.

While previous Liberal governments had committed Canada to Afghanistan and expanded its responsibilities in the more dangerous south in late 2005, the new minority government of Conservative Stephen Harper, elected in January 2006, was soon taking criticism for what armchair generals and political pundits now referenced in language reminiscent of America's long struggle in Vietnam, or the Soviet Union's in Afghanistan. From Liberals especially the charges were disingenuous, but heavy casualties in September 2006 during the Canadian-led Operation Medusa in the Panjwai district added a dose of public emotionalism to the political and military debate over the effectiveness and duration of the mission.

▲ There were pleasant moments for soldiers in Kandahar province, and Afghan children, charming and cheerful, provided many of them. This Van Doo was making friends in August 2007.

Afghanistan was a leading news story through all of 2007, a year in which it seemed that only Conservatives even vaguely recalled the events that had led Canadians to Afghanistan in the first place. The year ended in a government-appointed public commission, chaired by former Liberal deputy prime minister and foreign policy hawk John Manley, to advise Ottawa on the possible length and character of the mission beyond early 2009. The report in early 2008 cautioned against the risks of precipitate withdrawal, but urged more coalition help for Canadians in the south, more military capability, and greater attention to non-military efforts in the supposedly comprehensive diplomatic and developmental, as well as military, campaign then underway. More importantly, for a government anxious to maintain international commitments while removing Afghanistan as a domestic policy irritant, the report opened the door to gradually reducing Canada's combat role in the south in favour of greater civil support functions elsewhere. The government's decision, after surviving a confidence vote in the House of Commons in March 2008, to extend Canada's role into 2011 but to end it thereafter, came in the context of the Manley Commission's helpfully ambiguous recommendations. It also came amid the constant pillorying of government representatives for Afghanistan's seemingly endless war and hopeless corruption, and NATO's inability to generate the strategy or force structure sufficient to win within a reasonable time frame.

Afghanistan was the Canadian Forces' principal mission for most of the first decade of the twenty-first century, and the government's main foreign policy preoccupation in the same period. Contrary to the stubbornly persistent view, especially evident in the deeply anti-military quarters of the political left, that the war had eroded a proud peacekeeping tradition and decades worth of Canadian foreign policy neutrality, it was completely in keeping with previous overseas commitments and past articulations of Canadian interests. Indeed, unlike Korea, the first Persian Gulf War, South Africa, or either world war, the Afghanistan mission came in response to an unprovoked attack on North American soil in which Canadian citizens in substantial number had died. And, also unlike most past Canadian conflicts, it had a consistently evident—if inconsistently pursued—civil development quotient all but completely absent from past wars, and rarely a key aspect of past peace support operations either. Afghanistan was demonstrably not peacekeeping, however, a point on which both hawks and doves would readily agree, and the jarring media images of dead and wounded Canadians, firefights, Afghan civilians killed or wounded in coalition air strikes, and the war's mounting financial cost affected public perceptions to greater or lesser degree. The war exposed difficult operational and technical deficiencies, tensions in the defence-diplomacy-development troika that guided (at least nominally) Canadian policy, and, in rare cases, lacklustre leadership. In often-sustained operations under always-wretched conditions, the war also found Canadian forces in all service elements to be among the finest and most effective warriors in the coalition. This was no mean feat, given the military's relative underfunding by successive Canadian governments, and the rank and file's near-total lack of combat experience for roughly half a century.

Canadian public opinion proved far more divided on the wisdom of continuing the war itself than on the character of those who fought it. The evidence of popular pride and support for Canadian military personnel was higher during the Afghanistan conflict than at any point since the 1940s. Remembrance Day services across the country witnessed record attendance; a groundswell of public interest in military affairs fed social agencies in supporting military personnel and their families; and an exhibition produced by the Canadian War Museum drew the largest visitor total, nearly 200,000, in that institution's 130-year history. The return of fallen soldiers from overseas, at times feared by government officials who saw them as lightning rods for negative press coverage, became occasions for mass demonstrations of empathy and grief, opportunities for critical public connections between the civilian and military worlds that the secretive, overseas Cold War or distant peacekeeping missions had seldom provided.

In 2009, American officials discussed with Canadian counterparts on several occasions the future of NATO operations in Afghanistan, expressing guarded optimism that Canadian combat commitments would continue beyond 2011. This would be in keeping with US President Barack Obama's focus on Afghanistan in the second year of his mandate, and the redirection of American combat forces from Iraq after a previous surge had helped restore a modicum of peace and stability to that war-ravaged country. There was no departure during the year on Canada's part from its long-announced intention to end its mission in 2011. Growing evidence from a parliamentary budget officer that the financial costs of the war were vastly exceeding Ottawa's previously announced estimates imparted a brutal financial logic to the continuing debate. Whether Canada should stay, leave, or stay in a different role remained a leading topic of public discussion into early 2010, as another army battle group of some 2,600 young Canadians prepared to depart for Kandahar. After the usual Christmas recess of 2009, the Harper government prorogued Parliament until March 2010, an unusual decision that critics attributed to the government's fear of public scrutiny over revelations that Canadian Forces had in the past remanded prisoners to Afghan custody, where they had allegedly been tortured. At the end of the month, Prime Minister Harper confirmed that no troops would remain after the 2011 end of the mission. What else might stay in theatre was unclear. SEE ALSO: CANADA–UNITED STATES DEFENCE RELATIONS; HARPER; HILLIER; WAR ON TERROR.

READING: Janice Gross Stein and Eugene Lang, *The Unexpected War: Canada in Kandahar* (Toronto, 2007); Lee Windsor, David Charters, and Brent Wilson, *Kandahar Tour: The Turning Point in Canada's Afghan Mission* (Fredericton, 2008).

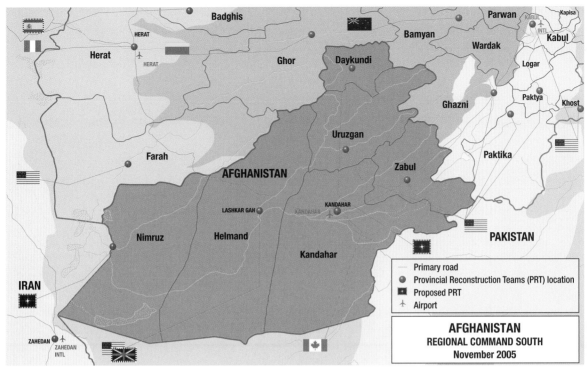

The map shows provinces and cities of Afghanistan, with markers:

- HERAT
- Herat
- HERAT (airport)
- Badghis
- Ghor
- Daykundi
- Bamyan
- Parwan
- Kapisa
- KABUL INTL
- Kabul
- Wardak
- Logar
- Ghazni
- Paktya
- Khost
- Uruzgan
- Farah
- AFGHANISTAN
- Zabul
- Paktika
- Nimruz
- Helmand
- LASHKAR GAH
- KANDAHAR
- KANDAHAR
- PAKISTAN
- Kandahar
- IRAN
- ZAHEDAN
- ZAHEDAN INTL

Legend:
- Primary road
- ● Provincial Reconstruction Teams (PRT) location
- ▦ Proposed PRT
- ✈ Airport

AFGHANISTAN
REGIONAL COMMAND SOUTH
November 2005

▲ The International Security Assistance Force was truly international, but not all countries fought. Canada, based in Kandahar, did.

Agira, Battle of (1943). Agira is a small mountain town in central Sicily overlooking the valley of the Salso River. In July 1943, it lay astride the route of Canadian forces driving hard eastwards toward Adrano, a strategic position near Mount Etna. A battalion of German panzer grenadiers with tanks and assault guns defended the town's western approaches, including several ridges around the tiny village of Nissoria. Two brigades from Major-General Guy Simonds's 1st Canadian Division, with massive air and artillery support, ground into the German defences in three days of heavy fighting from 24 July, as Britain's so-called Malta Brigade, assigned to Simonds for this battle, approached Agira from the southeast. Three costly and largely unsuccessful attacks around Nissoria ended in the early hours of 28 July, with Canadian troops of the Edmonton Regiment in possession of "Grizzly," the last substantial defensive position west of Agira. The town was about to be shelled that afternoon when a forward observation officer reported—wrongly—that German forces had fled the town. The barrage was cancelled and two companies of the Princess Patricia's Canadian Light Infantry entered Agira to cheering crowds; the companies then almost immediately came under fire from left-behind pockets of the enemy. Two hours of stiff house-to-house fighting ensued before the town was liberated. The five-day battle, the biggest for the Canadians in Sicily, cost 438 casualties. Agira is the site of the Canadian War Cemetery in Sicily with 490 graves, including 13 from the Royal Canadian Air Force. SEE ALSO: SICILIAN CAMPAIGN; SIMONDS.

Aid to the Civil Power. Provincial or local authorities can request assistance from the Canadian military in times of emergency. But Aid to the Civil Power should not be confused with standing federal powers over the national armed forces or with the

▲ The site of the largest battle for 1st Canadian Division in Sicily, Agira, lay in rough terrain that seemed designed for mule trains, and the Canadians were quick to employ them.

employment of the military in time of war in support of home front or civilian assistance operations.

Constitutional authority for national defence in Canada rests with the federal government. However, based on British practice, provisions have long existed for both municipal and local authorities to call on the armed forces for assistance in preserving law and order in the face of temporary emergencies, whether natural or man-made. Indeed, for much of Canada's early national history, the federal government itself considered the principal role of the militia (and, later, the small Permanent Force) to be the upholding of domestic authority while leaving external defence principally—and with great over-optimism—to Great Britain. The Canadian military's role in granting Aid

to the Civil Power echoed that of British forces in assisting colonial governments prior to Confederation in 1867. Through many decades in which municipal and provincial police forces—where they existed at all—were small, poorly trained, and under-equipped, local authority for law and order usually entailed tacit reliance on soldiers to respond to large-scale events or violent demonstrations.

For much of the period from 1867 to the 1930s, such requests for Aid to the Civil Power focused on labour disputes in which local governments in support of manufacturing or business interests called for military assistance to protect property or operations from striking workers. In the absence of a large professional military, the deployments fell to militia units. The command and administration of these units were highly partisan and often controlled by those same entrepreneurs who had prevailed upon local politicians to request intervention in the first place. Militia soldiers served alongside members of the paramilitary North West Mounted Police, the national police force, during the Winnipeg General Strike in 1919, for example, and assisted local authorities in scores of violent confrontations in the mining, lumbering, and industrial sectors in regions from Cape Breton, Nova Scotia, to the British Columbia interior. The troops' limited professionalism and poor training led to frequent charges of brutality. They were at the same time often extremely effective in suppressing unrest, not to mention far cheaper for local authorities than special constables or private security guards. In no case did federal military forces supplant or other-wise suppress local political authorities in the resolution of crises.

In the 1920s, Ottawa removed the ability of local magistrates to call directly upon federal troops for this kind of aid. Provincial attorneys general would henceforth be solely responsible, and local authorities would have to appeal through them to solicit federal help—a move that made the provinces accountable for moderating the enthusiasms of local mayors, magistrates, and business leaders. This helped to de-politicize the process and to ease long-standing tensions between organized labour and local militia units. However, there were other factors that reduced the need for local governments to request federal resources, including the growing size and professional capabilities of municipal and provincial police forces. Requests for aid were far less frequent after the 1930s, but they still occurred. Federal forces assisted several times after 1945 in suppressing prison riots, for example, and once during a police strike. The Quebec government famously called for aid during the 1970 October Crisis, in the face of two political kidnap-pings by the Front de Libération du Québec (FLQ), and did so again in 1990, when a dispute at Oka involving land developers, the provincial police, and First Nations communities led to an armed standoff and the threat of widespread violence. The

city of Toronto's request in 1999 for military assistance in response to a heavy snowstorm, foolishly endorsed by the province of Ontario, led to the deployment of several hundred reservists with armoured personnel carriers and brooms and shovels, and a generous helping of national ridicule for Mayor Mel Lastman. Efficient administration and the city's own workforce could have cleared the streets without calling in the army.

Perhaps the largest category of requests for Aid to the Civil Power in recent decades, entreaties from local police forces via their respective provincial ministers for special tactical equipment, vehicles, or logistical support, was codified in 1996 under the Canadian Forces Assistance to Provincial Police Forces Directions (CFAPPFD). This arrangement saw military assets employed during several high-profile standoffs involving First Nations and local authorities in the 1990s.

Other than the military-police liaison noted above, the right of provincial authorities to request military assistance in response to emergencies is incorporated in the National Defence Act, passed in 1922, which created the Department of National Defence. Part VI of the Act, "Aid of the Civil Power," permits attorneys general to petition Canada's senior military official, the chief of the defence staff (CDS), for military aid "where a riot or disturbance occurs or is considered as likely to occur." The CDS is obliged to execute the request, but remains responsible for determining the appropriate nature and level of the military's response. The provisions of the Act then establish the broad contours of a relationship between senior provincial authorities and the CDS, who conducts military operations on the direction of provincial authorities, but they do not delineate with clarity the role of the federal government vis-à-vis the military, or the relationship between higher federal and provincial authorities.

The federal government's own powers in case of domestic emergency expanded during World War I with passage of the War Measures Act (1914). It invoked the Act in both world wars and again during the 1970 October Crisis, in each case sparking long-term historical controversy over the moral, ethical, and political implications of curtailing civil liberties in response to security concerns. In 1970, the federal response—deeming the terrorist incidents an apprehended insurrection and invoking the Act to declare a federal emergency in a single province—might be said to have supplanted the military-provincial relationship outlined by the National Defence Act and demonstrated the continuing sweep of federal powers. Political reaction to the military deployments of 1970 and to the arrests and detentions of terrorist suspects that marked the crisis led to an extended review of federal emergency legislation, despite the disciplined and professional performance of the troops. The Emergencies Act that eventually replaced the War Measures Act in 1988 divided potential emergencies into four categories—public welfare, public order, international emergency, and war—and, while preserving for the federal government broad powers under the latter two categories, made the invocation of emergency aid subject to the Canadian Charter of Rights and Freedoms. It also limited Ottawa's ability to declare an emergency in a single province and left unclear the relationship between federal powers under the Emergencies Act and provincial access to military aid under the National Defence Act. The latter continues to permit provincial authorities to define the circumstances under which they might request federal military Aid to the Civil Power, while the former prohibits the extension of federal emergency power into provinces that have not explicitly asked for it or where no other federal law appears capable of resolving the problem.

The deployment of the military as Aid to the Civil Power has taken on new dimensions in recent years in light of the increased fear of catastrophic terrorism, pandemics, and other unprecedented emergencies. In addition to concerted and widespread efforts to protect critical infrastructure and to coordinate the planning and operations of federal, provincial, municipal, and non-governmental agencies, military capacities have also improved, especially in the area of counterterrorism. Provinces retain the right to request military Aid to the

Civil Power in response to emergencies; the federal government retains the right to provide military aid, in a range of circumstances, whether or not a province has officially requested it. SEE ALSO: OCTOBER CRISIS; OKA CRISIS; WAR MEASURES ACT.

READING: Eric Lerhe, "Civil Military Relations and Aid to the Civil Power in Canada: Implications for the War on Terror," Conference of Defence Associations Institute Graduate Student Symposium, *Security and Defence: National and International Issues* (Kingston, ON, 2004).

Air Board. The federal government established the Air Board in 1919 to assume control of all flying within Canada and to establish a small non-permanent air force. Its authority extended to both civil and military aviation, but was mainly regulatory. This was in response to duties assumed by Canada under the International Convention for Air Navigation, part of the peace treaty that had ended World War I. Under its chair, A.L. Sifton (former Alberta premier and a Cabinet minister in Sir Robert Borden's Union Government), the seven-member board created and ran the Canadian Air Force (CAF), a part-time air militia with a nominal strength of over 30,000. Headquartered at Camp Borden, Ontario, the CAF's main task from 1920–1922 was to provide month-long refresher courses every second year to former air crew, using surplus aircraft, equipment, and hangars supplied to Canada by Britain. Other Air Board operations included forest fire patrols, aerial photography, anti-smuggling flights, communications, and transportation. Its duties were subsumed by the new Department of National Defence in 1923.

Airborne Units. The 1st Canadian Parachute Battalion, formed in 1942, became part of the British 6th Airborne Division's 3rd Brigade and fought with great distinction in Normandy in 1944, dropping ahead of the seaborne landings to secure strategic points behind the Germans' coastal defences, and again at the crossing of the Rhine River in 1945. The First Special Service Force, administratively the 2nd

Canadian Parachute Battalion, was a Canadian-American unit that trained in the United States, landed at Kiska in the Aleutians, and then fought in Italy and southern France; its Canadians returned to First Canadian Army in 1944. After World War II, the 1st Canadian Parachute Battalion disbanded, and a Special Air Service unit took form in 1947. With rearmament after 1950, the three regular force infantry regiments each developed an airborne battalion as part of the Mobile Strike Force, primarily charged with the defence of Canada. In 1968, the Canadian Airborne Regiment (CAR) took shape, based at Edmonton and later at Petawawa, Ontario. The CAR saw service in Cyprus, most notably during the 1974 Turkish invasion during which it suffered two dead and several wounded in and around Nicosia airport. By 1979, each of the regular infantry regiments provided the CAR with personnel for a company-sized commando, and it was with this organization that the regiment deployed to Somalia in 1992 in a large peace enforcement mission. The killing of Shidane Arone, a Somali teenager, by airborne soldiers, and subsequent events related largely to ill discipline led in 1995 to the disbanding of the regiment, an action unprecedented in Canada as, essentially, governmental punishment for the unit's presumed misdeeds. In recent years, airborne capability has gradually been reintroduced to the army's three regular infantry regiments, with one airborne company per regiment. SEE ALSO: PEACEKEEPING; SOMALIA AFFAIR; WORLD WAR II.

READING: Bernd Horn, *Bastard Sons: An Examination of Canada's Airborne Experience, 1942–1995* (St Catharines, ON, 2003).

Air Force Organization. After World War II, the Royal Canadian Air Force organized itself into functional commands—Training Command, Air Transport Command, Air Materiel Command, Air Defence Command, and, as designated in the North Atlantic Treaty Organization after 1951, 1 Canadian Air Division. Maritime Air and Tactical Air were also at first labelled groups but eventually became commands. This structure ended with the unification of Canadian air, land, and sea units into the single-service

Canadian Forces in the late 1960s. In 1975, a reconstituted Air Command began operations in Winnipeg in a move seen by some as an end to the unified force and a return to a single service. Under Air Command were Fighter Group, Air Transport Group, Maritime Air Group, and 10 Tactical Air Group. In 1997, the groups combined into 1 Canadian Air Division, Air Command's headquarters shut down, and control of the force passed to the chief of the air staff in Ottawa who, in 2009, established 2 Canadian Air Division in Winnipeg to command air force training and doctrine.

Air Marshals, World War II. A tiny prewar service, the Royal Canadian Air Force (RCAF) met major challenges in World War II in expanding to become one of the Allies' principal strike forces against Germany and Italy in the European theatre. RCAF commanders ran a complex, fast-growing network of squadrons and commands around the world, and also managed the issues raised by thousands of individual Canadians serving in Royal Air Force (RAF) squadrons. A critical aspect of this work throughout the war was the handling of human resources and, in particular, finding and retaining trained, effective leaders for the RCAF's massive establishment.

Because of the way Canadian aircrew were dispersed throughout Royal Air Force squadrons, and because No. 6 Bomber Group only became operational on 1 January 1943, the number of senior Canadian officers overseas was relatively limited. Not until October 1940 did the RCAF have an air vice-marshal in Britain, the air officer in chief, L.F. Stevenson. After him came Air Marshal H. "Gus" Edwards—tough-talking, nationalistic, and the leading proponent of the "Canadianization" of the nation's air contingents overseas by concentrating Canada's personnel into distinctively RCAF formations. Edwards, whose title changed in July 1942 to air officer commanding-in-chief, RCAF overseas, continued in this post until the end of 1943 when he was replaced—for being too aggressive in pressing his case—by Air Marshal Lloyd Breadner, formerly chief of the air staff in Ottawa. (Breadner's successor in April 1945 was L.O. Johnson.)

At No. 6 Group, the RCAF's key operational posting, the first commander was Air Vice-Marshal G.E. Brookes, whose time in command lasted from October 1942 (before No. 6 became operational) to February 1944. His successor, the officer usually given credit for the bomber group's eventual successes after a long period of heavy casualties and overwhelming technical and operational challenges, was Air Vice-Marshal C.M. "Black Mike" McEwen, a tough disciplinarian. All these senior officers were World War I pilots. (A list of the other RCAF senior staff overseas can be found in Appendix B to B. Greenhous et al., *The Crucible of War, 1939–1945* [1994].)

In Canada, the lead RCAF position was the chief of the air staff (CAS). From December 1938 through to May 1940, the CAS was Air Vice-Marshal George Croil who had served in the Royal Flying Corps in World War I. Croil, who had once flown with Lawrence of Arabia, had been staff trained in Britain between the wars. Quiet, calm, and a good administrator, Croil was pushed upstairs to become inspector general by the new minister of national defence for air, C.G. Power, when he took over in May 1940. Croil's successor was Breadner, another World War I fighter pilot who had been staff trained in Britain. Promoted to air chief marshal on retirement in 1945, Breadner managed competently the RCAF's huge wartime expansion, helped notably in running the British Commonwealth Air Training Plan by (BCATP) Air Vice-Marshal Robert Leckie, the air member for training. Leckie was a British-born World War I pilot in the Royal Naval Air Service who came to Canada in 1919 as director of flying operations for the Air Board. His huge success at the BCATP led him to be named Breadner's successor as chief of the air staff in 1944, a post he held until 1947. (Other RCAF senior posts in Canada are detailed in Appendix A to W.A.B. Douglas, *The Creation of a National Air Force* [1986].) SEE ALSO: AIR BOARD; BOMBER COMMAND CONTROVERSY; BRITISH COMMON-WEALTH AIR TRAINING PLAN; CANADIANIZATION; ROYAL CANADIAN AIR FORCE; WORLD WAR II.

Aitken, William Maxwell, 1st Baron Beaverbrook (1879–1964). A financier and business entrepreneur,

the Ontario-born, New Brunswick–raised Aitken was a powerful representative of Canadian interests in Britain during World War I and a member of Winston Churchill's Cabinet during World War II.

Aitken made his initial fortune in Canada, but moved to Britain in 1910, where he was knighted the following year. A close friend of fellow New Brunswicker Andrew Bonar Law—the only Canadian to be prime minister of Britain (1922–1923)—Aitken represented the government of Canada at the front throughout the war. As the "Canadian Eye-Witness," he sent reports "wired from the trenches" (though in fact ordinarily compiled in London) and wrote a three-volume, bestselling account of the conflict, *Canada in Flanders*, to inform Canadians of the nature of the struggle. He was also responsible for the Canadian War Records Office, established on a shoestring budget in 1915, which he gradually expanded into a wide-ranging and effective documentary unit to record Canadian activities during the war and to remind British authorities of Canada's impressive contributions. He was made a peer in 1917, taking the name "Beaverbrook" after a stream near his Canadian home, and in 1918 became Britain's first minister of information in charge of all propaganda operations at home and abroad. His office pioneered the use of photographic propaganda for posters and recruitment campaigns, published a range of famous authors (including H.G. Wells and Rudyard Kipling), and used cinema newsreels to communicate news and government messages. He resigned from Cabinet in the fall over a jurisdictional dispute with the Foreign Office.

While running the Canadian War Records Office, he established the Canadian War Memorials Fund to provide a lasting visual record of Canada's role in the war through paintings, photographs, and films. The fund commissioned scores of artists who painted hundreds of pieces, the collection coming to Canada only after the armistice. One of the world's great collections of war art, it was held by the National Gallery until 1971 and then the greater part of it was transferred to the Canadian War Museum. A similarly impressive collection of several thousand war photographs is held by Library and Archives Canada.

⌃ Max Aitken, Lord Beaverbrook, during World War I.

Beaverbrook was Britain's leading newspaper magnate in the interwar years and, during World War II, he held several British Cabinet appointments. Beaverbrook continued to run his financial empire after the war, wrote several books, and became one of Canada's leading philanthropists. The unparalleled record of Canadian activities compiled under his auspices during World War I remains an essential starting point for serious research on the conflict, whether in art, film, photography, or print. SEE ALSO: PROPAGANDA; WAR ART.

READING: David A. Richards, *Extraordinary Canadians: Lord Beaverbrook* (Toronto, 2008).

Alabama Claims. The *Alabama* was a warship of the Confederate States of America constructed in Britain during the American Civil War. Before being sunk in 1864 by the USS *Kearsarge* off the coast of France, the *Alabama* had inflicted substantial losses on US shipping, seizing or sinking nearly 60 vessels. American claims for compensation from Britain for having allowed the vessel to be built and launched in violation of British neutrality laws were initially extravagant. These claims were based on the charge that commerce raiding by the *Alabama* and other vessels built in Britain had prolonged the war by many months, and that this prolongation had cost Washington more than $2 billion. The case prompted some American calls for the annexation of all or part

of Canada in compensation should a large settlement not be forthcoming. However, negotiators in 1871 agreed to international arbitration that resulted the following year in a $15.5 million settlement in gold to the American side.

Alaska Boundary Dispute. This dispute over the border of the Alaskan panhandle, stretching south along the British Columbia coast, resulted in a decision favourable to the United States. It also resulted in widespread disappointment in Canada at Britain's apparent failure to support the Canadian position on an international tribunal established to resolve the impasse.

After purchasing Alaska from Russia in 1867, the United States claimed possession of the coastline in a continuous stretch, unbroken by the deep inlets or fjords that ran into the interior and unaffected by the location of coastal or offshore mountains that appeared to form the boundary in a vaguely worded 1825 treaty between Russia and Great Britain. Canada claimed several of these inlets, including Lynn Canal, which gave access to the Yukon; here the discovery of gold in 1897 prompted a massive population influx and raised issues of regional jurisdiction, law enforcement, and border security. A Joint High Commission failed to resolve the boundary issue in 1898–1899. Canada sent troops, the small Yukon Field Force, into the goldfields to enforce its sovereignty. In 1903, an international tribunal of three Americans, two Canadians, and one Briton ruled in favour of most aspects of the American claim when the British representative, Lord Alverstone, the Lord Chief Justice of England, accepted Washington's position. The incident convinced some Canadians of the requirement for control of their own foreign policy and for a time soured relations with both the United States and Great Britain. SEE ALSO: CANADA–UNITED STATES DEFENCE RELATIONS; LAURIER.

READING: Norman Penlington, *The Alaska Boundary Dispute: A Critical Reappraisal* (Toronto, 1972).

Alaska Highway. Built in 1942 and 1943 from Dawson Creek through Fort St John and Fort Nelson, BC, and

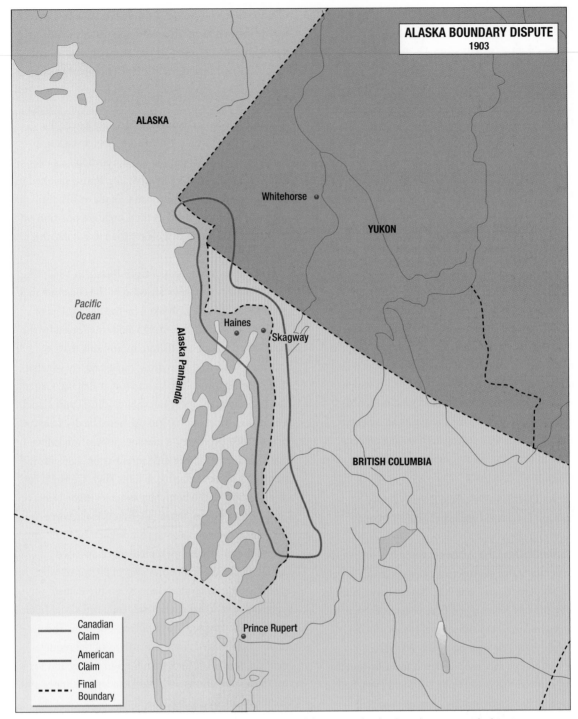

ALASKA BOUNDARY DISPUTE
1903

ALASKA

Whitehorse

YUKON

Pacific
Ocean

Alaska Panhandle

Haines

Skagway

BRITISH COLUMBIA

Prince Rupert

	Canadian Claim
	American Claim
----	Final Boundary

▲ Access to the sea was the issue in the Alaska Boundary Dispute, and the US won the day through international arbitration.

Watson Lake and Whitehorse in Yukon Territory to Delta Junction, Alaska, 150 kilometres southeast of Fairbanks, the road (also known as the Alcan Highway) became necessary—in Washington's eyes especially—because of the Japanese threat to the US Territory of Alaska and the Aleutian Islands.

The idea of a highway to Alaska had been alive for years, and British Columbia Premier Duff Pattullo had long been an advocate. The Canadian government had been far cooler to the proposal, worrying that a land link through Canadian territory could only increase US influence in BC and make Canadian neutrality impossible in the event of a war between the United States and Japan, a major concern of Canada's interwar military planners. Once the attack on Pearl Harbor in December 1941 had brought Canada and the United States into the war against Japan, these fears ended, and the Canadian government quickly embraced the idea of a highway providing that the United States agreed to pay its full construction cost and to turn over the Canadian portion of the road six months after the end of the war.

Building the road was a major feat of construction, undertaken by 11,000 US Army engineers (one third of them black soldiers) and up to 16,000 civilians. A total of 2,237 kilometres of pioneer road was carved out over rugged mountainous terrain and through muskeg and permafrost in just eight months at a cost of $148 million. Construction began in March 1942 and the road was dedicated on 20 November, although it could not be used by general vehicles until 1943; even then it was frequently impassable, not least during the spring melt of 1943 when 40 bridges washed away. The presence of large numbers of soldiers and outside civilians had a major impact on First Nations communities in the Northwest Territories and Yukon, resulting in widespread epidemics and other diseases, as well as problems with prostitution and alcohol. Some estimates suggest that the native population fell by as much as 50 percent as a result of this massive military presence.

Also developed in conjunction with the highway was Canol, an oil field development at Norman Wells, Yukon Territory, along with

▲ Carved out of the wilderness by US Army engineers in 1942–1943, the Alaska Highway was a rough road of strategic importance for the war against Japan.

associated pipelines to supply Alaska's fuel needs by a safe, inland route. The location of the Northwest Staging Route—a chain of airfields to ferry aircraft to the Soviet Union under the American Lend-Lease agreement, and also used to supply fuel needs for the highway project and for Alaskan military bases—helped determine the highway's curves and diversions. At the end of the war, the Canadian government purchased all assets of both developments, as well as taking over the Alaska Highway route on Canadian land, guaranteeing that there could be no future US territorial claims against Canada. The Canadian Army assumed responsibility for maintaining the Canadian portion of the route until 1964 when British Columbia and the federal Department of Public Works took over. SEE ALSO: CANADA–UNITED STATES DEFENCE RELATIONS.

READING: K. Coates and W. Morrison, *The Alaska Highway in World War II: The US Army of Occupation in Canada's Northwest* (Norman, OK, 1992).

Alberta Field Force. During the Northwest Rebellion of 1885, the Alberta Field Force was created under the command of Major-General Thomas B. Strange, a capable retired British artillery officer who had settled in the West after service in Quebec City and Kingston. Strange led his column of three weak militia battalions and a few North West Mounted Police north from Calgary and met Big Bear's band of Cree warriors at Frenchman's Butte, northwest of Battleford, on 28 May. Recognizing the strength of Big Bear's position, Strange refused to permit a major attack and Big Bear won the day, though inconclusively. Strange's militia, now reinforced by some of General Frederick Middleton's troops, followed the Cree northwest to yet another inconclusive skirmish at Steele's Narrows on 2 June. By now Big Bear's warriors were starting to desert, and the Cree leader surrendered on 2 July.

Alderson, Edwin Alfred Hervey (1859–1927). Alderson enlisted in the British army in 1878 and saw service in colonial wars, including the South

African War during which he had Canadian troops under his command. In 1914 as a lieutenant-general, he was appointed to command the Canadian Division and subsequently took command of the Canadian Corps. A competent but uninspiring officer, Alderson had terrible difficulty dealing with the interference of Canada's militia minister, Sir Sam Hughes, in command and equipment matters. After the corps' failure at the battle of St Eloi in April 1916, General Sir Douglas Haig sacked Alderson, who soon became inspector general of the Canadian Forces in England. His replacement was Lieutenant-General Sir Julian Byng.

Allard, Jean Victor (1913–1996). The Quebec-born Allard, a decorated veteran of World War II and the Korean War, became the first francophone to serve as chief of the defence staff (CDS). He joined the Non-Permanent Active Militia in Trois-Rivières in 1933 and served from 1939 to 1945 in a variety of

▲ Brigadier Jean Victor Allard in 1945.

staff positions in Canada and combat commands overseas. An astute leader and creative tactician, he led with great distinction the Royal 22e Régiment (the Van Doos) for more than a year in Italy, and commanded a brigade in northwest Europe from March to August 1945. After the war, he was Canada's military attaché in Moscow for three years, and later commanded the Canadian brigade during the closing stages of the Korean War. He led a British division in Germany from 1961 to 1963, an unusual posting for a Canadian officer. In 1965 he became the first head of Mobile Command, essentially a remodelled Canadian Army including both air and ground units.

Allard's stint as chief of the defence staff coincided with the tumultuous reorganization of the Canadian military into the unified Canadian Armed Forces. This was a controversial move driven by mercurial defence minister Paul Hellyer, with whom Allard enjoyed a good working relationship—unusual among the period's soldiers. These years also saw expanded use of the French language within the heavily anglophone command and organizational structure of the Canadian Forces, a cause Allard had personally championed since at least 1951. He proved as skilful in this highly politicized environment as he had once been in field command, and he is remembered both as the officer who unified the Canadian military and as the one who began to make it bilingual by creating a French-language army brigade, as well as an air squadron and a warship's crew. He retired in 1969 and later published his memoirs, one of the very few Canadian generals ever to have done so. SEE ALSO: BILINGUALISM IN THE CANADIAN FORCES; FRENCH-LANGUAGE UNITS; QUEBEC AND THE MILITARY.

READING: Jean V. Allard, *The Memoirs of General Jean V. Allard* (Vancouver, 1988).

Alliances, Canadian. A small country with a large territory, Canada has always relied on imperial protection or, after Confederation, external alliances for its security. It contributed to them too, to greater or lesser degree, since the late nineteenth century. A major combatant in two world wars, and a ranking middle power thereafter, Canada fought the Cold War with many other allies in Western Europe and with one, its principal one, in North America. It struggled in its other commitments to minimize the costs of a military alliance on one hand with growing continental integration on the other, sometimes relishing the plaudits received from its exercise of leadership abroad, and at other times straining unhelpfully at the limits of its own history, identity, and economic ties.

France's failure, ultimately, to fend off British power in the New World made Canada's first real ally Britain. From the end of the Seven Years' War in 1763, British North America, from Newfoundland to Vancouver Island, was defended by a smattering of British army units, Royal Navy ships, and locally raised regular forces or part-time militia. Residents of the various colonies understood that, in the event of crisis, Canadian defence, as part of the Empire, depended almost entirely on British resources; in return, most—almost all outside of the mostly French-speaking population of Quebec—understood the necessity (and desirability) of, in turn, supporting Britain's wars abroad. This imperial connection was hardly the sober analysis of a mutually entwined foreign policy. "Canada" existed only as a dependency of the British Crown after its conquest from France, not as an independent international actor. Ties of culture, blood, and identity were enormously powerful. Dissent and occasional disagreement notwithstanding, for Canada to have evinced any other kind of relationship with Great Britain in the decades after 1867 would have been, for most Canadians, unthinkable. Growing "Canadian" (and *Canadien*) forces in the nineteenth century had helped to alter gradually this relationship, leading to Confederation and partial autonomy in 1867 for some of Britain's North American dependencies, but the connections between Empire and colony would remain strong well into the mid-twentieth century, with decisive effects on Canadian activities abroad.

The role of British power in Canadian affairs, and the corresponding vulnerability brought to Canada by virtue of its British connections, were demonstrated during Britain's wars with the young American Republic. British authority attracted American attack during both the Revolutionary War in the 1770s and the War of 1812. Britain's army and navy nevertheless kept American forces at bay in each case, while the British navy swept the seas of French ships during the wars with France, ending with the defeat of Napoleon I in 1815. Britain strongly reinforced its garrisons in Canada during the American Civil War (1861–1865) as a precaution against attack from the national (or Union) government in the North, and maintained troops in Canada until 1870–1871, with naval and military bases at Halifax and Esquimalt for another 30 years thereafter. Canada's contribution to its own defence in this period was small—a tiny Permanent Force after Confederation, and a militia that had little training or equipment. Nonetheless, Canada did contribute to British wars: building the Canadian Pacific Railway that could, Canadians boasted, speed British troops from Europe to Asia; sending the Nile voyageurs to the Sudan in 1884; and dispatching substantial contingents to the South African War after 1899. Still, Canada was a consumer of security, and not a provider of it to Britain, until 1914. The two world wars would alter dramatically this relationship.

Automatically at war whenever London said so, Britain's legal entry into World War I made Canadian territory, ships, and commerce the legitimate target of overseas enemies. It did not determine the nature or extent of Canada's response, which would certainly be large. While much of French Canada, many recent immigrants—especially from European territories governed by empires Canada was about to fight—and rural families whose livelihood might not survive the absence of their men at the front, ranged from lukewarm to bitterly opposed to the implications of imperial unity, these were by far the minority voice. Canadians, like almost everyone else in 1914, raced anxiously to the colours in defence of king and country, led by tens of thousands who had been born in the British Isles. Hard-pressed by German arms in Europe and parts of Africa, and by Ottoman troops in the Middle East, Britain would solicit and receive massive military assistance from most of its principal dependencies and former colonies during the Great War. The effort transformed the Empire. Canada's Prime Minister Borden was among the ex-colonials who saw two truths coinciding: the necessity of a maximum military effort in defence of shared values and what he perceived as joint interests; and the logical consequence that sacrifice on the battlefield would lead to a more mature imperial relationship of mutual obligations and acknowledged autonomies.

The defeat and dismemberment of the German, Austro-Hungarian, and Ottoman empires by 1918, and the implosion of the Russian empire from 1917, marked the war's cataclysmic effect on the international system; Britain avoided a similar calamity, but 1918 found its finances in ruins, its population drained, and its Empire in the first stages of an irrevocable transformation. Canadian indignation at Britain's apparent presumption of its military support during the short-lived Chanak crisis (1922) heralded the shape of things to come: in any serious threat to the Commonwealth, Canada could not fail to come to Britain's aid, but the assumption of an automatic response, especially around the peripheries of imperial interests, was insulting to Ottawa and foolish for London. The national autonomy that Chanak presaged was in many ways confirmed by the Statute of Westminster (1931), which guaranteed to the dominions in law the freedom of manoeuvre their contributions at Gallipoli, the Somme, and Passchendaele had already earned them in practice— the right to decide their own foreign policy and, within the reasonable limits imposed by blood and memory, to pick their own battles. As Canadian security prospects had once depended on the ability of British ministers to spare resources for North American climes, so too did British fortunes now rest more firmly on the domestic squabbles of far-off former colonies and the deliberate nurturing of shared Commonwealth interests.

Canada responded in the interwar period to its dearly bought international profile by withdrawing from the world. Eschewing most forms of military security co-operation, demobilizing its army, and remaining studiously aloof from tawdry British issues, Canada also helped to undermine through indifference the fledgling League of Nations and displayed little save studied disinterest in the crumbling of the international system. It entered World War II after a week of delay during which the pretext of a parliamentary debate served well the domestic political agenda of a prime minister anxious not to repeat the domestic divisions of World War I. Canada entered the war a firm ally of Great Britain and, soon, of the peacetime colossus that was the United States, but it adhered closely at first to a profile that Prime Minister Mackenzie King hoped would keep losses low and contributions minimal. The success of enemy forces, especially in defeating France by the summer of 1940, transformed the alliance and Canada's formerly limited role within it.

With Britain on the verge of defeat in 1940 and 1941, the war forced Canada in its own national interest into an alliance with the United States, and toward a more massive mobilization of troops, weapons, food, and industrial output. Britain's economic, military, and political weakness obliged Canada to look to its own security, something only the US could guarantee after 1940. For its part, the US needed to be sure that Canada would not become a route through or over which an enemy could strike, whether in the Atlantic or the Pacific. These realizations led to the Ogdensburg Agreement of August 1940 and the creation of the Permanent Joint Board on Defence. Canadian forces would operate at war under largely British command (and sometimes, especially at sea, commanding the fleets of other nations), but with little voice—by choice—in the strategic direction of the struggle, save for the deployment and tasking of its own formations. US–Canadian interests would see major efforts in the construction of roads and pipelines along the Pacific Coast into Alaska; extensive co-operation in the North Atlantic; the presence of thousands of American troops in Canada and Newfoundland; and, by war's end, the preparation of a Canadian force, with mostly US equipment, to assist in the war against Japan. Physically, by 1945 Canada's armed forces had started to take on the look and feel of those of the United States; diplomatically, it was soon clear, after the Herculean efforts of Russia and the United States

in defeating the Axis Powers, where precisely postwar international power would reside.

The enduring finality of the wartime transformation of Canada's principal alliance from Great Britain to the United States is more evident in retrospect than it was at the time. That was partly due to the enormous sympathy for Britain's heroic wartime role and the charisma of Winston Churchill, who Canadians largely (and correctly) believed had saved the world. Well into the 1950s, Conservative leaders especially would lament the continental fixation they saw in Ottawa's postwar diplomacy and what they considered the unfortunate neglect of a European, principally British, heritage. Suez in 1956 was considered in some quarters the devious abandonment of Canada's historic partners, Britain and France, and not the shining moment of international good citizenship it has since more commonly become.

Of postwar enemies, however, there was far less doubt. The defection in September 1945 of a cipher clerk at the Soviet embassy in Ottawa was one of several incidents nudging postwar Canada toward the unprecedented assumption of peacetime alliance obligations. Embraced in the late 1940s by a new, internationalist prime minister and a cadre of brilliant, influential foreign service officers, a more active Canadian role, in part in response to Soviet antagonism, led to its becoming a charter member of the North Atlantic Treaty Organization (NATO) in 1949 and to a steadily deepening relationship with the United States to defend North America. Ogdensburg in 1940 marked the start of a continental alliance that resulted, in 1957–1958, in the creation of the North American Air Defence Command, linking the two nations' air forces and early warning systems against any continental attack. In Europe, Canadian troops returned in the early 1950s as part of NATO's forward defences against the Red Army, serving first under British command in northern Germany and, somewhat later after a highly symbolic reassignment, under American command farther south. Canadians who had hoped that NATO membership might be a counterweight to the bilateral relationship with Washington would be continually disappointed. NATO, its democratic decision-making structure notwith-standing, was Washington's security guarantee to a weak assembly of European powers ravaged by war and diminished by self-doubt. It was also Washington's primary tool in opposing Soviet adventurism. Even Europe's postwar recovery and later pseudo-unification could not outweigh the predominant fact of the alliance: it was a weapon for the exercise of American interests and the projection of its power into central Europe. It was not a multilateral talk-shop in which Canadian diplomats could dodge American supremacy while courting Europe's favour. It still isn't. In Brussels as in Ottawa, the United States remained the West's only superpower.

If the growing pre-eminence of the United States in Canadian alliance politics was one of two primary developments in the postwar years, Canada's commitment to international security through co-operative multilateralism was the other. A congenial joiner of diplomatic initiatives great and small, and leader of a few, Canada, as a member of the United Nations, soon found itself supporting collective security from Kashmir to the Congo, and from Korea to the Golan Heights. Goodwill missions and short-term peace-keeping deployments were not alliances to any substantial degree, but Canada's involvement with United Nations mandates made the blue beret, and later the blue helmet, so synonymous with Canadian diplomacy that it might have appeared as though Canada's major security partner was the UN, and its only international purpose peacekeeping. This was so patently untrue as to be ridiculous—even the rationale for most peacekeeping missions lodged firmly in the grim logic of Cold War crisis management—but Canada's only real alliance, NATO, was far away and little witnessed, while its only real defence partnership, NORAD, operated quietly from secret mountain fortresses and icy northern listening posts. After the Cuban Missile Crisis of 1962, NORAD's political implications—a near-unified warning and mobilization system that could bring the world to nuclear war with little involvement by Canada's own political leaders—were almost as difficult to contemplate as its possible failure in the event of another real crisis. The Canada–US partnership served

American interests by keeping its hemispheric defence policies beyond the realm of formal scrutiny by European allies and Canada's by leveraging its more limited power in a joint organization where it could exercise influence well beyond its weight. The UN served multiple interests too: at Suez (1956), Canadian action helped to prevent a split between the US and the Anglo-French invaders of Egypt and a potentially catastrophic rupture in the Western alliance at a critical juncture in the Cold War; in Cyprus (1964), Canadian troops helped to avert a war between Greece and Turkey, both members of NATO, that could have destroyed the alliance outright.

But it was, and remains, the American alliance that drove policy, even on occasions when political leaders disagreed. During the first Gulf War, Canada participated in large part because of the need to preserve US goodwill; its non-involvement in the Vietnam War was made easier by Canada's fortuitous presence on the International Control Commission set up in Indochina in 1954. During the second Gulf War, Canada avoided participation, choosing instead to deploy troops to Afghanistan, but that commitment, as frequently happens to junior alliance members, grew into a major, long-term affair. Afghanistan and the earlier preventive deployments of forces after the 9/11 terrorist attacks on the United States had been occasioned by NATO's invocation of the collective defence protocols contained in Article V of the North Atlantic Treaty. The first time in NATO's history that the alliance had responded in this way, by invoking its founding charter, the subsequent war in Afghanistan also enjoyed UN support as well as, at first, endorsement from most elements of Canadian and international civil society. At no previous time in Canada's history of alliance politics had the full spectrum of Canadian security obligations—to NATO, to NORAD, and to the international community as represented by the UN—so precisely or so dramatically converged. See also: Canada–United Kingdom Defence Relations; Canada–United States Defence Relations; North Atlantic Treaty Organization; Peacekeeping.

Reading: C.P. Stacey, *Canada and the Age of Conflict*, 2 vols. (Toronto, 1977, 1981); David G. Haglund,

The North Atlantic Triangle Revisited: Canadian Grand Strategy at Century's End (Toronto, 2000).

Amherst, Jeffrey, 1st Baron Amherst (1717–1797). One of Britain's most successful eighteenth-century generals, Amherst commanded the armies that finally conquered New France during the Seven Years' War (1756–1763). He entered the army at a young age and served in a cavalry regiment in Ireland before seeing active service on the continent during the War of the Austrian Succession in a series of staff capacities. He was a protegé of Major-General Sir John Ligonier, one of Britain's most capable soldiers, and later an aide-de-camp to the notoriously ineffective Prince William, Duke of Cumberland. He served in Britain and in Germany again during the early phases of the Seven Years' War in a senior administrative capacity with Hessian troops. When Ligonier replaced Cumberland as commander-in-chief in 1757, he gave the still untested Amherst command of a large expedition against the French fortress of Louisbourg on Île Royale (Cape Breton Island). Amherst sailed from England in May 1758 and met his fleet and army (which had already sailed from Halifax) in early June just off Louisbourg. After a dangerous landing to the west of the fortress on a well-defended shore, Amherst conducted a deliberate, European-style siege, aided by the close co-operation of Admiral Edward Boscawen, commanding the British fleet. The French surrendered on 27 July, in the face of overwhelming force and the murderous fire of British gun batteries that had gradually encircled

⌃ Painted in 1761 to please the British public, *The Charity of General Amherst* showed the conqueror of New France feeding the inhabitants of Montreal and commemorates an event that never happened.

their positions. The terms included the capitulation of French troops on Île Saint-Jean (Prince Edward Island), several hundred kilometres away.

Amherst garrisoned Louisbourg and then dispersed his forces, sending some against French settlements in the Saint John River valley and others to Île Saint-Jean, while he took five battalions to aid the commander-in-chief of British forces in North America, James Abercromby, who had been defeated by Montcalm at Fort Carillon (Ticonderoga, NY). Amherst later returned to Halifax where he learned in early November that Abercromby's defeat and subsequent inaction had led to his dismissal and recall to England and to his own promotion as Abercromby's replacement. He then went to New York to begin preparing for the following year's campaign.

The 1759 campaign saw three forces moving against French Canada. James Wolfe, who had served under Amherst at Louisbourg, received command of the forces directed against Quebec, while Amherst led a large force up Lake Champlain toward Montreal. A third force headed west to take Fort Niagara and establish a presence on Lake Ontario. Amherst proceeded with great caution against a vastly inferior—but skilfully retreating—French force, insisting on the construction of a small naval fleet on the lake and the construction of complex defences at Crown Point, New York, before moving too far north. By the time his preparations were nearly completed, word had arrived of the success of Wolfe at Quebec a month earlier and, fearing a large French concentration at Montreal in front of him, he deferred a further advance until the following year.

The campaign of 1760 ended the French presence in Canada. Advancing again in three columns from Quebec, Lake Champlain, and Lake Ontario—the latter under Amherst himself—the British force that arrived outside Montreal outnumbered its French defenders by approximately eight to one. The city surrendered on 8 September. Amherst denied the garrison the honours of war, and the French burned their colours rather than see them captured. Amherst sent troops on several Caribbean expeditions before the war's end, and in 1762 commanded William

Amherst, his younger brother, to recover St John's, Newfoundland, captured in a recent French raid. The quick campaign, ending in a sharp battle on the heights overlooking the town, proved the last battle of the Seven Years' War in North America. He left the continent for England in November 1763, never to return. Called by historian C.P. Stacey "the organizer of victory," Amherst had, aside from several sieges, never fought a battle. SEE ALSO: CONQUEST, THE; SEVEN YEARS' WAR.

READING: W.M. Fowler, Jr, *Empires: The Seven Years' War and the Struggle for North America, 1754–1763* (Vancouver, 2005).

Amiens, Battle of (1918). Allied forces won a major victory at Amiens, France, from 8 to 11 August 1918 at the outset of a combined arms offensive that would end World War I. The surprise attack was spearheaded by Canadian and Australian troops after several weeks of planning and counter-intelligence operations. German General Erich Ludendorff later called the opening day, which drove back German forces across a broad front, "the black day of the German army." Canadian forces suffered several thousand casualties, more than 4,000 on the first day alone, but achieved one of the war's most complete victories. Their 13-kilometre advance on 8 August was one of the longest single-day Allied advances of the war. Amiens proved to be the beginning of the "Hundred Days," a series of near-continuous battles in which Allied forces, including the Canadian Corps, repeatedly defeated the German armies along the Western Front, setting the stage for the armistice of 11 November 1918.

Anglo-Japanese Alliance. Motivated by mutual fear of Russian expansion, Britain and Japan signed a treaty of alliance in 1902 that bound each to come to the aid of the other in the event of war with another state. Renewed twice in subsequent years, the treaty's immediate effect was to help neutralize France during Japan's ensuing war with Russia in 1904, as coming to Russia's aid would have meant war with Britain. Japan honoured its treaty obligations by going into World

War I in support of Britain, with ships of the Imperial Japanese Navy also serving in the Mediterranean against German submarines, and coming to Esquimalt, British Columbia, on naval patrols of the North Pacific.

The wartime utility of the Japanese alliance from a Canadian perspective was tainted by fear of postwar immigration—the so-called yellow peril—and by concerns that Japanese competition with the United States might lead to a conflict in which British imperial forces would be compelled to fight alongside the Japanese against America. Few Canadians were sanguine at the prospects of successfully defending Canada against American invasion in the event of war. Prime Minister Arthur Meighen raised this concern forcefully at the Imperial Conference of 1921, where it connected with Whitehall's own emerging views. Despite complaints from Australia and New Zealand, Britain concluded that American friendship mattered more than Japan's. The alliance effectively ended in 1921 with the signing of a four-power treaty that sought to improve security relations in the Pacific by establishing naval limits for the United States, Great Britain, Japan, and France. It formally lapsed in 1923. SEE ALSO: CANADA–UNITED KINGDOM DEFENCE RELATIONS; CANADA–UNITED STATES DEFENCE RELATIONS.

Annapolis Royal (Port Royal). Located on Nova Scotia's Annapolis River, this town, founded by French settlers in 1606, changed hands several times during the French–English conflicts of the seventeenth and eighteenth centuries and was destroyed completely in 1613 by Samuel Argall, an English sea captain. A French fort, constructed here from 1687 and greatly expanded in the early 1700s, defeated two invasions from New England before falling for good to British forces in 1710 during the War of the Spanish Succession. The town was Nova Scotia's capital for several decades, until the founding of Halifax in 1749. It was garrisoned continuously by British troops until 1854. It was from here that British authorities coordinated the brutal deportation of French Acadians in the 1750s. The restored Fort Anne became Canada's first National Historic Park in 1917.

Anse au Foulon (Wolfe's Cove). British forces landed at this cove, just up the St Lawrence River from Quebec, on the early morning of 13 September 1759 during the Seven Years' War. After a force of light infantry had climbed the steep cliff and overpowered a much smaller French detachment, the army of Major-General James Wolfe landed and marched up a path from Anse au Foulon to the Plains of Abraham above. British victory in the ensuing battle led to the capture of Quebec.

Argentia Conference (1941). Held four months before the United States had entered World War II, this first and secret meeting between British Prime Minister Winston Churchill and US President Franklin Delano Roosevelt took place on British and American warships anchored off Argentia, Newfoundland, from 9 to 12 August 1941. The discussions led to what would soon be called the Atlantic Charter, a broad statement of war aims and preferences for a postwar political and economic settlement, as well as steps toward the coordination of American and Allied war production and strategy. Canada was neither invited nor informed in advance of the conference, a source of substantial frustration to Prime Minister Mackenzie King, not least because the meeting took place in Newfoundland, which he considered a Canadian sphere of interest, even though it was not yet part of Canada. The Atlantic Charter is often considered a critical first step toward the creation of the postwar United Nations.

Armistice. The armistice that ended World War I came into effect at 11:00 a.m. on 11 November 1918, the eleventh hour of the eleventh day of the eleventh month. In the final hours of the war, units of the Canadian Corps had entered Mons, a symbolic accomplishment as the British Expeditionary Force had retreated from there four years previously. The armistice, celebrated in all of the victor nations, was followed by the protracted negotiations leading to the Versailles Treaty in 1919. The anniversary of the war's end on 11 November is now known as Remembrance Day in

▲ Philip John Bainbridge's watercolour, painted in 1838, shows Anse au Foulon (or Wolfe's Cove), where the British climbed to the Plains of Abraham in September 1759.

Canada, where it is commemorated in national, provincial, and local ceremonies.

Aroostook War. In 1839, a long-simmering dispute along the poorly defined border between Maine and New Brunswick led to the mobilization of militia forces on both sides and threatened wider hostilities between Britain and the United States. At stake for British interests were lucrative timber rights, the largely French-speaking communities in the Madawaska area, and the vital year-round transportation route along the Halifax Road from New Brunswick to Quebec. The escalating crisis, involving border transgressions, arrests, and the militarization of the Aroostook region with troops, forts, and armed outposts, soon led to the deployment of regular troops from both sides. Maine created its own county to administer the area, but Washington and London, neither side wanting war, referred the dispute as part

of a broader package of border irritants to international arbitration. In the Ashburton–Webster Treaty of 1842, New Brunswick received some 13,000 square kilometres of the disputed area (or about 40 percent of its claim). The border was surveyed, mapped, and marked by 1847, the agreement dividing permanently many of the region's original settlers.

Arras, Battle of (1917). The World War I battle of Arras, France lasted from 9 April to 16 May 1917 and included, at its outset, the spectacular Canadian capture of Vimy Ridge, an important height of land overlooking the Douai Plain. British troops attacked north and south of the city to draw German attention from an impending French offensive farther south and to occupy higher ground prior to breaking through the German lines into more open territory farther east. The opening days of the attack, which had been preceded by extensive mining operations, led to impressive gains, especially at

▲ Crowds in all Allied nations, including these revellers in London, England, celebrated the end of World War I on 11 November 1918.

Vimy and along the Scarpe River, but the offensive failed to break through in any sector and soon bogged down amid heavy casualties and German counterattacks. The French offensive to the south also failed, leading subsequently to mass disobedience and outright mutiny in many French regiments. See also: Vimy Ridge.

Arrow, Avro, CF-105. The A.V. Roe Company (Avro), established in Toronto in 1945, began work on civilian and military jet aircraft, its expansion closely tied to Canadian rearmament after 1950. The company developed the CF-100 (Canuck) fighter, and in 1953, after the chief of the air staff proposed the development of a supersonic all-weather interceptor, the Cabinet agreed that Avro should produce two prototypes by

December 1953. The engines, armaments, and electronic systems were to be secured elsewhere, only the airframe to be designed and developed in Canada. In 1954, the government asked for 11 prototypes and placed a pre-production order for 29 aircraft at a cost of $190 million. No suitable engine could be found, however, and the government agreed that the Iroquois engine could be designed in Canada. Although costs continued to escalate, the Royal Canadian Air Force argued that no existing twin-engine aircraft could perform the task of intercepting Soviet bombers in the Far North. The Liberal government of Louis St Laurent, alarmed by the cost of the project, nonetheless decided in December 1955 to limit the Arrow's development until a proven design had emerged.

Only 11 aircraft were to be produced, with costs limited to $170 million over the next three years.

The Arrow was to have been armed with the American Sparrow missile, but the United States Navy cancelled its production, and no Canadian decision was made regarding its replacement for the Arrow. Ottawa then reduced the prototype production to eight aircraft. When the government of Progressive Conservative Prime Minister John Diefenbaker took power in June 1957, it discovered an expensive project (more than $300 million expended to that time) with a growing web of unresolved problems. In October, the Chiefs of Staff Committee recommended the purchase of 29 more aircraft and development of the Sparrow missile, and the Cabinet agreed. The first Arrow, a beautiful-looking machine, flew on 25 March 1958, just as estimates of the project completion costs reached $874 million. The cost for each aircraft was now stratospherically high, and efforts to increase the production run—thereby lowering unit production costs—by selling the Arrow abroad foundered. No other country, and especially not the United States to which large sales had been hoped, would buy the obviously excellent but expensive and untested interceptor. The Chiefs of Staff Committee recommended scrapping the project in the summer of 1958, the senior officers fearing that the ever-rising costs of the Arrow would absorb so much of the defence budget that other projects for all three armed services would need to be scrapped. The Cabinet hesitated, knowing that job losses in Toronto especially would be severe if the production lines shut down.

Finally, on 17 February 1959, the Cabinet agreed to cancel the Arrow, which had been intended as a

Canadians considered the CF-105 Avro Arrow a triumph of Canadian design and engineering. But the interceptor was expensive, no other nation would buy it, and the Diefenbaker government scrapped it.

nuclear-armed interceptor. Canada would instead secure Bomarc surface-to-air missiles from the United States to carry its nuclear warheads. The public announcement on 20 February led A.V. Roe's management, in a bloody-minded fit of rage, to fire 14,000 workers that same day. The media and Diefenbaker's political opponents at once accused the government of selling Canada short by scrapping a world-leading aircraft, a claim still passionately made half a century later by defence commentators, air enthusiasts, and aging engineers. In fact, the government had had little choice—once no foreign sales could be made, the Arrow was doomed, its development and production costs simply too expensive for a small power to sustain.

The CF-105 undoubtedly was a fine interceptor with flying characteristics equal to or better than those of the best aircraft of its day. But it had two engines and required a crew of two, both drawbacks, and the requirement that Canada design and produce the airframes, engines, and weapons systems was simply too much for Canada's talented but limited postwar defence infrastructure to handle efficiently. Almost immediately after its cancellation, myths began to circulate. The Americans had done the deed, some claimed, fearful that the Arrow was better than their own aircraft industry's products and that, as a result, they had blocked foreign sales. In fact, comparable aircraft were under development in the United States, their cost about one-tenth that of the Arrow; moreover, the US government had seriously considered offering to pay for some squadrons of Arrows for the RCAF to help out the Canadians. The myths persisted, as myths so stubbornly do, their sketchy evidence raised to "fact" in plays and television films, and in a series of conspiracy thesis books, lent credence by the proud but mostly unsubstantiated claims of former pilots, workers, and amateur sleuths. The reality was that the Arrow cost too much to be a front-line fighter in the early Cold War, but just enough to be an iconic touchstone of counter-factual history. SEE ALSO: DIEFENBAKER; MILITARY AIRCRAFT; NUCLEAR WEAPONS.

READING: Greig Stewart, *Shutting Down the National Dream* (Toronto, 1988).

Artificial Moonlight. During operations in Normandy in July and August 1944, Lieutenant-General Guy Simonds, commanding II Canadian Corps, created artificial light for troops attacking at night by bouncing searchlight beams off low cloud cover. The concept was familiar to anti-aircraft gunners, who had used searchlights to create artificially bright conditions since World War I, but was a novelty as applied to land warfare. The technique proved of debatable value, helping to guide troops to their destinations but also leading occasionally to disorientation among soldiers unprepared for its use and, worse, illuminating friendly troops for the enemy. It was later used several times in Allied attacks in both northwest Europe and in Italy, notably at the Gothic Line. German prisoners claimed the tactic was of marginal value save as a nuisance weapon.

ASDIC. Supposedly an acronym for the Allied Submarine Detection Investigation Committee, but apparently a name created as part of a cover story put out by the British Admiralty in 1939, ASDIC was a British sound-ranging device used in anti-submarine warfare. Building on World War I and interwar experimentation, ASDIC—or Sonar (an acronym for Sound Navigation and Ranging), as it came to be known in the United States—let warships track and attack enemy submarines with some success. Allied vessels equipped with one of the half-dozen types of ASDIC sets used during the war sank 246 German submarines (U-boats). Canadian companies produced 2,600 ASDIC sets for the Royal Canadian Navy and other fleets.

Atlantic, Battle of the. Great Britain depended on seaborne commerce for its survival, receiving two-thirds of its food, 30 percent of its iron ore, 90 percent of its copper and bauxite, 95 percent of its oil, all of its rubber, and 80 percent of its soft timber from abroad. If the supply lines were cut, Britain would be forced to surrender. German knowledge of this potentially fatal vulnerability, based in part on the submarine campaign against the British Isles during World War I, had informed its interwar naval planning and the deployment of naval resources at the

▲ ASDIC, or Sonar, painted here on the corvette HMCS *Drumheller,* enabled surface ships to track underwater U-boats.

outset of war in 1939. The Battle of the Atlantic was thus a decisive struggle, one mainly of German submarines (U-boats) against Allied supply convoys and their escorting warships.

In World War I, the German U-boats had come close to cutting the sea links between North America and Britain, and only the institution of the convoy system later in the war and the development of better anti-submarine warfare techniques and tactics had allowed Allied naval forces, led by the Royal Navy, to prevail. When the first convoy of World War II left Halifax for Britain on 16 September 1939, the German naval campaign had already claimed its first casualty, the passenger liner SS *Athenia*, sunk on 3 September just west of Ireland. The *Athenia*'s sinking shocked public opinion in all Allied countries and was the harbinger of much worse yet to come, but Allied prospects in the

coming struggle were improved by factors not yet appreciated by either the confident Germans or the soon-to-be hard-pressed Allies. Despite the lessons of the earlier war, interwar German planning, in part as a result of Hitler's infatuation with major surface ships, had diverted considerable resources away from cost-effective submarines and into expensive cruisers and battleships that would, presumably, raid Britain's coastal waters and challenge the Royal Navy with their speed, destructiveness, and inherent flexibility. The German navy, fortunately for the Allies, had fewer than 60 operational submarines on the outbreak of war, only 14 of which were at sea at any one time. For its part, the Royal Navy started the war with ASDIC, a sound-ranging system that let it track submarines, a large but unpre-pared fleet, and the support of smaller Commonwealth navies, including Canada's.

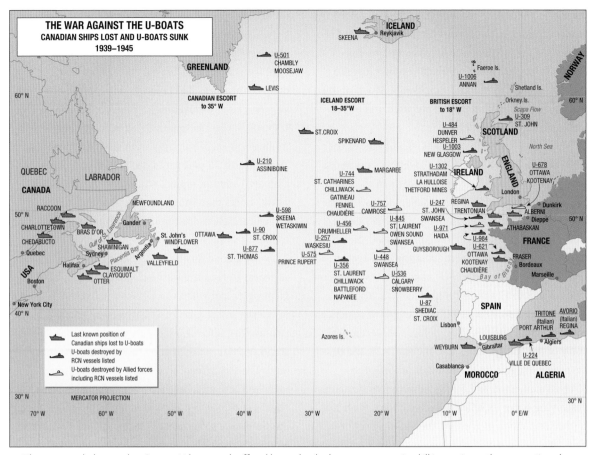

ICELAND
Reykjavik

SKEENA

GREENLAND

NORWAY

U-501
CHAMBLY
MOOSEJAW

Faeroe Is.

U-1006
ANNAN

Shetland Is.

LEVIS

CANADIAN ESCORT
to 35° W

ICELAND ESCORT
18–35°W

BRITISH ESCORT
to 18° W

Orkney Is.
Scapa Flow
U-309
ST. JOHN

SCOTLAND

60° N

ST.CROIX

SPIKENARD

U-484
DUNVER
HESPELER
U-1003
NEW GLASGOW

North Sea

QUEBEC

LABRADOR

CANADA

NEWFOUNDLAND

U-210
ASSINIBOINE

U-744
ST. CATHARINES
CHILLIWACK
GATINEAU
FENNEL
CHAUDIÈRE

MARGAREE

U-1302
STRATHADAM
LA HULLOISE
THETFORD MINES

IRELAND

ENGLAND

U-678
OTTAWA
KOOTENAY

London

RACCOON

50° N

CHARLOTTETOWN

CHEDABUCTO

Quebec

BRAS D'OR

SHAWINIGAN

Sydney

Halifax

ESQUIMALT

CLAYOQUOT

OTTER

Gander

St. John's

OTTAWA
WINDFLOWER

VALLEYFIELD

Gulf of St. Lawrence

Placentia Bay

Argentia

U-90
ST. CROIX

U-877
ST. THOMAS

U-598
SKEENA
WETASKIWIN

U-456
DRUMHELLER
U-257
WASKESIU

U-575
PRINCE RUPERT

U-757
CAMROSE

U-356
ST. LAURENT
CHILLIWACK
BATTLEFORD
NAPANEE

U-845
ST. LAURENT
OWEN SOUND
SWANSEA

U-448
SWANSEA

GUYSBOROUGH

U-247
ST. JOHN
SWANSEA

U-971
HAIDA

U-536
CALGARY
SNOWBERRY

REGINA
TRENTONIAN

U-984

U-621
OTTAWA
KOOTENAY
CHAUDIÈRE

Dunkirk

ALBERNI
Dieppe

ATHABASKAN

FRANCE

FRASER
Bordeaux

Marseille

Bay of Biscay

50° N

USA

Boston

New York City

40° N

Azores Is.

U-87
SHEDIAC
ST. CROIX

Lisbon

SPAIN

WEYBURN

Casablanca

LOUISBURG

Gibraltar

MOROCCO

TRITONE
(Italian)
PORT ARTHUR

AVORIO
(Italian)
REGINA

Algiers

U-224
VILLE DE QUEBEC

ALGERIA

Last known position of
Canadian ships lost to U-boats

U-boats destroyed by
RCN vessels listed

U-boats destroyed by Allied forces
including RCN vessels listed

30° N

MERCATOR PROJECTION

70° W   60° W   50° W   40° W   30° W   20° W   10° W   0° E/W

30° N

▲ The RCN struggled to combat German U-boats, and suffered losses, but had many successes, its skill improving as the war continued.

German U-boat losses outpaced new construction well into 1940. Nonetheless, the *Kriegsmarine* (navy) high command, its submarine fleet led by Admiral Karl Doenitz, took advantage of the fall of France to move its U-boat bases onto the Bay of Biscay on the Atlantic coast. With easier access to the Atlantic, longer cruising times, and freedom from the constant British aerial threat over the North Sea, in the last half of 1940, German submarines destroyed 1.5 million tonnes of Allied shipping. The Germans also began to develop and perfect "wolf pack" tactics in which the first submarine to sight a convoy contacted others nearby, and all launched coordinated torpedo attacks. (U-boats carried up to 21 torpedoes and had a powerful deck gun, used to finish off crippled merchant vessels.) In addition to being a clash of ships, sailors, and weapons, the Battle of the Atlantic

was thus also one of naval construction as each side raced to build vessels in greater number and better quality.

Success in the naval war also depended greatly on math and science. From June 1940 until May 1941, when British cryptanalysts at Bletchley Park in England, building upon earlier breakthroughs by Polish intelligence experts, first partially cracked the enemy's naval codes and began to provide what was called "Ultra intelligence," most of the early advantages lay with the Germans, who had also enjoyed some success in reading British wireless messages regarding convoy departures. The rate of Allied ship losses at first outpaced the new construction of merchant ships, with some convoys suffering truly horrific losses as the Royal Navy, its primary immediate task being the defence of the British Isles against invasion, could spare relatively small resources for the North Atlantic. In the convoy battles after the fall of France, Allied forces would lose heavily, forcing Britain to create a more permanent escort force to protect the vital transatlantic crossings. Much of this work would soon fall to the unprepared and as yet under-armed Canadians.

The Royal Canadian Navy (RCN), with fewer than 2,000 regulars in 1939, had no corvettes operational until early 1941 and little capacity early in the war to produce the number of trained sailors that would be needed by the rapidly expanding fleet. The RCN's Commodore Leonard Murray commanded the Newfoundland Escort Force (later the Mid-Ocean Escort Force) from May 1941, a force that would grow by mid-year to 12 full escort groups of nearly 40 warships, and even more with the arrival of American warships from late 1941, just before the December entry of the United States into the war. It would be a desperate struggle. In the first half of 1941, the U-boats sank another 1.5 million tonnes of shipping, destroying some 13 Allied ships for each U-boat lost. In the second half of the year, the losses were cut in half, although convoys continued to suffer heavily. In September 1941, one slow convoy, numbered SC42, lost 15 ships, and another was severely damaged, or one quarter of the merchant vessels that had set sail. At least 203 merchant sailors died in the explosion of their ships or by drowning, and the 70,000 tonnes of supplies lost included 21,600 tonnes of grain, 9,800 tonnes of chemicals, 9,300 tonnes of fuel oil, and more than 10,000 tonnes of lumber. This, a Royal Navy officer said, was "an appalling tale of disaster;" and it was not the only one.

Moreover, German U-boat construction was now hitting high gear and, in January 1942, there were 91 operational boats. Six months later, Doenitz had 331 U-boats, of which 141 were operational. The 50 on patrol at any one time represented a four-fold increase from the start of the war. America's entry into the war against Hitler in December 1941, after months of stretching both international credulity and international law by operating with Allied forces in an undeclared naval war against the U-boats, did not

immediately improve the Allies' prospects. German U-boats moved in close to the eastern seaboard where naval traffic was brilliantly silhouetted against the light from American coastal cities, which civil defence measures had failed to dim, and where most vessels were not travelling in protected convoys. The U-boats in this "killing time" sank more than 3 million tonnes of shipping in the first six months of 1942, almost 70 percent of it off the East Coast where convoys were not organized until the end of April. The U-boats then moved their operations to the Caribbean where they sank an additional 840,000 tonnes of shipping.

Some Canadians had been smug about American slowness in reacting to the U-boat menace, but gloating ended when the U-boats in May 1942 began operating in the Gulf of St Lawrence. Over the next two-and-a-half years, U-boats would sink 23 Allied ships, including the Sydney to Port-aux-Basques ferry, the ss *Caribou*, in October 1942, killing 375 men, women, and children. The ship losses were relatively minor, but the panic produced was not, and the Canadian government closed the St Lawrence to all transatlantic shipping on 9 September 1942, limiting coastal convoys to essential traffic. This increased the country's already overburdened rail traffic, strained resources at Halifax, and amounted to a German naval victory on Canada's doorstep. Most of the submarine attacks took place in 1942 and 1944, the last one in November 1944, when HMCS *Shawinigan* was torpedoed. The U-boats, despite patrols by the RCN and RCAF, suffered no losses in the Gulf of St Lawrence.

The climax of the Battle of the Atlantic came in the first months of 1943. Doenitz's *Kriegsmarine* now had at least a hundred U-boats at sea, and the Royal Canadian Navy, its ill-equipped escort vessels strained beyond endurance and its training not yet up to the mark, had to be largely pulled out of the struggle for retraining and re-equipping. The Admiralty had become so concerned about the performance of the four Canadian mid-ocean groups in convoy battles during the fall of 1942 that it asked the Canadian government to allow the

⌃ Merchant sailors were unsung heroes in the Battle of the Atlantic. These survivors of a U-boat sinking reached St John's on 15 September 1942, aboard the corvette HMCS *Arvida*.

groups to be redeployed to the eastern Atlantic on the routes between Britain and the Mediterranean. This brought the RCN ships under direct Royal Navy control at British bases so they could get better equipment and refresher training from experienced British crews. As a result, all but one of the Canadian groups were absent from mid-ocean convoys for much of the period from February to late April 1943. The RCN, however, did well against the U-boats on the UK–Gibraltar run and in providing escorts for the Allied invasion of North Africa in November 1942.

And there was still a 500-kilometre gap in the air coverage in the North Atlantic off Greenland, the so-called Black Pit. The Royal Canadian Air Force's

Eastern Air Command made heroic efforts to fill it with its operations from Newfoundland, but long-range aircraft, most deployed for strategic bombing raids against Germany, were in short supply. The RCAF wanted an aircraft with a minimum cruising speed of 150 knots, at least 20 hours' endurance, and a depth charge load of at least 1.5 tonnes. RCAF efforts to persuade the Anglo-American political and military leadership to divert such aircraft to the essential task of convoy protection were inexplicably and repeatedly ignored, until success was finally achieved in November 1942 in London and at the Atlantic Convoy Conference in Washington in March 1943. Even then, it took time to supply and train RCAF

The Battle of the Atlantic was horrific for merchant navy crews. The SS *Eurymedon*, torpedoed in September 1940, lost 29 dead. Here, some of its survivors come alongside the destroyer HMCS *Ottawa*, which would itself be sunk two years later. The convoy in which *Eurymedon* had been travelling lost six ships.

squadrons with Liberator B-24 aircraft. In February 1943, the U-boats, which could crash-dive in 30 seconds if they spotted an aircraft, sank 63 ships; in March, they destroyed 108.

At the Atlantic Convoy Conference, the RN, RCN, and USN altered their command structures. The RCN's Murray, now a rear-admiral, took over the Canadian North-west Atlantic Command, head-quartered in St John's, Newfoundland, with respon-sibility for convoy protection from 47° west and south to 29° north, or from north of New York City and west of the 47th meridian. Admiral Murray now had control of Royal Canadian Navy, Royal Navy, and United States Navy assets; he also at last controlled the resources of the RCAF's Eastern Air Command.

This unified Allied command was a vote of confidence in the Canadian navy and a sign that the tide had begun to turn. Access to the German naval codes, finally cracked completely by March 1943, was a very real advantage for the Allied navies. So too was the huge American (and the lesser but significant Canadian) construction program for merchant ships that, by November 1942, had begun to outpace the rate of ship losses inflicted by the U-boats; in 1943 alone, the US built 20 million tonnes of shipping. Canada built 410 merchant ships during the war. Other Allied advantages included the development of better sonar (as the Americans called ASDIC); the introduction of short-wave radar that could find the low profile of U-boats on the surface; new weapons such as Hedgehog, an array of depth charges that could be launched ahead of an escort ship; the gradual provision of more escorts as Canadian construction programs provided corvettes and frigates; the closing at last of the air gap with very long-range Liberator bombers; and the introduction of aircraft carriers on escort duties. The Allies also increased the size of convoys, permitting an increase in the number of escorts from six to nine. In May 1943, Allied warships sank 41 U-boats, and the enemy losses remained high despite the Germans' perfection of "wolf pack" tactics. The German losses could not be sustained for long, notwithstanding their extraordinary construction rate and their introduction of longer-range and snorkel-equipped U-boats.

By the beginning of 1944, the Germans had been all but forced to abandon their North Atlantic anti-convoy operations because of Allied predomin-ance. Only 26 U-boats entered or patrolled in Canadian North-west Atlantic Command's area of responsibility in 1944 and 1945, and Ultra intelligence helped locate them and suppress their activities. The RCN, RN, and the RCAF now bore almost the entire responsibility for the escort of convoys, a role continued until the end of the war. The loss of merchant tonnage was, as the RCN official history notes, "too little to have any strategic impact," but the destruction of five RCN escort ships in the last stages of the war was "grievous and embarrassing."

The Battle of the Atlantic, fought between small escort ships and the U-boats, with the merchant vessels and Britain's transatlantic lifeline as the prize, was a decisive Allied victory. More than 25,000 merchant ships went safely across the North Atlantic in escorted convoys, and the Allies sank 788 U-boats with some 32,000 crew while the Germans destroyed 2,232 ships of 11.9 million tonnes, killing 40,000 sailors. Some 2,000 Canadians in the merchant marine died at sea. Incredibly, the *Kriegsmarine* had 463 U-boats in service at the German surrender in May 1945, many now equipped with the snorkel under-water breathing system that had first been used at the end of 1943.

The Royal Canadian Navy's share in the battle had been important. Despite all its teething troubles, the RCN had accounted for 47 U-boats and provided half the escorts for the Mid-Ocean and Western Local Escort Forces. Canadian North-west Atlantic Command was the sole theatre of war commanded by a Canadian, and the Royal Canadian Air Force provided almost all the air coverage from the Maritimes and Newfoundland. SEE ALSO: CANADIAN NORTH-WEST ATLANTIC COMMAND; CONVOYS; CORVETTES; MURRAY, LEONARD; ROYAL CANADIAN NAVY; ST LAWRENCE.

READING: W.A.B. Douglas (et al.), *No Higher Purpose*, vol. 2, part I, and *A Blue Water Navy*, vol. 2, part II, of *The Official Operational History of the Royal Canadian Navy in the Second World War* (St Catharines, ON, 2002, 2007); W.A.B. Douglas, *The Creation of a National Air Force*, vol. 2 of *The Official History of the Royal Canadian Air Force* (Toronto, 1986); Roger Sarty, *Canada and the Battle of the Atlantic* (Montreal, 1998).

Atlantic Convoy Conference (1943). Representatives of the American, British, and Canadian navies met for 12 days in March 1943 in Washington to discuss the increasing threat posed by German U-boats to Allied success in the Battle of the Atlantic. After discussion on the command, organization, tactics, and equip-ment at their disposal, the Allies agreed that the Royal Canadian Navy, anxious to assert an increasing

national presence in the war at sea, should take charge of convoy protection in the Canadian North-west Atlantic Command area under Rear-Admiral Leonard Murray from 30 April. This would be the sole theatre of war under Canadian command in World War II.

Auger de Subercase, Daniel d' (1661–1732). A French military officer who served with distinction in New France from 1687, Subercase was governor of Plaisance (Placentia), France's small Newfoundland colony on the west side of the Avalon Peninsula, and the governor of Acadia from 1706. In Newfoundland, he mounted a damaging expedition against St John's and British outposts in Conception and Trinity Bays in 1705, capturing several towns and destroying supplies, ships, and cannon, but failing to capture the main fort at St John's. He was made governor of Acadia on the strength of his energetic performance in Placentia, and immediately set about improving the defences of Port Royal, his capital. Subercase defeated two major British attacks in 1707 during the War of the Spanish Succession (1701–1714), but was forced to surrender three years later when besieged by a force several times larger than his own. On his return to France, he faced court martial for losing the colony, but was acquitted and retired from military service.

Autobiography, Military. Few veterans in Canada have committed their memories to paper in any organized fashion. Fewer still have shaped their military experi-ences into epistolary cautions or explanations for the ages in the form of full-length autobiographies—stories of their lives and times, as opposed to snippets, letters, or fractured recollections of specific people, issues, or causes.

Of these latter, there are a great many indeed. Most colonial officers, whether French or British, and nearly all of those in the regular forces of the new Canada were literate, as were many of their troops. Hundreds created and circulated written accounts of their lives and experiences in some form or other; others were produced as letters or diaries or "true tales" by family members, descendants, or historians after the fact. Unpublished letters, diaries, and manuscripts are even more numerous, but these can be of little help to the lay reader to whom, even in an age of digitized records and on-line documents, they often remain physically inaccessible and intellectually disjointed. When lacking the context and explanatory narrative that good autobiography usually provides, unpublished work waits for its discovery and contextualization by the spelunking of full-time historians, whether professional or amateur. Personal experience then speaks to posterity only through the medium of second-hand sages, with the authority of having been interpreted, edited, and nuanced by those who were not.

This weakness in Canadian military literature, and its resulting impact on knowledge and understanding of the military past, is more easily described than it is explained. The relative dearth of military autobiography is a substantial impoverishment to the exploration of leadership and operations, and leaves the personal record of wartime experience with frustrating gaps. Air and naval warfare, home defence, senior command in all periods, the Cold War, Korea, women in war, First Nations, and peacekeeping are among the most notable weaknesses. Memoirs, diaries, and collections of letters exist in abundance for the world wars, and in lesser but still quite substantial numbers for the eighteenth and nineteenth centuries, but rarely in published form, and—among older accounts—almost none remain in print. If the Northwest Rebellion of 1885 were taken as a case in point, key personalities either died before writing their own reflections on life and war (Louis Riel), were illiterate and spoke only through an interpreter (Gabriel Dumont), or left no autobiography at all, save campaign accounts of limited scope, as in the case of Sir Frederick Middleton, who commanded government forces and compiled his later notes from a series of military lectures. Sam Steele's *Forty Years in Canada* is perhaps the best more or less comprehensive account of a soldier's life from this era. Lesser examples abound, but few of lasting historical or literary value. George Denison—author,

militia booster, and member of a prominent and influential Ontario family, as well as autobiographer—speaks of many things, of which one at least is military service.

D. Peter MacLeod's definitive history of the battle of the Plains of Abraham at Quebec in 1759, *Northern Armageddon*, published in 2008, tells a similar tale from the previous century. MacLeod relies heavily on autobiographical material, but not on actual autobiography. Of the scores of primary accounts he ferreted out from a decade or more of intensive primary research, most are unavailable to the casual student or history buff without access to a major archive. The journal of John Knox, for example, a captain in the 43rd Regiment of Foot, on which MacLeod relies extensively, often as his only witness, was published in 1769. Of the nearly five pages of published primary sources listed in his bibliography, few are real autobiographies in the sense of a post-hoc recitation and evaluation of the writer's life and times by the writer him (or her) self. The same is true of most accounts of the War of 1812, the rebellions of 1837–1838, the western campaigns of 1870 and 1885, and the South African War.

Reasonable hypotheses are not difficult to construct. A small Permanent Force and part-time militia produced few professional soldiers or men-of-letters in arms; the absence of major conflicts after 1814 provided little to write about in any case; and the market for military tales in underdeveloped, sparsely populated Canada hardly compared to that of London, Washington, or Paris. Adventure stories and celebratory biography were produced often and sold well, but to whom would Canadian military autobiography have appealed in the nineteenth century, when curious readers could have followed the lives of Napoleonic-era generals and admirals, the explosion of personal memoirs from the American Civil War, and, increasingly, historically tinged fiction, or the recollections of heroes from India, the Crimea, or the exotic battlefields of the Sudan? British literature was the mark of breeding, culture, and the well-read, not poorly produced Canadian tomes by minor local politicians or part-time farmer-soldiers. Canadian participation in the South African War produced a minor outpouring of breathless (and often self-serving) personal accounts, of which W.E.B. Morrison's, a gunner and future general, is a memorable exception, but it nowhere matched the avalanche of British material.

World War I—longer, fiercer, and immeasurably more costly—was a far cry from any previous Canadian experience. It was Canada's first literary war, one in which official historians, painters, propagandists, and photographers documented the nation's great effort in arms, and from which came torrents of letters, memoirs, and diaries. Whether officially inspired or personally derived, the literature was vast, uneven, and achingly incomplete. In recent years, major secondary works, notably the award-winning volumes of Tim Cook, *At the Sharp End* (2007) and *Shock Troops* (2008), and reprint series like those from Vanwell Books in St Catharines and CEF Books in Ottawa, have revisited or republished the best of these contributions, but of readable, reliable, or essential autobiography there remains remarkably little. Among the rank and file, Will Bird's several volumes stand out for their poignancy, sophistication, and raw emotion, but even Bird's unsurpassed *Ghosts Have Warm Hands* is more memoir than autobiography, leaving—as most such contributions do—the events of war dangling, and sometimes, disconnected from lives lived before and after the conflagrations they recount.

Senior officers from the Great War would write even less than the men they commanded, a welcome trait if one thought the horrors of that conflict fit only for interment with the millions of unfortunate dead, but a grand misfortune for the study of history and for the reputations of those who led Canadians so well for so long. Sir Arthur Currie, Canada's greatest general, left his battles and explanations to biographers who were more or less slow in coming; most of his senior comrades had even less to say. A handful, including E.L.M. Burns, would later write of their time in both world wars, but the commanders who fought Hitler would prove no less tongue-tied than those who bested the Kaiser.

General H.D.G. Crerar would not see even a biography for half a century. Guy Simonds, his principal subordinate and chief competitor, has seen venom, ridicule, and near-hagiography in published surveys of his service, but is waiting still for a modern biographer or editor to explain his brilliance and punctilio to modern officers and the reading public; his incomplete draft memoir remains unpublished. The rank and file were both more productive and more gripping. Volumes by Farley Mowat, George Blackburn, and Charlie Martin rank among the finest military memoirs in any country in any period.

Senior naval and air force officers were, if anything, even more reticent with the pen than army counterparts. World War II produced classic and compulsively readable accounts by Hal Lawrence, Alan Easton, James Lamb, and Murray Peden, but not one by a senior officer of any rank. Postwar work by official historians and Department of National Defence–funded think tanks have for many years been reconstructing personal narratives from scratch, publishing in collective biographies chapter-length accounts of the senior leaders who brought victory in 1945. Almost to a person, to most contemporary Canadians they are, sadly, a vast list of nobodies. Korea did no better, and if any non-military reader of this entry can name more than one autobiography from any armed service produced during the Cold War, it is a mark of rare alchemical brilliance indeed. Jean Victor Allard's essential autobiography is the best of a thin lot, and also one of the few French-speaking authors to have brought his story outside the barracks.

The relative anonymity of the people who fought Canada's wars has little to do with their character and much to do with the social milieu from which citizen-armies sprang, and then fast returned. No serious military history was taught in Canada until well into the late twentieth century, no publishing houses aspired to disseminate it, and little funding was available for its study. Biography was widely dismissed in the academy as the study of dead white males; autobiography, as the self-serving inventions of the risible old characters themselves. A lingering anti-intellectual malaise permeated Canada's small peacetime military, a quaint but acidic holdover from a century of militia fantasies, anti-professional bias, and actuarial prudence. There was no easy place for the thinking officer or the sharp-penned sailor, and few outlets for their works. Historian George Stanley was more right than wrong in calling Canadians an unmilitary people, at least as judged by its literary reflections on war, peace, and security and the recollections of those central to a military past. In the end, people as individuals decided, en masse, not to write, publish, or espouse, but the idea of "military autobiography" as a lucrative or necessary field would have been as mildly foolish a proposition to most Canadian warriors in ages past as it might be to Toronto publishers in more recent days.

The miasma of post–Cold War conflicts into which Canadians have been drawn since 1989 has produced much civilian debate and little military elucidation. Three senior officers—Generals Roméo Dallaire, Lewis MacKenzie, and Rick Hillier—have authored excellent accounts of their years in service, a welcome break from the past silence of their peers, but no sailors or fliers still, and remarkably few of the rank and file. A historiography of Canada's military autobiography would be a grim, brief, and thankless read. In its absence, there are few biographies to fill important gaps, little certainty of the motivations and knowledge of key historical actors at critical junctures, and bigger challenges in reconstructing basic narratives from which greater, more analytical surveys can with confidence proceed. The field is not empty, but it is roomy enough for more.
SEE ALSO: BIOGRAPHY, MILITARY; RESEARCH AND WRITING.

Auxiliary Services. During World Wars I and II, Canadian service organizations provided assistance to members of the armed forces. The Salvation Army (nicknamed the Sally Ann), the Young Men's Christian Association (YMCA), the Knights of Columbus, and other organizations created hostels in Canada and overseas, ran canteens, screened films, and provided quiet spaces where soldiers could read or write a letter. The Salvation Army, the soldiers' favourite, sent five chaplains overseas in World War I, ran canteens that offered hot drinks and snacks, raised funds in Canada to send comfort packages with socks, underwear, and other necessities to the troops, and assisted returned personnel. So valuable were the services provided in World War I that in 1939 the government created the Canadian War Auxiliary Service with the Sally Ann, the YMCA, the Knights, and the Canadian Legion as authorized service providers. Eventually each organization specialized, the Salvation Army, for example, in providing canteens, both fixed and mobile, and showing films. Sally Ann personnel accompanied Canadians to Sicily, Italy, and Normandy. (The Canadian Red Cross had a different status because of its obligations under the Geneva Convention. It too ran hostels in Britain.) After World War II, the military intended to offer auxiliary services on its own, found it could not do the job well, and the Salvation Army duly served alongside troops in NATO from 1952 until the withdrawal of Canadian troops from Europe in 1993.

Aviation, Military. Canada was relatively late in creating military aviation during and after World War I, and only became a major air power and aircraft producer during and immediately following World War II. It retained a varied, but steadily diminishing, military aviation industry during and after the Cold War, with fewer aircraft, bases, and personnel, although several key capabilities are currently under review in light of global instability following 1989 and the aging nature of many platforms.

Entering World War I in 1914 as part of the British Empire and with no air force of its own, Canada sent some 22,000 young men into aerial combat with British units and built more than 1,200 planes and flying boats for other Allied forces. The lure of flight so brilliantly dangled by prewar literature, magazines, and the sheer novelty of the technology enticed clerks

▲ The Canadian military gave service organizations a place at the front, and the YMCA, as in this October 1916 scene, was quick to fill it. The "Y" and the "Sally Ann" were hugely popular with the troops.

and farm boys who had never actually seen planes to enlist eagerly for air force service. Most would never see flight, serving instead as mechanics, armaments experts, or administrative staff in sites from Canada to France, but many would actually fly, discovering in their rickety, failure-prone airframes a fatality rate incomparably higher than anything experienced on the ground. In the trenches, the romance of flight was nevertheless secure, the blind optimism felt by many soldiers in the advantages to mind and body of soaring among the clouds ensuring a steady supply of applicants for the daring life of the flyer. No one could say that Canadians had no knack for it: by war's end, several of the Allies' leading aces were Canadian, including Billy Bishop, William Barker, and Raymond Collishaw.

After the war, a small interim air force trained aircrew and flew a hodge-podge of trainers, flying boats, and second-hand British aircraft, prior to the establishment of the Royal Canadian Air Force (RCAF) in 1924. The civilian nature of most interwar flying was paramount, however, and the rise of Nazi Germany and militarist Japan in the early 1930s saw Canada and its fledgling air force with barely a few dozen combat aircraft, most of them antiquated. In mid-1939, as the world hurtled toward war, barely a squadron's worth of Hawker Hurricanes was available to uphold Canada's share of wartime burdens. Most of what the country did have soon poured into the Battle of Britain, the first of many intensive—and not always successful—battles against an enemy far stronger and more capable in the war's early years than most prewar commentators had predicted.

Expansion during World War II was rapid, multifaceted, and quantitatively impressive. A government that at first hoped to fight in Europe with someone else's troops, and preferred not to fight in Asia at all, envisaged naval and air contributions to be easier and less costly than immediate ground force commitments. The British Commonwealth Air Training Plan (BCATP), which would make of Canada the "aerodrome of democracy," expanded from a limited liability commitment into a decisive contribution to the war, training tens of thousands for overseas service. An embryonic manufacturing plant would spew out some 15,000 planes and employ legions of home front workers, many of them women. Dozens of combat squadrons flew against enemy submarines, military targets, defensive installations, and cities, and struck at naval forces, secret weapons plants, factories, and railways. In addition to those serving with Canadian units, many thousands of Canadians served in British forces as well, in theatres of war from the North Pacific to the Burmese frontier, from Ceylon to Italy, from the British Isles to the Caribbean. Perhaps a quarter of the Commonwealth's overall air strength was Canadian, including those in Bomber Command, whose hammer blows against the German war machine, so costly and unsuccessful at first, had by 1945 shattered Germany's cities and helped to bleed white its costly air defences. The war expanded Canada's manufacturing plant and technical knowledge immensely, dotted the map with control towers, runways, and aerodromes that would form the basis of a postwar transportation network, and created a vast pool of skilled engineers, administrators, and flyers.

The postwar force would clearly be smaller. No one, save perhaps the most wild-eyed defence planner, of which there were a few, envisaged the sky-darkening fleets of 1944–1945, but it would be a potent force nevertheless, created from impressive advantages of people, plant, and skill. Rapid demobilization and the seeming hostility of political leaders toward even a moderately robust postwar capacity conjured a far harsher future. Not for the last time, economic pressures and shortsightedness augured for paying off warships, grounding expensive aircraft, and deleting army establishments. Air and sea power were critical potential deletions; in preserving maximum military flexibility for a country about to embark for the first time on major peacetime commitments abroad, they represented large budgetary savings but great operational risk.

The Cold War fortuitously intervened. In mobilizing for the return of a large Canadian contingent to Europe in the early 1950s, after the formation of the North Atlantic Treaty Organization in 1949 and the outbreak of war in Korea in 1950, Canadair of Montreal turned out thousands of the highly capable F-86 Sabres for Canadian and other air forces, while A.V. Roe, or Avro, developed the CF-100 Canuck, a successful long-range interceptor and the first military aircraft designed and built entirely in Canada. For a time, Canada maintained more fighter squadrons in Western Europe than did the United States. Ground-based radar and warning installations crept, ribbon-like, across the continental tundra to watch for Soviet bombers and, later, missiles, moving by stages ever farther northward as the warning time for long-range attack shrank from hours to mere minutes. Missile and drone research occupied battalions of scientists, many of whom had played leading roles in the research and development triumphs of the secret war of atoms and radio waves, narrowly won, against the totalitarian states.

It would not last. The relentless march of project development costs, high-technology infrastructure, and ever more expensive weapons platforms was not something that small countries, industries, and air forces could easily or indefinitely sustain. The cancellation of the Avro Arrow, a Canadian-designed interceptor of unprecedented capability, complexity, and—as the project evolved—cost, was an epic blow for an aviation industry that, a decade earlier, had measured its output in thousands of aircraft, and not the few score promised from the Arrow's production line. Thousands of fired workers fled to other industries, or other countries, as Canada began the first of many purchases of aircraft, helicopters, and aviation technologies from abroad, most of them from the United States. Some aircraft would still be built under licence at Canadian plants, and many other components assembled there, but the relative and inexorable decline of military aviation as an industry tracked loosely its fate as a military capability as well.

In Europe, as in North America, the gradual erosion of aircraft, squadrons, and personnel commenced not long after the Korean War, the singular event that had sparked a brief, and unique, post-1945 expansion. Part of this was the consolidation of technologies and capabilities into more versatile and more potent modern airframes, but part too was due to Canada's gradual military retrenchment from NATO Europe and the successive downgrading of continental air defence, both of which were central features of defence policy in the later 1960s and 1970s. The unification of the air force with the army and navy into the single-service Canadian Forces in 1968 promised greater administrative efficiency but little by way of extra people, machines, or missions. As the Cold War lengthened, stubbornly surviving the much heralded but false promise of détente, aircraft grew old and were cannibalized or grounded, while training time diminished under the scurrilous logic of budget efficiencies. Continental air defence was largely assigned to American-built computers in the joint Canadian-American North American Air (later Aerospace) Defence Command (NORAD), or to American fighter squadrons; in Europe, two or three Canadian squadrons now protected the country's ground brigade that could once have called upon a dozen for close tactical support.

In 1982, Canada purchased the CF-18 Hornet, a major modernization of the fleet with substantial industrial benefits for Canadian companies. It is still flying more than a quarter of a century later, with combat service in the Persian Gulf (1990–1991) and Kosovo (1999), though in fewer numbers as aircraft have crashed, were used for supplies, or mothballed as entire squadrons were grounded. Domestic high-tech aviation industries or branch plants have, in recent years, provided combat helicopters, drones, weapons systems, and space-related research and development to the Canadian Forces, which retains and will modernize aircraft for long-range transport, maritime patrol, and, in eventually replacing the CF-18, for air-to-air and air-to-ground combat. Military aviation has played a major role in the war in Afghanistan, although mostly, from the Canadian side, in the areas of transportation, logistics, and reconnaissance. Somewhat embarrassingly for a leading industrial nation, domestic political debate, despite Afghanistan and the continuing threat of airborne terrorism, has at times contemplated major structural reductions to Canada's military aviation capacity. At present, Canada is in a developmental partnership with the United States and several other countries to explore acquisition of the controversial and wickedly expensive Joint Strike Fighter, its funded participation having already resulted in hundreds of millions of dollars in contracts to Canadian companies, universities, and research groups. SEE ALSO: ROYAL CANADIAN AIR FORCE.

READING: Brereton Greenhous and Hugh Halliday, *Canada's Air Forces, 1914–1999* (Montreal, 1999); Jonathan Vance, *High Flight: Aviation and the Canadian Imagination* (Toronto, 2002).

Aviation, Naval. Canada's navy formed a Royal Canadian Navy Aviation Service in September 1918 to carry out anti-submarine patrols on the East Coast, but the service, never really operational, ceased flying in 1919. The 12 flying boats given to Canada by the United States Navy that had operated them from Nova Scotia passed to the government's Air Board. Naval air operations were officially dead until a World War II study in 1943 recommended that the Royal Canadian Navy (RCN) get back to flying, and the wartime RCN duly assumed responsibility for two Royal Navy (RN) carriers, HMS *Nabob* and *Puncher*. The aircrews were RN, but many Canadians had been trained as air and ground crew by the RN and formed the nucleus of Canadian naval aviation. The posthumous Victoria

Cross won by RCN Lieutenant Robert Hampton (Hammy) Gray, flying a Corsair from HMS *Formidable* during the last days of the war against Japan, formed a major part of RCN naval history.

Formally reconstituted in September 1945, RCN naval aviation began operations from HMCS *Warrior*, a carrier returned to Britain in 1947 in exchange for HMCS *Magnificent*. With a Naval Air Station at Dartmouth, Nova Scotia, the RCN created two carrier air groups flying Sea Furies, Fireflies, and Avengers, and trained for an anti-submarine warfare role at which it became very efficient. The "*Maggie*" was paid off in 1956 and replaced by HMCS *Bonaventure*, with its angled flight deck and steam catapults. The "*Bonnie*" carried 34 aircraft—Banshees, Grumman Trackers, and helicopters (after 1964, Sea Kings). It too became extremely proficient in working with RCN destroyers at anti-submarine work. Refitted in 1966, *Bonaventure* became a casualty of armed forces unification and budget cuts, and was retired from service in 1970.

By that time, RCN naval aviation had disappeared along with the navy as a separate service, the air component being swallowed into the new Maritime Command. In 1975, a further reorganization took place, passing control of all aircraft to Air Command, headquartered at Winnipeg. Specialized maritime squadrons thereafter operated under Maritime Air Group, the four long-range patrol squadrons flying Argus aircraft and, from 1980, CP-140 Auroras. Maritime Air Group had bases at Comox, BC, and Greenwood, NS, with helicopters on major ships and at Canadian Forces Bases at Shearwater, NS, and Patricia Bay, BC. After 1997, control of maritime air passed to the Air Force's 1 Canadian Air Division. SEE ALSO: ROYAL CANADIAN NAVY.

READING: J.D.F. Kealy and E.C. Russell, *A History of Canadian Naval Aviation, 1918-1962* (Ottawa, 1965).

Bagot, Sir Charles (1781–1843). The British government appointed Bagot, a former Member of Parliament, as minister to the United States in 1815. His most notable achievement was to negotiate the Rush-Bagot agreement (formalized in April 1817) that greatly reduced naval forces on the Great Lakes and Lake Champlain, a matter of substantial importance in the wake of the War of 1812. Bagot also negotiated and resolved boundary issues during his time in Washington. He would later serve as governor-in-chief of Canada from 1841 to 1843.

Barker, William George (1894–1930). Fighter pilot "Billy" Barker was one of the leading air aces of World War I, credited with 53 kills. Born in Dauphin, Manitoba, he enlisted in the army in late 1914 and served overseas as a machine-gunner through early 1916 when he transferred into the Royal Flying Corps. He qualified as an observer first, then commenced pilot training in early 1917. Barker, a notoriously daring and competent flyer, won the Victoria Cross for an action in October 1918 in which he engaged in combat with more than a dozen enemy aircraft over

▲ Lieutenant-Colonel William Barker, VC, with his Sopwith Snipe.

the Canadian lines near Valenciennes, France, shooting down four despite being wounded multiple times.

Barker was a wing commander in the newly established Canadian Air Force (CAF) in the early 1920s and commander of its training base at Camp Borden, Ontario. He was later the CAF's first acting director and highest ranking officer until the establishment of the Royal Canadian Air Force in 1924. He engaged in a string of less than successful civilian ventures after resigning from military service in 1926, battling alcoholism and, probably, post-traumatic stress disorder. At the time of his death in a plane crash in 1930, Barker was the president and general manager of Montreal's Fairchild Aircraft. He remains Canada's most decorated soldier.

READING: Wayne Ralph, *William Barker, VC* (Toronto, 2007).

Batoche, Battle of (1885). Batoche was the capital of Louis Riel's provisional government during the Northwest Rebellion of 1885. On 9 May, Major-General Frederick Middleton and some 800 men of the Northwest Field Force attacked the Metis' elaborate rifle pits around the small town, located approximately 45 kilometres south of Prince Albert. Gabriel Dumont, the Metis' top field commander, had wanted to fight a guerilla war against the Canadian force, using his soldiers' superior mobility and knowledge of the country, but Riel, convinced that God had ordained a victory at Batoche, insisted on defending the village. Dumont conceded to his leader and dug in his 300 men to resist Middleton's force, which included artillery and a hastily purchased Gatling machine gun. An attempt by the Metis to capture the guns failed when the Gatling gun drove them away. On 12 May, after probing attacks and sustained shelling had inflicted heavy casualties on the defenders and pulverized the town, a Canadian flanking column drew away enough of Dumont's men, who were desperately short of ammunition, to succeed in a headlong charge at the main defences. This was the

only decisive battle of the Northwest campaign, but it effectively ended the rebellion. Riel surrendered several days later on 15 May, and Dumont fled to the United States. SEE ALSO: DUMONT; NORTHWEST REBELLION (1885); RIEL.

READING: Bob Beal and R.C. Macleod, *Prairie Fire: The 1885 Northwest Rebellion* (Toronto, 1993).

Battle Honours. The practice of awarding battle honours to units that distinguished themselves in campaigns goes back centuries; the first British battle honour dates to 1695 and the first Canadian honour to the Fenian Raids of 1870. Canadian regiments that fought in the Northwest Rebellion of 1885 and served in or sent men to the South African War proudly emblazoned "South Africa" or "Batoche" or "Paardeburg" on their regimental colours (though these honours were only authorized in 1933). The practice became widespread and tightly controlled after World War I when firmer rules were put in place. Then, as after the 1939–1945 war, Department of National Defence committees had to decide which units received recognition after consultation with Great Britain and other allies on battle nomenclature. The British, for example, did not want to have "Hitler Line" on their colours, so as not to glorify the Führer. The Canadians, however, convinced that they had broken the Germans' Italian fortifications south of Rome, were less squeamish. The result uncharacteristically was that the British used the names of nearby Italian towns and Canadian units inscribed "Hitler Line" on their colours. The post–World War II awards committee also decided that defeats such as Dieppe and Hong Kong merited battle honours. The rules in place offered battle honours only to cavalry, armoured, and infantry units, and World War I and II honours were limited to ten to each regiment, with units deciding which honours to place on their colours. The practice continued during the Korean War, with the Princess Patricia's Canadian Light Infantry, for example, being recognized for its battle at Kap'yong (and also by the award of a United States Presidential Citation). As reserve units disappeared or amalgamated in the postwar period, successor regiments inherited their battle honours and continued the traditions of the disbanded regiment.

The Canadian Forces (CF) adopted new criteria in 2007 in an effort to merge navy, army, and air force precedence. The new CF Battle Honours Committee used these criteria to review Canadian aerial operations over the Balkans in 1999, leading to the award of the battle honour "Kosovo" to 425 and 441 Tactical Fighter Squadrons. Battle honours will undoubtedly be awarded for many of the struggles around Kandahar in 2006 during the war in Afghanistan (2001–present).

Beaumont Hamel, Battle of (1916). Beaumont Hamel, a small village in the Somme region of northeastern France, was the scene of a disastrous attack by troops of the Newfoundland Regiment against German positions in July 1916 during World War I. Plagued by miscommunication and by lack of clear intelligence on the German positions at the edge of a low rise overlooking the scene of their intended attack, the Newfoundlanders moved forward to their jump-off positions fully exposed to German machine-gun and small-arms fire that had not been stilled by the Allies' preliminary barrage. Attacking with other troops of the 29th British Division, the Newfoundlanders were slaughtered, losing 710 killed, wounded, and missing from a total of 801 engaged. It was the bloodiest day in Newfoundland's military history, and one of the bloodiest in percentage terms for any unit in the history of the British Empire. Casualties on this, the first day of a massive and generally unsuccessful British offensive along a much longer front, affected virtually every Newfoundland community and played a key role in the island colony's conscription debate the following year. The reconstituted unit was later bestowed the title "Royal" and fought several other major actions later in the war, before undertaking occupation duties in Germany. Beaumont Hamel battlefield is now one of the best preserved sites along the Western Front. It sits on ground maintained by Parks Canada on behalf of the people of Canada and Newfoundland and Labrador. The site includes several cemeteries, the remains of the regiment's trench lines, an interpretation centre, and a

The emblem of the Royal Newfoundland Regiment, the great Caribou stag at Beaumont Hamel overlooks Newfoundland's most famous, and tragic, battlefield.

magnificent caribou memorial with the names of the island's fallen. SEE ALSO: NEWFOUNDLAND, WORLD WAR I; ROYAL NEWFOUNDLAND REGIMENT.

READING: G.W.L. Nicholson, *The Fighting Newfoundlander: A History of the Royal Newfoundland Regiment* (2nd rev. ed., Montreal, 2006).

Beaver Dams, Battle of (1813). After the British victory at Stoney Creek in early June 1813, the Americans retreated to Fort George where they were harassed by British and Mohawk forces. The Americans, determined to end the harassment, on 24 June sent a force of 500 infantry with some cavalry and artillery against the British position at Beaver Dams, near present-day Thorold, Ontario.

Forewarned by Laura Secord, 46 British regulars and some 100 Mohawks and 300 Caughnawagas under the overall command of Lieutenant James FitzGibbon laid a trap that saw the native warriors surround the US column after a fierce struggle in which both sides sustained losses. His tiny British contingent in reserve until then, FitzGibbon persuaded the Americans, fearful of slaughter at the hands of the "savages," that surrender was their best course and got his way, some 480 soldiers laying down their arms. He later reported that "not a shot was fired on our side by any but the Indians. They beat the American detachment into a state of terror, and the only share I claim is taking advantage of a favorable moment to offer them protection from the tomahawk and scalping knife." The warriors had carried the burden of the fight and the day, and the British victory ensured that the Americans remained hemmed in at Fort George. Laura Secord became one of Canada's oldest and most cherished military heroines.

SEE ALSO: SECORD; WAR OF 1812.

Beurling, George Frederick (1921–1948). "Buzz" Beurling, born in Verdun, Quebec, was one of Canada's most successful wartime fighter pilots. After trying unsuccessfully early in World War II to join the Royal Canadian Air Force (RCAF), which rejected him as academically unqualified, he crossed the Atlantic on his own to join the Royal Air Force (RAF). With two German aircraft "kills" to his credit, the RAF posted him as a sergeant pilot to Malta in May 1942. The island, under siege by the German and Italian air forces, offered him constant action, and he quickly ran his kills to 28 or 29 (the calculations are in dispute) before he himself was shot down and wounded in October. After a return to Canada to recover and to be feted (10,000 people turned out in Verdun arena to cheer him), Beurling, now a flight lieutenant, returned to England and served in RCAF Squadrons Nos. 403 and 412 and shot down three more Luftwaffe aircraft. His superb eyesight and steadiness under pressure made Beurling an extremely accurate shot. But he was also undisciplined, including while in combat, and the RCAF released this "lone ranger" in August 1944. Beurling had been awarded the Distinguished Flying Medal and bar, the Distinguished Flying Cross, and the Distinguished Service Order, second only to the Victoria Cross for a junior officer. In early 1948, he joined the fledgling Israeli Air Force for $1,000 a week and died in an air crash in Rome en route to the Middle East.

READING: Brian Nolan, *Hero: The Buzz Beurling Story* (Toronto, 1981).

Big Bear (c.1825–1888). Born near Fort Carlton, Saskatchewan, Big Bear (or Mistahimaskwa) was an Aboriginal leader in the Prairie River region and, in the early 1870s, headed a large group of 65 Cree

▲ George F. "Buzz" Beurling, 1943.

▲ Big Bear in 1885.

Field Force, he fought in neither battle. He surrendered on 2 July 1885. Tried for treason, Big Bear served two years of a three-year term in penitentiary, was released in 1887, and died soon after. SEE ALSO: NORTHWEST REBELLION.

Bilingualism in the Canadian Forces. At its formation in the new Dominion, the Canadian military was, for all practical purposes, a unilingual English organization. Francophone militia units in Quebec might have used French in the mess and the armoury, but communications with other units and with headquarters in Ottawa proceeded in English only. This practice, along with many other factors, had predictable effects on enlistment for the South African War and World War I. The formation of the 22nd (French-Canadian) Battalion in 1914—that its name was in English is revealing—and its distinguished role at the front during World War I served to spur Quebec's military ardour, but not sufficiently to swell enlistments in what was seen as an anglophone army. Nor did the interwar years change much—not until 1928 was the name Royal 22e Régiment adopted for Canada's one Permanent Force francophone unit—and communications within the army remained in English. The air force and navy for their part made no gestures at all to francophones. World War II, which saw a French-speaking Royal Canadian Air Force (RCAF) squadron and a half-dozen French-speaking army units overseas, also changed little in the military's structure, traditions, or linguistic preferences.

Although Collège militaire royal de St-Jean opened in 1952 to educate and train junior officers, it was not until General Jean Victor Allard became chief of the defence staff in 1966 in a time of flux caused by the coming unification of the armed forces that real change began. Allard could take advantage of the report of the Royal Commission on Government Organization that had commented unfavourably on the plight of francophones in the military; the temper of the times, with pressure added by the creation of the Royal Commission on Bilingualism and Biculturalism and rising separatism in Quebec, also made action possible and necessary. Allard persuaded the

lodges and more than 500 people. He refused to sign Treaty No. 6, a proposed agreement between the Crown and the First Nations of central Saskatchewan, until forced to do so by his people's hunger and destitution in 1882. Big Bear worked to unite the northern Cree in the vain hope of winning concessions from Ottawa, but he lost control of many of his warriors to militants who seized the opportunity of Louis Riel's rebellion in 1885 to attack settlers at Frog Lake, killing nine of them. Reluctant to fight, and counselling non-violence, Big Bear was a consistent voice for peace and negotiation in the First Nations camp. Though with his warriors in two inconclusive skirmishes against the Alberta government to create French Language Units (FLUs) in all three environments (a brigade in Valcartier, a CF-5 air squadron in Bagotville, and the destroyer escort NCSM *Ottawa*), and the Official Languages Act of 1969 designated Canadian Forces units as English, French, or bilingual. The Defence White Paper of 1971 then committed the government to ensure that French-speaking officers and other ranks had representation in all ranks and trades proportionate to their numbers in the general population.

Such a policy was not well-received by many anglophones in the Canadian Forces (CF), and there were the inevitable complaints that some received promotions for their linguistic ability rather than their military skills. But over time, the complaints died away. In 1988, the Canadian Forces adopted a universal approach to bilingualism, aimed at having all who served able to function in both languages. This proved impractical, not surprisingly, and the present policy is functional bilingualism: those who must be bilingual to do their job are required to be so. By 2007, all the serving general officers in the CF had met the required standard for fluency in their other official language, while 85 percent of colonels/navy captains and higher had also done so. Francophones made up 24 percent of CF officers, 28 percent of the generals and admirals, and 28 percent of other ranks. The stress on bilingualism begun by Allard more than 40 years ago has largely succeeded, though there were still complaints as late as 2008 that CF training discriminated against francophones. SEE ALSO: ALLARD; QUEBEC AND THE MILITARY.

READING: Jean Pariseau and Serge Bernier, *French Canadians and Bilingualism in the Canadian Forces 1763–1969,* vol. 1; *1969–1987,* vol. 2 (Ottawa, 1993–1994).

Bill 80. The National Resources Mobilization Act of 1940 permitted home defence conscription but forbade compulsory service overseas. Pressure for overseas conscription in English Canada, in the media, from the Conservative Party (led from November 1941 by the pro-conscription former prime minister, Arthur Meighen), and within the

Liberal government's caucus and Cabinet began to increase dramatically after Japan entered the war in December 1941, and Prime Minister Mackenzie King decided that a conscription plebiscite might release his government from its restrictive pledges on the use of military manpower. The 27 April 1942 plebiscite, however, resulted in heavy support for conscription in English-speaking Canada and massive opposition to it in French Canada, thus leaving King on the horns of a very Canadian dilemma. The prime minister's answer was Bill 80, a parliamentary measure introduced in May 1942 to end the restrictions on where conscripts might be deployed. But because King simultaneously made clear that his policy remained "not necessarily conscription, but conscription if necessary," he weathered the storm by staying essentially in the same place he had been before the plebiscite, though now with his hands untied for the future. In Quebec, the feeling was one of betrayal, one of broken promises, and King's francophone public works minister, P.J.A. Cardin, resigned. In English Canada, the reaction was one of outrage that the prime minister had weaseled away from a vote that on a national basis was solidly for conscription, and his minister of national defence, J.L. Ralston, threatened to quit, submitting a resignation letter that King refused to accept—for now. Nonetheless, King held his country, caucus, and Cabinet largely together. In fact, in the spring of 1942, no Canadian divisions were in action and army casualties were few, thus making conscription almost wholly unnecessary except for symbolic reasons. This situation would change by November 1944, and King, when driven by necessity, did impose a measure of conscription for overseas service. SEE ALSO: CONSCRIPTION; KING; RALSTON.

READING: J.L. Granatstein and J.M. Hitsman, *Broken Promises: A History of Conscription in Canada* (Toronto, 1977).

Billion-Dollar Gift. By early 1941, Great Britain's munitions, materiel, and food needs in Canada in World War II were much greater than its ability to pay in dollars. At the same time, the United States'

Lend-Lease program allowed the British to get American supplies "free." In other words, as British negotiators politely pointed out to their Canadian counterparts, why should they pay Canada for what they could get for free from the United States? Added to the mix in a complicated military-diplomatic-political problem was Canadian loyalty to Britain and national admiration for the way the British had stood up to German aggression through the opening years of the war, plus a good deal of self-interest and concern at the political impact of job losses if British purchases in Canada dried up. The answer was a generous "billion-dollar gift" in 1942, along with a $750 million interest-free loan, intended to take care of Britain's requirements in Canada for 15 months. Anglo-Canadians glowed with pride at the gift, but many French-Canadians did not like the idea of siphoning money to the former colonial government, especially at a time when taxes were taking more and more of Canadian incomes. When London used up the loan and the gift much quicker than expected, the next tranche of help was called Mutual Aid, while public relations messages stressed that other Allies would receive Canadian help as well. SEE ALSO: WAR FINANCE.

READING: R.B. Bryce, *Canada and the Cost of World War II: The International Operations of Canada's Department of Finance, 1939–1947* (Montreal, 2005).

Biography, Military. Serious military biography in Canada is almost a contradiction in terms, although several recent monographs and the ongoing *Dictionary of Canadian Biography* (DCB), a project of unprecedented scholarship and vision, are important exceptions.

The relative weakness of military biographical study is not a question of primary records, although in many cases scholars have been stymied by access restrictions to personal papers, by the failure of many key figures to maintain diaries or autobiographical records, and by the logistical challenges of conducting research in a very large country with a very small number of sources of funding for military research. There is also little tradition in Canada of training or instruction in the biographical arts, and

little patience for it as an appropriate method of honing the research or writing skills of young graduate students. Recent biographies of H.D.G. Crerar and Bert Hoffmeister, both World War II generals, were doubly rare in having originated as doctoral projects and been concluded as readable tomes. One on Paul Triquet, VC, an equally valuable but less readable effort, represents the best and the worst of biographical publishing: a dedicated author pushing forward an important story, and the decline in editing standards and marketing support that all good stories nevertheless demand.

Simpler explanations for the weakness of Canadian military biography as a field might be the broader, and arguably parlous, state of military history itself, the difficulty of biography as a literary proposition, and the weak commercial market for personal military narrative. Political biography, economic biography, indeed any biography deemed by the academic establishment to be primarily the province of dead white males might all be said to suffer from similar afflictions. But no subset of the biographical field is potentially as tainted for granting committees or conference organizing teams as the lives of former warriors. A handful of military autobiographies have recently defied this stricture, but it is of note that a commercial press has published each one, a competent shadow author or editor has played an important role in every case, and each text has been torn from the headlines of the most recent war. Would any of them be marketable 20 or 30 years later as works of serious history instead of military journalism laced with polemics? It would be an exceedingly unlikely bet. The egregious prose and flip judgments of much military biographical work has not endeared the field to serious readers either: not all generals were giants nor soldiers titans. In the ceaseless bleat of military historians—or of non-historians who write reams of historical doggerel unfazed by lack of skill—to be taken seriously by their peers, it would help at times simply to write better history, or to expose politely those who do not.

Not all areas of military biography should be thought of in the same way. In some respects, the market, fed by an endless stream of enthusiastic and productive pens, is doing extremely well. A traditional emphasis on tales of frontier courage, military heroism, and patriotic sacrifice has transformed Montcalm, Wolfe, Laura Secord, Tecumseh, Winnie the Pooh (originally a Canadian infantry mascot during World War I), John McCrae, and many other historical figures, real and imagined, into icons of Canadian military history. Collectively, powerful biographies of Canadian soldiers have also had an impact on the popular imagination, most notably in Pierre Berton's *Vimy*, a work less truthful, poignant, or inspiring than the personal histories on which it was based, but immensely successful nonetheless. Fiction—Timothy Findlay, Jack Hodgins, Alan Cumyn, and many others—has provided a small army of memorable figures in a variety of hues, as has children's or young adult literature, the focus of which tends to be on a young person or adult hero over-coming, rather stoically in most cases, the endless travails of war. Soldiers, including Montcalm and Wolfe, were part of a major renovation to the perma-nent gallery of the Canadian Museum of Civilization in Ottawa, which deals with historic personalities, while several recent television programs have elevated military biography to the popular reality show format, in one case following the descendants of former military personnel as they rediscovered the lives and wars of their ancestors.

Of scholarly biography, however, there remains little. The lives of the politically great—prime minis-ters, especially—have fared better, and from these it is often possible to contextualize the choices and parameters faced by men and women in uniform. Laurier still awaits a royal treatment, for example, but Macdonald, Borden, King, Diefenbaker, Pearson, and Trudeau, among the country's most influential leaders, have all been subject to expert scrutiny, as have many of their key lieutenants. Senior ministers and manda-rins of World War II and the Pearson-Trudeau years have been especially well covered, with many senior bureaucrats, from defence ministers to clerks of the Privy Council, sometimes receiving monograph-length treatments on their own. The great wars have

fared better than those either before or since, though not as well as one might reasonably expect. Unlike American writing, which seems capable of nurturing a robust historiography on even the most hapless of regimental colonels, or British history, in which both illustrated nonsense and 500-page doorstoppers pour forth from wealthy popular presses in print runs in the tens of thousands, Canadian coverage has just scratched at the lives of senior officers and not much else.

Biography has accumulated slowly in the broad area of colonial warfare. Outside of battle studies and campaign accounts for the specialist market—many of them, especially those by Donald G. Graves and Carl Benn, excellent—the field is generally devoid of credible modern accounts. A 50-year-old volume on Count Frontenac by W.J. Eccles is still the class of its field, while *Louisburg Portraits* (1982), an award-winning work for young adults by popular historian Christopher Moore, is among the most insightful and enjoyable works of Canadian history. Wolfe has had several biographers, though few have exceeded the now-aged account in the DCB by the late C.P. Stacey. More writers have been interested in Wolfe's death, and depictions of same, than in his extraordinary life, imperial accounts of heroism and tragic loss having now fallen victim to Canadian political proprieties and the cardinal difficulty of remembering anything British in a country that is partly, and increasingly, not. Recent battle accounts have diminished his accomplishments in any case: in Peter MacLeod's version of the Quebec campaign, *Northern Armageddon*, he is noteworthy, in the continentally decisive clash of arms, as the doomed general who bungles least.

Other DCB accounts are equally strong, and the volumes, which now cover subjects who have died between the years 1000 and 1930, are the essential starting point for any serious biographical research on soldiers in this period. Most of them are by leading scholars and, while many could use an update, the consistent quality of the style, content, and bibliographical citations are unparalleled in any comparable work of collective biography. The on-line *L'Encyclopédie de l'histoire du Québec*, in contrast, is wildly unreliable—its Wolfe entry, for instance, dates from 1915. Military biography from British North America, the Confederation period, and the Boer War fares little better than the more distant colonial past. The one essential volume spanning the period is Desmond Morton's *The Canadian General: Sir William Otter* (1974), a work that covers more territory in Canada's military past, from the Fenian Raids to the 1920s, than almost any other. *Ministers and Generals* (1971), a previous work by Morton, is not biography at all, but in charting the relationship between military and political figures in the first decades after Confederation, includes more biography than almost any other work dealing with this period.

World War I is not much better served. Sir Arthur Currie, one of the war's great generals by any measure, wrote little himself but was much feted by others. The biography by A.M.J. Hyatt, which could use an overhaul and reprinting in light of intervening scholarship, remains a model of analysis, brevity, and scholarly impact nevertheless. John Swettenham's excellent three-volume epic on A.G.L. McNaughton is now 40 years old and Hyatt's opposite in terms of conciseness and crispness of narrative. Sir Julian Byng, who also commanded Canadians overseas, has a solid biography by Jeffery Williams. Ron Haycock studied Sir Sam Hughes, Borden's mercurial militia minister. Tim Cook, an award-winning historian who writes with a journalist's flare and a populist's skill, will soon review the Currie-Hughes relationship in an eagerly anticipated volume. Minor figures, including a few battalion commanders and brigadiers, have received occasional attention, often in the pages of *Canadian Military History*, a quarterly produced by Wilfrid Laurier University, or in the annual military history conference hosted by the same school each spring. Patrick Brennan of the University of Calgary has assembled impressive data on the full list of Canadian generals throughout World War I and presented his findings in several venues, but there is no monograph yet, as much as it is needed. Sandra Gwyn's social portrait of Ottawa at war, *Tapestry of War* (1992), will long remain the standard by which these things are judged. Such highpoints notwithstanding, the roster is short and the products thin from a highly literate country that sent nearly 700,000 of its citizens to war 90 years ago.

World War II is better served. In addition to leading political figures such as Charles Power, C.D. Howe, Ernest Lapointe, and James Gardiner, J.L. Granatstein's *The Generals* (1993) is the standard and often-cited text on the military side, a book that presented a collective biography of every general during the war. The research included the assembly of biographical files on subjects who had, quite literally, never been assessed in print before. With similar dossiers at the Directorate of History at the Department of National Defence, the manuscript collections at Library and Archives Canada, and the biographical files on officers, soldiers, and war artists maintained by the Canadian War Museum, are the starting points for biographical research in this period, just as the DCB would be for work on individuals before 1930. A handful of senior officers addressed themselves to posterity from among those who had served in this period, including Maurice Pope, George Kitching, and E.L.M. Burns, as well as a host of sailors, flyers, and soldiers in memoirs, collections of letters, and diaries. In addition to this rich vein of memoir material, and a thin skein of useful autobiography, a half-century of work by official historians has created important biographical files, financed biographical research, and woven individual narratives into a rich, subtle account of Canadians at war. Having completed work on the army's official history some years earlier, research in recent decades has concentrated especially on the navy and air force, spawning—in addition to monumental works of operational history—ongoing publications on command, leadership, and personality. *Warrior Chiefs* (2001), edited by Stephen Harris and Bernd Horn, included 17 biographical essays on both well-known and lesser-known figures. Raymond Brutinel, Jean Victor Allard, and Admiral Harold Grant received treatment, for example, along with Currie, Crerar, and General Roméo Dallaire.

A biography of H.D.G. Crerar finally arrived in 2007, but most of his senior colleagues are still waiting. A potential subject's earning a Victoria Cross or becoming a governor general has helped to inspire writers (Reginald Roy on George Pearkes, or Robert Speaight on Georges Vanier), as has becoming a senior minister (David Bercuson on Brooke Claxton) or a prime minister (Pearson, Diefenbaker), but few other endorsements seem to work on discriminating authors. There are thrilling exceptions. Doug Delaney's biography of Bert Hoffmeister, *The Soldier's General* (2005), may be the best military biography of a Canadian soldier ever written; Michael Whitby's edited work, *Commanding Canadians: The Second World War Diaries of A.F.C. Layard* (2005), would make a very good case as the finest ever written by,

and about, a sailor who led Canadians. The University of British Columbia Press, Canada's leading publisher of serious military titles, produced both volumes in conjunction with the Canadian War Museum in a wide-ranging series called *Studies in Canadian Military History*. Tony Foster's *Meeting of the Generals* (1986) and Robert Calder's wonderful family narrative, *A Richer Dust* (2004), are examples of excellent books that deserve wider readership. There are very few reliable biographies of Canadian military figures since 1945, however—none of consequence on Korea, peacekeeping, or the Gulf War, and none (yet) on Afghanistan. Carol Off's *The Lion, the Fox and the Eagle* (2001), although seriously flawed, is one of a depressingly small handful to come even close.

▲ William Avery "Billy" Bishop, VC, in 1917.

Historian Desmond Morton wrote in 1992 that "perhaps it is a fair reflection of the falling esteem for biography and the low estate of senior officers and the sparsity of many of their papers that adequate biographies of Rear-Admiral Murray, Generals Crerar, Foulkes, and Simonds, and Air Marshals Edwards, McEwan, and Breadner are nowhere even on the horizon." In the nearly 20 years since, only Crerar from this list has received a comprehensive treatment, and Simonds a mildly entertaining hagiography (*The Price of Command* in 1994). SEE ALSO: AUTOBIOGRAPHY, MILITARY; RESEARCH AND WRITING.

Bishop, William Avery (1894–1956). Billy Bishop was Canada's leading fighter ace of World War I and one of the most decorated military personnel in Canadian history. Although later historians questioned some of his kills, Bishop remains one of history's deadliest combat pilots.

Born in Owen Sound, Ontario, Billy Bishop went to the Royal Military College (RMC) in 1911, failed, and repeated his first year, leaving RMC when World War I began. He joined the Mississauga Horse, went overseas with the 7th Canadian Mounted Rifles in June 1915, and then transferred to the Royal Flying Corps in 1915 where he trained initially as an observer. He made it to France in early 1916, injured his knee, and returned to Britain. After retraining as a pilot and winning his wings in November 1916, he went to France the next March and established himself quickly. Bishop was a superb shot and, if not a natural flyer, a ruthless, aggressive combatant who sought action, and his score of enemy aircraft shot down mounted quickly. On 2 June 1917, he made a single-handed early morning attack on a German airfield and claimed to have destroyed three German aircraft. Although there were no witnesses and although some have questioned the veracity of his account, Bishop won the Victoria Cross (VC) for this exploit, adding it to his Distinguished Service Order and bar, his Military Cross, and his Distinguished Flying Cross. By June 1918, Bishop had 72 kills, including five on one day, the highest number among Canadian and Imperial pilots. Two months later, now

a lieutenant-colonel, he went to England as a staff officer to help organize the fledgling Canadian Air Force. After the war, Bishop set up a short-lived aviation company and worked in business in Britain and Canada. In World War II, as an honorary air marshal, he assisted with Royal Canadian Air Force recruiting. Bishop wrote a wartime account, *Winged Warfare*, in 1918; his son wrote his biography, *The Courage of the Early Morning*, in 1966.

John Gray with Eric Peterson wrote *Billy Bishop Goes to War*, a much praised and frequently staged musical in 1978 that brought Bishop back to public attention. But his reputation soon was assailed in a 1982 National Film Board production, *The Kid Who Couldn't Miss*. The production claimed he had faked his VC-winning raid. The charge caused a furor and sparked protests from veterans groups and in Parliament. More serious was the well-researched volume by Brereton Greenhous, *Brave Flyer, Bold Liar: The First World War Exploits of Billy Bishop, VC* (2001), which carefully dissected Bishop's claims and subjected them to a cold-hearted analysis. Bishop's courage and flying skill remain unquestionable, and more recent historians, including David Bashow, have upheld Bishop's kill totals.

Bomarc Missile. The Progressive Conservative government led by John Diefenbaker in 1959 announced its decision to cease work on the Avro Arrow, an advanced interceptor aircraft designed to operate in the North to defend Canada against Soviet bombers. Instead, the nation's airspace was to be protected by two squadrons of Bomarc missiles based at La Macaza, Quebec, and North Bay, Ontario. The Bomarc (an acronym for Boeing Michigan Aeronautical Research Center) was a surface-to-air nuclear-tipped missile with a 600-kilometre range. By 1962, however, the Diefenbaker government had begun to face opposition within the Cabinet, the bureaucracy, and the public over arming Canadian forces with nuclear weapons, and the prime minister's inability to decide on the government's course had become apparent. The nuclear problem worsened during the Cuban Missile Crisis of October 1962

▲ Based in Ontario and Quebec, the Bomarc surface-to-air missile was to destroy attacking Soviet bombers and protect the industrial heartland of North America.

when, the Bomarc installations still unready and unarmed, the government dithered over putting the Canadian military on alert and, by its public indecision at a moment of obvious crisis for the Unites States, greatly angered the administration of John F. Kennedy. Early in 1963, the Cabinet splintered over the nuclear issue, the government lost a confidence motion in the House of Commons, and Diefenbaker subsequently lost power in the April 1963 election. Liberal Prime Minister Lester Pearson, who had initially opposed the acquisition of nuclear weapons, campaigned for them in the election and, upon his election, duly armed the Bomarcs. The missiles were not removed from service until 1971. See also: Diefenbaker; Nuclear Crisis (1962–1963).

Bomber Command Controversy. Canadian participation in the combined bomber offensive against the Axis powers during World War II has been an intermittent source of public controversy since 1945.

Veterans of the campaign shared in the disappointment of British comrades over the way in which their treatment by political authorities, the press, and public opinion appeared to have been informed more by postwar debates over the morality or ethics of area bombing than by the exigencies of total war, the nature of the enemy, or the technologies of the day. The publication in the early 1960s of Britain's official history of the campaign supported the interpretation that strategic bombing had not delivered on its war aims, despite the heroism and professionalism of its crews and the hammer blows delivered late in the war to almost all aspects of German industry and military infrastructure. In this, it echoed key findings of the voluminous *Strategic Bombing Survey* published just after the war in the United States and based in large part on bomb damage assessment and interviews with many key participants, both German and Allied. Other works, including the memoirs of Germany's wartime production coordinator, Albert Speer, and comments in the diaries of Joseph Goebbels, the German propaganda minister, suggested more than one interpretation. As seen by Bomber Command's supporters, Speer and Goebbels appeared to confirm that resources poured into air defence had critically weakened the German war effort. As read by critics of the campaign, such postwar memoirs demonstrated the resiliency of the Nazi war machine and its relative imperviousness to air attack until very late in the war, by which time defeat in Russia and the West had rendered Germany's end inevitable.

Canadian veterans' organizations joined other international groups in supporting appropriate recognition for the "bomber boys" and in reacting to the steady stream of publications, for and against the bombing effort, appearing in subsequent decades. No longer merely a question of historical evidence or respect for aging veterans, the issue was partly overtaken by related postwar issues, including nuclear weapons, the treatment of civilians in wartime, international and humanitarian law, and the politics of memory as a political issue among Cold War allies and enemies. The construction in London of a statue of Sir Arthur Harris, the campaign's wartime

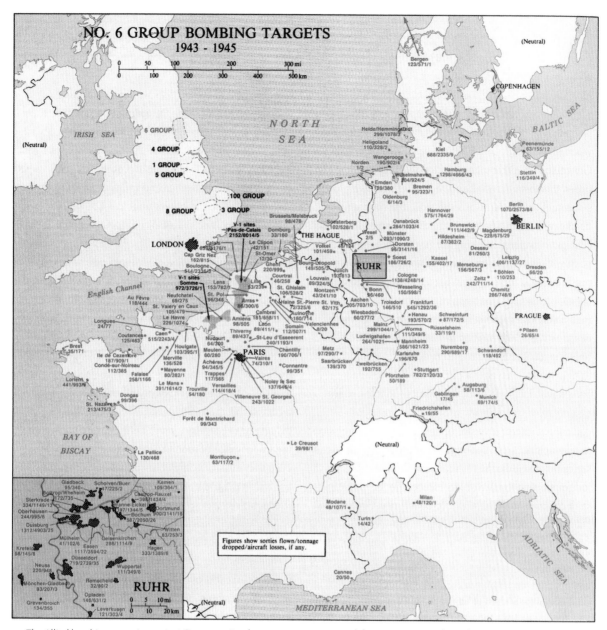

The Allied bombing campaign against Germany stirred postwar controversy, and the RCAF, its targets shown here, was not exempt.

commander, became a focal point for many years' worth of frustration, antagonism, and competing historical claims. The work was deemed by veterans to be a long-overdue gesture of respect for the 55,000 air force personnel, including 10,000 Canadians, who had died in Bomber Command. The Queen Mother unveiled the privately funded monument in 1992 amidst emotional, grateful veterans and their families, but to the catcalls of jeering protestors who expressed

repugnance that "Butcher" Harris, so named by German propagandists, would be honoured for his role in what many had since come to consider a war crime. The Harris monument, immediately placed under police guard to prevent defacement, presaged a renewed round of public debate over the air war and those who had led it. It did not lead to either the issue of a campaign medal for strategic bombing veterans or to a publicly funded memorial to their service, both of which would remain important veterans' projects for many years to come.

Projects surrounding the war's fiftieth anniversary revisited continually the nature and effectiveness of the air war. In Canada, a television production called *The Valour and the Horror* (1992) generated a massive campaign of protest from veterans and many historians when one episode, *Death by Moonlight*, on the Bomber Command offensive made a series of charged and, at times, unsubstantiated claims regarding Harris, air force personnel, and the air war in general. The spectacular debate resulted in hearings in the Senate, an unsuccessful civil suit by veterans seeking public damages for their portrayal, and a massive media campaign against the producers and the Canadian Broadcasting Corporation (CBC), which had aired the film. It pitted free speech and media advocates against veterans, historians against peace activists, and politicians against the public broadcaster. The film's producers defended vigorously their product, even after a CBC internal review had agreed with critics to some key points—that the series had not lived up to broadcast standards and had committed interpretive sins of omission and commission at several junctures. A companion illustrated book to the series was so riddled with errors and uninformed judgments that it more or less escaped public notice and sank quickly into a well-deserved obscurity. On the Internet and in university courses on history, communications, and journalism, debate over the program is still very much alive some 20 years later; the producers, Brian and Terence McKenna, still bristle at the suggestion of any historical or interpretive weaknesses in any aspect of their work.

The publication in 1994 of the third volume in the official history of the Royal Canadian Air Force during the war, *The Crucible of War, 1939–1945* was perfectly timed to aggravate a half-century long and entirely unresolved debate. A monumental work of scholarship, the multi-authored work repeated the broad outlines of the arguments of British official historians 30 years previously, arguing that Bomber Command had essentially failed to meet its objectives in a campaign marked by Harris's obstinacy and bloody-mindedness, and by the effectiveness and ingenuity of German defenders in finding ways to counteract the stunning ferocity of Allied air attack. Whereas most works of official history are consigned immediately to obscurity except among historians and military buffs, *The Crucible of War, 1939–1945* was a minor sensation, selling well but attracting unwanted attention to the Department of National Defence's military history unit. While professional historians were divided over the volume's depiction of the air campaign, with some questioning the existence and utility of the unit that had produced it and others upholding its scholarship, independence, and political courage, the enthusiastic endorsement of the book by the McKenna brothers as a scholarly vindication of their main points helped to divide historians against air veterans in ways that had not been true of the earlier controversy. Some veterans, and a few pro–Bomber Command historians, lobbied Ottawa for a direct repudiation of the department's historical section, which was substantially reduced in the 1990s in both budget and personnel. Not for the first time, the Bomber Command debate was partially recast in the aftermath of the official history as a dispute between history and heritage, free speech and the importance of memory, historians and veterans. If even the military's official historical unit could not be trusted to get the story straight after 50 years of study, then who could?

The Valour and the Horror and the awareness it raised of military history and contentious issues in Canada's military past provided a rallying cry for veterans anxious over their historical legacy and public representation. It also helped to spur both serious history and popular coverage of military events at a time when many public commentators were lamenting the state of history education generally, and military and national history in particular. The controversy helped to galvanize the veterans' movement into a more potent force on public policy issues, while polarizing some positions around competing schools of thought, often pitting the veterans' perspective against that of professional historians. Most of all, the dispute supported the old adage that the only bad publicity was no publicity at all. In 1994–1995, with the onset of major World

War II anniversaries, media networks conscious of the public drubbing their sector had received over the recent controversy, during which most media outlets had lined up publicly with the embattled producers and the CBC, authorized blanket coverage of commemorative ceremonies from France (1994) and the Netherlands (1995). It was the most publicized series of military events since the war. The anniversaries sparked a series of popular and academic books, educational projects, and on-line commemorative initiatives, and encouraged veterans groups to continue large-scale public campaigns for recognition, profile, and remembrance. The parade of veterans en masse at Apeldoorn in 1995 (and again in 2005), to the tearful adulation of Dutch civilians and throngs of grateful children, was perhaps the most moving military spectacle since VE Day. Veterans and their supporters, including many leading historians, would soon play key roles in campaigns to reinvigorate the presence of Canadian military landmarks in Europe, to repatriate an Unknown Soldier to the National War Memorial in Ottawa, and to raise funds for a new Canadian War Museum.

The Museum, a major federal project in downtown Ottawa and the national museum of military history, opened to great public acclaim in May 2005, another important anniversary year. A 130-year-old institution, the Museum's reopening in a purpose-built structure represented the renewed attention given in Canada to military subjects and, for many veterans, overdue acknowledgement of their role in the making of the country. An earlier museum renovation proposal involving a Holocaust memorial gallery within an existing building had sensitized veterans to public history projects: their complaints that it would detract money, attention, and respect from their own role in favour of an increasing emphasis on the Holocaust led to Senate hearings, a change in museum management, and, ultimately, a groundswell of public support for an entirely new building.

Even there Bomber Command veterans would soon find fault. Within a much larger gallery devoted to Canada's World War II air campaign, a single text panel on the "Enduring Controversy"

immediately attracted the ire of veterans and some family members of former Bomber Command personnel. The 70-word text, which appeared near several photographs of bombed German railway yards, cities, and defence installations, made reference to the continuing controversy over strategic bombing's morality and effectiveness, and noted that its success was severely limited until very late in the war. Veterans mounted a spirited campaign, with a letter-writing effort directed at federal politicians, to have it changed. Media coverage was almost entirely in favour of the museum standing its ground. Historians were slightly more divided, but generally agreed on the overall quality of the museum's presentation and on the truthfulness of its key points regarding the bomber offensive. Some museum and arts community professionals repeated their positions during *The Valour and the Horror* affair, arguing that the museum had the right to its voice and interpretations; others speculated that greater consultation with veterans groups or more inclusive language could have defused the controversy from its outset. A small handful of graduate students in history and museum studies used the debate as the basis for major papers or theses, most without ever having interviewed key participants in any aspect of the discussions, and without citing the primary records generated by years of staff work, correspondence, and evaluation.

After more than two years of public debate and several failed efforts at compromise, veterans' groups and museum officials were again called to Senate hearings in spring 2007 that ended, predictably, in the museum being asked to revise the panel in a way consistent both with history and the feelings of veterans' groups who had expressed outrage at what they took to be the museum's slanderous treatment of their service. Responding, the chair of the museum's Board of Trustees asked museum managers to revise the text, which was redrafted and installed in late 2007. The museum's chief executive office, Joe Geurts, departed during the crisis for unconfirmed reasons that press accounts nevertheless speculated were directly related to his stand in defence of the original panel. The revised, much longer text panel incorporated wording that had already been present elsewhere in the exhibition, while retaining the critical points regarding the continuing controversy surrounding the bombing campaign. Several quotations were removed to make way for the expanded panel, but otherwise no aspect of the exhibition was changed.

The issue receded as a leading news item soon after the new text was installed, but the Bomber Command debate, unsurprisingly, continued. Several editorials, blogs, and a handful of eminent historians assailed the museum for having surrendered to interest group pressure, and a few were at pains to deconstruct the new text, subjecting it to particular criticism over its wording on the effectiveness of the effort. Others were more sanguine, seeing little in the revised wording (except length) that would differentiate it from the previous text. Veterans' organizations were generally content with the newer version, but some former critics remained dissatisfied, calling for a boycott of the institution, the firing of its key staff, the removal of additional material (including an image of dead Germans) from the display, and the placement of the museum under the control of military and veterans' groups. A monograph on Harris that appeared in 2009, written by University of Toronto scholar Randall Hansen, a witness at the 2007 Senate hearing, was fiercely critical of Harris, the bombing campaign, and the museum's decision to alter its text panel. An excellent but opinionated tome, it received mixed reviews.

Borden, Sir Frederick William (1847–1917). Born in Nova Scotia and trained as a physician at Harvard University, Borden invested wisely and became wealthy. He was a militia stalwart and a local politician, winning election to Parliament as a Liberal in 1874 (where he remained, except for five years from 1882 to 1887, until 1911). Prime Minister Wilfrid Laurier brought him into the Cabinet in 1896 as minister of militia and defence, and Borden, who sent troops to the Yukon in 1899 to preserve order, worked to increase the appropriations for and efficiency of the

▲ Sir Frederick Borden in 1905.

Canadian militia. His major task was the raising and dispatch of contingents to the South African War (1899–1902), in which his son would be killed in action. After the war, Borden struggled with the British-appointed general officer commanding the militia (GOC) to Canadianize the nation's military forces, changing the legislation to permit Canadians to serve as GOC, creating a Canadian general staff, and forming a Militia Council that extended civilian control of the nation's military forces. He also agreed to take control of the British naval bases at Halifax, NS, and Esquimalt, BC, ending Britain's long military place in Canada. Less successfully, Borden decided to arm the militia with the Ross rifle, a weapon that worked well on the rifle ranges but failed in action during World War I. The Conservative government (led by his cousin Sir Robert Borden) named Camp Borden, Ontario, after him in 1916 to honour his successful tenure as militia minister. SEE ALSO: MILITIA; ROSS RIFLE.

READING: Carman Miller, *A Knight in Politics: A Biography of Sir Frederick Borden* (Montreal, 2010).

Borden, Sir Robert Laird (1854–1937). Sir Robert Borden was Canada's prime minister during World War I and the leading Conservative politician of his era. He expanded Canada's wartime contributions into a vast, costly military and industrial effort that contributed to success on the battlefield, political crisis at home, and the postwar attainment of autonomy within the emerging British Commonwealth.

Born in Grand Pré, Nova Scotia, and trained as a lawyer, Borden taught school and then practised law in Kentville and Halifax until he won election to the House of Commons as a Conservative in 1896. At a time when Sir Wilfrid Laurier's Liberals reigned supreme, he became party leader in 1901 as the least objectionable figure to the powerful Tories. There were several attempts to displace him but, again because aspirants to the Conservative leadership often had more enemies than allies, he somehow survived. One caucus colleague, Sam Hughes, said in 1911 that Borden was "a most lovely fellow; very capable, but not a very good judge of men or tactics; and is gentle hearted as a girl." Still, he opposed reciprocity with the United States in 1911 and won power in the election

▲ Sir Robert Borden addressing Canadian troops at Seaford, England, August 1918.

of that year. In Opposition, as a staunch imperialist, he had supported Laurier's plans to establish a Canadian naval service. As prime minister, he proposed instead a huge contribution of $35 million to Britain to build three dreadnought battleships for the Royal Navy. His legislation split his caucus, angering his French-Canadian supporters, but it passed the House only to run into a blockade in the Liberal-controlled Senate where it died in 1913.

When war came in August 1914, Canada as a colony was bound by Britain's decision to fight. The nation was completely unprepared for war, but Borden immediately committed the country in a whole-hearted way. His minister of militia and defence, Sam Hughes, cobbled together a division for overseas service with rapidity and much disorganization. That disorganization was soon evident elsewhere when contracting for army supplies and horses was besmirched by Hughes's cronyism. Faced with a major scandal in the making, Borden in 1915 managed to get Joseph Flavelle, a Toronto businessman, to clean up the mess by creating an Imperial Munitions Board to handle wartime purchases in co-operation with London. Flavelle succeeded in this objective, and Canada's war industry began to produce the goods. It took a hesitant Borden until late 1916 to finally tire of Hughes, but Borden then forced Hughes out of the government.

War finance, with its huge burdens, also preoccupied the government. Britain had been counted on to pay most of Canada's war costs, but within months the impossibility of this became clear. Borden's government began borrowing on Wall Street for the first time in 1915, raised vast sums by selling war bonds to Canadians, imposed (low) income taxes in 1917, and by that year had put rationing in place, in part to emulate US actions and to justify getting imports of scarce goods, metal, and coal from the Americans. The anti-reciprocity leader of 1911, Borden a few years later had been forced to recognize the continental forces that bound North America.

As a war leader, Borden showed his mettle. Once Hughes had been removed, once the organization of the nation's growing military forces had been sorted

out, Borden went to England for the Imperial War Cabinet and Conference in early 1917 and pushed for more for Canada in recognition of its substantial front-line role. He wanted more autonomy and a bigger role in shaping imperial policy, and he received much that he had sought. Resolution IX at the conference declared that the dominions were "autonomous nations of an Imperial Commonwealth" with a "right … to an adequate voice in foreign policy and in foreign relations."

After the taking of Vimy Ridge in April 1917 and after its horrendous casualties that could not be replaced by voluntary enlistment, Borden returned home and, his hesitancy gone, steeled himself to impose conscription. He knew that French Canada, nowhere near as committed to the struggle as were English Canadians, would oppose this measure so, in an effort to mitigate racial tension, he offered a coalition to Laurier, who refused. Rebuffed, Borden nonetheless introduced his Military Service Bill on 11 June 1917, telling Parliament that "If we do not pass this measure, if we do not provide reinforcements, if we do not keep our plighted faith, with what countenance shall we meet [the soldiers] on their return?"

Parliament passed the War Time Elections Act and the Military Voters Act that effectively gerrymandered the electorate, all but guaranteeing Borden a re-election victory by hiving off the immigrant vote and giving women relatives of soldiers the franchise. Creating a coalition was no easy task, but he persisted despite great odds. By late 1917, he had fashioned a Union Government by drawing in provincial Liberals, and his coalition handily won the election of December 1917, capturing a huge majority of English Canada's seats. That victory was achieved in large part by Borden's running a blatantly anti-Quebec campaign and making pledges to farmers that they and their sons would not be drafted, pledges he broke in the spring of 1918 after the Germans launched their great offensives in March. Winning the war required conscription and more men, Borden believed, and everything else including electoral fairness, Canada's unity, and the survival of the Conservative Party, now despised in Quebec, was secondary. Tough, determined, but completely lacking in charisma, the stubborn Borden bullied the country through the war, and overseas the Canadian Corps' four divisions did not want for reinforcements despite terrible casualties. He used the nation's military contributions to win Canada a seat at the Peace Conference at Versailles in 1919 and at the new League of Nations.

By 1920, Borden had been worn down by his efforts, and he left office in July. The Conservative Party did not recover in Quebec until 1958, long after his death, but Borden wrote his memoirs, delivered important lectures on constitutional matters, served as an elder statesman, and never truly received his due as one of the nation's great leaders because of his divisive tactics. SEE ALSO: CONSCRIPTION; HUGHES; QUEBEC AND THE MILITARY; WAR FINANCE; WAR INDUSTRY; WORLD WAR I.

READING: R.C. Brown, *Robert Laird Borden: A Biography*. 2 vols. (Toronto, 1975, 1980).

Bougainville, Louis-Antoine de, Comte de Bougainville (1729–1811). Born in Paris, de Bougainville studied and wrote on mathematics. He joined the French army in 1750 and became aide-de-camp to General Montcalm in 1756. He fought at Oswego and at Lake Champlain and was wounded at Carillon. By 1759, he was a colonel and, during General Wolfe's attack on Quebec, he had the task of keeping open the lines of communication between Montreal and Quebec. He continued to fight the British after Montcalm's death, but with the surrender of New France in 1760, he became a prisoner of war. His subsequent career in the French navy and as an explorer was notable.

Bourassa, Joseph Henri Napoléon (1868–1952). A grandson of Louis-Joseph Papineau, Bourassa was born in Montreal and first won election to Parliament as a Liberal in 1896. He opposed Sir Wilfrid Laurier over the dispatch of Canadian troops to fight in the South African War (1899–1902), resigning his seat in protest, arguing that the Boers posed no threat to Canada, and claiming that the government had set an unwise precedent by agreeing to participate.

Increasingly convinced that Laurier had become a tool of British and Canadian imperialists, Bourassa opposed creation of a Canadian navy, seeing in this a precursor to conscription. In a by-election in Drummond-Arthabaska in 1910, Bourassa successfully put a *nationaliste* candidate into the field against Laurier's man and won on the naval issue. The next year, co-operating gingerly with Robert Borden's Conservatives, Bourassa helped drive Laurier from power. The two francophone leaders partially rejoined forces in 1917 when, both opposing conscription for World War I, they lost the election to Borden's Union Government. Through his newspaper *Le Devoir*, Bourassa remained an important figure through World War II, once more opposing conscription for overseas service and working for the "non" side in the plebiscite of 1942. SEE ALSO: CONSCRIPTION; QUEBEC AND THE MILITARY.

READING: Joseph Levitt, *Henri Bourassa on Imperialism and Biculturalism* (Toronto, 1970).

Bren Gun Scandal. The John Inglis Company of Toronto won contracts to build Bren light machine guns for Britain and Canada in 1938. The contracts had not been tendered, leading Ontario Conservative politician George Drew to launch massive attacks against the Mackenzie King government in Ottawa. A royal commission set up to investigate Drew's charges found no evidence of corruption but did report unfavourably on contracting procedures in the Department of National Defence. As a result of the report, the government established a Defence Purchasing Board in 1939 that enforced competitive bidding for defence contracts. The Inglis Company eventually produced some 200,000 Bren guns for Canadian and Allied forces in World War II.

British Commonwealth Air Training Plan (BCATP). The BCATP (or Empire Air Training Scheme as it was called in Britain until June 1942) made Canada, in US President Franklin Roosevelt's famous phrase (actually suggested by L.B. Pearson), "the aerodrome of democracy." There was much truth in this statement, given that the plan trained 131,533 aircrew,

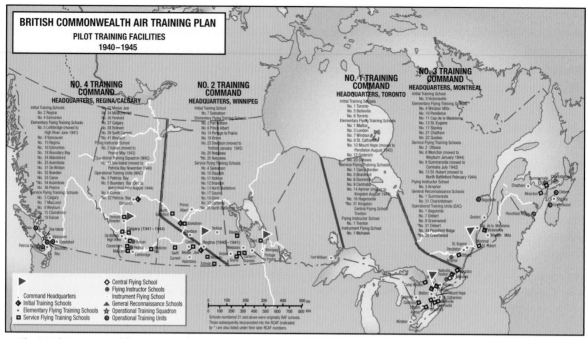

▲ The British Commonwealth Air Training Plan, its bases located all across Canada, produced vast numbers of aircrew and had a huge economic impact on communities.

some half of all those who served in the British and Dominions' air forces during World War II.

Discussions between Britain and Canada had taken place sporadically for some years before the outbreak of war in September 1939. Britain wanted to recruit and train Canadian pilots for the Royal Air Force (RAF) in Canada, but Prime Minister Mackenzie King was reluctant to agree, apparently because such arrangements would prejudice Canada's ability to decide if it wished to join a British war. In truth, King knew that Canada would go to war, but he worried about the political effect of such a peacetime military arrangement on his support in Quebec. Once the war began, attitudes in Ottawa began to change.

The idea of a great wartime Commonwealth air training plan appears to have originated with the Australian and Canadian High Commissioners in London, Stanley Bruce and Vincent Massey, and to have been picked up by the Air Ministry and the United Kingdom government. Mackenzie King, approached by London, agreed to discussions, in substantial part because in the limited liability war he

wished to fight air training could become the major part of Canada's war effort, a role that would minimize casualties and thus prevent a second conscription crisis like that of World War I.

Anglo-Canadian negotiations on the training plan, held in Ottawa from October to December 1939 and involving representatives from Australia and New Zealand as well, were complex and difficult. King wanted Britain to agree that the BCATP would be Canada's major contribution to the war, and he eventually got his way. For their part, the British wanted Canada to pay a large proportion of the costs, far more than the King government believed possible, and London also hoped to see all BCATP graduates assigned to the Royal Air Force, something Canada could not accept. Matters were not helped by Lord Riverdale, the British negotiator, who sometimes presumed too much, leading King to write in his diary, "Amazing how these people from the Old Country seem to think that all they have to do is tell us what is to be done." Nevertheless, on 17 December 1939, Mackenzie King's 65th birthday, the agreement was signed.

It was an ambitious program with training similar to that given by the Royal Air Force, with Initial Training Schools to offer the classroom basics of aeronautics, Elementary Flying Training Schools to instruct pilot trainees, Service Flying Training Schools to provide advanced techniques such as night and formation flying, and specialist schools to train air observers, bombers and gunners, air navigators, and wireless operators. Each month, 520 pilots with elementary training and 544 with service training, 340 air observers, and 580 wireless operators/air gunners were to graduate and proceed to Operational Training Units, mostly located in Britain. Canada was to supply the great majority of trainees. Pilot graduates were to be sergeants, with a number of the best graduates being commissioned as pilot officers.

Canada could retain 136 pilots, 34 navigators, and 58 wireless operators/gunners from the graduates each month for its Home War Establishment squadrons. Almost all of the first Canadian graduates, however, were to serve as BCATP instructors rather than to be posted overseas or to home squadrons. And Article XV of the agreement specified that Dominion graduates were to be assigned to an unspecified number of squadrons of their own air forces under RAF operational control, the number to be determined later. In practice, most of the BCATP graduates were assigned to RAF squadrons, leading to the substantial battle later fought by Minister of National Defence for Air C.G. Power over "Canadianization" and the creation of Royal Canadian Air Force (RCAF) squadrons overseas.

The original plan required large numbers of one- and two-engine aircraft for training: 702 Tiger Moths and Fleet Finches, 720 North American Harvards, 1,368 Avro Ansons, and 750 Fairey Battles. Great Britain agreed to supply most of these planes. Some 33,000 military personnel and 6,000 civilians were estimated to be required as instructors and administrative or maintenance staff in the different BCATP facilities, a huge challenge for the Royal Canadian Air Force, which had only 4,000 regulars in 1939. Part of the shortfall was met by using civilians from airlines and flying schools as trainers.

The December 1939 agreement, estimated to cost $607 million, was to expire in March 1943. Britain would provide $218 million in equipment and other costs. Canada was to pay $313 million, Australia and New Zealand the remainder. Alterations to the scheme soon raised the Canadian share by $40 million. The 1939 scheme specified that the BCATP would need buildings and airfields for 64 schools. BCATP airfields usually included a 813-metre main airstrip and two secondary ones arranged in a triangular pattern. Some of the training sites selected were already developed, needing only some additional buildings. On the other sites, extensive construction work was required, a large task with 8,300 buildings to be erected. Canada's wide-open spaces had made it the logical location for such a scheme.

In February 1940, the BCATP was placed under Air Commodore Robert Leckie, an able RAF officer who had served in Canada and who transferred to the RCAF (where he would later become chief of the air staff). Four regional commands were created to implement the plan with headquarters in Toronto, Montreal, Calgary, and Winnipeg. By 1 September 1941, the 16 Service Flying Training Schools required were in operation, seven months before the scheduled date. By the end of 1941, all the schools had been built, except for one bomber/gunner school not yet required. A total of 36,609 trainees had already passed through or were in the BCATP at the time.

One of the great difficulties became the supply of training aircraft. The Battle of Britain, beginning in the summer of 1940, forced Britain to keep every suitable aircraft on hand, thus making the provision of training aircraft to the BCATP impossible. Canada had to find an alternate source of supply, and C.D. Howe, the minister of munitions and supply, decided Canada would build its own version of the Avro Anson, modified with a US-made Jacobs engine, and other aircraft. It took money, time, and effort but, during the war, Canadian industry produced more than 8,000 Anson, Harvard, Tiger Moth, Finch, and Cornell trainer planes. Other aircraft were imported from the United States.

As the war developed, the planning for the 1939 BCATP came to be seen as too small by half. Almost 11,000 aircraft flew out of BCATP stations, while 104,000 civilians and military personnel administered and serviced 94 schools at 231 sites across Canada ranging from Victoriaville, Quebec, to Stanley, Nova Scotia, and to Pearce, Alberta. Building and running BCATP training stations poured money into and created jobs in small communities; Yorkton, Saskatchewan, for example, estimated that a thousand jobs at its training station would produce a monthly payroll of $100,000, a huge sum for a town that had struggled to survive the Depression. The total cost of the BCATP, by the time it closed down operations on 31 March 1945, had reached $2.2 billion, and Canada, its gross domestic product expanding rapidly during the war, paid $1.6 billion of that sum (and waived an additional $425 million owed by Britain in 1946).

Canadian graduates of the BCATP numbered 72,835, Royal Air Force 47,406, and Australia and New Zealand provided most of the remainder. (Almost 4,000 of the foreign BCATP trainees married Canadian women.) The BCATP trained 72,374 pilots, 25,646 of whom served in the RCAF and staffed some 85 RCAF squadrons that flew in every theatre of war. Approximately 3,000 trainees were killed in training accidents in Canada, a terrible toll; every week from 1942 to 1944, the years the BCATP was in full flight, saw a dozen trainees die. The vast majority of the more than 17,000 members of the RCAF who died in World War II were BCATP graduates.

Some 26,000 personnel who began training as aircrew did not graduate, most because they could not master the academic side of the training or found they could not handle the stress of flight. Most of these men subsequently served in their air forces in non-flying roles. There were also about 1,700 who began training too late to complete it before the BCATP closed down in March 1945. And there were those Canadian airmen who, for whatever reason, did not graduate and who found themselves enlisted in the army, getting their inoculations a second time and relearning foot drill and how to salute. One was Paul Hellyer, later the minister of national defence, from 1963 to 1968. His experiences of the rigidity of inter-service boundaries made him believe that a unified single service might perform better. SEE ALSO: CANADIANIZATION; ROYAL CANADIAN AIR FORCE; WORLD WAR II.

READING: W.A.B. Douglas, *The Creation of a National Air Force*, vol. 2, *The Official History of the Royal Canadian Air Force* (Toronto, 1986).

Brock, Isaac (1769–1812). Born in Guernsey, Brock joined the British army in 1785 as an ensign. He served in the West Indies, in Europe, and in Canada from 1802 where his efforts notably strengthened the defences of Quebec. Eight years later, he was posted to Upper Canada and in 1811 promoted to major-general and named administrator of the province. Brock thus was in command of both the military and civil arms of government when war with the United States began in June 1812. Brock had been making efforts to strengthen the militia, and he had planned to strike at American territory. He seized the initiative at once, capturing the fort at Michilimackinac, a victory that won the British the support of local First Nations. The Americans soon invaded Canada from Detroit, but Brock chose to

▲ Isaac Brock, painted in 1805.

attack Detroit itself, threatening the US lines of communication, a threat that cowed the weak American commander to retreat from Canada and then into surrendering. Brock's two victories bolstered the hitherto weak morale of Upper Canada's residents, many of them recent American immigrants who had not been quiet in expressing their sentiments. "The militia have been inspired by the recent success with confidence," Brock wrote, and "the disaffected are silenced."

With the western flank secure for the moment, Brock turned his eye to the Niagara frontier where, with only one regiment of British regulars and some Incorporated Militia, his troops were spread very thin. The Americans, mainly militia, crossed the Niagara River on 13 October, and Brock led his men into action at Queenston Heights, trying to drive them from a commanding position that threatened the British line. A tall man at six feet, two inches, Brock made a good target, and a rifle shot to his chest killed him instantly, casting much doubt on his supposed last words: "Push on, brave York volunteers." (His uniform, a bullet hole clearly visible, is on permanent display in the Canadian War Museum in Ottawa.) The battle seemed to be lost, the British in retreat, until Major-General Roger Sheaffe arrived with a thousand men from Fort George and, with a single volley and war whoops from accompanying Mohawk warriors, drove the Americans off the heights. Most of the survivors were forced to surrender at the river's edge.

Brock had been knighted four days before his death for his victory at Detroit. In Canada, his successful defence of the Province was marked by the erection of a large monument in 1824. Blown up in 1840, the monument was replaced by the present one that towers above Queenston Heights. See also: Queenston Heights; War of 1812.

Reading: J.M. Hitsman, *The Incredible War of 1812* (rev. ed., Montreal, 1999).

Brown, Arthur Roy (1893–1944). Born in Carleton Place, Ontario, Brown served as a fighter pilot with the Royal Naval Air Service and the Royal Air Force in World War I. He scored 10 victories over the Western Front, winning the Distinguished Service Cross and bar, but his reputation rests on the widespread belief that he shot down Manfred Freiherr von Richthofen, the famous German "Red Baron," in April 1918. The claim is not fully substantiated, some historians giving credit to an Australian machine-gunner firing from the ground. Brown was severely injured in an air crash a few months after the Richthofen battle and left the air force in 1919.

Brutinel, Raymond (1872–1964). Brutinel, born in southern France, immigrated to Canada in 1904 and made his fortune as a speculator in the West. At the outbreak of World War I, he conceived the idea of a motorized machine-gun unit, persuaded prominent political figure and businessman Sir Clifford Sifton of the utility of this idea, and went to the United States to acquire Colt .30 machine guns and specially made

▲ Brigadier-General Raymond Brutinel in World War I.

armoured cars from the Autocar Company in Ardmore, Pennsylvania. He began recruiting some 120 officers and men in Ottawa on 24 August 1914 and, by mid-September, had his vehicles and guns. The Autocar Machine-Gun Brigade, No. 1, with eight armoured vehicles, proceeded overseas with the Canadian Division, and to France in June 1915 under the name of the 1st Canadian Motor Machine Gun Brigade. Brutinel's beliefs in mobility, concentration of fire, and indirect fire, and his conviction that machine guns could have decisive impact on the battlefield, were innovative. They remained largely unproven until his brigade, expanded with three additional batteries all now equipped with Vickers machine guns, played an important role in stopping the great German offensives in March 1918. Before then, Brutinel's gunners had been used in dismounted roles, but his expertise was nonetheless highly valued—he became the Canadian Corps machine-gun officer in 1916 and commander of the Canadian Machine Gun Corps as a brigadier-general in 1918. Brutinel developed the corps' doctrine for the use of machine guns. He returned to France after the war. SEE ALSO: CANADIAN CORPS; WORLD WAR I.

READING: Yves Tremblay, "Brutinel: A Unique Kind of Leadership," in Bernd Horn and S. Harris, eds., *Warrior Chiefs: Perspectives on Senior Canadian Military Leadership* (Toronto, 2001).

Budget, Defence. Except in wartime or in times of great peril, Canadian governments have been loath to spend money on defence. The enemies abroad were far away, and the British and American navies would intercept them if they tried to attack North America. The potential enemy nearer to home, the United States, was so much bigger and more powerful that there was no point in spending on an inevitably futile effort at defence. With minor variations and exceptions, those were Canadian attitudes for most of the country's history.

In the years before Confederation, Canada relied on Britain for its defences, its tiny budgetary appropriations supporting the militia, which was always untrained and ill-equipped. After Confederation

and after Britain pulled its troops out of Canada (except for Halifax and Esquimalt), defence spending remained small, not rising above $1 million until the Northwest Rebellion of 1885 pushed expenditure to $5 million. Not even the gradual creation and expansion of the Permanent Force changed matters much, the bulk of government expenditure still going to support the militia, an area rich in government patronage. Still, after 1896 and the energetic efforts of Sir Frederick Borden as minister of militia, defence expenditure rose steadily, and by 1910 was at $9 million out of a total government expenditure of $122 million. During World War I, spending, of course, escalated dramatically—from $72 million in 1914 to $173 million in 1915, $312 million in 1916, $344 million in 1917, and $439 million in 1918. But with the return of peace, defence expenditures fell rapidly—to $18 million in 1921, $15 million in 1926, $13 million in 1933 at the nadir of the Depression, and, in 1938, with war clouds gathering, to only $38 million. World War II expenditures again were huge: $126 million in 1939, $1,268 million in 1941, $4,242 million in 1943, and $2,942 million in 1945. Once again there was a drop-off with peace, but only to a low of $196 million in 1947. The coming of the Cold War, the creation of the North Atlantic Treaty Organization (NATO), and the Korean War raised "peacetime" defence spending to unprecedented levels: $787 million in 1950, $1,959 million in 1952, $1,838 million in 1955, and $1,538 million in 1960. At its Cold War peak in 1952, Canadian defence spending was just under 8 percent of gross domestic product (GDP).

But Canada was becoming a social welfare state, expensive and popular programs such as Family Allowances, the Canada Pension Plan, and, soon, Medicare competing for scarce funding with much less popular defence expenditures. The Diefenbaker government tried to hold the line on defence spending as did Lester Pearson's, but Pierre Trudeau's Liberal government froze military spending, limiting it to approximately $1.7 billion for three years from 1968. That lowered defence spending to 2 percent of GDP, a figure that Canada would never achieve again, as expenditures rose relatively slowly while the GDP increased, pushed along by inflationary tendencies.

Under pressure from Canada's NATO allies, Trudeau did eventually raise defence spending, but the percentage of GDP devoted to the military continued to decline while inflation took its toll. The Mulroney government pledged to fix matters after 1984 but made them worse. The defence budget in 1993 was $12 billion and, after Jean Chrétien's government's deficit-fighting cuts, was $9.25 billion in 1998. Such cuts could only be achieved by slashing personnel and letting equipment grow obsolete. The situation was such that Liberal Prime Minister Paul Martin in 2004–2005 pledged more spending, and his successor, Conservative Stephen Harper, added to his totals. By 2009–2010, defence spending in Canada was some $21 billion, much the highest amount ever in dollar terms, but still only 1.2 percent of GDP.

Burns, Eedson Louis Millard (1897–1985). "Tommy" Burns was arguably the most interesting and complex Canadian general officer of World War II. Born in Westmount, Quebec, and nicknamed after a Canadian champion boxer, Burns graduated from the Royal Military College in 1915 and proceeded quickly into the hell of the trenches as a front-line signals officer in the 4th Canadian Division. He ended the war as a captain with the Military Cross, but his mother believed that the war had squeezed the life out of him and aged him prematurely.

Burns joined the Permanent Force where he helped to develop the techniques of air photo survey that mapped much of Canada (and for which he received the Order of the British Empire in 1935), and he earned a reputation as a proficient staff officer after his British Army Staff College training at Quetta, India. In his spare time, he wrote for H.L. Mencken's *American Mercury* under a pseudonym, Arlington B. Conway, producing regular pieces on military subjects. He sarcastically denounced those who still believed that cavalry were useful and noted that if intelligent men served in the infantry "it is unlikely they would long submit to being used as it is intended to use infantry." Burns also wrote short stories, plays, and a novel, and, an ambitious soldier, he published articles in the *Canadian Defence*

▲ Lieutenant-General E.L.M. Burns as UNEF commander, wearing a uniform he designed.

Quarterly, notably a piece that led a junior officer, Guy Simonds, to engage him in a spirited debate on the proper use of tanks. In a Permanent Force without any armour, this was great stuff by two future corps commanders. After attending (but not completing) the Imperial Defence College (IDC), Lieutenant-Colonel Burns was one of the few Canadian officers marked for high command.

World War II began while Burns was between terms at the IDC. He reported to the High Commissioner's office in London and became its senior military officer until Harry Crerar arrived to set up Canadian Military Headquarters. Burns then worked well for Crerar, who had him promoted to colonel, but Burns had a run-in with J.L. Ralston, the defence minister, that likely stopped him from being offered command of the armoured division forming in Canada in December 1940. Instead, he was named brigadier-general staff of the Canadian Corps in England but, still in Canada, spent much time in Montreal helping to develop the Ram tank. On these trips, Burns began an affair with a woman he met there, notwithstanding his wife and daughter living in Ottawa. This became important when Brigadier Burns, now in England at corps headquarters, wrote his mistress indiscreet letters commenting on the war and Canadian and Allied political and military personalities that attracted the censors' attention. Only Harry Crerar's friendship stopped his being sacked; instead, he was reduced in rank and returned to Canada—where he resumed his affair in Montreal. For a dour, cynical man who never seemed to smile or laugh, Burns led an interesting secret life.

He made his way back up the military ladder despite all. In February 1942, he became a brigade commander in the 4th Canadian Armoured Division and, the next year, commander of 2nd Canadian Infantry Division. In January 1944, he took over the 5th Canadian Armoured Division serving in Italy as part of I Canadian Corps under Crerar; before he could lead it in action, Crerar, departing for England to become First Canadian Army commander, tapped him to become his successor. Lieutenant-General Burns was on the way to the top; indeed, Crerar said that if anything happened to him, Burns should become army commander.

His first test came in May 1944 when the British Eighth Army attacked the Gustav and Hitler Lines that protected the route north to Rome. Burns's two divisions had a key role in the assault, the 1st Canadian Division opening a hole in the line and the 5th Armoured exploiting it. The casualties amounted to more than 7,000 killed, wounded, and ill in three weeks of gruelling battle, but the complaints against Burns arose over the huge traffic jam on the one road through the Liri valley for which he—and not the British commanders who had made a plan that took an army up a single highway—took the rap. General Oliver Leese of 8th Army tried to get Burns fired, but the Canadian high command, notably General Kenneth Stuart, chief of staff at Canadian Military Headquarters in London, and Crerar, refused to agree. So Burns continued to command and, in August and September 1944, I Canadian Corps assaulted the Germans' Gothic Line and broke it in the most brilliant Canadian military operation of World War II. There were kudos for Burns and a Distinguished Service Order, but also complaints;

his division commanders, Generals Christopher Vokes and Bert Hoffmeister, saw him as "depressing, diffident, and unenthusiastic." Vokes privately wrote that Burns "lacks one iota of personality, appreciation of effort or the first goddamn thing in the application of book learning to what is practical & what isn't." This time Crerar could not protect him, and Burns had to go, his victory on the Gothic Line notwithstanding.

The rest of Burns's war was anti-climactic, as he took command of Canadian rear area units in northwest Europe as a major-general. In 1945, he was seconded to the Department of Veterans Affairs, eventually becoming deputy minister in 1950. He published a study of Canadian manpower policy during World War II that was compelling in its analysis, but he toiled in comfortable obscurity until 1954, when he accepted the post of commander of the small United Nations Truce Supervisory Organization that operated on the borders between Israel and its Arab neighbours. Wearing a uniform of his own design, reportedly acquiring an Israeli mistress (who apparently spied on him for her government), Burns was the man on the spot when the 1956 Arab-Israeli War erupted and the Anglo-French invasion of Egypt began. After Lester Pearson's proposal for a United Nations Emergency Force (UNEF) won agreement at New York, Burns became UNEF's commander. As such, he brokered the arrangement that saw Canada—humiliated because Egypt refused to accept the Queen's Own Rifles as a component of UNEF—provide logistics, air, and reconnaissance units instead.

Burns's UNEF role, from which he retired in 1959, won him the recognition at home that his war service did not. He had even received a promotion to lieutenant-general in 1958 and, after his return from the Middle East, the post of adviser on disarmament in the Department of External Affairs with the rank of ambassador. In 1970, he published *General Mud*, his very good memoir of his service in two world wars.

An able and intelligent man, Burns suffered from some disabilities in personality that made him less effective than he had to be to command successfully. But his successes with I Canadian Corps in Italy ought to have won him praise rather than the abuse and demotion he received. SEE ALSO: CRERAR; ITALIAN CAMPAIGN.

READING: J.L. Granatstein, *The Generals: The Canadian Army's Senior Commanders in the Second World War* (Toronto, 1993).

By, John (1779–1836). A British military engineer, as a lieutenant and captain, By served in Canada from 1802 to 1811, working on the strengthening of Quebec's fortifications. He then served in the Peninsular War and in England. In 1826, after some years on half-pay, standard practice at the time, he was promoted to lieutenant-colonel and named the superintending engineer for the construction of a canal system that would link the Ottawa River and Lake Ontario by way of the Rideau and Cataraqui river systems. The canals were intended to create an alternate supply route to that of the St Lawrence River, too easily threatened by the United States. Constructing the Rideau Canal took five construction seasons, and it was expensive (£800,000 in all) and labour intensive. When By returned to England in 1832, however, the work was done. Bytown, later Ottawa, grew up around his headquarters.

Byng, Julian Hedworth George, Viscount Byng of Vimy (1862–1935). Born in England, the son of a somewhat impecunious earl, Byng joined the British army's cavalry in 1883 and served in India, the Sudan, and in the South African War. After staff and command posts, he led a cavalry division in the opening months of World War I, served at Gallipoli, and then commanded a corps on the Western Front. In May 1916, Lieutenant-General Byng (to his surprise) received command of the Canadian Corps, carefully assessed its weaknesses and strengths beginning with the shambles at the battles of St Eloi and Mount Sorrel and then on the Somme, and began

▲ Lieutenant-General Sir Julian Byng, April 1917.

the process of turning it into one of the premier Allied formations. Byng had the strength to fight off the more outrageous ideas of Sir Sam Hughes, the minister of militia and defence, and he promoted officers on merit. He directed the great and successful Canadian attack on Vimy Ridge in April 1917 and, soon after, as a full general, took command of Third British Army in the field and pioneered the use of tanks at Cambrai. Byng had become extraordinarily popular with the Canadian troops, so much so that they styled themselves the "Byng Boys." His gruff concern for his men's welfare, his competence in the field, and his absence of "side" had endeared him to the corps, and his appointment as Canadian governor general in 1921 was very well received. Byng ran into difficulty with Prime Minister Mackenzie King, however, falling victim to his political wiles during the "King-Byng" constitutional crisis in 1926, and he was much embittered at Canadian politicians by the time he returned to Britain to become Commissioner of the London Metropolitan Police. Byng was made a field marshal in 1932. SEE ALSO: CANADIAN CORPS; CURRIE; HUGHES; WORLD WAR I.

READING: Jeffery Williams, *Byng of Vimy: General and Governor General* (London, 1984).

Cabinet Defence Committee. In August 1936, the Mackenzie King government established a Cabinet Defence Committee that met only infrequently. At the outbreak of war in September 1939, King set up an Emergency Council, replacing it in December with the Cabinet War Committee, which had minutes and follow-up procedures, innovative measures at the time. After the war, the Cabinet Defence Committee was reconstituted, and it has continued under various titles as the Canadian government's senior defence body.

Cabinet War Committee. The organization of the work of Cabinet ministers in Ottawa was rudimentary until the coming of World War II forced change. Before September 1939, a Cabinet subcommittee on defence

▲ Mackenzie King (front row, centre) and his Cabinet War Committee, the ministers who directed Canada's extraordinary war effort, shown in 1943.

met infrequently; the name was changed on 5 September, just prior to Canada's declaration of war on the 10th, to the Defence Committee of Cabinet with a membership consisting of the prime minister, the (acting) finance minister, and the ministers of national defence, justice, and mines and resources. By 15 September, the name had changed once more to the Emergency Council (Committee on General Policy), and the government leader in the Senate had been added to the membership. Finally, on 5 December 1939, the Cabinet War Committee (CWC), established by Order-in-Council (PC 4017 1/2) replaced it. The CWC remained the key directing committee of the Canadian government through to the end of the war, its membership initially consisting of the prime minister (Mackenzie King), the ministers of justice (Ernest Lapointe, then Louis St Laurent), finance (J.L. Ralston, then J.L. Ilsley), national defence (Norman Rogers, then Ralston), and mines and resources (T.A. Crerar), as well as the Senate leader (Raoul Dandurand). The CWC increased in size on 27 May 1940 to include the minister of munitions and supply (C.D. Howe) and the minister of national defence for naval services (Angus L. Macdonald). The minister of national defence for air (C.G. Power) joined later. Other ministers participated as required, but the whole Cabinet met infrequently, as the CWC held 343 wartime meetings. Also present for CWC meetings were the clerk of the Privy Council and secretary to the Cabinet (Arnold Heeney) and the undersecretary of state for external affairs (O.D. Skelton and, after his death, Norman Robertson); other officials, including the chiefs of staff, attended when necessary. Heeney, the clerk and secretary, imposed order on the work of the CWC, drafting the agenda, taking and keeping minutes, providing documents, and ensuring that there was follow-up on decisions taken. SEE ALSO: WORLD WAR II.

READING: J.L. Granatstein, *The Ottawa Men: The Civil Service Mandarins, 1935–1957* (Toronto, 1982).

Caen (1944). This Norman city was the centrepiece of German defences at the eastern edge of the Normandy beachhead established by Allied forces after D-Day, 6 June 1944. The historic city, the medieval seat of William the Conqueror, had almost been entered by some Allied troops on 6 June, as planners had hoped; however, as the German panzer divisions rolled toward the coast and enemy resistance stiffened, Canadian and British forces were stopped short of their original objectives to the north and west. They would not get into Caen for more than a month. For the next several weeks, Canadian and British troops battered against the Germans holding the city's outskirts, with heavy artillery and air bombardments gradually flattening entire sections of the city and many of its principal buildings. Casualties on both sides mounted, but the Germans, including elite SS panzer units, held firm. The plan of British commander General Bernard Montgomery, which seems somewhat clearer in his memoirs than it did at the time, was to hold the bulk of German armour on the Anglo-Canadian front around Caen, making it easier for the Americans to advance inland farther west. The resulting attacks by Montgomery's forces tried to fix the enemy in place, a costly holding action, in other words, to enable success on the American front in exchange for British and Canadian losses at Caen. In early July, the 8th Brigade of General Rod Keller's 3rd Canadian Infantry Division, with the Royal Winnipeg Rifles of 7th Brigade, British and Canadian tanks, and aircraft, struck toward the town of Carpiquet and its airport. The attack brought the Canadians, suffering heavy casualties, into the town, which they fortified, but they succeeded in capturing only a portion of the airport. German counterattacks on 5 July were repulsed in fierce fighting, but the Canadians were under constant and effective enemy artillery bombardment for the next several days as British troops began pushing against Caen from the north. The Canadians finally took the airfield on 9 July as part of a general attack on Caen with four other British divisions, preceded by a heavy air raid by nearly 500 Allied bombers. The Canadians took Buron and Authie and finally moved into the ruined centre of the old town on 9 July, 33 days after its planned liberation. Among the leading units were the Sherbrooke Fusiliers and the Stormont, Dundas, and Glengarry Highlanders. In addition to some 500 casualties in and around Carpiquet on 4–5 July, the Canadians lost 1,200 more during the battles at Caen on 8–9 July, including 547 in the 9th Canadian Infantry Brigade that had led the assault. It would be more than a month before the Canadians and British finished off the Germans south of the city and, with US forces, finally sealed the Falaise Gap. SEE ALSO: NORMANDY.

Camp Borden. Established as an army training base in 1916 and named in honour of Sir Frederick Borden, the camp is located some 80 kilometres northwest of Toronto in sandy, poison ivy–covered soil. In 1917, the Royal Flying Corps established a training station there, which the Royal Canadian Air Force took over in 1924. Several Permanent Force training schools set up at Camp Borden in the 1930s, and during World War II, an estimated 185,000 men and women, soldiers and flyers, trained there. The infantry, armoured corps, army service corps, and medical corps trained officer cadets there during the Cold War. Now called Canadian Forces Base Borden, the establishment is the Canadian Forces' largest trades training station.

Camp X. Located on a 111-hectare farm on Lake Ontario between Oshawa and Whitby, Ontario, from December 1941, Camp X was the site where Western Hemisphere recruits chosen as spies and saboteurs for Britain's Special Operations Executive (SOE) received ten weeks of initial training; training was also provided to the US Office of Special Services in World War II. Run by the Canadian-born Sir William Stephenson's British Security Coordination from its headquarters in New York City, Camp X's training staff came from SOE. Stephenson's organization, charged with coordinating Britain's manifold intelligence activities in the Western Hemisphere, provided money and administration. The Canadian military took care of auxiliary services. Properly known as Special Training School (STS) 103, the camp drew the great bulk of its trainees from Canada and the US, both nations with people from a rich mix of ethnicities who could be trained for service in German-occupied Europe. Much mythology continues to flourish around Camp X, continuously burnished by acolytes of Stephenson, the "man called Intrepid." Its role was important as a training station, as a symbol of British-American intelligence

co-operation, and, not least, because it was the site of Hydra, a secret radio station handling British transatlantic intelligence communications. Although Camp X closed as a training centre in 1944, Hydra's operations kept the site going into the Cold War. Camp X served temporarily as the secure hiding place for Igor Gouzenko, the Soviet cipher officer whose defection in Ottawa in September 1945 helped to reveal the extent of Soviet spying operations in North America, and their likely knowledge of British and American atomic secrets.

READING: L.P. Hodgson, *Inside Camp X* (Toronto, 1999).

Canada–United Kingdom Defence Relations. Britain had responsibility for the defence of Canada, and Canada had no responsibility for its own defence, beyond its citizens' militia service, until the political union of Upper and Lower Canada in 1840, a responsibility that government and the citizenry, not for the last time, largely shirked. Governments refused to spend much money to secure Canada's borders and, even after Confederation, defence was not taken seriously. Few believed that Canada could defend itself if the United States made up its mind to attack; of those who believed that Britain would send troops in Canada's defence, some doubted that they would arrive in time to make a difference. The British regularly tried to persuade Canadian governments to improve the tiny Permanent Force and the militia, to strengthen fortifications, and, after 1900, to create a navy. They made these efforts because Canada was part of the Empire and potentially a source of troops for a future war.

The South African War, the first major test of the imperial bond, offered some comfort to the pro-imperialist crowd while simultaneously pointing to troubles ahead. English-Canadian opinion demanded participation while French Canadians, seeing in the Boers an oppressed people much as they thought of themselves, had little interest. The government of Sir Wilfrid Laurier caved in to the pressure for participation and dispatched troops who performed well. A precedent was set. Laurier's successor, Robert Borden, more imperialistic by nature, tried to offer money for Britain to build three dreadnoughts to help counter Germany; this plan failed to get through the Liberal-dominated Senate. But Borden put Canada extensively into World War I, raising 620,000 troops by voluntarism and conscription, and the Canadian Corps overseas proved a formidable fighting force. The war effort sped Canadian autonomy, fostered nationalism, including *Canadien* anti-war nationalism, and, with its terrible losses, encouraged many Canadians in their belief that no war could be worth fighting.

Borden's successor, Arthur Meighen, worried that the Anglo-Japanese Alliance might put Canada into war with the United States, and pressed successfully for London to escape this pact. Meighen sounded nationalistic here but he, like Borden before him, favoured a common imperial foreign policy. It was Mackenzie King who set the pattern for the next three decades—one of autonomy, no peacetime military commitments to Britain, and, when war did come, of eventual wholehearted participation. King forced the Empire to become the looser Commonwealth, and he secured recognition that the dominions had independence in foreign policy, recognized by the Statute of Westminster in 1931. To King, as to many others in 1939, independence was at least partly a formality, despite Westminster: Canada went to war when Britain did (one week later, in fact), because not doing so would have been unthinkable.

British and Canadian troops used the same equipment (much of it now supplied by Canadian factories), wore the same uniforms, and fought the same way during World War II under British generals who were not always impressive. Canada gave generous financial assistance to Britain and, except on rare occasions, did not object to Prime Minister Winston Churchill acting as if he always spoke for Canada on Allied strategy or treating the Dominion as a mere source of manpower. The ties of sentiment remained close, naturally enough after the wartime experience, but the Anglo-Canadian alliance by 1945 had largely been superseded by the Canada–US relationship. There was a new superpower and Canada, sharing North America with it, had no choice other than to adjust to the new reality. Britain and Canada nominally continued their wartime alliance, co-operated in the North Atlantic Treaty Organization (NATO), and exchanged intelligence information. Canada remained a member of the British Commonwealth and Canadian troops in NATO (until 1970) and in Korea served within larger British formations. But Britain after 1945 was no longer a Great Power, and the Canadian alliance with Britain after World War II was more rhetorical than real.
SEE ALSO: BORDEN, ROBERT; KING; SOUTH AFRICAN WAR; WORLD WAR I; WORLD WAR II.

READING: C.P. Stacey, *Canada and the Age of Conflict,* 2 vols. (Toronto, 1977, 1981).

Canada–United States Defence Relations. Canada and the United States began their relations in conflict. Even before the 1776 Declaration of Independence, the British colonies in what would become the United States of America had sent an invading army to Montreal and Quebec. That attack failed, but the Americans won their freedom from Britain. In the civil war that had pitted citizens of the Thirteen Colonies against each other as well as against the Crown, the losers—the Loyalists—flooded north into British North America. The United States tried again in 1812 to seize Upper and Lower Canada, failing thanks to good British generalship, skilful naval leaders, First Nations allies, and the Americans' own weaknesses in training, strategy, and command.

What followed came to be described in the early twentieth century as a hundred years of peace along an undefended border, but this was hyperbole. The Canadian rebels of 1837, for example, sought refuge in the United States, and some, with American supporters, launched armed raids into Canada. Confederate soldiers operating from near Montreal attacked St Albans, Vermont, during the US Civil War and robbed the town's banks. The Canadian courts amazingly let them go free—with their loot. The Irish-American Fenians sought to liberate Ireland by attacking British-controlled Canada after the Civil War, sending "armies" into Quebec and Ontario, and threatening New Brunswick and Manitoba. Every time the United States and Britain argued over foreign policy, Canadians braced, and occasionally actually prepared, for US invasion. In 1895, an argument over Venezuela's boundary, for example, turned into war talk in Washington and across the United States, but this time Britain placated the eagle, pledging never to go to war with the Americans.

Britain's long rapprochement with the United States left Canada increasingly vulnerable. A gold rush in the Klondike made the mountainous North and the boundaries of Alaska's panhandle, hitherto a frozen wasteland, into vital national territory and a possible precursor for military conflict or outright war. Canada dispatched North West Mounted Police and a good part of its tiny Permanent Force to Whitehorse as a Yukon Field Force to keep order and to demonstrate its willingness to maintain its sovereignty by force. US President Theodore Roosevelt had firm intentions of his own, what he called "ugly intentions," and he posted 800 soldiers to the region as well. An arbitration panel, a British judge holding the deciding vote, opted for the US position on the so-called Alaska Boundary Dispute, a clear indication, if Canadians had chosen to read it properly, that a fearful but practical Britain had abandoned Canada to the American sphere of influence. Outraged Canadians vilified the arbitrator more than they did Britain, and dutifully went off to war in 1914 as colonial citizens of the Empire.

Canada sent hundreds of thousands to war from 1914 to 1917, but the United States remained neutral, entering the conflict only in early 1917. Washington's entry eliminated Ottawa's nagging fear of raids or invasion by German or Irish sympathizers from south of the border, and increased defence co-operation between the two countries, especially in naval patrols along the eastern seaboard against German U-boats. The United States Navy (USN) sent six wooden "submarine chasers" to join the Canadian navy's tiny, ineffective anti-submarine vessels. USN seaplane units soon arrived at Halifax and Sydney, and co-operative defence of North America began. The war ended in November 1918; so did defence co-operation.

In fact, Canadian and American defence planners soon began to prepare war plans against one other. The US Army War College regularly studied how to invade Canada as part of a war with Britain. In Ottawa, Colonel James Sutherland Brown, the director of

military operations and planning, travelled by auto into the United States to calculate the best invasion routes if Canada had to launch spoiling attacks while awaiting British reinforcements. More seriously, Brown's staff prepared plans on how best to preserve Canadian neutrality if the United States and Japan went to war. How could Canada stop Japan from securing a toehold on the British Columbia coast? How could it prevent the United States from attempting the same tactic or "defending" Canada against Japanese invasion, whether Canada wanted to be defended or not?

All this strategizing ended for good when President Franklin Roosevelt and Prime Minister Mackenzie King began meeting and talking after 1935. The threat of war in Europe and Asia was increasing, and Roosevelt, his own nation weakly defended, worried that Canada's almost complete lack of defences provided an open back door into the United States. In January 1938, Roosevelt personally arranged secret conversations between the Canadian and US chiefs of staff. Nothing resulted from this first ever peacetime meeting of the two militaries, but it was followed just months later by Roosevelt's pledge in Kingston, Ontario, that the United States "will not stand idly by" if Canada were to be menaced by another empire. Surprised by this statement, Mackenzie King nonetheless promised a few days later that Canada would not allow the United States to be attacked via Canadian territory. When Canada went to war in September 1939, the United States stayed neutral; but once France fell to the Nazis, and Britain seemed on the verge of defeat, those words in 1938 took on real meaning.

The two leaders met at Ogdensburg, New York, in mid-August 1940 and changed their nations' defence relations forever. The Permanent Joint Board on Defence began to plan for the defence of North America. The United States instantly tried to gain control of the Canadian military; Canadians stoutly resisted and would only pledge co-operation. The situation was clear: as a result of the Ogdensburg meeting, Canada would do the maximum it could to help Britain, stripping its defences in Canada to that end because it was certain the United States would defend it *in extremis*. For a half century or more, Britain's power to help Canada had been in reality all but non-existent; now, there was no doubt that it was gone forever, and that Canada had a new protector. Soon, Canada received some of the destroyers the United States gave the Royal Navy in the "destroyers for bases deal"; it was not long before US troops were placed in some of those bases in Newfoundland where Canada had troops of its own. By September 1941, the United States still neutral, a USN admiral had command of the anti-submarine war being run out of St John's. After Pearl Harbor brought the United States into the war in December 1941, British, Canadian, and American ships worked closely together to win the Battle of the Atlantic.

America's emergence as a great power and key participant in the war shrank Canadian status in Washington's eyes. When the United States was neutral and worried about its own defence, Canada mattered. When Britain and the United States sat down to plan the war, Canada suddenly was just another dominion, one for which Britain could and should speak. This did not sit well with Ottawa, which lobbied to get a military mission in Washington and tried with limited success to get a voice in the economic aspects of the war. Still, Canada was of some importance to the United States, if only as territory. The Japanese seized control of some of the Aleutian Islands off Alaska in 1942, which led to US pressure to build a highway through Canada to Alaska. Canada agreed to the demand, and thousands of US Army engineers poured into British Columbia and the Yukon in 1942 to blast a pioneer road through the mountains and muskeg in record time. Canadian soldiers joined with GIs in 1943 in an invasion of Kiska Island, only to find that the Japanese had left secretly a few days before. That was the first large-scale army co-operation between the two nations; the creation of the 1st Special Service Force, a combined American and Canadian unit that fought in Italy and southern France, was another. In the fighting in Germany in early 1945, a US Army corps served under First Canadian Army for some time, yet another landmark. Many Americans came to Canada to train as fliers under the British Commonwealth Air Training Plan before American entry into the war. Many chose to remain with their

RAF (Royal Air Force) or RCAF (Royal Canadian Air Force) squadrons after their country joined the fight.

There were also now American airfields, weather stations, and soldiers galore on Canadian territory, so much so that Canadians joked that the telephone operators at American headquarters in Edmonton greeted callers with "Hello, US Army of Occupation." Pressed to act to restore Canadian control (amazingly, by the British High Commissioner in Ottawa, who seemed to be the first to notice the situation), the King government appointed an army general to show the flag and at war's end purchased all the American installations on Canadian soil. Significantly, however, Canada's post–VE Day army participation in the war against Japan was to be an infantry division, organized, trained, and equipped along US Army lines that would invade the Japanese home islands as part of a huge and potentially horrific US assault. The two atomic bombs made this Canadian role unnecessary by forcing imperial Japan's capitulation, but if Canadians assumed that after VJ Day they could revert to prewar somnolence, they were wrong.

The coming of the Cold War with the Soviet Union almost instantly made this clear. Igor Gouzenko, a Soviet cipher officer who defected in Ottawa in September 1945 with a bag of incriminating documents, demonstrated the extent of Soviet suspicion of the West. Canada decided to maintain the wireless intercept stations it had created during the war and switched its targets to Moscow and its friends, and the Permanent Joint Board on Defence—its permanence never in doubt—had its force and focus renewed. By 1948, Canada, Britain, and the United States were talking about the need for a new alliance to resist Soviet pressure and, in April 1949, they signed the North Atlantic Treaty with the Netherlands, Belgium, Luxembourg, France, Italy, Norway, Denmark, Iceland, and Portugal. Canada had hoped it could merely supply its European allies with World War II equipment but, once the Korean War began in June 1950 and the Soviet Union appeared to Western capitals to be entering a more aggressive phase, Canada began a major rearmament, pushed by the United States.

American pressure led Canada to send a brigade group to Korea and another for NATO (North Atlantic

Treaty Organization) service in West Germany, along with an air division of fighter aircraft. At sea, the Royal Canadian Navy (RCN) expanded rapidly and redeveloped its World War II expertise in anti-submarine warfare. The RCN and RCAF soon had close ties with their US counterparts—the natural tendency was to bond with the leaders in technology and tactics; the Canadian army, however, preferred to remain closer to the British, putting its brigades in Korea and Germany under British command, where the latter would remain for nearly 20 years before moving south to serve under American command. Canada–US linkages nonetheless were close and growing as the Cold War worsened. Faced with the threat of Soviet bombers attacking North America with nuclear weapons, the RCAF and the American air force wanted as much warning time and air defence coordination as possible. This led to the construction of three radar warning lines on Canadian soil, with most of the costs paid by the United States. It led to the Defence Production Sharing Agreement of 1958 that encouraged the US military to buy more from Canada and to the achievement of a long-term balance in each nation's sales to the other. It led as well to the North American Air Defence Agreement of 1957–1958, which created a joint headquarters in Colorado Springs to control North American skies. A Canadian was always the deputy commander of NORAD (North American Air/Aerospace Defence Command).

Many observers feared that Canadian independence had been compromised; even more thought such co-operation served both nations' interests. When the Cuban Missile Crisis erupted in October 1962, Canadians discovered that Bomarc missiles in Canada were unready to receive their nuclear warheads—in part because of prime ministerial dithering—and that Prime Minister John Diefenbaker had delayed and delayed again to put the RCAF's air defences on alert in conjunction with his American ally. The resulting crisis, a moment in which Canadian reliability as a friend and ally had been called into question, effectively brought down the government. Canadians could be prickly nationalists but, in the face of a real Soviet threat, they believed Canada needed to work with its

▲ Soldiers of the 1st Special Service Force, a joint American-Canadian unit, take Germans captive in Italy in January 1944.

superpower neighbour. Had they known that the RCN put to sea during the Cuban crisis without government authority to assist the USN in tracking Soviet submarines, their reaction might have been different.

Lester Pearson's Liberal government, elected in 1963, accepted the nuclear warheads over which Diefenbaker had worried, and vowed to restore good Canada–US relations. It was not to be, thanks to rising economic nationalism in Canada and the Americans' unpopular Vietnam War. Washington wanted Canada to deploy troops to Vietnam, but Canada had already agreed to serve on the International Control Commission monitoring the "peace." It could not simultaneously be a peacekeeper and a war fighter; moreover, Pearson disliked US tactics in the war, even going to Philadelphia to urge President Lyndon Johnson to stop the bombing in a public speech that (rightly) infuriated the president. Still, Canada could be useful to the United States. In 1960 it sent peacekeeping troops to the Congo, then a theatre in the Cold War, and it put infantry into Cyprus four years later, thus helping to prevent a war between NATO allies Greece and Turkey that could have destroyed the alliance. (A grateful President Johnson supposedly agreed to the Auto Pact as a reward for Canadian help.)

Relations grew even testier when Liberal Pierre Trudeau took office in 1968. Trudeau was almost as suspicious of the United States as he was of the USSR, and believed in keeping equidistance as much as possible. He also distrusted the military, believed that Canada's defence effort cost too much, and wanted to get Canadian troops out of NATO, although he later settled for reducing the military commitment to Europe by half. The tensions that resulted with Washington were long-lasting. Trudeau did grudgingly concede that the United States could test cruise missiles over Canada and, later in his long time in office, to increase defence spending, but his term marked a nadir in postwar bilateral relations. Brian Mulroney's Progressive Conservative government, elected in 1984, re-established the relationship, much too closely (or so nationalists infuriated by his 1989 Free Trade Agreement charged). As the world changed with the USSR's collapse and the end of the Cold War, Canada agreed to participate (in a very limited way) in the first Gulf War in 1990–1991 as part of a US-led coalition, and Mulroney's government became an active player in other American-led initiatives, including those in the former Yugoslavia and in Somalia.

Jean Chrétien's Liberals, swept to power in 1993 in a huge backlash against Mulroney's style and his pro-American policies, aimed to establish a cooler relationship with the United States and largely succeeded. There was a cut in defence spending of some 30 percent, and the Canadian Forces were chopped to 60,000 across all ranks over several years. This meant that beyond benign United Nations peacekeeping, Canada could do almost nothing effective abroad as equipment aged and troop strength dropped. Canadian defence, de facto, fell to the Americans, something that nationalists and pacifists—both groups with large numbers in Canada—did not grasp. After the al Qaeda attacks on New York and Washington in September 2001, defence mattered once again.

The Canadian government scrambled furiously to keep trade moving across a now-defended border as President George W. Bush made American homeland security his top priority while he prosecuted the War on Terror abroad. In late 2001, Ottawa agreed to send an infantry battalion to fight with American troops against al Qaeda and Taliban forces in Afghanistan— the planning locus for the 9/11 attacks—as the government attempted successfully to evade a commitment to participate in Bush's attack on Iraq the next year. The Chrétien government and its successor, led by Paul Martin, refused to join in a US anti–ballistic missile defence program, angering Washington. But Ottawa won some points when it placed troops in Kabul on a quasi-peacekeeping mission, and in 2005, Martin's short-lived Liberal government changed the mission to war fighting as part of the United Nations–authorized and NATO-led mission. The Canadian commitment to Kandahar of more than 2,500 soldiers was the largest since Korea, and it was most definitely not peace-keeping. Critics in Canada charged that participation in the War on Terror, George Bush's War (as it was often sneeringly portrayed), was not in Canadian interests, but the Conservative government of Stephen Harper, in power from early 2006, accepted the Kandahar commitment, increased it to 2,800, and lengthened it to 2011. Harper also began to spend large sums on defence, buying long-range transport aircraft, new armoured vehicles, artillery, and trucks (though acquisitions in the United States were being hampered by the US's International Traffic in Arms Regulations, which were intended to restrict access to military technology to individuals from a long list of nations working in countries such as Canada). He also pledged a "Canada first" policy that would put troops and ships into the Arctic to bolster Canada's claims against those of the other Arctic powers, including the United States; as the ice melts, commercial shipping increases, and mineral, oil, and gas reserves become accessible.

The Canada–US defence relationship has been long and contentious. Inescapably, the two nations are as joined together as the continent they share. Their defence requirements remain, in North America at least, all but indistinguishable. As Roosevelt and King realized in 1938, the United States defends Canada because it must, and Canada acquiesces because not doing so would be foolish in peace and suicidal in war. Canada is strategic geography for the United States, and the United States is the strategic bulwark—and, most of the time, financial succor—for Canada. Whether missiles, bombers, or car-bound terrorists, attacks on one can come with little warning through the political jurisdictions of the other. What may be prudent at home can be contentious abroad, however, the range and complexity of Washington's security arc far exceeding the parameters or interests of Canada's own. NATO unites both countries in the joint defence of the North Atlantic area and, in Afghanistan, areas well beyond that; but no other venue, least of all the United Nations, impels security co-operation to any similar degree. The two powers sometimes disagree, within normally reasonable limits, in international forums from New York to Geneva, and occasionally part company even on the conduct of war. Canadian nationalists score cheap points from American failures abroad while sheltering under its defence umbrella; American nationalists lash Canada for its social policy and disloyalty in Iraq. Both countries' soldiers serve, and often die together, in the hills of Afghanistan. The migration of Canada from colony to dominion to American ally, the result of a century and more of war, politics, and economic evolution, has been the principal trajectory of Canada's alliance posture since Confederation. It will not change soon. SEE ALSO: AFGHANISTAN WAR; ALASKA HIGHWAY; KING; NORTH AMERICAN AIR DEFENCE AGREEMENT; OGDENSBURG AGREEMENT; PERMANENT JOINT BOARD ON DEFENCE.

READING: Robert Bothwell, *Alliance and Illusion* (Vancouver, 2007).

Canadian Air Force. Sir Robert Borden's tiny Canadian Air Force, established in the closing months of World War I and taking form in Britain at the armistice, disbanded in mid-1919. In 1920, the newly-established Air Board authorized a small air force that became permanent thanks to the National Defence Act of 1922. In 1924, it acquired the name of the Royal Canadian Air Force. That name persisted until the unification of the three services in 1968 when the name reverted to that used at the air force's founding a half-century before.

Canadian Armed Forces/Canadian Forces. The Canadian Forces Reorganization Act, which became

law on 1 February 1968, ended the legal existence of the Royal Canadian Navy, the Canadian Army, and the Royal Canadian Air Force. In place of three separate services, the act created a single unified service with land, air, and sea "environments;" in place of the traditional navy blue, khaki, and light blue uniforms, all members of the new Canadian Forces would wear dark green. As defined in the National Defence Act, "the armed forces of Her Majesty raised by Canada … consist of one Service called the Canadian Armed Forces."

The reorganization of the three services had already begun on 1 April 1966 with the creation of six functional commands: Mobile Command, Maritime Command, Air Transport Command, Air Defence Command, Training Command, and Material Command. The land and air forces committed to Europe for service with the North Atlantic Treaty Organization continued as before, though they would now be called Canadian Forces Europe. Over time, the organizational structure of the military altered as the environments sought and secured more control over their activities. By the end of the twentieth century, the "Canadian Forces" (CF), as the military is most commonly called, primarily consisted of Maritime Command, Land Force Command, and Air Command, the main force generators for all missions or deployments. Each of the environments again had its own distinctive uniform, only the land forces continuing to wear the greens introduced in 1968. There remained unified support services, the so-called purple trades because they blended navy and air force blue with army green. The post–Cold War evolution of the CF saw the introduction of additional commands, including Canada Command, responsible for the defence of Canada; Canadian Expeditionary Force Command, responsible for military forces sent abroad; and Special Operations Forces Command, responsible for the military's growing complement of Special Forces. These commands, employers of the forces created by the three environments, were not universally hailed, but nonetheless took form after 2005 while the CF was heavily engaged in Afghanistan and during the term of General Rick Hillier as chief of the defence staff.

Canadian Army (Regular). Canada's permanent, or standing, land forces before World War II were known by a variety of names, but from World War II simply as the Canadian Army, the strength of which was fixed at 25,000. This was a small number compared to what the generals had expected after the efforts made during the war, but still it was by far the largest Permanent Force in the nation's history up to that time. The Cold War, the Soviet threat, the creation of the North Atlantic Treaty Organization (NATO), and the Korean War combined to oblige the government to increase military strength and to dispatch troops to Korea and to Europe. By 1952, the Canadian Army (Regular), which is not to be confused with the part-time soldiers of the militia, had 52,000 officers and other ranks, including a brigade in action in Korea and another in West Germany with NATO. Additional commitments soon arose—officers for peace observation missions in Palestine, Kashmir, and Indochina, and major United Nations deployments to Egypt after the Suez Crisis of 1956, to the Congo in 1960, and to Cyprus in 1964. Professional, highly trained, and well-equipped, the army of the late 1950s was arguably the best Canada ever fielded. But the increasing costs of defence equipment, the rapid pace of technological change, and the fervent desire of governments to spend money on more popular vote-catching policies squeezed defence budgets and eroded force size. By the mid-1960s, with the integration and, later, unification of the army, navy, and air force as government policy, it seemed clear that the heyday of military professionalism had ended. The Canadian Army (Regular) disappeared in 1968 when unification of the Canadian Forces became law.

READING: J.L. Granatstein, *Canada's Army: Waging War and Keeping the Peace* (Toronto, 2002).

Canadian Army Nursing Service. The first four Canadian nurses were professional nurses from Winnipeg who accompanied the Northwest Field Force during the Northwest Rebellion of 1885. After the battle of Batoche, which effectively ended the rebellion, seven additional nurses joined the staff of the general hospital created to treat the sick and wounded. In 1899 when Canada sent an infantry battalion to South Africa, four professionally trained nurses accompanied the contingent receiving, from 25 January 1900, the status of junior officers. They were not permitted to go into the field; instead, they worked in British army general hospitals, instructing hospital orderlies. As casualties mounted, especially from disease, these constraints disappeared. Led by Nursing Sister Georgina Fane Pope, the Canadian nurses of the First Contingent proved valuable, and more nurses arrived with subsequent contingents. On 1 August 1901, the Department of Militia and Defence formally organized the Canadian Army Nursing Service with a Permanent Force component comprising the nurses who had served or were serving in South Africa, plus a reserve component of qualified nurses working in Canada and available for military service. When the Army Medical Service reorganized in 1904, the reserve establishment increased to 25. At the beginning of World War I, there were five Permanent Force nurses and 57 on the reserve list, but wartime strength at its peak reached 3,141 with 1,886 serving overseas by 1917. In all, 53 nursing sisters died in service, including six killed when their hospitals were bombed, 14 drowned when a U-boat sank a Canadian hospital ship, and 18 who died of disease. In the interwar years, the Nursing Service came under control of the director general of medical services at army headquarters; in World War II, when 3,656 nursing sisters enlisted, and afterwards, the service was an integral part of the Royal Canadian Army Medical Corps.

READING: G.W.L. Nicholson, *Canada's Nursing Sisters* (Toronto, 1975).

Canadian Army Occupation Force (CAOF). At the end of World War II, the First Canadian Army provided a division-sized force of 18,000 as part of the Allied occupation of Germany. (There was also an air force contingent of 13 squadrons, later reduced to 11.) Commanded by Major-General Christopher Vokes, and with its units named after those that had served in 3rd Canadian Infantry Division, the Canadian Army Occupation Force consisted of volunteers and soldiers with low priority for repatriation to Canada. It was

⌃ Nursing sisters of the Canadian Expeditionary Force, much as these two shown in May 1917, frequently served close behind the front lines.

withdrawn in 1946 over the pronounced objections of Great Britain, which saw Canadian troops in Germany as freeing British troops for postwar colonial missions elsewhere. Ottawa had no interest in assisting London in this way, and rushed to repatriate its forces amidst a string of increasingly serious incidents overseas involving ill discipline, theft, corruption, and sit-down strikes. A separate deployment saw an infantry battalion serve in Berlin for most of July 1945.

Canadian Army Organization. The Canadian Army was and is organized into corps and regiments. The corps have historically encompassed the arms and services of the army: the arms mean essentially the combat arms, and include infantry and cavalry, as well as armour, artillery, signals, and combat engineers; the services are essentially those functions that support the combat arms and the military as a whole, including supply and transport, ordnance, electrical and

mechanical engineers, medical and dental professionals, and much else that an army needs to operate. Reorganization has grouped most of the services except medical and dental (which are unified for the three services into the Canadian Forces Medical Service) into an all-encompassing logistics category.

At the regimental level, the infantry and armour are grouped into units of battalion size (700–1,000 each), with the present three regular infantry regiments, the Royal Canadian Regiment, the Princess Patricia's Canadian Light Infantry, and the Royal 22e Régiment, each having three battalions. The armoured regiments of the regular force are the Royal Canadian Dragoons, Lord Strathcona's Horse, and the 12e Régiment Blindé. The artillery regiments are all from the Royal Canadian Horse Artillery. Signals units are organized in squadrons, engineers in combat engineer regiments, and logistics in service battalions. The army in Canada is organized into three brigade groups, each with three battalions of infantry, an armoured, engineer, and artillery regiment, a service battalion, and a signals squadron. All units are under-strength except on deployment when numbers are made up with reservists and soldiers posted in from other regular units. Canada itself is divided into four administrative land force areas encompassing the West, Ontario, Quebec, and the Atlantic region. At the top of the pyramid is the chief of land staff, based at National Defence Headquarters in Ottawa.

The current army structure is similar to that of the mid-twentieth century, but much smaller and considerably more complex. The army during the two world wars operated in divisions and brigades that were organized into corps and, during World War II, into a field army of two corps plus thousands of support troops. During World War I, infantry had been organized into companies, battalions, and brigades that were then grouped into divisions and a corps with supporting artillery, engineers, and other services attached, plus additional brigades of artillery, engineers, and cavalry. After 1945, the army adopted a brigade group organization to send troops to Korea and for North Atlantic Treaty Organization (NATO) service in Europe. No full brigade group has deployed on active service ever since, with the notable exception of West Germany, where a brigade formation remained in place until 1993. In recent decades, and especially since the end of the Cold War and the advent of complex war fighting and peace enforcement missions within much larger multinational formations, the standard deployment structure has been the battle group. This force of 2,500–3,000 personnel, one-third to one-half the size of a standard brigade, is normally based around a reinforced infantry battalion with armoured, artillery, engineer, medical, and other units attached. The much larger brigade groups in Canada have tended to become more administrative formations as time passes, much as divisional formations, after World War II, gradually gave way to brigades.

The militia or army reserve is organized in a fashion similar to that of the regular army with arms and services organized into brigade groups. For example, 31 Canadian Brigade Group in southwestern Ontario comprises the 1st Hussars and the Windsor Regiment from the Armoured Corps, the 11th and 56th Field Artillery Regiments, 31 Combat Engineer Regiment, the Royal Hamilton Light Infantry, The Lincoln and Welland Regiment, the 4th Battalion, Royal Canadian Regiment, the Royal Highland Fusiliers, the Essex and Kent Scottish, and the Argyll and Sutherland Highlanders, as well as three service battalions. The militia brigades get into the field for brigade exercises only in the summer. All are under-strength but serve as the basis for mobilization in time of crisis.

Canadian Army Pacific Force (CAPF). Canada agreed in principle to commit ground forces to the war against Japan at the Quebec Conference in September 1944, a decision confirmed by the Cabinet War Committee in November. The Mackenzie King government, however, had no desire to see Canada's soldiers help Britain restore its Asian colonies; instead, the Canadian contribution was to be deployed with US forces. The division-sized force was to be made up of volunteers, most of them from First Canadian Army, then fighting in Europe, each of whom would receive 30 days of leave in Canada prior to the start of training. In other words, no home defence conscripts were to be obliged to serve in Asia as the conscription issue continued to divide Canadians at home and damage the King government. The CAPF was to be organized into regiments, not brigades, and to be trained and equipped on American lines to simplify logistics and avoid command problems. Intended to participate in the invasion of the Japanese home islands, widely expected to be both difficult and bloody, the division—commanded by Major-General Bert Hoffmeister who had been the highly successful commander of the 5th Canadian Armoured Division in Italy and the Netherlands—adopted the names of units of the 1st Canadian Infantry Division. There were ample volunteers for the CAPF (more than 75,000 in all) and training was underway in Canada and the United States when Japan's surrender in August 1945 after the atomic bombings of Hiroshima and Nagasaki made its deployment unnecessary. The force quickly disbanded, much to the politicians' relief. SEE ALSO: CANADA–UNITED STATES DEFENCE RELATIONS.

Canadian Army Special Force (CASF). Announced by the St Laurent government on 7 August 1950, the CASF was to be raised to meet Canadian obligations to the United Nations in Korea. Assembled as part of the army's Active Force, the CASF was composed of 18-month volunteers with a leavening of regulars. The recruitment was hasty, but the 25th Canadian Infantry Brigade was in place by November under command of Brigadier John Rockingham. It went to Korea in 1951. The Special Force designation was rarely used once the brigade had been formed. SEE ALSO: KOREAN WAR.

Canadian Coast Guard (CCG). Formed in 1962, the civilian Canadian Coast Guard has 2,400 sea-going personnel operating 114 vessels. Its origins date to the creation of the Department of Marine and Fisheries in 1868 and, from 1936, the marine responsibilities of the Department of Transport. In 1995, the CCG amalgamated with the Department of Fisheries and Oceans Canada and, in 2005, became a Special Operating Agency of that department. The CCG, which is unionized, helps ensure safe waterways, enforces fishing regulations, and assists in sovereignty protection. It also runs the Canadian Coast Guard College in Sydney, NS.

Canadian Corps. Arguably the pre-eminent fighting formation in Canadian military history, the Canadian Corps constituted the nation's army in France and Belgium in World War I. When the Canadian Division of the Canadian Expeditionary Force departed Valcartier for England in September–October 1914, no one expected either a long war or a further major commitment of Canadian troops. But the course of the war, the development of trench warfare with its heavy losses, and the huge casualties suffered by the Canadian Division at Ypres in April 1915 quickly made clear that more men were required. The arrival of the 2nd Canadian Division in France in 1915 led to the creation of the Canadian Corps on 23 September 1915, initially under British Lieutenant-General E.A.H. Alderson. Two more divisions, the 3rd and the 4th, arrived on the continent in 1916 to bring the corps to its full strength. Other Canadian units—a cavalry brigade, two motor machine-gun brigades, and forestry and railway troops—

were not always attached to the corps but were for all practical purposes part of it. The corps would operate as part of a British field army throughout the war.

The Canadian corps began to realize its full fighting potential when Lieutenant-General Sir Julian Byng took command in May 1916. A British officer, Byng resisted patronage appointments from Canada and replaced failures with the meritorious and battle-tested. He inspired the troops with his modest demeanour and led the corps through the terrible battles on the Somme. The victory at Vimy Ridge in April 1917 was his, and he left soon after to take command of an army, his successor the 1st Canadian Division commander, Arthur Currie. Lieutenant-General Currie did not inspire his troops as Byng had, but he led them to victory with skilful planning at Hill 70 and in the appalling conditions at Passchendaele. Currie refused the British suggestion to split the corps' strong divisions into a two-corps army, seeing no gain in fighting efficiency from this and considerable damage to Canadian esprit de corps. He insisted on retaining his four-battalion brigades when the British, short of men, reduced theirs to three. At the same time, he increased the corps' complement of artillery, engineers, machine guns, and trucks and paid special attention to logistics, leaving a gifted British officer, Brigadier-General G.J. Farmar, in charge of this crucial area. The corps under Currie was a learning organization, one that sought lessons, practised its tactics, and proved innovative in the use of its weaponry and materiel and human resources.

In what was undoubtedly the high point of Canadian arms during the war, Currie's organization began the Hundred Days' offensive with a huge victory at Amiens on 8 August 1918; the corps followed this with an unbroken string of triumphs that saw the Canadians smash the Hindenburg Line, ending the war on 11 November 1918 at Mons, Belgium, where the British had first faced the Germans in 1914. Under Byng and Currie, the Canadian Corps became an elite formation of shock troops, always fighting where the going was hardest. Currie fostered the corps' nationalism by resisting British efforts to use the Canadian troops on a piecemeal basis.

In all, some 424,589 officers, nursing sisters, and men served overseas with the corps, a number that includes those who served in the Royal Flying Corps, the Royal Naval Air Service, and the Royal Air Force. Deaths from all causes in the Canadian Corps (including Canadian prisoners of war) were 53,584, while those wounded in action numbered 138,001. There were in addition 21,471 non-battle injuries. See also: Byng; Currie; World War I.

Reading: G.W.L. Nicholson, *Canadian Expeditionary Force, 1914–1919* (Ottawa, 1962); Tim Cook, *At the Sharp End: Canadians Fighting the Great War, 1914–1916,* vol. 1 (Toronto, 2007), and *Shock Troops: Canadians Fighting the Great War, 1917–1918,* vol. 2 (Toronto, 2008).

Canadian Defence League. Established in 1909 as "a non-political association to urge the importance to Canada of universal physical and naval or military training," the League was a lobby aiming to arouse interest in Canadian defence. It called for universal cadet training for all males between ages 12 and 18, followed by two years militia summer training. Concentrated in Toronto, it never achieved widespread support and, by 1914, had largely faded.

***Canadian Defence Quarterly**. The Canadian Defence Quarterly,* or cdq, was a military journal launched in 1923 that served as an important forum for professional military debate and discussion in the interwar period. Future generals Kenneth Stuart, E.L.M. Burns,

▲ The Canadian Corps paid special attention to supply, planning, and battle preparation. Ammunition stockpiles were a key to battlefield success.

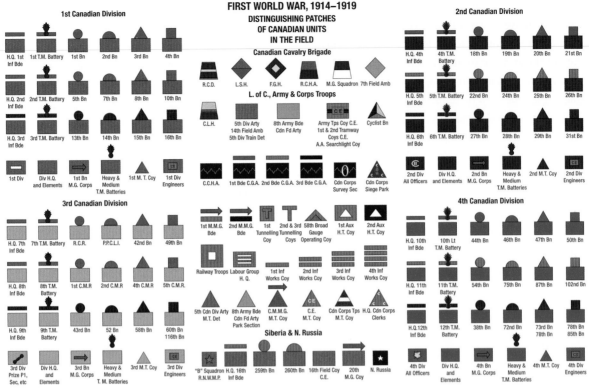

FIRST WORLD WAR, 1914–1919
DISTINGUISHING PATCHES OF CANADIAN UNITS IN THE FIELD

▲ The Canadian Corps' distinguishing flashes allowed soldiers to identify their own and their comrades' units and divisions.

and Guy Simonds were among its contributors—and Stuart its editor—before the journal ceased publication on the outbreak of war in 1939.

It was not revived in 1945, as the army, navy, and air force launched their own separate and largely forgettable publishing efforts (the *Canadian Army Journal* was, from 1947 to 1965, an important exception) as mixtures of celebratory service news and in-house military affairs. Armed forces unification in the late 1960s saw the publication of separate journals cancelled and their replacement by the glossy new tri-service journal, *Sentinel* (*Sentinelle* in French). No defence publication in the tumultuous post-unification period could have been expected to give consistent voice to critical opinions on defence issues or to spark unwanted debates, and *Sentinel* did not try. Issues as divisive as unification itself, budget shortfalls, the growing obsolescence of Canadian equipment, or national strategy within the western alliance amidst Vietnam, 1960s social unrest, growing Soviet and

Chinese military power and global influence, a violent separatist movement in Quebec, and changing views of Canada's role in the North Atlantic Treaty Organization (NATO) challenged many of the fundamental tenets of Canada's military and security posture. *Sentinel* remained glorified advertising copy for a military unaccustomed and largely unwilling to address in a serious way the nature of its own operating environment, and Canada, alone among the major democratic powers, lacked a serious forum for professional or scholarly debate and critical inquiry dedicated to military security issues.

A revived *Canadian Defence Quarterly* would attempt to play this role. Run as a commercial journal by the publishing company of William Baxter under the editorship of air force veteran, journalist, and political scientist John Gellner, the new CDQ launched in 1971 was slick, bilingual (*Revue canadienne de défense* in French), and cautiously aggressive in tackling issues of contemporary relevance, longer-term strategic importance, and military history. Gellner's editorship would be the longest and best in the CDQ's sometimes tortured history. Baxter's early support when the journal was losing money and struggling to establish itself against service suspicions and the absence of capable writers with the courage actually to write was not equalled in the 1990s when defence department budget reviews, strategic realignments, and grousing over content presaged first the withdrawal of key elements of institutional support, and then the journal's cancellation. Defence officials at times complained that CDQ was too virulent in its critiques of defence policy; defence academics sometimes whined that it was essentially an official journal in which real scholarship was seldom to be found. Thicker skins and perspectives not born of ideology or contempt might have led to greater charity in the respective camps. To the end in 1998, CDQ remained a useful contribution to Canadian defence and security analysis and is still widely consulted via on-line databases and archival collections. Its incisiveness and writing standards rarely matched that in complementary but competing publications such as *International Journal, International Security*, or the *Royal United Services Institution Journal*, but it was for close to 30 years a must-read for students (and practitioners) of Canadian military and security affairs, and a regular venue for the publication of defence papers by senior public officials, military officers, and academics. Several key staff from CDQ in its later years, including former editors John Marteinson and Martin Shadwick, moved to *Canadian Military Journal/Revue militaire canadienne* when it was established in 2000 as the professional journal of the Canadian Forces and the Department of National Defence.

Canadian Expeditionary Force (CEF). The CEF is the collective name given to the military structure created in 1914 in which some 620,000 Canadians served overseas during World War I. Its principal military formation was the Canadian Corps, a unit that, by mid-1916, had grown to four infantry divisions and tens of thousands of support troops. The CEF also included a range of other combat and non-combat units, administrative and headquarters personnel, and training establishments that were not part of the corps itself. It did not include the many thousands of Canadians who served as part of British units, nor those who served in the navy, merchant marine, or Royal Air Force. The CEF, in other words, was Canada's wartime army overseas. The CEF's structure and status in relation to politicians at home (or in London) and commanders at the front caused confusion and occasional controversy throughout the war. An administrative headquarters in London would answer at first to the minister of militia and later a reorganization to the Cabinet itself. Canada's senior field commander in charge of the Canadian Corps answered for military operations to a British general on the continent but, for the politics and administration of his command, to a Canadian minister in London. SEE ALSO: CANADIAN CORPS.

READING: G.W.L. Nicholson, *Canadian Expeditionary Force, 1914–1919* (Ottawa, 1962).

Canadian Forces Bases. Military and naval bases and forts originally took form at strategic points, aiming to defend them from attack. But as external land and sea threats declined, bases located on valuable real estate tended to be sold off. In urban areas, they gravitated to the suburbs where land was cheaper, to scrub land that had little value, or to areas that were in need of the employment a military installation could provide. After Unification in 1968, many bases were consolidated and took the designation of Canadian Forces Bases (*Bases des Forces Canadiennes*) or CFBS (BFCS). As of 2010, the major CFBs are Bagotville, Quebec; Camp Borden, Ontario; Cold Lake, Alberta; Comox, British Columbia; Dundurn, Saskatchewan; Edmonton, Alberta; Esquimalt, British Columbia; Gagetown, New Brunswick; Goose Bay, Newfoundland and Labrador; Greenwood, Nova Scotia; Halifax, Nova Scotia; Kingston, Ontario; Moose Jaw, Saskatchewan; North Bay, Ontario; Petawawa, Ontario; Shearwater, Nova Scotia; Shilo, Manitoba; St Hubert, Quebec; St John's, Newfoundland and Labrador; Suffield, Alberta;

Trenton, Ontario; Valcartier, Quebec; Wainwright, Alberta; and Winnipeg, Manitoba.

Canadian Forces College (CFC). Originating as the Royal Canadian Air Force's War Staff Course in 1943, the Canadian Forces College at Armour Heights in Toronto changed and developed through the Canadian military's postwar transformations. Unified in 1968, the Canadian Forces (CF) needed staff officers, and the college trained captains and majors for such roles, using a curriculum that featured lectures by outside "experts." Now with a much-increased civilian academic staff and higher academic standards, the CFC is operated by the Canadian Defence Academy, which is responsible for "professional development and life-long learning" for the CF. The college offers a variety of courses, including the Command and Staff program for majors and lieutenant-commanders, the Advanced Military Studies course for senior officers, the National Security Studies course for newly promoted general officers, and a Command and Staff program for reservists. As many as 30 foreign students from Western and, increasingly, from Asian militaries attend the CFC each year. Academic standards are maintained by the Royal Military College in Kingston, Ontario, which also can award a master of defence studies professional degree to CFC graduates who complete an add-on curriculum.

Canadian Forces Reorganization Act. Introduced in Parliament by defence minister Paul Hellyer on 4 November 1966, passed in April 1967, and proclaimed on 1 February 1968, this act unified the Canadian Armed Forces, ending the life of the Canadian Army, the Royal Canadian Navy, and the Royal Canadian Air Force as separate services. Unification's aim was to save money for equipment

▲ These gunners serving an 18-pounder with the Canadian Siberian Expeditionary Force were part of a futile Western effort against the Red (communist) side in Russia's civil war.

purchases by eliminating triplication and combining functional operations. SEE ALSO: UNIFICATION.

Canadian Intervention in the Russian Civil War. A Bolshevik-led revolt against Russia's tsarist regime led to domestic civil war, the withdrawal of Russia from World War I against Germany, and the intervention of several Western powers plus Japan on the loyalist (White) side. At the request of Britain, Prime Minister Sir Robert Borden agreed to send Canadian troops to Russia to aid British and Allied forces early in 1918. Communism frightened the capitalist Allies, but their overall aim was to keep Russia in the war; if Russia signed a separate peace, Germany could deploy more troops to the Western Front. There was also concern that masses of supplies shipped to the tsar's armies might fall into Red hands. Like other powers, the Canadian government, moreover, had an eye on potential economic and trade gains in Siberia.

The lead elements of the Canadian Siberian Expeditionary Force (CSEF) sailed from British Columbia ports in October 1918. While most of the 4,197 members of the 16th Canadian Infantry Brigade who served in the CSEF were volunteers, some had been drafted under the provisions of the Military Service Act, and francophone conscripts briefly mutinied in Victoria on 21 December 1918, just before they sailed. At Vladivostok, Canadians co-operated with Japanese and American units in attempting to train anti-Bolshevik forces and to guard supply and rail lines in western Siberia. They were almost always hampered by shortages of munitions and supplies and by the lack of clear political direction for their activities. Other Canadians served at Archangel and Murmansk in Russia's far north, east of the Finnish frontier, where the 16th Canadian Field Artillery Brigade with 497 officers and other ranks fought to deny these key northern ports to Bolshevik forces. Still more Canadians, including fighter ace Raymond Collishaw, fought against the Bolsheviks in the vicinity of the Black Sea. Nineteen Canadians died in Siberia or at sea, and eight gunners were killed in northern Russia. The Canadian government, fearing that it had made a

political blunder in committing its forces and aware the campaign in Russia had little political support back at home, withdrew all the troops between April and September 1919. SEE ALSO: BORDEN, ROBERT; WORLD WAR I.
READING: Benjamin Isitt, *From Victoria to Vladivostok: Canada's Siberian Expedition, 1917–1919* (Victoria, BC, 2010).

Canadianization. When Britain and Canada agreed to the British Commonwealth Air Training Plan (BCATP) in December 1939, Article XV of the agreement covered the disposition of dominion graduates from the scheme. The article said that they were to be assigned to an unspecified number of their own air force squadrons under operational control of the Royal Air Force (RAF), the precise number of squadrons to be determined later. In practice, however, most of the BCATP graduates were assigned directly to RAF squadrons, a thorny problem for the government of Canada.

Prime Minister Mackenzie King wanted Canadian fliers to be under Canadian control: why should the Royal Canadian Air Force (RCAF) be any different than the navy or army? That made sense, but King also wanted the British to pay the costs of RCAF squadrons overseas in return for London's share of the costs of the BCATP. The British objected to this because they believed that dominion units should be paid by the respective dominion and because they knew they would need to provide ground crew for any RCAF squadrons. In January 1941, Canada and Britain agreed that up to 25 additional RCAF squadrons would be formed from BCATP graduates and that Canadians serving with the RAF would wear Canadian uniforms. That was a step forward, but C.G. Power, the minister of national defence for air, properly wanted to see senior RCAF officers get command positions overseas and he wanted large RCAF formations, better aircraft (Lancaster bombers instead of Wellingtons, for example), and to see all Canadian BCATP graduates get commissions, unlike the RAF's policy. In difficult negotiations spearheaded in Britain by the blunt Air Marshal Gus Edwards, Canada made some headway

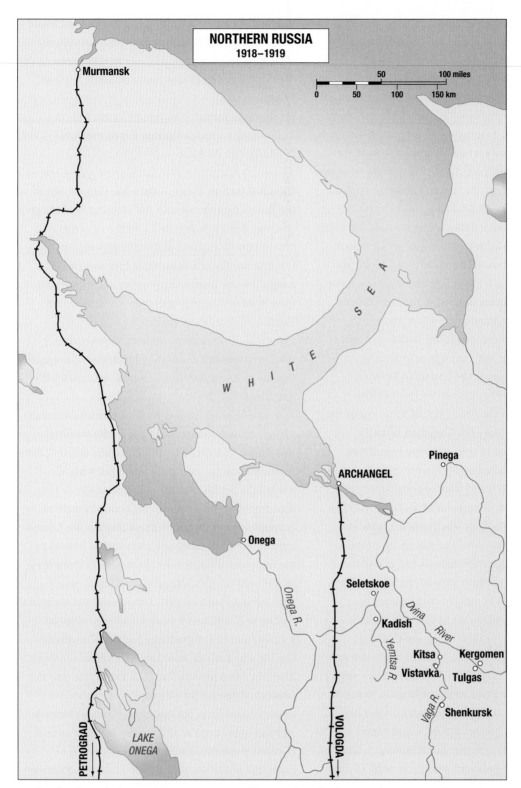

NORTHERN RUSSIA
1918–1919

Murmansk

50   100 miles

0   50   100   150 km

WHITE SEA

Pinega

ARCHANGEL

Onega

Onega R.

Seletskoe

Dvina River

Kadish

Yemtsa R.

Kitsa   Kergomen

Vistavka   Tulgas

Vaga R.

Shenkursk

PETROGRAD

LAKE ONEGA

VOLOGDA

The Allies dispatched troops to Russia in 1918 nominally to guard supplies but, in truth, to try to topple Lenin's Bolshevik government.

and began to assert more control over its overseas air personnel, though this policy astonishingly led some colonial-minded Canadian media to complain that Canada was trying to break up the Empire. One result of the process, known as Canadianization, was the formation of No. 6 Bomber Group; another was wilful RAF resistance to re-mustering Canadians in its own squadrons into those of the RCAF. Those Canadians already serving in established RAF crews, often with others from all across the Commonwealth, frequently preferred to remain with their mates; newer Canadian aircrew usually preferred to serve with Canadians and under Canadian command. While a very large number of RCAF aircrew remained in RAF squadrons, by war's end, there were 48 RCAF squadrons overseas. SEE ALSO: BRITISH COMMONWEALTH AIR TRAINING PLAN; POWER; ROYAL CANADIAN AIR FORCE; WORLD WAR II.

READING: B. Greenhous, et al., *The Crucible of War, 1939–1945: The Official History of the Royal Canadian Air Force,* vol. 3 (Toronto, 1994).

Canadian Navy Organization. The nation's naval organization has always been dictated by Canada's presence on the Atlantic and Pacific Oceans and by the historic focus on Britain and Western Europe. From the origins of the Royal Canadian Navy in 1910, ships have operated in East and West Coast squadrons from Halifax and Esquimalt respectively, which remain the navy's principal bases today. In wartime, and especially during World War II, Canadian naval organization reflected a far larger fleet, wider operational responsibility, and a broader mix of ships and aircraft. The navy assumed primary responsibility for a vast ocean area during the latter stages of World War II, and operated vessels (including aircraft carriers) or squadrons simultaneously in the Atlantic, North Sea, English Channel, Mediterranean, and North Pacific. The bulk of the fleet today remains based in Halifax, as it has been historically, with regular deployments alongside ships of the United States Navy and other North Atlantic Treaty Organization (NATO) allies in the North Atlantic, the Mediterranean, and the Caribbean. The Canadian navy plays a leading role in NATO's standing patrols,

and has maintained a presence with coalition partners in the Indian Ocean and Persian Gulf region for much of the past 20 years. Canada's limited naval capacity in Arctic regions leaves it with no substantial permanent presence or capability in the Far North. The navy's present organization consists of Maritime Fleet Pacific and Maritime Fleet Atlantic. The Naval Reserve is headquartered in Quebec City and has 26 units across the country. All respond to direction from the chief of the maritime staff based at National Defence Headquarters in Ottawa.

Canadian North-west Atlantic Command. At the Royal Canadian Navy's (RCN) request, the Atlantic Convoy Conference of February and March 1943 reallocated responsibilities for the war against German U-boats in the Battle of the Atlantic. As a result, Canadian North-west Atlantic Command came into being on 30 April 1943 under the RCN's Rear-Admiral Leonard Murray. Headquartered at St John's, Newfoundland, Murray's ships (and the aircraft of the Royal Canadian Air Force's Eastern Air Command, which only reluctantly and under Allied pressure agreed to be placed under RCN control) had responsibility for convoy protection from 47° west and south to 29° north, or from north of New York City and west of the 47th meridian. The creation of this command meant that the United States Navy commander at Argentia, Newfoundland, in command of the Newfoundland Escort Force since September 1941 (before the United States was at war), now operated under the control of a Canadian commander-in-chief. This sat well with Canadians, their nationalism spurred by the war. Although the RCN continued to have serious difficulties in fighting the war in the North Atlantic until late in 1943, the creation of this important theatre, the only one in World War II under Canadian command, was the first Allied recognition of the RCN's growing size and stature. The government declared that the "Canadian Navy can have no higher purpose" than to fight the enemy in the North Atlantic. "We have come to look upon [this task] as a national responsibility for Canada and one which geographically and strategically we are well placed to undertake."

See also: Atlantic; Murray, Leonard; Royal Canadian Navy.

Reading: W.A.B. Douglas, et al., *A Blue Water Navy: The Official Operational History of the Royal Canadian Navy in the Second World War, 1943–1945,* vol. 2, part 2 (St Catharines, ON, 2007).

Canadian Officers Training Corps (COTC). Founded in 1912 at McGill University, the COTC spread through Canadian universities during World War I. The scheme prepared young officers for military service and strove to inculcate a sense of responsibility for national security. The COTC continued through the interwar period, World War II (when, under the terms of the National Resources Mobilization Act, all fit male university students were required to enrol in the COTC or be subject to call-up), and the Cold War, training officers for the militia. It died in 1968, however, as a result of the combination of declining enlistment by COTC graduates in the militia, unification, and anti–Vietnam War sentiment. The Royal Canadian Navy operated a similar scheme, the University Naval Training Divisions (always abbreviated to "Untidies"), and the Royal Canadian Air Force ran a University Reserve Training Program. The end of these programs contributed to a massive disconnect between educated Canadians and the Canadian Forces. In recent years, a small alliance of educators, private citizens, and former graduates has sought to have the programs reinstated.

Reading: Robert Spencer, "Military Training in an Academic Environment," *Canadian Military History* (Autumn, 2009).

Canadian Patriotic Fund (CPF). The idea of raising money to provide assistance to soldiers' families and the wounded had originated in Canada during the War of 1812. A Patriotic Fund, created in 1900 during the South African War, raised large sums and still had $76,000 on its books at the outbreak of World War I. This residue passed to a new fund, established by Parliament on 22 August 1914, which limited itself to providing monthly grants to soldiers' families. Headed

▲ This Canadian Patriotic Fund poster sought donations to help soldiers' families during World War I.

by Montreal businessman H.B. Ames, CPF branches sprang up all across the country. In all, the fund raised almost $47 million. In 2009, the True Patriot Love Foundation, a new organization, began a campaign to raise $1.75 million to assist military families.

Canadian Rangers. During World War II, the Canadian army created the Pacific Coast Militia Rangers to keep watch on sparsely populated areas along the British Columbia coast. An estimated 15,000 had served in this organization by 1945. Two years later, Ottawa established the Canadian Rangers to take on the same task across the country and, by the 1970s, had concentrated its activities on the Far North. Equipped with .303 rifles, distinctive red sweatshirts and caps, compasses, radios, and—more recently— Global Positioning Systems, the Rangers undertake sovereignty patrols, exert a military presence, and

▲ The Canadian Rangers are reservists who serve as guides to the Canadian Forces and as Canada's eyes and ears in the Far North.

by the National Museum of Man from the late 1950s and, in the late 1980s, by the Canadian Museum of Civilization that succeeded the National Museum. The War Museum today remains part of the Canadian Museum of Civilization Corporation, a crown agency established in 1990.

The current museum on LeBreton Flats in the west end of Ottawa opened in May 2005, on the sixtieth anniversary of VE Day. It combined the collections once held at Vimy House, an old municipal garage, and 330 Sussex Drive, a former archival building that had been converted into a crowded, three-storey exhibition space, research library, and workshops. Commencement of the new building project had followed by more than a decade a federal task force report that had judged the country's military museums, including the Canadian War Museum, highly inadequate. A subsequent proposal to renovate the old Sussex building in part by the inclusion of a new wing devoted to the Holocaust was ultimately rejected. World War II veterans led a broadly based campaign against the project, which they feared would detract attention from Canadian military history and the remembrance of those who had served in uniform. The government of Liberal Prime Minister Jean Chrétien later authorized a new building entirely, situating it in the downtown precinct near other national public buildings, including Library and Archives Canada, instead of in the eastern suburbs near the old Rockcliffe air base and the current Canada Aviation Museum, as initially planned.

The Canadian War Museum's holdings include several hundred thousand objects, ranging from approximately one-third of the 94 Victoria Crosses won by Canadians since the nineteenth century to some 13,000 pieces of war art. The latter, mostly from the official war art programs of the world wars and several smaller efforts in the postwar period, rank among the largest and best war art holdings in the world. The War Museum also boasts one of the country's finest research collections and specialist libraries, and contains the strongest collections of military medals, uniforms, firearms, vehicles, and artillery in the country. Responsible to the

assist members of the Canadian Forces on operations and in training in remote areas. Organized into patrols and patrol groups, the 4,400-strong Ranger force consists of reservists, mostly Inuit, Dene, or members of other First Nations. The Junior Canadian Rangers, a northern youth training scheme, originated in 1996. Canadian Ranger strength is set to increase to approximately 5,000 by 2012.

READING: Ken Coates et al., *Arctic Front: Defending Canada in the Far North* (Toronto, 2008).

Canadian War Museum (CWM). The Canadian War Museum is Canada's national museum of military history and the largest and most visited military museum in the country. Established in the early 1880s with a small collection related mainly to the Canadian militia, it acquired substantial collections of weapons, uniforms, and archival material from the Canadian military after both world wars and operated from the War Trophies Building in Ottawa, a federal government site, during the 1940s. It was maintained

Department of Canadian Heritage, not the Department of National Defence, it is a tri-service museum covering all aspects of Canada's military past, from the first recorded instances of death by organized human violence on Canadian soil to the most recent Canadian conflicts. With approximately 450,000 visitors per year, it is the second most-visited federal museum in Canada, second only to the Canadian Museum of Civilization, its sister institution.

Canadian Women's Army Corps (CWAC). At the outbreak of World War II, many women joined unofficial groups to train for military service. Constant pressure from these groups and a growing shortage of male recruits led the Canadian Army on 13 August 1941 to agree to form the CWAC. Women between 18 and 45 with at least Grade 8 education could join. The corps initially was not a formal part of the army nor subject to military discipline, an indication of the army's reluctance and nervousness at putting women in uniform, but, on 13 March 1942, necessity (and the evident success of the CWACs in a variety of assigned roles) forced an end to this administrative confusion, and the Canadian Women's Army Corps became a recognized component of the Canadian Army. Pay initially was two-thirds that of men of equal rank, but this was raised to 80 percent in 1943. The CWACs enlisted 21,624 women who served eventually in 55 army trades, including drivers, cooks, clerks, telephone operators, and messengers—but most performed military variations of office work in Canada, the United States, Britain, and, from the spring of 1945, with First Canadian Army in

▲ These members of the Canadian Women's Army Corps, shown arriving in Britain in 1942, would do every kind of military work except combat.

northwest Europe. While CWACS may have been discriminated against in terms of pay (although less so than in most wartime civilian jobs), male and female veterans of the armed forces received equal benefits under the terms of the Veterans Charter. SEE ALSO: WOMEN IN THE MILITARY; WORLD WAR II.

READING: Ruth Roach Pierson, *"They're Still Women After All": The Second World War and Canadian Womanhood* (Toronto, 1986).

Canal du Nord (1918). The forced crossing of the Canal du Nord in late September 1918 during the Hundred Days' campaign was arguably the best battle fought by Sir Arthur Currie's Canadian Corps in World War I.

The 37-metre-wide canal behind which German forces had retreated after a string of defeats and withdrawals in previous weeks blocked the route to Cambrai and was among the last well-prepared positions along this portion of the Western Front. Firmly held by the Germans on its eastern side, it was a strong tactical obstacle that had been incorporated into Germany's Hindenburg Line and latticed with barbed wire, dugouts, and firing pits. It was also surrounded by marshy ground on both banks, and the area had been deliberately flooded to make it impassable for advancing troops. To the south, a dry, 3,700-metre portion of unfinished canal offered better prospects in the initial assault, but it was an exceedingly confined front and just as heavily defended. Currie nevertheless decided to attack a portion of this dry section, which would mean funnelling 50,000 troops onto a very narrow axis against prepared enemy positions and well-sited guns, and then—assuming the break-in battle proved successful—fanning them out again after breaching the eastern bank to consolidate the gains and prevent immediate counterattack in a crowded, shallow salient. Currie's superiors had their doubts about the feasibility of this plan, and Currie knew he might be fired if it failed. On 27 September 1918, after days of meticulous preparation, the 1st and 4th Canadian Divisions moved across the canal, Currie's engineers providing bridges and ramps to get men and vehicles up and over the east bank.

The surprise attack, supported by a heavy rolling barrage, brought the Canadians into and through the German positions and beyond the defensive belt edging the canal. By 1 October, the Canadian Corps with nearby British divisions had achieved most of its objectives, smashing the last organized German defences in front of the Canadian Corps and taking 7,000 prisoners. By the time the Corps was relieved on the Canal du Nord front on 11 October, it had suffered 20 percent of its strength killed, wounded, and missing.

The Canal du Nord battle showed Currie and the corps at their best, and that even a well-organized, highly successful World War I victory could only come at heavy cost. The commander's complicated plan had been transformed into orders that the corps' officers and men carried out. Massive artillery support; the specialized supplies to cross the canal; the weapons, ammunition, and food to sustain the attack—everything needed had to be in the right place at the proper time. The plan, the staff work, the logistics, and the fighting skill of the men all meshed properly; in 1915 or 1916 or even 1917, this would have been impossible to achieve with the resources and skills then at hand. Still, while Canadian troops fought quickly across the canal and into Bourlon Wood beyond, the speed with which German defences reappeared and the difficulty of moving their own supporting elements forward delayed the fall of Cambrai by another week and a half. SEE ALSO: CANADIAN CORPS; CURRIE; HUNDRED DAYS.

READING: Shane Schreiber, *Shock Army of the British Empire: The Canadian Corps in the Last 100 Days of the Great War* (Westport, CT, 1997).

Canloan. In late 1942, the British army had run short of junior officers, just at the time that Canada, having disbanded two home defence divisions, found itself with a surplus. The resulting Canloan scheme let Canadian junior officers volunteer to serve with the British, and 623 infantry and 50 Ordnance Corps officers did so, most of them subalterns, but some 80 of them captains. After refresher training in Canada, the first draft arrived overseas in April 1944, and all were soon in action in northwest Europe, Italy, and a few in Southeast Asia. With almost all serving in front-line units, the Canloans suffered a horrific casualty rate of 75 percent (456 men in total), including 128 killed in action. Canloans served with great distinction around the world, and one rose to command a battalion.

READING: Wilfrid Smith, *Code Word Canloan* (Toronto, 1996).

CANUSA. The Canada–United States Agreement on Signals Intelligence came into effect in 1949. It defined terms for the exchange of signals intelligence and was a de facto component of the UKUSA agreement that linked Britain, the dominions, and the United States in intelligence co-operation.

Carignan-Salières Régiment. Dispatched from France in 1665 in response to calls for protection against Iroquois attacks, the regiment's 1,200 soldiers, under Alexander de Prouville, Sieur de Tracy, defended New France. The troops built a string of forts along the Richelieu River, blocking the major attack route from the south, and launched a disastrous mid-winter expedition against the Iroquois in February 1666 that resulted in heavy losses. A summer attack was more successful. The regiment was recalled to France in 1667 after the Iroquois came to terms, but some 450 soldiers chose to remain in the colony, many marrying newly-arrived "filles du roi" (daughters of the king). The presence of so many additional soldier-settlers was an enormous boost to New France's capacity for self-defence. SEE ALSO: FRENCH-IROQUOIS WARS.

READING: M. Wyczynski, "New Horizons, New Challenges: The Carignan-Salières Regiment in New France, 1665–1667," in Bernd Horn, ed., *Forging a Nation* (St Catharines, ON, 2002).

Carleton, Guy, 1st Baron Dorchester (1724–1808). Born in Ireland, Carleton joined the British army in 1742 and became a protegé of James Wolfe who brought him to Canada as his quartermaster and engineer in 1759. Carleton commanded a battalion on the Plains of Abraham and suffered a head wound. In 1768, the government in London named him captain general and governor-in-chief in Quebec where he ruled in ways designed to win support from the French-speaking inhabitants, a matter of some importance as the revolution in the Thirteen Colonies began in what would later become the United States. Carleton managed the defence of the colony with minimal support from the French-speaking militia, and beat off an American attack on Quebec on 31 December 1775. Despite being criticized for not pursuing the retreating enemy with sufficient vigour, he still received a knighthood for his efforts and, in

▲ An officer of the Carignan-Salières Régiment.

▲ Guy Carleton, 1st Baron Dorchester.

1782, received the appointment of commander-in-chief in North America. Unfortunately, Carleton had to lead the evacuation of New York and effectively presided over Britain's defeat in the American Revolution. He became the governor of British North America in 1786 and remained so until 1795. SEE ALSO: QUEBEC (1775).

READING: J.M. Hitsman, *Safeguarding Canada, 1763–1871* (Toronto, 1968).

Caroline Affair. In the aftermath of the failed 1837 Rebellion in Upper Canada, supporters of William Lyon Mackenzie set themselves up on Navy Island in the Niagara River where they received aid, supplies, and reinforcements from allies on the American side. The small steamer *Caroline*, based at Schlosser, New York, a small landing with little more than a warehouse and a tavern, made regular runs to the island for this purpose, crossing back and forth over the British-American boundary in doing so. A group of Canadian militia led by a Royal Navy officer crossed by boat to the American side and stormed aboard the ship at dockside on the night of 29

December 1837; in the ensuing gunfight, two Americans were killed and several others wounded. The Canadians cut the vessel's moorings, set it on fire, and let it drift toward—and over—Niagara Falls. Sensationalized American news reports, which soon treated the British-Canadian raid as a cause for war, sometimes showed the *Caroline* with doomed sailors jumping from its blazing decks as it headed toward destruction. In Canada, the operation was cause for considerable celebration; in the United States, it saw calls for the raising of troops to defend the border. On both sides, senior officials sought to ensure that local clashes between Canadian rebels and their American supporters did not drag Britain and the United States into war.

Tensions between Britain and the United States as a result of the *Caroline* incident were not settled until the Webster-Ashburton Treaty of 1842 and the associated exchange of diplomatic notes that accompanied it. In these, essentially, Britain apologized for the raid and the United States for the provocation the rebel supply operation had represented, while the ship's owner was not compensated for the loss of his property. In recent years, the settlement of the *Caroline* incident has become an important point of international law. By agreeing that the use of American territory and property for abetting illegal military actions against British North America created the conditions for the legal use of force in retaliation, the US position has been cited as a precedent in support of the doctrine of anticipatory self-defence. This is sometimes known as pre-emptive attack, or "the Bush Doctrine," after President George W. Bush. SEE ALSO: REBELLIONS OF 1837–1838.

READING: K.R. Stevens, *Border Diplomacy* (Tuscaloosa, AL, 1989).

Caron, Sir Adolphe-Philippe (1843–1908). Born in Quebec City and trained as a lawyer, the ambitious Caron entered Parliament as a Conservative after winning an 1873 by-election. Sir John A. Macdonald appointed him minister of militia and defence in November 1880 before he was 37 years old. Although

Sir George-Étienne Cartier.

November 1885. Caron continued to serve as militia minister until 1892 when he became postmaster general. SEE ALSO: NORTHWEST REBELLION (1885).

READING: Desmond Morton and R.H. Roy, eds., *Telegrams of the North-West Campaign, 1885* (Toronto, 1972).

Cartier, Sir George-Étienne (1814–1873). Born in St Antoine, Lower Canada, Cartier practised law at Montreal and worked with John A. Macdonald to create Confederation. He was Macdonald's Quebec lieutenant and the minister of militia and defence from 1867 until his death. As minister, he put in place the new nation's Militia Act in 1868, established the foundations of its army, dealt with the Red River Rebellion in 1870, and responded to the withdrawal of the British garrisons from Canada in 1870–1871.

Casualties. Casualties in Canada's wars have been roughly commensurate with the country's evolving international role and the changing nature of warfare itself. Dwarfing by many orders of magnitude the brief campaigns of Canada's early national period, heavier casualties in the twentieth century have sparked bitter division, intense pride, and inconclusive mathematics.

The Canada that emerged in 1867 from the Confederation of several struggling British colonies was not rich in military tradition and almost completely unfamiliar with the human cost of major wars. The British conquest of New France in 1763, the result in part of a vicious scorched earth campaign against French settlements along the St Lawrence River valley, had been followed by a half-century of relative peace. American rebels pierced briefly Canada's imperial defences during the American War of Independence, but weather, incompetence, and the Royal Navy combined to seal the expedition's fate. Francophone militias, once the mainstay of security for vulnerable Canadian communities along remote waterways and trade routes, declined under a light but still unwelcome British yoke; anglophone militias grew steadily with the spread of Loyalist communities, though more as social clubs than as military bulwarks, their operational competence rarely tested. The

Caron had no military experience, he had few qualms about clashing with General Richard Luard, the British-appointed general officer commanding the militia. Luard wanted increased professionalism and to control appointments, but the nationalist (and patronage-conscious) minister believed he was in charge and prevailed. Caron, in 1883, increased the tiny Permanent Force's budgets and strength, established infantry training schools, and showed substantial energy during the Northwest Rebellion of 1885. The minister organized the nearly 8,000-strong force sent west, arranged logistical support, improvised a field ambulance, and struck arrangements with the Hudson's Bay Company and the Canadian Pacific Railway Company to assist the expedition. Caron also encouraged Quebec militia units to participate in the campaign. His efforts were recognized by the award of a knighthood in near-incessant frontier violence of France's colonial period was not repeated under British rule, the diplomacy of which managed largely to pacify or displace First Nations while moving the boundaries of settlement inexorably westward. Military casualties in French North America were frequent, numerous, and a lethal threat to the entire colony; in British North America, they were infrequent, light, and well within the Empire's capacity to absorb.

It was this unpromising mixture of weak militias with limited military experience, British regulars, First Nations warriors, and the Royal Navy that turned back Washington's uncoordinated, sometimes amateurish, forays during the War of 1812. Canada remained British after the Treaty of Ghent (1814), but as a defended outpost made increasingly untenable by America's growing population, military power, and continental ambitions. Political violence was hardly absent from daily life, but military violence—against internal dissent or external challenge—was uncommon, save for 1837–1838, when a short, forlorn uprising in Upper Canada and a more broadly-based rebellion in Lower Canada were both suppressed with vigour by imperial troops and local militias. A political total war in which defeat would have been tantamount to American annexation, the War of 1812 fed momentarily Britain's interest in constructing more robust Canadian defences. More lastingly, it stoked Canadians' unhelpful fantasy that martial character and militia strength, with minimal help from other sources, had triumphed over marauding American hordes. Neither the militia martyrs of 1812 nor the effort to suppress the Lower Canadian Patriotes of 1838 contributed much to securing the rudiments of an effective Canadian defence in the long term. Both events, however, exaggerated public impressions of the military qualities of the Canadian citizen, the extent of past sacrifice, and the irrelevance or undesirability of continued reliance on Britain for military succor. Proportionately, far more had died in defence of New France than of British North America, but the enduring myth from both empires across two centuries was similar: that part-time levies were the true stuff of popular legend and military success.

Metropolitan commanders—distant, unsympathetic, untrustworthy—had presumably expended local lives in causes to which they remained maddeningly uncommitted, and abandoned the locals when the going got tough.

It was about to happen again. The grim logic of Britain's nineteenth-century retreat from its military responsibility for Canada was broadly analogous to the abandonment of Quebec by France a century before, though one was voluntary and the other forced. In each case, the metropolitan centre had bigger wars to fight, greater interests to defend, and better prospects for success elsewhere. That few had died in Canada's early post-Conquest colonial wars did not obscure the fact that they might at some future point, and that precious resources had been drained from Britain's war against Napoleon to defend unnamed villages in the Canadian hinterland. Might the Americans try again? Could victory be repeated a second time? Local memorials from the War of 1812 were focal points for civic pride, collective delusion, and misplaced faith in British resolve. Memories of conquest and political ostracism in French Canada did not bode well for the unity required to fend off serious attack. Rising American power tested Canadian patience with the obvious insufficiency of its defensive resources and stirred memories of past heroism, but not the investments required to raise troops, build forts, and fortify a long, porous land frontier. The prodigious efforts of British military engineers were magnificent, effective, and ultimately futile. Five years after the first fearful, tentative steps toward political union, Canada was independent, vulnerable, and busy extending paramilitary control into a vast and disorganized West; British military power was at the beginning of the end of its long North American mission; and a handful of Metis and Aboriginal resisters in Manitoba were about to force upon Ottawa an avowedly imperial role of its own in the deadly suppression of regional dissent.

The resulting campaigns of 1870 and 1885 were not large or costly by most military standards, but they confirmed the broad contours of a political fissure that would scar Canadian politics for a century and more.

Red-coated troops suppressing French-speaking or Aboriginal forces were a metaphor of disunion and injustice for those predisposed to dissatisfaction with the power balances of Confederation that more moderate voices, then as since, could only with difficulty dispel. The successful mobilization of Dominion troops in 1885 and their clumsy, decisive victory reinforced other preconceived notions, not least the dangerous fallacy that part-time soldiers were adequate for a full-time job. Government losses in 1885 were sacrifices to national unity, military pride, and imperial justice; Metis and Aboriginal dead joined Montcalm and the Patriotes of 1837–1838 as casualties of political oppression in a divided state. It would not be the last time that the casualties of war stoked opposite sides in corrosive political debates.

The costs and consequences of nationhood were inflamed by competing charges of imperial hubris and ethnic disloyalty. Five hundred dead and wounded during the South African War (1899–1902) from a series of small volunteer contingents was an unconscionable butcher's bill for those opposed to Britain's overseas entanglements, but a necessary— even natural—outcome for boosters of imperial solidarity and the natural obligations of a rising military power. Canada's first national attempt to export security abroad was indelibly tainted by its national unity travails at home—foreign policy was domestic policy "with its hat on," as a later prime minister would declare. Was Canada independent or not? And did independence even matter when London asked a still predominantly anglophone country for support on a matter of life and death?

World War I (1914–1918) deepened such cleavages, on a vast human scale and with effects reaching into virtually every community. With approximately one percent of the Canadian population dead and another three percent wounded or injured, the war left a bitterly divided country in its wake, victorious and filled with justifiable pride in shared accomplishment, but also raw and in many ways embittered, its social divisions sourly affirmed by the horrors of Ypres, Passchendaele, and scores of lesser slaughters. Casualties overseas were the primary impetus for a

searing conscription debate at home in which equality of sacrifice, ethnic venom, religious hatred, and regional jealousy flourished unchallenged by leadership and unmindful of consequence. The political casualties were immediate and long lasting. The Liberal Party of Canada was annihilated by a pro-conscription coalition that made military service the one true virtue. Itself unelectable soon afterwards as the country rode its collective grief into a period of economic turmoil and epic disunity, "Union" government was a tainted sobriquet for the alleged excesses of misplaced patriotism. In the aftermath of more than 60,000 dead, even Canada's best general, Sir Arthur Currie, was accused by opponents at home of needlessly sacrificing Canadian troops at Mons, Belgium, in the war's final days. The charges were silly, partisan, untrue—and shamefully representative. But if the generals had not caused this mess, who had?

Peace was perhaps more tortuous in retrospect than at the time. The tickertape that flew in Halifax, Toronto, Montreal, and Vancouver; the crowds lining docksides and railway sidings; the frenzied national reunion of a fighting country with its fighting sons belied the soon-common postwar image in literature and the arts of sleazy civilian ingratitude and forlorn sacrifice. Wartime censorship had not shielded the country from casualty lists, grisly battlefield photos of dirty faces and eviscerated landscapes, and the steady flow of broken men to towns and cities across a land shorn of innocence in a war devoid of hope. But the reality of war competed with the necessity to find, embrace, and defend meaning. What had it all been for? Pride in martial accomplishment, satisfaction in the scale and impact of national contribution, and—among veterans especially—the intangible bonds of shared peril were deep, real, and not easily suppressed. Memorials, cemeteries, and the lure of absent loves made secular pilgrims of a generation to sites both local and, with increasing frequency, international. Commemorations celebrated victories and losses both, even as remembrance—of the brutality of war itself and the misfortune of its occurrence—crept more steadily into acts that were no longer of armistice or victory alone. The opening of Walter Allward's Vimy Memorial in 1936 witnessed an unprecedented outpouring of national pride in military service and honouring of a nation's dead; three years later, within months of the outbreak of another war, similar emotions greeted the dedication of a national war memorial in Ottawa. The idea that Canada was born on Vimy Ridge was powerful, restorative, and affirming for the generation that had experienced the war, whatever their reflections on its cost. Prime Minister Sir Robert Borden was hardly crass or disingenuous in suggesting, in insisting, that the dead and wounded of Flanders and the Somme were proof of Canada's maturation and precursor to the country assuming its proper place in world affairs; the obvious counterpoint—what price victory?—was no less a clarion cry for those tagged with disloyalty, or worse, for their critiques.

The lesson of the trenches was salutary for the postwar generation, however they weighed the dead and missing in the calculation of victory versus cost, autonomy versus commitment. Nowhere was this truer than among federal Liberals emerging successfully from the war's political wreckage: military commitments abroad entailed casualties, and casualties overseas meant political division at home. It was not quite an anti-war, much less an anti-British, philosophy, though it was predictably read as such by conservative nationalists, pro-defence lobbyists, and much of anglophone Canada. Fear of casualties, a healthy enough motivator for any government, conditioned powerfully Ottawa's early response to the outbreak of war in Europe in 1939. Naval, air, and economic commitments preceded any large-scale ground forces, the latter being developed in earnest only after Axis forces had pushed Britain to the brink of catastrophic defeat. The course of events spawned ironic punishments: intended at first as low-cost alternatives to the feared severity of ground combat, naval and air units were fed into gruelling wars of attrition in which merchant ships and bomber crews were initially decimated. An army waiting, for much of the war, in England would eventually get its turn but, by the collapse of Hitler's Reich in May 1945, total dead in all services would number less than 45,000, or

just three-quarters the total from the previous war. The wait in England, the reprieve from battle, essentially had reduced the toll.

The cause in World War II had been clearer, the casualties fewer, and the political dislocation at home less intense, but total war had unfolded in the twentieth century twice in much the same way. Even in the area of compulsory service, history repeated itself as excessive army casualties in attritional campaigns in Italy and northwest Europe led to conscription for overseas service in the final months of the war.

No subsequent war has tested Canadians to this extent. More than one million military enlistments made World War II the greatest in Canadian history, while its veterans and survivors benefits, programs, and entitlements—added to the costs of fighting, supply, and reconstruction—made it easily the most expensive. The unambiguous war guilt and violent depravity of Canada's principal enemies imparted moral clarity and psychic comfort to grieving families and returning veterans, but the scale of war and the intensity of conflict on land, sea, and in the air permanently altered most aspects of Canadian public affairs. Postwar debates, in scholarship as much as politics, would critique, at first tentatively but soon with growing confidence, the effectiveness and human cost of various campaigns, battles, and technologies, including in their purview the deaths of enemies as well as friends in the war's spiralling violence, but never its standing as what the American historian Studs Terkel had famously dubbed a "good war." Of no other conflict in the nation's history could this unambiguously be claimed.

A half-century of Cold War saw the ebb and flow (but mostly ebb) of standing commitments abroad against the latent power of the Soviet-led Warsaw Pact. Hundreds of training deaths passed largely unnoticed among the general populace in the rush to, and later from, postwar prosperity and the recurrent malaise of national unity debates. Potential combat commitments, notably in Korea, were always reviewed with one eye on cost and the other on the political implications of casualties, but even Korea—at several hundred dead and at least one thousand wounded in a broadly multinational and clearly justified cause—was for most United Nations troop contributors a far cry from the horrifying tolls of earlier wars. Peacekeeping deaths in ones and twos, and sometimes more, sparked occasional debate, though nothing more damaging than the political contests over the missions themselves. It is worth remembering that Suez (1956) for many Conservatives was an indecent abandonment of France and, more importantly, Britain, and hardly the national triumph for compromise and diplomacy it has since justifiably become.

The politicization of death in war is hardly new in Canada, as noted above, but national interest—and media coverage—of post–Cold War peace support operations has raised it to a high and occasionally tawdry art. Unlike the major wars of the twentieth century, when the dead were buried abroad in Commonwealth military ceremonies with those of Allied nations, combat fatalities from the complex and often violent missions since 1989 have been returned to Canada for burial, followed by media every step of the way. The merits of this strategy are debatable from either side, although the positive effects of reuniting the fallen with grieving loved ones suggest an efficacy and social responsibility that outweigh the logistical or public relations objections occasionally voiced by military officials or politicians. The historical reason for greater discretion—the presumed effect on American public opinion of body bags returning from the costly, controversial war in Iraq—is not as easily dismissed, but the lessons of history have here been confused with broader social cleavages in the American public, broader opposition to the war itself, and ideological debates on the role and influence of the contemporary media. Canadian public opinion for most post–Cold War missions abroad does not appear to have been specifically or regularly affected by the occurrence of casualties, although the longer-term impact of casualty and fatality reporting is harder to assess. During the war in Afghanistan (2001–present), the Conservative government of Stephen Harper thought the issue sufficiently sensitive to attempt banning publicity for the return of Canada's war dead, only to overturn the decision in response to the

ferocious response of the media, public opinion, the political opposition, and military families. Canada's Afghanistan war dead now follow a highly publicized route home, usually through a major military air base, along local roads by motorcade, and to home towns for widely covered local services. The outpouring of public respect and national grief that such caravans have occasioned is absolutely unique in Canadian history, occasions both for the relentless exposure of the human tragedy of war and for the support extended by Canadians to those who serve in their name. Such momentary expressions have been accompanied by a nation-wide "support the troops" effort that includes yellow ribbons, car decals, fundraising, and a wear-red-on-Friday campaign.

The precision of such efforts is determined by the accuracy of current combat accounting and by the one-to-one relationship, in name, of a Canadian death in war to the route home and circumstances of his or her interment. The same is not true of non-fatal casualties, where statistics remain disputed (or unreleased) and the social or political impact of higher casualty totals may affect exponentially public perceptions of the mission. This is not a new phenomenon. Counting casualties in war is an inexact science, despite the progressive development of comprehensive personnel records, grave registries, and systems to adjudicate pension claims. Battlefield carnage and the destruction of or simple inability to locate human remains, the vagaries of wartime administration, and the failure of personnel to report injuries incurred during military service are among the more common impediments to effective tabulations.

Even when deaths and injuries can be enumerated accurately, differences persist in how wars are defined, when their start and end dates are calculated, and who is to be included in the total. What is a war death, for example, when no war has actually been declared, as in Korea, the Persian Gulf, or Afghanistan, or when a zone of conflict is ambiguously defined, as in former Yugoslavia? What is a military casualty when a mission includes auxiliary or paramilitary services, such as police, firefighters, or civilian professionals working for the armed forces? Merchant sailors during World War II had the highest casualty rate of any wartime service, but were long excluded from wartime casualty totals, largely because of opposition from armed forces veterans who insisted that merchant sailors' civilian terms of work and pay levels should make them ineligible for military pensions and benefits. Similar issues of mathematics and political sensitivity surround the counting of Canadians in the armed forces of other countries, notably Commonwealth countries or the United States in the two world wars and Korea. Determining who is a casualty can sometimes depend on determining who is a veteran, and such definitions morph over time in response to issues far beyond the confines of good record-keeping or systematic administration. The best example, the inclusion of Newfoundland in Canada in 1949 and the folding of formerly imperial benefits and casualty numbers into the national totals, was perhaps the most skilfully handled; other issues, including the status of skilled civilian labourers, non-national employees (for example, on overseas peace support missions), or foreigners in Canadian service are less easily resolved.

The quality or nature of an injury or death, and when or how it is reported or treated, can also create impediments to accurate—or consensually inaccurate—totals. Counting wounds on the battlefield is easier to determine at the time than in retrospect because most wounds require treatment and most treatment requires some form of medical intervention. In simple terms, battlefield doctors and aid stations probably had a far better, if sometimes intuitive, sense of casualties and casualty rates than contemporary historians sifting through and comparing war diaries, letters, and nominal rolls. Counting them afterwards depends on a long chain of record-keeping, administrative competence, and historical scholarship that is more difficult the farther in time one moves from the event. It can also assume that contemporary language and social mores equate with those in the past, making it easy to compare categories that may have altered since the documents were originally compiled. Does a casualty list, for

example, include those impacted, or killed, by non-combat related causes, including accident, disease, or self-inflicted wounds? Does it include those affected multiple times as multiple casualties? Or, as in the case of communicable diseases, which soldiers were often reluctant to report for reasons ranging from embarrassment to fear of disciplinary consequences, are entire categories of 'casualty' poorly known because their nature carried severe social stigma? The contemporary US military distinguishes between casualties that result in a person being absent from duty for more than 72 hours ("heavily wounded"), and less than 72 hours ("lightly wounded"), but does not release public details on disease or other non-combat-related conditions.

These issues are far more complex than might at first appear. A soldier who steps on a mine in Afghanistan and dies in the resulting explosion is clearly a fatality of the war. One who dies in a vehicular accident in Kabul probably is as well. But what if the mine explosion or the accident occurs during training in Alberta, where soldiers are preparing for deployment, or in downtown Toronto, on the way to a hockey game? What about injuries or deaths on the home front or in peacetime? A soldier who dies when his armoured vehicle rolls over on an icy Bosnian road in the 1990s is surely a casualty of the conflict in former Yugoslavia, but what of one killed the same day in a training accident in New Brunswick, or a car crash on Highway 401? A category not addressed in any comprehensive way in historical combat statistics relates to mental stress and injury, an ever-broadening rubric that includes post-traumatic stress disorder. Some estimates of mental casualties from current high-tempo military operations, whether reported or not, range up to 30 percent of those deployed, a staggering figure. If such a figure was applied retroactively to veterans of the battle of Vimy Ridge or the Hundred Days' campaign that concluded the same war, the official count of Canadian wartime casualties would nearly triple: at Vimy alone, the number would rise to nearly 27,000 overall instead of the previously accepted total of 10,600.

In the table that follows, the statistics on dead and wounded include these totals only where an official estimate has been provided. The Government of Canada released some statistics related to post-traumatic stress disorder from Afghanistan, for example, but no such figure exists from South Africa or World War I, when the category of illness was neither recognized nor counted. The statistics as a whole reflect broadly accepted totals used by most reputable sources, but casualty rates have tended to grow over time, as groups formerly not considered combatants have been added to the list of veterans eligible for appropriate forms of government compensation. The Books of Remembrance, located in the Peace Tower on Parliament Hill in Ottawa, use numbers that are considerably larger than those assembled by the official historians of either world war. These reflect the inclusion of those who died up until the Books' own cut-off dates, which in each case is longer than that normally accepted as the last day of the war (April 1922 for World War I and October 1947 for World War II). Neither larger figure includes Newfoundlanders or merchant sailors. The statistics on war wounded, much less war injured or sick, are even more difficult to pin down, both because of differences in calculating a war's end date and the lack of consistently reliable numbers from official sources. Figures on post-traumatic stress disorder released by Canada in early 2010, for example, give the number of former personnel, including members of the Royal Canadian Mounted Police, who were receiving disability support from Veterans Affairs Canada from approximately 2002, when Canadian ground units entered the Afghanistan war in substantial numbers. They did not specify the number of these attributable to service in Afghanistan or other missions (Haiti, for

instance) or the number of military versus non-military personnel. Even a conservative interpretation of these numbers would suggest that Canadian forces in Afghanistan have suffered 2,000 or more psychological casualties.

The numbers of dead and wounded remain sources of pride and consternation, disappointment and deep respect. And in the case of Afghanistan, where Canadian troops remain deployed in a combat role until at least early 2011, they continue to creep higher. Where known or estimated, these given here include the numbers of Newfoundlanders and merchant sailors. They also use the Books of Remembrance instead of the lower numbers contained in other sources.

One should approach these numbers with great caution. In Afghanistan, for example, where the total reflects fatalities known as of late June 2010, the number for wounded (529 as of February 2010) and injured (913) does not include an additional 2,200 personnel known to have been collecting disability benefits due to Afghanistan service. The reasons for these have not been disclosed, but it seems reasonable to suppose that some of the "wounded and injured" are included in this total, and that several hundred others remain unaccounted for. It is also known that since 2001, when the first Canadian personnel deployed to the Indian Ocean region, until late 2009 the number of Veterans Affairs clients claiming benefits as a result of post-traumatic stress disorder climbed from 389 to nearly 8,200. It is not clear what portion of this number derived from the Afghanistan war, although it also seems reasonable to assume that the percentage is high. There is no accurate tabulation of Canadians killed or injured due to military service during the Cold War, although several hundred died in aircraft accidents, fires, or vehicular crashes, and no

	Date	Dead	Wounded or Injured	Total
South African War	1899–1902	277	252	529
World War I	1914–1918	68,656	176,380	245,036
World War II	1939–1945	47,200	54,414	101,614
Peace support operations	1946–2010	116	Unknown	Unknown
Cold War	1949–1989	Unknown	Unknown	Unknown
Korean War	1950–1953	516	1,558	2,074
Afghanistan	2001–2010	151	1,442	1,592

reliable count of wounds or injuries due to service in international peace support missions.

The statistics on military casualties have been almost as sensitive and divisive as the conflicts from which they arose. The dead are easier to count, and more difficult to refute, but the wounded, injured, or diseased are far more problematic. In some periods, they were scarcely counted at all; currently, their numbers are watched religiously, as proof of a gradually succeeding mission in Afghanistan, or as tangible evidence of a Vietnam-like imbroglio for the government of the day. Psychological casualties, and the legitimacy with which they are increasingly viewed, are altering the way in which war's social costs are assessed. Ramp ceremonies overseas and the progress of fallen soldiers along major transportation routes back in Canada have personalized the costs of war to Canadian citizens in unique ways, leading to widespread popular support for military personnel and their families. The longer-term impact of such public intimacy with death and the human cost of war—in politics, diplomacy, or popular culture—remain to be seen.

Censorship. Canada named Lieutenant-Colonel Ernest Chambers to the post of chief censor in World War I to control sensitive military information in the media. Overseas, the military controlled journalists' access to the front and censored their reportage. The system applied in Canada was more severe than in most countries and even increased in rigour after the armistice in November 1918, thanks to fears of Bolshevism. In all, 253 publications faced suppression, 90 percent of them US-based and two-thirds of them in the ethnic press. On occasion, Chambers censored material published freely in Britain on the grounds that Britons, nearer the fighting, could be told things that might upset Canadians.

In World War II, the system established under authority of the Defence of Canada Regulations was more sophisticated, but overseas soldiers' letters were subject to vetting, and Canadian press reporting—like everyone else's—was controlled by regulations laid down by the Supreme Headquarters Allied Expeditionary Force. The results frequently seemed like propaganda more than reportage. Back in Canada, although censorship was nominally voluntary with the media observing a list of restrictions, the chief censor and a Censorship Coordination Committee in the Department of National War Services watched the press very closely. Ottawa forced one Communist newspaper to cease publication in November 1939. Foreign publications also came under scrutiny, the *Saturday Evening Post* especially being viewed as anti-British in the first years of the war. The government in both wars had to be particularly careful with French-Canadian opinion, which was cool to Canada's involvement in the conflict and, after 1940, not unsympathetic to Vichy France. Newspapers like *Le Devoir* were cautioned on occasion. Military censorship in conflicts since 1945 has ordinarily focused on matters of operational security. In recent wars, reporters have travelled with military units to the front or on deployments for extended periods, acquiring close access to military personnel in exchange for some surveillance of their footage and reports back home. The advent of new media including personal cellular phones, miniature video recorders, and satellite communications has made any kind of censorship more difficult. The Internet and the many ways in which information can be almost immediately shared has also made it difficult to limit the spread or breadth of information transfer once a story has first appeared. Countering this has been the geographical remoteness of many recent battlegrounds and the difficulty faced by news organizations in sustaining reporters in the field in areas such as central Africa, the Balkans, or Afghanistan. Often by default, military-supplied news is the only news on offer in the critical initial stages of reporting.

READING: Jeffrey Keshen, *Propaganda and Censorship during Canada's Great War* (Edmonton, 1996); Claude Beauregard, *Guerre et Censure au Canada, 1939–1945* (Sillery, QC, 1993).

CF-100 Avro Canuck. The Canuck, designed by A.V. Roe (or Avro) Canada, was the first jet fighter designed and built in Canada. The all-weather,

▲ Designed and produced by A.V. Roe, the CF-100 "Canuck" was the mainstay of Canada's air defences from 1953 to 1962.

twin-engine interceptor (also known as the Clunk) entered service in 1953 after a long development period. The Canuck compensated for its relatively slow speed with a short take-off distance, a good rate of climb, and excellent performance characteristics in bad weather and at night. These traits made for effective performance in its principal role with the North American Air Defence Command (NORAD), the interception of Soviet long-range bombers over the continental North. Several Royal Canadian Air Force (RCAF) squadrons also flew Canucks in Europe from 1956 to 1962. Most of the production run of 692 aircraft went to Canada, but Belgium purchased 53. The aircraft was to have been replaced in Canadian service by the CF-105 Avro Arrow, but cancellation of the controversial and expensive Arrow program in 1959 led to the purchase in 1961 of the American-designed CF-101 Voodoo and the gradual retirement

of the Canuck fleet. One RCAF squadron continued to use the CF-100 for reconnaissance, training, and electronic warfare until 1981.

READING: Larry Milberry, *The Avro CF-100* (Toronto, 1981).

Champlain, Samuel de (c.1570–1635). A key figure in the making of French Canada, Champlain came to New France in 1603. His widespread explorations and his creation of alliances with local First Nations, intended to protect nascent French settlements, led inevitably to conflicts with the Iroquois, initially in 1609 where Champlain awed the natives with his arquebus, killing two chiefs. After other battles, Champlain suffered wounds in an unsuccessful attack on an Iroquois fort south of Lake Oneida in 1615. The English, led by David Kirke, captured him in 1629 after successfully laying siege to Quebec and reducing its inhabitants to starvation. Champlain returned as governor of a restored New France in 1633. His efforts laid the foundations of the colony of New France.

Reading: David H. Fischer, *Champlain's Dream* (Toronto, 2008).

Chateauguay, Battle of (1813). In October 1813, the United States sent two large forces northward, hoping that by seizing Montreal and severing British North America along the line of the St Lawrence River, it could force the surrender or abandonment of imperial troops in Upper Canada. Poorly coordinated and suffering from serious problems of supply, leadership, and training, the columns were defeated in detail by smaller British forces, one at Chateauguay in late October and the other at Crysler's Farm the following month.

The American troops headed for Chateauguay numbered some 4,000 and were commanded by Major-General Wade Hampton. They moved from Burlington, Vermont, across Lake Champlain to Plattsburgh, New York, and then up the Chateauguay River where a smaller British and Canadian force under Lieutenant-Colonel Charles Michel de Salaberry had assembled to meet them. After many of his New York units refused to cross into Canada, Hampton was left with perhaps 2,600 troops against 1,600 British, the latter consisting of de Salaberry's Canadian Voltigeurs (*Voltigeurs Canadiens*), local militia, Canadian Fencibles (a regular unit raised in Lower Canada), and some Mohawk warriors. On 25 October, Hampton sent a 1,000-strong column to try to outflank de Salaberry, who had fortified a position at a river bend with an abatis and arrayed his troops in a series of mutually reinforcing positions. The outflanking column got lost in the night but found itself in front of de Salaberry's positions the following morning, 26 October, when it was driven back by the defenders' musket fire. Another 1,000 Americans advanced in line toward the British position but, without having brought their cannon into action against the enemy's field fortifications, were driven back by musket fire as well. Short of supplies, demoralized by bad weather, and thinking they faced a much larger British force, the Americans withdrew toward Plattsburgh having suffered approximately 75 killed, wounded, and missing, to British losses of fewer than 20. In retreating south, Hampton ignored an order to join the second American column near Ogdensburg, which would soon share his command's ignominious fate—utter defeat at the hands of a badly outnumbered British force. The battle of Chateauguay saved Montreal and made de Salaberry a Canadian folk hero, his feat embellished by early accounts that his men had defeated an American force perhaps 20 times their own number. See also: Crysler's Farm; War of 1812.

Reading: J.M. Hitsman, *The Incredible War of 1812* (rev. ed., Montreal, 1999).

Chief of the Defence Staff (CDS). This post, the top military appointment in the Canadian Forces, came into being in 1964. Defence minister Paul Hellyer, who was set on integrating and then unifying the three services, gave the CDS responsibility for the control and administration of the Canadian Forces. In addition to being the military's senior officer and commander, the CDS is also the government's senior military adviser on matters of national defence and often attends Cabinet meetings when the prime minister desires military counsel. The role has sometimes led to conflict or miscommunication with that of the deputy minister, the senior civil servant responsible for departmental administration and accountable to the elected minister. Powerful deputy ministers have sometimes been accused of imposing on the prerogatives of the CDS in his command function as head of the armed forces; powerful CDSs have sometimes been seen as challenging civilian control of the military by undermining the minister or courting access directly to the prime minister. The position of CDS has often rotated between senior members of the three services—army, navy, and air force—although historically officers from the army (usually the largest service) have predominated.

Reading: Douglas Bland, *Chiefs of Defence: Government and the Unified Command of the Canadian Armed Forces* (Toronto, 1997).

Chiefs of Staff Committee. Formed in January 1939 just prior to the outbreak of World War II, the Chiefs of Staff Committee brought together the chief of the general staff, the chief of the naval staff, and the chief of the air staff to provide advice to the minister of national defence. In 1951, defence minister Brooke Claxton added a chairman to the committee, initially General Charles Foulkes, in an attempt to secure unity of direction in military planning. As the appointment suggested, unified decision-making had hitherto been illusory, each chief striving for a bigger share of the budget. The appointment of a chairman did not solve matters. The Chiefs of Staff Committee disappeared along with the individual service chiefs when defence minister Paul Hellyer created the post of chief of the defence staff in 1964 and set Canada on the road to armed forces unification. SEE ALSO: FOULKES.

Chippawa, Battle of (1814). During the closing stages of the War of 1812, an American force of more than 3,500 under Major-General Jacob Brown defeated a smaller British force of some 2,100 commanded by Major-General Phinias Riall near Chippawa Creek, just west of the Niagara River. The American force, consisting mainly of well-drilled regular infantry and artillery, supported by several hundred militia and Iroquois warriors, crossed the frontier to capture Fort Erie on 3 July and then moved north toward Chippawa Creek. They pushed back smaller British forces sent to delay their advance, but encamped south of the British positions along the river, which had been fortified with earthworks and artillery. Thinking that much of the American force opposing him consisted of poorly prepared militia, and not realizing that Fort Erie had fallen (which might have delayed some of the Americans as a besieging force), Riall moved out from his strong defensive position on 5 July and crossed Chippawa Creek moving south. The main battle was preceded by fierce fighting between light infantry, militia, and First Nations warriors on each side as they sought to control the forested areas just inland and to the west of cleared ground along the Niagara River. British forces suffered heavily against larger American units

in this fighting, but managed to control much of the area until late in the day, eventually shielding the right flank of the main force as it withdrew northward.

Riall led his own regulars and artillery into the fields between the forest edge and the edge of the Niagara River to meet a brigade of Americans commanded by Winfield Scott, a future American commander-in-chief. Other American troops were marching to the scene or encamped behind Scott's position, but the main clash would occur between approximately 1,400 troops per side. The battle saw two opposing lines of regulars firing at one another with muskets and artillery, as skirmishing and sniping continued in the woods along the battlefield's western flank. Scott's guns succeeded in blowing up a British ammunition wagon and, after heavy losses on both sides from close-range musket fire, an American force of 300–400 managed to outflank the British line on the right, forcing the redcoats to give ground. Under severe pressure and with many of his senior officers killed or wounded, Riall withdrew back across the Chippawa. A serious pursuit by the Americans might have destroyed his army entirely. American losses numbered approximately 325 (out of 2,100 or so engaged in the battle), while the British lost about 500 (from a similar number of 2,000 or so who had fought on 5 July). British troops eventually retreated to Fort George after Brown turned the Chippawa position by crossing the creek upstream from the British fortifications. The armies would meet again at Lundy's Lane, an even bloodier battle, several weeks later.

The victory of American regulars over British regulars at Chippawa was an important stage in the professional development of the United States Army, and a nasty surprise for British commanders accustomed in many other battles during the war to facing poorly trained militia under mediocre senior officers. SEE ALSO: LUNDY'S LANE; WAR OF 1812.

READING: J.M. Hitsman, *The Incredible War of 1812* (rev. ed., Montreal, 1999).

Chrétien, Joseph Jacques Jean (b.1934). Born in Shawinigan, Quebec, Jean Chrétien was a lawyer when first elected to the House of Commons as a Liberal in 1963. He held junior portfolios under Lester B. Pearson and many more senior ones under Pierre Trudeau, including finance and justice. He left Parliament in 1986 but returned in 1990 as Liberal leader, then won three consecutive majority governments.

Chrétien came to power with Canada facing huge deficits, and his government brought the fiscal situation under control by dramatic cuts in federal spending, not least in national defence. One of his first acts was to scrap a major—and already signed—helicopter contract. The symbolic cancellation fulfilled a campaign promise that the Liberals would not sanction expensive military acquisitions in the aftermath of the Cold War, but legal fees and contract cancellations cost the government hundreds of millions of dollars. The decision also left the Canadian Forces to fly obsolete Sea Kings into the second decade of the twenty-first century. The government later replaced aging search-and-rescue helicopters with essentially the same model that the Liberals had cancelled. The defence budget fell (in constant 1992–1993 dollars) from $11.8 billion when Chrétien took office to $9.5 billion four years later, and the strength of the Canadian Forces dropped from 75,900 in 1994 to just above 60,000 in 1999.

In many ways, the Chrétien government carried through on the broad outlines of policies first broached in a serious way by Pierre Trudeau, Chrétien's old mentor and former boss, 20 years previously. It sought consciously a peace dividend from the termination of the Cold War, tried at various times to distance itself from both the United States and the North Atlantic Treaty Organization (NATO), re-emphasized Canada's role within the United Nations (UN), and cut or cancelled equipment replacement contracts that promised to modernize some aspects of the Canadian Forces. It brought the Canadian army brigade and air group home from duty with NATO in Europe, fulfilling an earlier promise by Progressive Conservative Prime Minister Brian Mulroney, but leaving Canada poorly represented (and little trusted) in alliance councils. It ended a new military commitment to humanitarian intervention in Somalia and a 30-year-old one in Cyprus, while over time substantially increasing that in the former Yugoslavia to 1,000 in 1995 and 1,200 in 1996; an additional 1,300 soldiers were committed to NATO's Kosovo Force in 1999. Chrétien's government deployed troops to Haiti and sent a commander and some staff officers to the ill-fated United Nations force in Rwanda as well as to other UN operations. There was nothing wrong with these commitments except that the Canadian Forces, its numbers and budgets dropping and its equipment aging, could not readily fulfill them without great strain. By 1999, Canada had 4,500 troops overseas or more than 20 percent of the army's trained strength, amply fulfilling the Department of Foreign Affairs' view that what Canada needed was "peace police."

Chrétien was more open than most previous prime ministers in his depictions of military assets as bargaining chips in international diplomacy, and in espousing a "boy scout" role for Canadian diplomacy that seemed to embrace serious action only when there was little danger of additional cost or longer-term commitments. Canadian missions were numerous, risky, and continuous in the Chrétien years, but marked by a decided reluctance to face casualties, invoke force, or support deployed troops in dangerous situations. As NATO moved toward greater activism in former Yugoslavia, Canadian voices generally urged caution; when fighting seemed possible in Kosovo, Canada sent aircraft but no troops; when rhetorical outbursts regarding security in central Africa risked actually having to do something there, Canada balked. All the while, Canadian security initiatives on anti-personnel landmines, the possession of nuclear weapons, international criminal justice, and other files encrusted the critical Canadian-American security relationship with awkwardness and distrust.

The 9/11 attacks on the United States in 2001 increased the military's deployment tempo even further and took Canada into the War on Terror, the navy deploying to the Middle East, the air force basing its old Hercules aircraft there, and the army dispatching a battalion of the Princess Patricia's Canadian Light Infantry (PPCLI) to Afghanistan to work with a US division against the Taliban and al Qaeda. With 2,500 soldiers in Afghanistan in 2002, the military's leadership decided it could not replace the PPCLI there; simultaneously, the air and naval contingents were all but at their limit. In June 2003, the navy announced a "pause." But the army would get little rest. The Chrétien government, trying to avoid a commitment to the war against Iraq in 2003, instead sent troops back to Afghanistan in a UN-authorized but NATO-run force. This led one general at National Defence Headquarters to resign in protest. The Afghan commitment had much in its favour, but the Canadian Forces had too few personnel to manage easily such an indefinite commitment, along with its other deployments.

Jean Chrétien's political success—three majorities in three elections—was supreme. His effect on the Canadian Forces was all but disastrous. No prime minister in Canadian history has used the Canadian military more while supporting it less. SEE ALSO: AFGHANISTAN WAR; SOMALIA AFFAIR; WAR ON TERROR.

READING: Jean Chrétien, *My Years as Prime Minister* (Toronto, 2007).

Citadel, Halifax. Constructed on Citadel Hill overlooking Halifax, NS, construction of this star-shaped British fortification—officially called Fort George—began in 1828 on the site of several earlier defensive works. It was the centrepiece of a series of defensive works known as the Halifax Defence Complex. By the time the Citadel was completed in 1856, advances in artillery and naval technology had begun to render the fort obsolete, although its defences and armaments were subsequently improved to defend against rifled enemy cannon instead of older

▲ The centrepiece of a chain of forts protecting Halifax, the Citadel, shown here in 1918, sat atop Citadel Hill and commanded the area with its guns.

smoothbores. The city's defences were also reinforced for better protection against threats from the sea as well as threats from overland. The Citadel was garrisoned by British troops until 1906 when Canadians took over. It was garrisoned by Canadian soldiers during both world wars, and is now a National Historic Site. The Citadel was never attacked.

Citadel, Quebec City. The Quebec Citadel sits on Cape Diamond (Cap Diamant) high above the city overlooking the St Lawrence River. While some of its fortifications date to the French regime during the late seventeenth century, British forces constructed most of the current fort from 1820 to 1831. Garrisoned by the British army until 1871, the Citadel later served as headquarters for the Canadian Army's Permanent Force artillery school and, after World War I, for the Royal 22e Régiment. It had been intended to ward off American attack, whether overland or by sea, or to serve as the last

bastion of defence for troops who had been driven from Quebec and nearby areas by enemy forces. Like the smaller citadel at Halifax, constructed some years later, it was never attacked. The Citadel has been used as the governor general's summer residence since 1872.

Civil Defence. Civil defence is the passive defence of civilian targets against attack with the aim of saving lives and minimizing damage. During World War II, Canada set up an Air Raid Precautions organization to prepare urban centres for air attacks if any came. The mission saw thousands of Boy Scouts, students, and home defence troops watching from rooftops across Canada for German bombers that never came.

During the Cold War, the risk of air attack was real and potentially catastrophic, first from piloted bombers and then from long-range missiles. Major-General F.F. Worthington began Civil Defence Canada under defence department auspices in 1948, Canada's first

▲ The Quebec Citadel, sited high above the St Lawrence on Cap Diamant, was the heart of the British garrison in Canada. British troops, including these soldiers of the 60th Regiment, departed Canada for good in 1871.

peacetime civil defence organization. Its task was greatly complicated by improvements in strategic bombing and by the development of nuclear weapons: the bombers could fly higher, move faster, and come with less warning than their World War II counterparts, while missiles reduced warning time to minutes and, especially with increases in payload (their destructive capacity) and number of warheads, quickly outpaced the ability of defensive measures to absorb a serious attack. Civil defence remained important as a focus of public morale, and quite possibly to help a government's senior leaders ride out attack in deep underground bunkers, but in the nuclear age the idea of a successful defence of civil society would slowly become a contradiction in terms.

It was still worth a try, but the seriousness of Cold War civil defence efforts gradually diminished as western strategic thinking coalesced around the twin ideas of deterrence and mutually assured destruction (MAD). In the macabre logic of the nuclear world, the impossibility of surviving a nuclear war made defending against it redundant, and perhaps even dangerous: could preparing to survive Armageddon mean that one's enemy was actually planning to unleash it? Administratively, responsibility for surviving the unthinkable would prove well travelled and poorly developed. During the Korean War, the organization moved to the Department of National Health and Welfare. An interdepartmental working group in 1956 recommended creation of an Emergency Measures Organization (EMO) to plan for the continuation of government in the event of nuclear attack, to designate and construct air raid shelters, to collect and stockpile emergency supplies, and to plan for evacuations from urban areas. EMO urged Canadians to build bomb shelters in their backyards; few did. EMO absorbed Civil Defence Canada in 1957 and was succeeded in turn by Emergency Planning Canada in 1974 and by Emergency Preparedness Canada in 1986. There were many organizations, little money, and few realistic plans.

As the Cold War waned, planning for civil defence—neither comprehensive nor well coordinated

to begin with—lapsed even further, although defence against a virus, earthquake, or a power plant's nuclear meltdown seemed far more realistic than hiding in sewers from Soviet missiles. The al Qaeda attacks on New York City and Washington in September 2001 brought planning back to life, resulting in the creation of a new Department of Public Safety and Emergency Preparedness in 2003. The government of Conservative Prime Minister Stephen Harper passed the Emergency Management Act in 2007 that combined the coordination of all government emergency planning agencies in a new department, Public Safety Canada, with responsibility for "minimizing a continuum of risks to Canadians" ranging from terrorism to natural disasters. Disaster planning has recently been tested in a limited way by viral outbreaks, but not by external attack. The civil defence bureaucracy nonetheless employs at least 50,000, if one totals the relevant staff in each principal department and agency. In late 2009, the federal auditor general found in a review of Canadian emergency preparedness "that Public Safety Canada has not exercised the leadership necessary to coordinate emergency management activities, including protection of critical infrastructure in Canada." In 2010, the government announced plans to meet these criticisms.

Civil Liberties in Wartime. SEE CENSORSHIP; INTERNMENT; JAPANESE CANADIAN EVACUATION.

Civil-Military Relations. In Canada, as in most liberal-democratic states, civil control of the military means the control of the armed forces by civilians elected to Parliament acting in accordance with the laws of Canada. Civil control is intended to ensure that decisions and risks affecting national defence and the employment of the Canadian Forces are taken by politicians accountable to the people rather than by soldiers, officials, or others. In practice, therefore, the Cabinet, under the direction of the prime minister, is responsible and accountable to Canadians to control the military in all respects. The law gives politicians control over matters affecting the establishment, provision, and use of armed forces, while officers are allowed, under the direction of ministers, to control more strictly military matters including force standards and doctrine, discipline, the organization of units and formations, most promotions, and field operations. There is a narrow space between civil and military responsibilities, but it is sufficiently wide to permit ministers and officers to adjust to circumstances without crossing inappropriately into the other's domain.

Not a subject much discussed in Canada, relations between the military and government have occasionally been extremely difficult. British general officers commanding the Canadian militia who objected to patronage appointments or who believed that government spending on defence was too small regularly ran into problems. Major-General E.T.H. Hutton's efforts to force Canadian participation in the South African War and to shape the contingent might have seen him recalled at Ottawa's request had he not received a command in the field. During the conscription crisis in November 1944, pro-conscription commanders on the West Coast talked to the media despite orders to the contrary, and they and others threatened mass resignations if Ottawa did not send conscripts overseas. For their part, the politicians also egregiously interfered with the military, World War I militia minister Sam Hughes being the perfect example as he tried to get his friends and family commands in the field.

No one doubts that the civil government must set the policy and provide the funds and that it is the military's duty to carry out the policies and orders it receives. But the line of propriety has sometimes been difficult to define. In the 1962 Cuban Missile Crisis, Prime Minister John Diefenbaker delayed putting the Canadian military on alert. The Royal Canadian Navy, on the orders of its commander in Halifax, nonetheless put to sea to search for Soviet submarines. Did its obligations to its American ally and its fellow citizens outweigh its duty to follow the prime minister's orders? At roughly the same time, the Royal Canadian Air Force, anxious to see Canada get nuclear weapons, brought journalists and influential

Canadians to North American Air Defence Command headquarters in Colorado for briefings. Was this a violation of proper civil-military relations? And when defence minister Paul Hellyer pressed forward with his plans for integration and unification of the armed forces in the mid-1960s, Rear-Admiral William Landymore, commanding in Halifax, openly campaigned against the minister's plans. The minister demanded Landymore's resignation in 1966, but should he have been sacked immediately because he had manifested publicly his opposition? Did Landymore's duty to his sailors outweigh his duty to follow orders he believed dead wrong?

More recently, General Rick Hillier, while chief of the defence staff from 2005 to 2009, ran into difficulty because of his plain speaking, often pronouncing on commitments or their associated policies, and not just on the performance or operations of Canadian troops while doing them. Calling the Taliban in Afghanistan and other enemies of coalition forces "scumbags," for example, was understandable language for a soldier at war, but impolitic for the government's senior military adviser whose job included controlling the passions of troops in the field, maintaining standards of international law during the deployment, and denying to government or coalition critics unnecessary opportunities to critique the mission. It was an honest outburst, though embarrassing for the government. But did it also call into question proper relations between the military and the civil authority? It did not, or at least not immediately, but it certainly questioned the extent to which military authorities were exercising the predominant role in the war, and thereby defining its character, at a time when government officials were at pains to depict the mission's humanitarian and multi-faceted nature, the even-handedness of coalition troops in dealing with locals, and the care taken to adhere to the highest legal and ethical standards in the conduct of military operations.

No one's interest has been well served by public squabbling over civil-military issues. A senior officer who disagrees with government policy can argue the case with the minister, resign (in the event the argument is unsuccessful), and contemplate going public with his or her views. Politicians' responsibilities are less clear, given their necessary supremacy as elected officials in this relationship, but the pitfalls of handling poorly the military file have also been clear, even where—in peacetime, at least—military issues stir few voters. Shortchanging the military or sending it into action without proper training and equipment risks political opprobrium if things go wrong. The fallout from the 1990s mission to Somalia and the resulting military scrutiny after a series of criminal investigations and reviews reflected this possibility. While originating with a handful of soldiers in the Canadian Airborne Regiment, the after-effects included a lengthy public inquiry and, later, cross-Canada public hearings that castigated the federal government for failing to uphold its end of what amounted to a social contract with those in uniform by providing the proper leadership, training, and resources to enable the military to do its job. SEE ALSO: CONSCRIPTION; HELLYER; HILLIER; HUGHES; KING; SOMALIA AFFAIR; UNIFICATION.

Claxton, Brian Brooke (1898–1960). An Anglo-Quebecker, Brooke Claxton attended Lower Canada College and McGill University, then joined the artillery in 1916 during World War I. He rose to battery sergeant major, saw much action, and won the Distinguished Conduct Medal. He returned to Canada a convinced nationalist and a believer in the League of Nations and collective security. After completing his war-interrupted law degree at McGill in 1921, he earned a distinguished reputation in the Montreal bar and became an inveterate joiner, working with organizations such as the Canadian Club, the lobby for a national broadcasting system, and the Canadian Institute of International Affairs. In 1940, Claxton successfully contested a Montreal seat as a Liberal (where he was one of the first Canadian politicians to make extensive use of opinion polling) and in 1943 became Prime Minister Mackenzie King's parliamentary secretary. In 1944, he became the first minister of national health and welfare, responsible for implementing the family allowance scheme that had much to do with creating the welfare state and, not coincidentally, with the Liberals' 1945 election victory. After combining the service wartime defence ministries into a single department in December 1945, King appointed Claxton minister of national defence in 1946, charged with cutting wartime personnel and budgets and creating a small, economical peacetime military. In this post, which he held until 1954 under both King and Louis St Laurent, Claxton had substantial impact as Canada, having made the cuts, scrambled to create brigades and air squadrons for service in Korea and Europe, and to build its largest professional forces ever to meet the demands of the Cold War. The budget-cutter presided over defence spending that, by the time he left politics, was above 7 percent of gross domestic product. Secretive, prone to depression, overly sensitive to media criticism, Claxton overcame a succession of

▲ Brooke Claxton, minister of national defence, in 1951.

scandals, including charges that horses were on the army payroll and mutinies on several Royal Canadian Navy ships. In the latter instances, Claxton ordered G.S. Currie and Admiral Rollo Mainguy to report on what had gone wrong and to suggest remedies. Claxton built the army, navy, and air force into the most highly funded, well-trained, and well-equipped peacetime military Canada has ever fielded. He left politics in 1954, went into business as the head of Metropolitan Life, and then led the new Canada Council on its creation in 1956. See also: Korean War; World War II.

Reading: David Bercuson, *True Patriot: The Life of Brooke Claxton, 1898–1960* (Toronto, 1993).

Cold War. The Cold War between the Communist world and the capitalist West began in the closing months of World War II and continued until the collapse of the Soviet Union and Warsaw Pact after 1989. The standoff survived crises, wars, incessant spying, and relentless propaganda, sometimes threatening to erupt into full-scale hostilities. It always returned to a tense and suspicious status quo that each side preferred to the uncertainties of a great power war that would have risked nuclear annihilation. The Cold War's retrospective stability was not mere nostalgia bred of post–Cold War international uncertainties. The half-century of confrontation saw the gradual emergence of recognizable spheres of interest, norms of behaviour (and misbehaviour), methods of communication or signalling, and diplomatic tools that helped moderate the worst excesses of ideologues on both sides. Mutual antagonisms were sometimes shunted onto peripheral conflicts where interests might collide without escalation into global war. Rules and practices grew around military exercises, technological developments, and diplomatic practice—or regimes, in security parlance—that helped opponents and third parties to discern intentions and categorize risks. Peacekeeping evolved from crisis management to confidence-building measures, intended both to prevent international war, and to freeze in place implacable confrontations without ever spurring international peace. Deployments that were initially measured in months soon stretched into years, and then into decades. As armed forces grew, modernized, and prepared in deadly earnest to slaughter one another, the Cold War's militarization was tracked by growing interest in exploring arms control or mutual security protocols to reduce arsenals and facilitate trust. A non-aligned movement of neither ideological stamp sought manoeuvring room from the great geopolitical embrace, while itself sheltering a variety of thuggish miscreants, many of whom were not very non-aligned at all, and most of whom sought financial or other gain from competing power blocs. The Cold War was a balance of terror that teetered on a modicum of understanding: no side could likely survive war with the other, though each might sometimes be tempted to think the unthinkable.

The Cold War was rooted in the mutual antagonisms that separated the Soviet Union and world communism generally from capitalist Western states that saw state socialism of the Soviet type as an existential threat. The rickety social order of late nineteenth-century industrialism and the oligarchic power structures that supported it were vulnerable to and petrified of populist reform movements, and saw in all radical agendas the seeds of systemic revolution. Anarchists, socialists, communists: most were watched, bullied, or suppressed by state agencies in the West—often with extreme brutality—long before tsarist Russia succumbed to rebellion and coup d'état in 1917. The loss of a key wartime ally was one reason for Western intervention on the loyalist, or "White," side in the ensuing Russian Civil War; fear that the Russian disease was a political pandemic was the other. "Red" victory enshrined the Soviet Union as a powerful challenger state in a system run by cautious, war-weary, and vulnerable victors; it was also well outside the historical norms or societal understanding of the other great powers, and a continuing source of revolutionary agitation. On the Soviet side, the reasons for distrust were even more obvious: a record of Western invasion, interference, ostracism, and insult—the Russian as barbarian, primitive, ignorant—left Moscow predisposed to seeking allies abroad, building military capacity at home, and securing in between the strategic depth required for national self-defence. Conflicts along the fault line separating Soviet paranoia from Western insecurity were inevitable.

The Grand Alliance of World War II between the United States, Great Britain, and the Soviet Union was one of dire necessity with scant trust on either side. Hitler's invasion of the Soviet Union in June 1941, before German forces had brought Great Britain—and with it, the British Commonwealth—to heel was a strategic error second only to his declaration of war on the United States the following December. In rapid succession, Germany added to its enemies the world's two great leviathans, guaranteeing its own inevitable defeat and the preponderance of Soviet and American power for generations to come. The wartime alliance against the Axis was a crude marriage of convenience: the democracies, including Canada, provided vast quantities of material to the Soviet Union, whose Red Army devoured German armies wholesale on the Eastern Front. Stalin clamoured for greater Western efforts on the ground against Germany, while Western and Chinese forces fought Japan alone until the war's closing weeks in the Pacific. Stalin insisted on firm control over territories conquered by Soviet arms; Western governments sought in vain the return to power of pro-Western governments in exile or the imposition of local democrats in the postwar order. The mistrust grew more overt and potentially hostile at war's end, as Soviet and Western interests clashed in Poland, Greece, northern Iran, Norway, the North Pacific, and in the occupied areas of a defeated Germany. Evidence of widespread Soviet espionage against Western interests also played a role, including the defection of Igor Gouzenko, a cipher officer at the Soviet embassy in Ottawa, in September 1945. Gouzenko's documents demonstrated the existence of spy networks in Canada, with ramifications that reached into the United States and Britain. Western diplomats and intelligence officers struggled to define for their political bosses the true nature of the Soviet threat: Moscow was possessed of vast military capability, or so it seemed, but what were its intentions?

The Soviet Union's failure to leave those areas of Eastern Europe it had occupied during the war was a principal cause of friction. Had the war in Europe been fought to supplant one form of despotism in order to replace it with another? Britain's Winston Churchill needed little convincing of Moscow's relentlessly expansionist agenda, but others were less sure; the transformation of American policy from benign optimism under President Roosevelt to reluctant pessimism under Harry Truman was the defining moment in the early Cold War. Everywhere, it seemed, the last lights of hope were blinking out. The United Nations proved susceptible to paralysis by the Soviet veto in the Security Council, all but eliminating the prospect of an international order based on the rule of law helping to prevent global catastrophes. Western Europe—slow to recover from the war, demoralized, and fearful—watched the USSR blockade the divided city of Berlin and crush a latent pro-democracy movement in Czechoslovakia. The Russians pushed in Norway and Iran. There was civil war in Greece. Truman responded with the Marshall Plan, an expensive and aggressive attempt to rally the democracies with economic aid. He later adopted a policy that would become emblematic of the West's security posture throughout the Cold War: containment. The West gravitated slowly to one of the key lessons of the 1930s: in the face of capable, intransigent pressure, erstwhile allies would hang together or hang separately.

Political solidarity was a first step. Negotiations between several European governments over joint defence measures were paralleled by secret talks between Britain, Canada, and the United States. Ottawa's position was one of growing internationalism, led by Louis St Laurent, a new prime minister less worried by external ties than his predecessor, and by a coterie of talented, urbane foreign service mandarins who saw in effective diplomacy both the prospect of postwar peace and prosperity and a necessary counterweight in

Canadian affairs to the preponderant influence of the United States. The North Atlantic Treaty, signed in early 1949, created the North Atlantic Treaty Organization (NATO), a unique and unprecedented collective defence pact between ten European countries plus Canada and the United States. The guts of the treaty, Article V, pledged members to a collective response to external aggression; an ably negotiated add-on, Article II, framed largely at Canadian insistence, promised forms of mutual co-operation that might make the alliance something more than just a politico-military pact. Events would conspire to make it a military agency first.

The outbreak of war in Korea in June 1950, half a world away but nonetheless a war authorized by Moscow and with the concurrence of Communist China, sped Western rearmament. After Korea, NATO evolved rapidly into something far more than a political statement: it grew with members' commitments of army, navy, and air force units and the integrated command structures to lead them in the field. These would take many years to develop, but NATO's European-based forces evolved from a mere tripwire that would present an attacker with the danger of an early nuclear response, into a shield force of several million that might, under optimal circumstances, have defeated an aggressor before the nuclear button could be pushed. The latter was a pipe dream in 1950, as Canada embarked on the greatest peacetime rearmament in its history, sending army brigades, ships, and aircraft to Korea and to NATO Europe simultaneously in 1950–1951, and increasing the armed forces overall by tens of thousands. For most of the following decade, Canada would be a substantial player in alliance counsels, with a large air force and a substantial ground contingent in Europe. When NATO sought to review its decision-making and consultative processes in 1956, and the role of smaller powers within the organization, one of the three "Wise Men" appointed to the task was Lester B. Pearson who, as foreign minister, had originally signed the treaty for Canada.

The Soviet threat in these years was real enough that Canada's first peacetime deployments received general public approval, even though Ottawa's defence spending soared to almost 8 percent of gross domestic product by 1952. NATO-wide, the story was the same. In early 1952, the alliance pledged to create some 90 divisions for service in Europe, about half as ready-divisions, and the rest capable of being mobilized in less than 30 days. Europe's stumbling economic recovery rendered this quadrupling of NATO's military effort a fiscal impossibility, but the numbers grew steadily just the same. In 1955, with the Federal Republic of Germany's membership in NATO, they were set to grow even more; by the mid-1980s, German numbers would be nearly 50 percent of NATO strength along the critical Central Front. The immediate impact of West Germany's NATO membership was more sobering: the Soviet Union countered by creating the Moscow-dominated Warsaw Pact, a military alliance of its European satellites.

The conventional balance was only one aspect of the Cold War standoff. Both sides readied themselves for war and armed themselves with nuclear weapons and the long-range bomber fleets, missiles, and submarines to deliver them to enemy targets. In Europe, NATO defence soon depended on smaller-yield "tactical" nuclear weapons to compensate for the Red Army's preponderance in conventional (non-nuclear) weaponry and its sheer weight of numbers. In North America, vulnerability to Soviet attack forced close co-operation of Canada and the United States, the creation of radar warning lines, and the development of sophisticated air defences. Continental defence merged, more or less seamlessly, in the North American Air (later Aerospace) Defence Command in 1957–1958. The Arctic became strategic real estate, sovereignty patrols and surveillance missions grew in number and importance, and Canada co-operated with allies, including Australia and New Zealand as well as NATO partners, in the sharing of all kinds of intelligence. In Europe, the dividing line between East and West having settled along what Winston Churchill had famously called an Iron Curtain, running from northern Norway to the Mediterranean and beyond, reaching into the Caucasus at Turkey's Soviet frontier, a tense watch bristling with weapons hardened into place. Elsewhere, the interests of East and West clashed as they jockeyed for strategic advantage, sought allies and proxy states to secure their interests or fight local wars, and supported competing sides in power struggles over land, minerals, or political power. A complicating factor was always China, where the Communists had emerged victorious in the late 1940s from a civil war that left a rump Nationalist government on the offshore island of Taiwan; the Communists had the land, the people, and the growing military might, but the Nationalists had American support and, for more than two decades, international recognition and legitimacy. In Central Europe, powerful armies observed one another warily, conducting exercises to test readiness and show resolve while nervous that preparedness be misrepresented as preparation for war. In Korea, the armistice in 1953 left a devastated peninsula divided into armed camps, the North sheltering under Communist protection, the South under that of the United States. As the main potential battlegrounds for East-West conflict stabilized, tensions spread laterally around the globe.

There were recurring periods of less tension. Joseph Stalin's death in 1953 created some optimism, but his successors, as during the Suez Crisis of November 1956 and the simultaneous brutal Soviet repression of the Hungarian revolution, threatened to unleash their missiles against the West. An American spy plane was shot down over Russia, its pilot trotted before the international media by gleeful Soviet officials after the United States had refused to acknowledge that any over-flights had occurred. The Soviets put nuclear missiles into Cuba, a Communist state since a successful revolution put Fidel Castro in power in 1959, and the United States—which had its own missiles in Turkey—reacted with sloppy indignation and political vigour, a dangerous mixture. Dumb luck and adroit diplomacy helped end the nuclear showdown (the Cuban Missile Crisis) after a 13-day cliffhanger during which many thought the Cold War would end in red-hot nuclear salvos. The Soviets withdrew their missiles, in exchange for the later face-saving withdrawal of US missiles from Turkey. In the West's greatest postwar test of will and solidarity, Canada's intestinal fortitude had, from the Americans' perspective, been found wanting. John Diefenbaker's government, already at odds with the Americans and with domestic public opinion for its reluctance to accept nuclear warheads for the weapons it had ordered, was grievously wounded by the Cuban crisis. Accused of dithering and disloyalty in a moment of clear threat, it was defeated in Parliament and in a subsequent election, losing to a Liberal party that promised decisiveness, integrity, and nuclear weapons. Canada would not dispose of its last nuclear weapons until the 1980s.

Through the 1960s, prosperity, social tensions, and the growing stability of the East-West confrontation led many Western states to re-evaluate their military postures, and to redirect defence budgets into social policy or other forms of non-military spending. The armed truce survived serious crises in the Middle East and Czechoslovakia; Soviet and Chinese interests clashed in central Asia; and US leadership of the Western alliance was increasingly called into question by the war in Vietnam. Pierre Trudeau, Canada's slick, groovy, socially conscious prime minister from 1968, in many ways embodied the period's growing critique of status quo international politics and the sometimes ill-considered alternatives the times appeared to demand. He reviewed Canadian defence policy and cut the country's NATO contribution in half, a plan that received a harsh response from Canada's allies who had just watched the USSR crush the "Prague spring" that had seemed to be bringing change to Czechoslovakia. He might have done more, withdrawing Canada even further from the Western camp, had senior cabinet ministers, notably foreign minister Mitchell Sharp and defence minister Léo Cadieux, not intervened and reminded him of the practical value of the NATO shield, the necessity of solidarity, and the value of Canadian membership to overall national interests. Trudeau was a devotee of détente, a false dawn of better East-West relations that rose and fell in the 1970s, buoyed by President Richard Nixon's visit to Communist China in 1972 and by international recognition—including Canada's—of one of the world's bloodiest and most repressive dictatorships, and later crushed by the Soviet Union's invasion of Afghanistan in 1979.

The 1980s sidelined Trudeau's brand of internationalism, amidst both a deepening Western retrenchment against Soviet adventurism and a rising tide of popular unrest with the nuclear arms race and the risks posed by nuclear proliferation. NATO's decision to deploy new nuclear missiles into Europe in the early 1980s, in partial response to the growing strength of Soviet nuclear forces, prompted massive popular protest and, in Canada, a long (and unsuccessful) campaign against the testing of American cruise missiles over Canadian territory. When the jittery Soviet Union shot down a civilian Korean airliner in 1983 with much loss of life, the tragedy helped galvanize Western hardliners like Ronald Reagan and Margaret Thatcher into massive rearmament and growing defiance of the old certainties of Cold War politics. Trudeau, near the end of his political life, launched an abortive peace mission that took him around the globe. Brian Mulroney's Progressive Conservatives would sweep two elections in his wake, promising greater solidarity with allies, and more troops and equipment for the Canadian military. It was coincident with the Cold War's swan song. A hawkish defence policy review produced by the Mulroney government in 1987 read—and looked—as though it had been produced in the 1950s Pentagon. Brimming with colourful bar graphs and pie charts warning of Soviet strength and NATO weakness, it poured rhetorical fuel onto the dying embers of the Cold War. A few of the weapons systems it promised would eventually appear, bolstering the long-suffering Canadian Forces against post–Cold War uncertainties; most, including the promise of nuclear-powered submarines, were soon the footnotes of history, curious remnants of a bellicosity as unusual in Canadian military history as it had been untimely and improbably expensive.

The beginning of the end was the coming to power in Moscow of Mikhail Gorbachev in 1985. Intelligent, younger than the geriatric leaders he succeeded,

Gorbachev had visited Western Europe and Canada as a rising Soviet minister, and understood how ideology and incessant military spending had crippled the Soviet economy and social structure. Foolish enough to believe that he could change the system from within, leaving a modernized but more prosperous Soviet Union in his wake, but courageous enough to try, Gorbachev embarked on a campaign of internal reform and external rapprochement that would sweep away both his country and the Cold War in less than half a decade. A succession of summits with Reagan and his successor, George H.W. Bush, essentially brought the historic struggle to a close, and spawned unprecedented international agreements on the reduction of nuclear and conventional weapons. The Berlin Wall, erected in 1961 to stop East Germans fleeing to freedom, came down in 1989, the Communist regimes of Eastern Europe collapsed of their own dead weight, the Warsaw Pact dissolved, and the Soviet Union fragmented and struggled, unsuccessfully, to remake itself as a collection of quasi-democratic states. NATO remained, searching for a new role, while its constituent states took their peace dividends and reduced their militaries. Canada retrenched from the Cold War as though it had been an unfortunate accident, acknowledging the uncertainty of what events might come while embracing the savings derived from what had ended. Military planners would continue to defend the requirement for a balanced and capable all-arms force for years thereafter, but cost-cutting federal governments now pushed the Canadian Forces toward more constabulary roles, elevating the chimera of peacekeeping into the ersatz grail of an increasingly on-the-cheap security policy. Canada withdrew forces from their permanent NATO deployments in Europe in 1993–1994, ending a nearly 50-year commitment over the loud grumblings of many allies; even as the bases closed, thousands of Canadians redeployed under United Nations command to a hodge-podge of international security missions in former Yugoslavia, a weakly stitched multi-ethnic, non-aligned country that proved another casualty of post–Cold War transition. In Asia, China soon began to make over its controlled economy into an almost-capitalist one; although it made threats at Taiwan, the centre of power of the Kuomintang the Communists had defeated in 1949, too many Chinese were making too much money to risk outright war.

The Cold War had been the seminal conflict of the second half of the twentieth century. The democracies had been victorious. Europe had been liberated from Moscow's control, and the Soviet Union and its makeshift alliance, the Warsaw Pact, destroyed. NATO staggered into the new century searching for missions, adding new Eastern European states with near-indecent haste, and bitterly divided between a continental European bloc toying publicly with the alliance's postmodern irrelevance and an Anglo-American pillar—supported by many of the new members for whom the old bogeyman, Russia, had really not changed all that much. Devastating wars in Central America, Vietnam, Korea, and the Middle East had never led to a general shooting match between East and West during the long Cold War watch, but millions were dead and entire regions blighted by landmines, unemployed warlords, and growing great power disinterest. Trillions of dollars had been siphoned into history's longest and costliest non-war. Canada had been by turns enthusiastic and demure, steadfast and unreliable, rarely punching above its weight but never entirely abandoning the match. A founding member of NATO, it had sometimes been found absent at critical junctures, its long retreat from international military commitments gradual enough to be officially denied but persistent enough to be noted. SEE ALSO: ALLIANCES, CANADIAN; NORTH ATLANTIC TREATY ORGANIZATION.

READING: Robert Bothwell, *Alliance and Illusion* (Vancouver, 2007).

Collective Security. The idea that aggressors could be deterred or defeated if all other nations combined against them found its first practical expression in the covenant of the League of Nations. That pledge failed in practice because almost all states, including Canada, proved unwilling to accept the obligations that collective security required. The United Nations (UN), created in

the closing days of World War II, tried to manage the idea better, and mounted a collective response to the Korean War in 1950 and in a large number of later peacekeeping operations. But the UN could be paralyzed by the vetoes held by the world's great powers in the Security Council, and the idea of "coalitions of the willing" outside the UN took hold in the later twentieth century as a substitute for, and occasionally as a complement to, UN actions. Sometimes the UN authorized action (as in the Gulf War of 1991); other times, the UN refused to give authorization and others proceeded in any case (as in the war against Iraq in 2003). The North Atlantic Treaty of 1949 was another attempt to ensure collective security, in this case by binding its members in a common front against the Soviet Union, the combined strength of which was intended to deter Soviet adventurism. The alliance created by the North Atlantic Treaty was first and foremost a political pact, but one that also contained a clear military—or collective defence—component, a clause in the treaty that bound member states to come to the aid of one another when attacked by an outside force. This clause was triggered for the first time in September 2001 after terrorists attacked several targets in the United States. The alliance's creation also enabled member states to discuss mutual security concerns and to take joint action outside of the United Nations, and without subjecting critical decisions to the veto power of the Soviet Union in the Security Council.

Collective security—joint efforts to promote peace, international order, and the safety of one's interests through combined action—is sometimes conflated with or opposed to collective defence—joint action to guarantee the military defence of one's people, territory, and interests in the event of external attack. The differences are more than academic. The North Atlantic Treaty Organization can be thought of as a members-only collective security agency that has a collective defence mechanism at its heart; the United Nations might be viewed as a collective security agency that has no functioning collective defence mechanism. A running critique of both agencies has been that neither plays a sufficient role in ensuring *co-operative*

⌃ Lieutenant-Colonel Raymond Collishaw, 1918.

security—the gradual reshaping of competing security interests into forms of peace, order, and common security shared by, and sustained through, the efforts of all international actors. SEE ALSO: NORTH ATLANTIC TREATY ORGANIZATION.

Collège militaire royal de Saint-Jean (CMR). Opened in 1952 at the historic military installation at Saint-Jean-sur-Richelieu to add a francophone dimension to Canada's military colleges, CMR initially offered a preparatory year to cadets with junior matriculation and followed this with two years of university-level study and training before sending its bilingual graduates to the Royal Military College (RMC) in Kingston for a final two years of work. In 1985, the college won the right to award degrees and, in 1988, to offer graduate programs. With the end of the Cold War and subsequent budget cuts, the

government of Jean Chrétien closed CMR in 1995, though a "prep" year, preparing francophones for RMC, continued. In 2007, CMR reopened (with its own board of governors) with some 200 cadets studying there for one or two years, depending on the program they intended to follow at RMC.

Collishaw, Raymond (1893–1976). Born in Nanaimo, BC, Collishaw joined the Fisheries Protection Service, the precursor to the Royal Canadian Navy, as a cabin boy at age 15. When World War I began, he travelled to England to join the Royal Navy and, by 1916, was a pilot with the Royal Naval Air Service (RNAS). Collishaw became its highest scoring ace and the Canadian with the second-highest number of aerial victories with 60. He was awarded the Distinguished Service Order and bar, the Distinguished Service Cross, and the Distinguished Flying Cross. Later transferred to the Royal Air Force (RAF), he ended the war as a lieutenant-colonel. Collishaw commanded a squadron in the Russian Civil War, remained in the RAF, and during World War II, led No. 204 Group in the Western Desert. He retired in 1943 as an air vice-marshal.

Commission on the Defences of Canada. Established by the governor general, Lord Monck, to advise on what was necessary in terms of fortifications and defences to protect the Province of Canada, the commission of six officers reported in September 1862. The focus of any attack from the south, they maintained, would be Montreal, but new fortifications should be built between Sarnia, on the Michigan frontier north of Detroit, and Lévis, Lower Canada, at a cost of £1.6 million. The key to defending the colony was to secure naval supremacy on the Great Lakes, to create a large militia, and for Britain to provide some 130,000 regular troops. As with most such reports, nothing happened. The Canadian government rejected compulsory training for the militia because, it said, "No probable combination of regular troops and militia would preserve our soil from invading armies." Except during World Wars I and II, Canadian troop strength has only approached such numbers—briefly—in the mid-1950s, at the height of the Cold War.

Commission on the Defences of North America. Established by the Duke of Wellington to report on what was necessary to defend British North America, the commission of engineer officers under Sir James Carmichael Smyth reported in 1825. It recommended 21 different defensive works ranging from major fortresses at Montreal, Kingston, Niagara, and Halifax to a number of lesser works on likely attack routes from the south. Notably, the commissioners called for canals on the Ottawa and Rideau Rivers. The estimated cost of implementing all the recommendations was £1.65 million, a figure that created hilarity at Westminster. All that Parliament would approve was £56,000 to construct the Rideau Canal. Cost overruns boosted this expenditure, and later periods of tension with the United States led to building some of the fortifications recommended in 1825. A Halifax-to-Montreal military road had also been proposed, but cost, political infighting, and lack of interest prevented its commencement for many years, by which time intercolonial railways were its principal competition as a security-enhancing mode of communication.

READING: Gary Campbell, *The Road to Canada: The Grand Communications Route along the St John River to Quebec* (Fredericton, 2005).

Committee of Imperial Defence (CID). Established in 1904 by the British government, the committee combined the Cabinet Defence Committee and the Joint Naval and Military Committee and created a permanent secretariat. The CID was to consider all questions of imperial defence from the points of view of the British services, the dominions and colonies, and India. Many Canadian leaders saw the committee as a centralizing force intended to limit the Dominion's autonomy and to serve British interests.

Commonwealth War Graves Commission (CWGC). Created in 1917 as the Imperial War Graves Commission to build and maintain cemeteries and to provide perpetual care for the British Empire's war dead, the commission's name was changed in 1960. The CWGC maintains 23,000 sites in more than 150 countries and commemorates 1.7 million war dead, including some 760,000 whose names were listed on memorials because their remains could not be identified. With more than 110,000 dead in 75 countries, Canada contributes 10 percent of CWGC costs each year. All the cemeteries are superbly maintained, each grave marked with a uniform headstone without regard to rank, race, or creed. The stones show religious symbols—a cross or Star of David, where the deceased's religion is indicated in personnel records—and frequently include a phrase or two from parents, spouses, or children.

READING: Eric McGeer, *Words of Valediction and Remembrance: Canadian Epitaphs of the Second World War* (St Catharines, ON, 2008).

Conquest, The. General James Wolfe's victory on the Plains of Abraham on 13 September 1759, General

Sai Wan Cemetery in Hong Kong is one of many war cemeteries maintained by the Commonwealth War Graves Commission. Some 280 Canadian soldiers are buried here.

Jeffrey Amherst's taking of Montreal on 8 September 1760, and the subsequent cession of New France to Britain in the peace treaty of 1763 collectively comprise The Conquest. To France, the loss of the colony was important but not critical. To the 76,000 Canadiens, almost all of whom remained in Canada after the war, the change in colonial masters was significant indeed, for many the beginning of a long struggle for religious, linguistic, and cultural rights that continues to this day, especially in Quebec. The Conquest has long achieved the power of cherished myth, the actions—real and imagined—of British (and, later, Canadian) governors becoming the explanation in Quebec nationalist accounts for every failure, underachievement, or misapprehension in Quebec's history under non-francophone rule. The Conquest was a powerful image in the development of Quebec's separatist movement in the latter half of the twentieth century, and sensitivity to representations of the British period remains strong. In 2009, federal officials cancelled a proposed re-enactment of the battle of the Plains of Abraham to mark the event's 250th anniversary on land maintained by the National Battlefields Commission after vocal protests by pro-sovereignty groups. SEE ALSO: QUEBEC (1759).

READING: Fred Anderson, *Crucible of War: The Seven Years' War and the Fate of Empire in British North America, 1754–1766* (New York, 2000).

Conscientious Objectors. Anyone who refuses military service for reasons of conscience, religious belief, or opposition to being placed in a situation where the killing of others might become necessary, is a conscientious objector. Canada had admitted Doukhobors and immigrants from the "peace churches" before World War I with the understanding that they would not be required to perform military duties, but under the strain of war those guarantees were not always honoured. Others, facing military service because of Canada's 1917 conscription act, argued for exemption on religious or moral grounds. Some were conscripted nonetheless, 163 were jailed, and, widely perceived as "slackers," few received much public support. By mid-1919, 40 "conshies" were still behind bars, but most were released at much the same time as the demobilization of members of the Canadian Expeditionary Force at war's end. In World War II, the state was more understanding, but more than 12,000 conscientious objectors were obliged to perform what was called Alternative Service Work at camps across the country.

READING: Amy Shaw, *Crisis of Conscience: Conscientious Objection in Canada during the First World War* (Vancouver, 2008).

Conscription. The compulsory enlistment of civilians for military service dates back to the French regime in Canada where *habitants* were obliged to turn out to help defend their settlements. Under the British, the Sedentary Militia, required to muster one day a year, was similarly a precursor to conscripting citizens for service in the event of need. Such measures were tolerated, primarily because they were largely ignored. In the twentieth century, however, conscription for overseas service was contentious in the extreme. The creation and imposition of conscription legislation sparked, in each world war, some of the fiercest and most divisive political debates in Canadian history.

In World War I, Canada initially raised the Canadian Expeditionary Force (CEF) by voluntary methods, and these proved sufficient from 1914 into early 1917. But the terrible casualties in the trenches began to outpace recruiting and, after a visit to Britain

and France in the spring of 1917 around the time of the Vimy Ridge victory, Prime Minister Sir Robert Borden came to believe that compulsory service had to be imposed to sustain the ranks of the Canadian Corps with at least a hundred thousand troops. The British also pressed Canada to act. To Borden, the war was a sacred cause that had to be won, but he knew that French Canadians did not share this attitude, and understood that imposing conscription would certainly create a political crisis of historic proportions. He tried to avoid it by inviting Liberal leader Sir Wilfrid Laurier to join him in a coalition that would impose compulsion, but the francophone Laurier

World War I recruiting posters reflected the assumptions of English-Canadian propagandists, in this case, that historical imagery derived from New France would encourage French-Canadian enlistment. Their failure by 1917 helped make conscription more likely.

feared that such an act would irretrievably split the country and destroy his own standing in Quebec.

Borden then moved ahead, introducing his own Military Service Bill, drafted by Arthur Meighen, the solicitor general; this passed into law in August. The Act declared that all men between the ages of 20 and 45 were liable for military service, unless they fell under various grounds for exemption. Determined to prevail, Borden then gerrymandered the electoral rolls with the Military Voters Act (MVA) that let soldiers who could not remember their constituency vote generically for the government or the opposition. Their votes would be allocated where needed. Also, the Wartime Elections Act (WTEA), again drafted by Meighen, gave the vote for the first time to women—but only to women with relatives in the military. The WTEA also removed the vote from naturalized enemy aliens. The MVA and the WTEA encouraged those English-speaking Liberals who had been reluctant to join a Union Government under Borden to do so; they could see the electoral writing on the wall. In December 1917, Borden's Union Government won a huge victory by painting Quebec as disloyal and cowardly, and the government, completely excluding francophones, implemented conscription. The first men reported for military training in January 1918.

Of those eligible for call-up, well over 90 percent sought exemption, every case being heard and decided by local tribunals. In all, 401,882 men registered and, by the end of the war, 124,588 had been taken on strength with the CEF. But only 24,132 had arrived in France by the armistice of 11 November 1918, and how many had actually been incorporated into CEF units is unclear. Still, 24,000 men was more than a division's worth of reinforcements, enough to sustain the entire four divisions of the Canadian Corps for some time in battle; the remainder of the conscripts at home could have kept the CEF fighting well into 1919 had the war gone on.

While conscription had obvious military advantages, as a political measure it was a disaster. It helped Borden to win re-election in 1917 in a brutally racist election that alienated Quebec from the Tories for 40 years. It produced a major riot in Quebec City, put down by troops sent in from Toronto, that left four dead and some 150 injured. It left English Canadians believing their French-speaking compatriots were a race of traitorous cowards. It infuriated farmers to whom Borden had promised exemptions from military service for their sons in the election campaign and then reneged when the Germans mounted their spring offensive in 1918. It alienated labour groups too, whose members believed that wealth should also be "conscripted," placing the burden of the war more equitably on the rich who they believed had profited from the conflict. And its dire political consequences shaped the nation's military personnel policies in World War II.

During the interwar years, the memory of conscription was deliberately kept alive by the Liberal party, which in Quebec pointed to the Conservatives and to Arthur Meighen as those with the blood of conscripts on their hands. But it was Liberal Prime Minister Mackenzie King who had to deal with military personnel issues in World War II, and he demonstrated more care for the concerns of Quebec than had his World War I predecessor. To King, the avoidance of conscription required keeping the army small and ill equipped, and putting most money in the late 1930s into the navy and air force for the defence of Canada, as he believed neither service likely to incur in a future war the huge casualties that might require conscription to maintain military strength. In March 1939, with war looming, King pledged that no government led by him would impose conscription for overseas service, a promise repeated in September, when he took Canada into war, and again in the election campaign of early 1940 that gave him a huge majority.

But wars unfold as they will, not necessarily as politicians wish. The fall of France in June 1940 led many English Canadians to begin calling for compulsory service, and the Liberals responded by passing the National Resources Mobilization Act (NRMA) that called for registration and home defence conscription. The term of service initially was for 30 days, soon increased to 120 days and, eventually, to the duration of the war. This was a half-measure, of course, but as few Canadian soldiers were yet in action, it left matters more or less quiescent until November 1941 when former prime minister and current pro-conscription Senator Arthur Meighen returned as Conservative leader. The entry of Japan into the war on 7 December 1941 added fuel to the fire, and many of the ministers in King's Cabinet by now favoured conscription for overseas service.

The prime minister's response was to call for a non-binding plebiscite in April 1942 to release the government from its past commitments restricting the methods of raising personnel for military service. (The plebiscite call likely helped lead to Meighen's defeat in the York South by-election in Toronto in February 1942.) The plebiscite, in effect, asked all of Canada to release the government from the pledges it had made to Quebec. It outraged francophones, led to the creation of *La Ligue pour la défense du Canada* that out-organized the feeble "oui" campaign in Quebec and produced a massive vote (72.9 percent) against conscription in the mostly-French-speaking province. In the rest of Canada, the vote was heavily for King's position, except in francophone areas and in heavily ethnic areas. With Quebec so staunchly opposed to Ottawa's position, the prime minister appeared trapped.

He resolved the dilemma in true King fashion, introducing Bill 80 that deleted from the NRMA the clause limiting the service of conscripts to Canada alone, at the same time telling the nation that his policy was "not necessarily conscription but conscription if necessary." In effect, nothing had changed despite the plebiscite result, leading the Conservative opposition to say, parroting Gilbert and Sullivan, that "yes is but another and a neater form of no." So it seemed. Such were the competing views of King's political manoeuvring that he faced resignations from both sides of his own Cabinet. The minister of public works, P.J.A. Cardin, resigned in protest of Bill 80 that he feared would ultimately mean conscription. The minister of national defence, J.L. Ralston, threatened to do so too because he believed King did not mean to impose conscription, but stayed.

Meanwhile, the war went on. Canadians lost heavily at Hong Kong in December 1941 and at Dieppe in August 1942, and casualties began to mount after the invasions of Sicily and Italy in 1943, and higher still after the Normandy invasion put the rest of Canada's overseas divisions into the fight in June 1944. The army general staff had assured King that there were sufficient reinforcements to keep the front-line units up to strength but, because they used outdated British wastage calculations and failed to factor in the heavy proportion of infantry casualties, by late summer 1944, First Canadian Army faced a deficit of trained infantry replacements. After some expedients had been tried and failed, defence minister Ralston returned to Canada from a trip to the front in October convinced that the only remaining source of infantry reinforcements was the home defence (NRMA) army of 60,000 conscripts in Canadian camps. Of these, not more than 37 percent were francophones, but English Canadians naturally believed that all so-called Zombies were Québécois and called loudly for their being shipped overseas.

A huge political crisis ensued that divided the country and threatened the government's survival. King fired Ralston and put General A.G.L. McNaughton, the former commander of First Canadian Army (relieved by Ralston in late 1943) in his place. The general believed he could persuade NRMA conscripts to volunteer for overseas service, but he failed dismally. Generals in Canada began to get restive, threatening to quit their posts; Cabinet ministers began to plot King's overthrow or their mass resignation. His political antennae quivering, King acted decisively on 22 November 1944, deciding to order 16,000 conscripts, the estimated shortfall in infantry reinforcements, overseas. That silenced the generals and quieted the ministers, except for air minister Charles Power, a Quebec City Member of Parliament, who resigned. As Power's departure suggested, the Quebec response was harsh to what was seen as yet another betrayal; English Canadians, most of whom had long wanted conscription, took no pleasure in the belated government decision. King survived in the House of Commons.

The prime minister had clearly delayed the inevitable as long as he could, however much the front-line units might have suffered from fighting the Germans with thinning ranks and rushed replacements. The anger in Quebec subsided quickly, helped along by the government decision that only volunteers would go off to the Pacific to fight Japan, and Quebec gave King his margin of victory in the 1945 election. Although some of the 16,000 deserted or threw their rifles away, and despite a serious mutiny in the Terrace, British Columbia, camp, there was less difficulty than might have been expected in getting the conscripts overseas. Only 2,463 conscripts reached the front lines before the German surrender; by almost all accounts, they performed well in action. In fact, because First Canadian Army was largely out of the line from November 1944 to early February 1945, the reinforcement system managed to catch up, and conscripts, ironically enough, were not really necessary by the time they began to arrive.

The events of World War II should have ended considerations of conscription in Canada, but the army's planners in June 1945 nonetheless produced a plan for a peacetime army of 56,000 to be sustained by a form of universal military training that would see men from 18.5 to 19.5 years of age enlisted for 12 months of military training. Trained conscripts then would be required to serve in the militia, and this reserve force was to provide the personnel for any future emergencies. This military plan took into account everything except the political reality of a nation that had barely survived three conscription crises, and the King government promptly killed it.

When the Cold War began in earnest and Canada raised troops for the Korean War and for service with the North Atlantic Treaty Organization in Western Europe, the idea of conscription returned. The francophone lawyer Louis St Laurent was prime minister, and he had supported King in his wartime recruitment policies, including those of November 1944. By late 1950, with the Soviet Union looking aggressive and World War III seeming a distinct possibility, the Cabinet had already decided that, in the event of war,

Canada should have conscription at once. The cards for a national registration had already been printed and plans drafted. Would Quebec be upset? The journalist who had privately asked defence minister Brooke Claxton this question in early 1951 received an unguarded but revealing answer: "With this Prime Minister," Claxton replied, "we can do anything in Quebec." Certainly the St Laurent government spent huge sums on defence and built up the regular army, navy, and air force to historic levels. But there is little in Canadian history—and nothing in contemporary opinion polls—to suggest that conscription would have been any more palatable in the 1950s in Quebec than it had been in 1917 or in 1942 and 1944. Claxton's bluff was never called. In subsequent decades, veterans' organizations and service groups continued to call periodically for some form of universal service, unsuccessfully and with little or no public support. See also: Borden, Robert; King; Quebec and the Military; Ralston; St Laurent.

Reading: J.L. Granatstein and J.M. Hitsman, *Broken Promises: A History of Conscription in Canada* (Toronto, 1977).

Convoys. Convoys are groups of merchant ships sailing together under the protection of naval vessels. Long used to offer economical and efficient defence against sea raiders, convoys had fallen out of favour until the huge losses caused by German U-boat attacks during World War I forced the British Admiralty to reinstitute their use in 1917. The convoy system, coupled with the cracking of German naval codes, began almost immediately to reduce losses. As a result, when World War II began, the system came into use at once. Halifax became the main North American port where convoys formed, and the merchant ships sailed out under the protection of corvettes, frigates, and destroyers, one escort group handing off its convoy to another until the British Isles—or Murmansk or Gibraltar or other ports—were reached. Convoys ordinarily moved in a giant rectangle, their speed that of the slowest ship. The most vulnerable and valuable vessels, including oil tankers, would be in the centre, surrounded by other

▲ Grouped together, merchant ships could be better protected by their naval escorts. This World War II convoy (c.1940), forming up in Halifax's Bedford Basin, faced a hard voyage across the North Atlantic to British ports.

merchant ships and the naval escorts, the latter using radar or sonar to try to pinpoint attacking enemies, whether ships, submarines, or aircraft.

The success of the convoy system obliged the U-boats to alter their tactics. Instead of attacks by a single submarine, the German navy, or *Kriegsmarine*, turned to "wolf packs" of up to a dozen U-boats that could savage a convoy protected by relatively few escorts. Convoy SC-42 in September 1941, protected only by a single Royal Canadian Navy destroyer and three corvettes unequipped with radar, lost 16 ships out of 64. By early 1943, the Germans had some 200 U-boats at sea and were inflicting heavy losses—in March, the Germans sank 103 merchant ships. But the closing of the North Atlantic air cover gap, the development of

escort carriers, new sonar devices, and better depth charges, along with more and better trained escort ships and the cracking of the enemy's codes, swung the balance to the Allies before the end of 1943.

Convoy protection and the anti-submarine warfare that it required was a principal occupation of Canadian forces in the North Atlantic Treaty Organization (NATO) throughout the Cold War. New York, Halifax, and other ports were the main assembly points for convoys that would have reinforced NATO Europe in the event of hostilities against the Soviet-led Warsaw Pact. Canadian surface ships, submarines, and aircraft would have ranged far into the North Atlantic in advance of convoy formations, possibly carrying the fight well into the North Sea and Arctic waters accompanying United States Navy carrier battle groups. They would also have helped to screen the Greenland–Iceland–United Kingdom, or GIUK, gap against Soviet submarines moving from their northern bases into attack positions in the mid-Atlantic or off North America's eastern seaboard. Convoy battles in World War III would have been complicated by Soviet long-range aircraft with their anti-ship missiles, and by the possibility that nuclear weapons might be used to devastating effect against groups of ships at sea. Canadian regular and reserve personnel trained intensively on convoy organization, especially in Halifax, and fleet units practised with NATO allies, especially Britain and the United States, in large multinational squadrons. While most transatlantic convoys would likely have been routed to the British Isles, as in past wars, it was also possible that they would have gone to ports in western France, or up the English Channel to such continental ports as Antwerp or Rotterdam. SEE ALSO: ATLANTIC; COLD WAR; ROYAL CANADIAN NAVY.

READING: Marc Milner, *North Atlantic Run* (Toronto, 1985).

Copp, Terry (b.1938). A long-serving and charismatic professor at Wilfrid Laurier University and the founder of the Laurier Centre for Military Strategic and Disarmament Studies, Copp is the leading scholar of Canada's military role in World War II and an influential advocate for military history in both military and civilian post-secondary education. His work on battle exhaustion, published in 1990; his study, *The Brigade*, on the 5th Canadian Infantry Brigade (1992); and his two important volumes on the Canadians in Normandy, *Fields of Fire* (2003) and *Cinderella Army* (2006), have led to a reinterpretation of Canadian soldiers' effectiveness in 1944 and 1945. Copp's interest in the battlefields of northwest Europe has also led to the creation of battlefield memorials, the conduct of tours for teachers and students, and the publication of invaluable battlefield guides to Canadian participation in both world wars. He is the founder of a quarterly journal published by the Laurier Centre in co-operation with the Canadian

War Museum; entitled *Canadian Military History*, it is Canada's leading journal of military history.

Corvettes. The main anti-submarine ship used by the Royal Canadian Navy (RCN) in World War II, the corvette was a very small warship. Displacing 950 tonnes and about 65 metres in length, the "Patrol Vessel, Whaler Type" had a range in its first iteration of 6,400 kilometres at 12 knots. (Later versions had almost double the range.) Maximum speed was only 16 knots, but with its shallow draft the ship was manoeuvrable and, equipped with depth charges dropped from two stern chutes or launched from throwers on each side, could catch and destroy U-boats. The corvette's armament was a four-inch gun, a 2-pound pom-pom, machine guns, and, later, two or more Oerlikon 20mm guns. Late-war corvettes carried Hedgehogs that could throw a pattern of 24 63-pound depth charges some 200 metres ahead of the ship, hitting the water in a 40-metre wide circular pattern. The Hedgehogs, which only exploded on contact with an underwater object, were vastly more effective and accurate than the conventional depth charge. They doubled the chances of a kill, and could be controlled by ASDIC (a device to track enemy submarines) without interfering with its operation. The standard crew for a corvette was 47, and the initial estimated cost when the design was first proposed in Britain in 1938 was only £90,000.

The first 64 Canadian *Flower* class corvettes were ordered in February 1940 as part of a naval construction program for 90 ships of different types at a cost of $49 million; some of the corvettes built in Canada were intended to go to the Royal Navy in a swap for *Tribal* class destroyers for the RCN. Basic in design as they were, the corvettes posed a challenge for Canadian shipyards that lacked experience in building warships. The task was somehow managed, and the first 14 corvettes made their way unarmed to Halifax before the end of the year. By war's end, 107 had been built in Canadian yards on the East and West Coasts and on the Great Lakes at an average cost of just under $600,000. The RCN sailed 123 corvettes, of which 12 were larger *Castle* class corvettes from

▲ Small, cramped, under-powered, and lightly armed like HMCS *Frontenac*, seen here, the corvettes were the workhorses of the Royal Canadian Navy in World War II.

Britain. Nine RCN corvettes were lost during the war, while Canadian corvettes participated in the sinking of 15 U-boats.

Designed for use in coastal waters, the corvettes had not been built for mid-ocean work—they had an open bridge, for example, a serious disability in winter weather. But in the desperate early years of World War II, the corvettes had to sail well into the Atlantic to protect the critical convoys that kept North American supplies going to Britain. They were unstable in the rough North Atlantic, and could ice up so much in winter seas that they threatened to tip. They were crowded, especially so as more ratings were put aboard to handle extra equipment and armament (which was usually very slow in being fitted on RCN ships), and the food provided from a tiny galley was uniformly dreadful. Adding to the difficulties as the RCN expanded fifty-fold in the course of World War II, most of the ship's company had never been to sea, and the officers, the very few regulars and reservists aside,

were almost as green. That the corvettes managed to put to sea at all was a triumph; that they did as well as they did in the early years of the war at sea and defeated the U-boats from mid-1943 onwards, was a miracle. If the Battle of the Atlantic was won, and it was, it was won in large part by RCN corvettes and those who sailed them. The last Canadian corvette extant, HMCS *Sackville*, is docked in Halifax as a memorial to those who served on the RCN's little ships. SEE ALSO: ATLANTIC; CONVOYS; ROYAL CANADIAN NAVY.

READING: Mac Johnston, *Corvettes Canada: Convoy Veterans of World War II Tell Their True Stories* (Toronto, 2008); Marc Milner, "The Humble Corvette," *Legion Magazine*, (May/June 2008).

Courcelette, Battle of (1916). The Canadian Corps was committed late to the British army's horrific Somme campaign, fighting around Courcelette in mid to late September 1916. The battle, sometimes called the battle of Flers-Courcelette, began on 15 September as British forces launched the last of three great offensives along the River Somme in northern France. It ended on 22 September. Fought on a 12-kilometre front by Britain's Reserve and Fourth Armies, the former of which included the Canadian Corps, the attack was notable because it featured the first use of tanks. The British put all 49 of their tanks into the battle, but only 15 worked well enough to get into action. Of six tanks that accompanied the Canadian assault, only one would reach its objective.

With two divisions, the Canadians had the right flank of the Reserve Army's assault and secured the village of Courcelette, much of the fighting carried out by the 5th Canadian Infantry Brigade of the 2nd Canadian Division, including the 22nd Battalion. Having stormed successfully the German positions south and west of Courcelette, the Canadians would repel 14 German counterattacks in clinging to sodden, shell-ravaged trenches in the hours to come. "If hell is as bad as what I have seen at Courcelette," Lieutenant-Colonel Thomas Tremblay of the Van Doos said, "I would not wish my worst enemy to go there." Additional Canadian units had advanced to the left of the 5th Brigade, pushing into a German entrenched position known as Fabeck Graben. But the advance of British forces farther along the line to capture objectives beyond the town of Thiepval left the partly secured Canadian position exposed on its left. The initial assault divisions would be relieved halfway through the battle by fresh formations, including the 1st Canadian Division, but there were no further substantial gains. The Canadian Corps suffered 7,230 casualties during the period 15 to 22 September, most of them in the Courcelette sector. In their three days at Courcelette itself, the 22nd, 25th, and 26th Battalions suffered more than 200 casualties each, or roughly 30 percent of their effective strength.

Crerar, Henry D.G. (1888–1965). The key leader of Canada's World War II army, Harry Crerar was born into comfortable circumstances in Hamilton, Ontario. He attended Upper Canada College and the Royal Military College, joined the militia artillery, and went to Valcartier in August 1914 as a captain. He proceeded overseas with the Canadian Division and served throughout the war, rising from a battery commander in 1915 to an acting lieutenant-colonel in command of the 3rd Brigade, Canadian Field Artillery and then to counter-battery staff officer for the Canadian Corps. His was an exemplary service, and he won the Distinguished Service Order and was mentioned in dispatches.

Encouraged by General Sir Arthur Currie and Brigadier-General A.G.L. McNaughton, Crerar decided to join the Permanent Force artillery as a major and soon became an acting lieutenant-colonel, a rank he would keep for almost 15 years in the tiny interwar army. But Crerar made his mark. He won a place at the British Army Staff College at Camberley and then served a stint at the War Office in London, getting to know the senior officers with whom he would later fight World War II. He punched his ticket at army headquarters in Ottawa, earning a reputation as an intelligent and able staff officer. He attended the Imperial Defence College, the requisite schooling for a rising star, and was an able director of military operations and planning in Ottawa. Then, at last

Lieutenant-General Harry Crerar (left) with Field Marshal Sir Bernard Montgomery in Germany, 1945.

a temporary brigadier, he became commandant at the Royal Military College in August 1938 and almost immediately began commuting from Kingston to Ottawa to put the final touches on the army's war mobilization plan. As much as anyone, Harry Crerar was responsible for ensuring that the Permanent Force's officers had control of the wartime Canadian army, at least at the outset.

Crerar's wartime rise was quick. He became brigadier general staff at Canadian Military Headquarters in London, which he proceeded to organize. His task was to work out the relations between Ottawa and the War Office and to make arrangements for the arrival, training, and employment of Canadian troops. In July 1940, the war going disastrously wrong for the Allies, Crerar returned to Ottawa as vice-chief of the general staff and, quickly made a major-general, as chief. He created the country's home defence conscription scheme, in effect, to put flesh on the bones of the National Resources Mobilization Act, establishing the 30-day training scheme, then expanding it to 120 days, then expanding it once more to extend for the duration of the war. More importantly, he managed the raising of the volunteer army for overseas, a frenetic process that saw new divisions and supporting units formed with rapidity. It was Crerar who, in late 1941, produced the plan that created the First Canadian Army of five divisions and two armoured brigades and persuaded the government that this could be done without conscription for overseas service.

It was also Harry Crerar who sent troops to Hong Kong in the autumn of 1941, a deployment that was initiated when he met with the outgoing British commander in the Crown colony, Major-General A.E. Grasett, with whom he had attended RMC more than 30 years before. When the request came from London for one or two battalions for Hong Kong, Crerar was willing, and the politicians went along. There were errors in the preparation and equipment of the Hong Kong force, but the Royal Commission created to investigate matters after the expedition's catastrophic defeat laid not a finger on Crerar. By the time the commission began its work, Crerar, now a lieutenant-general,

had been posted to England where he took over command of I Canadian Corps as part of First Canadian Army, led by his old friend, General McNaughton.

Without experience commanding troops in the field in World War II, Crerar knew he needed to establish his reputation. He worked hard to become close to General Bernard Montgomery, who led South Eastern Command under which the Canadians served. He sought Monty's advice on training and on personnel and, as a result, promoted a number of promising younger officers and fired senior officers who were too old or too inefficient for modern war. He also led his corps on some tough exercises and did well, winning Montgomery's important, but fleeting, approval.

The officer responsible for Hong Kong, Crerar also made the key decisions that sent Canadian troops on the Dieppe raid. McNaughton was on sick leave and Crerar was acting commander of the Canadian Corps in early 1942. He knew that Canadians at home were upset that their troops had seen no action in the European war; he knew the politicians worried about a public relations disaster if the United States might get its troops into action before the Canadians; and he could see that his troops' morale in England was suffering from the widespread impression that Canadians would never fight. On hearing rumours of planning for a big raid, he lobbied to have Canadians mount it, got his way, and saw the 2nd Canadian Infantry Division selected. Operation Rutter, scheduled for early July 1942, had to be scrubbed because of enemy air attacks and inclement weather, but Operation Jubilee, the same raid on Dieppe with less heavy air and naval support, went ahead in August with Crerar's blessing. Once again, the debacle at Dieppe hurt him not at all. He at once argued that the lessons learned made it worthwhile, a position held to afterwards, all practical evidence to the contrary, by every senior officer involved.

Meanwhile Crerar worried about First Canadian Army under McNaughton. A brilliant scientist and a man with much charisma, McNaughton was no trainer, no successful judge of men, and no tactician. He failed badly on one big exercise and the British began to have serious doubts about him. Crerar actively fed this impression, talking with his old Staff College and Imperial Defence College cronies, dining with the Canadian High Commissioner, and passing his concerns to visiting Ottawa ministers. He was skilful enough in the way he did this that he remained on good terms with McNaughton, and managed to secure a posting to command I Canadian Corps in Italy at the same time that McNaughton's competence for high command erupted as a major Anglo-Canadian issue, resulting in his ouster. After a brief time leading the corps in Italy, Harry Crerar was back in England in March 1944 as army commander, preparing for D-Day.

First Canadian Army was, like other armies, essentially a support organization, allocating resources to the corps and divisions that fought the battles. Crerar did not determine necessarily who won or lost, but his task was to guide, encourage, support, and coordinate. He had considerable difficulties in this role, in part because of a longstanding difficult relationship with Lieutenant-General Guy Simonds, commander of II Canadian Corps, and he quickly developed another with Lieutenant-General John T. Crocker of I British Corps, serving in his Army in Normandy. And above Crerar, there was Montgomery, now leading 21 Army Group. Crerar bore some responsibility for these tenuous relationships, but these did not stop 3rd Canadian Division from landing on Juno Beach on D-Day and playing a major role in establishing and securing the beachhead. Crerar's First Canadian Army headquarters did not become operational in Normandy until 23 July, but he had already clashed with Montgomery. As army commander, Crerar was responsible to Ottawa for the operational employment of all Canadian troops wherever they might serve. Completely ignoring the way the Empire had evolved, Monty thought this meddlesome and improper, and had become convinced that Crerar was a nitpicking legalist and nationalist. The Canadian held his ground and prevailed, but the grudge-holding Montgomery was unhappy with the length of time taken by the Canadians to close the Falaise Gap (a delay caused in part because Monty had not assigned sufficient British divisions to assist Simonds's II Canadian Corps in its

push south from Caen), and he became even more upset with Crerar after his 2nd Canadian Division liberated Dieppe. Called to a meeting at Montgomery's headquarters on 3 September, Crerar chose instead to attend a parade and commemorative service at Dieppe, an event of great and symbolic Canadian importance. Furious, Monty told Crerar "our ways must part," then appeared to realize that only the government in Ottawa could replace Crerar, not a British commander, and backed off. Relations, already bad, never recovered.

Crerar did not command his army in the difficult Scheldt battle, anemia and dysentery forcing him to take sick leave and turn over the reins to Simonds, a better general and one in whom Montgomery had confidence. When he returned to health, Crerar, now promoted to full general, led First Canadian Army in the operations to clear the territory to the west of the Rhine (with British and American corps under his control) and then over the Rhine. In April 1945, with I Canadian Corps having come to northwest Europe from Italy, Crerar's reunited First Canadian Army liberated the Netherlands.

Harry Crerar had fought two wars against the Germans. He delegated Lieutenant-General Charles Foulkes of I Canadian Corps to take the enemy's surrender in Holland because he did not want to be in the same room as Nazi officers, and he ordered that his soldiers who died on German terrain be buried in the friendlier soil of the Netherlands. Unemotional on the surface, Crerar felt matters deeply. Having planned the demobilization of his great force, Crerar returned to Canada to cheers but no adulation. He deserved some. He was unquestionably the man who had built the wartime army, shaped it, and led it in its greatest battles. He was less a great field commander than a careful administrator, a skilled participant in the bureaucratic battles that had to be fought, a cautious nationalist dealing with the remnants of a declining Empire, and a man of enormous personal ambitions that he largely realized. A complex figure, Harry Crerar was arguably a better commander than the Canada that had ignored its armed forces during the interwar years deserved. SEE ALSO: DIEPPE RAID; FIRST CANADIAN ARMY; HONG KONG; WORLD WAR II.

Reading: Paul Dickson, *A Thoroughly Canadian General: A Biography of General H.D.G. Crerar* (Toronto, 2007).

Crow's Nest, The. The Crow's Nest was a "seagoing officers' club" in St John's, Newfoundland, established in 1942 to serve the city's teeming population of Allied naval personnel. Occupying the vacant upper floor of what had been a shabby downtown warehouse (now a provincial heritage building) and reachable by 59 rickety wooden steps up its exposed western side, the club was soon a mainstay of wartime naval life, memorable to all and visited by most. It closed briefly in 1945–1946, but reopened as "The Newfoundland Officers' Club—Crow's Nest" with patron and founder Sir Leonard Outerbridge as its first president. The club is home to a substantial collection of military artifacts and memorabilia, the most famous of which is the periscope from the World War II German submarine *U-190*, installed in 1963 and later restored to its wartime condition. Now known as the Crow's Nest Officers' Club, it remains in its original location, arguably Canada's most famous naval "establishment."

Crysler's Farm, Battle of (1813). During the War of 1812, a large American force under Major-General James Wilkinson had moved north from Sackett's Harbor and then down the St Lawrence River toward Montreal. As part of a two-pronged offensive against Canada, they intended to meet there with a second column of 4,000 troops, led by Major-General Wade Hampton, advancing north from Plattsburgh, NY. Three weeks into an advance hindered by bad weather, poor leadership, and British gunboats and harassing militia, Wilkinson learned that Hampton had been defeated earlier at Chateauguay, and sent word for Hampton to join him by marching overland toward Cornwall. Hampton declined to do so, leaving Wilkinson on his own moving cautiously downriver, past British positions on the north shore and pursued by a small British force that had hastened by boat from Kingston to Prescott after it became clear that the Americans were headed to Montreal and not Kingston, as originally thought.

With some troops ashore on the Canadian side of the river and moving east, Wilkinson also detached a smaller force to face west against the British who had moved up from Prescott, reinforced by troops from the garrison there. On 11 November, the Americans, numbering perhaps 2,500, moved against the smaller British force of British and Canadian regulars, militia, and a few native warriors, amounting in all to under 1,200. The Americans, adding men piecemeal to their advance, attacked across muddy ploughed fields—now underwater near present-day Morrisburg, Ontario, on the St Lawrence River—carefully chosen by the British commander, Lieutenant-Colonel Joseph Morrison, and were cut to pieces, losing around 450 men against British casualties of 190. After a sharp and confused engagement, the Americans withdrew, barely saving most of their artillery from British capture. The debacle, as well as news that Hampton had refused to come to Wilkinson's aid, forced the Americans to retire into winter quarters south of the St Lawrence. The defeat at Crysler's Farm, combined with the defeat of Hampton's army at Chateauguay, had been the United States' last significant chance to take Canada. The defeat of Napoleon in 1814 permitted Britain to reinforce its North American possessions with several thousand troops and extra ships, sailors, and military engineers. See also: Chateauguay; War of 1812.

Reading: J.M. Hitsman, *The Incredible War of 1812* (rev. ed., Montreal, 1999).

Cuban Missile Crisis. In October 1962, the United States discovered that the Soviet Union was constructing missile bases in Fidel Castro's Cuba. A tense confrontation that brought the world close to nuclear war followed, ending only when the Soviets on 27–28 October agreed to dismantle and remove their missiles. The incident had special importance in Canada because Prime Minister John Diefenbaker, informed of the US decision to blockade Cuba just before President John F. Kennedy announced it publicly, refused to bring Canada's armed forces to a high alert state, instead wondering publicly whether the issue should be referred to the United Nations for inspection and verification. In effect, he had averred

▲ The world came very close to nuclear war during the 1962 Cuban Missile Crisis. Most Canadians supported the United States' position, but these McGill University students protested outside the US Consulate in Montreal.

openly that he did not believe what Washington had told him. The Royal Canadian Navy put to sea from Halifax on its own nonetheless, destined to assist US warships by relieving them for blockade duties off Cuba, and defence minister Douglas Harkness defied the prime minister in readying the air force and army accordingly, without his boss's concurrence. Diefenbaker did not relent until the evening of 24 October, with the North American Air Defence Command (NORAD) moving to its second-highest alert status and his defence minister imploring him to action; as late as the Cabinet meeting that morning, Diefenbaker had refused to commit. When his hesitation was revealed, the Canadian public response was very critical. Kennedy's reaction was fury, and Canadian-American relations, already difficult because Diefenbaker could not make up his mind to accept nuclear warheads for the Bomarc missiles he had ordered and was having installed in Canada, reached a historic nadir. Diefenbaker's belief that Canadian membership in the North American Air Defence Command entitled him to more notice was sound enough. His inability to understand the unusual gravity of the Cuban crisis and the mutual expectations created by joint Canadian–American command arrangements was not. Nearly 40 years later, when terrorist attacks on several American locations sparked a heightened alert by all NORAD forces, Canadian units moved seamlessly into action alongside American allies. SEE ALSO: CANADA–UNITED STATES DEFENCE RELATIONS; NORTH AMERICAN AIR DEFENCE COMMAND.

READING: Peter T. Haydon, *The 1962 Cuban Missile Crisis: Canadian Involvement Reconsidered* (Toronto, 1993); Denis Smith, *Rogue Tory : The Life and Legend of John G. Diefenbaker* (Toronto, 1995).

▲ Canada's greatest commander, Lieutenant-General Sir Arthur Currie, returning to Canada with his son, 1919.

Currie, Sir Arthur William (1875–1933). Canada's greatest military commander, Currie was born in Strathroy, Ontario, and moved to British Columbia in 1894. He taught school, and later ran a successful real estate and property speculation business in Victoria until he was wiped out in the 1913 crash. His true avocation was the military. He had joined the militia in 1893 as a private, and established a reputation for energy and efficiency, so much so that by 1909 he was commanding officer of the 5th Regiment, Canadian Garrison Artillery. In 1913, as his business failed, he took command of the 50th Regiment, a new infantry unit, and made the terrible error of diverting $10,800 from regimental funds to help cover his own losses. This theft, which remained unknown for some time, hung over Currie's head for many years.

He must have seen the coming of war in 1914 as an escape from his troubles. Currie was a friend of Garnet Hughes, the son of Canada's militia minister, and, at Valcartier, the elder Sam Hughes selected Currie to command the 2nd Canadian Infantry Brigade. Currie took the brigade to England, survived the muddled training on Salisbury Plain, and went to the continent in March 1915. At the battle of Ypres the next month, during which the Germans first used gas, Currie's performance was mixed. In the chaos of battle for the first time, he issued orders from his headquarters and cobbled together a fluid defence that bent but did not crack. At one point, Currie personally went to the rear to seek reinforcements and was severely chastised by a British officer for leaving his post. This was a minor error, one Currie would not make again. He did succeed in gathering up stragglers who returned with him to the lines.

By September 1915, the 2nd Division of the Canadian Corps already formed, Currie had taken command of the 1st Canadian Division. When Lieutenant-General Sir Julian Byng took over the Canadian Corps in May 1916, he quickly realized that Currie was the best of his commanders, and sent him to study French tactics at Verdun in December 1916. Currie's report pointed to good reconnaissance as the key, along with efforts put into familiarizing every soldier with the objectives sought and then practising each soldier's role. Maps and photographs went down to platoon level, and each of the French infantrymen could operate every infantry weapon—and those belonging to the Germans as well. The French relied on fire and movement, with infantry consolidating on captured positions and fresh troops, moving in rushes and leading the assault forward, employing machine-gun fire and grenades to keep the enemies' heads down. Thanks in part to Currie's advice, the Canadian Corps reorganized, its companies now made up of four platoons, each of four sections, and each employing fire and movement. Officers stressed individual initiative, and platoons became more self-reliant, a policy that brought specialists, like Lewis gunners, bombers, and rifle grenadiers, back into the

platoon and made it capable of integrated action. Currie's division took all its objectives at Vimy and, when Byng was promoted, Currie became his obvious successor. He was soon to be knighted, making him Lieutenant-General Sir Arthur Currie.

This was a small miracle. Currie was a militia officer in a British-controlled colonial army that scorned amateurs. He was also notably pear-shaped with his heavy body looking awkward on pipe-stem legs. He had no moustache, not much of a chin, and cut no figure in Douglas Haig's army. But he was intelligent, could learn from his mistakes, tried to avoid casualties, and had the personal courage that demanded he do his own reconnaissance. And, despite the incident of 1913, he was an honest, moral

▲ Lieutenant-General Sir Arthur Currie in a war cemetery, 1919.

man. What he was not was a charismatic inspiration to his men, and his awkward words to them were generally stiff, obtuse, and little appreciated. Byng had enraptured the soldiers, but Currie, a shy man, bored them, and this made him unpopular.

But he was a great commander. At Hill 70, just after taking command of the corps, he argued for his own plan, not the army commander's, got his way, and, by taking the high ground, forced the Germans to launch repeated counterattacks that the Canadians destroyed. At Passchendaele, he argued strenuously against the Canadians being committed but, obliged to obey, insisted on more preparation time and more resources, after which his troops took the ridge and the ruins of the village. The British urged the Canadians to split the corps into two, but Currie, seeing no advantage to this, rejected the idea. Instead, he strengthened his infantry battalions, added more artillery, engineers, machine guns, and logistical support, and made the Canadian Corps a force with the striking power of a small army—"the shock army of the British Empire," a later historian correctly called it. The high point of his career, the pinnacle of Canadian military achievement, came during the Hundred Days that began on 8 August 1918 and lasted to the armistice. Currie's corps smashed the Germans at Amiens, broke the Drocourt-Quéant Line, crossed the Canal du Nord, cracked the Hindenburg Line, took Cambrai and Valenciennes, and ended the war where the British had begun it, at Mons, Belgium. The casualties had been terrible, but the achievements were enormous.

Currie's soldiers received great acclaim in Canada, but Currie, though heaped with honours by the Allies, did not. Some of his wealthy officers paid off his debt to the Crown for the misappropriated funds from 1913, relieving him of one burden. But there was another. Angry that his son had not received command of a division in the corps, Sam Hughes, fired as a minister but still a Member of Parliament able to say anything in the House, attacked Currie repeatedly, shamefully arguing that the general's own vanity had led to casualties at Mons. A decade after the war, Currie fought a libel suit against a newspaper on this issue and won, but with a judgment of only $500.

Promoted to general on his return to Canada in 1919, he served briefly as inspector general until, in 1920, he became principal of McGill University, a post he would hold until his death. SEE ALSO: CANADIAN CORPS; HUGHES; WORLD WAR I.

READING: A.M.J. Hyatt, *General Sir Arthur Currie* (Toronto, 1987).

Cut Knife Hill, Battle of (1885). West of Battleford, Saskatchewan, on the Poundmaker Reservation, Cut Knife Hill was the site of a battle on 2 May 1885 during the Northwest Rebellion. A "flying column" of some 390 Canadian regulars, North West Mounted Police, and militia under Colonel W.D. Otter clashed with a smaller number of Cree and Assiniboine warriors under Chiefs Poundmaker and Fine Day. Intending a punitive expedition, Otter quickly found himself all but surrounded and pinned down in a poor defensive position while the warriors used ground and cover to good advantage. After several hours of fighting and 22 casualties, including 14 killed, Otter was able to withdraw to safety, in substantial part because Poundmaker forbade his men to pursue the retreating Canadians. SEE ALSO: NORTHWEST REBELLION; OTTER; POUNDMAKER.

Dallaire, Roméo A. (b.1946). Born in the Netherlands to a Canadian soldier and his Dutch spouse, Dallaire attended the Collège militaire royal de Saint-Jean and the Royal Military College, graduating as an artillery officer. By 1991, he was a brigade commander at Valcartier, QC, and in 1993–1994 as a major-general he was the force commander for United Nations troops in Rwanda. Because of lack of personnel, restrictive rules of engagement, and a global failure of political will, the United Nations Assistance Mission for Rwanda (UNAMIR) was unable to prevent Hutu militants from murdering some 800,000 Tutsis over approximately 100 days, the worst example of mass murder and war crimes in post–Cold War history. The frustrating experience shattered Dallaire, who would wage an increasingly public battle with post-traumatic stress disorder (PTSD) in later years, one that played an important role in bringing this affliction to public attention in the context of complex, violent, and often disastrous peace enforcement missions. Dallaire assumed several senior posts after returning to Canada, and played a leading role in officer professional development. Appointed assistant deputy minister human resources (military) at National Defence Headquarters in 1998, Dallaire left the army in early 2000 to write his memoirs. *Shake Hands with the Devil* (2004) became an international bestseller and a major film. Dallaire became a public figure of note, vocal in causes related to humanitarian intervention, child soldiers, and African security issues. In 2005, the Liberal government of Prime Minister Paul Martin appointed him to the Senate, where he sits as a Liberal representing the province of Quebec. SEE ALSO: PEACEKEEPING.

READING: Carol Off, "Do the Right Thing! Lieutenant-General Roméo Dallaire in the 1990s," in Bernd Horn and S. Harris, eds., *Warrior Chiefs:*

Perspectives on Senior Canadian Military Leaders (Toronto, 2001).

D-Day. D-Day was the World War II term for the day an invasion was to proceed, with H-Hour being the precise time of landing. D-Day, however, has come to symbolize the invasion of Normandy, France, on 6 June 1944 by American, British, and Canadian forces.

The decision to invade at Normandy, made at the Quebec Conference in August 1943, put US General Dwight D. Eisenhower in overall command with British General Bernard L. Montgomery as ground forces commander. The assault, a huge and extraordinarily complex combined operation called Operation Overlord, had to put five infantry divisions and armoured units from three nations on five separate beaches, in addition to dropping three airborne divisions on the flanks and inland of the landing beaches. Thousands of aircraft and ships had to be coordinated, troops and supplies properly positioned, and an elaborate deception program maintained. By 1944, the Allies had gained some experience in mounting invasions on a defended shore, and the lessons of earlier amphibious landings, including the disaster at Dieppe in August 1942, had been digested: heavy air and naval bombardment was a requirement; the assault should proceed over open beaches and not at a defended port (this required the creation of an artificial port, or Mulberry, so troops and supplies could be unloaded in the immediate follow-up to the D-Day assaults); and the employment of specialized landing craft and armoured vehicles were essential.

The five invasion beaches—dubbed Gold and Sword for the British, Juno for the 3rd Canadian Division and the attached 2nd Canadian Armoured

Brigade, and Utah and Omaha for the Americans—had been well prepared for defence by the energetic German commander, Field Marshal Erwin Rommel. The Allies, by attacking in bad weather and not at the Pas de Calais, the closest point to England, where the enemy had expected the invasion to come, secured tactical surprise, but pre-invasion bombing was less successful than hoped. Landing craft foundered on enemy obstacles and mines or were sunk by shelling; heavy seas caused delays, drownings, and chaos; and naval crews made errors in putting the infantry ashore at the wrong landing points. Enough determined troops made it onto the beaches in good order to make the invasion a success. Allied airpower had secured complete command of the skies, and few German torpedo boats or destroyers troubled the massive invasion fleets with their accompanying escorts. Though the enemy reacted more slowly with counterattacks than Allied planners had feared, fighting was hard on all the beaches, the Americans at Omaha Beach experiencing the worst sustained resistance. Casualties were heavy, but far lighter than had been predicted. The Canadians lost 340 killed, 574 wounded, and 47 taken prisoner. By 12 June, despite heavy fighting and strong German armoured counterattacks, the Allies had united their bridgeheads into a continuous front stretching almost a hundred kilometers long and reaching 24 kilometres inland. SEE ALSO: JUNO BEACH.

▲ Equipped with bicycles, most of which were soon thrown away, soldiers of the 3rd Canadian Division ready themselves to land on Juno Beach, 6 June 1944.

⬆ General John de Chastelain inspects a guard of honour, 1989.

READING: C.P. Stacey, *The Victory Campaign* (Ottawa, 1960).

de Chastelain, Alfred John Gardyne Drummond
(b.1937). Born in Romania, the son of a British oil engineer who came to Canada in 1955, John de Chastelain graduated from the Royal Military College in 1960. An infantryman, he served in Canada, the Middle East, and with the North Atlantic Treaty Organization (NATO) where he led the 4th Canadian Mechanized Brigade Group from 1980–1982. He became vice-chief of the defence staff in 1988, and chief of the defence staff (CDS) the next year. His tenure coincided with the end of the Cold War, the Oka crisis, and the first Gulf War, as well as declining budgets and troop reductions. The government appointed de Chastelain ambassador to the United States in 1993, but Prime Minister Jean Chrétien recalled him to Ottawa to be CDS again the next year, the only officer ever to have been appointed twice to this position. De Chastelain's second appointment as CDS coincided with a report into the Somalia mission of 1992–1993, during which Canadian troops had tortured to death a Somali teenager, the controversial report blaming de Chastelain for a failure of command. As revelations continued about the conduct of the Canadian Airborne Regiment before, during, and after the ill-fated Somalia deployment, the Chrétien government took the unprecedented decision of disbanding the regiment entirely, over the objections of the CDS. De Chastelain, who had offered his resignation over the Somalia fallout and was refused by the prime minister, handled with tact and decisiveness media suspicions of a severe rift in civil-military relations as a result of the affair. After stepping down in 1995, at the government's behest he became involved in the Northern Ireland peace process, serving with substantial success from 1997 as chair of the Independent International Commission on Decommissioning, a body directed to encourage paramilitary groups to give up their weapons.

Defence Lobbies. *See* PREPAREDNESS GROUPS.

Defence of Canada Regulations (DCR). An interdepartmental committee of civil servants drafted the regulations in 1939 and, under the authority of the War Measures Act, the government proclaimed them on 3 September 1939, one week before Canada declared war against Germany. The DCR gave the government sweeping powers to control dissent, monitor the media, and protect the nation against subversion; it used the regulations to intern suspect Germans and Italians, immigrants and Canadian citizens alike, to outlaw the Communist Party and intern many of its members, and, in the summer of 1940, to outlaw the Jehovah's Witnesses in a move designed to mollify Roman Catholic Quebec. In early 1942, Ottawa used its powers under the DCR to order the evacuation of Japanese Canadians from the British Columbia coast. Provincial governments, notably Ontario's Mitch Hepburn government, also used the regulations to act against trade union organizers.

Defence Production Sharing Agreement (DPSA). Negotiated by the Diefenbaker government in 1958, this agreement with the United States aimed to achieve a long-term balance in defence purchases by each country from the other. The DPSA exempted Canadian firms from some aspects of "Buy American" legislation and allowed competition on equal terms with US companies. A related Defence Development Sharing Agreement extended the provisions to development efforts. The DPSA continues to give broader access to the US defence market than does the North American Free Trade Agreement.

Defence Research Board (DRB). Established in 1947 with scientist Omand M. Solandt as its head, the DRB had responsibility for defence research in areas such as missile development, chemical warfare, and explosives, and primary responsibility for advising the Department of National Defence (DND) on technical and scientific matters. DND absorbed the board's functions and staff in 1974.

Defence Schemes Numbers 1–4. During the interwar years, the director of military operations and planning at Canadian army headquarters worked on plans for four eventualities. Scheme No. 1 outlined the steps necessary to defend Canada in the event of a war between Britain and the United States involving Canada, a possibility that was not as remote at that time as it might appear today. The plan called for limited offensives into the northern United States and a fighting withdrawal while Canadian forces awaited reinforcements from Britain. This plan was cancelled in 1931. Defence Scheme No. 2 involved the direct defence of Canada against Japan, but no plan was definitively developed as, in the early 1930s, the focus in planning changed to the protection of Canadian neutrality in the event of a war pitting the United States against Japan. Defence Scheme No. 3, first circulated in 1931, considered home defence and sending a large expeditionary force overseas. Approved by successive defence ministers in the governments of both Conservative R.B. Bennett and Liberal W.L.M. King, the scheme maintained that national defence required commitments beyond Canada's borders. This was the plan put into effect in September 1939. Defence Scheme No. 4, never completed, called for sending a small expeditionary force to participate in imperial campaigns or wars; its incomplete planning suggests that army planners gauged correctly the unlikelihood

that contemporary political leaders would ever endorse such a throwback to colonial schemes.

READING: Stephen J. Harris, *Canadian Brass* (Toronto, 1988).

Defence Structure Review (DSR). In 1974, the Trudeau government, faced with what seemed to be an end to Cold War détente and Canada's declining military capabilities, ordered a Defence Structure Review to find ways of meeting the country's military commitments on a fixed defence budget. Conducted by a committee of senior officials and officers, the DSR put the military's operational needs first and called for additional funding forcefully enough that the Liberal government agreed to increase capital expenditures by 12 percent a year for five years. The review, completed in several stages—Canadian Forces tasks, force structure and the capability to perform specific missions, and the weapons systems and funds needed to conduct these missions—came at a time when the Trudeau government was reviewing, under some pressure, its commitments to the North Atlantic Treaty Organization (NATO). In part, this pressure was military-related, but it was political too, tied to a possible way of facilitating Trudeau's "Third Option" in foreign policy by building linkages with major European states, most of which remained unhappy with Canada's defence cuts earlier in the decade. By late 1975, Canada announced that it would retain and re-equip its existing forces in NATO Europe, with directions emerging from the DSR that would impact defence procurement and capabilities for many years to come. These would ultimately include the purchase of Leopard I main battle tanks, the CP-140 Aurora long-range maritime patrol aircraft, the *Halifax* class of modern patrol frigates, and the CF-18 fighter-bomber. Trudeau's Liberals would not be in office when many of the effects of the NATO-oriented DSR came to fruition in the late 1980s. The contrast between the Canada-centric defence review of the early Trudeau years and the NATO-driven procurement strategy of later years was a source of policy confusion and political criticism for the government in office for much of the latter period. After 1984, Progressive Conservative Brian Mulroney would reap some political benefit when systems actually ordered in the Trudeau years came into service.

Demobilization. Coming home from war is almost as complicated as getting there, perhaps even more considering that morale among military personnel is generally high on the way over but prickly and decidedly impatient while waiting to come home. Demobilization is not simply the opposite of mobilization, though it shares many of the same characteristics in its demands on resources, administration, and communications. It is, in the end, a massive human movement telescoped into a relatively short space of time and dependent for its success as much on group psychology as logistics. It also occurs precisely as the bonds of military discipline begin to erode in citizen armies raised temporarily for war. Canada demobilized awkwardly but well after World War I and, having considered carefully the lessons of the first war, even better the second time around.

Discussions on how best to demobilize the Canadian Expeditionary Force began in 1916 at the Department of Militia and Defence in Ottawa and the Ministry of the Overseas Military Forces of Canada in London. The decision was to begin to demobilize as soon as the armistice was signed, the first troops to be released being units in Canada. Original estimates had been that it might take as long as 18 months to bring home the overseas forces. Some two-thirds had returned within five months, however, and, within a year, repatriation was all but complete. The major difficulties came from the shortage of shipping and from the professed inability of Canadian railways to transport more than 25,000 soldiers a month (a number later raised to 45,000 after government pressure). In the Canadian Corps, units returned as entities; otherwise, the principle of first in, first out was followed wherever possible. Each soldier chose a destination in Canada and received free transportation to it, obtained a War Service Gratuity, and was given demobilization leave. The Department of Soldiers' Civil Re-establishment, created in February 1918, had plans in place to give veterans who wanted to farm long-term loans. There were also pensions, medical treatment,

and vocational training, but veterans' organizations remained dissatisfied. Rioting by troops awaiting repatriation embarrassed Ottawa and infuriated Britain. Scapegoats were charged, more ships found, and the Canucks shipped back from whence they came.

Demobilization after World War II also occurred far more quickly than expected. By the end of March 1946, ten months after VE Day, the Royal Canadian Navy reported that it had discharged 76,905 officers and men, the Royal Canadian Air Force 147,263, and the army 342,361. The army, with the largest numbers, used a point-score system to determine the order of return to Canada—2 points for each month of Canadian service, 3 points for each month overseas, plus 20 points for those who were married or had dependent children. The system worked more equitably than that of World War I, but led to conflict between military commanders, who saw great value in their units returning as recognizable entities, and political leaders who faced growing pressure to bring home the longest-serving soldiers first. General H.D.G. Crerar was the leading exponent of the former view; the first minister of veterans affairs, Ian

⌃ Getting soldiers home from overseas wars is always difficult. These 3rd Canadian Division men boarded ship in Britain in March 1919 on their way back to Canada.

Mackenzie, a loud proponent of the latter. A riot among army troops in England and several sit-down strikes by impatient air force personnel marred an otherwise fast-moving and efficient system. As in 1919, protesting troops helped spur better organization and, most important of all, the availability of additional ships for transatlantic crossings. The latter was a chronic problem in 1945, as shipping priority had been given to troops and equipment moving from the European war to the Pacific theatre for action against Japan.

In Ottawa, the Department of Pensions and National Health, formed in 1928, had begun demobilization planning in December 1939. Far more generous than in World War I, benefits under what was called the Veterans Charter came to include rehabilitation grants, a clothing allowance, out-of-work grants, and cash payments depending on length of service, the last a product of the Department of Veterans Affairs, established in 1944. Educational or vocational training could be had and, if a veteran chose not to take them, he or she—women received the same benefits as men—could take re-establishment credits instead that could be used to start a business or buy a home. There were pensions for the disabled and for dependants of those killed, and medical care for the wounded and injured. Veterans' organizations asked for more, but there was general agreement that Canada had done well for its veterans. SEE ALSO: VETERANS' ORGANIZATIONS; WORLD WAR I; WORLD WAR II.

READING: Dean F. Oliver, "Canadian Military Demobilization in World War II," in J.L. Granatstein and P. Neary, eds., *The Good Fight: Canadians and World War II* (Toronto, 1995).

Department of Defence Production (DDP). Established in 1951 to direct the rearmament induced by the Korean War and the intensifying Cold War, the department's first minister was C.D. Howe. Working closely with the Department of National Defence, DDP placed contracts for military equipment until its winding down in 1969, its functions then assumed by the Department of Supply and Services. The latter

was, in turn, superseded by Public Works and Government Services Canada in 1993.

Department of National Defence (DND). The department was created by authority of the National Defence Act (1922) and established on 1 January 1923. With modifications and amendments such as the Canadian Forces Reorganization Act (1968), the National Defence Act remains the department's primary enabling legislation, defining the roles and responsibilities of the organization, the minister, the deputy minister, and the chief of the defence staff. The new department amalgamated the Department of Militia and Defence, the Department of Naval Service, and the Air Board, placing the three armed services under a single minister. It continues to exist as such, though during World War II the navy and air force had ministers of their own. There has also frequently been an associate minister of national defence. DND has one of the largest budgets and, with its military and civilian personnel, the largest staff of all federal departments. As the largest federal employer, it is a highly visible presence in many communities, including Ottawa and the National Capital Region.

Initially, a civilian deputy minister handled management while the service chiefs directed their forces. In 1951, a chairman of the chiefs of staff was put atop the military hierarchy to bring greater coordination; with the integration of the armed forces in 1964, this title changed to chief of the defence staff. In 1972, the department's military and civil branches merged at National Defence Headquarters with a coequal deputy minister and chief of the defence staff operating under the minister. The deputy minister is the department's senior civil servant, responsible for policy, resources, interdepartmental coordination, and international defence relations; the chief of the defence staff handles the command, control, and administration of the Canadian Forces (a separate legal entity from the department), and military strategy, plans, and requirements. Both answer to the minister of national defence, an elected Member of Parliament appointed by the prime minister. The lines of

▲ HMCS *St Laurent*, seen here, was the lead ship in the class, commissioned in 1955.

responsibility between deputy minister and chief of the defence staff have not always been clear. Claims that the civilianization of the department have essentially neutered the military's senior commander and subordinated the position to the deputy minister are more numerous than those critiquing the chief of the defence staff's role in policy-making and increasingly unfettered access to the prime minister, with attendant worries over the strength of Canada's civil-military balance. The Department of National Defence is headquartered in downtown Ottawa alongside the Rideau Canal.

Department of Naval Service. Created on 4 May 1910 to run the newly created Canadian navy, the department was led by the minister of marine and fisheries who took the additional title of minister of

naval service. In February 1922, the King government transferred the ministerial powers to the minister of militia and defence; both offices disappeared with creation of the Department of National Defence on 1 January 1923.

Destroyer Escorts. Similar to but smaller than destroyers, these ships were used primarily for anti-submarine warfare. The seven *St Laurent* class destroyer escorts, or DDEs, designed in Canada in 1949 and completed from 1955 onwards, had a superb, modern appearance, as did the seven *Restigouche* and six *Mackenzie* class ships that followed. Most were converted to carry helicopters with the addition of flight decks and hangars. The original DDEs of the *St Laurent* class displaced 2,227 tonnes, could make 28 knots, and carried a crew of

249. They were armed with two twin 3-inch guns, two 40-millimetre guns, homing torpedoes, and two anti-submarine mortars. To sailors, they were "Cadillacs."

READING: M. Davis, "The St Laurent Decision," in W.A.B. Douglas, ed., *The RCN in Transition, 1910–1985* (Vancouver, 1988).

Destroyers for Bases Deal. President Franklin Delano Roosevelt and Prime Minister Winston Churchill agreed in August 1940 to trade 99-year leases on British bases in the West Indies and Newfoundland, not yet part of Canada, for 50 old American destroyers. With World War II going very badly for the Allies, with Germany occupying the Low Countries and France and preparing for an invasion of Great Britain, the arrangement made sense for both parties. The destroyers could help protect the British Isles at the moment of maximum danger; the bases would let Roosevelt safeguard the neutral United States in the event it was drawn into the war. At Ogdensburg, New York, the same month, Roosevelt sounded out Prime Minister Mackenzie King on letting the United States establish bases on Canadian soil, but King, anxious to protect Canadian independence, stoutly rejected the idea. A number of the American destroyers nonetheless came to the Royal Canadian Navy, and the Canadian and American forces, both with troops and ships based in Newfoundland, eventually learned to co-operate

▲ Britain traded bases to the United States for 50 obsolete destroyers in 1940. The Canadian navy received its share, including HMCS *St Croix*, seen here.

well together. The Americans kept forces in Newfoundland after Confederation in 1949, as was their right; their last base at Argentia closed in 1994.

SEE ALSO: CANADA–UNITED STATES DEFENCE RELATIONS.

Destroyers, *Tribal* Class. The Royal Navy developed this destroyer type during the 1930s in response to the building of large "super" destroyers by other naval powers. These heavily-armed, fast, short-range ships were much larger than previous British destroyer types, including those used by the Royal Canadian Navy (RCN), essentially being the equivalent of light cruisers. The RCN had asked for such ships as early as 1938 but was unable to get government concurrence; it acquired its four wartime *Tribals*—HMCS *Athabaskan, Haida, Huron,* and *Iroquois*—from British shipyards, ordering them in 1940–1941 as a prelude to building a big-ship fleet.

Tribals in service with the RCN during World War II had an average displacement of 2,000 tonnes, carried six 4.7-inch guns in three double turrets as main armament, and were also equipped with two 4-inch anti-aircraft guns, four 2-pound pom poms, and six 20-millimetre guns, as well as four 21-inch torpedo tubes. They had a top speed of 36 knots and ordinarily carried 14 officers and 245 other ranks. These destroyers were not primarily intended for anti-submarine escort service (although they could engage in anti-submarine warfare), but as fleet-type destroyers to participate in gun and torpedo actions against enemy ships or shore installations. The RCN *Tribals* saw action early and often during the war, including the dangerous Murmansk run to northern Russia, but were most noted for their service in the English Channel from the spring to the fall of 1944 in support of the Normandy invasion. *Athabaskan* was lost in one of these actions, while *Haida* earned a superb reputation. During World War II, four additional *Tribals* were laid down at Halifax. When completed after the war, they were the largest and most sophisticated warships yet to emerge from Canadian shipyards. The four—HMCS *Micmac, Nootka II,*

▲ *Tribal* class destroyers were big, powerful ships. HMCS *Iroquois*, shown here, was built in the UK as were the three additional wartime RCN *Tribals*. Four more, built in Canada, came into service after the war.

Cayuga, and *Athabaskan II*—entered service between September 1945 and January 1948 and soon were converted to anti-submarine and anti-aircraft ships. They and their surviving wartime sister ships formed the backbone of the RCN in the late 1940s and early 1950s until the arrival of the *St Laurent* class of destroyer escorts. Six *Tribals* saw service during the Korean War (1950–1953), used primarily for fleet escort duty, minesweeping, and attacks on coastal targets in North Korea. The last of the *Tribals*, HMCS *Athabaskan II*, was paid off in April 1966. See also: Atlantic; Royal Canadian Navy.

Reading: E.C. Meyers, *Tribal Class Destroyers of the Royal Canadian Navy, 1942–1963* (Victoria, BC, 2006).

Detroit, Battle of (1812). In July 1812, General William Hull led an American army to the present site of Windsor, Ontario, as the beginning of his offensive against Upper Canada. Abandoning the operation a few weeks later on 7 August, Hull returned to Fort Detroit where he soon found himself under siege by British regulars, Canadian militia, and native warriors led by Major-General Isaac Brock. Hull believed his forces to be greatly outnumbered and feared that the First Nations warrriors threatened his supply lines. When Brock moved against the fort on 16 August and used his artillery to bombard the Americans, Hull promptly surrendered the fort, his 2,500 troops, and the relief army that was coming to his aid. The capitulation greatly encouraged the Canadians and prevented western Upper Canada from occupation in the first year of the war. SEE ALSO: BROCK; WAR OF 1812.

DeWolf, Harry George (1903–2000). "Hard over Harry," as he was called by his sailors on HMCS *Haida* in World War II, was the most decorated Royal Canadian Navy (RCN) officer of the war. Born in Bedford, Nova Scotia, and trained at the Royal Canadian Naval College from which he graduated in 1921, DeWolf served in Royal Navy ships until 1925 when he returned to the tiny interwar RCN. A man who struggled against seasickness for his entire naval career, DeWolf held a number of sea and headquarters posts until, in 1939, he became the captain of HMCS *St Laurent*, one of the navy's handful of destroyers. He saw extensive service in the North Atlantic until, in 1943, he took over *Haida*, a brand new *Tribal* class destroyer. His ship escorted Murmansk convoys but won its great reputation in the English Channel and off France in the months before and after D-Day, sinking 14 enemy vessels and risking its own destruction by rescuing survivors from its sister ship, HMCS *Athabaskan*. After the war, DeWolf commanded RCN aircraft carriers and served in Ottawa and Washington. He became a vice-admiral and chief of the naval staff in 1956 and served until his retirement in 1961. SEE ALSO: DESTROYERS, *TRIBAL* CLASS.

Dextraze, Jacques Alfred (1919–1993). One of Canada's greatest fighting soldiers, Dextraze, born in Montreal, enlisted in the Fusiliers Mont-Royal (FMR) in 1940 as a private. By 1942, he was serving as a junior officer in England, and he then commanded an infantry company in Normandy in 1944. Promoted to lieutenant-colonel, he led the FMR through the rest of the war, winning two Distinguished Service Orders for his courage and earning the respectful nickname "Mad Jimmy." He left the army in 1945 but rejoined on the outbreak of war in Korea where he commanded the 2nd Battalion of Le Royal 22e Régiment, again with distinction. Dextraze served as chief of staff to the United Nations Operation in the Congo and, in 1964, directed the rescue of civilians there. In 1972,

▲ Harry DeWolf aboard his ship, HMCS *Haida*, in May 1944.

after service as a brigade commander and in Ottawa, "Jadex," as he had become known, became chief of the defence staff, a post he held for five years. He was instrumental in persuading the reluctant Liberal government of Pierre Trudeau to acquire new equipment for the military, most notably Leopard I main battle tanks, and he was the military representative on the influential Defence Structure Review of 1974–1975. SEE ALSO: DEFENCE STRUCTURE REVIEW.

Diefenbaker, John George (1895–1979). Born in Neustadt, Ontario, Diefenbaker went west with his family in 1903. He studied at the University of Saskatchewan, then enlisted during World War I. His brief military career ended in England when a combination of neurasthenia and a training accident led to his repatriation. Diefenbaker practised law with some substantial success, but failed in repeated efforts to enter politics until, in 1940, he bucked a Liberal trend and won election to Parliament as a

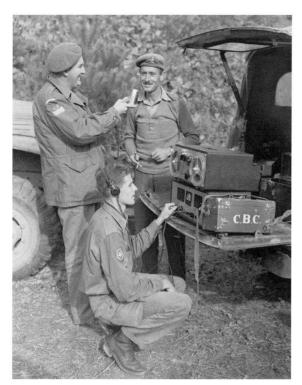

▲ The charismatic J.A. "Mad Jimmy" Dextraze (right) being interviewed by the Canadian Broadcasting Corporation in Korea, 1951.

Conservative. In 1956, his party selected him as leader, and the next year, in the greatest upset in Canadian political history, he won a minority victory over Louis St Laurent. In 1958, in a second election, the Conservatives scored the largest majority to that time.

Defence questions tormented Diefenbaker during his six years as prime minister. He took Canada into the North American Air Defence Agreement in his first days in office, following the advice of General Charles Foulkes, the chairman of the Chiefs of Staff Committee, and his new defence minister, General George Pearkes. The Cabinet Defence Committee had not yet been formed, and the Cabinet was not consulted about the decision. The issue soon turned messily political as the Liberals, who knew the file, peppered the government with questions they would not have asked had they been in power.

Two years later, the Conservatives rightly scrapped the Canadian-designed fighter-interceptor, the CF-105 Avro Arrow, its development costs spiralling out of control, and opted to acquire nuclear-armed Bomarc surface-to-air missiles from the United States. The government mishandled the Arrow announcement, and massive layoffs of a highly skilled workforce came at once at A.V. Roe's plant outside Toronto. The Bomarc decision hung over Diefenbaker's head for four years while the bases were under construction in northern Ontario and Quebec, enough time for opposition to nuclear weapons to develop. The government was especially vulnerable because it had already agreed to accept nuclear weapons for the army and air forces serving with the North Atlantic Treaty Organization (NATO) in Europe.

The Department of External Affairs opposed nuclear weapons; BC's minister, Howard Green, led the fight in Cabinet with advice from his officials. The defence minister, now Douglas Harkness, wanted the weaponry, but he was less skilful in the bureaucratic and political infighting, and Diefenbaker, indecisive, was not sure if he should take the warheads required by missiles he had already ordered and which alone would make the missiles effective. The election of 1962 reduced the Tories to a minority, Diefenbaker broke his ankle and was in constant pain, and the Cuban Missile Crisis in the autumn saw him at his wavering worst. The Soviet Union had been discovered putting nuclear missiles in Fidel Castro's Cuba, and the administration of President John F. Kennedy reacted with controlled fury, imposing a blockade—called, for sake of legal appearances, a quarantine—on Cuba and putting its forces on high alert. Under the North American Air Defence (NORAD) agreement, Canada was entitled to information and notice, and a senior Kennedy emissary had briefed Diefenbaker. But he became furious at Kennedy, decided Canada had been slighted, and refused to order the military to go on alert in the greatest crisis of the Cold War. The Bomarc bases were not complete and the Royal Canadian Air Force's (RCAF) fighter-interceptors had no nuclear weapons, but the Royal Canadian Navy could put to sea to track Soviet submarines. Again Diefenbaker refused to order the alert, but the navy left Halifax on its own, and Harkness quietly implemented the alert without the prime minister's approval.

When word inevitably got out, Diefenbaker's standing in the Cabinet, caucus, and country suffered. Public and private pressure from Washington increased, and the government fell apart in February 1963, ministers resigning amid talk of political coups. The Conservatives suffered defeat on a vote of confidence. Indecision on the nuclear issue had destroyed Diefenbaker, and he lost the April 1963 election. His viciously anti-American campaign, however, held the Liberals under L.B. Pearson to a minority government. "The Chief," as Diefenbaker was always known, remained as Leader of the Opposition until 1967, a powerful, divisive force in Parliament and the country. SEE ALSO: ARROW, AVRO; FOULKES; NUCLEAR CRISIS (1962–1963); PEARSON.

READING: Denis Smith, *Rogue Tory: The Life and Legend of John G. Diefenbaker* (Toronto, 1995).

Dieppe Raid (1942). On 19 August 1942, nearly 5,000 soldiers from the 2nd Canadian Infantry Division and the 1st Canadian Armoured Brigade, along with 1,075 British commandos and Royal Marines, plus 50 United States Army Rangers, struck at Dieppe, France, in a major raid. The result was a debacle, a horrific disaster that left the beaches covered in dead and wounded, with many hundreds marched away as prisoners. The controversy over Dieppe began at once and continues largely unabated.

The idea of a large raid on the French coast originated in Combined Operations Headquarters, commanded by British Admiral Lord Louis Mountbatten. The planners wanted to test out the theory and practice of amphibious warfare and to determine if a defended port could be seized. That was the main tactical reason. The Americans, in World War II only since December 1941, also wanted to create a second front on the European continent as soon as possible, a goal that Moscow, bearing the full brunt of the war against Germany on the Eastern Front, also wanted desperately. The raid could be viewed as a test of the invasion concept. In Canada,

some politicians, including defence minister J.L. Ralston, wanted their troops, some in Britain for more than two years, to get into action to gain experience in battle and to appease a public clamouring for heroes; overseas, some Canadian senior officers knew their restless soldiers needed action, and the troops themselves, tired of being asked by English friends if they would ever fight, largely shared that opinion.

Thus, in the winter of 1942 when Lieutenant-General Harry Crerar, acting as the commander of the Canadian Corps while General A.G.L. McNaughton was in Canada on sick leave, heard rumours that Mountbatten was planning a major raid, he demanded that the British chiefs of staff select Canadians for the task; it would be good for morale, he judged. By the time McNaughton returned to England in April 1942, the British had agreed and, on the advice of Lieutenant-General Bernard Montgomery, the commander of South Eastern Command under whom the Canadians served, had chosen the 2nd Division for the job. Montgomery thought it the best-trained Canadian formation, and believed Major-General J. Hamilton Roberts, its general officer commanding, was the best of the Canadian division commanders.

Canadian officers from that point forward had a large share in planning the operation. The decision not to bomb the town before the raid, for example, was agreed to by Roberts and his staff, presumably because ruins might interfere with the progress of tanks. Mountbatten's headquarters continued to be heavily involved, and so too was Montgomery who had the "go/no go" responsibility. When Operation Rutter, the original raid scheduled for the first week of July 1942, had to be scrubbed because of bad weather and a German air attack on the raid's ships in port, it was Montgomery who made the decision. In the interval between Rutter and the renewed operation, now dubbed Jubilee, Montgomery left for the Middle East to a command in North Africa. The 2nd Division's destiny would be very different, and the decision to let loose Operation Jubilee came from Mountbatten, McNaughton, Crerar, and Roberts. The commanders knew that soldiers would have talked in

Canadian POWs were marched through the streets after the surrender at Dieppe, excellent fodder for German propaganda.

the pubs about the cancelled raid on Dieppe in July; they banked on the likelihood that the Germans would not believe that the same troops would attack the same target a month later. There is no evidence that the Germans knew Jubilee was coming. Whether Mountbatten had the authorization to mount Jubilee when he did has been challenged; if not, he ought to have been cashiered.

The Dieppe plan called for just under 5,000 troops drawn from the infantry battalions of the three brigades of the 2nd Division and an armoured regiment from the 1st Canadian Armoured Brigade (along with the British commandos) to assault the town and surrounding areas from the sea. Covered by 74 squadrons of fighters and fighter-bombers overhead and eight destroyers, a sloop, and a gunboat offshore, infantry from the Essex Scottish and the Royal Hamilton Light Infantry (RHLI), accompanied by tanks of the Calgary Regiment, would land on the beach in front of the town. To the east at Puys, the

Royal Regiment of Canada and three platoons of the Black Watch would land on a tiny beach under a steep cliff. At Pourville, to the west of Dieppe, the South Saskatchewan Regiment and the Queen's Own Cameron Highlanders were to disembark, after which the Camerons would move eight kilometres inland to attack an airfield and a German headquarters. The floating reserve was the Fusiliers Mont-Royal. The Commandos' task was to eliminate German batteries east and west of the three main landing areas. The raid's intention was to take Dieppe quickly, establish a defensive perimeter, and hold it just long enough to permit the destruction of harbour facilities. The raiders were then to depart by sea. No heavy bombing had been allocated to soften up the defences, and the Royal Navy declined to assign battleships to support the assault—the Admiralty deemed the English Channel too risky because of its proximity to so many German airfields. The German defences at Dieppe were in the hands of the 302nd Infantry

Division, but ample reserves of additional troops were close by.

The raiders boarded their landing craft on 18 August and set sail that night. Very quickly, everything unravelled, starting with the flotilla running into a German coastal convoy. The firing offshore alerted the German coastal defences, removing the element of surprise on which much depended. The Royal Navy landed the Canadians on Puy's Blue Beach 35 minutes late and they could easily be seen by two platoons of Germans on the beach and in a pillbox on the cliff overlooking it. Three waves of attackers from the Royal Regiment of Canada and the Black Watch were cut to pieces, and only a few intrepid survivors made it to the top of the cliff. Those still alive on the beach surrendered at about 8:30 a.m.; those atop the cliff held out until the late afternoon.

At Pourville's Green Beach, the situation was only marginally better. The South Saskatchewan Regiment landed on time in darkness and achieved surprise, but the Royal Navy landed part of the unit in the wrong place. One company, properly landed, met its objective. The rest, trying to cross a bridge over the River Scie faced withering fire from the Germans perched on the high ground to either side of the landing beach. The South Saskatchewan's commander, Lieutenant-Colonel Cecil Merritt, then led his troops across by sheer force of will: "Come on over, there's nothing to it," he said, standing up and swinging his helmet. Merritt then led attacks up one of the hills with his troops, joined by some of the Queen's Own Cameron Highlanders (who had landed with their pipers playing). The bulk of the Camerons moved inland nearly 2,000 metres until they encountered very heavy opposition and withdrew to the beach. The landing craft to pick them up were there, as planned, but very few of the survivors could reach them through the hail of German machine-gun fire. Merritt stayed to organize the defences that let those who made it get away. He was taken prisoner and soon received the Victoria Cross.

The real disaster was in front of Dieppe itself on Red and White Beaches. The enemy, hearing the firing from Puys and Pourville, was at the ready when the Canadians approached the shore. The only advantage the attackers had was the air force attack on the cliffs to the east of the beaches and strafing by Hurricanes of the beach defences. The infantry landed while the Germans tried to collect themselves after the air attack, but the Calgary's new Churchill tanks arrived late and managed to do little, many failing to get over the seawall, others unable to move on the baseball-sized stones that made up the beach. Only three tanks eventually reached the Esplanade where they did damage to the enemy. Without effective fire support, the infantry took heavy casualties from Germans firing from the cliffs and from the fortified casino at the west end of the beach. Some of the Royal Hamilton Light Infantry broke through the Germans' wire and made it to the casino, which they cleared. A handful of brave men made it into the town. Like most of the RHLI, the Essex Scottish, raked by fire from the east and west headlands, died or fell wounded where they had landed. The carnage now was compounded when garbled messages from the beach that suggested success led General Roberts, the Canadian commander, to send in the reserve battalion. The Fusiliers Mont-Royal landed at 7:00 a.m. and met only slaughter. Few made it off the beach.

The results were horrific. The Royal Regiment suffered 524 casualties and managed to get only 65 of its number back to England. Among the other regiments, losses were almost equally heavy: the Royal Hamilton Light Infantry lost 480 and extracted 217; the Essex, 530 while bringing home just 52; the Queen's Own Cameron Highlanders lost 346 and brought home 268; and for the South Saskatchewans, the grisly numbers were 339 and 353. The Calgary Tanks were only slightly better off, losing 174 while 247 made it back to Britain. At least half of those who returned to England had never landed. In all, the Canadians lost 56 officers and 851 other ranks killed, 586 wounded, and 1,946 taken prisoner. Only 2,200 returned to England, including many wounded. British army and Royal Marine casualties numbered 275. The Royal Navy had 28 percent of the ships it deployed sunk, and lost 550 officers and ratings. The

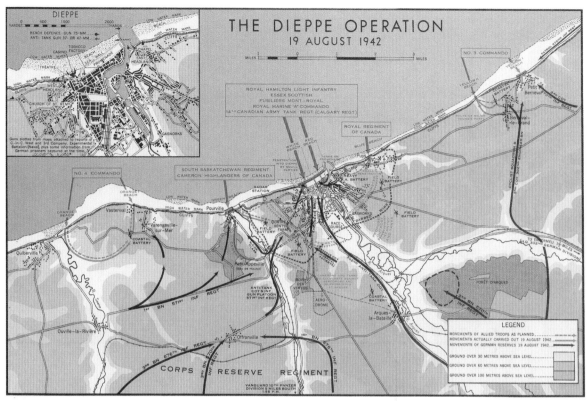

The Dieppe debacle cost the 2nd Canadian Division heavily, but the generals claimed its lessons made D-Day in June 1944 successful.

Royal and Royal Canadian Air Forces lost 106 aircraft, the heaviest loss in a day since the war began, and suffered 67 casualties. The Luftwaffe had 48 aircraft destroyed. German losses in all were under 600. Dieppe was a terrible disaster, a historic blunder of bad planning.

What had gone wrong? The only accurate answer to this question is "everything," although some things were more influential than others. Raiding France was a useful tool for the Allies to force the enemy to keep troops in the West rather than in Russia, and—arguably—it was good to test invasion theories. But it was a mistake to remount a once-cancelled operation. It was an error not to have heavy bombing precede the assault and a huge blunder to fail to have big naval guns firing offshore. It was foolish to depend so completely on surprise above all, and more foolish still to go on with the attack once surprise had been lost. It was stupidity to attack a

defended port where cliffs dominated the beaches—where else would the Germans put their firepower?—and to land on a beach in front of Dieppe where the shingle impeded the tanks' progress, on which a successful advance into the town depended. Dieppe was not on the far side of the planet, but a day trip that hundreds of English visitors had taken every day for decades. The lack of good sense and the failure to apply simple intelligence to the plan by Mountbatten's staff, Montgomery, and the Canadian planners were monumental. Of the senior commanders, Roberts became the lone scapegoat and was sacked some time after the raid. Crerar, Montgomery, and Mountbatten continued their wartime careers unaffected by the disaster. The distinguished British historian, David Reynolds, fingered Mountbatten as "responsible for the shambles" and characterized him aptly as an "egregious political climber" who had

▲ The Commonwealth War Graves Cemetery at Dieppe, France, holds the remains of 948 Commonwealth troops, including 707 Canadians.

already been "so absurdly over-promoted." A sailor with the best of royal and political connections, Mountbatten was likely immune from firing. He ought to have been demoted, at least, after Dieppe; instead, a year later, he became Supreme Allied Commander for Southeast Asia.

Dieppe was a lesson on how not to mount an amphibious assault. It was also a model of artful propaganda and shameless self-promotion as Mountbatten and other senior commanders, experts at public relations with media lines prepared in advance in case of failure, claimed at once that it was a success and a great learning experience. In light of the successful D-Day landings two years later, they would claim that it had been an invaluable armed tutorial

that had now paid off. General Crerar did much the same. Understandably perhaps, so have many Dieppe survivors, not wanting the lives of their friends to have been thrown away for nothing.

Did the lessons learned in Operation Jubilee pave the way for D-Day, 6 June 1944? It is doubtful. Early versions of the plan had incorporated most of the elements—and deemed them essential to success— that later foul-ups and service infighting had gradually removed. Air superiority, bombing support, and heavy naval gunfire, along with armour support, surprise, and speedy movement from crowded, vulnerable beaches were broadly accepted as the ingredients for successful amphibious operations, even by Dieppe's own planners. The dreadful results of Dieppe may have emphasized the obvious, but it was hardly the wheel reinvented. The raid did caution against over-optimism, however, and it raised the bar considerably in planning any future landing on German-held coasts. It offered critical lessons in scale, coordination, unity of effort, and the irreplaceable element of surprise, as well as a host of more tactical lessons on beach assault, combined arms warfare, and the extreme demands of seaborne landings. Even at Normandy, where the weight of the Allied assault makes comparisons with Dieppe tenuous at best, the scorecard was mixed. Heavy bombing was terrific for friendly morale, and for disorienting temporarily German defenders, but it was wildly inaccurate and not hugely successful in destroying beach defences. Naval gunfire was much better, but command of the sea and air were not advantages enjoyed in 1942, so the comparison is unhelpful. D-Day saw better landing craft and specialist armoured vehicles, and the assault troops were better trained, but these would likely have been true even if Dieppe had never happened. And instead of landing at a fortified port, the D-Day invasion went in over open beaches and the Allies brought their port, the Mulberry, with them. Some lessons were heeded, but most had been learned years before and long taught at staff colleges or ought to have been common sense. The blunders that created the debacle at Dieppe were and remain inexcusable, and most of the blame must be placed on the British military. The historian Max Hastings's judgment in his *Finest Years: Churchill as Warlord 1940–45* (2009) is brutal but correct: " ... a sense of institutional incompetence overlay the débacle. The invaders bungled the amphibious assault in every possible way .... After almost three years of war, Britain was incapable of conducting a limited surprise attack against an objective and at a moment of its own choice." SEE ALSO: CRERAR; MCNAUGHTON; RALSTON.

READING: Brian Loring Villa, *Unauthorized Action: Mountbatten and the Dieppe Raid* (Toronto, 1989); Denis and Shelagh Whitaker, *Dieppe: Tragedy to Triumph* (Toronto, 1992).

Disarmament. A cause that has always engaged Canadians, disarmament was frequently discussed during the interwar period, a time when Canada was already effectively disarmed. It became a major governmental and political issue with the development of nuclear weapons—which Canada had chosen not to build or acquire—and effective delivery systems in the late 1950s. The campaign against nuclear weapons for the Canadian military, spearheaded by the Voice of Women and the Combined Universities Campaign for Nuclear Disarmament, played a major role in bringing down John Diefenbaker's government. Paradoxically, L.B. Pearson's Liberals, initially opposed to nuclear weapons, switched sides and won the 1963 election, agreeing to accept the warheads. Under both Diefenbaker and Pearson, a Canadian ambassador for disarmament, initially Lieutenant-General E.L.M. Burns, participated in constant, largely fruitless negotiations in various international forums. Disarmament would be principally a great power affair, but Canadians—in government and in civil society—would play important roles throughout the long Cold War and after.

The Nuclear Non-Proliferation Treaty of 1968 aimed to limit the spread of nuclear weapons, and talks between Moscow and Washington (Strategic Arms Reduction Treaty [START]), begun in 1969, eventually produced limitations on anti-ballistic missile defences and two treaties (START I in 1991 and START II in 1993) that imposed limits on nuclear warhead stockpiles. The end of the Cold War lowered tensions, but proliferation has proceeded nonetheless, as countries such as Israel, South Africa, India, and Pakistan developed their own nuclear weaponry, and others such as Iran and North Korea sought to do so. This increased the risks of catastrophe, as did the development of other weapons of mass destruction. Canadians participated in most rounds of NATO–Warsaw Pact conventional arms reduction talks in Europe, in the development of controls on the international transfer of missile technology, and in substantial efforts to control anti-personnel land-mines, cluster munitions, and the global trade in small arms. Canada's goal in 2009—"the total elimination of all nuclear, chemical, and biological weapons and … effective controls on their means of delivery"—remains a noble pipe dream, and one not always in accord with the views of its nuclear-armed allies, the United States, Britain, and France. Canadian support for non-proliferation and the reduction and elimination of nuclear weapons has sometimes created tension in terms of its membership in NATO and NORAD, especially given the nuclear umbrella under which the Western alliance ultimately shelters. It remains a principle objective of Canadian policy, however, and Canada is a respected member or active supporter of most international arms control agencies. It also shares intelligence and advice with other powers in the monitoring of treaty compliance on issues that affect its interests. One of only a handful of countries to have done so, Canada unilaterally disarmed itself of nuclear weapons in the 1970s and 1980s, and has also voluntarily destroyed its stockpiles of chemical weapons and anti-personnel landmines, the latter in compliance with the Ottawa Treaty. SEE ALSO: OTTAWA TREATY.

READING: Albert Legault and Michel Fortmann, *A Diplomacy of Hope: Canada and Disarmament, 1945–1988* (Montreal, 1992).

Distant Early Warning Line. The Distant Early Warning, or DEW, Line, announced in 1954 and completed in 1957, consisted of a chain of radar, warning, and control stations stretching across the northern Arctic from Baffin Island to Alaska. Along with the more southerly Pinetree and Mid-Canada Lines, the US- and Canadian-built DEW Line aimed to detect incoming Soviet bombers as they flew to continental targets. The rapid emergence of intercontinental ballistic missiles, submarine-launched missiles, and cruise missiles weakened the line's usefulness. The North Warning System, another joint project designed to detect low-flying missiles and aircraft, similarly lost utility with the end of the Cold War and the collapse of the Soviet Union.

Divisions, Army, World War I. Canada raised and maintained four infantry divisions for front-line

service overseas during World War I. The 1st Canadian Division (originally called the Canadian Division) formed from the men called up by militia and defence minister Sam Hughes and gathered at Valcartier, Quebec. It trained on Salisbury Plain in England and went to Flanders in March 1915. The 2nd Canadian Division began to form in Canada in October 1914, proceeded overseas in the spring of 1915, and crossed the English Channel toward the front in September. The 3rd Canadian Division took shape overseas primarily from battalions and supporting units already there late in December 1915; the 4th Canadian Division formed similarly in April 1916. A 5th Canadian Division also took shape in England but it did not deploy to France, its specialists sent to bolster the other four fighting divisions and its infantry battalions broken up and used as reinforcements from the beginning of 1918. The four divisions in France formed the Canadian Corps. Other Canadian units included engineers, railway troops, medical personnel, and a full brigade of cavalry, though some of these—notably the cavalry—existed outside the structure of the corps.

The organization of each of the divisions featured three brigades with four infantry battalions per brigade. By the end of the war, after repeated reorganizations, each division had two brigades of field artillery, each with four batteries of guns, three battalions of engineers, a signal company, three trench mortar batteries, a battalion of machine guns, three field ambulances, an ammunition column, and a divisional train of the Canadian Army Service Corps. The personnel strength of a division was approximately 18,000, but a division was almost never at full strength due to casualties and those soldiers away on courses or on leave.

Division commanders were major-generals who, in action, almost always had been successful brigadier-generals. Corps commanders, lieutenant-generals, ordinarily were drawn from successful division commanders. Arthur Currie, to cite the best Canadian example, was a good brigade commander promoted to

▲ Designed to provide maximum warning of a Soviet bomber attack, the DEW line relied on advanced radars, like this one at Cambridge Bay in 1958.

command a division and, when an opening occurred, promoted once more to corps command.

READING: G.W.L. Nicholson, *Canadian Expeditionary Force, 1914–1919* (Ottawa, 1962).

Divisions, Army, World War II. As in World War I, the Canadian army was organized into divisions overseas; in World War II, however, the divisional organization was also used at home for units charged with the defence of Canada.

The home defence divisions were numbered as the 6th, 7th, and 8th Divisions. The 6th Division, formed in May 1942, had responsibility for the defence of Vancouver Island, a task it continued until the end of 1944. The 7th Division, also formed in May 1942 and

in operation until October 1943, acted as a general reserve for the Maritimes and was commanded from Debert, Nova Scotia. The army created the 8th Division in July 1942 to defend northern British Columbia. Headquartered at Prince George, the division functioned until October 1943.

Overseas, Canada fielded five divisions, the 1st, 2nd, and 3rd Canadian Infantry Divisions and the 4th and 5th Canadian Armoured Divisions. The 1st Division took shape in October 1939 and proceeded to England where it remained until detailed for the invasion of Sicily in July 1943. This division fought in Italy until, early in 1945, it moved to northwest Europe. The 2nd Division, authorized in May 1940, served in Britain, fought in the Dieppe raid, and took

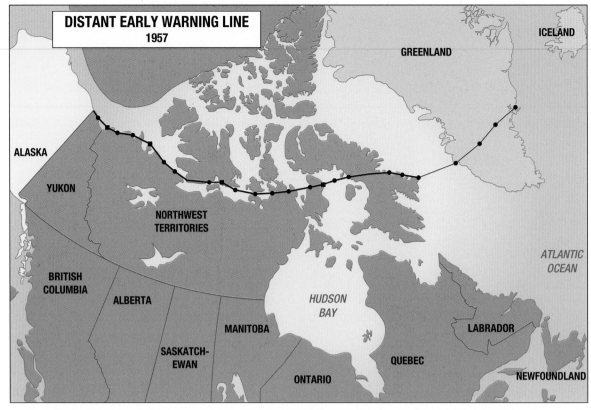

DISTANT EARLY WARNING LINE
1957

ICELAND

GREENLAND

ALASKA

YUKON

NORTHWEST
TERRITORIES

ATLANTIC
OCEAN

BRITISH
COLUMBIA

ALBERTA

HUDSON
BAY

MANITOBA

LABRADOR

SASKATCH-
EWAN

QUEBEC

NEWFOUNDLAND

ONTARIO

▲ Located in the high Arctic, the DEW Line provided maximum warning of any Soviet bomber attack against North America.

part in the Normandy campaign and in the fighting in northwest Europe. The 3rd Division, created in October 1940, served in Britain until D-Day when it spearheaded the Canadian share of the invasion, landing at Juno Beach. This division then fought to the end of the war in northwest Europe. The 4th Canadian Armoured Division, initially raised as infantry and converted to armour, was authorized in June 1941, served in Britain, and fought in Normandy and northwest Europe. The government authorized the 5th Armoured, dubbed the "Mighty Maroon Machine," in March 1941 and it served in Britain, Italy, and northwest Europe.

All the Canadian overseas divisions formed part of First Canadian Army from its formation in April 1942. The 1st Division and the 5th Armoured operated as I Canadian Corps in Italy and then in northwest Europe; the 1st Canadian Armoured Brigade formed an administrative part of the corps though it

often fought with British forces. The 2nd and 3rd Divisions and the 4th Armoured Division formed II Canadian Corps in Britain and northwest Europe, along with 2nd Canadian Armoured Brigade.

Infantry divisions overseas had three infantry brigades, each with three infantry battalions and an armoured reconnaissance regiment. Armoured divisions had an armoured brigade of three regiments and either one (4th Armoured Division) or two (5th Armoured Division) infantry brigades, as well as a reconnaissance regiment. Each infantry division had three artillery regiments, an anti-tank regiment, and a light anti-aircraft regiment; armoured divisions had two artillery regiments, one self-propelled, and anti-tank and anti-aircraft regiments. The infantry divisions had four engineer companies, signallers, transport companies, field ambulances, and other specialist services; armoured divisions had similar component units.

An infantry division at full strength numbered 18,376 officers and other ranks, of which infantry made up 8,148, artillery 2,122, supply and transport 1,296, engineers 959, medical 945, signallers 743, and other specialist units the remainder. An armoured division had approximately 15,000 all ranks, but this would vary depending on the number of its infantry brigades. For all practical purposes, no unit was ever at full strength; certainly this was true for units in action.

Division commanders were major-generals (two stars in current terminology) who, in action, almost always had been successful (one-star) brigadiers. Corps commanders, all (three-star) lieutenant-generals, ordinarily were successful division commanders. The army commander was a (four-star) general.

READING: C.P. Stacey, *Six Years of War: The Official History of the Canadian Army* (Ottawa, 1955).

Dollard des Ormeaux, Adam (1635–1660). An officer and garrison commander at Ville-Marie, Dollard had come to New France in 1658. At the end of April 1660, he led a party of 17 French, 40 Hurons, and 4 Algonquins on an expedition to the Ottawa River. At Long Sault on 2 May, he ambushed a force of 300 Iroquois that he likely believed intended to attack Ville-Marie. The ambushers then found themselves besieged in a decrepit palisade on a hill, without ammunition or water, and with little food. After several attacks had been repulsed over a week, the Iroquois called in 500 more warriors, the Hurons deserted, and the surviving defenders, perhaps five, were tortured and killed, some eaten. The facts are lacking or confusing, but during the nineteenth century the story of Dollard became a nationalist paean to French Canada's survival against all odds. SEE ALSO: FRENCH-IROQUOIS WARS.

Dominion Arsenal. Established in 1882 by the federal government in Quebec City as the Cartoucherie de Québec to produce cartridges and shell casings, in 1901 the name changed to the Dominion Arsenal.

During World War I, a second factory opened in Lindsay, Ontario, the hometown of Minister of Militia and Defence Sir Sam Hughes. Additional facilities opened during World War II and, in 1945, the Crown corporation, Canadian Arsenals Ltd., took over management. The original Quebec site, located in Artillery Park, closed in 1964.

12e Régiment Blindé. In 1968, defence minister Léo Cadieux formed this armoured regiment to help ensure that francophone units had their place in the army, linking to a militia regiment at Trois-Rivières, Quebec, from which the Three Rivers Regiment in World War II had come. The regular force 12e, located at Canadian Forces Base Valcartier as a component of Ve Brigade, has served in the North Atlantic Treaty Organization (NATO), on a wide variety of peace support operations, and in Afghanistan.

Drocourt-Quéant Line. A heavily fortified and well-defended portion of the Germans' Hindenburg Line, located north of St Quentin, west of Douai, and just east of Arras, France, the Canadian Corps attacked the Drocourt-Quéant Line on 2 September 1918. The 1st and 4th Canadian Divisions led the attack against the enemy's concrete bunkers and machine-gun posts and broke the defences on a nearly 7,000-metre front. Skilfully planned and led by the Canadian Corps commander, Lieutenant-General Sir Arthur Currie, the assault forced the Germans to withdraw east of the Canal du Nord on 3 September. The Canadians lost more than 5,600 killed and wounded in the attack that Currie considered the highlight of the corps' Hundred Days, "one of the finest performances in all the war." SEE ALSO: CANADIAN CORPS; CURRIE; HUNDRED DAYS.

Drummond, Sir Gordon (1772–1854). Born in Quebec, the son of a British officer, Drummond joined the British army in 1789 and fought in the wars against Napoleon. As a lieutenant-general, he served in Canada from 1808–1811, but was in Ireland when the War of 1812 began. Taking command in Upper Canada at the end of 1813, he found US troops in control of the Niagara and Detroit areas with much of southwestern Upper Canada evacuated. He moved against the Niagara frontier, crossed into the United States, and re-took control of the peninsula. Imposing martial law on Upper Canada so he could secure the food he needed to feed his men, he also launched a naval attack on Oswego, New York, to destroy US Navy supplies. But his subordinate Major-General Phineas Riall lost at Chippawa in early July 1814 and Drummond, through his own exertions at the front and some good luck, narrowly defeated the Americans at Lundy's Lane a short time later. Pressing forward, Drummond then attacked the enemy's fortified camp near Fort Erie, suffered heavy casualties, and withdrew. The arrival of the British fleet swung the advantage back to Drummond and the Americans retreated back to US territory. Drummond then succeeded Sir George Prevost in command in the Canadas on 3 April 1815, and it fell to him to implement the terms of the Treaty of Ghent ending the war with the United States. Personally courageous and aggressive, Drummond had markedly improved the British position in Upper Canada during his months in command. He departed Canada in 1816 with a knighthood. SEE ALSO: WAR OF 1812.

READING: J.M. Hitsman, *The Incredible War of 1812* (rev. ed., Montreal, 1999).

▲ The first battle of the Northwest Rebellion of 1885, sketched here, took place in March at Duck Lake, where Louis Riel's forces killed or wounded 23 North West Mounted Police and settlers.

▲ The most famous of World War I soldiers' troupes, the Dumbells were formed in the 3rd Canadian Division.

Duck Lake, Battle of (1885). Duck Lake, located some 50 kilometres southwest of Prince Albert, Saskatchewan, and midway between Louis Riel's headquarters at Batoche and the North West Mounted Police camp at Fort Carlton, was the site of the first battle of the 1885 Northwest Rebellion on 26 March. The Metis, led by Riel and Gabriel Dumont, inflicted 23 casualties, including ten dead, on a small Canadian force of North West Mounted Police and settlers led by Superintendent L.N.F. Crozier. Riel's victory and the small losses his men suffered (though the Dumont family lost one killed and three wounded) guaranteed that his rebellion would gather strength. See also: Northwest Rebellion.

Dumbells. A World War I concert troupe formed by men of the 3rd Canadian Division under the direction of Merton Plunkett, a YMCA entertainment officer, the Dumbells performed skits and songs, featuring female

impersonators, at and behind the front lines. The troupe earned great acclaim, so much so that in 1918 it staged a four-week run at the Coliseum in London. After the war, the Dumbells performed in North America, doing cross-Canada tours until they failed financially in 1932.

Dumont, Gabriel (1837–1906). Born at the Red River, Dumont was a Buffalo hunter who had moved west to the vicinity of Fort Carlton, Northwest Territories, before the outbreak of Louis Riel's first rebellion in 1870. As the head of the strongest faction of Metis in the Northwest, he led the group that invited Riel in early 1885 to return from the United States to head a new agitation for rights and land. Dumont became the "adjutant-general of the Metis nation," in effect, Riel's field commander in the Northwest Rebellion. His tiny army of 300 surprised the Canadians at Duck Lake and Fish Creek, both victories, though costly ones because they used up ammunition and lost horses that

▲ Gabriel Dumont after the Northwest Rebellion.

gave the Metis their mobility. Two weeks after Fish Creek, the Canadian forces laid siege to Batoche, Riel's capital, where Dumont's men had entrenched themselves in well-prepared rifle pits. The weight of forces, the Canadians' artillery, and a Gatling gun made the result inevitable. Dumont fled to the United States where he joined Buffalo Bill Cody's Wild West show. He returned to Canada after the amnesty of 1886 and wrote his memoirs. Dumont believed that Riel's strategic error in not fighting a guerilla war had lost the Metis the fight, and he was sharply critical of the local clergy for not supporting the uprising.

SEE ALSO: NORTHWEST REBELLION; RIEL.

READING: George Woodcock, *Gabriel Dumont: The Métis Chief and His Lost World* (Edmonton, 1975).

Eccles Hill, Battle of (1870). In late May 1870, fear of renewed raids into Canada by the army of the Fenian Brotherhood, Irish Americans opposed to British rule in North America, led to the mobilization of militia units in New Brunswick, Ontario, and Quebec. Under John O'Neill, a party of 400 Fenians with one cannon crossed into Quebec from Vermont on 25 May. At Eccles Hill, local militia, farmers, and militia reinforcements from Montreal, under the overall command of Lieutenant-Colonel William Osborne Smith, had gathered to meet them. The Canadians kept up a harassing fire on the small Fenian force for several hours, and then advanced, scattering the invaders in a panicked retreat. The Fenians suffered a number of casualties (accounts vary on how many), while the militia suffered no losses. A second Fenian attack two days later at Trout River, 15 kilometres west of Eccles Hill, was no more successful, the defenders this time having their own artillery. SEE ALSO: FENIAN RAIDS.

Emergencies Act. Passed by Parliament in 1988 to replace the War Measures Act, this legislation is subject to the Charter of Rights and Freedoms and provides for compensation for those who might suffer as a result of designated emergency situations. The Act established four categories of emergencies: public welfare (for example, floods or storms); public order (such as threats to national security); international; and war. In case of war, the Emergencies Act authorizes the government to give any order it believes "necessary or advisable." Provisions of the Act ensure parliamentary scrutiny of government action and impose time limits on the powers exercised.

Emergency Management Act. The threat of nuclear attack on Canada led the Diefenbaker government to create the Emergency Measures Organization (EMO) in 1959 to expand the nation's civil defence. Emergency Planning Canada followed EMO in 1974 and was in turn replaced in 1980. After other alterations in organization and following the al Qaeda terrorist attacks on the United States in 2001, the Harper government passed the Emergency Management Act in 2007, putting the measure under a minister of public safety with the aim of strengthening readiness and improving the coordination of federal agencies in response to crises. SEE ALSO: CIVIL DEFENCE.

Enlistments. Canadian enlistments for the South African War (1899–1902) numbered 8,372, including a battalion of the Royal Canadian Regiment raised to garrison Halifax, some 1,200 enlisted for the South African Constabulary, and unofficial privately raised units such as Lord Strathcona's Horse. Only 3,500 Canadian soldiers served in the war at Canadian government expense, the remainder being paid by Britain.

During World War I (1914–1918), naval enlistments were approximately 9,000, while the Canadian Expeditionary Force enrolled 619,636 men and women, a figure that includes conscripts, nursing sisters, and those serving with the Royal Naval Air Service, the Royal Flying Corps, and the Royal Air Force. Figures for Newfoundland enlistments and for those who served in the Merchant Marine are occasionally added to these totals.

In World War II (1939–1945), the Royal Canadian Navy enrolled 106,522 officers, ratings, and women; the Canadian Army enlisted 730,159 men and women, including those conscripted; and the Royal Canadian Air Force enlisted 249,662 men and women. Once again, Newfoundland and Merchant Marine enlistments are sometimes added to these totals.

The Korean War (1950–1953) saw the Canadian Army enlist 21,940 for Korean service, although several thousand more served there after the armistice; 10,208 of these enlistees joined the Canadian Army Special Force raised specifically for the war. The Royal Canadian Navy enlisted 3,621 personnel for Korea. In addition to transport crews flying from North America, a small number of air force personnel also served in Korea, including 22 fighter pilots who flew in American squadrons. SEE ALSO: NEWFOUNDLAND AND WORLD WAR I; NEWFOUNDLAND AND WORLD WAR II.

Equipment, Army. The technology of war has changed dramatically over the last century, and the Canadian Army has tried to keep up. At the time of Confederation, the army moved by horsepower, its cavalry used swords and lances, its artillery was primitive, and its infantry relied on rifles for its firepower. By the time of the Northwest Rebellion of 1885, the Gatling gun had added a firing capacity vastly greater than the rifle to the military repertoire. Nonetheless, the army that went to South Africa in 1899 and to France and Flanders in 1915 was recognizably the same as that of 1867.

World War I altered everything. Motorized transport supplemented the horse and, by the end of the war, had all but supplanted it as the preferred troop and materiel carrier. The development of the tank, an armoured vehicle able to move on the muddy, wired battlefield, presaged a war of movement, as did Raymond Brutinel's Mobile Machine-Gun Brigade. The soldier's basic weapon, once the Ross rifle went to the scrap heap, was the reliable Lee-Enfield rifle, firing a .303 bullet that was also used in the Lewis machine guns that, by late 1916, were available at the platoon level, and the Vickers guns that were concentrated in machine-gun battalions. Stokes mortars proliferated, as did the Mills bomb or grenades, arguably the infantryman's weapons of choice. Artillery—ranging from 18-pounders to 60-pounders and including guns and howitzers—added to its range and explosive power, and did most of the killing. Gas, heavily used by the Canadian Corps and everyone else along the Western Front, demanded that respirators become a vital piece of personal kit.

World War II personal equipment was a visible continuation of that of the 1914–1918 war, but trucks and jeeps were everywhere and the horses mostly gone (donkeys would still be used in mountainous terrain). The tank increased greatly in power, armament, speed, and numbers, most Canadian units in action using the American-designed Sherman, while armoured cars undertook reconnaissance. The artillery used the quick-firing 25-pounder gun as its standard weapon. Platoon weapons came to include anti-tank weaponry, like the PIAT (projector, infantry, anti-tank), mortars, and the Bren light machine gun which, with three to a platoon of infantry, was omnipresent. The Lee-Enfield rifle was still used and the Sten submachine gun soon became standard equipment, even though it was notoriously unreliable. Communications equipment, telephone and radio, improved substantially. The Universal Carrier (or Bren Gun Carrier), a tracked vehicle, came into use, and General Guy Simonds conceived the idea of an armoured personnel carrier, a tank chassis with the turret removed, to carry troops into action protected by armour on all sides.

The army that fought in Korea and trained for the Cold War in West Germany and Canada again looked much like that of World War II, although it evolved gradually from the look and feel of a British army to one more closely resembling the Americans. British Centurion tanks were the main battle tank into the 1970s until their replacement by German-made Leopards. The "deuce-and-a-half," the 2 1/2 tonne truck, carried the army's loads, and the Lee-Enfield rifle remained the personal weapon into the late 1950s, until superseded by the North Atlantic Treaty Organization (NATO) standard FN 7.62mm rifle. American equipment increasingly replaced the British patterns Canada had used. The American helmet replaced the uncomfortable British "tin hat." The advent of Honest John nuclear surface-to-surface missiles in the 1960s meant the arrival of the nuclear battlefield, forcing soldiers to spread out on the battlefield lest a single nuclear strike destroy entire formations. The acquisition of American M113 armoured personnel carriers gave mobility and protection, the 105mm artillery piece became standard, and the helicopter appeared as a troop carrier and for reconnaissance.

By the end of the Cold War and the early years of the twenty-first century, the Canadian army had adopted the C7A1 assault rifle and the C6 general purpose machine gun, employed TOW anti-tank guided missiles, and operated a range of anti-air missiles, from hand-held to those carried on mobile armoured vehicles. Soldiers in Afghanistan drove Leopard C2A6 tanks, acquired for Afghan use, and operated a variety of armoured vehicles, most notably the LAV III, a Canadian-designed armoured personnel carrier, with a 25mm chain gun and a coaxial machine gun; the LAV could carry three crew plus seven infantry. The new artillery weapon was the ultra-light 155mm M777, capable of astonishing accuracy at long ranges. Soldiers wore uniforms with an innovative series of digitally-created camouflage designs and, in operations, personal armour and night-vision goggles. Light, medium, and heavy trucks handled logistics for the troops, while Griffon helicopters provided air mobility, as did the bigger Chinook helicopter, abandoned in the early 1990s but reacquired after Afghanistan showed their continued utility. The army may not have been completely computerized, but it was increasingly sophisticated in its ability to gather and employ intelligence data quickly on and off the battlefield.

Esquimalt, BC. Located on the southeast coast of Vancouver Island very near Victoria, Esquimalt has been a naval base since the 1850s, and the site was enhanced by the construction of Royal Navy dry docks there in the 1880s. The base spawned a number of coastal defence sites and fortifications along nearby headlands and likely avenues of enemy attack. Britain tried regularly from the 1870s to persuade Canada to take over responsibility for the defence of the base; in 1906, Canada finally did so. Esquimalt had some importance in World War I when German raiders sporadically operated in the Pacific, and much more in later years. In the 1930s, World War II, and the Cold War, Esquimalt was the focal point of Canada's West Coast defences. Canadian Forces Base Esquimalt employs 4,200 military and 2,200 civilian workers on its 42 square kilometres and is home to MARPAC or Maritime Forces Pacific, the navy's Pacific fleet.

Examination Unit. Established by the Department of External Affairs on 9 June 1941 with its budget concealed in the estimates of the National Research Council, the Examination Unit initially had the task of eavesdropping on communications to and from the Vichy France legation in Ottawa. The first head of the unit was the American Herbert Yardley, an accomplished cryptographer who was *persona non grata* in Washington and London following the publication of his book on American interwar spying on Japan's codes. By the time Yardley had been relieved and Canada had broken relations with Vichy the next year, the unit's work had expanded to include the interception of German messages to and from South America and the decoding of Japanese wireless traffic. Simultaneously, the three armed services had established their own intercept units, later combining them in the Joint Discrimination Unit (JDU). The Examination Unit, scheduled for shut down after VE Day, instead merged with the JDU on 1 August 1945 and continued as such until 3 September 1946 when the new Communications Branch, National Research Council, began operations, its mandate directed at intercepting the signals traffic of the Soviet Union and its allies. The Communications Branch was the forerunner of the present Communications Security Establishment.

READING: Kurt Jensen, *Cautious Beginnings: Canadian Foreign Intelligence, 1939–1951* (Vancouver, 2008).

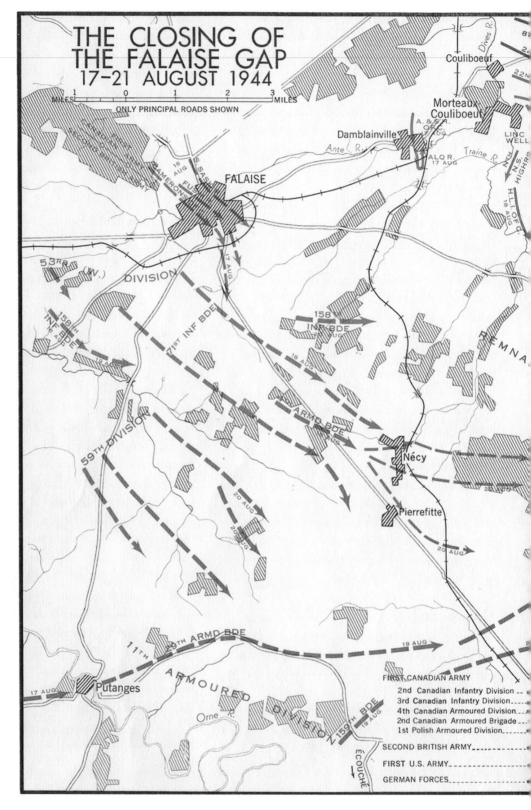

THE CLOSING OF THE FALAISE GAP
17–21 AUGUST 1944

MILES 1 0 1 2 3 MILES
ONLY PRINCIPAL ROADS SHOWN

Couliboeuf

Morteaux
Couliboeuf

Damblainville

Ante R.

Traine R.

Dives R.

A. & S.H.
OF C.

ALQ R.
17 AUG

LINC
WELL

N.S.R.

H.L.I. OF C.
18 AUG

FALAISE

53RD (W.)   DIVISION

71ST INF BDE

158
INF BDE

ARMD BDE

REMNA

59TH DIVISION

Nécy

Pierrefitte

20 AUG

20 AUG

19 AUG

11TH   59TH ARMD BDE

ARMOURED   DIVISION

159TH BDE
19 AUG

Putanges

17 AUG

Orne R.

ÉCOUCHÉ

FIRST CANADIAN ARMY

2nd Canadian Infantry Division
3rd Canadian Infantry Division
4th Canadian Armoured Division
2nd Canadian Armoured Brigade
1st Polish Armoured Division

SECOND BRITISH ARMY

FIRST U.S. ARMY

GERMAN FORCES

⌃ II Canadian Corps played a critical role in closing the Falaise Gap, but only after thousands of Germans had escaped.

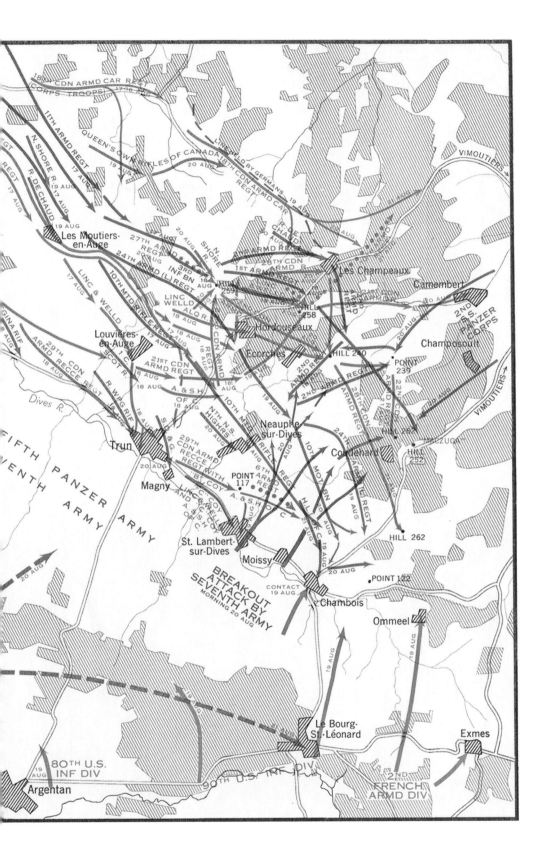

18TH CDN ARMD CAR REGT
CORPS TROOPS 17-18 TC

11TH ARMD REGT
N. SHORE R 17 AUG
R. DE CHAUD

QUEEN'S OWN RIFLES OF CANADA 19TH CDN ARMD CAR
19 AUG
20 AUG
ENFIELD BY GERMANS 19 AUG

VIMOUTIERS →

Les Moutiers-
en-Auge
19 AUG

27TH ARMD
REGT
20 AUG
24TH
ARMD (L) REGT
3RD CDN
INF BN 18
AUG

28TH CDN
1ST ARMD R
HILL
259

Les Champeaux

Camembert

2ND
S.S.
PANZER
CORPS

Louvières-
en-Auge
1 C.
SCOT R

LINC WELLD
ALQ R.

10TH MTD RIFLE REGT
18 AUG

HILL
258

Hordouseaux

Ecorches

HILL 240

Champosoult

POINT
239

LINC & WELLD
17 AUG

29TH CDN
ARMD RECCE REGT
18 AUG
R WPG RIF
18 AUG

21ST CDN
ARMD REGT
18 AUG
A. & SH
OF C.
18 AUG

CDN ARMD
REGT
18 AUG

10TH MTD
2ND ARMD REGT
28TH CDN
22ND CDN
ARMD REGT

VIMOUTIERS →

Dives R.

NTH N.S.
HIGHRS.

Neauphe-
sur-Dives

24TH ARMD
REGT
10TH MTD BN.

HILL 262

Trun
20 AUG

29TH
CDN ARMD
RECCE
REGT WITH
B COY
LINC & WELL
AND A & SH OF C
"B" COY A. & S.
POINT
117

S. & G.

6TH ARMD
REGT

Coudehard

HILL
252

Magny

LINC WELL
AND A & SH OF C

POINT
117

A. & SH OF C

HILL 262

HILL 262

St. Lambert-
sur-Dives

Moissy

BREAKOUT
ATTACK BY
SEVENTH ARMY
MORNING 20 AUG

CONTACT
19 AUG

Chambois

20 AUG

POINT 122

Ommeel

FIFTH

PANZER

SEVENTH

ARMY

ARMY

80TH U.S.
INF DIV
19 AUG

Argentan

90TH U.S. INF DIV

Le Bourg-
St.-Léonard

2ND
FRENCH
ARMD DIV

Exmes

19 AUG

Falaise, Battle of (1944). The Allies invaded France on D-Day, 6 June 1944, and established themselves inland. But progress into Normandy was slow and, despite a massive buildup of forces, the British, American, and Canadian troops were held in check by strong German resistance, much of it from panzer (tank) divisions concentrated in the Anglo-Canadian sector in front of the city of Caen. By 25 July, the US forces to the west had at last begun to break out of the bocage, but the Germans, rather than with-drawing to the east as good sense might have suggested, instead decided by the end of the first week of August to strike at the Americans. The enemy thrust, Operation Luttich, provided the Allies with the possibility of a great envelopment: if the British and Canadians could force their way south toward the town of Falaise, severing the east-west roads along which the Germans would have to retreat, they might be trapped in a pocket, pinned against US forces coming from the west and south-west, and destroyed or forced to capitulate.

But to get to Falaise was a major challenge, one that fell mostly to II Canadian Corps, commanded by Lieutenant-General Guy Simonds. From their firm base in Caen, the city captured only after long, arduous fighting, the Canadians moved south, their night attack, Operation Totalize, moving off on 7 August. A product of Simonds's fertile tactical brain, Totalize employed improvised armoured personnel carriers (Kangaroos) and huge columns of armour and infantry steered by radio beams and under artificial moonlight created by bouncing searchlight beams off the clouds. Unfortunately, Allied bombing support fell partly on the Canadians, causing hundreds of casualties and resultant confu-sion, and enemy resistance remained vigorous, the

defenders galvanized by the energy of Kurt Meyer, the commander of the 12th SS Panzer Division.

With Operation Totalize at best a partial success and with increasing pressure from General Montgomery to close the gap, Simonds tried again on 14 August. Allied bombing errors once more disrupted the plan, Operation Tractable getting off to a somewhat ragged beginning because of casualties to Canadian and Polish troops. Most objectives none-

▲ Canadian armour on the move in the Norman summer of 1944. Note the tightly packed column, evidence of the Allies' complete command of the air above the battlefield.

theless fell to the attackers and, by 16 August, with Falaise now in the hands of the 4th Canadian Armoured Division, the gap between Canadian and US forces moving on Falaise from the southwest was less than 30 kilometres. The pocket finally was sewn shut on 21 August when Canadian troops relieved the Poles holding off enemy attacks from east and west a few kilometres southeast of Falaise, but not before tens of thousands of the enemy had escaped. Even so, German casualties were huge, amounting to as much as half of their strength in Normandy. The roads around Falaise were littered with the dead and with German armoured and horse-drawn equipment, the stench such that pilots flying above the carnage claimed they could smell the death below.

The Falaise Pocket was a huge but partial victory. British and American historians have pointed fingers at Canadian slowness in reaching Falaise. There is some truth to the complaints—the 4th Canadian Armoured Division and the 1st Polish Armoured Division were new to action and their commanders might have performed better. But the critics neglect the ground south of Caen that favoured the enemy, the tremendous power of German anti-tank guns, and the calamitous impact of two bombing support operations that went awry with terrible results. Montgomery's decision not to add British troops to the southward push is also almost inexplicable. As historian Terry Copp has demonstrated, these factors and the very high casualty rates suffered by the 2nd and 3rd Canadian Infantry Divisions and the 4th Canadian Armoured Division testify to both the severity of the fighting and the efforts made by the Canadians to close the gap. SEE ALSO: NORMANDY; SIMONDS.

READING: Terry Copp, *Fields of Fire: The Canadians in Normandy* (Toronto, 2003); Brian Reid, *No Holding Back: Operation Totalize, Normandy, August 1944* (Toronto, 2005).

Fenian Raids. The Fenian movement began in 1857 when Irish Americans began to organize to help Ireland win its independence from Great Britain. The aim of the large and influential paramilitary group—by the end of the American Civil War it numbered 10,000—was to harass or even liberate British North America. Either way, this presumably would force London to send more troops overseas, in theory weakening Britain's hold on Ireland and thus speeding independence. The first Fenian raid in April 1866, an attempt to seize Campobello Island in New Brunswick, was broken up by US troops. The one achievement of the abortive raid was to encourage hesitant New Brunswickers to consider the benefits of Confederation with other British North American colonies. The next attack came across the Niagara frontier on 1 June 1866 where, at Ridgeway, a force of several hundred or more Fenians scored a victory against militia units but failed to follow up their advantage and retreated back to the American side of the line where most were arrested and interned. An attack on Canada East at Pigeon Hill and Mississquoi was even more ineffective, and the Fenian menace subsided for some time. In May 1870, the Fenians again launched raids over the Quebec-Vermont border at Eccles Hill and Holbrooke's Corners and once more made no headway. US authorities blocked a final raid planned for Manitoba the next year, intended to fan the sparks struck by the Red River Rebellion (1870). Despite the fact that large numbers of Fenians had served in the US Army during the just-ended Civil War, the raids were comic opera, largely a military farce. They did, however, illuminate the weaknesses of the Canadian militia, and strained the loyalty of some Canadian Irish Catholics. The threat to Canada during and after the Civil War, including the Fenian raids, led to a considerable strengthening of the British garrisons, contributed to the political process that resulted in Confederation in 1867, and strained Anglo-American relations.

READING: H. Senior, *The Last Invasion of Canada* (Ottawa, 1991); J.M. Hitsman, *Safeguarding Canada, 1763–1871* (Toronto, 1968).

First Canadian Army. The First Canadian Army was the largest ever Canadian field formation, the nation's major military effort in World War II. The army at its

▲ Militia from the 13th Royal Regiment from Hamilton, Upper Canada, who guarded the frontier in 1865 against attacks from the Fenian Brotherhood.

creation consisted of two corps, I and II Canadian Corps, their constituent divisions, and armoured brigades and other units. For most of the war, the great majority of the soldiers in First Canadian Army were Canadian, but units of other nationalities—British, Polish, Belgian, Dutch, and American—also served under Canadian command. From the time Army Headquarters moved to Normandy and into operations in July 1944, for example, the two formations under its control were II Canadian Corps and I British Corps. At one point, during the great struggle for control of the Scheldt estuary in late 1944, Canadian troops were actually in a minority in First Canadian Army. The often-multinational force also relied on British heavy artillery and logistical support.

Formed in Britain in April 1942 under General A.G.L. McNaughton's command, First Canadian Army's normal complement at full strength was the 1st, 2nd, and 3rd Canadian Infantry Divisions and the 4th and 5th Canadian Armoured Divisions, along

with the 1st and 2nd Canadian Armoured Brigades. This formidable force encompassed 42 infantry battalions, 12 armoured regiments, 45 batteries of field artillery, and an array of specialized units. McNaughton's permanent successor in command when he was relieved in December 1943 was Lieutenant-General H.D.G. Crerar; when he became ill in the fall of 1944, Lieutenant-General Guy Simonds took command for a few months.

The army served with distinction throughout the fighting in Europe, a result that might not have been predictable given the paltry size of the prewar force— merely 4,000 regulars and a largely untrained militia—and the absence of senior officers with field command experience. The growing pains caused by such a small professional cadre would continue throughout the war, but the army eventually produced highly capable commanders, staff officers, and warriors, who operated effectively together through one of the most gruelling land campaigns in Western military history. First Canadian Army's principal problem was not its military acumen—as some British brass occasionally claimed—but its political status as Ottawa's principal tool for war fighting, and the government's extreme aversion to high casualties that might create the necessity for conscription. It had a second problem as well, at least for its British colleagues and more senior commanders: General McNaughton's insistence on keeping the Canadians together so that, under his command, the army might be what he described as a dagger pointed at the enemy's heart. McNaughton's insistence on organizational unity, derived in part from the lessons of World War I, might have helped Ottawa dodge the risk of heavy combat losses a while longer if he had been a better field commander with the full support of his British commanders, but he was not that leader and the British were not that patient. The bookish Canadian proved less than able on field exercises that brought him unfavourable reviews and, by 1943, he had lost his superiors' confidence. McNaughton's resistance to sending divisions into action meant that battle experience for commanders and soldiers alike was slow in coming, once again something that curbed British enthusiasm, and it was not until Ottawa's pressure to have Canadian participation in the attack on Sicily in July 1943 (the Dieppe debacle a year earlier notwithstanding) that 1st Canadian Division saw sustained action. That Italian commitment, soon expanded to a corps, demonstrated clearly that McNaughton had lost the struggle; shortly thereafter, he lost his job.

General Harry Crerar, whose highly capable sniping had helped seal McNaughton's fate, inherited First Canadian Army as a field army in name only, with its principal fighting formations separated by half a continent of German-occupied territory. Most army-sized formations would share this difficulty from time to time, with divisions or corps detached to other commanders or even theatres of war, but the Canadian case was unusual, and it meant that Crerar would take a smaller and more polyglot force into Normandy than most of his senior colleagues. That he led it capably and with a string of hard-fought victories to its credit, from the Falaise Pocket through to the clearing of the

Channel ports and the Scheldt estuary and the liberation of the Netherlands, was a credit to his organizational and administrative talents, and to those of the commanders and senior staff officers with whom he served. Canadian troops from Italy would later be reunited with First Canadian Army in the closing months of the war, integrated more or less seamlessly into the largest and most powerful striking force ever commanded by a Canadian in war. Fighting almost continuously from Sicily to Italy to Normandy and beyond, the Canadians suffered heavy casualties in return for their prominent role in the European campaigns of 1943–1945, triggering the conscription debate, decision, and ensuing controversy that early-war Canadian policy had so desperately striven to avoid. First Canadian Army would never enjoy the public notoriety of the British Eighth or the American Third Army, nor perhaps the esprit de corps and self-assuredness of such formations, but it was by 1945 a ruthlessly potent, reliable, and professional organization that measured its successes in liberated countries. Crerar had played the pre-eminent military role in creating this ambitious and unprecedented strike force; there was more than minor justice in him leading it to victory. SEE ALSO: CRERAR; MCNAUGHTON; SIMONDS.

READING: J.L. Granatstein, *Canada's Army: Waging War and Keeping the Peace* (Toronto, 2002).

I Canadian Corps. The corps was formed in Britain in July 1940 from the 1st and 2nd Canadian Infantry Divisions and first commanded by Lieutenant-General A.G.L. McNaughton. Its primary role was the defence of England against German invasion, a very real possibility after the fall of France in June 1940. By 1943, unhappiness in Canadian political and public circles at the lack of action for Canadian troops (the disasters at Hong Kong and Dieppe notwithstanding) led Ottawa to insist, over McNaughton's opposition, that the 1st Canadian Division participate in the invasion of Sicily, along with the 1st Canadian Armoured Brigade. Political pressure soon demanded that the 5th Canadian Armoured Division join in the Italian fighting too as part of a new I Canadian Corps, commanded briefly by Lieutenant-General Harry

Crerar, and then successively by Lieutenant-Generals E.L.M. Burns and Charles Foulkes. The corps fought its way though the Hitler and Gothic Lines, earning a fine reputation but suffering heavy casualties, until it was moved to northwest Europe to participate in the liberation of the Netherlands in the last months of World War II. SEE ALSO: BURNS; FOULKES; ITALIAN CAMPAIGN; MCNAUGHTON.

Fish Creek, Battle of (1885). During the Northwest Rebellion of 1885, units of Major-General Frederick Middleton's militia column moving north along the South Saskatchewan River toward Louis Riel's capital of Batoche came under attack on 24 April. A group of some 150 Metis and native warriors led by Gabriel

Dumont surprised the column at Fish Creek. Using cover to good advantage and firing from trenches dug into a coulee, Dumont's troops fought the larger Canadian force to a standstill with sniper fire from its concealed positions. After a day's fighting, with his ammunition running low and several of his men having deserted, Dumont decided to withdraw. The militia suffered heavy casualties, about one in six of the 300 present, and Middleton withdrew his inexperienced troops to the south, his advance delayed for two weeks. Dumont's men lost four dead. SEE ALSO: DUMONT; MIDDLETON; NORTHWEST REBELLION.

Fisheries Protection Service of Canada (FPS). The Department of Marine and Fisheries, beginning in

Sailors of the Fisheries Protection Service, around 1900 or so, the precursor to Canada's navy.

1870, operated armed schooners to prevent foreign vessels poaching in Canadian waters. The ships were crewed by merchant sailors, some of whom after 1901 received training in gunnery. In 1903–1904, the FPS acquired two steel ships armed with rapid-firing guns, and more crew received rudimentary training on the Canadian Government Ship *Canada*. When the Canadian Naval Service took form in 1910, the vessels of the Fisheries Protection Service transferred to the navy. The director of the Service from 1908, Rear-Admiral Charles Kingsmill, then became director of the naval service. SEE ALSO: KINGSMILL.

Flanders Fields. *See* "IN FLANDERS FIELDS."

Flank Companies. Major-General Isaac Brock faced a difficult task in attempting to defend Upper Canada in the event of a war with the United States. Shortly before the outbreak of the War of 1812, he persuaded the colony's assembly in 1811 to allow him to raise and train two flank companies from each militia regiment, or 2,000 troops, either volunteers or men chosen by ballot. They would serve while most of the colony's personnel reserves, the aptly named Sedentary Militia that trained once per year, stayed home.

Flavelle, Sir Joseph Wesley (1858–1939). Born in Peterborough, Canada, Flavelle made his fortune as president of William Davies Co., a major pork packer, as owner of the Robert Simpson Co., and as a bank chairman. During World War I, he took control of the Canadian munitions industry when it was wracked by scandal and inefficiency, thanks to Minister of Militia and Defence Sir Sam Hughes's lax management and rampant cronyism. The Imperial Munitions Board, as directed by Flavelle, became a huge empire that ran factories, negotiated labour agreements, and effectively had a foreign policy of its own, dealing with Britain and the United States on sales of munitions and supplies. Tough, aggressive, imperious, Flavelle did not receive the credit to which he was entitled other than a baronetcy in 1917; instead, he was damned as the "Baron of Bacon" for the William Davies Co.'s alleged war

profiteering. SEE ALSO: IMPERIAL MUNITIONS BOARD; WAR INDUSTRY.

READING: Michael Bliss, *A Canadian Millionaire: The Life and Business Times of Sir Joseph Flavelle, Bart., 1858–1939* (Toronto, 1992).

Foreign Enlistment Act. Passed into law on 10 April 1937, this act prohibited Canadian citizens from enlisting in the military forces of, or rendering assistance to, the enemies of a friendly foreign state. It allowed the government to apply the act to any case where there was armed conflict, civil or otherwise, although its application to civil wars would prove extremely difficult to interpret. The original measure aimed to prevent Canadian volunteers from fighting in the Spanish Civil War. Thousands served anyway. It was a factor in the personal decisions of many Canadians during the American war in Vietnam, as Vietnam as a whole was considered a friendly state, which technically made Canadians enlisting in US

⬆ Sir Joseph Flavelle.

forces subject to federal prosecution. The act, revised since 1937, remains in force, though it is seldom invoked.

Fort Frontenac. This fort was constructed by Governor Frontenac in 1673 at the mouth of the Cataraqui River near Kingston, Ontario. The French briefly abandoned the fort in 1689 after a siege by the Iroquois, but quickly restored it as a keystone of their power on Lake Ontario. Fort Frontenac served as the arsenal for the French navy at the beginning of the Seven Years' War, but the British captured it in 1758 and garrisoned it as a major base during the War of 1812. It relied on British army heavy artillery and logistical support. The Tete du Pont barracks, built near the fort's site, were used by the Canadian army for staff courses, housed the National Defence College after World War II, and are still used by the Canadian Forces for instructional purposes.

Fort Garry. Built in 1822 at the forks of the Red and Assiniboine Rivers, Lower Fort Garry was a Hudson's Bay Company trading post and the administrative centre of its massive Rupert's Land territory. The fort was located in what is now Winnipeg. It was destroyed by floods in 1826 and rebuilt in stone upriver as Upper Fort Garry. Louis Riel bloodlessly seized Fort Garry during the Red River Rebellion (1870) after the Hudson's Bay Company transferred Rupert's Land to Canada.

Fort George. Located at Niagara-on-the-Lake on the Canadian side of the Niagara River, the fort was built by British engineers between 1796 and 1799 after Jay's Treaty obliged them to withdraw from Fort Niagara on the American side. British forces used the fort as their headquarters on the Niagara Peninsula. The US army took Fort George in May 1813 after a fierce battle during the War of 1812, but the British recaptured it in December and held it for the rest of the war. After the war, Fort George fell into ruins and was not rebuilt until restoration began in the 1930s to convert it into a historic site.

Fort Henry. Built during the War of 1812 to protect the outlet from Lake Ontario to the St Lawrence River, Fort Henry was reconstructed between 1832 and 1837 to defend the Rideau Canal. The fort is a large, star-shaped structure, the largest fortification west of Quebec City, and British regulars garrisoned it until the British army withdrew from Canada in 1871. Canadian troops used the fort for another two decades, but it was abandoned until World Wars I and II when it was used to house prisoners of war. It is now restored as a historic site.

Fort Saint-Jean. The fort was one of five erected by the French in the valley of the Richelieu River in the 1660s to counter Iroquois attacks. The precise location of the first Fort Saint-Jean, built in 1666 and abandoned in 1672, remains unknown. In 1748, engineer Gaspard-Joseph Chaussegros de Léry constructed a new fortification 40 kilometres southeast of Montreal comprising a wooden stockade built on piles, 3.5 to 4 metres tall, flanked by bastions at each corner with firing slits for cannons. The French destroyed the fort just prior to the surrender of New France to the British in 1760, but Governor Guy Carleton ordered it rebuilt in 1775. Almost at once, it was subject to attack by American forces and, after a siege of 45 days that delayed the American advance on Montreal, surrendered. Following the rebellion of 1837–1838, new fortifications were built on the site that, since 1952, have formed part of the Collège militaire royal de Saint-Jean.

Fort York. Constructed in 1793 by Lieutenant-Colonel John Graves Simcoe on the north shore of Lake Ontario on the present site of Toronto, Fort York came under American attack twice during the War of 1812. In 1813, the attackers destroyed the fort and much of the town, though many Americans, including their commander, died when a magazine exploded. Allegedly in retaliation for the sack of York (and other Canadian towns), British troops later burned Washington, DC. A restored Fort York, surrounded by an expressway and new construction, remains as a historic site.

Foulkes, Charles (1903–1969). Born in England, Foulkes came to Canada as a youth, briefly attended the University of Western Ontario, and joined the militia in 1922. He transferred to the Royal Canadian Regiment in the Permanent Force in 1926, served in various posts, and attended the British Army Staff College, but was still a captain on the outbreak of war in 1939. His wartime rise was spectacular. By the time of the invasion of France in June 1944, Foulkes led the 2nd Canadian Infantry Division; during the subsequent campaign, he briefly served as acting commander of II Canadian Corps. Foulkes was not highly esteemed by Lieutenant-General Guy Simonds, II Corps' commander, but was a favorite of Lieutenant-General Harry Crerar, in command of First Canadian Army, a relationship that led to his command of I Canadian Corps in Italy in November 1944. As a lieutenant-general, Foulkes led his

▲ Lieutenant-General Charles Foulkes in 1945.

formation through to the end of the Italian campaign and, after the corps' transfer to northwest Europe, through the liberation of the Netherlands in spring 1945, when he accepted the German surrender in that theatre.

Selected over Simonds (on Crerar's recommendation) to become chief of the general staff at war's end, he presided over the postwar demobilization of the army and then its very substantial strengthening for the Cold War, North Atlantic Treaty Organization (NATO) service, and the Korean War. A skilled political operator, Foulkes became the first chairman of the Chiefs of Staff Committee in 1951, a post he held until resigning in 1960. The most powerful military bureaucrat in the nation's military history, Foulkes played a major role in dealing with the US military and with Canada's NATO allies. He almost single-handedly persuaded Minister of National Defence George Pearkes and the Diefenbaker government to accept the North American Air Defence Agreement in 1957 and to acquire nuclear weapons for Canadian forces in Canada and Europe. These decisions, explicable in light of Cold War realities, caused major difficulties for Diefenbaker. They also set Canada on the path of increasing defence coordination, and continental defence integration, with the United States. SEE ALSO: CLAXTON; DIEFENBAKER; I CANADIAN CORPS; SIMONDS.

READING: Sean Maloney, "General Charles Foulkes: A Primer on How to be CDS," in Bernd Horn and S. Harris, eds., *Warrior Chiefs: Perspectives on Senior Canadian Military Leaders* (Toronto, 2001).

French-Iroquois Wars. Warfare among First Nations in eastern North America was endemic before the arrival of European colonists. Nonetheless, the sporadic small wars that pitted the French against the Iroquois Confederacy through most of the seventeenth century constituted a major challenge to the security of the struggling colony of New France. The Mohawk, Oneida, Onondaga, Cayuga, and Seneca nations actively sought access to fur-trapping areas and fought against other First Nations in order to maintain them. The French, supporting the Huron and Algonquin and advancing their own imperial and commercial interests, found themselves at war and, to help protect their allies and their own settlements, built forts and provided arms.

The Iroquois were fierce fighters and the conflict had many of the trappings of what would later be called total war—the near-total mobilization of resources on both sides for extended periods in order to wage a pitiless campaign against the enemy's home front and armed forces. Iroquois raids destroyed forts, settlements, and enemy encampments, their war parties often killing French missionaries living among their allies. French settlements, in turn, were on a near-constant war footing, with all residents more or less under arms, small stockades or fortified points being erected in many locations as places of refuge in the event of sudden attack. Between 1642 and 1653 especially, the Iroquois laid waste to Huron, Neutral, Abenaki, and other nations before accepting a peace treaty with the French. The peace failed, fighting began anew, and France sent the Carignan-Salières Régiment on punitive expeditions against Mohawk villages. That produced another treaty in 1667 that lasted more than a dozen years, but war flared up again in 1680 and was subsumed in a larger Anglo-French conflict, culminating in a major Iroquois raid on Lachine in 1689. The inevitable French reaction resulted in Count Frontenac's last sorties against the Iroquois. Not until the Great Peace of 1701 did the Iroquois finally agree to remain neutral in the struggle between Britain and France for control of North America. SEE ALSO: DOLLARD DES ORMEAUX; FRONTENAC.

French Language Units (FLUs). In 1968, Minister of National Defence Léo Cadieux won Cabinet authority to designate some units in the newly-unified Canadian Forces (CF) as French Language Units in an effort to retain francophone personnel and improve recruiting. NCSM *Ottawa* was the first FLU, followed by the air force's No. 433 Squadron. One-third of the Canadian Airborne Regiment was also designated and, after 1969, the Ve Brigade at Valcartier, Quebec, was the largest French-speaking formation. The language question continued to

bedevil the CF which, in 1988, adopted a universal approach to bilingualism—everyone was to be bilingual. After this inevitably failed, in 2008 the CF adopted a functional approach with language determined by the function and location of a unit. Units are now designated English Language, French Language, or Bilingual, and serve "clients" appropriately. All senior officers must be bilingual in order to achieve promotion, a requirement that is sometimes followed in theory alone. SEE ALSO: ALLARD; BILINGUALISM IN THE CANADIAN FORCES; QUEBEC AND THE MILITARY.

Frenchman's Butte, Battle of (1885). On 28 May 1885 during the Northwest Rebellion, soldiers from Major-General Thomas B. Strange's militia column confronted some 200 native warriors, most from Big Bear's band but led by war chief Wandering Spirit, dug in at Frenchman's Butte, some 45 kilometres northwest of present-day Lloydminster. Strange had 300 soldiers and one cannon, but the natives' rifle fire from their superior positions pinned down his men and prevented a Canadian attempt to outflank their positions. Fearing he might be surrounded, Strange withdrew without having sustained any casualties. Big Bear surrendered on 2 July and was sentenced to a jail term; Wandering Spirit was executed. SEE ALSO: BIG BEAR; NORTHWEST REBELLION.

Frigates. Late in 1940, the Royal Navy called for a ship that could protect convoys in mid-ocean against U-boats, a task the corvette was not intended to fulfill. The frigate, originally known as a twin-screw corvette, was larger with longer range and, in World War II, the Royal Canadian Navy (RCN) eventually operated ten British-built and 60 Canadian-built *River* class frigates. They entered service in 1943–1944 and became the mainstay of the RCN. In the early 1950s, the RCN modernized the 21 frigates that then remained in service until the late 1960s. In 1977, in the aftermath of the Defence Structure Review, planning began for a wholly new frigate with advanced anti-submarine warfare and anti-aircraft capabilities, a class capable of playing a decisive role in any conflict at sea with increasingly

The Canadian navy has a dozen *Halifax* class frigates, modern, powerful ships that play a multiplicity of roles. HMCS *Ville de Québec*, shown here, has been part of the fleet since 1993.

effective Soviet air and naval forces. In 1983, the government placed contracts for six ships and, in 1987, for six more *Halifax* class frigates; the first, HMCS *Halifax*, came into service in 1992. The ships, much bigger than *River* class ships or wartime destroyers, displaced 4,750 tonnes, could make 31 knots and travel as far as 7,100 nautical miles without refuelling, and had a crew of 229. The frigates carried a helicopter, had an anti-submarine role, carried anti-air and anti-ship missiles, and were armed with a 57mm deck gun and a 20mm Phalanx close-in weapon system. The *Halifax* frigates remain the Canadian navy's main vessels. The Harper government has provided $3.1 billion in mid-life modernization and service life extension projects.

Front de Libération du Québec (FLQ). The FLQ was a terrorist organization organized in cells that aimed to "free" Quebec from Canada by fomenting a violent revolution. Small in number, the FLQ's members began their campaign by blowing up mailboxes and attacking federal institutions, perpetrating hundreds of small attacks. Police investigations broke up the organization, but new recruits managed to keep the FLQ alive. In October 1970, the FLQ kidnapped James Cross, the British trade commissioner in Montreal, and another cell then kidnapped and murdered Pierre Laporte, Quebec's labour minister. The so-called October Crisis led Pierre Trudeau's federal government to invoke the War Measures Act, intervening with troops in Quebec and temporarily suspending civil liberties. Initial public revulsion at the murder and kidnappings eventually turned to concern that Ottawa had overreacted. The FLQ did not revive after the crisis. SEE ALSO: OCTOBER CRISIS; TRUDEAU; WAR MEASURES ACT.

Frontenac, Louis de Buade de Frontenac et de Palluau (1622–1698). A soldier, Frontenac secured appointment as governor general of New France in 1672. Quickly grasping the western fur trade's potential profitability, he established Fort Frontenac on Lake Ontario with a view to expanding the colony's influence. Putting up small forts to the west and south put Frontenac in conflict with the powerful Iroquois, who had expansionist aims of their own. He also faced difficulties with cautious politicians in Paris who worried that he might bring France into conflict with England and its colonies farther south, and who fretted over his wrangling with other colonial officials. They recalled Frontenac in 1682, and he did not return to New France until 1689, this time with orders to fight the Iroquois who had attacked the settlement at Lachine in force. Frontenac's attack on towns in New York led to confrontations with the English and Sir William Phips's attack on Quebec in 1690. Frontenac faced down this assault, and a guerilla war with the Iroquois followed. In 1696, now very old, he led a full-scale campaign against the Iroquois, burning villages and crops. By 1698, the Iroquois, their strength worn down by years of incessant fighting, sued for peace. Plagued by charges that he was subsidizing his fur trade activities with military funds, Frontenac died before he could be recalled again to France. He was unquestionably the driving force in the consolidation of seventeenth-century New France. SEE ALSO: FRENCH-IROQUOIS WARS.

READING: William Eccles, *Frontenac: The Courtier Governor* (Toronto, 1959).

▲ Count Frontenac as imagined in 1890.

Garrisons, British. After New France fell to Britain in 1763, the captured territory needed to be garrisoned, first to keep the French Canadians in check, and second to guard against increasingly restive American colonists. Major garrisons at Halifax, Quebec City, Montreal, Kingston, York, London, Amherstburg, and later at Esquimalt amounted in all to about 7,000, except in times of crisis. In each location, the presence of British troops had important effects—by attracting commerce and spending money on local goods, by building roads, ports, or canals, and by settling with their families on adjacent land during or after their military service. In some areas, notably Quebec City and Montreal, the redcoats were sometimes the unwelcome reminders of historical outcomes the locals would have preferred to forget; in others, they were a stabilizing presence essential to the development of secure trade, the maintenance of peace, and the deterrence of crime. Garrisons aided local political authorities in times of trouble as well, and were as often turned on troublesome workers or local hooligans as on American adventurers or invading rebels. Palpable tensions between local militia leaders and snooty garrison commanders often clouded the obvious: that British regulars were British North America's only real line of defence against any serious military threat. Troop levels increased in times of trouble or outright attack, but were drawn down as soon as decently possible thereafter, the army's globe-trotting regiments then shipping out to home, the Caribbean, India, or wherever else the Union Jack was temporarily in jeopardy.

Permanent garrisons were expensive as standing forces and dangerous for the promises of future support they seemed to imply to local rulers in the far-flung corners of the Empire. If Canada was attacked by Russia, France, or the United States, would London send 10,000 troops, or 100,000, to join the few dispersed garrisons already on hand that would be wrangling local militia forces in mounting a probably forlorn defence? The growing population and economic strength of the larger colonies made many in Britain question the rationale of its own forces acting as the over-the-horizon reinforcement pool for prosperous polities that were or should be, more or less, allies.

The doubt was especially acute for Canada, which faced not some minor local potentate but an increasingly powerful American goliath. The War of 1812 had been a near-run thing. Could Britain, Canada, and a cobbled together coalition of First Nations allies ever repeat it? The American Civil War saw Union (Northern) power grow by leaps and bounds, at first convincing Britain that diplomatic recognition for the rebellious Confederate (Southern) power would be foolhardy, and later implanting firmly the idea that a successful defence against what might in a crisis amount to hundreds of thousands of battle-hardened American troops was a fantasy-turned-nightmare. British wobbliness on the subject of defending Canada against American depredations was not the only factor leading to imperial support for Confederation and the downsizing of British military obligations in North America, but it was far from unimportant. By 1867, a new nation had sprouted on Washington's northern frontier, one from which Britain's military presence was fast retreating, the redcoats' role in quashing Fenian renegades and Manitoba rebels notwithstanding. By 1871, all the troops had departed except for those at Halifax and Esquimalt, and they too were gone in 1905–1906. Britain might still come to Canada in some future hour of need, but what of Canada's now assisting

Britain? For a half-century and more after Confederation, this would be a principal tenet of Canadian military affairs—whether and by how much the colony should support the mother country, in South Africa, in Europe, in the Mediterranean, or in the provision of ships and other forms of support to British interests. In two world wars, Canadian troops would help to garrison Britain. British aircrew would train in Canada in the twentieth century, and army units would use Canadian territory for brigade-size exercises for most of the Cold War, but the age of the garrisons had long past. SEE ALSO: CANADA–UNITED KINGDOM DEFENCE RELATIONS.

READING: J.M. Hitsman, *Safeguarding Canada 1763–1871* (Toronto, 1968).

Gas Warfare. The use of poison gas by German forces at the second battle of Ypres in April 1915 caught its Allied victims by surprise. French colonial troops, its first targets, retreated in disorder after suffering heavy casualties. The ground-hugging chlorine, released from cylinders that had been hauled to the front and carried by the wind toward the Allied lines, seeped into trenches and firing positions clogged with waiting troops, eating at the lung tissue of soldiers unprotected by any form of anti-gas device. As wretched, choking waves of Algerians and Moroccans stumbled toward the rear, the success of the assault caught both sides by surprise. German units moved slowly forward to consolidate on the old French positions and to probe the gap created in the Allied lines; the Canadian Division's troops shifted left to protect their flank and prevent a wider break through, launching several determined but costly counterattacks. Two days later, now defending an exposed salient, the Canadians were hit by gas as well. Just days after its first widespread use, the new weapon was no longer a surprise, but it was a gruesome, frightening weapon against which no Allied troops at the time had an effective defence, save for the unreliability of the weapon itself. It was utterly dependent on wind speed and direction, and therefore a great danger to the side that used it, and it persisted on the battlefield, infecting trenches and shell holes

that were the objectives of attacking troops. The Canadians suffered 6,000 casualties in holding tenaciously to most of their positions, but a new and fearsome weapon had joined the war.

All sides would use it. Using canisters at first, and later shells, and with ever-more sophisticated chemical compounds, every major belligerent proceeded to violate the Hague Convention by using poison gas as a weapon of war. Massive British shell production began in 1916, despite the ambiguous results of their own use of gas in offensive operations, while gas training schools, special gas combat detachments, and gas medical units proliferated along the front. Like other armies, the Canadian Corps protected its soldiers with increasingly sophisticated gas masks and breathing devices (for soldiers and for horses), and developed the medical and rehabilitative procedures to treat gas casualties during and after battle. The Canadian Corps Gas Services, established in May 1916, was an indication of the extent to which gas weapons, and protection from them, had become a normal part of military doctrine by the middle of the war. In Canadian use, gas became principally a weapon for counter-battery work, fired by the artillery at enemy gun positions to render them inoperable for the duration of an attack, suppressing them, in effect, by spreading poisonous fumes in and around the gun line. By the battle of Amiens in August 1918, 20 percent of the shells fired in counter-battery work by Canadian units were gas shells, which were also used extensively to fire ahead of a captured position, screening it from counterattack. As the German experience had revealed in 1915, gas was at least as good at denying an enemy the ability to occupy or pass through an area of ground as it was in actually killing enemy troops.

Most major powers continued to develop gas weapons—as well as deadlier nerve agents—in the interwar period, and all prepared to defend against them, but the combined horror of chemical weapons and their dubious tactical advantages contributed to their rarely being used during World War II. Japanese forces used chemical weapons in China, as did the Italians in Abyssinia in the 1930s. They were also deployed by Allied and Axis forces to the fighting

First used in World War I, gas warfare was more terrifying than militarily effective, especially as both sides improved their countermeasures and developed better defensive equipment. Here, German prisoners assist Canadian wounded from the battle of Amiens in August 1918 to the rear, all but one wearing masks.

fronts as a possible retaliatory weapon, but never fired. At the end of the war, many chemical weapons were dumped at sea by Allied warships, including some by Canadian vessels off Canada's East Coast. Canadian wartime chemical weapons research was concentrated at an experimental station established in Suffield, Alberta, in 1941, originally as a British scientific facility operated by the Canadian Army, but run after the war entirely by Canada. Chemical and other types of weapons research continued there afterwards, making Suffield—which remains an advanced research facility—a principal focus of protest by disarmament and peace groups. Among the subjects of postwar research was the airborne deployment of chemical defoliants, used widely by US forces during the Vietnam War; the testing of the most famous of these, Agent Orange (as well as other dioxin-based sprays), at Canadian Forces Base Gagetown, New Brunswick, during the 1960s would be revealed publicly 40 years later, prompting civil litigation against the Department of National Defence for medical ailments allegedly caused by the toxins.

Canada continues to conduct research on anti-gas and chemical weapons defences but maintains no such weapons of its own, save those used for research purposes. It is a signatory to the Chemical Weapons Convention, which it ratified in 1995. Older stocks of Cold War–era chemical weapons have now been safely destroyed. Chemical (and nuclear and biological) countermeasures remain regular parts of military training, and terrorists have used lethal gas in mass civilian attacks. During the Gulf War (1991), Iraqi forces possessed vast chemical weapons stockpiles that Iraqi leader Saddam Hussein regularly threatened to use, and Canadian and other coalition troops carried NBC (nuclear-biological-chemical) protective clothing to guard against them. Despite several false alarms, no chemical attack ever came. Civilian police forces, paramilitaries, and counter-terrorist forces maintain limited stockpiles of non-lethal gas for use in selected emergencies.

READING: Tim Cook, *No Place to Run: The Canadian Corps and Gas Warfare in the First World War* (Vancouver, 1999).

Gays and Lesbians in the Canadian Forces. Before 1988, homosexuals had been barred from military service, a legal fiction borne of societal norms that had never prevented them entirely from serving, and many had, often at great personal risk and under conditions of overt harassment. The Charter of Rights and Freedoms and the Canadian Human Rights Act made discrimination against gays and lesbians illegal and, in October 1992, the Federal Court ruled that barring homosexuals from the Canadian Forces (CF) violated the Charter. The chief of the defence staff then said that "inappropriate sexual conduct by members of the forces, whether heterosexual or homosexual" would not be tolerated. A study in 2000 found that the Canadian Forces' policy was working: it was "not universally embraced" but did appear to be "universally accepted." From 2005, CF chaplains performed same-sex marriages on military bases, and Palm Centre, a California gay issues think tank, said Canadian Forces policy led those of the 25 nations that permitted gays and lesbians to serve. SEE ALSO: SEXUAL DISCRIMINATION.

READING: G. Kinsman and P. Gentile, *The Canadian War on Queers: National Security as Sexual Regulation* (Vancouver, 2010).

Generals, World War I. In a recent study of the general officers of the Canadian Corps, Patrick Brennan noted that of the 48 who led Canadians from mid-1916 to the end of the war, seven were British regulars. Of the 41 remaining, three-quarters were Canadian-born with an average year of birth of 1873 and an average age at war's end of 42. There were only three francophones; only two of the English-speaking were Roman Catholics, while some 62 percent were Anglican. All the general officers had prewar military experience—nine in the Permanent Force, 27 in the militia, and a dozen had Boer War service. Most were middle class by origin and in their prewar lives: 12 were from the professions, many were in business, and only two were farmers. One was killed in action, one taken prisoner; another was killed after transferring to the British army. Some won promotion on merit, some by Minister of Militia and Defence Sir Sam Hughes's patronage, some by both.

It is striking that the key staff positions overseas were filled by British officers. The Canadian Corps' brigadier-general, general staff, the senior planner, was always a British regular. The deputy adjutant and quartermaster general, the corps' logistician, was British through to the end of the war; so too was the commander of heavy artillery until 21 October 1918. The general officer commanding the Canadian Corps was British until Arthur Currie took over in June 1917; the first commander of the Canadian Division was British, again until Currie took over in September 1915. A British officer commanded the Canadian Cavalry Brigade for most of the war and several infantry brigade commanders were British. The Canadian generals seem to have done well by learning how to command when in command; they could not have managed, however, without staff officers and other senior colleagues from the British army.

The corps' commanders were Generals E.A.H. Alderson and Julian Byng, both British regulars, and Currie. The 1st Division's commanders were Alderson, Currie, and A.C. Macdonell. The 2nd Division's commanders were Sam Steele, R.E.W. Turner, and H.E. Burstall. The 3rd Division's were M.S. Mercer, killed on 2 June 1916; L.J. Lipsett, killed while later commanding a British division; and F.O.W. Loomis. David Watson led the 4th Division.

In Canada, the chief of the general staff was Major-General W.G. Gwatkin; four general officers in turn filled the post of adjutant general, two the post of quartermaster general, and two served as master general of the ordnance. In Britain, the chief of the general staff of Canadian Forces to the end of the war was General Turner and the adjutant general was P.E. Thacker. Two officers filled the post of quartermaster general and four, one of whom was a colonel, the director general of medical services. A table of all senior appointments can be found in Appendix A to G.W.L. Nicholson, *The Canadian Expeditionary Force, 1914–1919*. For a nation that had scarcely any trained military at all at the beginning of the war, the Canadian Army was well served by its senior commanders. SEE ALSO: CANADIAN CORPS; CANADIAN EXPEDITIONARY FORCE.

READING: Patrick Brennan, "Byng's and Currie's Commanders," *Canadian Military History* (Spring 2002); G.W.L. Nicholson, *The Canadian Expeditionary Force, 1914–1919* (Ottawa, 1962).

Generals, World War II. Canada had 68 officers who held the rank of major-general or higher in World War II. Of those, 53 were born in Canada, 11 in Britain, and three in British colonies or to officers on imperial service. Only seven were Roman Catholic and only six were francophone. Relatively few of the generals—only 21—had university degrees, though many, like Harry Crerar, E.L.M. Burns, Guy Simonds, and Christopher Vokes, had graduated from the Royal Military College, which did not offer degrees until well after the war. Most were born in the 1880s; just two were born after 1910. Of the 68, 39 came from the Permanent Force (PF) and 22 from the infantry. But those data include all the senior officers, not only those who led troops in the field. The typical battlefield general was a PF captain or major in his mid-thirties at the beginning of the war with ten to fifteen years' service, likely including a stint at the British Army Staff College. A few were not typical—those officers from the militia who rose to command divisions in the field, such as Bert Hoffmeister, Bruce Matthews, and Holly Keefler.

In the first years of the war, all the division, corps, and army commanders (except for Simonds and C.R.S. Stein) based in Britain had served in the 1914 war and were mostly in their fifties. Senior British officers such as Bernard Montgomery thought their age and lack of training disqualified them from field command in high tempo warfare. Andrew McNaughton, successively the commander of the 1st Canadian Division, I Canadian Corps, and First Canadian Army, had ability, but British generals were not impressed with his performance on exercises, his choice of subordinates, and his nationalism. His successor in command of First Canadian Army was the politically astute H.D.G. Crerar who had initially impressed British commanders but who, by late 1943, had fallen afoul of Montgomery.

I Canadian Corps' commanders in Britain were McNaughton and Crerar; the commander of II Canadian Corps was E.W. Sansom. 1st Canadian Division's commanders in Britain were McNaughton, George Pearkes, VC, and H.L.N. Salmon, the officer killed in an aircraft crash on his way to be briefed on the Sicily invasion where he was to command his division; 2nd Division's were Victor Odlum, Crerar, J.H. Roberts, Simonds, and E.L.M. Burns; 3rd Division's were Sansom and C.B. Price; 4th Armoured's were L.F. Page and F.F. Worthington, the latter the "father" of the Armoured Corps; and 5th Armoured's were Sansom and Stein.

Few of these officers could be considered unqualified successes. Sansom, Pearkes, Odlum, and Price all drew British scorn. Page and Worthington were replaced because of their age. Roberts, who had commanded the 2nd Division at Dieppe, was, in effect, made the scapegoat for the disaster of August 1942, though his relief came some time later. Stein inexplicably rose to command a division and, clearly in over his head, was relieved quickly.

Canada's operational commanders at army and corps level all had spent the early war years in Britain in training. Harry Crerar was the only commander to lead First Canadian Army in its operations in northwest Europe, though Guy Simonds ably filled in for him when he fell ill. In Italy, I Canadian Corps was briefly led by Crerar, then by E.L.M. Burns who directed operations against the Hitler and Gothic Lines with success but was nonetheless relieved of command because of his inability to get on with his superiors and subordinates. His successor, Charles Foulkes, had his own personality and command defects, but was a brilliant army politician who capped his war by taking the German surrender in the Netherlands and then becoming the postwar chief of the general staff in Ottawa. Guy Simonds led II Canadian Corps in northwest Europe with great success and had the high regard of British and American commanders, the sole Canadian who did. He was a difficult subordinate, however, and he and Crerar did not get on. The division commanders on operations, all younger men, were: 1st Canadian Infantry Division, Simonds, Christopher Vokes, and Harry Foster; 2nd Canadian Infantry Division, Foulkes and Matthews; 3rd Canadian Infantry Division, Rod Keller, D.C. Spry, and Keefler; 4th Canadian Armoured Division, George Kitching, Foster, and Vokes; and 5th Canadian Armoured Division, Simonds, Burns, and Hoffmeister, the latter arguably the best field commander the army produced. Except for the three militia officers named above, all came from the PF.

In Britain, the key staff appointment was the senior combatant officer (until 1943), a position held by Crerar and then P.J. Montague, the only militia officer to reach the rank of lieutenant-general in World War II. The post's title changed later in the war to the chief of staff, Canadian Military Headquarters. Kenneth Stuart, who had been chief of the general staff in Ottawa and later took the blame for the reinforcements shortage in 1944, filled it for some time, followed by Montague.

In Canada, the chief of the general staff was the army's lead appointment. The incumbents were T.V. Anderson, Crerar, Stuart, and J.C. Murchie, all Permanent Force officers. There was also an array of senior staff officers, a mix of regulars and militia. (Their titles and names are listed in Appendix F of C.P. Stacey, Six Years of War.) Home defence divisions were led by militia officers: 6th Division, A.E. Potts and H.N. Ganong; 7th Division, P.E. Leclerc, the only francophone to command a division; and 8th Division, Ganong. All these officers had served in Britain before being returned to Canada to take up their commands. The commanders of Atlantic Command were W.H.P. Elkins and L.F. Page; of Pacific Command, R.O. Alexander, Pearkes, and Worthington. All were Permanent Force officers.

The remarkable point is that Canada's tiny Permanent Force and ill-equipped, ill-trained interwar militia produced officers who could command an army, two corps, and five divisions in operations with competence. There were failures, officers who had to be relieved of their posts, but that was true in every other army as well. More impressive were the successes. Crerar was no Napoleon, nor a Patton, a Rommel, or an Eisenhower, but he led First Canadian Army very creditably. Simonds was a master planner and an innovative thinker and tactician. Matthews, a militia artillery officer, and Hoffmeister, a militia infantry officer, were probably the two best division commanders, able men who planned carefully, led by example, and cared for their troops. As in World War I, Canada was well served by its generals. SEE ALSO: CRERAR; FOULKES; MCNAUGHTON; MILITIA; PERMANENT FORCE; SIMONDS.

READING: J. L. Granatstein, The Generals: The Canadian Army's Senior Commanders in the Second World War (Toronto, 1993); C.P. Stacey, Six Years of War (Ottawa, 1955).

Goddard, Nichola Kathleen Sarah (1980–2006). The first Canadian female combat soldier to be killed in action, the first Canadian woman to be killed by enemy action since World War II, Captain Nichola Goddard died near Panjwai, Afghanistan, on 17 May 2006, four years to the day after her graduation from the Royal Military College. Born in Papua, New Guinea, where her father was a teacher, Goddard was a member of the 1st Regiment, Royal Canadian Horse Artillery, serving as a forward observation officer with the 1st Battalion of the Princess Patricia's Canadian Light Infantry. Lieutenant-Colonel Ian Hope, the commander of Task Force Orion in which she served, described her leadership as "a superb mix of cheerfulness and competence." She died when two Taliban rocket-propelled grenades struck her armoured vehicle.

▲ Captain Nichola Goddard, Kandahar, 2006.

Captain Goddard was buried in the National Military Cemetery in Ottawa and awarded a posthumous Meritorious Service Medal. Goddard's husband, Jason Beam, was the first widower to receive the Silver Cross, hitherto presented only to mothers or widows of Canadian war dead. SEE ALSO: AFGHANISTAN WAR.

Gothic Line. Extending across Italy from La Spezia in the west to Pesaro on the Adriatic, the Gothic Line was German Field Marshal Albert Kesselring's last major defensive line in northern Italy. The Germans retreated to the Gothic Line after the fall of Rome on 5 June 1944 and made it into a formidable barrier of carefully sited concrete bunkers, mines, artillery, and machine-gun nests protected by belts of barbed wire and the difficult mountainous terrain of the Appenines. In August, the British Eighth Army moved to the Adriatic coast and prepared to breach the line, the central task falling to I Canadian Corps commanded by

Lieutenant-General E.L.M. Burns. The surprise attack on 25–26 August, based on information Major-General Bert Hoffmeister, commander of 5th Canadian Armoured Division, had uncovered on a reconnaissance, caught the Germans napping and pressed them back to their main defensive works. Another assault on 30 August had driven them a further 24 kilometres north by 3 September, forcing the enemy, all too often the tough soldiers of the German 1st Parachute Division, back to their third defensive line. It took three weeks of hard fighting for the Canadians to push beyond the last mountain defences and to liberate Rimini on 21 September, making the Gothic Line battles arguably the most significant Canadian military victory of World War II. The attack northwards beyond the German lines stalled, a result of rain and mud and the brilliant defensive tactics of Kesselring's soldiers. The cost to the Canadians was heavy: 4,511 casualties in action and another 1,005 evacuated because of illness or battle exhaustion. Although Burns's men had won the victory, he was sacked the next month. SEE ALSO: BURNS; I CANADIAN CORPS; ITALIAN CAMPAIGN.

READING: Mark Zuehlke, *The Gothic Line: Canada's Month of Hell in World War II Italy* (Vancouver, 2003).

Gouzenko, Igor Sergeyevich (1919–1982). An officer in the Red Army working at the Soviet Union's embassy in Ottawa, Gouzenko had the task of coding messages. He defected on 5 September 1945, carrying with him substantial information that proved that Soviet military intelligence (GRU) was running spy rings in Canada, and he also knew details of some operations in the United States. After some difficulty in persuading Canadian officials to believe him, he and his family were hidden away, and eventually a 1946 Royal Commission investigated his allegations. The British and American governments followed closely the unfolding case, and Gouzenko's information fuelled the suspicion quickly hardening into the Cold War. He lived under another identity for the rest of his life, later writing a memoir and a novel. SEE ALSO: COLD WAR.

READING: Amy Knight, *How the Cold War Began* (Toronto, 2005).

Great Peace of Montreal. After a century of recurring warfare, France and some 40 First Nations negotiated a treaty on 4 August 1701 and began five decades of peace. There had been a treaty between France and the Iroquois in 1700, but the French aimed for a more comprehensive pact. Some 1,300 Iroquoian envoys (and several hundred First Nations warriors who were allies of the French) then came to Montreal in the summer of 1701 and, after much ceremony and discussion, achieved the Great Peace. The Iroquois, battered by Frontenac's campaigns against them and weakened terribly by disease, secured the right to trade on equal terms with the French and English and to have access to hunting grounds north of Lake Ontario. The French and their native allies secured their communities against attack by the fierce and militarily capable Iroquois, without hindering colonial expansion into non-Iroquoian territory. The treaty also represented the acknowledgement by New France of the sovereignty and political rights of First Nations signatories, the diplomatic power of the Aboriginal peoples, and the growing military strength of New France. SEE ALSO: FRENCH-IROQUOIS WARS; FRONTENAC.

READING: Gilles Havard, *The Great Peace of Montreal of 1701: French-Native Diplomacy of the Seventeenth Century* (Montreal, translated, 2001).

Gulf War (1990–1991). In response to Iraq's invasion of Kuwait on 1 August 1990, the United States organized an international coalition, including European and Middle Eastern countries, to force Iraqi dictator Saddam Hussein to retreat. Prime Minister Brian Mulroney joined many other world leaders in condemning the invasion, offering Canadian naval assistance to the US-led naval blockade in the Persian Gulf. Three old destroyers (HMCS *Athabaskan*, *Restigouche*, and *Terra Nova*) and

▲ Canada played a small role in the Gulf War that liberated Kuwait in 1991. This Canadian military hospital was one piece of the Canadian Forces' contribution.

a supply ship (*Protecteur*) hurriedly prepared for service and sailed on 24 August. The small task group handled more than a quarter of the naval interceptions by the multinational fleet and, after the coalition struck back at Iraq in January 1991, the Canadians directed a multinational Combat Logistics Force comprised of ships from ten navies. The army, however, was in such a decayed state that it could not provide a credible force for Gulf War service, not even from the under-strength brigade in Europe with the North Atlantic Treaty Organization (NATO). The government offered a CF-18 fighter squadron on 14 September, which flew patrols over the naval blockade beginning 8 October. The coalition sent its aircraft and troops against Saddam in January 1991. The Canadian fighters were not initially allowed to participate, though they could provide air cover after 1 February and attack ground targets from 24 February. Canada had also agreed to send a field hospital on 24 January.

The Iraqis folded quickly with heavy casualties. Coalition losses were few, and there were no Canadian casualties. The war revealed the parlous state of the Canadian Forces, the continued utility of maintaining a capable navy, and the growing requirements for transportation and logistical support for units deployed outside the confines of the traditional NATO area as part of coalition actions. The war, fought under United Nations auspices, nevertheless sparked the usual political scuffles in Canada over its defence relationship with Washington, militarism, peace, and the balance in Ottawa's Middle East diplomacy between Israel (against which Iraq launched missile attacks during the conflict) and the Arab states. It also marked the onset of more than 20 years of Canadian military deployments to the Persian Gulf and Indian Ocean region. SEE ALSO: ALLIANCES, CANADIAN; CANADA–UNITED STATES DEFENCE RELATIONS; MULRONEY.

READING: Jean H. Morin and Richard H. Gimblett, *Operation Friction: The Canadian Forces in the Persian Gulf, 1990–1991* (Toronto, 1997).

Sir Willoughby Gwatkin as chief of the general staff, 1918.

Gwatkin, Sir Willoughby Garnons (1859–1925). Born in England, Gwatkin joined the British army in 1882. He served in Canada from 1905 to 1909 as director of operations and staff duties at militia headquarters. Seconded permanently to Ottawa in 1911 as a colonel, he drew up the mobilization plan for raising an expeditionary force for overseas service, the plan later scrapped by Minister of Militia and Defence Sam Hughes at the outbreak of World War I. Gwatkin became chief of the general staff (CGS) in 1913 and had the complex task of dealing with Hughes, mobilizing the huge Canadian Expeditionary Force, eventually enlisting conscripts, and planning for repatriation and demobilization. He retired as CGS in 1920 and then became an air vice-marshal and inspector general of the new Canadian Air Force before retiring in 1922. SEE ALSO: HUGHES; MOBILIZATION; WORLD WAR I.

Haida, HMCS. The last survivor of the 27 *Tribal* class destroyers built for Britain, Australia, and Canada during World War II, *Haida* was commissioned into the Royal Canadian Navy (RCN) in August 1943 and put to sea under Commander Harry DeWolf. The ship served as an escort on Murmansk convoys, then made its reputation in the months before and after the D-Day invasion of 6 June 1944, working against German E-boats and destroyers in the English Channel and French coastal waters. *Haida* destroyed 14 vessels, including two destroyers, a U-boat, a minesweeper, and other small craft, and took part in the rescue of survivors from HMCS *Athabaskan*, her sister ship, sunk on 28 April 1944. After World War II, the destroyer underwent conversion to an anti-submarine warfare destroyer, served two tours during the Korean War from 1952 to 1954, and remained in RCN service until 1963. The decommissioned *Haida* then went on display

⌃ The most famous Canadian warship, HMCS *Haida* established its reputation in 1944 under Commander Harry DeWolf. Pictured here after the war, *Haida* is now berthed in Hamilton harbour.

at the Toronto waterfront, where it was a main attraction of the Ontario Place amusement park until 2002. Purchased by Parks Canada and substantially restored to her appearance in the period from roughly 1949 to 1951, *Haida* now floats in Hamilton harbour as a National Historic Site. See also: Destroyers, Tribal Class; DeWolf.

Haldimand, Sir Frederick (1718–1791). Born in Switzerland, Haldimand served in the Prussian and Dutch armies until 1756, when he transferred to the British army. He served against the French during the Seven Years' War and became military governor of Trois-Rivières from 1762 to 1763. After years of service in Florida and the Thirteen Colonies, London named him Governor of Quebec in 1777, a post he held through the American Revolution. His task was to hold Quebec, and he worked hard to prevent French Canadians from siding with the Americans and their French allies. After the British defeat in 1783 and the independence of the United States, he had responsibility for settling Mohawks and United Empire Loyalists on British territory, a task he handled well despite constant allegations (as he had faced since 1756) that, as a Swiss, his loyalty was less than certain. See also: Seven Years' War.

Halifax. Founded in 1749, Halifax was a British military and naval base of great importance during the colonial conflicts that ended in the defeat and occupation of New France, and during the American Revolution that soon followed. Canada assumed responsibility for the city's defences in 1906, and in both world wars and the Cold War, Halifax would be a principal naval base, a logistical and command centre, a training establishment, and a major convoy assembly point. The Royal Canadian Navy used Halifax as its main East Coast port from its founding in 1910. The city suffered horrific damage as a result of the 1917 Halifax Explosion. In May 1945, the end of World War II sparked an infamous riot in which disgruntled sailors and others ran roughshod through the downtown core, damaging businesses and fighting with military police and shore patrols. Halifax remains the home port for the Canadian navy's East Coast fleet of nearly 20 vessels, and—by military population—the country's largest military establishment. See also: Citadel, Halifax; Halifax Explosion; Halifax Riot.

Halifax Explosion (1917). On 6 December 1917, the Norwegian ship *Imo*, carrying relief supplies for Belgium, collided with the French munitions ship *Mont Blanc* in The Narrows of Halifax harbour at 8:40 a.m. Some 25 minutes later, the French vessel's cargo of 2,750 tonnes of explosives ignited, producing the greatest man-made explosion in history to that time. A major convoy port and naval base in World War I, Halifax was devastated. Approximately 1.3 square kilometres in the north end of the city had been virtually levelled by the blast and by the fires that swept through the ruins. Across the harbour, Dartmouth was also hit hard. The sound of the blast could be heard as far away as Prince Edward Island. The cold and snow of a hard winter compounded the survivors' suffering. The toll was horrific: close to 1,500 dead at once and another 500 in the days that followed, along with 9,000 injured out of an urban population of approximately 50,000; 13,500 buildings destroyed or badly damaged; and the cost of the destruction an estimated $35 million. Relief efforts initially had to be improvised with intact hospitals jammed and doctors' offices full of the wounded, but soon help from across eastern Canada and New England poured in, amounting in all to $30 million. The city's reconstruction was aided by the Halifax Relief Commission, incorporated in April 1918, which continued in operation until June 1976. Rumours of sabotage remain unproven to this day; the young Royal Canadian Navy, responsible for movement control and ship inspections in Halifax's fiercely busy harbour, took the blame. Naval operations resumed soon afterwards.

Reading: John G. Armstrong, *The Halifax Explosion and the Royal Canadian Navy: Inquiry and Intrigue* (Vancouver, 2002).

Soldiers search for survivors in Halifax, Nova Scotia, after a massive explosion in December 1917 left 2,000 people dead, 9,000 injured, and much of the city in ruins.

Halifax Riot (1945). On VE Day, 8 May 1945, the people of Halifax set out to celebrate the end of World War II in Europe. Businesses, restaurants, stores, and taverns closed, some because their employees left to take the day off, whether authorized or not. Neither civil nor military authorities had planned much for the historic occasion, and the result was chaos. On leave and with nothing to eat or drink, soldiers, airmen, sailors, and female service personnel attacked and sacked Keith's Brewery and raided government liquor outlets, taking an estimated 65,000 bottles. The crowd, now well lubricated and out of control, began to trash downtown shops, restaurants, and taverns, strewing broken glass and shop contents across teeming streets from which all order had disappeared. There was fighting, rape, and widespread destruction of property; soon, three rioters were dead and 200 more were under arrest.

The lack of victory planning by military or civil authorities was a convenient scapegoat for deeper issues. Halifax had been a city of 65,000 civilians in 1939 that had 60,000 service personnel added to it during the war. Rents soared, amenities grew scarce, liquor was expensive and hard to acquire under primitive consumption laws, and gouging landlords and shopkeepers who preyed on service personnel became objects of ridicule and the focus of growing hatred. Through a long war in a bustling, expensive, and sometimes unfriendly city, resentments festered. The riot was, in part, the sailors' way of striking back. Several of the arrested received lengthy prison terms, a government inquiry blamed poor discipline in the Royal Canadian Navy, and Rear-Admiral Leonard Murray, in command, unjustly took the rap.

READING: Stanley Redman, *Open Gangway: The (Real) Story of the Halifax Navy Riot* (Hantsport, NS, 1981).

Harkness, Douglas Scott (1903–1999). Born in Toronto, Harkness farmed and taught school in Alberta until World War II when he served overseas, winning

▲ Servicemen and women rioted in Halifax on VE Day, 1945.

the George Medal. Elected to Parliament in 1945 as a Progressive Conservative from Calgary, he became agriculture minister in 1957 in the Diefenbaker government. Named defence minister in 1960, he called for Canadian forces to be armed with nuclear weapons, a stance that brought him into conflict with Secretary of State for External Affairs Howard Green and, when Diefenbaker could not decide on his course, with the prime minister. In October 1962 during the Cuban Missile Crisis, Harkness quietly defied his leader, putting the forces on alert despite direct orders not to do so. It was the most serious rupture in Canadian civil-military relations, and in the executive control of the military, in Canadian history. In February 1963, amidst Diefenbaker's continuing inaction on nuclear weapons, Harkness resigned from

Cabinet, his departure helping to bring the government down. Harkness ran successfully in the 1963 election, won by Lester Pearson's Liberals, and held his seat until 1972. SEE ALSO: CIVIL-MILITARY RELATIONS; CUBAN MISSILE CRISIS; DIEFENBAKER; NUCLEAR CRISIS (1962–1963).

Harper, Stephen Joseph (b.1959). Born in Toronto, Stephen Harper moved to Alberta and worked for the Reform Party, and was a rising star in the resurgence of Western-based Conservative populism in the 1990s. He won election to Parliament in 1993 and again in 2002, capturing the leadership of the short-lived Canadian Alliance in 2002. Harper then forged a union with the Progressive Conservative Party, becoming the leader of the new Conservative Party of Canada in a convention in 2004. He won the federal elections of 2006 and 2008, forming minority governments.

As prime minister, Harper was markedly more pro-American, pro-Israel, and pro-defence than his Liberal predecessors, often invoking what he considered past inaction or lack of commitment in explanation for policies that were sometimes precipitous and almost always contentious. After having supported while in Opposition the participation of Canadian troops in the 2003 American-led invasion of Iraq, he also supported the war in Afghanistan and skilfully managed to get parliamentary approval—working with the Liberal Opposition—to extend the mission there until 2011. His Canada First defence strategy, announced in 2008, contained plans for an expensive and substantial re-equipment of the Canadian Forces, for more personnel and for a greater emphasis on the defence of Arctic sovereignty. The Harper government built on the 2004–2005 reinvestment in defence by the government of Liberal Paul Martin by increasing military spending in Canada to over $20 billion by fiscal 2009–2010. Few post-1945 governments had been as avowedly pro-defence, and increases in defence spending of up to 14 percent per annum, levelling out only slightly to 2010–2011, had not been seen since the Korean War. The new equipment in hand or on order by early 2010 included tanks, armoured vehicles, artillery, C17 heavy lift aircraft, C130J Hercules transports, and Arctic Offshore Patrol Vessels. Other projects seemed to be stalled by an unwieldy procurement process and the economic downturn that began in late 2008, including new fighter aircraft, new or refurbished supply ships, logistics trucks, and replacement helicopters for the air force's venerable Sea Kings. Public support for the men and women of the Canadian Forces remained high, in part due to the visibility of military and military heritage initiatives during Harper's time in office, but Canadian casualties in Afghanistan and repeated instances of the corruption, torture, and ineffectiveness of the Kabul government had, by 2010, begun to weaken support for Harper's policies. See also: Afghanistan War; Hillier; North, Defence of the.

▲ Paul Hellyer as associate defence minister, 1957.

Reading: William Johnson, *Stephen Harper and the Future of Canada* (Toronto, 2006).

Hellyer, Paul Theodore (b.1923). Born in Waterford, Ontario, Hellyer served in the military during World War II, at first in the Royal Canadian Air Force and later, after the release of excess aircrew, in the army. His treatment during this process, in which he was re-mustered and inoculated by army doctors for the second time, left a lasting impression of military inefficiency and needless bureaucratic overlap. After the war, Hellyer became a successful property developer, won election to Parliament in 1949 as a Liberal, and served briefly as associate defence minister in the last year of the St Laurent government. In Opposition, he was instrumental in persuading Liberal leader Lester Pearson to renounce his resistance to nuclear warheads, a change that contributed materially to the Conservatives' defeat. After the 1963 election, Hellyer, as defence minister and recalling his wartime experience, launched on a process to integrate and later unify the three armed services—army, air force, and navy—as a singular, tri-service military.

The creation of the Canadian Forces in 1968, and the eradication of the old service identities, generated one of the greatest defence crises in Canadian history. Many senior officers resigned, lobbyists sprang into action, parliamentary opposition raged, veterans and service groups protested, and the wheels of efficiency, as seen by Hellyer, ground onward. The minister stubbornly persisted, convinced that he was correct in his desire to reduce the triplication of committees and functions as a way to get more money for equipment. He was correct in assuming that such reforms would improve administrative efficiency, eliminate waste, and increase the defence department's accountability, but either disingenuous or foolishly optimistic in his promise that Liberal governments of this era would funnel extra monies to defence. Hellyer left the defence portfolio in 1967, just before unification's implementation. He failed to win the leadership race to replace Pearson in 1968, and resigned from the Trudeau government the following year. His subsequent political career was checkered. While individual service identities—most notably the return to distinctive service uniforms for the air force and navy—later followed, the Canadian Forces nominally remains a single-service military under a chief of the defence staff. SEE ALSO: INTEGRATION; UNIFICATION.

READING: Paul Hellyer, *Damn the Torpedoes!* (Toronto, 1990).

Hill 70, Battle of (1917). The Canadian Corps, now commanded by Lieutenant-General Sir Arthur Currie, received orders to capture Lens, France, a coal-mining town dominated by Hill 70, on 7 July 1917. The limited attack was intended to divert German attention from other fronts. Currie studied the terrain, saw the flaw in his orders, and argued strongly enough to secure a change: he would take Hill 70, make Lens indefensible unless the enemy recaptured it, and from its commanding heights beat off German counterattacks. Bad weather delayed his well-planned, two-division attack until 15 August, but the Canadians held most of their objectives after the first day, at a cost of 3,500 casualties.

Enemy counterattacks, as Currie had predicted, crashed against the Canadians for the next several days, all of them crushed by well-laid artillery and machine-gun fire and by the strong positions occupied by Currie's confident, capable infantry. The battle saw the extensive use of gas shells, flame-throwers, and burning oil drums to create smoke screens. A Canadian attack on Lens was later repulsed, with heavy loss on both sides. Currie called Hill 70 the corps' "hardest battle," but it was also the first time that a Canadian general had persuaded his superiors that he had a better way to fight a battle. By early fall, the Canadian Corps had been transferred to the Ypres sector in preparation for its role in the Passchendaele campaign. Six Canadians earned the Victoria Cross at Hill 70, including Corporal Filip Konowal, the only Ukrainian Canadian to receive the honour. Hill 70 cost the Canadian Corps 9,200 killed, wounded, and missing. SEE ALSO: CANADIAN CORPS; CURRIE.

Hillier, Rick J. (b.1955). Born in Campbellton, Newfoundland and Labrador, Hillier served in the militia before graduating from Memorial University under the Regular Officer Training Program. He joined the Armoured Corps and served in Canada, with the Canadian brigade in Germany as part of the North Atlantic Treaty Organization's standing forces, in former Yugoslavia, and at National Defence Headquarters in Ottawa. He led a Canadian-based brigade group, directed military operations during the 1997 Winnipeg flood and the 1998 ice storm in Quebec and Ontario, and in 1998 became deputy commander of a US armoured corps in Texas. He then commanded a multinational division in Bosnia-Herzegovina, and in May 2003 became chief of the land staff and, shortly after, commander of the International Security Assistance Force in Afghanistan.

Appointed chief of the defence staff in February 2005, Hillier helped persuade the government of Paul Martin to increase its Afghan commitment substantially and to begin the process, carried on by the successor government of Stephen Harper, of re-equipping the Canadian Forces (CF). A charismatic leader much loved by his soldiers (if not always by

▲ General Rick Hillier (right) in Afghanistan, 2007.

sailors or fliers), Hillier was notably, and refreshingly, outspoken, a candour that sometimes drew criticism that he was prone to overstepping his boundaries as a military commander, using the court of public opinion to conduct discussions with his employer over issues of support for the troops, defence budgets, and operational freedom of action. He was occasionally criticized for being army-centric in his views, despite his successful articulation to government of the need for several major naval and air force projects, and for positions that led Canadian forces into increasingly close alignment with those of the United States. His earlier support for wheeled fire-support vehicles for the army, instead of new or better main battle tanks, the defenders of which he had caustically disdained, was rendered suspect after the army's experience in Afghanistan, which later resulted in the deployment of tanks. Hillier tackled head-on Canada's stubborn fixation with peacekeeping, and constantly reiterated the CF's principal purpose as a fighting organization, though one with many roles. He contributed to making the CF more popular with the public than it had been in decades, explaining consistently and well to widespread audiences, including the federal Cabinet, the Canadian Forces' many missions and requirements, emphasizing repeatedly and with great passion the centrality to Canadian interests of the work and professionalism of those men and women under his command. Hillier initiated a major reorganization of the military command structure, improved Canadian military relations with its principal allies, and presided over a more capable, more confident armed forces than any predecessor of the last generation. He left his CDS post on 1 July 2008, one of the most successful, capable, and highly regarded soldiers in Canadian history.

READING: R.J. Hillier, *A Soldier First* (Toronto, 2009).

Hindenburg Line. Running from Arras to the River Aisne near Soissons, France, the Hindenburg Line, built by 65,000 troops after September 1916, was a formidable system of German defences. The line featured concrete bunkers, used reverse slopes where possible to protect against artillery fire, and incorporated up to four separate but interconnected trench systems. In early 1917, the Germans surprised Allied planners by withdrawing into these new positions, shortening their front in the west and permitting better defence in depth, while leaving more divisions available as reserves to reinforce threatened sectors. The retreating Germans destroyed buildings, bridges, railway tracks, and other infrastructure as they withdrew. In September 1918 during the Hundred Days, the Canadian Corps was among the formations that attacked the Hindenburg Line. The first assault against the Drocourt-Quéant section on 2–3 September broke the line and forced the enemy to retreat to the east. The corps then attacked the well-defended Canal du Nord on 27 September in a brilliant manoeuvre, crossing it and pressing on toward Cambrai, a key road and rail junction, which the Canadians took on 8–9 October. Cracking the successive defences of the Hindenburg Line was, arguably, the greatest victory in Canadian military history. The casualties incurred, almost 31,000 from 22 August to the fall of Cambrai, reflect the fierceness of German resistance, even in the closing weeks of the war. See also: Canadian Corps; Currie; Hundred Days.

Hitler Line. The Adolf Hitler Line and the attached Gustav Line protected the southern approaches to Rome from the advancing Allied armies during World War II. The 1st Canadian Division went on the attack on 16 May and, on 23 May 1944, the two divisions of I Canadian Corps, fighting together for the first time under Lieutenant-General E.L.M. Burns, struck the enemy line. The concrete bunkers, tank turrets sunk into concrete, mines, machine guns, and wire facing the Canadians were intact and fully garrisoned. The 1st Division's troops cut a breach in the line into which poured the tanks and infantry of the 5th Armoured Division. Hard fighting in crossing the three rivers on the attack route resulted in 7,000 killed, wounded, and taken prisoner, but the Germans broke and the pursuit north began. The British Eighth Army's headquarters nonetheless complained that the Canadians had caused a massive traffic jam on the one good road that ran north through the Liri valley and thus slowed the advance. US troops liberated Rome on 4 June. See also: Burns; Italian Campaign.

Hochwald Forest, Battle of the (1945). A densely wooded forest sitting on a long ridge in front of Xanten, Germany, the Hochwald was the objective of Operation Blockbuster on 26 February 1945. In a night attack spearheaded by the 2nd and 3rd Canadian Infantry Divisions of II Canadian Corps, the Canadians employed Kangaroo armoured personnel carriers and tanks to carry infantry forward under artificial moonlight. The Germans, defending their own soil, resisted with great ferocity, inflicting heavy casualties. It took two days for the infantry to get into the Hochwald itself, advancing slowly amidst a warren of bunkers, wire, and mines. The forest was finally cleared on 4 March and Xanten fell on the 8th; by 10 March enemy resistance west of the River Rhine had been all but eliminated. See also: Simonds.

Home Front, World Wars I and II. With its population of some eight million and with only a rudimentary industrial base, Canada was completely unprepared for war in August 1914, unprepared psychologically, militarily, and organizationally. No such conflict had happened before, and no one in government or out could have contemplated the reality of the next four years of war. Those who thought ahead in that summer of 1914 envisaged a few short, sharp battles on land, the triumph of Britain's Royal Navy at sea, and a triumphal march into Berlin led by the French, Russian, and British armies. The only question in most minds was whether the Canadian volunteers would get to the front in time to test their mettle before the German Kaiser's Prussian hordes had run up the white flag in precipitous surrender. The justness of the cause was unquestioned and Canada, as a British colony, was in the war at once, bound legally by Britain's declaration of hostilities. Even in Quebec, especially Montreal, where pro-imperial sentiment found less popular traction and fewer vocal advocates among francophones, there seemed initially to be little doubt. Across the country, young Canadians hurried to sign up, hustled along by uncompromising appeals to patriotism and by the moral certitude of a just cause and an imminent victory.

The economy was in the doldrums when war began, and the inevitable interruptions of trade made matters worse. It took a year or more before the war-induced boom began to take hold, grain exports increased, and the first munitions were sold. Canada's production of artillery shells, after November 1915 wholly controlled by the Imperial Munitions Board, would amount to over $1 billion worth, a huge sum by any standard. The war eventually created labour shortages as men went into the army and factories went on double shifts, and workers, male and female, came to the cities from rural areas. That, in turn, created a farm labour shortage that left farmers, struggling to plant and then bring in crops that could command good prices for once, desperate for help. Wartime inflation pushed up the price of food, leading city dwellers, many of them earning better wages than before the war, to curse farmers for their financial opportunism and supposed failure to enlist for military service. The wartime calls for "A New National Policy" of lower tariffs and the postwar rise of farmer progressivism had their roots in this strain.

Women went into factories in large numbers during World War I. This painting by G.A. Reid shows workers at the Russell Motor Works in Toronto.

Another factor was conscription. To farmers, compulsory military service meant that even less labour would be available for their use. Their argument that food was as much a war-winning weapon as armaments was true enough, but it received little broader credence in the feverish atmosphere of 1917. Victory then was everything, and Canada needed every recruit it could possibly find to be at the front. Including French-speaking Canadians? That was a problem. Quebec, while happy enough to operate war factories, was not sending volunteers to the army in anything like the numbers of English Canada. There were no hard data available for public discussion, but none truly believed that francophone volunteers amounted to more than 25,000 or so, if that. Québécois nationalists noted, with some justice, that Canada's enlistment figures were badly skewed: it was the British-born who were enlisting, they argued, and not the English-speaking Canadian-born. Moreover, the language of the army was English, there were almost no French-speaking senior officers, Minister of Militia and Defence Sam Hughes was an Orangeman who hated Catholics, and the real threat to French Canada lay in Ontario where Regulation 17 forced English on French-speaking children. Why should French Canadians enlist to fight the Prussians when it was in Ontario that the French language was actually threatened? The passage of the Military Service Act in August 1917 and the imposition of conscription split the country. The farmers won sweeping exemptions just before the election; the francophones did not. Both would be called up wholesale when the Germans' 1918 offensives threatened to win the war. For good measure, the Borden government guaranteed itself election victory when its Military Voters Act and its Wartime Elections Act gave the vote to soldiers to use where most helpful for the government, took away the votes of recent immigrants, and granted them to women relatives of soldiers. The December 1917 election also hit a new low in racism, Quebec being damned as a slacker province and Liberal leader and anti-conscription stalwart Sir Wilfrid Laurier as the Kaiser's henchman.

The vote for women may have been an election-winning tactic in 1917, but it was also implemented in recognition of the role women had played in the war. Working in factories, replacing men as tram drivers, knitting socks for soldiers, or working in the fields, women had earned the vote. Other social reforms also moved quickly forward in the hothouse atmosphere of the war. Prohibition was necessary so scarce alcohol could be used for munitions. Income taxes came into place to make those who earned most carry their share of the war's costs. Implemented in 1917 after the Americans came into the war and imposed it on their citizens, food rationing in theory meant that scarce goods could be more equally shared. And the state intruded into hitherto forbidden areas: for example, as venereal disease spread rapidly, keeping men from the front, Ottawa and the provinces entered into their first shared cost program to counter it.

The war created an enormous gap between those at home and those who fought. The bitterness of returning soldiers in 1919, their rage against the French Canadians, the immigrants, the profiteers, the slackers, embittered Canadian life for a generation. It divided city from country, French from English, worker from management, and young from old in ways that sparked regional resentment, political division, and social and labour conflict. This was true even as Canadians celebrated justly their achievements in arms, the return of their heroes, and the role claimed by the Dominion in imperial affairs as the result of its wartime efforts. Remembrance and commemoration were civic duties even as tight-fisted governments shrank the military, reduced budgets, and struggled to ensure that payments to veterans did not crush the exchequer. Close-lipped old soldiers might choose to forget the war that those who were not there never understood, but its scars and impacts echoed through the interwar period just the same. Conscription in World War II was an issue precisely because of the memories of World War I. Because of the 1914–1918 experience, the public and the government had some sense of what might be expected.

Canada in 1939 was still caught in the Great Depression with unemployment high and the economy groaning. There was no enthusiasm anywhere for the coming war, certainly not in French Canada or on the farms across the nation. The wave of public enthusiasm that greeted the Munich agreement of September 1938—the pact that stripped the Sudetenland from Czechoslovakia in a triumph of Anglo-French appeasement—demonstrated that such sentiments were far more widely shared than in 1914. There was also growing fear that appeasement would not be enough. The very real sense that Adolf Hitler and the Nazis were a menace to democracy increased sharply when Hitler tore up the September agreements by marching into Prague in March 1939. War in Europe was coming; Japanese expansion in China and its growing naval power suggested, especially to those living along the vulnerable West Coast, that it might not be long in engulfing the Pacific either.

The public's attitude at the beginning of the war in Europe in September 1939 was one of fearful resignation. The memory of the terrible casualties of World War I hung heavily over the country, and in Quebec the scars of the 1917 conscription crisis were still fresh. For Prime Minister Mackenzie King, the wartime task was to bring Canada into and through the war undivided, or at least substantially less divided than in the earlier struggle. He had to bring Quebec along as Canada entered the war against Germany, while managing the enthusiasms of more imperialistic Canadians who would, then as before, press Ottawa for automatic commitments and maximal efforts on behalf of the mother country. He could not—and did not want to—dissociate Canada from the British position, nor could he endorse it so closely or so soon as to divide his party, his base of support in Quebec, or his ability to conduct the war at home. The Statute of Westminster of 1931 made Canada autonomous in foreign policy, but the statute's powers had yet to be tested. King's answer in September 1939 as British and French ultimatums to Germany for its retreat from an invaded Poland expired and the great powers marched again to war, was to call Parliament, permitting

Canadians, at least nominally, to decide if their country should join the war. The result of the discussion was preordained and entirely academic, given his party's strength in the House and the Conservatives' united support for hostilities, but the week-long delay, leading to a declaration of war on 10 September, one week after Britain, demonstrated autonomy, appeased the imperialists, and mollified—more or less—critics in Quebec. Whether the country's national interests were yet at stake in a war in Europe was another question entirely.

In effect, Canada had played no part in prewar diplomacy, and went to war when Britain did for much the same reasons as in 1914. The nature of the German regime (and that of Italy and Japan as well) would become truly apparent only later, despite growing public evidence, much of it disgracefully ignored in Canada as elsewhere, of the plight of Europe's Jews. The extent and pace of fascist ambitions could no longer be denied in September 1939, however, and these surely were worth opposing, even for former proto-isolationists like King. Anglo-Canadian opinion would never have countenanced non-involvement in any case, and King was always aware of the strength of this view. A wily prime minister had made a wise call at the right time for the right reason; that he could have done no less was beside the point. Political adroitness notwithstanding, entering the war was one thing; fighting it was another.

Mackenzie King's war was initially to be one of "limited liability." Canada would do its part but it would not risk tearing itself asunder by virtue of its effort, as it had in World War I. The prime minister would have preferred not to send an army division overseas early in the struggle, but his Cabinet insisted. Even so, King forced the British to agree that the British Commonwealth Air Training Plan (BCATP), huge and expensive as it was, would be Canada's primary role. Nor would there be any conscription for overseas service. King had promised this in March 1939 (as had the Opposition leader, Dr R.J. Manion), and he repeated it in September. These attitudes persisted into the spring of 1940, long enough for the Liberals to be re-elected in a landslide. But the

Germans swallowed Denmark and Norway in April and stunningly crushed the Low Countries and France in May and June. Britain was now alone, Canada and its 11 million people now its major ally. The budget caps on war expenditures came off, the economy began to hum, and Canada was wholeheartedly in the war. C.D. Howe, hitherto the transport minister, became the minister of munitions and supply, and "C.D." provided the galvanizing spark. He would become Canada's "minister of everything."

He did not have much to work with. There were at least 400,000 unemployed and one million on relief in 1939, while only 3.8 million had gainful employment, 2 million of those in agriculture. The gross national product (GNP) was $5.6 billion, and government spending was in the range of $680 million a year. The war altered matters dramatically: the GNP in 1945 was

$11.8 billion, more than double the prewar figure. Unemployment had disappeared and 5.1 million people had work, with 3.2 million in industry. The manufacturing sector had almost doubled in size, and war industry at its October 1943 peak employed 1.2 million men and women or 13.3 percent of the population over 14 years of age. And, of course, 1.1 million men and women served in the wartime armed forces.

The government needed money to pay for the war's costs, and increased taxes provided much of it. Ottawa's authority was constrained by the British North America Act's separation of powers between the federal and provincial governments—until the federal budget of 29 April 1941 announced Ottawa's intention to levy the taxes required to fund the war, paying to every province that agreed to surrender its

▲ In World War II, women did every kind of home front work. These women of the Queen Mary Needlework Guild mended clothing for soldiers overseas.

income, corporate, and succession taxes an annual payment equal to its previous revenues from these fields. This was to be a voluntary agreement, Ottawa pronounced piously, but any province that failed to agree could face the burden of saddling its citizens with double taxation. There were pro forma protests, but the provinces caved in. The Dominion-Provincial Taxation Agreement Act, 1942 formalized the deal. The government now had the taxation room it needed to fight the war. Excise, sales, and retail purchase taxes were increased or imposed. Raw tobacco faced a ten cents a pound levy, cigarette taxes increased from $5 to $6 a thousand; cameras, photographs, and radio tubes had a ten percent tax added to their cost, and a luxury tax on virtually all entertainment added 20 percent to the cost of movies and sporting events. A War Exchange Tax, ordinarily 10 percent, raised revenue and deterred unnecessary imports, thus preserving scarce US dollars.

The rates of corporation and income taxes increased dramatically. At the beginning of the war, a married man with two children paid no income tax at all unless he was in the upper brackets; if he earned $3,000, his income tax was $10. Four years later, after tax increases had squeezed hard, the $3,000 a year man was paying $334 in income tax and an additional amount of $1,200 in "compulsory savings," a surcharge in the form of a loan to be repaid at the end of the war. The ingenuity of the federal finance department was almost as unlimited as the government's need for money. Corporation taxes increased from 18 to 40 percent, generating $636 million—or nearly half of all corporate profits—in 1943. Excess profits taxes produced more revenue. All profits in excess of 116 2/3 percent of standard profits (the average of profit from the not-so-buoyant years from 1936 to 1939) were taxed at 100 percent. Corporations, however, were to receive a 20 percent rebate after the war. "No great fortunes," the finance minister said, perhaps with more optimism than was justified, "can be accumulated out of wartime profits." High corporate and personal taxes, while they did not stop some from getting rich out of the war, tried to ensure that a measure of equal treatment prevailed. So too did the freeze on prices and wages,

imposed in October 1941. From September 1939 to the imposition of wage and price control, the cost of living went up 17.8 percent; but, for the rest of the war, the increase was only 2.8 percent, the most successful record of fighting inflation among all the belligerents. Essentially, the managers of the wartime economy had learned from the errors of World War I: they taxed heavily and managed inflation, and the nation and the war effort benefitted. With all this money coming in, wartime spending in Ottawa reached well above $5 billion in 1945, almost nine times 1939 spending.

Production increased dramatically in every sector of the economy between 1939 and 1945. Good weather helped produce bumper crops of grain— 556 million bushels of grain in 1942, every bit of which found a market at home or overseas. Pork production more than doubled while beef rose by one-third and agricultural exports rose threefold. In the iron and steel industries, pig iron and steel ingot production more than doubled over the course of the war, and a nation that in 1939 had built no merchant ships, by 1944 had put 345 into the water; aircraft production reached 14,700 by the beginning of 1945; and Canada's auto plants turned out 45,710 armoured vehicles and 707,000 military trucks of all kinds. The Canadian army ran on these vehicles, and so too did much of the British army.

The total of war production in Canada was $10.9 billion by 1945, placing Canada fourth among the Allies with one-seventh of total Commonwealth production. The Canadian military used only a third of this bounty, and so rich had Canada become (and so short of hard currency to pay for anything were Britain and its Empire) that virtually all the remainder was given away as gifts to Britain, or as Mutual Aid to Britain and the Allies. Mutual Aid was the Canadian equivalent of the Americans' Lend-Lease, and in percentage terms was more generous. But there was self-interest here too: war production in Canada was an investment in full employment and in infrastructure-building at home.

Canada was at war, straining every sinew for victory but, extraordinarily, the country had never been so prosperous. There was work for everyone—

fathers, mothers, daughters—with as much overtime available in the factories as individuals could handle. Average wages increased dramatically, rising from $956 in 1938 to $1,525 in 1943. People had the money to eat better than they had during the Depression, even if food rationing put limits on what meat, butter, sugar, coffee, tea, as well as appliances, autos, gasoline, and other commodities were available. But if Canadians could not buy everything they wanted, they could save for the future. The government sold $12.5 billion in Victory Bonds that everyone purchased (down to children spending 25 cents on war savings stamps), and every bond drive was oversubscribed. At the same time, bank accounts increased, a cushion for the expected postwar downturn. Many flirted with the black market, trying to get meat or gas or auto tires, but the government's Wartime Prices and Trade Board kept careful watch on profiteers.

Everyone worried about their husbands, sons, and brothers in action overseas, but Canadians listened to the radio—Lorne Greene reading the CBC news was "the voice of doom" but Bert Pearl and "The Happy Gang" offered good fun and music—and their kids followed the adventures of "L for Lanky" about the crews of Bomber Command when they were not collecting tin cans, fruit baskets, or milkweed pods for recycling and war purposes. Teenage girls put on bobby socks while city boys wore zoot suits with big shoulders and an exaggerated drape in the pants that somehow defied clothing rationing, and some zoot-suiters fought with servicemen over girls. Most young people danced to swing at large dancehalls or listened to Glenn Miller records. Parents worried about their daughters having sex or, worse, an illegitimate child in an era before birth control was reliable, while others fretted over hasty wartime marriages and feared that divorce would rise high enough to shake the social order. A wife with a husband overseas worried that he was having affairs with English women (and later Italian, French, Belgian, Dutch, and German women). Their servicemen spouses feared that slackers and the "zombies," as home defence conscripts were called derisively, could be preying on their lonely wives.

Certainly there was immorality and many marriages foundered under the stress of long absence (some soldiers in the 1st Division were away from Canada for six years), but most, like Canada, survived.

Doctors made house calls (but in wartime people could pay their fees as many could not in the 1930s) and they received extra gas coupons and access to tires so they could do so. Comic books, called "Canadian whites" because scarce dyes went to war production, reached young boys and girls, most about superheroes fighting evil Nazis or Japanese militarists. Clergymen and social workers worried about how the absence of fathers overseas might affect the way children developed, and juvenile delinquency did show wartime increases, peaking in 1942. Life not only went on; it was better than before the war, even with almost everyone conscious of what was at stake.

The war changed Canada dramatically. Hundreds of thousands left rural Canada for the factories in the city, and housing in the cities and towns became a scarce and expensive commodity despite government rent control. Women began to work in war plants, sometimes bringing their babies along to daycare centres at the work site. The scarcity of men, serving in uniform, opened up jobs to women that had been unimaginable in 1939—from street car drivers to aircraft designers—and 1.4 million women were employed, a participation rate of almost one in three, at the wartime peak in 1945. When the war ended and the men came back, many, but not all, of those jobs disappeared. Later feminist scholars notwithstanding, most women wanted to escape the factory to have a home after the war, along with a husband and a family, and to live what was seen as a normal life. Labour participation rates for women never returned to their prewar levels just the same. For women as for men, the struggle had been transformative.

Unionization increased dramatically, with government clearing the way with an order-in-council (PC 1007 of 17 February 1944) that confirmed employees' rights to form unions and laid out the rules for defining and certifying bargaining units. Labour peace could keep vital production going, and where there were production bottlenecks and failures, one way around them was to create Crown corporations. A shortage of rubber? Set up a Crown company to produce synthetic rubber. Wood veneers for aircraft were in scarce supply? A Crown corporation could do the job. Machine tools? C.D. Howe's Citadel Merchandising could get them and make sure they went where they were most needed. In all, 28 Crown corporations came into being during the war, some manufacturing, some purchasing and distributing, others supervising and controlling. The establishment of Crown companies, operating with great flexibility outside the usual bureaucratic restraints, allowed for efficiencies. The Liberal government benefitted from all this economic success and public wealth. People complained and the Opposition suggested it could have done it all better, of course. But King and the Liberals seemed in control—and were.

There were still challenges to King's dominance. In September 1939, Premier Maurice Duplessis in Quebec called an election to protest what he saw as Ottawa's centralization of power, with the war as an excuse. King's Quebec ministers went into the fray and smashed the Union Nationale with their promises against conscription. In January 1940, Ontario Premier Mitch Hepburn complained that Canada was doing nothing in the war and his legislature passed a condemnatory motion that King used as an excuse for a snap election of his own. He won massively, happily for him just before the war in Europe turned against the Allies. King soon had to pass the National Resources Mobilization Act, implementing home defence conscription, and his government moved quickly to squelch (relatively minor) protests in Quebec by locking up Montreal's showboat mayor, Camillien Houde, who had encouraged his citizens not to register. The question of conscription did not go away, with a conscription plebiscite in April 1942 and a major government crisis the next month, as well as a genuine reinforcement shortage in the fall of 1944 that came close to bringing the government down. King bobbed and weaved and sent 16,000 home defence conscripts overseas, but he held the government and country together in a fashion that guaranteed him his place among Canada's great leaders.

King also used the wartime opportunity to begin to put social welfare measures into law. In 1940, he secured provincial consent to amend the constitution and put Unemployment Insurance on the federal government's books, knowing that wartime full employment could fill the coffers so that benefits could be paid out when (no one thought it was if) bad times returned with peace. In 1944, with the social democratic Co-operative Commonwealth Federation showing strength in the opinion polls and forming the government in Saskatchewan and the Opposition in Ontario, King's government passed a family allowance bill, giving mothers a monthly payment for each child; for many women, this was the first money of their own they had ever had, and it was intended to be used to buy milk, cribs, blankets, baby shoes, and a myriad of items that would keep farms and factories working after the war. This one scheme was to cost Ottawa almost half the total 1939 federal budget, an indicator of how the war had changed everything. And because Ottawa's mandarins feared a return of economic depression, there was a host of other plans designed to spend money to create jobs: a Veterans Charter to reward servicemen and servicewomen with clothing, money, and training; money for home building; money to convert industry to peacetime production; money for great public projects; money for everything. It worked—the economic downturn all had expected did not materialize, and Mackenzie King and the Liberals won the 1945 election, narrowly, to be sure, but deservedly just the same. SEE ALSO: BORDEN, ROBERT; CONSCRIPTION; HOWE; KING; WAR FINANCE; WAR INDUSTRY; WORLD WAR I; WORLD WAR II.

READING: Barbara Wilson, *Ontario and the First World War, 1914–1918* (Toronto, 1977); Jeffrey Keshen, *Saints, Sinners, and Soldiers: Canada's Second World War* (Vancouver, 2004).

Hong Kong, Battle of (1941). In August 1941, the just-relieved British commander of the Hong Kong garrison, Major-General A.E. Grasett, passed through

Ottawa on his way back to England. He visited the chief of the general staff, Major-General H.D.G. Crerar, a Royal Military College of Canada classmate, and told him that the Japanese army, then all but triumphant in China, could never fight successfully against white troops. Hong Kong, the message was, could defend itself if its garrison was bolstered, and its reinforcement would let Japan know that Britain took its Pacific possessions seriously. Not coincidentally, a few days after Grasett's arrival in London, the War Office—which surely knew just as well as Prime Minister Winston Churchill did that Hong Kong was indefensible—asked Canada to send troops to the Crown colony. "This action," London told Ottawa, "would strengthen garrison out of all proportion to actual numbers involved . . . ."

No one in Ottawa (Crerar possibly aside) wanted to send troops to Asia, *terra incognita* for Canada's army. There was a threat of war there, to be sure, but without any hard intelligence capability of their own and knowing only what London chose to tell them, most

Canadian officials and military staff believed that Tokyo's military government was rattling sabres and bluffing with its talk of war. But the Liberal government, already facing increasing calls for conscription and charges that Canada was doing too little to fight the war in Europe, did not want to hand the Opposition Conservatives the political gift that a refusal to meet London's request for troops would mean. The army staff received its orders: find troops for Hong Kong. No one on the staff believed the Canadians would need to fight, so attention focused quickly on two battalions that had recently returned from garrison duty in Jamaica and Newfoundland, respectively the Winnipeg Grenadiers and the Royal Rifles of Canada, the latter a Quebec City unit with a good representation of francophones. Neither battalion was fully trained or up to strength, but the headquarters staff believed the Hong Kong garrison posting would provide ample time for training to be completed for the original units and the reinforcement officers and other ranks who joined the force just prior to embarkation.

The battle of Hong Kong in December 1941 ended in the surrender of the surviving garrison. These Canadian soldiers had spent almost four years in vile conditions in Japanese POW camps, their release not coming until Japan's surrender in August 1945.

Under the command of Brigadier J.K. Lawson, a very competent officer who brought with him a brigade staff, the Hong Kong force of 1,973, plus two nursing sisters, sailed from Vancouver on 27 October 1941. Because of errors by staff officers in Ottawa, the vehicles and heavy equipment that should have travelled with the contingent did not reach Vancouver in time and were loaded on another vessel. This ship, carrying in all 212 trucks and carriers, would end up in the Philippines after war with Japan began on 7 December. The Canadian troops arrived in Hong Kong on 16 November and settled in, becoming part of a British and Indian garrison of 14,000. The Japanese, they were told, had few troops in the area, obsolete aircraft, and were overall quite poorly equipped. For its part, Japanese intelligence reported to Tokyo that the Canadians "are not excellent in character."

Orders to attack Hong Kong on 8 December had already been issued to the 38th Division of the Imperial Japanese Army, and it did so the day after Pearl Harbor. With stunning speed, the Japanese overran the British and Indian defenders holding the incomplete and undermanned "Gin Drinkers' Line" on the mainland, destroyed the handful of obsolete Royal Air Force aircraft, and quickly drove the defenders back onto Hong Kong Island. On 18 December, the Japanese staged a successful amphibious assault and began their final conquest.

The British had split the Canadian force on the island in two, leaving only the Grenadiers under Lawson's control. The Royal Rifles, serving under British commanders that they euphemistically described as "highly nervous...and very tired," defended their assigned locales tenaciously but were forced to retreat into ever-shrinking perimeters on the rugged terrain. The Grenadiers did so as well. The result was that Lawson's headquarters at the Wong Nei Chong gap was overrun on 19 December, and he and his staff, after "going outside to fight it out," died at the hands of the Japanese who lost an estimated 600 men in the attack on the Winnipeg unit. Company Sergeant-Major John Osborn of the Grenadiers earned a posthumous Victoria Cross when he saved men of his company by falling on a hand grenade. At roughly the same time, the Rifles' mascot, a Newfoundland dog named Gander, took in its mouth a grenade that had landed in the midst of a group of Canadians and ran off with it, saving the soldiers but dying in the grenade's explosion.

The battle now degenerated into savage Japanese attacks and gallant but fruitless and ill-coordinated British and Canadian counterattacks. The island's British commanders had lost control and hope and, with no prospect of relief, the surrender on Christmas Day was inevitable. The victorious Japanese went on a rampage, shooting and torturing prisoners, bayoneting wounded in their hospital beds, and raping and murdering military and civilian nurses. Canadian losses in the battle of Hong Kong were 290 dead and 483 wounded, an extraordinarily high casualty rate of almost 40 percent that bore testimony to the ferocity of the fighting and the effective resistance offered by ill-equipped and partially trained Canadian soldiers. The Japanese suffered some 2,100 casualties in 17 days of fighting.

There was worse to come for those taken captive. Although the treatment varied, on the whole the Japanese brutalized their POWs for almost four years, starving them, not providing medicines to the ill, and torturing any who caught their attention. A Canadian-born Japanese soldier, Kanao Inouye, was a prison guard and apparent Kempeitai secret police operative. The "Kamloops Kid," as Canadian soldiers called him when they discovered his British Columbia birth, took special delight in tormenting his former countrymen. He personally killed three and savaged many more, adding to the toll of 128 Canadian POWs who died in the Hong Kong cages. (Inouye was executed after the war.) Some of the POWs were moved to Japan where overwork, starvation, and maltreatment led to the deaths of 136 more. Liberation did not come until September 1945 after Japan surrendered. Of the 1,975 Canadians who had left Vancouver in 1941, just over 1,400 would return in late 1945, many suffering from debilitating diseases for the rest of their lives. Japan has yet to make amends for its appalling maltreatment of Allied prisoners.

The federal government in February 1942 created a Royal Commission under the chief justice of the

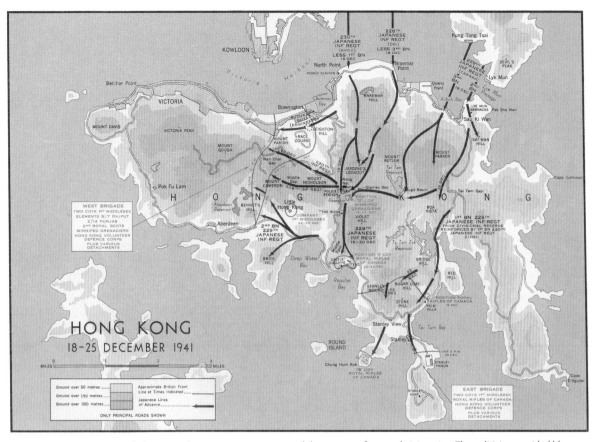

The disaster at Hong Kong led to a Royal Commission in Ottawa and the censure of army administration. The politicians avoided blame.

Supreme Court of Canada, Sir Lyman Duff, to investigate the failings in Canada that doomed the Hong Kong contingent. The only person censured was the quartermaster general, Major-General E.J.C. Schmidlin. After the war, the British commander at Hong Kong, Major-General C.M. Maltby, wrote a self-justifying report that was sharply critical of the Canadian units. Current historical scholarship tends not to support his complaints and, if any blame is affixed to Canadians, it is usually placed on the Canadian government for so casually sending troops to an indefensible island. The Canadian soldiers who fought at Hong Kong inflicted heavy casualties on the attackers and fought better than might have been expected of green troops. SEE ALSO: CRERAR; PRISONERS OF WAR.

READING: Brereton Greenhous, *'C' Force to Hong Kong* (Toronto, 1997).

Hose, Walter D. (1875–1965). Born at sea, Hose served in the Royal Navy for 21 years before transferring to the recently created Canadian navy in 1912. During World War I, he captained HMCS *Rainbow* on the West Coast. He later commanded anti-submarine warfare patrols and defences in the Gulf of St Lawrence in 1917–1918. He became Director of Naval Service in 1921, a post he held until 1934. As director, he struggled to secure a large enough budget to keep the Royal Canadian Navy alive, put time and effort into developing a naval reserve, and successfully fought off attempts to eliminate the navy altogether in 1933.

Howe, Clarence D. (1886–1960). Born in Waltham, Massachusetts, C.D. Howe came to Canada as a young man and did well building grain elevators. Elected to Parliament in 1935 as a Liberal, Howe quickly went into the Cabinet and established a reputation as a minister who could get things done. Prime Minister Mackenzie King put him in charge of the new Department of Munitions and Supply in 1940, and Howe at last had a challenge befitting his organizational talents. With money no object, Howe mobilized the Canadian economy to produce munitions—everything from Sherman tanks to *Tribal* class destroyers to Lancaster bombers flowed from the production lines. At the same time, Howe created government-owned Crown corporations to do what industry could not. In 1944, Howe took on the added post of minister of reconstruction, putting him in command of the conversion from war to peace, a task he handled with such skill that the transition was astonishingly smooth. Howe was close to Louis St Laurent, King's successor, and, with the creation of the North Atlantic Treaty Organization, the outbreak of the Korean War, and Canada's massive Cold War rearmament, became minister of defence production in 1951, once more charged with mobilizing the nation's industry. Again, he did the job well and, by the early 1950s, defence absorbed more than 7 percent of gross domestic product. Howe encouraged the development of the Canadian aircraft and shipbuilding industries and, among many projects, oversaw the construction of the CF-100 Canuck interceptor and the *St Laurent* class of destroyer escorts. He pushed development of the CF-105 Avro Arrow forward but, by the mid-1950s, even he had become alarmed at its escalating development costs. Howe might have killed the expensive project but, in 1957, John Diefenbaker's Conservatives unexpectedly defeated the Liberals, leaving Howe out of power after 22 years in the Cabinet. Tough, smart, creative, Howe had a transformative effect on Canada. SEE ALSO: HOME FRONT; WAR INDUSTRY; WORLD WARS I AND II.

READING: Robert Bothwell and William Kilbourn, *C.D. Howe* (Toronto, 1979).

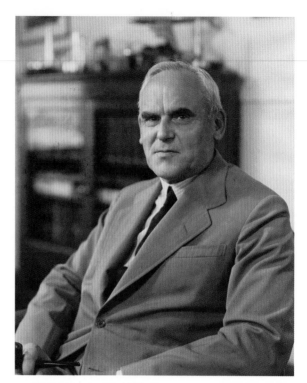

▲ C.D. Howe during World War II.

Hughes, Sir Samuel (1853–1921). One of the most colourful and contentious characters in Canadian history, Sam Hughes was born in Darlington, Canada West, and educated in Toronto. He was a property speculator, newspaper owner, Orangeman, and militia stalwart when he won election to the House of Commons in 1892 as a Conservative. Hughes believed that a Canadian farmer or shop clerk armed with a rifle was a better defender of his country than any professional soldier, British or Canadian, and his experiences in the South African War confirmed his opinion. A militia battalion commander, Hughes offered his unit for service, was rebuffed, and then finagled his way to South Africa as a staff officer. Somehow he secured command of a small force of irregulars and performed his service capably. But his refusal to follow orders, his attacks on British generals, and his shameless self-promotion in letters to the Canadian media led to his sacking. Hughes claimed he ought to have won two Victoria Crosses during the war, awards supposedly denied him by jealous professional officers.

A firm supporter of the Ross rifle as the right weapon for the Canadian militia, Hughes became minister of militia and defence in Robert Borden's government in 1911. His energy and drive led to a doubling of the defence budget and hence to improvements in the militia's training and armouries, and he supported planning for mobilization in the event of war. But when World War I began in August 1914, Hughes threw away the existing plans and mobilized a large force at Valcartier, Quebec, where no camp yet existed. The First Contingent of the Canadian Expeditionary Force was born in chaos, its equipment produced hastily, its officers chosen at the minister's whim. Still, it was a great achievement to get a Canadian division overseas in two months, albeit mostly

untrained and largely unequipped, and Hughes's knighthood in 1915 was far from undeserved. Where Hughes failed was in allowing his cronies to get their hands on contracts for everything from uniforms to horses to artillery shells. The resulting scandals caused huge difficulties for the government and led to the creation of the much more efficient Imperial Munitions Board.

Hughes's interference did not end at Valcartier. He considered himself Canada's war minister, wore his major-general's uniform, thought seriously about taking command of the Canadian Division himself, and continued to interfere with personnel and equipment matters. Long after the Ross rifle had failed in battle, he tried to force the Canadian infantry to use it. Soldiers threw it away and took Lee-Enfields

▲ Sir Sam Hughes comes ashore, 1916.

from dead British soldiers; when General E.A.H. Alderson, the Canadian Division commander, ordered the Ross to be withdrawn, Hughes put him on his "enemies" list. The minister's allies and appointees meddled in military matters in England, as well, and Hughes's recruiting system—or lack of system—in Canada led to battalions being recruited with the promise that they would see action under their officers, promises that experienced commanders at the front could not permit to be carried out. As a result, the battalions were broken up, and useless officers piled up in England.

Hughes's behaviour becoming increasingly erratic, the long-suffering Borden finally sacked him in November 1916 to the great relief of the Canadian Corps and his Cabinet colleagues. "The nightmare is over," one minister sighed; the "mad mullah" is gone, an officer overseas said. But Hughes was not finished. Lieutenant-General Sir Arthur Currie had refused to give Hughes's son, Major-General Garnet Hughes, a field command, leaving him in England as commander of the 5th Canadian Division. This created a long-lasting enmity, and Hughes began to attack Currie, sheltering behind his parliamentary immunity. Hughes charged that Currie's vainglory had led to unnecessary casualties at Cambrai in October 1918 and in the last few days of the war at Mons, Belgium. It took Currie ten years to overcome these spurious charges, and a libel trial in 1928 to put them to rest. By then, Hughes, who had become old and embittered, was dead from pernicious anemia. SEE ALSO: BORDEN, ROBERT; CANADIAN EXPEDITIONARY FORCE; CURRIE; MILITIA; WORLD WAR I.

READING: R.G. Haycock, *Sam Hughes: The Public Career of a Controversial Canadian, 1885–1916* (Waterloo, 1986).

Hundred Days, The (1918). Beginning on 8 August 1918, Lieutenant-General Sir Arthur Currie's Canadian Corps fought an extraordinary series of battles. The opening engagement, the battle of Amiens, saw the corps advance a dozen kilometres, blasting through the German lines. Georges Vanier of the 22nd Battalion said later: "We felt somehow

Beginning with a great advance on 8 August 1918, the Canadian Corps fought and won a succession of costly victories during the Hundred Days, including the liberation of a ruined Cambrai in October.

that the Germans were beaten and . . . hope stirred our hearts." The advance continued for two days more, then the Canadians halted, moved north to the Arras area, and, on 26 August, the assault began on the Hindenburg Line. The first area to fall was the heavily defended Drocourt-Quéant Line, after which Currie had to cross the Canal du Nord. The wide obstacle, flanked by flooded marshes, seemed impassable, but Currie found a dry section, sent the entire corps, greatly assisted by his engineer units, over it on a tight timetable on 27 October, and made his plan work. Experts consider the canal crossing the best example of the corps' professionalism. The corps then took Cambrai and, the enemy now on the run, liberated Valenciennes. On 11 November, the day the armistice came into effect, the Canadians were in Mons, Belgium, where the British Expeditionary Force had first met the Germans in August 1914.

The Hundred Days had been a triumph of Canadian arms, without question the most important effort ever made by Canadians in battle. The campaign was also hugely costly. Between 8 August and 11 November 1918, the corps suffered 45,835 killed, wounded, or captured, almost 20 percent of Canadian casualties for the entire war and 45 percent of the Canadian Corps' strength on the opening day, 8 August. The casualties of the Hundred Days were more than the First Canadian Army sustained in the entire campaign in northwest Europe in World War II from Normandy to VE Day.

The Hundred Days' campaign, in which the Canadian Corps played such a distinguished part, broke the back of Germany's forces along the Western Front and forced upon Berlin the armistice talks that would end the war. SEE ALSO: CANADIAN CORPS; CURRIE; DROCOURT-QUÉANT LINE.

READING: Shane B. Schreiber, *Shock Army of the British Empire: The Canadian Corps in the Last 100 Days of the Great War* (Westport, CT, 1997).

Hutton, Sir Edward Thomas Henry (1848–1923). Born in England and in the army from 1867, Major-General Hutton came to Canada in 1898 as general officer commanding the militia and complained vociferously about the inefficiency of the patronage-ridden militia. His minister, Frederick Borden, supported many of his reformist ideas but found him erratic, high-handed, and arrogant. At the outset of

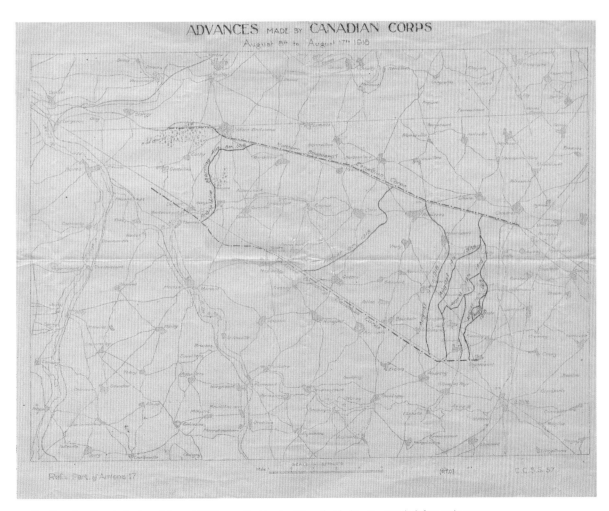

▲ The Canadian Corps' attack on 8 August 1918 began the Hundred Days that led to Germany's defeat in the West.

the South African War, he went behind the Laurier government's back to organize a contingent for the war, and the government had decided to demand his relief in 1900 when London offered him a command in South Africa.

Hyde Park Declaration (1941). Prime Minister Mackenzie King met with US President Franklin Delano Roosevelt at the president's home at Hyde Park, New York, on "a grand Sunday" in April. Canada's war effort had fallen into serious difficulty because war production had increased imports from the United States, and the nation, unable to convert its huge trade surplus in soft currency (such as sterling) into American dollars, could no longer pay for them. The two leaders agreed that the United States would import more raw materials from Canada, helping with the dollar shortage. At the same time, Roosevelt undertook that Britain's Lend-Lease account could be charged with the components sent to Canada for incorporation into munitions destined for the British Isles. In other words, an American engine destined for a fighter produced in Canada for Britain, for example, would not drain Canada's US dollar supplies. This declaration, made by the two leaders acting on their own, effectively freed Canada of financial concerns for the next four years of war and allowed the nation's war industries to make a huge contribution to Allied victory. At the same time, just as the Ogdensburg Agreement had linked the defences of the two nations, the Hyde Park Declaration tied together their economies as well. SEE ALSO: CANADA–UNITED STATES DEFENCE RELATIONS; WAR FINANCE; WAR INDUSTRY.

Imperial Munitions Board (IMB). Britain's Ministry of Munitions created the board in November 1915 to handle British orders for munitions and supplies in Canada, driven in part by shortages of artillery shells for its armies in France. Led by Toronto businessman and meat packer Joseph Flavelle, the IMB restored order out of the chaos created by Minister of Militia and Defence Sam Hughes, whose enthusiasms and political appointments had generated as much inefficiency and scandal as actual production. The board placed orders for shells, ships, and aircraft, and entered into agreements with US government departments after American entry into the war in 1917. It also established and ran its own factories when private industry would not or could not deliver the goods. In late 1916, for example, the IMB took over the Curtiss aircraft plant in Long Branch, near Toronto, renamed it Canadian Aeroplanes Limited, and operated it until the end of the war. The IMB was Canada's largest wartime employer, after the military itself. It was wound up in 1919. SEE ALSO: FLAVELLE; WAR INDUSTRY; WORLD WAR I.

READING: Michael Bliss, *A Canadian Millionaire: The Life and Business Times of Sir Joseph Flavelle, Bart., 1858–1939* (Toronto, 1992).

Imperial War Cabinet (IWC). British Prime Minister David Lloyd George convened the Imperial War Cabinet on 2 March 1917 to discuss matters relating to the conduct of World War I with the leaders of the dominions and India. Sir Robert Borden represented Canada, using his trip to London to visit troops at the front (and to decide to impose conscription). Borden described the Imperial War Cabinet as a "Cabinet of Governments. Every Prime Minister . . . is responsible to his own Parliament and to his own people." Borden also viewed it as "the genesis of a development in the constitutional relations of the Empire, which will form the basis of its unity in the years to come." There was a second session of the IWC in 1918.

READING: R.C. Brown, *Robert Laird Borden: A Biography,* vol. 2 (Toronto, 1980).

Imperial War Conference. Held at the same time as the Imperial War Cabinet in London from March 1917, the conference discussed imperial relations. Largely at Sir Robert Borden's initiative, the conference agreed to Resolution IX declaring that any postwar readjustment of constitutional relations "should be based upon a full recognition of the Dominions as autonomous nations of an Imperial Commonwealth" entitled to "an adequate voice in foreign policy" and "continuous consultation."

"In Flanders Fields." Quickly written by Lieutenant-Colonel John McCrae, a medical doctor serving with the artillery in the Canadian Division on 5 May 1915, upon the death of a friend in battle, "In Flanders Fields" almost instantly became the best-known piece of poetry of World War I. It was first printed anonymously in the British weekly magazine *Punch.* The poem's evocation of poppies led to their use as an international symbol of remembrance of war dead, while the poem itself has become synonymous with remembrance and is frequently a central feature of official ceremonies, commemorative events, and anniversaries. Though it has assumed a wide readership, in part as a literary reflection on the loss and, possibly, the futility of war, its lines clearly impart a sense of martial commitment to and faith in the Allied cause. It was this sense, and not the more pacific, and questionable, interpretation of later years, that ensured its wartime and postwar popularity and its incorporation into the military and veterans' canon as an act of remembrance.

Influenza Epidemic (1918). The "Spanish flu," as it was widely called because it was first identified in Spain, struck worldwide in 1918. The first cases among soldiers of the Canadian Corps were diagnosed in June 1918 and, according to the military's medical authorities, "owing to the excellent condition of the men, this disease made little headway." But it did not disappear and, in the autumn and winter of 1918 and into 1919, influenza cases in the Canadian Expeditionary Force numbered almost 46,000 with 776 deaths. Some suggest the disease first reached Canada among the crew on military transports from England in June 1918 and was retransmitted from Canada to England in September and October 1918. Others maintain that American soldiers passing through Canada en route to overseas brought the disease but, inevitably, the flu spread from soldiers to civilians. Soldiers in the Siberian Expeditionary Force shipped across Canada in late September 1918 carried influenza with them as they moved west. A typical case began with sudden weakness, pain, and chills. For those seriously affected, an army doctor stationed at Quebec wrote, coughing produced "quantities of blood stained expectoration or nearly pure dark blood…the face and fingers cyanosed, active delirium came on…the tongue [grew] dry and brown, the whole surface of the body blue, the temperature rapidly fell and the patient died from failure of the respiratory system." In all, between 50 and 100 million people died during the global pandemic, including an estimated 30,000 to 50,000 Canadians who succumbed to the pneumonia that developed in some 20 percent of those afflicted.

READING: M.O. Humphries, "The Horror at Home: The Canadian Military and the 'Great' Influenza Pandemic of 1918," *Journal of the Canadian Historical Association* (2005).

Inouye, Kanao (1916–1947). Born in Kamloops, BC, Inouye lived in Canada until going to Japan in 1935. During World War II, he served in the Imperial Japanese Army and the Kempeitai, the secret police, at the Shamshuipo prisoner of war camp in Hong Kong that held Canadians captured there in December 1941. The sadistic Inouye, dubbed "the Kamloops Kid" by the POWs, was notoriously cruel to the Canadians, three of whom died at his hands. As he was a British subject, his acts constituted treason, and a postwar military tribunal found him guilty. Inouye was executed on 25 August 1947. SEE ALSO: HONG KONG.

Integration. From 1963 on, Liberal defence minister Paul Hellyer aimed to eliminate waste resulting from the triplication of services in the armed forces. His Defence White Paper of 1964 introduced the concept of integration, expected to achieve financial and personnel savings by creating a better-coordinated force. Integration was generally well received, but it was soon followed by the more contentious policy of unification, which united the army, navy, and air force into the single-service Canadian Forces in 1968. SEE ALSO: HELLYER; UNIFICATION.

Internment. The forcible confinement of persons in wartime, internment was used by Canada in both world wars. During World War I, Germans, Austro-Hungarians, and subjects of the Turkish empire were deemed subject to internment if there were "reasonable grounds" to believe they might commit espionage or act illegally. In all, some 8,579 were interned in 24 camps across Canada, including 2,009 Germans, most of them army reservists. The internees also included 5,954 Galicians, as Ukrainians were then called, along with 81 women and 156 children who went voluntarily to the camps with family members. Very few of the latter were loyal to the Austro-Hungarian Empire, but the government's broad-brush approach swept them up anyway. While many were permitted to leave the camps when labour shortages arose in 1916, government internment operations incarcerated the innocent, divided families, and violated basic civil liberties. General Sir William Otter ran the camps for the militia department; in 1915, the justice department took over.

Before World War II, an interdepartmental committee of bureaucrats prepared the Defence of Canada Regulations that expanded the scope of internment. Anyone acting in a manner "prejudicial to the public safety or the safety of the state" could be interned, a description covering both enemy aliens and Canadian citizens. Lists of pro-Nazi Germans, Italian and domestic fascists, and Japanese Canadians suspected of readiness to assist Canada's enemies were in preparation before the war. By January 1941, 763 Germans, most of whom were members of Nazi front organizations, had been interned; 127 were freed after review. For Italians suspected of supporting Mussolini, the numbers were 586 and 105; in addition, 28 domestic fascists were interned, as was Camillien Houde, Montreal's mayor, who advised his compatriots not to adhere to the terms of the National Registration of 1940. Once Japan entered the war in December 1941, the police arrested 38 Canadian Japanese suspected of subversive intentions. Later, 720 more Canadian Japanese were interned at Angler, Ontario, a group that included pro-Japan supporters but also some Canadian Japanese who protested too loudly at the Canadian government's policy for forced evacuations from the Pacific Coast. At war's end, 425 internees remained at Angler. Not all Japanese Canadians were interned; the mass evacuation from the West Coast constituted in scale and racial undertones an unprecedented violation of civil rights and basic freedoms, but it was not internment. The later confiscation of Japanese Canadian property, without compensation or subsequent return, and federal plans to deport Japanese Canadians back to Japan after the war left indelible scars on Canada's conduct of the war, regardless of the underlying security issues that had helped to precipitate the removals.

World War II would see the establishment of 26 detention camps, most of which held prisoners of war and civilian internees sent by Britain to Canada. Most Canadian internees were at Petawawa, Ontario, or Angler, with responsibility for camp operations shared between the army and the department of the secretary of state. Foreign nationals in internment camps had their interests watched over by a "Protecting Power," which was Spain in the case of the Japanese, whose diplomats or representatives conducted visits and reported on the status of detainees. The International Committee of the Red Cross also played a role in monitoring conditions.

The Mulroney government in 1988 apologized formally for the treatment accorded Japanese Canadians after a long and difficult campaign for redress led mainly by Japanese Canadians themselves, often against considerable public and governmental indifference. The case was complicated politically by the continuing failure of the government of Japan to apologize for its horrific treatment of Canadian and Allied prisoners of war, and by the wanton violations of the laws of war committed by its troops with the full knowledge and active encouragement of its military and political leadership. Ottawa's eventual about-face offered financial compensation to Japanese Canadians interned or evacuated, including active supporters of Japanese aggression, a group never acknowledged by pro-redress claimants. A similar apology was given to interned Italian Canadians, including active fascists. Ukrainian Canadians also received an apology for their World War I internment. Although plans had been made to sweep up subversives in the event of World War III, no enemy aliens or suspected security risks have been interned in Canada under circumstances similar to those in either world war since 1945. SEE ALSO: DEFENCE OF CANADA REGULATIONS; JAPANESE CANADIAN EVACUATION; WAR MEASURES ACT.

Italian Campaign. After the successful invasion and conquest of Sicily in July and August 1943, the Allies turned their focus to the Italian mainland with the aim of driving fascist dictator Benito Mussolini out of power (which they did on 25 July) and Italy out of the war (the Italian surrender occurred on 3 September). If Germany now chose to defend the country, Allied strategists believed that the required reinforcements could only come from the Russian front, which would ease Moscow's burden in the suddenly two-front war. The Allies also believed that the Germans, as an occupying army in Italy and no longer allied with the

Italians, would face a restive population at their back. But Italian geography, mountainous and cut by rivers that ran across the country, heavily favoured the defence. The Allied advance up the Italian boot tied up more Allied than German resources, and Italy proved as incapable a guerrilla power as it had been a belligerent one. German forces, with limited reinforcements from other theatres, quickly lost command of the air and sea around the Italian peninsula but, on the ground, fought a bloody, superb defensive battle that consumed several Allied corps for the balance of the war.

Initially, the sole Canadian commitment to the campaign was the 1st Canadian Infantry Division, now battle experienced after its impressive debut in Sicily, and its accompanying 1st Canadian Armoured Brigade. As part of General Bernard Montgomery's British Eighth Army, the 1st Division under Major-General Guy Simonds came ashore at Reggio di Calabria on 3 September 1943 and began to press inland. Six days later, British and American troops assaulted Salerno, where they met fierce resistance. The Germans fell back slowly elsewhere, leaving rear parties to harass the invaders, planting booby traps and wreaking destruction on Italian towns and cities as they retired. The enemy's aim was to move into readily defensible, well-prepared positions south of Rome.

The Canadians had originally been expected to return to Britain after Sicily, bringing their battle experience to First Canadian Army, but now they were to be joined by 5th Canadian Armoured Division and I Canadian Corps headquarters, a substantial expansion in strength. The Allied Supreme Commander in the Mediterranean, US General Eisenhower, had not wanted another armoured division, preferring more infantry, but this political decision initiated in Ottawa (and made despite General McNaughton's protests that were so strong as to lead to his relief from command of First Canadian Army a few months later) had to be accepted. The new formations would not be in the field until early 1944, necessitating the expansion and continued maintenance of the long Canadian lines of communication to Italy. Meanwhile the 1st

Division, now under Major-General Christopher Vokes (Simonds moved laterally to lead the 5th Armoured), proceeed north to force the Moro River and seize the small Adriatic port city of Ortona.

This proved to be a bloody, difficult chore. The German defenders were paratroopers and panzer grenadiers, tough and efficient fighters. The surrounding terrain, cut with gorges and steep-banked rivers, required the Allies to halt and concentrate their forces repeatedly in order to cut through successive lines of naturally strong defences supplemented by guns, barbed wire, tank traps, and minefields. The Canadian infantry fought from farm building to farm building through a cold November and, on 6 December, they put their first troops across the flooded Moro River. The German resistance, supported by tanks, resulted in heavy Canadian casualties and the attackers' position across the Moro and atop the escarpment was not firm until 9 December. Worse was soon to come: as the Canadians closed on Ortona, the Germans prepared the town for a street-to-street defence, blowing up houses to stop Allied tanks and personnel carriers, creating ambushes and killing zones amidst the rubble, and latticing the debris with demolitions, booby-traps, and concealed positions.

First, the attackers had to breach "The Gully," a deep cut that the 90th Panzer Division chose as its main defence line south of the city. The Gully ran inland for 915 metres, a perfect obstacle to tanks, with German weapons pits dug into its banks that were all but immune to shelling. It took days of costly fighting to get over and around The Gully, and Captain Paul Triquet of the Royal 22e Régiment earned a Victoria Cross on 14 December for his role in seizing and holding Casa Berardi. Not until 21 December did the Canadians reach Ortona's outskirts, as The Loyal Edmonton Regiment began to fight its way through the streets. It was fatal to move into the enemy's prepared killing zones; the only way to take the city was to go house by house, block by block, using a "mouse-holing" technique of blowing holes in the walls of adjoining houses, clearing one house top to bottom, and then moving into the next one, leaving

German dead—and, all too often, Canadian dead too—behind.

On 25 December, Canadian infantry companies pulled back one at a time for a Christmas dinner in a ruined, roofless church—while one officer played carols on the organ—and then went back to the fighting. On the night of 27–28 December, the Germans silently, efficiently pulled out, leaving the ruined city to the Canadians and its Italian residents who emerged from cellars and caves to find only ruination. The 1st Division had lost 1,372 dead, many more wounded, and others with their nerves completely shattered. "Little Stalingrad," the media called it; certainly it had been the hardest fight the Canadians had yet seen, a pyrrhic victory that left the 1st Division spent, but a victory nonetheless, with Canadians on the battlefield and the Germans, temporarily at least, in retreat.

The campaign continued after a winter lull. I Canadian Corps, now led by Lieutenant-General E.L.M. Burns, moved secretly across Italy to the Liri Valley, near Cassino, to prepare to join the attack on the Gustav and Hitler Lines protecting Rome. The defences were strong—concrete bunkers, dug-in tank turrets, mines, wire, and a skilful, well-led enemy, and the valley was cut by the Liri, Gari, and Rapido Rivers that had to be crossed before the formidable defences of the Gustav Line could be assaulted. Initially, 1st Canadian Armoured Brigade supported the 8th Indian Infantry Division in crossing the Gari on assault boats, and then completed two Bailey bridges used by Canadian tanks on 12 and 13 May. During those days and on 14 May the bridgeheads expanded, while thrusts were mounted deeper into the German positions. On 15 May, the Three Rivers Regiment fought a particularly vicious battle near the town of Pignataro. Now in danger of being outflanked, the Germans were forced to withdraw to the Hitler Line.

The initial Canadian attack here by General Vokes's 1st Infantry Division went in on 16 May and the 5th Canadian Armoured Division, now led by Major-General Bert Hoffmeister, joined in the fighting a week later. On 24 May, the Westminster Regiment (Motor) forced a crossing of the Melfa River, and company commander Major John Mahony, despite three wounds, successfully organized and inspired the defence of the bridgehead against superior numbers of enemy infantry supported by armour and self-propelled guns. He was awarded the Victoria Cross.

Despite very heavy casualties (some 7,000 killed, wounded, and captured) and massive traffic jams on the single good road through the Liri valley, the Canadians made good headway, and their work and that of their Allies opened the road to Rome. Its capture by US troops, on 4 June, almost simultaneous with the D-Day invasion on 6 June 1944, made it the first Axis capital to fall. But for the Canadians and others in Italy, the focus in the media was now on France; the "D-Day Dodgers…in sunny Italy," as a British MP and a soldier song famously labelled them, would soon be all but forgotten.

Eighth Army headquarters and its commander General Oliver Leese had not been very pleased with the way General Burns and his corps staff had managed the recent battle, complaining about inexperience that had led to the traffic tie-ups. (It had not been the Canadians who planned Eighth Army's attack through a valley with one good road; that was Leese's doing, but Canadian inexperience made matters worse.) Efforts to break up the corps followed and failed, then an attempt to sack Burns, which also failed when General Ken Stuart, the chief of staff at Canadian Military Headquarters in London, refused to agree with making a Canadian the battle's leading scapegoat. Nonetheless, Burns was on notice.

The next major Canadian action came in August well to the north and on the Adriatic side of the peninsula. The Germans' Gothic Line protected the valley of the River Po, and it was a formidable obstacle built onto the high ground of the Appenines with concrete blockhouses, wire, mines, machine guns, and small units of tough, well-trained infantry and combat engineers. The Canadians had six rivers to cross, each well defended. But the I Canadian Corps was now an experienced formation, and when General Hoffmeister, doing his own reconnaissance,

⌃ In July 1944, soldiers liberate the village of San Pancrazio, Italy, where German troops had earlier massacred civilians.

saw that the first enemy defences seemed only lightly held, the scheduled attack was moved up by two days, and the 5th Canadian Armoured Division, "Hoffy's Mighty Maroon Machine," efficiently cracked the first line, almost encircling the German division opposite it and forcing its retreat. The rest would not prove as easy. From 30 August for more than a month, the Canadians battered their way forward, pushing a spearhead through the mountains to Rimini and beyond. In October, on the Savio River, Private "Smoky" Smith of the Seaforth Highlanders almost single-handedly stopped two German counterattacks against his regiment's bridgehead, destroying two tanks and killing or scattering a large body of the enemy. Smith won the Victoria Cross.

General Burns's I Canadian Corps had scored a signal victory, arguably Canada's most important one of the war, but Burns would not remain much longer in command to receive the kudos. This time, it was his division commanders, Vokes and Hoffmeister, who were unhappy with his dour personality and uninspiring leadership, and their complaints led to his ouster and replacement by Lieutenant-General Charles Foulkes (no less dour a personality) who came to Italy on 10 November from commanding the 2nd Canadian Infantry Division in France and the Low Countries.

Deteriorating weather paralyzed the advance (and the soldiers) in mud and cold. The final heavy fighting by the Canadians came on the Senio River north of Ravenna in January 1945. In February, I Canadian

ITALY
3 September 1943–25 February 1945

GULF OF GENOA

Genoa

EMILIA

Bologna

Reno

Senio

GOTHIC LINE

Ravenna

Pistoia

1ST CANADIAN CORPS

Pisa

Arno

Florence

Rimini

Tomba di Pesaro

Pesaro

TUSCANY

Siena

Arezzo

Metauro

Ancona

L. Trasimene

MARCHES

ELBA

Perugia

Tiber

UMBRIA

ADRIATIC SEA

CORSICA

Viterbo

LATIUM

WINTER LINE

Ortona

Villa Rogatti

ROME

ABRUZZI

&

SARDINIA

6th U.S. CORPS JAN 1944

Anzio

1ST CANADIAN CORPS

Liri

Ceprano

Sangro

Biferno

Termoli

Cassino

MOLISE

Campobasso

ADOLF HITLER LINE

Vinchiaturo

GUSTAV LINE

Volturno

Foggia

APULIA

78TH BRIT. DIV. & 4th ARMD. BDE. 22–23 SEP 1943

TYRRHENIAN SEA

Naples

CAMPANIA

Melfi

Bari

Salerno

FIFTH U.S. ARMY 9 Sep 1943

Potenza

Gulf of Salerno

LUCANIA

Taranto

1ST BRITISH AIRBORNE DIV 9 SEP 1943

GULF OF TARANTO

SICILY
10 July – 6 August 1943

Trapani

Palermo

Messina

Reggio

Marsala

Strait of Messina

CALABRIA

Sciacca

Agira

Leonforte

Regalbuto

Catanzaro

Valguarnera

Adrano

Piazza Armerina

Catania

Licata

Grammichele

BRITISH EIGHTH ARMY 3 SEP 1943

1ST CDN DIV

Augusta

SEVENTH U.S. ARMY 10 JULY 1943

Ragusa

Syracuse

Messina

Modica

Rosolini

Reggio

1ST CANADIAN DIVISION

Ispica

Pachino

BRITISH EIGHTH ARMY 10 JULY 1943

0 10 20 30 40 50 miles

0 20 40 60 60 km

0 20 40 60 80 100 miles

0 20 40 60 80 100 120 140 160 km

N

◣ I Canadian Corps fought in Italy for some 18 months and suffered more than 25,000 casualties in a gruelling campaign.

Corps began its move to northwest Europe where it was to join up with the remainder of First Canadian Army for the liberation of the Netherlands. Officers of the corps professed astonishment at the lavish scale of support the northwest European campaign had compared to what they had received in Italy.

The campaign in Italy had been gruelling and costly. It did tie down German resources, but it also used up more Allied troops and equipment than the enemy, on the defensive, had to deploy. The Germans, skilfully led by Field Marshal Albert Kesselring, had dragged out the costly campaign in a manner that served Nazi interests and inflicted heavy casualties. Some 92,757 Canadians served in Italy, of whom more than a quarter were killed, wounded, captured, or injured. Between the two divisions and the armoured brigade, there were 5,399 killed, 19,486 wounded, and 1,004 taken prisoner; another 365 died from other causes. SEE ALSO: BURNS; I CANADIAN CORPS; FOULKES; SICILIAN CAMPAIGN; SIMONDS.

READING: G.W.L. Nicholson, *The Canadians in Italy* (Ottawa, 1957).

Japanese Canadian Evacuation. Census figures showed 23,000 persons of Japanese origin in Canada in 1941, almost all living in British Columbia's coastal areas. Fishers and market gardeners for the most part, Japanese Canadians (and Chinese Canadians too) had stirred racist fears of the "yellow peril" in BC for 40 years or more, concerns that increased exponentially as imperial Japan became expansionist in the 1930s. Many Japanese Canadians actively took the side of an aggressive, expansionist Japan in its war in China, and their English-language newspaper published propaganda features supplied by the Japanese consulate-general in Vancouver. Such activities, legitimate in peacetime, looked very different as war approached. The federal government, sensitive to the concerns of the BC majority and worried about security, created a Special Committee on Orientals in 1940 that ordered Japanese Canadians to register with federal authorities

▲ After Japan entered World War II in December 1941, the Canadian government removed Japanese Canadians from their homes on the British Columbia coast to the interior.

and barred them from military service. No plans had been made for mass evacuation or internment in the event of war, though Canadian and US officials on the Permanent Joint Board on Defence in the fall of 1941 had considered the need for coordinated action in dealing with their Japanese communities.

After Japan's attack on Pearl Harbor, Hawaii, on 7 December 1941 and the fall of Hong Kong at the end of the month, public fears that Japan might attack the West Coast increased, and British Columbia media and political and military leaders demanded action from the federal government. Authorities had beached the community's fishing boats and seized its radios at once after the attacks on 7 December. Then, on 14 January 1942, although bureaucrats and military officials in Ottawa did not believe that the Japanese Canadians posed a threat to British Columbia, the government, pressed by the minister of pensions and national health, BC's Ian Mackenzie, decided to order all males of military age moved inland. As Allied defeats in Asia continued and as word spread of atrocities against prisoners of war and "fifth column" activities in the territories Japan had conquered, mounting public pressure led the government in February to order the evacuation of all Japanese Canadian men, women, and children, citizens and aliens alike, to makeshift inland towns. Ottawa, by this time, also knew from Allied intelligence sources (the United States had broken some Japanese codes and shared intelligence with the British who informed Canada through the High Commission in London) that the Japanese consulate-general in Vancouver had earlier been ordered to recruit spies to track Canadian naval and military movements. Canada's own intelligence sources on the West Coast were almost non-existent. This lack meant that the government had almost no knowledge of either the absence or presence of any spying or subversive intentions. The dearth of credible intelligence fed fears and proved very harmful to Japanese Canadians, the vast majority of whom had no hostile intent to Canada and many of whom wanted to serve (but were not permitted to do so until late in the war) in the Canadian military.

The government confiscated Japanese Canadian owned property (eventually selling it off at fire sale prices) and moved the Japanese Canadians well away from the coast over the next few months and into the BC interior. Men were put to work on road gangs or in the forests, though labour shortages soon led the government to encourage men and women to move eastward to manufacturing or farm jobs in central Canada and Alberta; many did. Several hundred men who resisted the evacuation and those who were adamant supporters of Japan ended up in an internment camp in Angler, Ontario, but the great majority of Japanese Canadians were not interned and (unlike the interned men) not under the eye of Spain, the protecting power for Japan's interests in Canada.

The Mackenzie King government, on 4 August 1944, decided to repatriate "disloyal" Japanese Canadians to the Japan most of them had never seen and later to encourage as many as possible of the remainder to go. In the end, 3,964 left Canada. Those who stayed, once the repatriation policy ended, re-established with great difficulty their lives in Canada, many east of the Rockies.

This was far from Canada's finest hour: a racist policy used to single out one ethnicity had no place in a war that was, in part at least, fighting against Axis racism. Public fears had spiralled out of control in British Columbia in early 1942, Japan's forces were advancing on every front, the number of soldiers in the province was small, military staffs feared that white soldiers might not act against white mobs that could attack Japanese Canadians, and the government believed it had to act. Nonetheless, the forced evacuation of Japanese Canadians from the West Coast remains an unprecedented violation of civil rights and basic freedoms; the confiscation of Japanese Canadian property and the removal of many Japanese Canadians to Japan afterwards left an indelible stain on Canada's conduct of the war.

After a long, successful campaign for redress by the Japanese Canadian community, Brian Mulroney's Progressive Conservative government issued a formal apology and offered monetary compensation four decades later. See also: Defence of Canada Regulations; Internment.

Reading: Ken Adachi, *The Enemy That Never Was: A History of the Japanese Canadians* (Toronto, 1968); Patricia Roy et al., *Mutual Hostages: Canadians and Japanese during the Second World War* (Toronto, 1990).

Jervois, William Francis Drummond (1821–1897). A military engineer, Drummond came to British North America in 1863 during the American Civil War to advise on colonial defences. He recommended improving fortifications at Halifax, Quebec City, and Montreal, but believed the Great Lakes could not be held, making defence west of Montreal impossible. Returning to Canada a year later, he tried to persuade the Canadian government to pay for the defences of Montreal and suggested building fortifications in Canada East that, if the Americans attacked, could help gain time for a strategic withdrawal eastward, the arrival of winter, and intervention by the Royal Navy. This report, in effect abandoning Upper Canada, caused natural concern, but not so much that the Canadian government was willing to spend money to try to improve matters. A British loan to build fortifications was diverted to railway construction and nothing was done. Canada relied on luck and the implicit belief that the United States would do nothing harmful.

Juno Beach. On D-Day, 6 June 1944, the British, American, and Canadian Allies returned to France with a huge landing on the Normandy coast. The

⬆ One of the five D-Day invasion beaches, Juno was assaulted by the 3rd Canadian Division and 2nd Canadian Armoured Brigade. Here, troops wade ashore at the village of Bernières-sur-Mer.

MAP 2

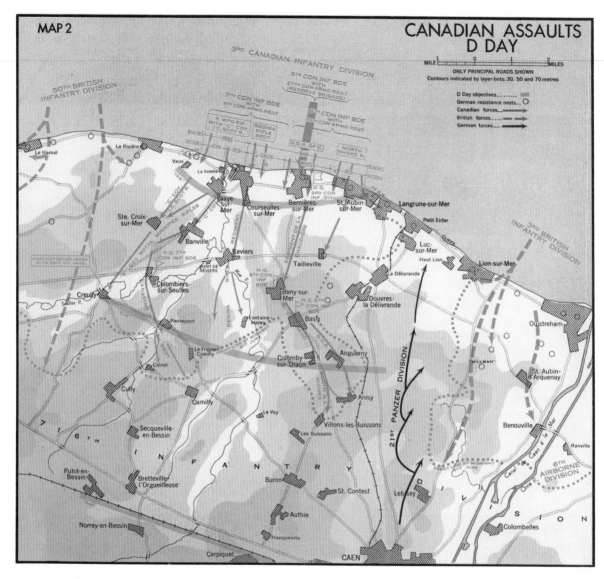

CANADIAN ASSAULTS D DAY

ONLY PRINCIPAL ROADS SHOWN
Contours indicated by layer-tints: 30, 50 and 70 metres

D Day objectives..........
German resistance nests...
Canadian forces.........
British forces.........
German forces....

▲ The 3rd Canadian Division landed in Normandy with other Canadian and Allied forces on D-Day, 6 June 1944. Its heavy casualties were nevertheless fewer than expected, and the division moved inland in good order.

Canadian component of Operation Overlord was the 3rd Canadian Infantry Division, commanded by Major-General R.F.L. Keller, supported by the 2nd Canadian Armoured Brigade. Its assigned beach, Juno, extended for roughly eight kilometres between Grave-sur-Mer and St Aubin-sur-Mer. Juno was one of five invasion beaches, with two each allocated to the British and Americans.

The Canadian plan of attack called for the 7th and 8th Brigades to land in the first wave, perhaps 3,000 soldiers in all touching down, and to consolidate the beachhead. Infantry and armour would then move up to 15 kilometres inland to take the high ground west of Caen. The 9th Brigade, the reserve, was to be ashore in time to help drive off expected German counterattacks. Heavy bombing, shelling from the sea, and the attackers' own artillery and tanks were to provide support.

The plan worked relatively well. Although the aerial bombing did not destroy defences manned by three battalions of the Germany's 716th Infantry Division, fire support from the sea was effective. The men in the first wave of landing craft, touching down just before 8:00 a.m., established themselves ashore, though not without difficulty as concrete bunkers along the shoreline remained intact. The defending German units were essentially wiped out. All Canadian battalions took their immediate objectives and then moved inland, some exceeding their intermediate objectives as well, but Caen itself would not be secured until July. Counterattacks from the 12th SS Panzer Division, delayed by air attacks and not as well coordinated as the enemy had hoped, began on 7 June. Canadian casualties on Juno Beach were 340 killed and 574 wounded, terrible enough, but about half what had been feared by the planners.

READING: Mark Zuehlke, *Juno Beach* (Vancouver, 2004).

⌃ Richard Jack, *The Second Battle of Ypres, 22 April to 25 May 1915*, 1917
oil on canvas, 371.5 x 589.0 cm
Canadian War Museum

❮ Mabel May
Women Making Shells, 1919
oil on canvas, 182.7 x 214.9 cm
Canadian War Museum

▲ Frederick Varley, *Some Day the People Will Return*, 1918
oil on canvas, 183.5 x 229.3 cm
Canadian War Museum

❮ James Wilson Morrice
Canadians in the Snow, 1918
oil on canvas, 274.8 x 365.7 cm
Canadian War Museum

▲ Frank Johnston, *Looking into the Blue*, 1918
watercolour and gouache on hardboard, 72.1 x 57.5 cm
Canadian War Museum

▲ Arthur Lismer, *Olympic with Returned Soldiers*, 1919
oil on canvas, 123.0 x 163.3 cm
Canadian War Museum

▲ Frederick Varley, *German Prisoners*, 1918–1920
oil on canvas, 127.4 x 183.7 cm
Canadian War Museum

Kap'yong, Battle of (1951). In April 1951, during the Korean War, Commonwealth troops including a battalion of the Princess Patricia's Canadian Light Infantry (PPCLI) fought a successful defensive battle against a far more numerous Chinese Communist force in the Kap'yong area northeast of Seoul, capital city of the Republic of Korea (ROK), or South Korea.

On 22 April, Chinese Communist forces launched a spring offensive against ROK and United Nations (UN) troops, one arm of their assault aimed at the Kap'yong Valley. After a ROK division broke and fled, the 27th Commonwealth Infantry Brigade, including the Canadians, moved into positions on hills 20 kilometres behind what had been the front. The 3rd Battalion of the Royal Australian Regiment occupied a

▲ In April 1951, the 2nd Battalion PPCLI fought off Chinese Communist forces near Kap'yong, South Korea. In this painting by Ted Zuber, a Korean War veteran, American aircraft drop supplies onto the Canadians' hill-top positions.

hill on the right of the UN line, while the 2nd Battalion of the PPCLI, commanded by Lieutenant-Colonel Jim Stone, dug in on Hill 677, five kilometres to the west, with a broad valley dividing the two units. The advancing Chinese juggernaut first hit the Australians, who withdrew only after an epic, costly defence that inflicted hundreds of casualties on the attackers. The Chinese then moved against the Canadians.

The Chinese attacked at 10:00 p.m. on 24 April, their charge heralded by bugles, whistles, and exploding mortar shells. One Canadian platoon had to abandon its position, but the company under attack held. At 1:00 a.m., the Chinese hit another company position, all but overrunning it until the company commander called for artillery fire on his own position. The New Zealand artillery regiment supporting the PPCLI obliged, dumping 2,300 rounds on the hill and killing many of the Chinese. At first light on 25 April, the Chinese withdrew, but the PPCLI, now cut off, had to ask for supplies to be airdropped in anticipation that the Chinese might renew the assault. They did not. The Chinese regiments at Kap'yong had been decimated by Canadian and UN firepower and soon fell back in disorder after the unsuccessful attack. The PPCLI, only in Korea for four months at the time, suffered astonishingly light losses of just 10 dead and 23 wounded in the battle and received a US Presidential Unit Citation for its efforts, as did the 3rd Battalion of the Royal Australian Regiment. The New Zealand gunners received a South Korean Presidential Unit Citation. The Commonwealth troops had helped blunt a major enemy offensive, despite having been outnumbered five to one. The Canadian Korean War Memorial Garden is now located nearby. SEE ALSO: KOREAN WAR; PRINCESS PATRICIA'S CANADIAN LIGHT INFANTRY.

READING: H.F. Wood, *Strange Battleground: Official History of the Canadian Army in Korea* (Ottawa, 1966); David Bercuson, *Blood on the Hills: The Canadian Army in the Korean War* (Toronto, 1999).

Kemp, Alfred Edward (1858–1929). A successful Toronto manufacturer of sheet metal, Kemp had been born in Clarenceville, Canada East. He won election to Parliament in 1900 as a Conservative, and Prime Minister Borden chose him to replace Sir Sam Hughes as minister of militia and defence in late 1916. Kemp began to restore order to the militia department, and the next year Borden sent him to London as minister of the overseas military forces of Canada, a post he held until 1920. Kemp's task overseas was similar to what he had done in Ottawa, rooting out Hughes's problematic or troublesome political appointees and fixing his inefficiencies. Kemp worked to give the Canadian Corps what it needed in order to fight effectively, and then presided over its demobilization and return home.

Khaki University. During both world wars, Canadian authorities overseas sought to ease the transition of military personnel to postwar civilian life—and to occupy them while they awaited repatriation—by offering a range of courses from basic literacy to higher education. Henry M. Tory, president of the University of Alberta, led the World War I–era Khaki University from 1917. It grew from religious and other classes offered by military padres and charitable organizations, and operated initially under the auspices of the Young Men's Christian Association. Some 50,000 military personnel took courses and the army took over the operation of the university in 1918, making it an essential element of training and personnel management in the Canadian Expeditionary Force. Courses included everything from carpentry and trades to agriculture, commerce, and literature. Several sites were established throughout England and some in France, while hundreds of other Canadian soldiers attended British educational institutions.

The World War II Khaki University began in 1945, led by Brigadier G.E. Beament, an Ottawa lawyer and staff officer in First Canadian Army. In intent and operation it was similar to that from World War I, designed to improve morale, occupy the troops, ease repatriation, and prepare returning personnel for the newfound rigours of civilian life. The university, run as a unit of Canadian Military Headquarters, offered first- and second-year courses in residence at a Junior College campus at Leavesden, England, and extension courses. It was disbanded in 1946.

▲ Prime Minister Mackenzie King, VE Day, 8 May 1945.

King, William Lyon Mackenzie (1874–1950). Born in Berlin (later Kitchener), Ontario, Mackenzie King was the grandson of the Upper Canadian rebel of 1837, William Lyon Mackenzie. Interested in social questions, he landed a government research job and the post of editor of the *Labour Gazette* in the just-created Department of Labour, where he would soon become deputy minister.

King built a formidable reputation as a young man on the rise. In 1908, he ran successfully as a Liberal in his hometown; a year later, Sir Wilfrid Laurier named him labour minister. Skill and determination in this job did not save him in 1911 when the Liberals, campaigning in support of free trade with the United States, went down to defeat at the hands

of Robert Borden's Conservatives. King himself lost his seat.

The next years were difficult. He had to find work and became a labour expert in the employ of American entrepreneur John D. Rockefeller, Jr, but the outbreak of war in 1914 made King's stay in the United States look almost unpatriotic. Why was he not in the army? In King's mind, there was no difficulty in dealing with this question. He was 40 years old in 1914, his parents were old and ill, and he had to help support his siblings. Critics then and later dismissed such arguments as self-serving, but the reasons had cogency. He would not have a military career, but instead maintained hope for one in politics. King ran as a Liberal in the December 1917 election, but lost.

He philosophically supported compulsory service, the election's major issue, but, when the Liberal party split on the question, facing a pro-conscription Union Government under Borden, King remained with Laurier. Despite King's defeat, that loyalty would later pay off handsomely.

The end of the Great War, with its terrible casualties and dislocation, produced unprecedented labour unrest in Canada. Rising prices, the return of the army, and government disorganization created a climate that occasionally verged on revolution. Mackenzie King, a genuine expert on labour questions, in 1918 published a wordy (and largely impenetrable) book, *Industry and Humanity*, that nevertheless marked him as a reform-minded centrist. With Laurier's death in February 1919 and the eruption of the Winnipeg General Strike in May, King seemed to be the man of the hour as Liberals gathered to select a new leader. There were better known candidates but none, other than King, who had both remained loyal to Laurier in 1917 and appeared to understand the complexity of postwar labour issues. The leadership became his when Québécois delegates voted for him en bloc, though it took three ballots to determine the outcome.

King had one primary goal: to reunite the Liberals' pro- and anti-conscription wings, in effect its Quebec and English-Canadian members. In the 1921 election, Prime Minister Arthur Meighen campaigned for a high tariff, but King ran against the Union Government's war record and on his own reputation as a conciliator, the man to bring French and English Canadians, farmers, workers, and industrialists together. The message worked, the Liberals capturing 116 seats, including all 65 in Quebec.

His initial successes as prime minister were on the international stage. A soft nationalist and a supporter of British ideals and the monarchy, King opposed British interference with Canada's autonomy and the arrogance of its colonial mandarins, understanding intrinsically that maintaining Canadian unity at home demanded an exquisite balance in the conduct of its affairs abroad. In 1922, Prime Minister Lloyd George had publicly asked for Canadian support for British military intervention at Chanak in Turkey before an official request had even reached Ottawa. A leader who had reduced the Canadian military to tiny numbers, King expressed outrage at this assertion of a common imperial foreign policy that he knew could tear his country apart, but in public said only that Parliament would decide. It was a clever dodge, as Parliament was not in session and he was not about to recall it, so no contingent sailed for Turkey. London fumed, French Canada applauded, and the crisis subsided. King then went to the Imperial Conference of 1923 intending to get autonomy recognized—as a self-governing dominion, King's Canada had to make its own policy and serve its own people's national interests. The British found the Canadian "obstinate, tiresome and stupid," but he ultimately prevailed: the conference recognized that the diplomatic unity of the Empire was a relic of the past. King's insistence on making foreign policy decisions in Canada had begun the process of turning the Empire into the Commonwealth.

King received scant credit from those Canadians who remained attached to Britain and, although he lost seats in the 1925 election, he clung to power desperately. The governor general, Viscount Byng of Vimy, eventually handed the prime ministership to Meighen, but the Conservative chief could not survive in the House of Commons or in the 1926 election. King returned triumphant but, when the Depression hit in the fall of 1929, King did little, and R.B. Bennett, the new Conservative leader who promised to blast his way into the markets of the world and create jobs, won election in 1930, just in time for history's greatest financial and economic catastrophe. King's timing could not have been better. By 1935 and the next election, his party's cry of "King or Chaos" resulted in a huge Liberal majority with 178 seats.

His position secure, King might have been expected to play a role in foreign policy as the world slid toward another world war, but he lent no support to tepid British or French efforts to rein in Germany. In his view, Canada had no stake in Eastern Europe, and the tensions at home between French and English Canadians, always exacerbated by the prospect of involvement in a "British" war, demanded that Canada speak softly. Nor did Canada have a big stick. The regular army, navy, and air force combined numbered only 10,000, the reserve forces were weak, and there was little modern equipment. It would not matter, if war came: King's preference for non-involvement had limits and his attitudes toward war and commitment were contingent, never categorical. Though misunderstood—and often deliberately misrepresented—at the time (and by many historians since), King's loyalties were unmistakable: if war came, Canada would fight. Visiting Germany in 1937, he told Adolf Hitler, the German dictator, that Canadians would swim the ocean if Germany went to war with Britain.

Canadians would fight in Europe, but they would surely be tested at home as well, and King worked assiduously to cultivate US President Franklin D. Roosevelt. The prime minister and the president were hardly close friends, and the disparity in their nations' power was substantial. But they respected each other as politicians, understood that geography obliged them to work together, and began to move their countries toward close co-operation in defence. Secret staff talks took place and, in 1938, Roosevelt informally put Canada under the American defence umbrella. When war came in 1939, the good relations established between the two leaders mattered.

The war was a testing time for King and Canada. By skilful manoeuvring, King kept the country united. He had desperately hoped to stay out of war—like most Canadians he had cheered the Munich agreement of 1938—but he and his Cabinet had decided that Canada had to join in if Britain fought; English-Canadian public opinion would demand nothing less. But King could decide the scope of involvement, and his instincts were for a war of limited liability and, as he had promised in March 1939, a war without conscription for overseas service. That pledge to Quebec was sincerely meant, but it would become a millstone. And when Britain went to war on 3 September 1939, King delayed Canada's own declaration for a week, time enough for Parliament to decide—a foregone conclusion but a useful tactic just the same—on its own to enter. Soon after, King began

the negotiations with Britain that led to the British Commonwealth Air Training Plan, a scheme that he had London declare to be Canada's major contribution to the war. For a brief time, it even seemed doubtful that a division of infantry would proceed overseas. Canada was in the war, reluctantly in Quebec, with limited enthusiasm in many other areas of Canada, but the country was decidedly in—and united. This was King's huge achievement.

The prime minister soon faced attacks from both the reluctant and the enthusiastic. In September 1939, Quebec Premier Maurice Duplessis used the war as an excuse for a snap election, charging that the federal government was centralizing power with emergency orders. Ottawa viewed this as an attack on national unity, and King's Quebec ministers, promising no conscription if Duplessis met defeat, entered the fray. Duplessis was duly smashed, and a Liberal government took power. Early in the New Year, Liberal Premier Mitchell Hepburn of Ontario, rabidly anti-King, charged that the federal government was doing nothing in the war and had his legislature condemn the war effort. King used this extraordinary action to justify his own snap election, catching the opposition completely unready. Again the government pledged itself against conscription, and scored a huge victory. King was in power with a fresh mandate when the fortunes of war turned against the Allies in April and May 1940.

From being a war of limited liability with the major Canadian effort directed to air training, Allied defeats in Europe made the conflict a struggle for the survival of democracy itself. Britain now stood alone in Europe with Canada its greatest (and geographically nearest) ally. It could not fall. There would be a vastly expanded Air Training Plan, a very large navy, and a bigger army than in the Great War. Britain's peril also emboldened pro-conscription forces in the country and in Cabinet, and King fought a long rearguard action to stave off the inevitable. The tactical retreat came in June 1940 when the National Resources Mobilization Act (NRMA) authorized home defence conscription for 30 days; this term soon stretched to cover the war's duration. In late 1941, pro-conscription pressure resulted in an April 1942 plebiscite that asked Canadians to release the government from its anti-conscription promises of 1939–1940. The government won, but French Canadians voted heavily "non." The NRMA was duly amended, but King pledged that the change meant "not necessarily conscription, but conscription if necessary," one of the most famous and deviously self-serving ambiguities in Canadian political history. It was also a classic King formulation that described his military recruitment policy with precision. Defence minister J.L. Ralston almost resigned over what he considered to be his boss's unconscionable lack of commitment in a time of crisis; one Quebec minister, P.J.A. Cardin, actually did resign, but for the opposite reason—the prime minister's callous disregard for past undertakings and his clear slide toward compulsory military service.

King held the party together for two years more until heavy infantry casualties in Italy and Normandy created a reinforcement crisis in the autumn of 1944. Aware that sending home defence conscripts overseas could jeopardize French-English unity at a time when the war was all but won, King sacked Ralston and appointed General A.G.L. McNaughton, the former commander of First Canadian Army, in his place. McNaughton tried and failed to persuade home defence conscripts to volunteer for the front and, after an agonizing three weeks, King reversed course and decided to dispatch 16,000 conscripts overseas. King prevailed in the Commons, and many Québécois eventually concluded that King had done his very best to hold off compulsory service.

He had similar success in his relations with Roosevelt. The defeats on the European continent in 1940 put Canada's safety in peril, not least if a defeated Britain had to surrender the Royal Navy. At the president's request, King found himself conveying American demands on the future of the British fleet to Prime Minister Winston Churchill. He also found Roosevelt pressing for a defence alliance in August 1940 (the Permanent Joint Board on Defence), and the Canadian agreed, first, because he had no choice, and second, because the alliance let Canada do its utmost to get troops and machines overseas without worrying about home defence. The change in imperial masters nonetheless proved fateful. So too was the shift in economic dependence to the United States. The war greatly expanded Canadian industry—and hence imports from the south. By early 1941, Canada was all but bereft of American dollars to pay for its purchases and, in April of that year, King went to Roosevelt's home at Hyde Park, NY, to plead his case. The result was an agreement that resolved the dollar crisis and let Canadian industry work flat out. The industrial effort, directed by the powerful C.D. Howe, was huge, and Canada offered Britain and the Allies billions in loans, gifts, and Mutual Aid.

Canadian-American relations were generally very good indeed with few of the battles that troubled relations with London. Those tended to revolve around Canada's assertion of its newfound strength. Although King never sought any role in Allied strategic decisions, he was determined that Canada's role in key areas where it had power be recognized. Arguing the so-called functional principle, King claimed a special place for Canada in food production, in resources, and in relief, all areas in which Canada's contributions were disproportionately large. Aided by a brilliant team in the Department of External Affairs, he acquired a seat on two of the Anglo-American Combined Boards.

At the same time, King at last began to implement social welfare. In 1940, he pushed unemployment insurance into law and, after 1943, established family allowances, allocated large sums for housing, created a Department of National Health and Welfare, and, in the Veterans Charter, crafted what was likely the best package of benefits for demobilized servicemen and women anywhere.

Canada's war record had been superb, putting more than 1.1 million men and women into uniform and generating a huge industrial and agricultural effort—and all without much inflation or a cut in living standards. For once, King deserved an election sweep, but the 1945 election was a tough fight. He prevailed narrowly, his cautious conscription policies earning him grudging support in Quebec and 127 seats in a House of 245. It was a victory nonetheless. King was now almost 71 years old and perceptibly failing, but there was no sign of his preparing to step down. There did appear to be a logical successor, the intelligent, fatherly French Canadian, Louis St Laurent, who King convinced to remain in politics at war's end, naming him secretary of state for external affairs in 1946.

There was no shortage of postwar concerns and issues. The expected economic downturn at war's end did not immediately occur, something attributable, at least in part, to government preparations, planning, and spending. What preoccupied King's last years in power, however, was the international stage. In September 1945, a Soviet cipher officer, Igor Gouzenko, defected from the embassy in Ottawa carrying documents proving that the USSR had run spy rings in Canada during the war. There were indications, too, in Gouzenko's material of espionage in high places in Washington and London. This affair, quickly communicated to the United States and the United Kingdom, showed that the Soviet Union remained an implacable foe of the democracies. A Cold War was coming. It was not something King welcomed, because of the unwanted commitments it might bring. He did not run from it either and, by 1948, King's officials were in secret discussions with London and Washington about the need for an alliance of democracies in the North Atlantic region to deter possible Soviet aggression.

It was also time for the aging King to go. After a Liberal Party convention selected St Laurent, King resigned his post on 15 November 1948. His legacy was a Liberal Party that had become Canada's "government party." It had held the centre of the road so skilfully and for so long under King's leadership, with a politics based on nationalism, national unity, and the development of new programs of social welfare, that opposition on the left and right had been disarmed. Internationally, the Commonwealth was in substantial measure his creation, and Canada's record in World War II, hugely impressive in personnel and production, was his as well. Unloved, maligned, and frequently misrepresented, Mackenzie King ranks as perhaps the greatest of Canada's leaders. SEE ALSO: CANADA–UNITED KINGDOM DEFENCE RELATIONS; CANADA–UNITED STATES DEFENCE RELATIONS; CONSCRIPTION; QUEBEC AND THE MILITARY; WAR FINANCE; WAR INDUSTRY; WORLD WAR II.

READING: C.P. Stacey, *Arms, Men and Governments: The War Policies of Canada, 1939–1945* (Ottawa, 1970); J.W. Pickersgill, *The Mackenzie King Record*, 4 vols. (Toronto, 1960–1970).

Kingsmill, Charles Edmund (1855–1935). Born in Guelph, Canada West, Charles Kingsmill joined the Royal Navy (RN) in 1869 and made a successful career as the captain of battleships. On a visit to Canada on HMS *Dominion*, he met Prime Minister Sir Wilfrid Laurier, was impressed by him, and in 1908 was offered the post of commander of the Fisheries Protection Service (FPS). The FPS was the basis of the Naval Service, soon the Royal Canadian Navy, created in 1910, its first ships two old RN cruisers crewed by borrowed RN sailors. The navy became a victim of competing Liberal and Conservative visions and was scarcely in existence when World War I began. Fearing that German U-boats would attack ships in Canadian waters, Kingsmill created a St Lawrence patrol out of FPS ships and purchased yachts and steel hull trawlers that met the need for a standing presence in Canada's home waters. By the end of the war, he had a large fleet of small ships and the beginning of a Naval Air Service. Knighted and promoted to admiral, in 1919 Kingsmill left the navy he had founded, his plans for postwar expansion defeated by a cost-conscious Union Government.

Kingston, Ontario. One of Canada's historic military sites, Kingston is located on the north shore of eastern Lake Ontario. Count Frontenac, the governor of New France, first fortified it in 1673 when he built a rough palisade at the mouth of the Cataraqui River. The fort was destroyed in 1689 and rebuilt in 1695 by the French, but it was easily taken by Lieutenant-Colonel John Bradstreet's British troops in 1758. Loyalist settlers, refugees from the newly created United States, flooded the area after 1783 when the town became the anchor of eastern Upper Canada's defences. During the War of 1812, it was the site of the most important naval shipyards on Lake Ontario and a principal concentration point for British forces guarding the St Lawrence River against American forces to the south. Fort Henry, constructed in the 1830s, defended Colonel John By's Rideau Canal, a great feat of military engineering that linked Lake Ontario with Montreal by way of Ottawa. British regulars garrisoned the fort until 1871. The Royal Military College of Canada opened in Kingston in 1876, and the city has been a military base continuously ever since, with military schools, Eastern Ontario Headquarters, the staff of 1st Canadian Division, the National Defence College, and the Land Forces Staff College all based there at various times. The latter two institutions were housed very near the site of Fort Frontenac, built more than 335 years before.

King William's War. *See* WAR OF THE LEAGUE OF AUGSBURG.

Kinmel Park Riots (1919). Once the armistice of 11 November 1918 had been concluded, the soldiers of the Canadian Corps wanted to return home as quickly as possible. But shipping was scarce, and the corps' leadership intended the troops to return home by battalions to ensure a disciplined repatriation and proper civic receptions when formed units returned to the communities that had raised them. There were understandable delays in demobilization and resentment that some conscripts might be getting home earlier than volunteers if units went as groups instead of as individuals according to length of service. This led to heightened tensions that erupted in a vicious riot/mutiny at the Canadian camp at Kinmel Park in northern Wales on 4 and 5 March 1919. The troubles were fuelled by alcohol but, tragically, five men died in the fighting and more than 30 were injured. There were other riots in mid-June at Witley in Surrey and at Epsom. The rioting and its alarmist coverage in the press led the British government to find hitherto unavailable shipping, and repatriation of the Canadians

sped up. Similar protests and sit-down strikes occurred in 1945–1946 as Canadians awaited repatriation after World War II, and a riot at Aldershot in early July 1945 resulted in serious property damage and several courts martial. SEE ALSO: DEMOBILIZATION.

READING: Julian Putkowski, *The Kinmel Park Camp Riots, 1919* (Clwyd, UK, 1989).

Kirke, Sir David (c.1597–1654). Born in Dieppe, France, one of five sons of an English trader, Kirke led a merchant-financed expedition in 1627–1628 to drive France out of its holdings on the St Lawrence. Kirke's ships seized a French supply vessel, and he dispatched an emissary to Quebec to demand its surrender from Samuel de Champlain, the governor. Expecting additional supplies from France, Champlain rejected the demand and Kirke sailed away, but not before he captured the French supply convoy. The next year, a second Kirke expedition against Quebec found New France near starvation, and this time Champlain had no choice except to surrender, which he did on 16 July 1629. France had its colony restored by the treaty of St Germain-en-Laye three years later. Knighted for his role at Quebec, Kirke soon became the first governor of Newfoundland and the co-owner of the island.

Kiska, Attack on (1943). The Japanese occupied Attu and Kiska, islands in the Aleutian chain off the Alaska Territory of the United States, in June 1942. The Americans staged an amphibious invasion of Attu on 11 May 1943 and, after a brutal struggle that produced almost 4,000 US casualties, recaptured the island on 29 May. Then it was Kiska's turn, the island occupied by some 8,000 Japanese in strong fortifications. This time 4,831 troops of the 13th Canadian Infantry Brigade, based in Pacific Command as part of the 6th Division and led by Brigadier Harry Foster, took part in the assault along with almost 30,000 US troops. The First Special Service Force, a combined Canadian and American unit, also took part. After heavy preliminary air and naval bombardment, the attackers landed on Kiska on 15 August 1943 only to find that the Japanese had pulled out secretly and silently on 28 July, though the attackers suffered casualties from

▲ In August 1943, US and Canadian troops attacked Kiska Island, earlier occupied by Japan, in the frigid Aleutian chain. The attackers found that enemy forces had secretly withdrawn.

friendly fire and even more from booby traps left by the enemy. One Canadian was wounded and four died. The 13th Brigade had substantial numbers of home defence conscripts enrolled under the National Resources Mobilization Act in its ranks, and this was the first time Canadian conscripts were deployed into what was expected to be battle, as Kiska was deemed to be North American soil. SEE ALSO: CANADA–UNITED STATES DEFENCE RELATIONS.

READING: Galen Perras, "Canada as a Military Partner: Alliance Politics and the Campaign to Recapture the Aleutian Island of Kiska," *Journal of Military History* (1992).

Korean War (1950–1953). The end of World War II in 1945 set the stage for a new kind of struggle, a Cold War between rival power blocs led by the United States and the Soviet Union. The outbreak of war in Korea in June 1950 deepened Cold War divisions and helped to militarize a global conflict of ideologies, political systems, and world views. It drew Canada more deeply into international security issues, under United Nations (UN) auspices in Korea and those of the North Atlantic Treaty Organization (NATO) in Europe.

The Cold War's immediate causes were strategic and ideological differences that had emerged between Moscow and the West during and immediately following World War II, although its roots stretched to the establishment of the Soviet Union itself. Suspicious of Soviet motives since the Russian Revolution of 1917, some Western countries feared that the defeat of Germany, Italy, and Japan by 1945 would encourage Moscow to extend its power in Europe, Asia, and the Middle East. The Soviet Union's wartime leader, Joseph Stalin, distrustful of Western governments for their anti-Communist policies, wanted a buffer zone of subordinate states between his country and potential enemies in the West that historically had displayed little reluctance in laying claim to Russian territory. Soviet forces battered their way into German-held Eastern Europe and, after Berlin's surrender, refused to leave; it was economically easier to billet the conquering army there than to bring it home to the devastated cities and burned-over farmlands of the Soviet Union. Soviet occupying forces proceeded to loot occupied territories of the industrial tools needed by the home country for postwar reconstruction. Local elites were disempowered, incarcerated, or simply shot, and pressure was brought to bear on bordering states—Norway, Iran, Turkey—to comply with Soviet presence, pressure, and strategic concerns. In April 1949, after several major international crises, 12 Western states formed the North Atlantic Treaty Organization (NATO) to deter potential Soviet aggression.

In Asia, US–Soviet relations also deteriorated. On the Korean peninsula, the surrender of Japanese forces in 1945 gave way to military occupation by the victorious Allies. Divided along the 38th parallel into an American sphere of influence in the South and a Soviet sphere in the North, Korea became a focal point of conflict as each side desired the country's unification under a government friendly to its own interests. The withdrawal of American and Soviet troops in 1948–1949 did not lead to reduced tensions. On Sunday, 25 June 1950, after receiving the green light from Beijing and Moscow, North Korea invaded the Republic of Korea (ROK), or South Korea.

▲ Canada committed a brigade group to the Korean War. Here, Sherman tanks of Lord Strathcona's Horse move forward.

The United States quickly moved to offer air and naval assistance to the South Koreans. The United Nations Security Council also voted to condemn the invasion and, later, to request the assistance of UN member states in restoring the prewar border. In early July, a British-sponsored resolution created a UN military command for the Korean "police action" commanded by American General Douglas MacArthur, one of the heroes of the Pacific war against Japan. In addition to ROK and American troops, which bore the brunt of the fighting over the next three years, the UN mission received support from more than 40 other countries. Australia, Belgium, Canada, Colombia, Ethiopia, France, Great Britain, Greece, Luxembourg, the Netherlands, New Zealand, the Philippines, South Africa, Thailand, and Turkey all sent combat forces; Denmark, India, Italy, Norway, and Sweden sent medical detachments or hospital ships.

After capturing most of the peninsula, North Korean forces suffered a devastating defeat when American troops outflanked them by landing at Inchon, far behind the front lines, in September 1950, a brilliant amphibious operation. By mid-October, MacArthur's advance deep into North Korea had triggered Communist Chinese intervention against the UN. Slipping secretly across the Yalu River on the North Korean–Chinese border over a period of several weeks, hundreds of thousands of Chinese "volunteers"—the Chinese were scrupulously disingenuous in disavowing their formal role, an involvement that has since been demonstrated conclusively by the release of period documents— struck south in early November, their attack precipitated in part by fear that MacArthur planned to carry the war across the Yalu and onto Chinese soil. The disciplined and agile Chinese divisions at first drove UN forces south in disorder. By early 1951, however, UN counterattacks had returned the front line roughly to the 38th parallel. Months of difficult truce negotiations, punctuated by heavy fighting, followed. On 27 July 1953, after many false starts, the combatants signed an armistice at Panmunjom. Nearly 60 years later, the peninsula remains divided

between a democratic South and a totalitarian (and communist) North.

Canada supported the United Nations effort in Korea but preferred, at first, to make only a limited military commitment. With relatively small and poorly prepared armed forces in 1950 after a half-decade of thorough demobilization, and few vital interests in Asia, Canadian policy-makers hoped that the conflict might be contained or limited. This would be easier, the Canadians hoped, if the United States could be persuaded to act militarily only under UN auspices. Although Canada had not lapsed back into near isolationism after 1945, as it had after 1918, and had played an important role in founding NATO in 1949, it was not yet prepared to play a leading role in global security. Memories of the Hong Kong disaster in 1941, when a hastily assembled Canadian force, part of the British garrison, was defeated and captured by invading Japanese troops, added an extra note of caution to any discussion of sending ground troops to Asia. Nevertheless, Korea appeared to demonstrate that Communism was an aggressive, expansionist power against which military force might be the West's only option. As former diplomat John Holmes later noted, "For those who assumed that participation in international institutions was going to be cheap, 1950 was a bad year."

Korea therefore became more than just a UN action to restore a disputed boundary. Particularly for American officials, it was an important test of Cold War loyalties. For Canada, its close relationship with the United States, strong support for the United Nations, and firm adherence to Western values (the democratically-elected government of South Korea was recognized by the United Nations) made it difficult to refuse the UN's request for assistance. Accordingly, in late June, Ottawa agreed to send three destroyers, HMCS *Cayuga*, *Athabaskan*, and *Sioux*, to serve under UN command during the Korean crisis, the first of eight warships and over 3,500 sailors that would eventually serve in the conflict. Later in July, the government also announced the assignment of No. 426 (Transport) Squadron, Royal Canadian Air Force, to the United States Military Air Transportation

Service to fly supplies and personnel between North America and Japan. The squadron would eventually fly 599 round-trip missions carrying 13,000 passengers and three million kilograms of freight.

With UN forces hemmed inside a shrinking perimeter near the port of Pusan in the southeast, these modest commitments came under increasing criticism from American, British, and UN authorities who pressed Canada in July and early August for ground troops as well. In Canada too, many voices criticized the Liberal government of Prime Minister Louis St Laurent for not doing more. Ottawa's reluctance stemmed in part from the sorry state of the postwar army. As H.F. Wood, the army's official historian of the Korean War,

later noted, "No ground forces of any significant size were ready." Postwar defence policy had simply not envisaged the possibility of a large, quick-reaction army formation for international security purposes.

On 7 August, the government finally relented, St Laurent authorizing the recruitment of the Canadian Army Special Force (CASF), a brigade-sized formation "specially trained and equipped to be available for use in carrying out Canada's obligations under the United Nations Charter or the North Atlantic Pact." Recruitment began immediately and in some confusion but, by 18 August, the chief of the general staff reported that sufficient men had enlisted to make the CASF operable. Many recruits had to be released

▲ Korea was an impoverished country during the war, and Canadian infantry, here passing civilians in a typical village, looked forward to "R and R" in Japan.

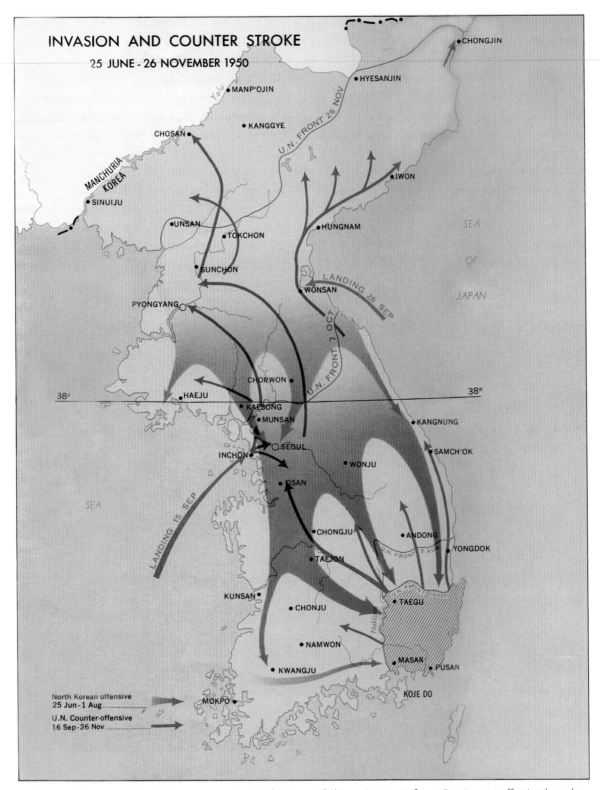

INVASION AND COUNTER STROKE
25 JUNE - 26 NOVEMBER 1950

CHONGJIN

MANCHURIA
KOREA

Yalu
MANP'OJIN
HYESANJIN

KANGGYE

U.N. FRONT 26 NOV

CHOSAN

SINUIJU

UNSAN
TOKCHON

IWON

HUNGNAM

SUNCHON

LANDING 26 SEP

WONSAN

PYONGYANG

SEA

OF

JAPAN

U.N. FRONT 7 OCT

38°   38°

CHORWON

HAEJU

KANGNUNG

KAESONG
MUNSAN

SAMCH'OK

INCHON

SEOUL

WONJU

LANDING 15 SEP

OSAN

SEA

CHONGJU

ANDONG

U.N. FRONT 15 AUG

YONGDOK

TAEJON

KUNSAN

U.N. FRONT 15 SEP

TAEGU

Naktong

CHONJU

NAMWON

MASAN

KWANGJU

PUSAN

KOJE DO

MOKPO

North Korean offensive
25 Jun - 1 Aug ....

U.N. Counter-offensive
16 Sep - 26 Nov ....

▲ The Korean War pitted United Nations troops against North Korean and Chinese Communist forces. Despite great offensives by each side, the result was a bloody, three-year stalemate along approximately the prewar north-south boundary at the 38th parallel. This map shows the front moving down and then back up almost the entire length of the Korean peninsula during the first six months of war.

on medical grounds and many others deserted. Of those who stayed, nearly half were World War II veterans and one in five were former non-commissioned officers. Brigadier John Rockingham, recalled from civilian life to command the brigade, was a superb officer who had won the Distinguished Service Order in the previous war. So had all three of his infantry battalion commanders, Lieutenant-Colonels J.A. Dextraze (Royal 22e Régiment), R.A. Keane (The Royal Canadian Regiment), and J.R. Stone (the Princess Patricia's Canadian Light Infantry). Subsequently, Canada's army contingent in Korea would be replaced, or rotated, twice more, with three successive brigade commanders, Brigadiers M.P. Bogert (April 1952 to April 1953), Jean Victor Allard (April 1953 to June 1954), and F.A. Clift (June to December 1954).

A Canadian Military Mission, Far East, was soon established in Japan to prepare for the troops' arrival and handle leave, logistics, and other administrative details, while Ottawa later placed additional troops from the regular army on active service for possible Korean duty. In the meantime, training for the Special Force continued, first in Canada and later at Fort Lewis, Washington. After the Inchon landing in September and the temporary liberation of South Korea, it appeared that few Canadians would actually be needed to fight in what seemed like a soon-to-be-concluded war, MacArthur himself intimating that only a token force might be necessary. Chinese intervention and the rapid UN retreat in late 1950 altered quickly this calculus and led to the dispatch of the 2nd Battalion, the Princess Patricia's Canadian Light Infantry, in November. After some additional uncertainty, the rest of the Special Force, now called the 25th Canadian Infantry Brigade, followed in early spring, arriving in Korea beginning on 4 May 1951 in time to help recapture UN positions around the 38th parallel for the third time in the war. The Patricias fought well at Kap'yong in April 1951 as part of a Commonwealth brigade, earning a US Presidential Unit Citation for their role in halting a major Chinese offensive. The battle set the tone for many more to follow. At Kap'yong, Canadian infantry and half-tracks

supported by mortars, New Zealand artillery, and American tanks, succeeded in holding a series of hilltop positions against a much larger Chinese force that attacked at night. By the winter of 1951–1952, positions like this stretched the width of Korea with each side jockeying for minor topographical advantage as peace talks moved ahead with excruciating slowness.

Intermittent fighting and aggressive patrolling extended right up to the armistice, punctuated by pitched battles for key hills and ridges. Between 22 and 26 November 1951, for example, Dextraze's 2nd Battalion, Royal 22e Régiment, suffered 63 casualties in repulsing a series of furious Chinese attacks near Hill 355. According to historian David Bercuson, the battalion's "D" Company commanded by Captain (Acting Major) Réal Liboiron, though heavily outnumbered, conducted "one of the finest defensive actions in the history of the Canadian army." In early May 1953, "C" Company, the 3rd Battalion, The Royal Canadian Regiment, similarly lost 26 killed, 27 wounded, and 7 taken prisoner in a pitched defensive battle; Korean soldiers attached to the battalion, or 'Katcoms' (Korean Augmentation Troops Commonwealth), suffered an additional 22 casualties. Between 3 May and the Panmunjom armistice, another 18 Canadians would die at the front.

UN forces, with superior air, sea, and artillery support, were generally content to remain on the defensive during this period of "static" war, patrolling actively but using firepower to crush enemy assaults instead of attacking aggressively themselves. This was a controversial strategy, blamed by some for prolonging the war and incurring, in the long run, greater UN casualties. On the other hand, any attempt to defeat North Korea and unify the peninsula by force risked a longer, even more costly war against China and, possibly, the Soviet Union. At a time when Western forces in Europe and elsewhere were weak and public opinion on the far-off Korean struggle was not united, a more assertive military strategy also had its liabilities. These considerations affected Canadian diplomacy. Appreciating that the war was an important trial for the new United Nations, Canadian policy-makers also tried to ensure that UN objectives would not be so ambitious as to preclude the possibility of a negotiated settlement. Exercising what political scientist Denis Stairs called the "diplomacy of constraint," Canada sought in particular, and with mixed success, to help moderate American policies that, at various times, seemed to risk broadening or prolonging the war and committing UN forces indefinitely to South Korea's defence.

As historian Greg Donaghy has argued, Korea "transformed the Cold War from a tense but fairly stable diplomatic standoff into a much more precarious and dangerous confrontation" that "altered completely the context in which Canadian foreign policy was developed and implemented." Fear of Soviet attack, pressure from the United States and other Allies, and Canadians' own sense of the global balance of power led to a major rearmament program in the early 1950s and the return to Europe, in 1951, of thousands of Canadian troops under NATO command. Washington's increasing concerns about a Soviet nuclear attack across the Arctic also heightened Canadian interest in questions of national sovereignty and joint US–Canadian planning for continental defence. A major military and diplomatic effort for Canada, Korea was just one component, albeit an important one, in the early history of the Cold War. Moreover, coming just five years after the massive efforts required during World War II, Korea generated vastly less public and media interest than the earlier struggle. Canadian battles, casualties, and the peace talks did receive press coverage, but the comparatively low level of attention accorded the war, in Canada and elsewhere, led to its being dubbed—inaccurately though understandably—a "forgotten war."

It is a description that sits especially poorly with Canada's more than 25,000 Korean War veterans (a further 7,000 Canadians would serve in Korea between the 1953 armistice and the final repatriation of Canadian personnel in 1957). Having fought a tough, resourceful enemy for three years under often appalling conditions, and suffered over 1,500 casualties in the process, their disgust with the manner in which Korea was often officially remembered—as a UN "police action"—gave birth to an active, effective veterans' movement and a continuing campaign for public recognition. For the first time, a United Nations army had intervened successfully to stem international aggression and Canadians had played an important part. SEE ALSO: CANADA–UNITED STATES DEFENCE RELATIONS; COLD WAR; KAP'YONG.

READING: Denis Stairs, *The Diplomacy of Constraint: Canada, the Korean War, and the United States* (Toronto, 1974); H.F. Wood, *Strange Battleground: Official History of the Canadian Army in Korea* (Ottawa, 1966); David Bercuson, *Blood on the Hills: The Canadian Army in the Korean War* (Toronto, 1999).

Kosovo (1999). The collapse of Yugoslavia in the 1990s led to declarations of independence by its component states and a vicious series of internecine conflicts. The tepid and, more or less, ineffective international political response to the lingering Balkan crisis, including the ethnic cleansing—often by massacre—of minority ethnic groups shocked global public opinion and led, by the mid-1990s, to a more robust international effort backed by military contributions from the North Atlantic Treaty Organization (NATO). NATO air strikes in 1995 helped establish the conditions for the Dayton Peace Accords later in the year that ended the fighting and established a series of rump states more ethnically homogenous than the federal, multi-ethnic former Yugoslavia.

The Republic of Serbia, one of Yugoslavia's successor states, emerged from the Balkan wars with continued ethnic tensions, unresolved economic and diplomatic challenges, and a leadership, under Slobodan Milosevic (a signatory at Dayton), little reconciled to the NATO-enforced postwar order. Tensions in the Serbian province of Kosovo, where a large Albanian majority had spawned a small but violent separatist group, led to the massive intervention of Serbian security forces and to inflated media accounts of atrocities, ethnic cleansing, and war crimes that, for Western audiences in particular, were eerily reminiscent of reports that had been ignored in former Yugoslavia earlier in the decade. After international efforts to end the crisis proved unsuccessful, in March 1999, NATO, alarmed at evidence of an escalating humanitarian crisis, began a

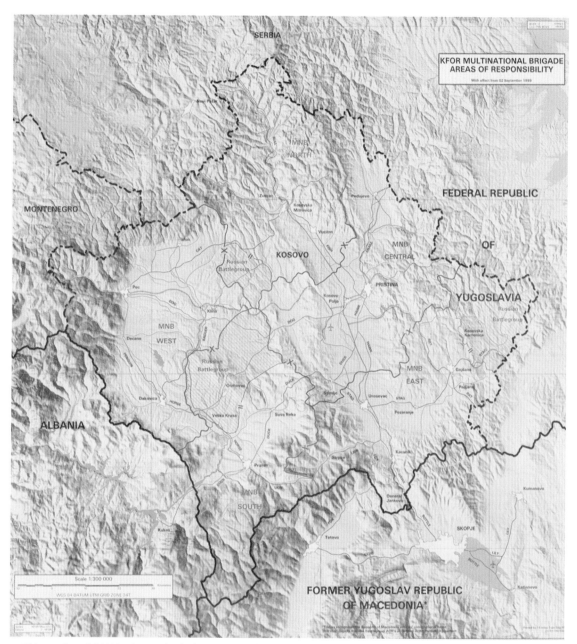

This map from fall 1999 indicates the deployment areas for the units of KFOR, or Kosovo Force, as well as those areas occupied by pro-Serbian Russian forces. NATO's military campaign resulted in the occupation of much of Kosovo, and tense showdowns with both Serbian and Russian troops.

substantial but carefully circumscribed bombing campaign against Serbian military and civilian infrastructure targets to force Belgrade to cease security operations in Kosovo. The campaign, largely conducted from high altitude and under stringent command-and-control restrictions to avoid collateral damage and limit civilian casualties, was both the product of Western liberal impatience at the international community's reluctance to intervene in supposedly sovereign issues, and the cause of large-scale public and political protest against Western militarism. It was also a source of debate among military professionals and analysts over the relative merits of air power and precision-guided munitions versus a ground campaign and the occupation of

enemy territory as the only sure way of imposing one's will on a determined enemy.

Canadian CF-18 aircraft, based at Aviano, Italy, participated in this three-month offensive and ultimately dropped 10 percent of the bombs that forced Milosevic to yield, though not before Serb resistance had proven remarkably impervious to NATO airpower, and Russian opposition to NATO action had threatened broad international repercussions for the West's intervention. The United Nations in June 1999 authorized a NATO-led Kosovo Force (KFOR) of some 50,000 to enter Kosovo to bring Serbian paramilitaries to heel, monitor Serbian withdrawal, and to disarm the ethnic Albanian separatist force known as the Kosovo Liberation Army. KFOR also aimed to help an estimated 850,000 refugees return to their homes. The Canadian Forces provided some 1,470 troops to KFOR—an infantry battle group, a reconnaissance regiment, engineer detachments, and helicopters. Most of the Canadian troops withdrew before the end of 1999, as Canada instead increased its commitment to the Stabilization Force in Bosnia-Herzegovina, another state created by the Dayton Accords and one then still under international supervision. Operation Kinetic—Canada's participation in KFOR—ended in 2000 although some Canadians remained in Kosovo into late 2002. KFOR itself remains in Kosovo in early 2010, its transitional mission substantially modified by Kosovo's unilateral declaration of independence in early 2008 after the failure of UN-brokered peace talks. Canada is among some 60 countries that have since recognized the new state, the status of which remains in doubt, its independence having been brought before the International Court of Justice by Serbia, supported by Russia and several other countries. In September 2009, Canada rejoined KFOR for the first time since 2002, sending a five-person Canadian Forces group to assist the new Kosovo Security Force in its equipment donor

Canada deployed troops into Kosovo in 1999 to ensure a Serbian withdrawal and to enforce peace. Trooper Eric Bennett is shown working on the surveillance system atop his Coyote armoured vehicle.

Lahr. Lahr was the main Canadian army base in Germany from 1970 until the withdrawal of Canadian Forces from their North Atlantic Treaty Organization (NATO) deployments in Europe in 1993–1994. It sat near the French border in Baden-Wurttemberg, conveniently close to the Canadian air force base at Baden-Soellingen. Lahr had been a major French base until that country announced its withdrawal from NATO's integrated military command in 1967, at which point Canadian air units—ejected, along with other NATO formations, from French airfields—replaced the French. After Pierre Trudeau's government slashed the NATO contribution in half as a result of the 1968–1969 defence review, Canada's badly weakened half-brigade group had to be moved from its front-line position in northern West Germany to NATO reserve at Lahr farther south. The revised mission also saw the Canadians move from British command under NATO's Northern Army Group (NORTHAG) to American command under the Central Army Group (CENTAG). Canadian Forces Base Lahr was formally decommissioned in August 1994.

Lake Erie, Battle of (1813). Control of the Great Lakes—and thus command of the most effective means of transportation around southern Upper Canada—was a critical element of the War of 1812. At Put-in Bay on the Ohio shore of Lake Erie on 10 September 1813, the United States Navy faced off against the Royal Navy. Led by Master Commandant Oliver H. Perry, the Americans won, sinking or capturing six British vessels, led by Commander Robert Barclay. Casualties on both sides were heavy. Significantly, the Americans had built all their warships in Lake Erie shipyards; the British, for their part, had managed to construct only one ship, the

Detroit, and that difference tilted control of Lake Erie to the United States. Perry's famous message said it all: "We have met the enemy and they are ours." American naval control of Lake Erie led to the recapture of Detroit and British defeat at the battle of Moraviantown, where Tecumseh fell, one month later. SEE ALSO: WAR OF 1812.

Laurier, Henry-Charles-Wilfrid (1841–1919). Born in St Lin, Lower Canada, educated in French and English, Wilfrid Laurier went to McGill College in Montreal in 1861 where he formed connections with Rouge political activists. Practising law by 1864, he opposed Confederation, writing newspaper articles against the formation of a new nation and calling for Quebec to be a separate entity. But once the Dominion of Canada existed, Laurier accepted it. He won election to the Quebec legislature in 1871 and then moved to the federal Parliament in 1874. A powerful orator and a strong intellect, Laurier began to make his mark. In 1885, he denounced Prime Minister Sir John A. Macdonald for executing Louis Riel, blaming the Northwest Rebellion on government neglect. "If [I] had been on the banks of the Saskatchewan when the rebellion broke out," he said, "[I] would have taken up arms against the government…." Less than two years later, Laurier was the leader of the Liberal Party. In 1896, he led his party into power, becoming Canada's first francophone prime minister.

To Laurier fell the task of deciding the ways in which Canada would participate in the South African War (1899–1902). English-speaking Canadians were moved by Imperial Britain's grandeur and believed that Britain was inevitably right in all she did; French Canadians often took the

▲ Sir Wilfrid Laurier in 1917.

This gesture was denounced in Quebec as too much and in many parts of English Canada as too little, but Laurier, splitting the middle, realized that English-Canadian imperialism had to be recognized. Before the war was over, more than 7,000 Canadians were to serve in South Africa.

Laurier also had to deal with another empire, the American. Gold had been discovered in 1898 in the Klondike and a flood of prospectors, many of them Americans, flooded the area. The government dispatched the small Yukon Field Force and the North West Mounted Police to keep order—and to prevent any American effort to seize the territory. That succeeded, but when an impartial commission, created to adjudicate the Alaskan boundary with Canada, reported in October 1903 and found against Canada's claims—the British judge had sided with the United States—there was outrage in Canada.

For years at colonial conferences in Britain, Laurier had resisted British efforts to create an Imperial Council or to gather contributions to the Royal Navy (RN) but, by 1909, Germany had begun to challenge the RN's supremacy. In Parliament in March 1909, Members of Parliament gave unanimous approval to a resolution calling for the establishment of a Canadian navy. Laurier's Naval Service Bill, introduced the next January, called for a navy of five cruisers and six destroyers, crewed by volunteers, that could, with parliamentary approval, fight with the RN in time of war. The Conservatives, led by Robert Borden, now argued instead for a cash gift to Britain to build three dreadnought battleships. French-speaking Conservatives, fearing that a navy eventually meant conscription, called for a plebiscite; outside the House of Commons, Henri Bourassa and his newspaper Le Devoir denounced Laurier. The opposition led to the Liberal candidate's defeat in a famous by-election in Drummond-Arthabaska, Quebec, in November 1910, proving the power of anti-conscription forces. The next year, Laurier's government was gone, defeated by Borden on the issue of reciprocity with the United States. In Quebec, the naval issue still roiled voters, and Laurier now found himself in Opposition. His first

opposite tack. Not all anglophones were blind to the martial excesses of Empire, nor were all francophones predisposed to dismiss out of hand the imperial tie. On his first visit to Britain as prime minister in 1897, Laurier had said: "If a day were ever to come when England was in danger, let the bugle sound and . . . though we might not be able to do much, whatever we can do shall be done by the colonies to help her." Was 1899 a moment of imperial danger? Laurier, sensitive to the competing pressures of Canadian opinion, struck a path of compromise—assistance to Britain but not unlimited support. He agreed to raise and arm a battalion of 1,000 volunteers with Britain assuming full responsibility for them from the time they reached South Africa.

great task was to defeat Borden's Naval Aid Bill, a six-month-long struggle won when the still Liberal-dominated Senate rejected the bill.

Then World War I fell upon the nation. While it was immediately clear that French Canadians were not moved by the struggle in the same way as most English-speaking Canadians, Laurier did his best to encourage enlistment and support for the war. He renounced partisan politics and proclaimed a political truce that did not last very long. In 1917, when Borden—desperate for recruits to reinforce the hard-pressed Canadian Corps—called for conscription, Laurier could not go along. He rejected Borden's offer that he serve in a coalition government, and continued to reject conscription, certainly without a vote on the issue, because he opposed compulsion and feared the divisions it would be sure to create. The Military Service Act passed through Parliament, the Military Voters Act and the War Times Election Act all but guaranteed the government an electoral victory, and Borden formed a Union Government in October 1917. He led it to a sweeping victory in the December 1917 election, Laurier taking only 20 seats outside Quebec. Canada had been split, just as Laurier feared.

Laurier died on 17 February 1919, Canada's "first gentleman" and one of its greatest political leaders. Though ultimately broken by the great tide of imperial sentiment that washed over Canada in the years from the outbreak of war in South Africa through World War I, his legacy was profound. In addition to his economic, social, and political impact, Laurier had created a tiny Canadian navy, enforced Canadian sovereignty in the turbulent northwest, supported the Empire without splitting the country over South Africa, presided over the gradual professional development of the post–South African War army, and fought hard though unsuccessfully against compulsory military service. SEE ALSO: CONSCRIPTION; QUEBEC AND THE MILITARY; ROYAL CANADIAN NAVY; SOUTH AFRICAN WAR; WORLD WAR I.

READING: Réal Bélanger, *Wilfrid Laurier* (Boisbriand, QC, 1986).

Pierre LeMoyne as portrayed on a World War II recruiting poster.

Leased Bases Agreement. *See* DESTROYERS FOR BASES DEAL.

Le Moyne d'Iberville, Pierre (1661–1706). One of the many sons of an indentured servant who had made his fortune in New France, Pierre Le Moyne launched repeated expeditions against the English on Hudson Bay to disrupt the Hudson's Bay Company's trade on behalf of the French Compagnie du Nord. He participated in the French-Sault-Algonquin raid on Schenectady, New York, in 1690 and, in the same year, captured York Fort, only to lose it and recapture it twice more, in 1694 and 1697. In a spectacular northern naval battle in July 1697 against three English ships, Le Moyne, aboard *Pélican*, sank the

English ship *Hampshire* near Hayes River and captured another. Le Moyne also fought against the English in Newfoundland in 1696, razing 36 coastal fishing communities, killing 200 residents, and taking some 700 prisoners. Le Moyne then headed back to Hudson Bay, upon which English forces soon recaptured his Newfoundland conquests. The Treaty of Ryswick in 1697 put his northern victories in doubt as well, and the trading posts on Hudson Bay eventually passed to England. Le Moyne's later exploits came in Louisiana and the West Indies, where he died in 1706.

Leopold Canal (1944). The canal separated German forces in the Breskens Pocket, south of the Scheldt estuary in Belgium, from the advancing Canadians during the initial stages of the battle of the Scheldt that aimed to clear the approaches to the critical port of Antwerp. In miserable weather on 6 October 1944, the 7th Infantry Brigade of the 3rd Canadian Infantry Division crossed the canal in assault boats under the cover of a massive canopy of ignited jellied fuel launched from 27 Wasp flamethrowers. They established two small bridgeheads, about 3 kilometres apart, on the north bank of the canal. Stiff German resistance from the first-class 64th Division and heavy counterattacks stopped any further advance for several days. On 9 October, the Canadians finally connected the two bridgeheads and, on 14 October, the Germans pulled back, the Canadians resuming their advance northwards to the estuary itself. Casualties for this operation amounted to 533 officers and other ranks.

Lévis, Francois Gaston de, Duc de (1719–1787). An able soldier, Lévis was Montcalm's second-in-command from 1756, defending the Lake Champlain route against British invasion. He played a role in the defence of Quebec until August 1759, when he went to Montreal to organize its defences. After Montcalm's death, he took command of French forces and, in April 1760, led a small, hastily assembled army down the St Lawrence from Montreal to attempt to retake Quebec. He soundly defeated a British force at Ste Foy and laid siege to Quebec, but

was forced to retreat when the Royal Navy reached the city. Lévis defended Montreal until forced to capitulate to vastly superior forces in September. He ended his military career as a marshal of France and a duke. SEE ALSO: SEVEN YEARS' WAR.

Ligue pour la défense du Canada, La. When the Mackenzie King government called a plebiscite on overseas conscription in January 1942, the Quebec reaction was one of outrage at what was perceived as a broken promise. The Ligue, formed by nationalists and led by journalist and intellectual André Laurendeau, took to the field to support the "non" side and had substantial success in mobilizing voters as the results on 27 April demonstrated, with 73 percent in Quebec voting "non." The Ligue later became the basis for the Bloc Populaire Canadien, a *nationaliste* political party.

Limited Liability War. Canada's massive commitment of personnel to World War I had resulted in terrible casualties and much political strife in Canada when conscription divided the nation. As war began to seem a real possibility once more in the mid-1930s, Prime Minister Mackenzie King determined that such divisions could not be allowed again to threaten Canadian unity. His policy was that a Canadian contribution to the coming war would be one of limited liability, one that would minimize casualties and thus eliminate any need for conscription. Canada was not a great power, its interests were not likely to be directly challenged, and the country did not need to tear itself apart once more. At the onset of war in September 1939, King only reluctantly agreed to dispatch an infantry division overseas, and all but forced London to agree, in December 1939, that Canada's contribution to the British Commonwealth Air Training Plan should be recognized as its major role in the war. But events do not always follow political wishes. With the fall of France in May–June 1940, the German aerial bombardment of Britain (the Blitz), and other military disasters, limited liability disappeared, replaced by a massive Canadian war effort and, later, conscription. SEE ALSO: CONSCRIPTION; KING; WORLD WAR II.

Lord Strathcona's Horse (Royal Canadians). This Canadian cavalry regiment was raised and equipped by Lord Strathcona (Donald A. Smith), Canadian High Commissioner in London, during the South African War, its men largely cowboys or members of the North West Mounted Police. The cost to Strathcona has been estimated at $1 million, a huge sum in 1900. Originally known as Strathcona's Horse, the regiment established a reputation during hard service on the veldt. Disbanded after the war, it re-formed on 1 October 1909 as Strathcona's Horse (Royal Canadians) and, on 1 May 1911, as Lord Strathcona's Horse (Royal Canadians). In World War I, the regiment initially served as infantry alongside the 1st Canadian Division and, later, as cavalry with the Canadian Cavalry Brigade where it distinguished itself at Moreuil Wood in March 1918. The regiment became part of the Permanent Force between the wars. In World War II, it fought as an armoured regiment of the 5th Canadian Armoured Brigade in the 5th Canadian Armoured Division and saw service in Italy and northwest Europe. Postwar, the regiment served in Korea, in Canada's NATO brigade in Germany, on numerous peacekeeping operations, and in Afghanistan in the early twenty-first century. It is based in Edmonton.

Louisbourg. A massive French fortification on the southeast coast of Île Royale (Cape Breton Island), Louisbourg was intended to dominate the Gulf of St Lawrence so as to guard Quebec and Montreal and to provide a base from which to raid the sea lanes to and from New England. Settled in 1713, with fortification beginning in 1719, fortress Louisbourg was a huge undertaking built primarily of stone and brick that took almost three decades to complete. It included a walled town, a seaport, and a military base; to counter it, the British established Halifax as a government centre and naval base. Despite its thick walls, the fortress was vulnerable to long-range shelling from across the harbour and from low hills close by to the west. In 1745, during the War of the Austrian Succession, besieged by a mixed force of New England militia and Royal Navy vessels, Louisbourg

▲ The great French fortress on Cape Breton, Louisbourg fell to the British in 1758. This sketch of the siege, painted four years later by Captain Charles Ince, details the scene.

▲ The British victory at Lundy's Lane in July 1814 kept Upper Canada safe from the Americans. This 1859 painting by Alonzo Chappel captures the ferocity of the fighting.

surrendered after six weeks. Returned to France at the end of the war despite protests from the American colonies, Louisbourg fell once more in July 1758, early in the Seven Years' War, after another six-week siege directed by Major-General Jeffery Amherst. Taking the fortress was the essential prelude to Britain's attack on Quebec the next year; Brigadier James Wolfe, who had distinguished himself at Louisbourg, would be promoted to command that assault.

The British victory at Quebec (1759) and the surrender of Montreal the following year ended French colonization in Atlantic Canada. Cape Breton itself remained under British rule when the war ended, and British engineers blew up Louisbourg in 1760–1761. Two centuries later, John Diefenbaker's government began to rebuild Louisbourg as a major historic site. SEE ALSO: AMHERST; SEVEN YEARS' WAR.

READING: A.J.B. Johnston, *Endgame 1758: The Promise, the Glory and the Despair of Louisbourg's Last Decade* (Lincoln, NE, 2007).

Lundy's Lane, Battle of (1814). On 3 July 1814, United States Army regulars attacked across the Niagara River and took Fort Erie. They then advanced north and won a fierce and bloody firefight at Chippawa, where Brigadier-General Winfield Scott, the outstanding American officer of the campaign against Canada, led one of the attacking brigades. The defeated British retreated to Fort George and, after manoeuvres by both sides and the failure of the US Navy to arrive in support of its ground forces, the British deployed at Lundy's Lane, a low ridge several kilometres north of Chippawa and just west of the falls. Commanded by Lieutenant-General Gordon

Drummond, the 3,000-plus British regulars and Canadian militia fought the Americans, roughly equal in strength and led by Major-General Jacob Brown, on 25 July.

British artillery, located in a cemetery in the centre of the British line, inflicted heavy casualties on Scott's brigade until American reinforcements charged and captured the guns in vicious hand-to-hand fighting. All the gunners were apparently killed, wounded, or captured. After organizing reinforcements, Drummond launched three successive counterattacks, all of which failed to retake the cannon, but both sides—each having lost more than 850 men in the five-hour battle—were spent. This was the bloodiest battle of the war in the Canadas. Generals Brown, Scott, and Drummond suffered wounds, attesting to the ferocity of the engagement. Catherine Lundy, the wife of Thomas Lundy whose home stood on the battlefield, handed out drinking water to thirsty redcoats and militia who had marched nearly 20 kilometres on that 25 July, and tended wounded soldiers in her kitchen.

The Americans, having demonstrated that their regulars could more than hold their own against the British, retreated with some British guns to Fort Erie and claimed victory. The British were left with the task of burning the dead men and horses from both sides in a huge funeral pyre. Drummond, in his report, put the best face possible on the result of the battle: "The enemy abandoned his camp, threw the greater part of his baggage, camp equipages and provisions into the rapids and having set fire to Streets Mills and destroyed the bridge at Chippawa, continued his retreat in great disorder toward Fort Erie." The result at Lundy's Lane ensured that Upper Canada remained in British and Canadian hands. See also: Drummond; Niagara Frontier; War of 1812.

Reading: J.M. Hitsman, *The Incredible War of 1812* (rev. ed., Montreal, 1999); Jon Latimer, *Niagara 1814: The Final Invasion* (Oxford, 2009).

▲ John McCrae, poet and soldier, in 1914.

McCrae, John (1872–1918). McCrae, born in Guelph, Ontario, served in the militia artillery there, taking a commission in 1893. He attended the University of Toronto and studied arts, beginning to publish poetry. He then attended medical school at university. He graduated in 1898 and interned in Toronto and at Johns Hopkins Hospital in Baltimore. When the South African War began in 1899, McCrae took an artillery battery from his hometown overseas. On his return to Canada, he left the militia. After teaching at McGill University and the University of Vermont

and practising at hospitals in Montreal, he joined the Canadian Expeditionary Force at the beginning of World War I, going overseas with the first contingent as brigade surgeon in the 1st Brigade, Canadian Field Artillery. At Ypres in April 1915, McCrae was in the thick of the struggle as he tried to help the thousands of Canadians killed and wounded by shellfire and gas. After conducting the burial service for Lieutenant Alex Helmer, a friend and former student, on 2 May, he quickly drafted the poem for which he is best remembered. "In Flanders Fields," published in London in December 1915 by *Punch*, almost instantly became famous and, after the war, the red poppies McCrae had observed amidst the carnage of the battlefield became the symbol of remembrance. McCrae was serving as the chief of medical services at No. 3 Canadian General Hospital near Boulogne, France, in January 1918 when, worn down by the continuous strain, he contracted pneumonia and meningitis and died. SEE ALSO: "IN FLANDERS FIELDS"; REMEMBRANCE DAY; WORLD WAR I.

Macdonald, Angus Lewis (1890–1954). A popular Liberal premier of Nova Scotia from 1933 to 1940, World War I veteran Macdonald was called to Ottawa to join Mackenzie King's Cabinet as minister of national defence for naval service in July 1940. Elected to Parliament in Kingston, Ontario, in a by-election, Macdonald built the Royal Canadian Navy (RCN) to its wartime strength of 100,000, a huge task considering the navy's tiny prewar numbers. The RCN understandably had problems with equipment and leadership, but Macdonald had little hesitation in firing those he believed had not performed well. A pro-conscription minister, he had a difficult relationship with his cautious prime minister, and a disillusioned Macdonald was happy enough to return to

△ Prime Minister Sir John A. Macdonald in 1890.

the premier's office in Halifax in April 1945; he remained premier until 1954.

READING: Stephen Henderson, *Angus L. Macdonald: A Provincial Liberal* (Toronto, 2007).

Macdonald, John Alexander (1815–1891). Sir John A., Canada's first prime minister, was born in Scotland and came to Canada with his parents when he was a child. He served briefly as a militia private during the 1837 rebellion in Upper Canada and, as a lawyer, defended several of the Patriot Hunters involved in the battle of the Windmill at Prescott, Upper Canada, in 1838. As a politician, he was avid for office, running for alderman in 1843 and for the Upper Canadian legislature as a Conservative the next year. In 1856, after years in Opposition and some time as a minister, he became the leader, the de facto co-premier, of the Upper Canadian section of the government of the Canadas. He would remain the leader of his party and of his government for the rest of his life.

Macdonald was a drinker, a trait that sometimes affected his political effectiveness. In 1862, his government introduced a bill to expand Canada's militia. Macdonald, who had created the post of minister of militia in 1861 and indeed took the office himself for a year, favoured the measure strongly, with a civil war underway in the United States and London and Washington exchanging threats and imprecations, but he ran into heavy weather in Parliament and the press. With the *Globe* noting that Macdonald was having "one of his old attacks," a widely understood reference to his drinking, the bill went down to defeat, and the government resigned. John A. would be out of office for two years.

But Confederation, his greatest success, was not far off. The end of the American Civil War, the threat of Fenian attacks (Macdonald again became militia minister from 1865 to 1867, the better to deal with the Irish-American raids), and the genuine fear that the United States might try to bind up its wounds by "liberating" British North America—all were used along with economic reasons to push and prod several of Britain's North American colonies together. The fears were not chimeras. Confederate soldiers used Canadian territory and contacts to raid St Albans, Vermont, in 1864, and were released from Canadian jails with their loot on a technicality. American fury was genuine, and the government called out 2,000 militia to keep order along the border, while Macdonald created a spy agency to collect information in the United States and at home.

The new government of post-Confederation Canada took form slowly. To be his militia and defence minister, Macdonald chose his closest colleague, George-Étienne Cartier, who negotiated the transfer of Rupert's Land from the Hudson's Bay Company to the new Dominion. With Macdonald ill with gallstones, it was also Cartier who handled the organization of the Manitoba Field Force that British Colonel Garnet Wolseley led to Manitoba in 1870. Most of the British military left Canada soon after the pacification of the Red River, but the government did nothing to replace them with a Canadian regular force.

Recovered, Macdonald served in 1871 as one of the British commissioners negotiating the resolution of the Anglo-American differences that had arisen during the Civil War. The Americans, among other things, wanted the right to fish in Canadian waters; the Canadians sought recompense for the Fenian attacks. The Americans won their point, and John A. received nothing in return. Stuck, Macdonald had to support the Treaty of Washington in Parliament in 1872. He soon found himself embroiled in the Pacific Scandal and out of office. He would remain in Opposition until 1878, his Liberal successor, Alexander Mackenzie, creating the Royal Military College in 1876.

Macdonald regained power in the 1878 election, campaigning on a protectionist tariff, and he retained his hold for the rest of his life. His government laid the foundations for a Permanent Force in 1882, setting up Infantry and Cavalry Schools of Instruction; the government thus had a few regulars to hand when Louis Riel led the Northwest into rebellion in 1885. Militia minister Adolphe Caron organized the largely militia force that moved west over the still-incomplete Canadian Pacific Railroad and, though stumbling in the field, the Northwest Field Force managed to defeat Riel's few hundred rebels and their Aboriginal allies. It was Macdonald who moved quickly to get Riel to trial and Macdonald who wanted him dead. "He certainly will be executed," the prime minister wrote privately, "but in the present natural excitement people grumble at his not being hanged off hand." Later, after Riel had been hanged, Macdonald argued that "I felt it would have been an act of political insanity to yield" to calls for clemency "simply because the man was of French blood."

Riel's execution cost Macdonald in Quebec, but he won re-election in 1887 and again in 1891, campaigning against reciprocal trade with the United States in his last election. "I am a British subject and British born," he said famously, "and a British subject I hope to die." He did in fact die soon after the election.

Macdonald had won the 1891 election with his "British subject" cry, but he had never been one willing to do whatever Whitehall had wanted. He had learned in Washington in 1871 that British interests would always prevail over Canada's if London saw a need to placate the United States and, though he acceded to General Wolseley's request in 1884 for voyageurs to assist the expedition intended to relieve General Gordon in Khartoum in the Sudan, he had no desire to help dig Britain out of holes of its own making. Certainly he was unwilling to spend money or lives to that end.

Macdonald was a Canadian, a nationalist first and only secondarily an imperialist. He was anti-American, as most Canadians of his era seemed to be, and he was a realist. Canada might have needed a bigger and better military, but other needs—economic, political, demographic—had to be met first. Still, his government had fended off the Fenians, put down two rebellions, and laid the foundations of the Permanent Force. SEE ALSO: NORTHWEST REBELLION; PERMANENT FORCE; RED RIVER REBELLION; RIEL.

READING: Donald Creighton, *John A. Macdonald: The Young Politician* and *The Old Chieftain*, 2 vols. (reissued, Toronto, 1998).

McEwen, Clifford Mackay (1896–1967). Born in Griswold, Manitoba, McEwen trained as a pilot in World War I. He shot down 27 enemy aircraft, most in action over Italy; a painting by V. Fitzgerald, now held in the Canadian War Museum, immortalized one of his victories. The much-decorated McEwen stayed in the air force after the war, becoming one of the first pilots to fly with the new Royal Canadian Air Force (RCAF). During World War II, his rise was rapid and, by 1941, he was the air commodore responsible for operations on Canada's East Coast, where he had difficulties dealing with bumptious US commanders, assigned there before the United States was in the war. In early 1944, Air Vice-Marshal McEwen took command of No. 6 Bomber Group (RCAF), then suffering from a high casualty rate and resulting morale problems. "Black Mike," as he became known, cracked down on ill discipline, frequently flew on missions with his 16 squadrons of Halifax and Lancaster bombers, and transformed No. 6's performance, turning it into one of Bomber

Major-General Lewis MacKenzie is depicted here by Gertrude Kearns with suitable power and defiance of pose, as he appeared in Sarajevo, 1992.

Command's most effective units. By the end of 1944, No. 6's casualty rate was the lowest in Bomber Command. He retired from the RCAF in 1946.

READING: David Bashow, "Four Gallant Airmen," in Bernd Horn, ed., *Intrepid Warriors* (Toronto, 2007).

MacKenzie, Lewis (b.1940). Major-General Lewis MacKenzie, born in Truro, Nova Scotia, served in the Canadian Forces (CF) for 36 years. His career was not unusual for soldiers of his generation: service in the NATO brigade in Germany and on a succession of peacekeeping tours in Gaza, Cyprus, Vietnam, Central America, and the former Yugoslavia. MacKenzie commanded the United Nations Observer Group in Central America (ONUCA) in 1990, and then was posted to the Balkans where he took command of Sector Sarajevo for the United Nations Protection Force (UNPROFOR) in 1992. He became an international celebrity when his troops forced open Sarajevo airport to relief flights. MacKenzie's blunt talk on television struck a responsive chord, given the international community's apparent inability or unwillingness to offer genuine help in response to Europe's greatest humanitarian crisis since 1945. He retired from the CF in 1993 to become a consultant and wrote a memoir, *Peacekeeper: The Road to Sarajevo*, which was a bestseller. He ran as a Progressive Conservative in the 1997 election, but lost. A charismatic figure, appearing regularly as a media commentator on international affairs, he remains arguably the best-known Canadian soldier of his time. He is an influential advocate of better care for military personnel and their families. SEE ALSO: PEACEKEEPING.

READING: Lewis MacKenzie, *Peacekeeper: The Road to Sarajevo* (Vancouver, 1993); Lewis MacKenzie, *Soldiers Made Me Look Good* (Vancouver, 2008).

Mackenzie-Papineau Battalion. This unit of the Spanish Republican or Loyalist forces battling nationalists led by the Fascist Generalissimo Francisco Franco during the Spanish Civil War (1936–1939) was named for the leaders of the Rebellions of 1837 in Upper and Lower Canada. Part of the International Brigades that rallied to the cause of the elected Spanish government, the battalion had perhaps 1,300 volunteers in all in its ranks (an additional 300 or more Canadians served in other units, many in the Abraham Lincoln Battalion raised by Americans) and fought in several major battles, suffering heavy casualties. Most of the volunteers were immigrants to Canada, and most (76 percent) were Communist Party of Canada members or active supporters, organized and funded by the party. Communists they may have been, but in a war where political factionalism was important to the Soviet Union that came to dominate the Loyalist side, the Mac-Paps had a well-earned reputation for political unreliability and for rejecting the authority and structure their commissars tried to impose. The unit formed in Spain in 1937 and incorporated all Canadians fighting in the country in late 1938. Its first Canadian commander was Edward Cecil-Smith, a competent soldier. In late

▲ William Lyon Mackenzie, years after the 1837 Rebellion.

was constantly frustrated by the refusal of British-appointed governors to introduce democratic changes. In December 1837, with rebellion underway in Lower Canada, he gathered his reform-minded supporters in an effort to overthrow the government and create an American-style democracy. Following his defeat at Montgomery's Tavern, north of Toronto, Mackenzie fled to the United States. He then tried to mount an invasion of Canada but was checked again at Navy Island in January 1838. Defeated and disillusioned, Mackenzie remained in the United States until 1850 when he returned to Canada after an amnesty. He soon was in Parliament again, but was largely a spent force. His grandson, William Lyon Mackenzie King, would have a more successful political career. SEE ALSO: REBELLIONS OF 1837–1838.

McNaughton, Andrew George Latta (1887–1966). Born in Moosomin, Northwest Territories, Andy McNaughton trained as an engineer at McGill University and joined the militia in 1909. He took an artillery battery overseas with the first contingent in 1914 and served with great distinction in the Canadian Division's first battles of World War I. Wounded twice, he became the key figure in developing the Canadian Corps' extremely successful counter-battery operations, using every means available—sound-ranging, air observation, flash spotting—to locate and destroy enemy artillery. At Vimy Ridge in April 1917, 83 percent of German artillery had been neutralized before the successful attack. By the armistice, Brigadier-General McNaughton had command of the corps' heavy artillery.

McNaughton stayed in the postwar Permanent Force, his rise quick. In 1922, he was deputy chief of the general staff (CGS) and in 1929, as a major-general, CGS. It was his bad luck to be in charge during the Great Depression when already small budgets all but disappeared, but he did his best to reorganize the militia, and he seized the opportunity to run unemployment relief camps for the R.B. Bennett government. The men, paid 20 cents a day and thus dubbed the Royal Twenty Centers, built military infrastructure across the country, airfields and landing

1936 and early 1937, Montreal surgeon Dr Norman Bethune also set up a mobile blood transfusion service, apparently the first of its kind anywhere, for the Loyalists.

The Canadian government noticeably disapproved of the Mackenzie-Papineau Battalion and the Communist Party's recruitment efforts, and passed the Foreign Enlistment Act in an effort to prohibit Canadians from fighting in foreign wars. At least 400 Canadians died in the Spanish Civil War, and many of the surviving Canadian veterans—the "premature anti-Fascists"—served in the military during World War II. SEE ALSO: FOREIGN ENLISTMENT ACT.

READING: Michael Petrou, *Renegades: Canadians in the Spanish Civil War* (Vancouver, 2008).

Mackenzie, William Lyon (1795–1861). Born in Scotland, Mackenzie came to Upper Canada in 1820 and soon started to publish *The Colonial Advocate*, a newspaper espousing governmental reform and attacking the Family Compact that ruled the colony. Elected to the Legislature, soon mayor of Toronto, he strips included. Unionized workers were not happy at seeing their work disappear, and most of those in the camps were bitter and felt exploited. Bennett put McNaughton, a genuinely scientific soldier, in charge of the National Research Council in 1935.

Prime Minister Mackenzie King found him there in September 1939 and gave him command of the 1st Canadian Division as World War II began. McNaughton took his division overseas in December and began to train to fill a spot in the British line in France. The German blitzkrieg that rolled across western Europe in mid-1940 changed those plans and, although some Canadians got to France in the forlorn hope of creating a new front after the Dunkirk evacuation, the 1st Canadian Division by July 1940 was among the best-equipped formations left in Britain. McNaughton soon commanded a corps and, by 1942, First Canadian Army, eventually consisting of two corps with three infantry and two armoured

A steely-eyed General Andrew McNaughton, portrayed on a Victory Bond poster.

divisions plus two more armoured brigades. The difficulty was that McNaughton—who had charisma to burn—turned out to be no field commander, failings demonstrated on Spartan, a large-scale exercise in 1943 under the disapproving eye of British commanders, and he fought with the British as well as with the politicians at home. McNaughton wanted his army to be kept together for the invasion of Europe, but the British—their doubts about the Canadian general growing—insisted that the troops and commanders had to get battle experience. The politicians, pushed by a public anxious for glory, wanted the same thing. In July 1943, over McNaughton's initial objections, the 1st Division went off to participate in the invasion of Sicily; I Canadian Corps headquarters and the 5th Canadian Armoured Division soon followed, again despite McNaughton's concerns over the break-up of his command. McNaughton had lost the deployment battle, and the British chief of the imperial general staff, General Alan Brooke, Canadian Generals Ken Stuart and H.D.G. Crerar, and Mackenzie King's defence minister, J.L. Ralston, saw to his removal by the end of 1943.

Mackenzie King had earlier considered McNaughton as a candidate for governor general but, when the reinforcement crisis of the fall of 1944 erupted, King tapped him to replace Ralston as defence minister. The new minister's job was to persuade home defence conscripts to volunteer for overseas service to provide the infantry reinforcements needed by units fighting in Italy and northwest Europe. McNaughton tried, was booed by Canadian Legion members at one speech, and failed to "convert" the conscripts. Faced with what looked like wholesale resignations of senior officers in Canada, he told King of his failure, and the prime minister, seeing the possibility of a generals' revolt, promptly decided to order 16,000 conscripts overseas. McNaughton went along but paid the price when he lost a by-election in Grey North, Ontario, in February 1945 (his wife's Catholicism played a major part in the contest) and then failed to win a seat in Moosomin, Saskatchewan, in the general election of June 1945. His political career was over.

McNaughton's public service was not yet done, however. He represented Canada at the United Nations, served on the International Joint Commission and the Permanent Joint Board on Defence and, near the end of his life, waged a notable fight against the proposed Columbia River Treaty between Canada and the United States.

A powerful figure, McNaughton had genuine scientific gifts and ample charisma. His men loved him in both world wars. But he did not have the temperament to be a successful commander in the mid-twentieth century where getting on with politicians and allies was critical. Nor did he have the tactical and strategic sense to fight battles, military and political, successfully. SEE ALSO: CONSCRIPTION; CRERAR; FIRST CANADIAN ARMY; KING; RALSTON.

READING: John Swettenham, *McNaughton*, 3 vols. (Toronto, 1968–1969); John Rickard, *The Politics of Command: Lieutenant-General A.G.L. McNaughton and the Canadian Army, 1939–1943* (Toronto, 2010).

Magazines, Military. The Canadian military has never been at the forefront of strategic thinking. It was modelled on the British armed forces and followed their lead. But repeatedly in the post-Confederation years, some bright sparks tried to publish magazines that might reach out to the militia or the Permanent Force—or sometimes both—and serve as a vehicle for debate and discussion on military topics. The first such nominally bilingual magazine, *The Canadian Military Review*, began in 1880 and lasted only until 1881. Much more successful was the self-proclaimed organ of the militia, *The Canadian Military Gazette*, which began publication in 1885 and lasted until 1948. This journal had good sources in its early years, perhaps even the British general officer commanding the Canadian militia, General E.T.H. Hutton, as, in October 1898, it leaked the militia headquarters' plans for sending a contingent to the South African War and greatly embarrassed the Laurier government.

If the militia had its own journal, then the Permanent Force wanted one too. *VRI Magazine*, begun in 1894, did not last long and was succeeded by the *United Service Magazine* which ceased publication in 1898. In 1900, *Military Topics: The Journal of the Canadian Militia* began monthly publication in Toronto but seems to have lasted only for three issues.

After World War I, the *Canadian Defence Quarterly* (CDQ), unofficially official and edited by an officer from the army general staff, began publication in 1923 and continued until the outbreak of World War II. CDQ served as a professional journal for the regular and reserve forces and reprinted articles from British, American, and other nations' military journals, but some Canadian officers such as Kenneth Stuart, CDQ's most important editor; Guy Simonds; and E.L.M. Burns wrote important think pieces in the journal. CDQ began anew as a private venture in 1971 (with a Department of National Defence subsidy) under the editorship of John Gellner. The end of the subsidy killed CDQ in 1998.

Following World War II, the services began publishing their own magazines. *The Canadian Army Journal*, started in 1947 and distributed to all officers, offered articles and book reviews on military topics, some specially written for it. *Crowsnest*, a similar magazine for the Royal Canadian Navy, and *The Roundel*, published by the Royal Canadian Air Force, began in 1948 and, like the army's magazine, closed down in 1965 as the Canadian Forces began the process of integration and unification. *The Canadian Army Journal* was revived in 1997 to disseminate Land Force doctrinal and training concepts, but also published book reviews and historical articles.

The chief of the defence staff authorized the publication of *Sentinel/Sentinelle* in November 1965 with the intent of assisting the transition of the three separate Canadian services into the unified Canadian Forces. The avowed aim was to foster better understanding between the sea, land, and air elements. The bilingual magazine, more a public relations vehicle than anything else, lasted until 1994 when it was the victim of budget cuts and, as the chief of the defence staff impenetrably explained, the need "to adapt our internal communication tools to the fast pace of today's life…."

In 2000, the Canadian Forces began publishing the bilingual *Canadian Military Journal/Revue Militaire Canadienne*, a fully illustrated quarterly produced on glossy paper. The CMJ featured opinion pieces and scholarly articles by serving members of the Canadian Forces and civilians, offered commentaries and book reviews, and engaged in debate. SEE ALSO: *CANADIAN DEFENCE QUARTERLY*.

Mainguy Report (1949). Rear-Admiral Rollo Mainguy was named to lead the commission of inquiry that studied dissatisfaction within the Royal Canadian Navy (RCN) in 1949 after several "mutinies" had broken out aboard three RCN ships, the aircraft carrier HMCS *Magnificent* and the destroyers *Athabaskan* and *Crescent*. Mutiny perhaps was too strong a word to describe the events—which lacked violence and were more akin to sit-down strikes or collective actions in the absence of an effective grievance resolution process—but the government, fearful of Communist Party influence, set up the inquiry. Mainguy and his colleagues Louis Audette and Lionel Brockington found no "subversives" in the RCN and no collusion, though they did see a connection between the three incidents. Their comprehensive recommendations, issued in October 1949, included greater Canadianization of the navy, notably the addition of *Canada* on uniform shoulder flashes, improvements in creature comforts for naval ratings, and a relaxation of the strict officer-ratings relationship that had been copied from the Royal Navy. SEE ALSO: MUTINIES, NAVAL.

READING: Marc Milner, *Canada's Navy* (2nd ed., Toronto, 2010).

Manitoba Force. The Manitoba Force of about 300 troops was formed from the militia who remained behind when Colonel Garnet Wolseley returned east from Manitoba in the late summer of 1870 after his Red River Expedition had put an end to the Red River Rebellion. It was the only effective Canadian military presence in the province and, in October 1871, turned out to defend Manitoba from a threatened Fenian attack. To reinforce the garrison, a second militia expedition consisting of some 212 militia and 60 canoe men was sent from central Canada in the late fall of 1871. They arrived within four weeks. The Manitoba Force remained responsible for law and order in the province until the North West Mounted Police took over in 1877.

Manley Report (2008). The Independent Panel on Canada's Future Role in Afghanistan reported on 22 January 2008. Created by Prime Minister Stephen Harper in 2007 and chaired by John Manley, formerly deputy prime minister in the Chrétien government, the panel's members were Jake Epp, Pamela Wallin, Derek Burney, and Paul Tellier, distinguished figures all. The report, while critical of some of the Conservative government's Afghanistan policies (not least its failure to provide medium helicopters for the Canadian contingent), appeared to take direct aim at Liberal leader Stéphane Dion, who wanted Canada out of its role in Afghanistan in 2009. Instead, the Manley Panel's recommendation for Canada to remain beyond that date helped the Harper government press the Dion Opposition into a parliamentary agreement to postpone the end of the Kandahar mission in its then-current form until 2011. There were, Manley said, "times when we have to be counted, times when it matters." SEE ALSO: AFGHANISTAN WAR; HARPER.

Medak Pocket (1993). The disintegration of former Yugoslavia into its component federal states at the end of the Cold War resulted in large-scale violence and a series of disjointed, often ineffective Western efforts to manage a peace process that warring factions on the ground refused repeatedly to respect. Conflicts in Slovenia and Croatia preceded the outbreak of savage fighting in Bosnia-Herzegovina, with nascent national armies and sectarian paramilitaries fighting neighbouring states, ethnic militias, and local warlords. The multi-ethnic Yugoslav National Army, divided and occasionally paralyzed by the competing claims on its loyalties, fought against breakaway separatist forces even as it eroded into a Serbian-Montenegrin rump, as rival factions in what amounted to a multinational civil war practised ethnic cleansing against one another. In the absence of residual federal authority, the successor states and often-powerful ethnic enclaves adhered generally to exclusive and exclusionary ethnic identities, despite centuries of multi-ethnic coexistence throughout the region. The level of violence as these new, unstable political entities—several were unrecognized as states—sought to expel, expunge, or suppress other factions, religions, or ethnic enclaves was on a scale not seen in Europe since World War II. The United Nations Protection Force (UNPROFOR), created in early 1992, deployed first into Croatia and then into Bosnia to try to maintain order and protect civilians.

In September 1993, Croatian forces launched an offensive against Serbian-held territory in the Gospic area, a salient captured in late 1991 and then defended mainly by troops of the breakaway Serbian republic of Krajina. A five-day battle saw Croatian troops secure several objectives within what was called the Medak pocket, while Serbian forces counterattacked there and in other areas, shelling Croatian towns, including Zagreb, the capital, with long-range artillery and surface-to-surface missiles. A UN-brokered ceasefire, agreed to by representatives of both Croatia and Serbian Krajina, led to the interposition of the 2nd Battalion of the Princess Patricia's Canadian Light Infantry (2PPCLI) under Lieutenant-Colonel James Calvin, and some French troops, between the factions, with a mandate to supervise the withdrawal of the Croatians to their pre-offensive lines, and the pullback of Serbian troops from the pocket. The Princess Pats, a regular army mechanized battalion with, at the time, a very high proportion of reservists in its ranks, had M113 armoured personnel carriers, TOW anti-tank missiles, and heavy mortars. Local Croat forces refused to let the Canadians enter the area, violating the ceasefire agreement, and fired on the Canadians' white-painted vehicles flying UN flags, resulting in a 15-hour firefight in which four Canadians were wounded, in exchange for perhaps 27 killed and many wounded on the Croatian side. Tough negotiations finally brought the fighting to an end, and the Canadians moved forward only to discover that the

Croats had been trying—unsuccessfully—to hide signs that they had killed Serbian civilians in several captured villages. The Croats had also raped girls and women, burned the villages and farmhouses, slaughtered livestock, and poisoned wells. Colonel Calvin's men documented the Croat crimes, hoping that International War Crimes prosecutions might follow. Two Croatian commanders finally went on trial 14 years later in The Hague in June 2007; one received a seven-year sentence while the other was acquitted. The Croatians still deny any crimes and claim they suffered no casualties in the action.

The Canadian government's suppression of news regarding the battle led to charges, when the story later appeared, that the impact of events in Somalia in 1993, where a local teenager had been tortured to death by Canadian troops, had prompted a formal blackout on military-related stories for fear of media publicity or potentially incriminating public scrutiny. It also appeared to reinforce the government's preference, and that of many public commentators, to see Canada's post–Cold War armed forces as a peacekeeping and not a war-fighting instrument of state. Non-government sources, notably journalists, were instrumental in bringing the Medak story to light, and in highlighting both the failure of UN troops to prevent local atrocities (the pocket had been adjacent to the UN-patrolled Sector South) and the effectiveness of a robust Canadian-French response to the Croats' refusal to recognize the eventual ceasefire. It was not until 2002 that a Governor General's Commendation was awarded to the members of 2PPCLI for their actions at Medak. The public struggles of several veterans of this battle with post-traumatic stress disorder are representative of the problems faced by many soldiers, diplomats, aid workers, and journalists in coming to terms with the horrific civil conflicts witnessed in the 1990s, and the frequent inability of international forces to help—even when in place and possessed of the requisite capacity. SEE ALSO: MULRONEY; PEACEKEEPING.

READING: Carol Off, *The Ghosts of Medak Pocket: The Story of Canada's Secret War* (Toronto, 2004).

Canada's shipbuilding industry boomed during World War II. Hundreds of Canadian-built merchant ships, including the ss *Grafton Park*, seen here at its October 1944 launch at United Shipyards Ltd. in Montreal, carried the vital trans-Atlantic cargo that kept Britain and Russia in the war.

Merchant Navy. In March 1918, late in World War I, the Canadian government ordered 63 ships to be built in Canadian yards for service in the Canadian Government Merchant Marine. None had been delivered by the time of the armistice in November, so the service was stillborn. *The Book of Remembrance* on Parliament Hill lists the names of 578 merchant sailors from Canada and Newfoundland who died in U-boat attacks; an undetermined number of Canadians serving on foreign-flagged vessels also died during the war because of enemy action.

Some two weeks before Canada declared war in September 1939, the government took control of Canada's 39 merchant ships and 1,450 sailors, all civilians, putting them under control of the Royal Canadian Navy. The first convoy for Britain left Halifax on 16 September. In the following months, a shortage of warship escorts and lack of air coverage across the entire North Atlantic led to heavy merchant ship losses

and an escalating shipbuilding campaign to outpace them. Canada's fleet increased to some 210 ships and 12,000 sailors by the end of the war, while Canadian shipyards also built 220 merchant ships for Britain. In addition, some 133 Great Lakes ships had to be pressed into North Atlantic service because of shipping shortages. Most Canadian merchant ships, operated by Park Steamships, a Crown corporation, were armed, and Royal Canadian Navy Reserve (RCNR) gunners, ordinarily seven ratings per ship, operated the weaponry and other communications or detection gear; merchant crews also supplemented the RCNR gunners as needed. Of the 16,000 Canadian and Newfoundland civilians who served on merchant ships, some 1,168 died at sea in the 82 Canadian ships that were lost to the U-boats. Another 461 Canadians died while serving on Allied or neutral merchant vessels sunk during the war. Eight women are included in the 1,629 merchant sailors lost to all causes, as are eight sailors who died while prisoners of war. During the Korean War, 12 Canadian flag merchant ships carried supplies to Korea, without loss.

Merchant navy veterans did not have status as war veterans until 1999, sixty years after the beginning of World War II. The Royal Canadian Legion and other veterans groups for years had opposed this due to differences in pay, status, and terms of service. Over time, the sailors received various benefits previously available only to members of the armed services; since 2000, merchant navy survivors have received all principal benefits accruing to other Canadian war veterans, as well as a $24,000 lump sum payment in compensation for the years they were denied.

A table listing all World War II Canadian merchant ships lost and casualties can be found at www.familyheritage.ca/Articles/merchant1.html. SEE ALSO: ATLANTIC; CONVOYS.

READING: F.B. Watt, *In All Respects Ready: The Merchant Navy and the Battle of the Atlantic, 1940–1945* (Toronto, 1985).

Mewburn, Sydney Chilton (1863–1956). A Liberal lawyer in Hamilton, Ontario, Mewburn served in the 13th Royal Regiment of the militia and rose rapidly through the ranks during World War I, his service only in Canada. A major-general by 1917, the pro-conscription Mewburn joined Sir Robert Borden's Union Government as minister of militia and defence in October 1917, won election to Parliament in December, and had the difficult tasks of enforcing the Military Service Act and bringing the soldiers back to Canada in 1919. He remained as minister until January 1920 and in politics until 1925. His son was killed in action in 1916.

Meyer, Kurt (1910–1961). An able soldier and a committed Nazi who had served on the Eastern Front and, according to British scholar Anthony Beevor, committed atrocities there, *Standartenführer* Kurt Meyer commanded the 25th SS Panzer-Grenadier Regiment that faced the 3rd Canadian Infantry Division on the Normandy beachhead in June 1944. In fighting on 7 June, the day after D-Day, the teenage soldiers of Meyer's *Hitlerjugend* regiment took prisoner several Canadians. After interrogating the Canadians at his headquarters at the Abbaye d'Ardenne, Meyer's men executed 23 of them. Later, more POWs, perhaps as many as 187 in all, suffered the same fate. Belgian resistance fighters captured Meyer, promoted on 14 June to command the 12th SS Panzer Division, on 6 September, several weeks after his division had been all but destroyed in the Falaise pocket. In December 1945, Canada tried Meyer before a military court for war crimes. The Waffen SS general predictably claimed that he was unaware that his soldiers had murdered the Canadians, but the tribunal found him guilty on three of five charges and sentenced him to death by firing squad. The commander of Canadian occupation forces in Germany, Major-General Christopher Vokes, commuted the death sentence to life imprisonment, his rationale being that Meyer had only indirect responsibility for the killings. Imprisoned at Dorchester Penitentiary in New Brunswick for almost nine years, Meyer was released in September 1954, and became a beer salesman in Germany. His later clients would include Canadian army messes at North Atlantic Treaty Organization bases in West Germany. SEE ALSO:

FALAISE; NORMANDY; PRISONERS OF WAR; WAR CRIMES.

READING: Kurt Meyer, *Grenadiers* (Mechanicsburg, PA, 2005); P.W. Lackenbauer and C. Madsen, *Kurt Meyer on Trial* (Kingston, ON, 2007).

Mid-Canada Line. A chain of eight sector control stations and 90 remotely operated radar sites built along the 55th parallel, the Mid-Canada Line was situated between the Distant Early Warning (DEW) and Pinetree Lines as part of the system of radar stations intended to detect attacking Soviet bomber forces. The Mid-Canada Line stretched from the Alaska border to the Atlantic Ocean and cost $250 million, paid entirely by the Canadian government as a contribution to continental defence with the United States. The radars, roughly 50 kilometres apart, utilized a system developed at McGill University—the so-called McGill Fence—and went into full operation in 1958 after a massive three-year construction process. Changes in technology quickly made the radar stations outdated, and the line shut down in 1964–1965.

Middleton, Sir Frederick Dobson (1825–1898). Born in Ireland and commissioned in the British army in 1842, Middleton was posted to Canada in 1868 for two years; while there, he married a French Canadian with whom he had two children. Middleton had much colonial experience and had served with distinction in the Indian Mutiny of 1857–1858, but was still a colonel nearing the end of his career when offered the post of general officer commanding the Canadian militia in 1884 at a local rank of major-general and pay of $4,000 a year. He was quick to accept.

Soon after assuming his post, Middleton organized and led the Northwest Field Force on its expedition against Louis Riel's Metis during the Northwest Rebellion of 1885. This was a large, complex operation across vast distances, a massive undertaking for Canada's small force. Middleton was pompous, cautious, and ponderous, and favoured his British staff officers over Canadians, rationally enough since the latter had almost no training. Some of his militia soldiers thought him too deliberate, even incompetent, in pursuing a vastly outgunned and outnumbered Metis force. However, most of the militia was poorly trained and badly led, the roads were poor and logistics uncertain, and caution may well have been the wisest course. As Middleton wrote, the loss of young soldiers "who thought they were going out for a picnic" in battle against the Metis horrified him.

Middleton divided his force of some 5,000 into three columns: Major-General T.B. Strange led the western column; Lieutenant-Colonel W.D. Otter the central one; and Middleton himself led the one farthest east. His column fought an indecisive engagement against the Metis at Fish Creek, where Middleton, rallying his green troops, repeatedly exposed himself to Metis fire before besieging Batoche, Riel's stronghold. There, some of his men forced his cautious hand when, after a desultory siege of several days, they broke ranks to rush the Metis positions and bring the battle to a close. Complete victory over Louis Riel, Gabriel Dumont, the Metis, and those few First Nations who had joined the rebellion soon followed, and Middleton received a knighthood in August 1885 and a gift of $20,000 from the Parliament in Ottawa.

He remained as general officer commanding but, in 1890, a parliamentary select committee determined that he had misappropriated furs confiscated from a Metis trader during the 1885 campaign, and damned him with the verdict that his actions had been "highly improper." This forced his resignation and return to England. Middleton had likely acted unwisely but, in his own view, he had been a victim of "this country of vain, drunken, lying & corrupt men." He spent his days from 1896 as keeper of the crown jewels in the Tower of London, the British government's undoubted way of telling Canada that, in its view, Middleton's honesty was unquestioned. SEE ALSO: CARON; DUMONT; NORTHWEST REBELLION; OTTER; RIEL.

READING: R.C. Macleod and Bob Beal, *Prairie Fire: The 1885 North West Rebellion* (Edmonton, 1984).

Military Aircraft. A vast country with more geography than people, Canada has been an aviation pioneer, with a history of industrial innovation, personal achievement, and scientific breakthroughs. The economic metrics of low population density and widely separated cities, however, have made aircraft development an intermittent project, its prospects greatest in times of war or heightened security threats, but difficult or impossible to sustain without the stimulus of imminent enemies or guaranteed sales to needy allies. Canadians have flown in hundreds of different types of aircraft, and the air force has owned almost as many: several have been designed and produced by Canadian plants to meet Canadian demands; many have been designed by others and made in Canada under license or partnership agreements; and others still have been made entirely offshore and flown as is, or purchased off the shelf. Only the main models are noted here.

Major-General Sir Frederick Middleton in 1885.

The Great War began just five years after the first powered flight in Canada. The Aerial Experiment Association's Silver Dart flew for almost a kilometre on 23 February 1909. Developmental progress in aviation was rapid thereafter and, in 1915, the Curtiss Aviation School opened in Toronto and began to train pilots, the new weapon already having proven itself in France and Flanders. There was no Canadian Air Force until very late in World War I, and it never saw action. Canadians nevertheless served in all the various British air forces, flying such early fighters as the BE-12, the Nieuport Scout, the de Havilland DH-2, the SE5A, and the Sopwith Camel, the most successful British fighter of the war. Raymond Collishaw, one of Canada's most successful aces, flew the ungainly looking Sopwith Triplane. Canadians also flew in bombers, notably the Handley Page VO100, the first heavy bomber flown by the Royal Flying Corps, and the Armstrong Whitworth FK8, in which Canadian A.A. McLeod won the Victoria Cross in 1918. Canadian pilots trained in Canada on the Curtiss JN4, the Jennie.

A second organization called the Canadian Air Force (CAF) came into existence in 1920, a part-time militia training scheme under the short-lived Air Board; the latter was absorbed by the new Department of National Defence in 1922–1923. The Royal Canadian Air Force (RCAF) was created in 1924, an organization that controlled civil flying and incorporated the work of the CAF and the Air Board. The first aircraft in Canadian hands, aside from some 50 German aircraft taken as war trophies, were a dozen Curtiss H2SL flying boats used by the United States Navy on anti-submarine patrols from Nova Scotia in 1918—and left behind as a gift when the war ended. Additional gifts came from Britain—11 Felixstowe F-3s, two Curtiss H16 flying boats, a Fairey IIIC seaplane, 62 Avro 504 trainers, 38 fighters of different types, as well as 12 airships, spare parts, and technical gear. With this the RCAF began its existence, and the H2SL, for example, was the RCAF's workhorse through the 1920s. Vickers Vikings, another flying boat, were purchased in the mid-1920s, and 30 Vickers Vedettes, designed for Canadian conditions, soon after, along with seven Varuna aircraft. Other float-equipped machines were also acquired as the RCAF devoted itself to Civil Government Air Operations. The hodgepodge nature of interwar aircraft reflected the generally sorry state of contemporary military funding, even as civilian air shows, the romance of flight in popular culture, and, gradually, civil aviation and related industries took hold. Of modern military aircraft, the RCAF had virtually none until the acquisition in 1927 of nine Armstrong Whitworth Siskins (a first-line RAF biplane fighter) and six Armstrong Whitworth Atlases (an army co-operation machine). These were the only military aircraft in the RCAF until ten more Atlases were purchased in 1934. In 1937, Canada acquired a handful of Blackburn Shark torpedo bombers, some Westland Wapitis, bargain-basement priced bombers, a few Avro 626 open cockpit fighters, and finally, in 1939, a squadron of Hawker Hurricanes, the first modern monoplane fighter in the RCAF.

World War II changed everything. At home, the RCAF ran the British Commonwealth Air Training Plan (BCATP), which used a wide variety of one- and two-engine trainers: the Tiger Moth, the Stearman, the Fleet Finch, the Yale and its cousin the Harvard, the Cessna Crane, the Anson, the Fleet Fort, the Fairey Battle, the Fairchild Cornell, and, at Operational Training Units, Hurricanes, de Havilland Mosquitoes, and Liberator bombers. The BCATP resulted in an extensive network of airfields, buildings, and transportation routes across Canada, and left behind thousands of trained aircrew, ground technicians, scientists, and maintenance personnel. Defence industries produced aircraft, weapons, bombs, and component parts, and trained the technical personnel who would play a leading role in postwar aviation firms, defence research, and military operations.

Overseas, RCAF aircrew flew in every aircraft used by the RAF. Bombers included the Bristol Bolingbroke, the Handley Page Hampden, the Vickers Wellington, the Douglas Boston, and the North American Mitchell B-25. The RCAF No. 6 Group in Bomber Command operated Wellingtons, Handley Page Halifaxes, and Avro Lancasters, including one squadron of Canadian-made Lancs. RCN pilots flew Fairey

Swordfish off Canadian-operated aircraft carriers, and Lieutenant Hampton Gray won a posthumous Victoria Cross flying a Vought Corsair over the Japanese home islands. Fighter pilots flew Hurricanes (seven squadrons overseas) and Supermarine Spitfires (14 squadrons), Curtiss Tomahawks (four squadrons), North American Mustangs, and Mosquitoes (four night fighter squadrons). The RCAF also flew maritime surveillance and bomber aircraft off Canada's East Coast and abroad, mainly using Consolidated Canso and Catalina boats, Liberator bombers, or Lockheed Hudson or Ventura aircraft.

After World War II, the RCAF moved into the jet era, first acquiring Vampire fighters and then the F-86 Sabres (many hundreds of which were made in Canada), which it sent to Europe for NATO service. The CF-100 was developed in Canada by A.V. Roe for home air defence (and some CF-100s flew in Europe as well), as was the abortive CF-105 Avro Arrow. Producing high-cost aircraft and their associated technologies for a relatively small air force with few guaranteed external markets doomed Canada's nascent military aircraft industry in the later 1950s, and the Arrow's controversial cancellation gutted, for a time, the domestic corps of engineers, designers, and research scientists responsible for earlier innovative projects. At its peak, however, the RCAF had some 750 operational fighter aircraft in the 1950s, while military research and development was also at the forefront of work on remotely piloted vehicles, missiles, and other related technologies. The CF-101 Voodoo, an American product, eventually replaced the CF-100, while overseas the CF-104 Starfighter (also American) took over from the Sabre and was itself replaced by the CF-18 Hornet (American again), of which Canada purchased 138, with 79 still available in 2008 for service. The CF-18s also handled home air defence duties when the Voodoo was retired. Paul Hellyer's unified Canadian Forces bought CF-5 tactical fighters, generally considered a costly error, but used for many years as the "aggressor squadron" against budding CF-18 pilots and as training aircraft. The RCN flew Fairey Fireflies and McDonnell Banshees from the carriers *Magnificent* and the *Bonaventure*. When

the recently refurbished "*Bonnie*" was paid off as a cost-cutting measure in 1970, the navy lost what air role it had left after unification.

The RCAF had no postwar bombers though it did use Lancasters on a variety of surveillance and spying missions. Maritime surveillance by Grumman Trackers, flown off RCN carriers, Lockheed Neptunes, the Canadair Argus, and the Lockheed CP-140 Aurora, remains a principal air mission; the old but still flying Auroras are destined for replacement, one imagines imminently. Helicopters included the now-aged Sea Kings and the new Cormorants; and for tactical use in support of the army, Twin Hueys as well as Kiowa, Chinook, and Griffon helicopters, some of which served in Afghanistan. The large, troop- and equipment-carrying Chinooks, foolishly sold off in the early 1990s, have been reacquired from 2008 for use in Afghanistan. Postwar transport aircraft included the North Star, the CC-130 Hercules, and, in 2007, four of the huge CC-177 Globemasters. Later variants of the Hercules were also to be acquired beginning in 2010. Canada is a participant in the international Joint Strike Fighter project, the product of which will eventually be the likely replacement for the CF-18, although, due to unit costs and other factors, few of the newer aircraft will see service. SEE ALSO: ARROW, AVRO; BRITISH COMMONWEALTH AIR TRAINING PLAN; ROYAL CANADIAN AIR FORCE.

READING: T.F.J. Leversedge, *Canadian Combat and Support Aircraft* (St Catharines, ON, 2007); John Griffin et al., *Canadian Military Aircraft ... 1968–1998* (St Catharines, ON, 2007).

Military Language. As with every profession, the military has its own language and forms of usage intended to limit access to outsiders, boost morale within the guild, and ease communications between professional peers. A peculiar mix of specialized diction, arcane acronyms, profanity, and tradition-derived euphemisms, military language ranges from the hopelessly anachronistic to the ruthlessly practical. At either end of this spectrum, whether the toasts and rhythms of a history-steeped mess dinner or the technical geek-speak that peppers on-air communications, it is at best frustrating and at worst indecipherable to non-military personnel and all but the most conscientious students of history. The organizational derivations of most such Canadian military language are British, with a few nods to the old French regime, layers of additional oddities added by successive wars and excursions abroad, and technical lingo grafted onto all by organizational strictures or scientific shorthand. There is specific language for the various branches of service too, much of it barbed—in jest or not—against sister services, and carefully honed, often humorous turns of phrase to describe anyone or anything other than one's own immediate comrades. Surface sailors may be "fish heads" to submariners, for example, or members of the armoured corps "zipper heads" to the other combat arms.

The British military from which the Canadian service essentially evolved had incorporated words and phrases from a variety of foreign lands over several centuries of colonial deployments, most notably from the Indian subcontinent. Khaki, for example, always pronounced "kar-key" in English intonation with a slightly exaggerated first syllable (and never "kackie," as Americans might say it), was the local word for the colour of light brownish yellow or deep beige (it literally meant "dusty" or "dust-covered") that uniforms turned when coated in dust and dirt along the sun-baked frontier; it was also the colour in which they were soon manufactured as a more practical alternative to crimson or scarlet. A "chit" (from "chitthi") was a written note or voucher, and in military slang it usually indicated that one had a note of permission. South Africa provided the word "laager" for an overnight encampment, something still used by armoured forces, as well as "commando." Bastardized French of the "kootchy-koo" variety was common in both world wars, the first of which also popularized terms such as "trench coat," "no man's land," and "over the top," all still used. The Afghanistan War has already injected new words and phrases into Canadian military speech, as has every major war before it: "sandbox," meaning Afghanistan itself, for example; "Opsec" or Operational Security,

information that could be of use to the enemy; and "rat lines," the routes through the mountains used by the Taliban.

World Wars I and II, Canada's major wars, poured words into the military's language. Ypres, where so many Canadians fought, was "Wipers." "Ack-ack" was anti-aircraft artillery, but "flak" to Allied aircrews, the short form of the German word for anti-aircraft gun. A safe, easy job was "cushy," probably from the French for "lying down." Dangerous weapons were humanized and identified from their sounds. The German grenade was a "potato-masher" because of its shape; some enemy shells were "whizz bangs" because of their sound, "Jack Johnsons" after the boxer, or "flying pigs." "M&V", or meat and vegetables, was the short form for the unappetizing tinned slop provided for meals (or MREs today, after the American-produced Meals—Ready to Eat, an unfortunate misnomer in many cases). The ever-present lice were called "cooties" while cigarettes were "coffin nails," which suggests that even in 1914 soldiers understood that cigarettes were harmful to health. The Royal Army Medical Corps, the British army's medical service, was abbreviated to RAMC, and soldiers usually translated this as "Rob All My Comrades," for the alleged habit of stretcher-bearers stealing from casualties. H-Hour indicated when an attack was to begin, while D-Day in World War II was the designated day for an invasion, or simply the day on which something was going to happen, and not only the invasion of France on 6 June 1944. A "tail-end Charlie"—or an "arse-end Charlie"—was a rear gunner on a bomber and sometimes that bomber had a "prang," an accident, or had "to ditch," crash-land in the water. Of course, "ops" could be "scrubbed," which meant flying operations had been cancelled for the day. Military Police were invariably referred to as "meatheads," and, adopting the US term from the Vietnam War, some Canadians called their infantry "grunts" or, more simply, PBI, for Poor Bloody Infantry. Naval traditions were generally British and drummed into young sailors with ferocious attention to detail, only marginally less so in the modern navy than the one that fought Hitler or the Kaiser.

Abbreviations were omnipresent and important enough that an understanding of them used to be a subject on officer promotion examinations. Bn, Bde, Div—battalion, brigade, division—more shorthand than acronym, are simple enough. Novices might easily decipher UN, NATO, NORAD, and JAG as well, but only the cognoscenti know the meanings and subtle evolutions of others, such as GSO1 (general staff officer, Grade 1), now in Canadian-adopted US parlance, G1 (the senior staff officer to a commander). Command and organizational clutter make any military sentence consonant heavy and clarity light. The CF (Canadian Forces), to start with the simplest one, is led by the CDS (chief of the defence staff), with the CAS, CLS, and CMS under command (the chiefs of the air, land, and maritime staffs respectively), who implement the CFDS (Canada First Defence Strategy) while also contributing resources to the CEFCOM (Canadian Expeditionary Forces Command) as part of the GWOT (global war on terrorism), in addition to resources deployed through the CANSOFCOM, DART, ISAF, the MINDSW, and half a dozen others, for Afghanistan alone. ISAF is the easiest of these to identify, if only because it is in the news virtually every day, but look up the rest and try to envisage them in a sentence, attempting to explain to the voters of Citizenville, Ontario, what Canada is up to in Asia. There is minor irony in DGPA, an effective linguistic cloaking device, actually referring to the defence department's directorate general of public affairs, whose website lists some 90 phone numbers, fax contacts, and emails, from coast to coast, but no succinct explanation of what the DGPA actually does. National Defence Headquarters in Ottawa is NDHQ, or "Fort Fumble" to gentle critics; North and South Tower have colloquial, and sometimes rhetorical, significance to insiders (they reference civilian-military tensions within the department). An ADM is an associate deputy minister in any department, but what was the ADM HR (MIL)? The current existence of an ADM HR (CIV) should help the curious to decode.

Acronyms and organizational shorthand are an occupational hazard in all complex bureaucracies, of course, and the military—in Canada or elsewhere—is probably no worse, or only marginally worse, than scientific organizations, universities, or other government departments. Some euphemisms are designed to conceal, however, though they derive from war's nasty business itself and the utility sometimes of softening the grim images of conflict with well-intended evasions. "Friendly fire" refers to your troops being fired on by your own weaponry or that of allies, and "collateral damage," often vilified as deliberate obfuscation, usually refers, without much dissembling, to the unintended killing of civilians during an assault or air attack.

And, of course, soldiers and sailors curse freely and fluently, bending both official languages into every imaginable contortion through the artful use of religious iconography and reverential phrases, as well as sex, bodily functions, and ethnic slurs. Every variant of the usual noun for human intercourse will be employed in every sentence, often more than once, making the FUBAR and SNAFU of earlier wars seem saintly by comparison. (YouTube can be a delightful source of modern soldier oratory.) Language often extends well beyond a coping device, morale builder, or indoctrination tool, however, to embrace or reflect attitudes that are crudely offensive and intentionally incendiary, as well as frequently being sexist, homophobic, and racist. The relatively recent presence of women in all military occupations and the official acceptance of gays and lesbians in the Canadian Forces have modified these traits but slightly.

Military Medicine. Before Canadians formed their own military units, British surgeons provided medical assistance to the wounded during battles on British North American soil. The standard of care was rudimentary, surgeons equipped with kits containing a saw, knife, scalpel, forceps, and tourniquets, and very little changed through the beginning of the twentieth century.

The origins of Canadian military medicine date to the years immediately prior to Confederation when militia units began to recruit their own doctors and stretcher-bearers. In 1866, Ottawa named a part-time medical staff officer, and militia exercises aimed to

△ Developments in military medicine reduced infection and saved soldiers' lives. Civilians, like this boy in France in June 1944, also received care when possible.

provide one doctor for every 400 soldiers. There was still no national military medical service but, with the Northwest Rebellion of 1885, the minister of militia and defence appointed the army's first surgeon general. To supplement the medical personnel who accompanied each unit of the Northwest Field Force, Ottawa mobilized two field hospitals and recruited professional nurses from Winnipeg. All medical personnel with the expedition, many from the medical faculties of McGill University and the University of Toronto, were under the supervision of the chief of the medical staff in the field, McGill's Dr Thomas

Roddick. After the battle of Batoche that ended the rebellion, Roddick set up a general hospital near the battlefield to treat the wounded and sick, and additional nurses soon joined his staff.

Although regiments still recruited their own medical personnel, the army took its first step toward a permanent medical service in June 1899, with the formation of the Army Medical Department and, when Canada dispatched an infantry battalion to South Africa later that year, three regimental medical officers and four professionally trained nurses accompanied the contingent. As of 25 January 1900, the nurses received the status of junior officers, but they were not permitted to go into the field. Instead, they worked in British army general hospitals, instructing hospital orderlies. As casualties mounted, especially from disease, these constraints disappeared. Led by Georgina Fane Pope of Prince Edward Island, the Canadian nurses of the First Contingent proved valuable, and four more nurses came out with the Second Contingent in the late winter of 1900. On 1 August 1901, the Department of Militia and Defence formally organized the Canadian Army Nursing Service with a Permanent Force (PF) component comprising the nurses who had served or were serving in South Africa and a reserve component of qualified nurses working in Canada and available for military service.

The South African War also led in January 1902 to the establishment of the 10th Canadian Field Hospital, sent with the Third Contingent, and its relative success encouraged creation of the Canadian Army Medical Corps (CAMC) in July 1904 with a PF component of eight officers and thirty-six other ranks. The reserve component included doctors, dental officers, and nursing sisters. By 1906, the Corps had been organized into field-deployable units and, after a 16-day exercise in 1911, developed its own procedures and policies. Much emphasis was placed on the need for sanitation, a lesson from South Africa where disease killed more Canadians than the enemy.

The 1st Canadian General Hospital (raised from the CAMC reserve) deployed to France in October 1914, well before other units of the Canadian Expeditionary Force, and began receiving patients on 21 October; four months later, when the Canadian Division arrived in Flanders, the hospital had already treated nearly 3,000 patients. The CAMC expanded exponentially as World War I went on. By 1918, the overseas medical establishment included dozens of field ambulance units, four casualty clearing stations, ten stationary hospitals, sixteen general hospitals, five special hospitals, and three convalescent hospitals. Much of the medical staff came from university teaching faculty. The numbers of wounded, most of them casualties caused by shellfire and machine guns, were enormous, and most moved from regimental aid posts to the advanced dressing stations, operated by the field ambulances, and then to casualty clearing stations, and from there to hospitals in the rear. The sick, also numerous, not least those suffering from respiratory diseases of all kinds, including Spanish flu in 1918–1919, followed the same path. By all accounts, the CAMC performed well, and it also pioneered the use of blood transfusions in the field. During the war 21,453 personnel, including 3,141 nursing sisters, served in the medical corps, which sustained 1,325 casualties, including 504 killed in action or who died of wounds, and 127 who died of disease. The latter included Lieutenant-Colonel John McCrae, MD, commanding officer of No. 3 Canadian General Hospital and author of "In Flanders Fields," the iconic Great War poem, who died of pneumonia and meningitis in January 1918. The Royal Canadian Navy, very small in size and mainly deployed in Canadian waters, provided medical care to its officers and ratings; it also operated five hospital ships to ferry more than 28,000 wounded and sick from Europe to Canada. Many Canadian medical personnel were on the HMHS *Llandovery Castle* that was sunk by a U-boat with heavy loss of life on 27 June 1918.

In World War II, the Royal Canadian Army Medical Corps (the "Royal" was added in 1919 in recognition of the Corps' wartime service), in addition to field ambulance units, operated five casualty clearing stations, twenty-eight general hospitals, three convalescent hospitals, and one general hospital specializing in neurology and plastic surgery. Nearly 35,000 men and women (including 3,656 nursing sisters) served in the RCAMC; 107 were killed as a result of enemy action and 491 wounded. Major RCAMC installations received about 84,000 patients, and achieved a recovery rate of 93 percent for wounded casualties and 99.91 percent for victims of disease, thanks in substantial part to the development of treatments such as sulfa and penicillin.

The Royal Canadian Navy deployed its own medical services during the war. The RCN medical establishment grew slowly at first, and the first naval hospitals opened only in 1941 at HMCS *Naden* in Esquimalt, British Columbia, and HMCS *Stadacona* in

⌃ The frequently-dreadful conditions in World War I's trenches made the work of stretcher bearers gruelling, as this photograph from November 1916 suggests.

Halifax, Nova Scotia; during the course of the war, the RCN opened seven more hospitals. From 1942 onwards, the RCN, which had hitherto relied on the Royal Navy, began training its own medical personnel. The navy lost nine medical officers, one nursing sister, and 16 ratings who were killed in action or died as a result of enemy action. The RCAF, too, began the war with no medical capability, but established a medical branch in late 1940 and developed a network of small airfield hospitals that extended across Canada through the Home War Establishment and the flying schools of the British Commonwealth Air Training Plan. By the end of 1944, there were 100 station hospitals in Canada and Newfoundland. The RCAF did not operate hospitals overseas, but many of its medical personnel served in Royal Air Force institutions.

After World War II, the three services continued to operate their own medical branches throughout the Korean War, in NATO, and on some of the larger peacekeeping missions. In Korea, 34 per thousand of the wounded would die, compared to 114 per thousand in World War I and 66 per thousand in the 1939–1945 war. Among those with diseases in Korea, 0.7 per thousand succumbed, compared to 5 per thousand in 1914–1918 and 0.9 per thousand in World War II. Treatment nearer the front, rapid evacuation, better hygiene, antibiotics, and blood transfusions—all contributed to a declining death rate.

In January 1959, the Department of National Defence unified the medical branches as the Canadian Forces Medical Service (CFMS), a precursor to the triservice unification that occurred in 1968.

In May 1969, the CFMS was authorized as a personnel branch of the CF, completing the administrative process of amalgamation. In 1995, the Canadian Forces Medical and Dental Services were united under the surgeon general who later became the chief of health services. By that point, the CFMS had become one of the victims of budget and personnel cuts with most of its military hospitals closed down. As early as 1990, the auditor general had suggested that CF operational needs might not be able to be met, and in Canada the military began to draw on civilian facilities for services provided in garrison in Canada. Such military medical resources as Canada retained were geared for operational deployments. The 1st Canadian Field Hospital, based in Petawawa, Ontario, joined British land forces and was deployed in the Saudi Arabian desert behind 1 (UK) Armoured Division during the Gulf War of 1990–1991. On 25 February 1991, the field hospital became fully operational. Five hundred and thirty personnel operated the hospital, which treated both British and Iraqi wounded.

Straitened though its circumstances were, the CFMS proved able to function well during the war in Afghanistan. In February 2006, more than 160 military medical personnel deployed to Kandahar. Their primary task was to establish a hospital to provide surgical treatment for severely injured patients. This hospital replaced the existing American facility but provided increased capabilities. The medical staff consisted of a general surgeon, an orthopedic surgeon, two anesthesiologists, an internist, a radiologist, an oral surgeon, and several family physicians. The hospital included a patient ward with nine beds and an intensive care unit with three beds, a blood bank, ultrasonography, digital radiography, laboratory services, and a CT scanner. Setting up this hospital involved the largest deployment of Canadian Forces Health Services personnel and equipment since the Gulf War.

To meet the challenge of a sudden increase in operational tempo, seven complete teams of medical and support staff were trained and deployed in rotation to 2009. Many members of the surgical staff were civilian doctors willing to serve abroad, in part, at least, because the experience gained in Afghanistan would be useful in treating future disasters in Canada.

SEE ALSO: AFGHANISTAN WAR; CANADIAN ARMY NURSING SERVICE; NORTHWEST REBELLION; SOUTH AFRICAN WAR; WORLD WAR I; WORLD WAR II.

READING: Gary H. Rice, *A Sketch of Military Medicine in Canada, 1867–2009* (Carleton Place, ON, 2009).

Military Music. Music has accompanied military forces for centuries. The French brought fifes and drums to Canada in the seventeenth century, and the British came with larger regimental bands. Canadian units of the volunteer militia after the mid-1850s began to form bands, the first apparently being the Independent Artillery Militia Company in Hamilton, Ontario, in 1856, which developed from the Sons of Temperance band. Bands played to mark the departure of troops to fight the Fenians in 1866, and, by 1869, the Queen's Own Rifles' band had 32 members, the 10th Royal Grenadiers a band of 40, and the Victoria Rifles of Montreal a band of 25. By 1880, almost all militia units had a band of some sort, and the 90th Regiment of Winnipeg's brass played for the troops in the field during the Northwest Rebellion of 1885. Regimental bands also performed at community functions and some, such as the Queen's Own, toured Canada and the United States. In 1898, the Royal Canadian Garrison Artillery Band formed at Quebec City under Bandmaster Joseph Vezina, with 25 musicians. The band was the first permanent one formed in the military forces of the British dominions.

At the beginning of World War I, no provision was made for bands, but units soon formed their own. A photograph of the 15th Battalion (48th Highlanders) taken in September 1914 at Camp Valcartier showed eight pipers, five drummers, and fifteen buglers. When Canadians went into action in 1915, several Highland battalions had pipers who played them into battle; one piper, James Richardson of the 16th Battalion, won a posthumous Victoria Cross at Regina Trench in 1916. There were also concert shows, and each of the Canadian Corps' four divisions produced one, as did some brigades and battalions. The most

⌃ Armies march to military music, and Canadian military musicians, like this brass band performing at a Victory Bond concert in World War I, were popular at home and abroad.

successful was the 3rd Canadian Division's Dumbells troupe that, under the lead of Merton Plunkett of the YMCA, entertained soldiers behind the front (and at the London Coliseum in 1918) and developed into a popular postwar vaudeville act.

In World War II, militia units were not allowed to enlist their bands for overseas service, though some units "smuggled" their bandsmen overseas as infantry. Pipers did not ordinarily lead soldiers into battle in World War II, but the Queen's Own Cameron Highlanders landed at Dieppe to the skirls of a piper, and the Canadian Scottish went ashore on Juno Beach to the sound of the pipes. Bands—136 in Canada and 69 overseas—and entertainment troupes soon formed in England and at home and, by 1942, the army had

some 5,000 bandsmen (and women in the Canadian Women's Army Corps' two bands) on strength. "The Army Show" and "Meet the Navy" were smash hits in Canada.

After 1945, military bands went through periodic reorganization and budget-slashing. In 1951, there were 106 militia bands; by 1980, there were just eight navy reserve bands, three air reserve bands, and thirty-two militia bands. Regular force bands numbered eight during the huge expansion of the army in the 1950s and nineteen by 1968; after unification, only seven remained. By 2007, there were two bands each for the army, navy and air force, and 52 in the reserves. The Central Band of the Canadian Forces, an air force band based in Ottawa, is the premier ensemble.

Military music remains popular with the Canadian public, as frequent tattoos and festivals demonstrate. Quebec City's 400th anniversary in 2008, for example, featured a military music festival that brought bands from the Czech Republic, Singapore, Chile, and South Korea, among others, to the city.

The music played by Canadian military bands has tended to be primarily that by British, French, German, and American composers. Much has come from the rich tradition of military music associated with British regiments that served in Canada or to which Canadian units are allied, and from American composers, not least of Broadway show tunes. Nonetheless, Canadian marches are very frequently played and the three regular force infantry regimental marches are all of Canadian composition. SEE ALSO: POPULAR MUSIC IN WARTIME.

Military Service Act (1917). On 29 August 1917, the Military Service Act was proclaimed into law, introducing conscription to Canada. The legislation decreed that all men aged 20 to 45 could be conscripted for overseas service as reinforcements for the Canadian Expeditionary Force (CEF). Prime Minister Sir Robert Borden had introduced the measure in the hope of obtaining 100,000 additional soldiers. The act became the key issue for Borden's Union Government in the December 1917 election, but it led to anti-conscription riots in Quebec and massive evasion and many exemptions from service there and elsewhere. Only some 24,000 conscripts made it to the CEF in Europe by the end of the war, but they provided the reinforcements needed to replace the heavy casualties of the Hundred Days. The conscripts in Canada would have been sufficient reinforcements for the Canadian Corps had the war continued into 1919. SEE ALSO: BORDEN, ROBERT; CONSCRIPTION.

READING: Roger Graham, *Arthur Meighen: The Door of Opportunity*, vol. 1 (Toronto, 1960).

Military Voters Act (1917). Passed on 20 September 1917 to aid Sir Robert Borden's government in the upcoming federal election, the act expanded the franchise among military electors. All British subjects on active service regardless of age, sex, or residence were given the right to vote. The act also allowed the government to allocate the votes of soldiers overseas who declared that they did not know their home constituency to those ridings where the government saw fit. This almost invariably meant to those ridings where government candidates needed them. The soldiers' vote favoured overwhelmingly—92 percent—Borden's Union Government in the December 1917 election, enough to take 14 seats away from the Liberals. SEE ALSO: BORDEN, ROBERT; CONSCRIPTION; WAR TIME ELECTIONS ACT.

READING: Roger Graham, *Arthur Meighen: The Door of Opportunity*, vol. 1 (Toronto, 1960).

Militia. The militia is a part-time, volunteer military force that helps to defend Canada. Some have viewed it as a reserve force to supplement the regular professional army in times of trouble; others have seen it as the backbone of Canada's military, trained by regulars, but with the primary mission of defending the country.

In New France, able-bodied males were organized into militia units under a locally elected captain, one of the few elected positions in the colony. Adapting to Aboriginal styles of forest warfare, the militia was used mostly as border raiders, attacking British frontier settlements, usually in conjunction with Aboriginal allies. The militia often served together with French regulars, although maintaining its more irregular fighting style.

The militia continued to exist after the conquest of New France, but it played little role in defending Canada against the 1775 invasion launched by the rebelling American colonies at the start of the Revolutionary War. With the arrival of the Loyalists after the British defeat, a number of militia units were established in the English-speaking colonies. They, along with some French-speaking militia units, fought alongside British regulars to defend Canada in the War of 1812. British regulars bore the brunt of the war, with the militia mainly handling labour and transport duties. The Canadian militia myth had it, however, that the sturdy Canadian yeomanry had beaten off the invader, assisted marginally by British regulars.

After the War of 1812, the militia languished in the British North American colonies. There was the Sedentary Militia, supposed to be composed of all the able-bodied males in the colony capable of being mustered at a moment's notice, but it almost always amounted to nothing. The lieutenant-colonel of the battalion located in and around Stanstead, Lower Canada, reported in November 1846 that "the Militia having been so long neglected in Stanstead I find I have no papers in my possession that will enable me to fill the blank return furnished with any degree of consistence…." After the Militia Act of 1855, an Active Militia was created, consisting of a nominal strength of 5,000 volunteers who were paid a small sum for their ten annual training days. But after an initial burst of enthusiasm, the Active Militia again usually proved to be poorly led and badly equipped. After Confederation, the Militia Act of 1868 established the Active Militia at 40,000 men and provided for a reserve militia, in effect a continuation of the Sedentary Militia. The latter never existed; training for the former usually consisted of little more than occasional night and weekend drills supplemented by a week-long militia camp every summer or so (less often for rural battalions). The country was also divided into a number of military districts for better militia organization.

In 1874, Canada appointed the first general officer commanding (GOC) the militia, the British officer Major-General Edward Selby Smith. The GOC's task was to lead the Canadian militia (including training it to operate in conjunction with the British army) and to maintain liaison with Britain, while also serving the minister of militia and defence. Only British officers were appointed until 1908. The GOC had a difficult task due both to the reluctance of the Canadian government to spend money on defence and its extreme sensitivity to anything it considered interference by an imperial officer in Canadian political affairs; such interference was inevitable when the GOC tried to get Canada to improve its own defences.

In 1882, the government established permanent militia schools to train militia officers. Attendance was made compulsory the following year but, despite this attempt to train militia officers to a respectable standard, patronage appointments undermined efficiency. Attempts by GOCs to eliminate patronage created constant friction with the government. Although a tiny Permanent Force (PF) took form in 1883, the militia—and not the regulars—was still looked upon as the backbone of Canada's military. This view was reinforced by the militia myth to such a degree that for a long time the term "Permanent Active Militia" was used to designate Canada's professional soldiers, "Non-Permanent Active Militia" being used for the militia itself. The PF remained tiny, such funds as were available going to the militia, and ministers like Sam Hughes who took office in 1911 hated the regulars. As a result, the vast majority of Canadian Expeditionary Force and Canadian Corps officers in World War I came from the militia, not the PF. Those who survived and learned on the job often performed brilliantly. Canada's greatest soldier, Sir Arthur Currie, was a Victoria militia officer.

The militia, like the PF, entered into the dark days of peace in 1919. Numbers fell and equipment grew obsolete, but a core of regular soldiers continued to train the militia, and the PF provided a nucleus around which the militia could form in time of war. The PF had also learned better how to prepare itself against the politicians, and in World War II regular officers secured most of the key positions at home and abroad. Once again, the militia formed the backbone of the Canadian Army, and again arguably the best Canadian field commander, Major-General Bert Hoffmeister, was a Vancouver militia officer.

The militia continued after World War II, but in a much-diminished role as a reserve force for the regulars. Since 1945, it has been reorganized several times as ministers attempted to redefine its role. In the late 1950s, fears of Soviet nuclear attack running high, the government tasked the militia with "national survival," essentially rescuing survivors from bombed cities. Scorned by militia stalwarts as "snakes and ladders" and as a denial of its fighting role, national survival hurt the militia's enrolment and eventually disappeared as a role. That demonstrated the militia's considerable political power, and it has continuously resisted attempts to eliminate its units and functions. Tension between the regulars and the reservists has been sufficiently intense and counterproductive, so in 1995 the government named a former chief justice of Canada, Brian Dickson, to chair a Special Commission on the Restructuring of the Reserves. The commission's recommendations on ameliorating tensions were largely adopted; its recommendations on consolidating smaller and weaker units were largely ignored.

The militia, though small in present-day Canada—some 21,000 (in autumn 2009) organized in approximately 120 units—has performed superbly in providing men and women to fill regular force positions in Canada and for overseas deployments. Militia soldiers made up more than 20 percent of some infantry battalions deployed to former Yugoslavia in the 1990s and an even higher percentage of some battle groups fighting in Afghanistan. Some roles, such as Civil-Military Cooperation (CIMIC) and PsyOps (Psychological Operations), are provided almost entirely by reservists. In other words, the militia remains an essential part of Canada's army. SEE ALSO: ACTIVE MILITIA; GENERALS, WORLD WAR I; GENERALS, WORLD WAR II; PERMANENT FORCE; SEDENTARY MILITIA; WAR OF 1812.

READING: Desmond Morton, *Ministers and Generals: Politics and the Canadian Militia, 1868–1904* (Toronto, 1970); Stephen J. Harris, *Canadian Brass: The Making of a Professional Army, 1860–1939* (Toronto, 1988).

Militia and Defence, Department of. Established by order-in-council on 1 July 1867 and given its statutory basis by the 1868 Militia Act, the Department of Militia and Defence had as its first minister Sir George-Étienne Cartier. The department had responsibility for all the country's militia and defence requirements, including personnel and equipment, and was thus a fertile field for patronage. Always understaffed and under-financed except in wartime, the often-troubled department was absorbed by the newly created tri-service Department of National Defence on 1 January 1923.

Militia Myth. Citizen-soldiers, part-time Spartans with innate martial virtues and natural prowess at arms, have defended Canada successfully for at least 200 years; when lazy, disinterested regulars shied from the duties or proved inadequate to the task, ready throngs of ten-feet-tall militia stalwarts dropped their rakes and ploughshares, raced into action, and saw off marauding First Nations warriors, Americans, or—in Europe—Germans. That, with a little emphasis added, is the militia myth that took form in Upper Canada during and after the War of 1812 when local citizens, notably York's leading Anglican cleric, John Strachan, denounced British commanders for their incompetence (he was not always without good reason in such charges) and came to the view that Loyalist militia had saved Canada from the American invaders. Egerton Ryerson, writing almost seven decades later, put the myth in its most extreme form, making explicit (if garbled) reference to the account by Herodotus of the campaigns of Thermopylae and Plataea: "The Spartan bands of Canadian Loyalist volunteers, aided by a few hundred English soldiers and civilized Indians, repelled the Persian thousands of democratic American invaders, and maintained the virgin soil of Canada unpolluted by the foot of the plundering invader."

In fact, it had been the well-trained British regulars of 1812, including several units raised in North America, who had borne the primary responsibility for successfully defending Canada, often working with First Nations warriors in doing so, and not the militia, which had been used primarily as a labour and transport force. Over time, the myth produced the further belief among Canadian political leaders, much of the press, and virtually all militia officers that a vigilant, well-armed militia, as opposed to a corps of professional soldiers, offered Canada's best defence. If the militia had been well-armed and well-trained, this might have been so, but it never was. The militia myth, moreover, was a self-fulfilling prophecy that provided a rationale for the government to direct its small resources toward the maintenance and training of the militia, rather than the tiny Permanent Force, which it did with a will. Sam Hughes, minister of militia and defence in the government of Sir Robert Borden, believed the myth implicitly, and this had a major impact on the creation and functioning of the Canadian Expeditionary Force in World War I.

Senior officers like General Sir Arthur Currie, a prewar militia officer who had served overseas, returned to Canada in 1919 convinced that the nation required an army of professionally trained regulars. Currie and his officers had learned on the job in the trenches, but they believed that the casualty toll might have been lower if there had been better prewar training. The politicians did not agree, and the interwar Permanent Force (PF) once again became a tiny, ill-equipped force. The Non-Permanent Active Militia, itself ill-equipped and untrained, became the basis for Canadian defence. Though the regular officers ensured that the senior command positions in the Canadian divisions that fought in World War II mostly went to members of the Permanent Force, this caused some resentment as the militia officers learned on the job. Brigadier William Murphy, a Vancouver lawyer who rose to command the 1st Canadian Armoured Brigade in Italy in 1944, probably had it right when he wrote in a letter home that "I feel I have got about as far as a militiaman can in this war." But Lieutenant-General Charles Foulkes, a corps commander who became chief of the general staff after the war, noted that 60 percent of division commanders, 75 percent of brigade commanders, and 90 percent of commissioned officers were militia. That was likely correct in 1945, but all the wartime chiefs of the general staff, all the army commanders, and all the corps' commanders had been PF.

Both regulars and militia officers remained exquisitely conscious of the divide between them, a gap that continues, more than six decades later, exacerbated by shortages in funding for both sides. So poisonous did relations between the two groups get by the mid-1990s that the government established a Special Commission on the Restructuring of the Reserves (SCRR), a former chief justice of Canada, Brian Dickson, at its head. Most of the commission's recommendations were put in place, and this perhaps helped smooth regular force-militia relations, although proposals to consolidate militia regiments into larger and more viable units were rejected. The resentment that the Department of National Defence, dominated by regulars, allegedly does not give full weight to reserve force qualifications or pay reservists at the same scale as regulars nonetheless persists. The militia myth, tailored slightly for modern conditions and more mundane fiscal debates, lives on. SEE ALSO: MILITIA; RESERVE FORCES; WAR OF 1812.

READING: James Wood, *Militia Myths: Ideas of the Canadian Citizen Soldier* (Vancouver, 2010); J.L. Granatstein, *Canada's Army: Waging War and Keeping the Peace* (Toronto, 2002).

Mobilization. Detailed plans for mobilization to be carried out by the country's militia districts had been prepared by Permanent Force staff officers at Ottawa headquarters prior to the outbreak of World War I. The minister of militia and defence, Sam Hughes, nonetheless discarded the plans after the beginning of the war and telegraphed militia units to raise volunteers and send them to Camp Valcartier, north of Quebec City, where a training camp had yet to be constructed. Hughes also decided that the men raised by militia units would be absorbed into numbered battalions, roughly grouped by geography. There was much chaos as a result of these radical revisions of the mobilization plans but, by September 1914, some 25,000 troops had arrived at Valcartier. From there, the first Canadian contingent of some 31,000 went to England in October 1914. New battalions of infantry, raised by individuals or organizations, took shape across the nation and provided units for subsequent overseas contingents. It took two years for the professional military planners to get a grip on the process Hughes had set in train and, until they did, the result was disorganization in Canada, in Britain, and, to a lesser extent, at the front. Most units raised in Canada after 1915 had to be broken up later in England; the troops would be used as reinforcements for existing battalions of the Canadian Corps. The officers could revert to lieutenants if they wished to go to the front; if not, they could remain in England.

^ A Toronto streetcar decked out to encourage recruits in World War I. Voluntary recruitment declined as the war dragged on, leading in 1917 to conscription.

The Borden government finally conducted a voluntary national registration in early 1917, prior to passing its Military Service Act in the summer. Implemented after a general election on 17 December 1917, conscription added further political difficulties to the problem of securing enough troops to replace casualties, though it did put some 100,000 into uniform by the armistice of 11 November 1918. Despite the politico-military problems, the Canadian Corps was never short of the reinforcements it needed to operate in the field.

The officers of the interwar Permanent Force swore that Hughes-style chaos would not recur, and careful plans for mobilization were in place well before the German invasion of Poland on 1 September 1939 began World War II. The army plan contemplated an expeditionary force organized on British lines that would eventually reach six divisions. The government had not been informed of this, but Brigadier Harry Crerar, the drafter of the plan, believed that it would agree to send at least one and possibly two divisions quickly overseas. Before its own declaration of war on 10 September, Canada mobilized the militia, air force, and navy. Canada's few destroyers were ordered to patrol the coasts, militia units began to patrol vital points on land, and aircraft went on alert on the East Coast. Mobilization orders to designated units for two divisions and a corps headquarters went out. However, Prime Minister Mackenzie King's government wanted a limited liability war effort, given Canada's financial situation and the prime minister's fear that a big war effort would bring conscription and national division. King himself would have preferred to send no army troops overseas and to focus Canada's war effort on the British Commonwealth Air Training

Plan, but public opinion (and his Cabinet) demanded an army contribution. One division was to proceed overseas later in 1939; the second would train in Canada. The fall of France in May to June 1940 took the lid off the war effort, and Canada began to send as many troops as it could overseas, eventually fielding First Canadian Army of five divisions and two armoured brigades, as well as home defence formations; the Royal Canadian Air Force expanded to a quarter million personnel and the Royal Canadian Navy to 100,000.

Ottawa handled the process of mobilization better after 1939 than in World War I. The National Resources Mobilization Act, passed in June 1940, authorized a national registration and home defence conscription. Following the national registration in August 1940, mobilization proceeded apace with all three services recruiting in an organized, methodical fashion and with conscription for home defence, operated in tandem by a National Selective Service organization and the army, bringing in recruits for training and trying to keep skilled workers where they might contribute most to the war effort. There were the inevitable problems but, by comparison with the Great War experience, mobilization in World War II was efficient and effective. Despite this, army planners substantially underestimated infantry casualties and, in the autumn of 1944, a shortage of reinforcements came close to bringing down the government.

Mobilization plans for the military and for industry existed during the opening years of the Cold War; indeed, the cards for a national manpower registration had been printed and stockpiled. But, as the nature of warfare changed in the nuclear era and after the Cold War ended, no one in Ottawa appeared to believe seriously that mobilization plans were needed. The Special Commission on the Restructuring of the Reserves called for such a plan in its 1995 report, as did other public studies and private reports. But nothing was done and, at present, in the early years of the twenty-first century, Canada apparently has no mobilization plan. SEE ALSO: CONSCRIPTION; HUGHES; KING.

Mons, Battle of (1918). The first clash of World War I between British and German forces took place in Mons, Belgium, in August 1914, and the British were forced to retreat. The war also ended there for the Canadian Corps in November 1918, the final stage in the Allied offensive that had started on 8 August at the onset of the Hundred Days' campaign that led to the defeat of the German army. Spearheaded by the 2nd Canadian Division, the corps liberated the city on 10 November and forced the Germans to retreat toward Antwerp the following day, 11 November, the day the guns fell silent on the Western Front. A trumped-up controversy later developed over whether the corps' commander, Sir Arthur Currie, had needlessly sacrificed men in this final assault of the war.

READING: Robert J. Sharpe, *The Last Day, the Last Hour: The Currie Libel Trial* (Toronto, 1988).

Montcalm, Louis-Joseph de, Marquis de (1712–1759). After a distinguished military career, Major-General Montcalm came to New France in 1756 to take command of all French troops at the outbreak of the Seven Years' War. His instructions, however, made clear that the governor, Pierre de Rigaud de Vaudreuil, was his superior. Montcalm was very much a European professional soldier: a vain, hyper-confident man, he believed his regular battalions could win battles with massed, disciplined firepower, and not with the guerilla tactics favoured by Vaudreuil, the Canadien militia, or the native warriors. The militia he considered an undisciplined rabble. Outnumbered and outgunned by British and British-American forces from the very start, Montcalm took advantage of his internal lines of communication to strike at and subdue British posts along Lake Champlain, thus denying his enemy overland access to the St Lawrence River Valley. His forces captured Fort Oswego in the summer of 1756, securing control of eastern Lake Ontario. The next summer, Montcalm laid siege to Fort William Henry on Lake George and took its surrender on negotiated terms. But his native allies killed prisoners and their women and children, despite guarantees of safe conduct. Though Montcalm likely could not have stopped the massacre, he

Soldiers of the 42nd Battalion pass Belgian civilians on the road to Mons in November 1918. Canadian troops ended the war where Britain had suffered its first great reverse in 1914.

did not appear to have tried too hard to do so. Montcalm then failed to follow up his victory by taking nearby Fort Edward and, as he might have done, advancing on Albany. The British received a respite, amassed a large force, and, in the summer of 1758, battered it to death against the log walls of Fort Carillon (Ticonderoga) on Lake George—yet another victory for Montcalm. The victory, however, led to bitter squabbles with Vaudreuil, both men telling tales to Paris about the other.

A capable and now proven tactician, Montcalm, promoted to lieutenant-general, could not stop the British under Major-General James Wolfe from arriving in the St Lawrence at the end of June 1759. Despite several inconclusive engagements, the siege of Quebec, and the levelling of the city by British artillery firing from Pointe-Lévy across the river, dragged on until Wolfe was able to place 4,400 troops on the Plains of Abraham on the morning of 13 September. The British sat astride Montcalm's lines of communication with Montreal but, that late in the season, they could not stay in Canada for longer than a few weeks more.

Montcalm then committed two major blunders. He ordered his men to leave the walls of Quebec and to attack, rather than to wait out General Wolfe and harass his inevitable retreat back to his ships. And second, he inexplicably ordered the attack before all available reinforcements reached him. The French troops in Montcalm's ragged line faced heavy British volleys, some of his militia took cover to reload, and the French line broke. Wolfe lay mortally wounded on the field, and Montcalm, joining in the retreat, was shot just as he entered the city; he died the next day. Quebec City surrendered shortly after.

▲ The Marquis de Montcalm, a capable general whose mistakes at Quebec in 1759 cost France an empire.

The sanctification of Montcalm, the effort to turn him into a great general, began at once and continues. His successor in command, the Chevalier de Lévis, more correctly wrote: "One must admit that we have been very unfortunate; just when we could hope to see the campaign end with glory, everything turned against us. A battle lost, a retreat as precipitous as it was shameful, has reduced us to our present condition, all caused by attacking the enemy too soon without mustering all the forces at [Montcalm's] disposal. I owe it to his memory to vouch for the honesty of his intentions,…he believed he was acting for the best, but unfortunately, the general who is defeated is always wrong." SEE ALSO: PLAINS OF ABRAHAM; QUEBEC (1759); WOLFE.

READING: D. Peter MacLeod, *Northern Armageddon: The Battle of the Plains of Abraham* (Vancouver, 2008).

Montgomery's Tavern. When the Lower Canadian Patriotes rose in rebellion during the fall of 1837, most of Upper Canada's British troops moved east to help

deal with them. William Lyon Mackenzie seized the opportunity to gather his supporters at Montgomery's Tavern, north of Toronto (on Yonge Street, just north of the present Eglinton Avenue), on 4 December to prepare to seize the capital. After skirmishes and parleys, some 1,000 loyal troops and volunteers moved out of Toronto to confront the 200 or so rebels at the tavern. After 20 minutes of musket and artillery fire, Mackenzie's men melted away, and constituted authority in Upper Canada was preserved. SEE ALSO: MACKENZIE, WILLIAM LYON.

Montmorency Falls, Battle of (1759). During the siege of Quebec in the summer of 1759, Major-General James Wolfe attempted to seize a redoubt at the falls, east of Quebec, in the hope that the French commander, the Marquis de Montcalm, would be drawn out of the city and into battle on unfavourable terms. In his desire for a decisive confrontation, Wolfe had failed to realize that the redoubt could be covered by fire from the French lines. When Wolfe changed his plan on the spot, opting for a frontal assault on the enemy entrenchments, he suffered a serious check. The abortive attack at Montmorency Falls on 31 July cost the British more than 200 killed and over 400 casualties in all.

READING: D. Peter MacLeod, *Northern Armageddon: The Battle of the Plains of Abraham* (Vancouver, 2008).

Moraviantown, Battle of (1813). The battle (sometimes called the battle of the Thames) was fought during the War of 1812 when disorganized and demoralized British troops, Canadian militia, and parties of Aboriginal warriors under General Henry Proctor retreated in the face of American forces advancing up the River Thames, north of Lake Erie. Under the command of William Henry Harrison, the Americans forced the smaller British force to battle on 5 October 1813 and Proctor's troops broke, leaving the natives—led by the Shawnee chief Tecumseh—to fight the Americans. Tecumseh was killed and some 400 British were taken prisoner. Although the British had been routed, the battle was inconclusive because General Harrison, his supply lines overextended and his militia unwilling to continue to serve, could not prolong his advance.

Moreuil Wood, Battle of (1918). On 21 March 1918, the German army mounted a huge offensive on the Western Front that aimed to end the war before the United States, which had entered the conflict a year earlier, could bring its full weight to bear in Europe. For the most part, the fighting bypassed the Canadian Corps, most of it taking place to the south of the Corps' main positions. The exception was at Moreuil Wood on the River Arve along the important Amiens-Paris highway where Lord Strathcona's Horse, the Royal Canadian Dragoons, and the Fort Garry Horse, the three regiments of the Canadian Cavalry Brigade commanded by Brigadier-General J.E.B. Seely, went into action on 30 March in a desperate bid to stop the German advance toward Amiens. The Canadian cavalry charges and desperate hand-to-hand fighting checked the enemy attack and temporarily drove German forces from the area of Moreuil Wood, although it changed hands again soon afterwards and was not finally secured (by French troops) until August 1918. Amiens did not fall and the Germans ceased their operation on 5 April, but the Canadian troopers suffered heavy casualties in one of the last cavalry engagements of the war.

Morton, Desmond Dillon Paul (b.1937). Born in Calgary, the son of an army officer and the grandson of General Sir William Otter who fought the Fenians, Louis Riel, and the Boers, Desmond Morton was educated at Le Collège Militaire Royal de St-Jean, the Royal Military College, Oxford University, and the London School of Economics. He served in the Canadian Army and later taught history at the Universities of Ottawa, Toronto, and McGill. He has written extensively on labour history, but is best known as a prolific and popular military historian, most of his works focusing on World War I (notably *Ministers and Generals*, *Fight or Pay*, *When Your Number's Up*, *Silent Battle*, *A Peculiar Kind of Politics*, and, with Glenn Wright, *Winning the Second Battle*). Morton also wrote a biography of his grandfather,

The Canadian General: Sir William Otter. He is the author of *A Military History of Canada*, the best one-volume account, frequently reprinted.

Mount Sorrel, Battle of (1916). On 2 June 1916, units of the 3rd Canadian Division, in action for less than two weeks, held positions atop Mount Sorrel in the Ypres Salient of Belgium when a massive German artillery barrage, combined with the explosion of four huge mines under its positions, almost wiped out the defenders. One of those killed was the division commander, Major-General Malcolm S. Mercer; also wounded and taken prisoner was Victor Williams, one of Mercer's brigade commanders. At the same time, the Germans launched a flanking attack against Canadian positions to the north. The Germans had little trouble taking the high ground and advanced almost a kilometre, and the Canadians suffered very heavy casualties. A Canadian counterattack the following day failed to retake the lost ground. Lieutenant-General Sir Julian Byng, the new Canadian Corps commander who had taken over on 28 May, then gave the task to the 1st Canadian Division under Arthur Currie. Major-General Currie planned his attack carefully, paying special attention to the use of artillery and smoke, and his assault went in on 8 June. In one hour, and with relatively few casualties, the Canadians regained almost all the position. The Germans counterattacked some days later, but Currie's men held. The fighting for Mount Sorrel cost the Canadian Corps some 8,000 casualties.

Mulroney, Martin Brian (b.1939). A fluently bilingual lawyer born on Quebec's North Shore, Brian Mulroney won the Progressive Conservative leadership in 1983 and a huge majority in Parliament in 1984. Mulroney had promised to rebuild and restore the Canadian Forces; after the cuts of the Trudeau years, its numbers were down to 82,000. He had also promised to work with Canada's allies, especially the United States, much maligned in Canada during the Trudeau years. But national finances were in bad shape and the Mulroney government's first budget cut defence spending rather than increasing it; the government also failed to meet Canada's pledge to the North Atlantic Treaty Organization (NATO) to increase defence spending by 3 percent per year before inflation. There were increases between 1986 and 1988, but they remained below the 3 percent target. Hopes for additional defence funds did not revive until Perrin Beatty, a young and enthusiastic defence minister, took over this position at the end of 1986. Beatty produced a markedly anti-Soviet 1987 White Paper that pledged a five-year funding plan and budget increases of 2 percent over inflation. It also promised new equipment for each of the services and a fleet of up to a dozen nuclear-powered submarines, seemingly directed at American ambitions in the Arctic as much as at the USSR.

But timing is everything, and it was not propitious for grand Canadian defence schemes. The emergence of Mikhail Gorbachev in Moscow, the fall of the Berlin Wall, the end of the Soviet empire, and the collapse of the USSR made the Beatty White Paper an instant relic. The commitment to NATO was cut by 1,400 troops in 1991, and the 1992 budget announced that the troops in Europe would be brought home in 1993. Troop strength continued to fall, equipment to age.

The post-1987 cuts notwithstanding, international politics remained decidedly non-peaceful. The Iraqi invasion of Kuwait in 1990 led to the formation of a great coalition under the United States. Mulroney was a fervent supporter, but Canada's army—only about 20,000 in all—was not in fit condition to join in, though the navy and air force participated in various ways. The Oka crisis at home, and Somalia, former Yugoslavia, and other crises abroad stretched resources and mocked the idea of a lasting peace dividend. At Oka in the summer of 1990, Mohawks faced off against Canadian soldiers in full glare of television lights; the Canadian Forces (CF) managed to restore order, but it was a tinderbox. In the former Yugoslavia, Canadians operated in a country splitting apart, with well-equipped armies and ruthless paramilitaries running amok. The United Nations created weak peacekeeping forces with weaker mandates, and some Canadians—notably Major-General Lewis MacKenzie in Sarajevo and the 2nd Battalion of the Princess Patricia's

Canadian Light Infantry in the Medak pocket—performed well. Others found only death, destruction, and post-traumatic stress disorder. Somalia was worse yet. The Canadian Airborne Regiment saw the discipline of some soldiers break down, a youth was tortured and murdered at Canadian hands, and there was dissembling and cover-up in the CF and the Department of National Defence. The mess would unravel after Mulroney's departure from office, but his government bore the primary responsibility.

Mulroney took the "peace dividend" and cut the CF, but the military was busier than ever with UN and other missions around the globe. Soldiers undertook one operation after another overseas, and personal relationships cracked as stress mounted and equipment broke down. Mulroney seemed unable to say "no" to the UN or to his international friends, and he stretched badly the Canadian Forces. Despite the promises of 1984 to remedy the CF's problems, Mulroney left matters worse than he found them.

READING: Brian Mulroney, *Memoirs* (Toronto, 2007).

Murray, James (1721–1794). During the Seven Years' War, Murray commanded a battalion at the siege of Louisbourg and served as one of James Wolfe's brigadiers at the Plains of Abraham. He commanded the British garrison at Quebec City over the winter of 1759–1760. In the spring of 1760, he was defeated by the Marquis de Lévis at Ste Foy but held Quebec because of the timely arrival of British warships. Murray was the military governor of Quebec from 1760 and became the first civil governor in 1764. He was removed in 1766 because his efforts to placate the French Canadians angered the handful of English-speaking Protestants in Quebec; this handful engineered his recall to England.

Murray, Leonard Warren (1896–1971). Born in Pictou County, Nova Scotia, Murray joined the first class of the Royal Naval College of Canada in 1911 at age 14 and served in World War I with the Royal and Royal Canadian Navies, and in the interwar period with both fleets. After service in Ottawa as director of naval operations and training, his operational

⌃ Rear-Admiral Leonard W. Murray during World War II.

commands during World War II included commodore commanding the Newfoundland Escort Force in 1941–1942, commanding officer Atlantic Coast in 1942, and commander-in-chief of the Canadian North-west Atlantic Command in 1943. In this latter post he had responsibility for all convoys and their defence north of 40° and east of 47°. With his combination of concern for his sailors and professional competence enough to satisfy the Royal Navy and the United States Navy, Rear-Admiral Murray was thus the only Canadian to command a theatre of war. Along with his theatre responsibilities, he ran the vast Halifax naval base. When VE Day celebrations in the Nova Scotia capital in May 1945 degenerated into a riot, naval officials and the federal government held Murray responsible and forced him

into early retirement. He moved to England, became a lawyer, and specialized in maritime law.

READING: Roger Sarty, "Rear-Admiral L.W. Murray and the Battle of the Atlantic," in Bernd Horn and S. Harris, eds., *Warrior Chiefs* (Toronto, 2001).

Mutinies, Naval (1949). In February and March 1949, three short-lived "mutinies" broke out on separate Royal Canadian Navy (RCN) warships. The incidents occurred aboard the destroyers HMCS *Athabaskan* on 26 February and *Crescent* on 15 March, and the aircraft carrier HMCS *Magnificent* on 20 March. The *Athabaskan* incident took place while the ship was in Manzanillo Harbour, Mexico, and involved the refusal of 90 of the ship's 196 sailors to perform routine duties for a period of about one hour. The events on the *Crescent* (which involved 83 out of 167 ratings) and the *Magnificent* (32 ratings out of 828) were similar. *Magnificent* was in the Caribbean at the time, *Crescent* at Nanking, China. Similar sit-down strikes or work stoppages had taken place during World War II on the destroyer *Iroquois* and in 1947 on the cruiser *Ontario*. As a result of all these "mutinies," the minister of national defence, Brooke Claxton, fearing that Communists might have secured a foothold in the RCN, established a commission of inquiry under Rear-Admiral Rollo Mainguy that reported in October 1949. The commission found that the incidents had occurred as a result of poor shipboard living conditions, the social gap between officers and ratings, and the tendency of RCN officers to emulate the Royal Navy's attitudes toward personnel. In effect, the report commented unfavourably on the leadership of the RCN's officers. The Mainguy Report recommended ways to ease these problems and urged the Canadianization of the RCN. SEE ALSO: MAINGUY REPORT.

READING: Marc Milner, *Canada's Navy: The First Century* (2nd ed., Toronto, 2010).

National Defence Act. Passed in 1922, the National Defence Act combined the Department of Militia and Defence, the Department of Naval Service, and the Air Board into a new Department of National Defence. The act subsequently has been modified as occasion required, but continues to define the organization and function of the department, the roles and responsibilities of its senior officials, and the relationship between the Canadian Forces (the military) and the civilian defence department. Shortly after the outbreak of World War II, Ottawa created additional ministers of national defence for air and naval services to handle the expanded forces, but these offices disappeared after the wartime emergency when responsibilities again centred on a single defence minister. The government of Lester Pearson amended the act in 1968 to authorize the unification of the armed services, and the Jean Chrétien government amended it in 1999 to incorporate changes to the system of military justice.

The act governs disciplinary matters in the Canadian Forces and deems Criminal Code offences to be service offences under the National Defence Act, thus making it the legislative authority for the prosecution of ordinary crimes in the military.

READING: Douglas Bland, *The Administration of Defence Policy in Canada, 1947 to 1985* (Kingston, ON, 1987).

National Defence Headquarters (NDHQ). Following the passage of the National Defence Act in 1922, the new Department of National Defence established its headquarters in Ottawa. When the armed forces expanded during World War II and Ottawa created the Ministries of National Defence for Air and Naval Services, three separate "temporary" buildings served as NDHQ. The minister of national defence, Brooke Claxton, reintegrated NDHQ after taking over in 1946. The combined military-civilian headquarters for the Canadian Forces and the Department of National Defence is now located in the Major-General George R. Pearkes Building in downtown Ottawa.

National Interests. Canadians have historically debated the chasms, real or imagined, between personal or collective values and the more mundane interests their governments might pursue. Passion, rhetoric, and the trappings of conviction notwithstanding, they have rarely evinced much sustained support for a values-based international security policy or the costs that such commitments of conscience might entail. Freedom, democracy, and a broad belief in a liberal, secular, pluralist society have sparked individual action and informed political positions, but the old realist cant of nations having no friends, only interests, has been as true in Canada as elsewhere since its creation as an independent state. A capable diplomatic corps has defended or advanced Canadian interests abroad consistently and well, sometimes educating political bosses on the unfortunate signals—and risky repercussions—of more mercurial pursuits. On the other hand, political leadership has often honed wish lists and self-important moralizing into decisive deployments of energy, intellect, or assets.

The continuity of such interests in Canada has been far more impressive than their variations, though critical evolutions have occurred. The assumption of greater imperial obligations in the late nineteenth century, the commitment (sometimes flaccid) to multinational causes in time of peace after World

War II, the accelerating integration of North American defence and security structures from 1940 onwards, or human security in more recent years have all marked significant departures in their time. Perhaps in retrospect, they were more evolutionary than revolutionary, but dramatic nonetheless, especially for those who opposed them. Over the longer term, however, it is easier still to identify national interests that have been more or less consistently espoused. These include the protection of Canadian territory and people; independence and national unity; economic growth and the prosperity and welfare of citizens; and co-operation with like-minded states in common pursuits at home and abroad. Other causes have come and gone—imperial unity, Western expansion, neutralism—while others great and small have dragged resources and commitments in unfamiliar and sometimes dangerous directions—continental integration, pacifism, the export of democracy, and a plethora of half-baked, poorly funded initiatives surrounding aid and development. But basic interests have remained, and Canadians, by any reasonable measure, have remained comfortable in espousing them.

Lists omit many of the subtleties occasioned by nearly 150 years of rolling priorities, competing policies, and clashing egos, but the centrality to Canadian interests of what remain essentially domestic concerns is a striking comment on a nation that has fought two world wars and a half-dozen major conflicts abroad, and one that remains a charter member of the world's greatest security alliance, the North Atlantic Treaty Organization (NATO). In short, Canadians go abroad when they must, stay home when they can, and are secure enough in Fortress America, the continent and not the country, to need regular convincing that the world requires them any other way. Nationalists of all stripes have grown so sufficiently capable at spinning the limitless perils of any competing conceit that even the terrorist attacks of 9/11 left many Canadians unconvinced that global terrorism posed an existential threat. It is, and always has been, a potentially lethal myopia, whatever its attractions. Does national unity really mean appeasement, or prosperity demobilization?

The historical pretzels required to buttress the case are Herculean, but they prosper just the same. The idea that illiterate fanatics huddled in musky Afghan caves constituted a dagger pointed at the heart of Ottawa defied decades of illogic, firmly believed, that Canada's only real security tasks were territorial protection, national unity, northern sovereignty, and an ever-rising Toronto Stock Exchange. And yet rational analysis of transnational terrorism, Islamic extremists, and weapons of mass destruction admitted few other conclusions than the relentless internationalism of modern-day threats to the national interest, challenging even Cold War orthodoxies about force structure and military deployments abroad and civil liberties at home. Sensible politicians—Liberals and Conservatives both, and there have been a great many of eloquence, conviction, and character in each camp—had known as much since at least 1914, but the struggle to pay dues, maintain alliances, and affirm interests has seen as much noise as nuance and far more wistfulness than wisdom. Debates about the Afghanistan War currently have this flavour, as though 9/11 had never occurred and the values of freedom, democracy, or pluralism could somehow be directed to prosper without regard for enemies or the dirty business of war.

Even homeland security, a fancy moniker for the state's most basic and historic duty, has been contested ground. Canada must keep its territory secure and protect its people, the basic task of any government, but how secure, against whom, and at what cost, given the vast expanse of the national domain? The infrastructure of state security is now the largest in Canadian history, most of it directed at smugglers, terrorists, or transnational crime, and relatively little directed at Russian bombers or their contemporary equivalents. Co-operation with the United States, the historic foe and indispensable ally, is the essence of good sense in this unavoidable pursuit, but the century-long dance between engaging with and distancing from Uncle Sam remains as vibrant now as during the reciprocity debates of 1911. Independence and sovereignty can only really be guaranteed by American power—and can only really be threatened by it too. Anti-Americanism is a national sport, the filaments of economic integration, cultural networks, and political alignments binding both countries notwithstanding. The United States poses no military threat, but a benign one of such power as to impact every aspect of the national life. Survival in this context is a relative term, as cultural nationalists in the present-day, and economic nationalists before that, have well understood; the vigorous protection of sovereignty, territory, airwaves, or print runs, and ensuring that the Canadian portion of North America is secure from outside incursion, are the baselines for sensible policies more easily envisioned than executed. Prosperity demands economic links, and sovereignty requires barriers. US administrations must never be permitted to make offers of "help" that could not be refused; likewise, they must never be predisposed not to offer help at all.

National unity is the other great balancing act. More difficult even than relations with Washington are relations with Quebec City or Edmonton. Threading the nation's linguistic and regional factionalism is the principal job description of any modern-day prime minister. It is a mistake to act against the will of any large region of the country, and an error not to act abroad if most of Canada wishes to do so. Squaring a circle might be easier, but managing this national interest carefully and properly is critical for any government. It has sometimes been read, even when handled expertly, as inconsistency, opportunism, or cynicism. Provinces, linguistic groups, First Nations, and, increasingly, cities demand international space and federal funds for their own parochial fixations. Who speaks for Canada and what are the nation's interests when a single Canadian can be represented at an international conference by many flags? Only one, the Maple Leaf, is constitutionally empowered to speak collectively abroad, but does this matter when interests have been split, shared, parcelled out, and auctioned off? Mackenzie King had an easier task in many respects than Stephen Harper: a domestic playing field with fewer constituencies, the battle lines between them more clearly defined than those between the hyphenated legions of

contemporary interests, each empowered by postmodern disdain for centralization, unity, vision, or purpose.

The pursuit of security abroad with like-minded friends as the essential background to prosperity or security at home was not the only possible outcome of spilled blood on foreign shores. Sir Robert Borden may have wished it so in World War I, and history flattered his efforts, but contemporaries were not so sure. The League of Nations failed. Europe was abandoned. The Empire found a rough hearing in interwar Canada, even though few doubted that a Britain imperilled would tug again at old heart strings, which would remain numerous enough to force the issue one more time. Peace was a value too great to forsake but too dear to fight for, save in the direst of circumstances. Interests demanded staying home and creating jobs, leaving to others the thankless tasks of democracy, diplomacy, or war. A century after Vimy, Amiens, or the living hell of Passchendaele, internationalism seems a far more certain outcome in pursuit of Canadian interests than in fact it ever was. Even a second global war left the issue temporarily in doubt. Were these Canada's wars? Was King wrong to have embraced limited liability as his first war strategy and rapid demobilization as his last?

The issue was not long in doubt. Globalization won out, not in the heady, all-things-are-new giddiness of the post–Cold War era, but in the fearful, tentative certainties of the building East-West struggle, when the road from security to alliance to commitment to capabilities led past graveyards of fallen warriors and outmoded assumptions. The route was tortuous at times, but quick and rail thin at others, the 1950s witnessing a head-long sprint to arms, allies, and overseas deployments. Canada's battlefields were abroad, or in northern skies watching for the contrails of Red-starred bombers, even in times of peace, the tense interlude from which Armageddon might spring in a mushroom cloud. Alliance entanglements brought strength in numbers, as much against canny Washington as cunning Moscow, and leveraged defence efforts into diplomatic influence, access, and respectability. It was a new game for an old concept:

Dedicated in 2001, the National Military Cemetery, situated within Beechwood Cemetery in Ottawa, is intended to become Canada's Arlington.

co-operation with friends and allies, and shameless dependence on them in most respects, to ensure survival and to enhance prosperity. Canadians would squabble at the margins, mostly about Americans and the nuclear weapons they had pioneered and owned in abundance, but they would remain remarkably consistent too. Having fought dictatorships and oligarchies in the past, they would oppose them in the future, understanding implicitly that liberty, democracy, and economic freedom were the finest guarantors against future instability. This privileging of domestic interests amidst consistent awareness of their reliance on world affairs has been the defining feature of the last seven decades of Canadian statecraft. Good relations with Washington are its linchpin; productive engagement with the rest of the world its necessary context (and appropriate balance). Ideologues and moralists would have it otherwise,

but few of those have been granted power, yet.

SEE ALSO: ALLIANCES, CANADIAN; CANADA–UNITED KINGDOM DEFENCE RELATIONS; CANADA–UNITED STATES DEFENCE RELATIONS.

READING: Michael Hart, *From Pride to Influence: Towards a New Canadian Foreign Policy* (Vancouver, 2008).

National Military Cemetery. Canada's National Military Cemetery was dedicated on 28 June 2001. The idea of Lieutenant-General Roméo Dallaire, then associate deputy minister human resources (military), the cemetery is located at Beechwood Cemetery (itself designated as the National Cemetery in 2009) in Ottawa with room for 12,000 graves. The cemetery is reserved for serving or honourably released members of the Canadian or Allied forces and merchant navy veterans. Burial expenses for serving members of the Canadian Forces are paid by the military. There is a ceremonial area and an adjacent National Memorial Centre, opened in April 2008, with a Hall of Colours (for laid-up regimental colours).

National Resources Mobilization Act (NRMA) (1940). Passed by Parliament in the immediate aftermath of the fall of France on 21 June 1940, the NRMA provided for the conscription of men for home defence. Initially, the call-up of unmarried men between the ages of 21 and 24 was for 30 days of training, but this was extended to 120 days in February 1941, and then extended again on 26 April 1941 for the duration of the war. Conscripts served in Canada and some later participated in the joint US–Canadian invasion of Kiska in the Japanese-occupied Aleutian Islands, off Alaska. Those conscripts who refused to volunteer for overseas service became the object of much public and political ridicule. They were known as NRMA men or, more derogatorily, Zombies. The act came under the Department of National War Services until 1942 when its administration was transferred to the Department of Labour. After the conscription plebiscite of 27 April 1942, the Mackenzie King government passed Bill 80 amending the NRMA to authorize the dispatch of home defence conscripts overseas. But, as King said, the policy remained "not necessarily conscription but conscription if necessary." Necessity did not arise until the autumn of 1944 when high casualties in Normandy, the Scheldt, and in Italy created a shortage of trained infantry reinforcements and obliged the government in late November to order overseas 16,000 of the 60,000 home defence conscripts in Canada who had not volunteered. Some 12,908 NRMA troops made it overseas, though only 2,463 went on strength of units of First Canadian Army before the end of the war. Reports suggested that the conscripts who saw action generally performed well; 69 were killed, 232 wounded, and 13 taken prisoner. SEE ALSO: CONSCRIPTION; KING; ZOMBIES.

National Selective Service (NSS). Established in October 1941 under the Department of Labour, National Selective Service controlled where Canadians

Designed by Vernon March, the National War Memorial was dedicated by George VI in 1939, just before another world war began. The monument now commemorates all Canada's war dead.

worked, when they could change jobs, and who was obliged to serve in the army in defence of Canada under the National Resources Mobilization Act. Males were covered initially; women from 20 to 24 years old came under the NSS's jurisdiction in September 1942. All employees had to give the NSS a week's notice to change jobs, and men aged 17 to 45 were barred from "non-essential" jobs including selling real estate, manufacturing luxury and recreational goods, and driving a taxi. This massive incursion of the state into Canadians' lives was an indicator of total war.

READING: Michael Stevenson, *Canada's Greatest Wartime Muddle* (Montreal, 2001).

National War Memorial. Located in the heart of Ottawa on Confederation Square, the memorial was dedicated by George VI on 21 May 1939. Designed by British sculptor Vernon March to honour the

Canadian dead of World War I, the cenotaph over time became the National War Memorial to those killed in World War II, Korea, peacekeeping and peacemaking operations, and Afghanistan, and is the site of the national ceremony of remembrance each year on 11 November. The Tomb of the Unknown Soldier, placed directly in front of the memorial and dedicated in 2000, added markedly to the symbolism and solemnity of the site.

Naval Aid Bill (1912). Prime Minister Robert Borden introduced the bill in December 1912 to authorize giving the then-huge sum of $35 million to Britain for construction of three dreadnought-type warships for the Royal Navy. This "emergency contribution" to the Royal Navy, offered when Germany's naval construction was in full swing, was as much for Canada's defence as Britain's, Borden argued, and he hoped it would give Canada a greater say in imperial defence policy. The Liberals fought bitterly against the measure since it would effectively end the Laurier government's naval program, initiated in 1910. Liberal domination of the Senate ensured their ability to kill the legislation, passed earlier in the House after Borden's Conservatives had imposed closure for the first time in Canadian parliamentary history, in May 1913. See also: Borden, Robert.

Naval Service Act (1910). At the 1909 Imperial Conference, British Admiralty officials told the dominion prime ministers that Britain needed help in its naval race with Germany. Prime Minister Sir Wilfrid Laurier's answer was the Naval Service Act of 1910. The act established the Department of the Naval Service and set up a small Canadian navy to serve with the Royal Navy (RN) in time of war. The act was unpopular both with imperialists, who believed it did not go far enough, and also with Quebec nationalists, who decried any military assistance to Britain and argued that having a navy might lead to conscription. The act was one cause of Laurier's 1911 defeat at the hands of Robert Borden, hurting his party in anti-conscription Quebec. Borden expressed his preference with the 1912 Naval Aid Bill, calling for a cash

contribution of $35 million to Britain to build three dreadnoughts. Before Laurier's government fell, however, the training cruisers HMCS *Niobe* and *Rainbow* had been acquired from the RN, marking the effective beginning of the Royal Canadian Navy. See also: Naval Aid Bill; Royal Canadian Navy.

Reading: Marc Milner, *Canada's Navy: The First Hundred Years* (2nd ed., Toronto, 2010).

Nelles, Percy Walker (1892–1951). The first entrant into what would become the Royal Canadian Navy (RCN), Percy Nelles, the son of a Permanent Force army officer, signed on with the Fisheries Protection Service as a cadet in 1908. He became a midshipman on HMCS *Niobe* in 1910, then went to the Royal Navy (RN) to complete his training. After holding a series of operational and staff positions in the RCN and RN, Nelles became chief of the naval staff in 1934 and fought successfully to keep the navy alive during the Great Depression. No dynamic leader, he nonetheless guided the RCN through the years of wartime expansion, taking it from some 2,000 regulars to a strength of 100,000 men and women. Although Nelles cannot be blamed for many of the RCN's shortcomings in the early phases of World War II (the product of too rapid growth), he perhaps did not press hard enough to acquire the latest anti-submarine warfare equipment for his vessels. Following a prolonged disagreement with the minister of national defence for naval services, Angus L. Macdonald, about this issue and the RCN's training standards, and a power struggle within the RCN, the minister fired Vice-Admiral Nelles in January 1944 and posted him to London the same year as senior Canadian flag officer overseas. He retired from the navy in 1945. See also: Atlantic; Royal Canadian Navy.

Reading: Roger Sarty, "Admiral Percy W. Nelles: Diligent Guardian of the Vision," in Michael Whitby, et al., eds., *The Admirals: Canada's Senior Naval Leadership in the Twentieth Century* (Toronto, 2006).

Netherlands Liberation (1945). After clearing the Rhineland and crossing the Rhine, the soldiers of First

^ Cheering civilians surround a Canadian-British column in Heiloo, Holland, on 8 May 1945. The photo, taken by local resident Gerard Visser, captures a scene repeated countless times across German-occupied Europe.

Canadian Army, now comprising I Canadian Corps (transferred north from Italy) and II Canadian Corps, turned their attention to the Netherlands toward the end of World War II. II Canadian Corps had the task of freeing northeast Holland and the German coast, while I Canadian Corps dealt with the western part of the country north of the Maas River.

In the first two weeks of April, the Canadians took Almelo and Groningen, Zutphen, Deventer, and Zwolle, and reached the sea on 18 April. II Corps then went into western Germany, crossing the Ems and attacking Emden and Wilhelmshaven. I Corps had the great cities of the Netherlands in its sector, including Amsterdam, Rotterdam, and The Hague, the residents of which were starving after the *Hongerwinter* (hunger winter). Food had run out, transport had broken down, and the Germans were unwilling to do anything to ease civilian needs. The Gestapo continued to hunt down and execute resistance elements, cracking down even harder in its last days in control.

I Canadian Corps took Arnhem in fierce fighting by 14 April, and the 5th Canadian Armoured Division liberated Appeldoorn on 17 April. The Germans fell back to their Grebbe Line but were persuaded on 28 April—largely because their leaders feared execution as war criminals—to permit airdrops of food, or "Operation Manna," as it was called. A few days later, the Germans allowed Canadian trucks to carry food through their lines. Finally, on 5 May, Lieutenant-General Charles Foulkes, the commander of I Canadian Corps, met with the German commander-in-chief, Colonel General Johannes Blaskowitz, in a hotel in Wageningen to arrange the capitulation. The German generals, one Canadian wrote, "looked like men in a dream, dazed, stupefied, and unable to realize that for them their world was utterly finished."

The Germans had resisted strongly until the capitulation. On 1 May, with Hitler a suicide victim in his bunker in Berlin, Canadians completed their attack on Delfzijl, a small port on the River Ems. The Cape Breton Highlanders, a unit that had fought through Italy, reported in its regimental history that it was its toughest fight of the war with 68 killed and wounded.

For the Netherlands, liberation by the Canadians after five years of occupation and repression was a cause for massive celebration. Dutch remembrance of the war remains a national event, a tradition passed through generations, the youngest of whom play an active role in maintaining cemeteries and honouring the Allies' war dead. They maintain a unique bond with former Canadian service personnel and their families, part of a special relationship between the two countries that has remained intact into the twenty-first century. See also: Crerar; First Canadian Army; Foulkes; Simonds; World War II.

⌃ Newfoundland's Thomas Ricketts, VC.

Reading: C.P. Stacey, *The Victory Campaign: The Official History of the Canadian Army, 1939–1945*, vol. 3 (Ottawa, 1960); D. Kauffman and M. Horn, *A Liberation Album: Canadians in the Netherlands, 1944–45* (Toronto, 1980).

Newfoundland, World War I. Newfoundland, a separate British dominion in 1914 and not yet a province of Canada, contributed 12,000 military personnel to Allied forces during World War I from a prewar population of 242,000. By 1918, some 35 percent of men aged 19 to 35 had served. More than 6,200 troops served with the dominion's principal contribution, the Newfoundland Regiment, which fought throughout the war as part of a British division. The Newfoundlanders served in the Middle East and fought in the Gallipoli campaign against Turkish troops before moving to the Western Front in early 1916. On the opening day of the Somme offensive, 1 July 1916, the regiment suffered 710 killed, wounded, and missing out of 801 present in a 30-minute attack on German positions near Beaumont Hamel. The reconstituted regiment, later given the title "Royal," participated in several other major engagements and undertook occupation duties in Germany after the armistice. In October 1918, one member of the regiment, 17-year-old Thomas Ricketts, earned the Victoria Cross, the British Empire's highest decoration for courage in the face of the enemy.

As in Canada, recruitment in Newfoundland became more difficult after the heavy casualties of 1916 and 1917. The creation of a new militia department along with a substantial propaganda campaign that featured special inducements for married men did not maintain troop strength. A Military Service Act, or compulsory service, became law in April 1918 after a bruising political fight similar in many respects to that in Canada the previous year. Largely Catholic rural districts dependent on fishing labour opposed conscription; mainly Protestant St John's, the capital and largest city, supported it. Labourers and unionists called for the conscription of wealth; the business class countered that conscription was the best means of sharing wartime burdens. The regiment overseas, having been reinforced in the spring with the last volunteers in the training depots, ended the war as a volunteer formation. The conscripts remained at home.

Great Britain's declaration of war automatically committed Newfoundland to the struggle, but the dominion government's patriotic response was genuine and popularly shared. The war temporarily muted political conflicts over religion, class, and the economy, and a new, bipartisan Newfoundland Patriotic Association (NPA) managed most aspects of the war effort. Women's groups, social organizations, and churches were the basis for a dense network of patriotic associations committed to veterans' welfare, overseas relief, and fundraising. A National Government replaced the NPA in mid-1917 amid the growing conscription debate and charges of war profiteering by wealthy merchants. It enacted the Military Service Act and governed until the armistice, but collapsed in May 1919.

Newfoundlanders served in several other forestry, naval, and military units, including nearly 2,000 in the colony's naval reserve, which recruited only from the ranks of sailors and fishermen. Many more sailed individually with British, Canadian, and American military and merchant vessels; of 500 known to have served as merchant sailors, more than 100 died. Several dozen women worked as nurses in the Volunteer Aid Detachment. The Great War was an unmitigated shock in the small colony, and few communities were unaffected by tragedy. SEE ALSO: BEAUMONT HAMEL.

READING: G.W.L. Nicholson, *The Fighting Newfoundlander: A History of the Royal Newfoundland Regiment* (2nd rev. ed., Montreal, 2006).

Newfoundland, World War II. The economic shocks of the interwar period had left Newfoundland a have-not dominion, governed by a British-appointed Commission of Government. Unlike Canada, which declared war one week after Britain did, London's declaration was legally binding on Newfoundland, so the small, struggling colony of 322,000 was at war on 3 September 1939. An Act for the Defence of Newfoundland had been passed two days earlier,

legislation similar to Canada's War Measures Act, and the commission prepared to defend the home front with locally raised units and set the economy on a war footing. There was no great urge to repeat the experience of World War I, in which an expeditionary infantry regiment serving overseas with British troops had earned a battlefield reputation at enormous human cost, especially at Beaumont Hamel. In this second world conflict, most Newfoundlanders in uniform would be with British or Canadian naval forces, while many thousands of other military-age recruits would stay home, working in war-related industries or at the soon-burgeoning American, Canadian, and British military facilities that would bring the dominion to full employment. Some 12,000 men and women from Newfoundland and Labrador would ultimately serve abroad, of approximately 22,000 who enlisted overall.

As in Canada, the fall of France in mid-1940 changed the complexion of Newfoundland's war. Canadian troops arrived, by invitation, to assume the lion's share of local defence duties, taking responsibility for the major airbase at Gander in the interior, building other sites at Goose Bay, Labrador, and Torbay, just outside St John's, as well as a large naval establishment at St John's itself. The Americans soon followed, taking 99-year leases on bases at St John's, Stephenville, and Argentia as part of the "destroyers for bases" deal negotiated between a struggling Britain and a still-neutral United States in August 1940. Seaplanes flew from Botwood, fighters from Torbay, and bombers destined for Europe staged through Gander. The friendly invasion of Allied troops would grow to many thousands by its high point later in the war, their money and infrastructure helping to transform dockyards, bases, and industries, as well as the social complexion of many of the dominion's major towns and cities through personal relationships, children, and wartime marriages. If Beaumont Hamel, the terrible slaughter of Newfoundlanders on the Somme on 1 July 1916, had been the historic metaphor of Newfoundland's World War I experience, the teeming harbour of St John's, with its squadrons of naval vessels and docks crowded with merchant ships and supply vessels, was probably most emblematic of World War II. The city and its residents were much favoured by Allied navies over other East Coast North Atlantic ports, with "Newfiejohn" (or "Newfyjohn") used often to designate it from Saint John, New Brunswick, another busy wartime port. Newfoundland's strategic geography made it a front-line base throughout the war in the struggle against German U-boats, with large sea and air units using the island as a base of operations. Naval battles raged around the island, merchant ships were sunk at the Bell Island iron ore docks in Conception Bay, and the sinking of the ferry ss *Caribou* on 14 October 1942 with 137 dead was a massive local tragedy.

Newfoundland raised troops for home defence, avoiding the infantry commitments that had led to conscription during World War I. It also raised a civilian forestry corps of several thousand that served overseas. The Commission of Government permitted British and Canadian forces to recruit in Newfoundland, and several thousand dominion residents signed up, including 3,000 in Britain's Royal Navy. Up to 10,000 Newfoundlanders may have served in merchant ships during the war. The British army grouped Newfoundland recruits into two regiments of artillery that would see service in North Africa, Italy, northwest Europe, or Britain, the 57th (Heavy Artillery) Regiment and the 166th (Field Artillery) Regiment, while the Royal Air Force channelled Newfoundlanders into the 125th (Newfoundland) Squadron, a unit of night fighters. A large and successful volunteer patriotic movement supported military efforts at home and abroad. Of the nearly 1,100 men and women from Newfoundland and Labrador who died as a result of wartime service, more than 330 were from the merchant navy.

⌃ Soldiers of the Royal Newfoundland Regiment training for home defence in World War II.

Newfoundland's economy sizzled throughout the war, with full employment, well-paying jobs, a constant influx of American dollars, and higher prices for some exports. An overheated economy bred its own problems, from inflation to housing shortages, and the presence of thousands of young men led to social pressures from petty crime to prostitution and venereal disease, but co-operation between Newfoundlanders and Labradorians and Allied garrisons marked the relationship far more than conflict. As a result of the war, Britain began the political process that would lead to the Confederation of Newfoundland with Canada in 1949.

READING: Peter Neary, *Newfoundland in the North Atlantic World, 1929–1949* (Montreal, 1996).

Newfoundland Escort Force (NEF). The Royal Navy (RN) and the Royal Canadian Navy (RCN) established the Newfoundland Escort Force (NEF), under the command of Commodore Leonard W. Murray, in May 1941 to counter German U-boats in the western Atlantic. Its western terminus was at the RCN's new base in St John's, Newfoundland, its eastern at Havfijordhur harbour, north of Reykjavik, Iceland. The NEF escorted merchant ship convoys from eastern Canada to the vicinity of Iceland, where it handed them over to escort vessels sailing from the British Isles. Six Canadian destroyers and seventeen corvettes, the first in the RCN and all crewed by untried sailors, reinforced by seven destroyers, three sloops, and five corvettes of the Royal Navy, were assembled for the force. Commodore Murray said in October 1941 that "the reputation of the RCN in this war depends on the success or failure of the NEF." Murray was right, and that reputation initially was poor as the corvette crews struggled to master their task. In February 1942, the NEF was reorganized as the Mid-Ocean Escort Force. The Royal Canadian Air Force provided air cover for the convoys as far out to sea as the aircraft could manage, which was only about 650 kilometres at that stage of World War II. SEE ALSO: ATLANTIC; MURRAY, LEONARD.

READING: W.A.B. Douglas et al., *No Higher Purpose: The Official History of the Royal Canadian Navy in the Second World War, 1939–1945*, vol. 2, part I (St Catharines, ON, 2002).

Niagara Frontier. The Niagara Frontier is the portion of the Niagara Peninsula lying closest to the United States that is bounded on the east by the Niagara River, on the north by Lake Ontario, and on the south by Lake Erie. Strategically located and the logical path for American invaders to follow in attacking Canada, the frontier was the scene of much sharp fighting during the War of 1812, including the battles of Queenston Heights, Forts Erie and George, Stoney Creek, Chippawa, and Lundy's Lane. Several important military posts were sited on the frontier, including Fort George and Fort Erie on the British side and Fort Niagara on the American side. Both sides fought bitterly for the forts garrisoned by regulars and militia. The British posts provided an important line of communication between the frontier and Fort York (modern-day Toronto). As a peninsula or salient jutting from British territory toward the United States and surrounded by large bodies of water on two sides, British possession of the frontier was always vulnerable to American naval power, which could carry troops to either flank of defences along the Niagara River itself. Both sides used naval power to guard against amphibious attack, launch raids, and transport troops and supplies. SEE ALSO: WAR OF 1812.

Nile Expedition (1884–1885). In 1884, Britain mounted an expedition up the Nile River from Egypt into the Sudan to relieve Major-General C.G. "Chinese" Gordon who was besieged in Khartoum by the forces of the Mahdi, a powerful Muslim religious leader opposed to Britain's presence in the region. Lieutenant-General Sir Garnet Wolseley commanded the expedition, which would have to overcome the Nile's cataracts as the troops moved upriver. Wolseley decided that Canadian boatmen—he called them voyageurs—such as those who had helped transport his Red River Expedition into the Canadian West in 1870, would be immensely helpful. The Canadian government gave Britain permission to recruit such a group, the first time a quasi-military Canadian force

↑ Frederick Villiers painted the Nile voyageurs who went to Africa in 1884 to assist the expedition sent to relieve General C.G. Gordon in Khartoum.

would serve overseas: 378 boatmen and several army officers signed on and went to Egypt under the command of Colonel F.C. Denison. Most of these men returned to Canada some six months later without having played any significant role in the expedition, given that their six-month contracts had expired. They refused to re-enlist despite an offer of increased pay. The remaining 89 men capably helped the expedition manoeuvre its heavy boats through the Nile rapids. Wolseley's troops successfully reached Khartoum, but not before the Mahdi's forces had seized the town and beheaded Gordon. The last of the Nile voyageurs left for Canada in March 1885. Sixteen of the Canadians died during this expedition, most from disease or drowning.

READING: Roy MacLaren, *Canadians on the Nile: 1882–1898* (Vancouver, 1978).

Normandy, Battle of (1944). The battle for Normandy opened with the D-Day landings of British, American, and Canadian forces on 6 June 1944, and ended with the closing of the Falaise Gap

in the third week of August. Elements of First Canadian Army played a significant role in the fighting throughout.

Canadian participation in the battle began on the night of 5–6 June as the 1st Canadian Parachute Battalion, part of the British 6th Airborne Division, took part in airborne landings near Benouville on the Caen canal, about halfway between the Bay of the Seine and Caen. Its task was to secure the left flank of the invasion and take the bridges across the canal and the Orne River that parallels it. The paratroopers secured their immediate objectives.

The main Canadian effort was launched on the morning of 6 June when the 7th Canadian Infantry Brigade of the 3rd Canadian Infantry Division, accompanied by the tanks of the 1st Hussars, landed on Mike sector of Juno Beach; at the same time, the 8th Canadian Infantry Brigade, along with the Fort Garry Horse, landed east of there on Nan sector. The 9th Canadian Infantry Brigade and the Sherbrooke Fusiliers constituted the floating reserve. Commanding the 3rd Division was Major-General

R.F.L. Keller. Until Lieutenant-General H.D.G. Crerar's First Canadian Army was able to assume control of Canadian formations in Normandy on 23 July, the Canadians fought under the command of Second British Army and 21st Army Group, commanded by General Sir B.L. Montgomery.

The initial Canadian objective was the stretch of beach from St Aubin-sur-Mer on the east through Bernières-sur-Mer to Courseulles-sur-Mer on the west. This constituted Juno Beach, sandwiched between Sword Beach to the left and Gold Beach to the right, both of which were assaulted by British troops. Farther to the west lay Omaha and Utah beaches, assigned to American troops. The Canadian attackers, faced with two companies of German infantry, many in concrete bunkers, took their beach objectives and moved inland, overcoming German defences while incurring casualties that, while heavy, were substantially less than planners had feared.

Montgomery's original plan called for a deep, rapid thrust by armour early in the invasion, with the capture of the city of Caen and the rolling country beyond as the major objective. Although the Allies enjoyed overwhelming air superiority and the support of naval guns firing from ships offshore, the terrain, crisscrossed with ridges and wooded slopes, dotted with orchards, small towns, and clusters of farm buildings, greatly favoured the defence. German Panther and Tiger tanks were far better than the Shermans used by Allied units, while armoured tank destroyers and anti-tank guns took a fearsome toll on Allied vehicles as they moved across open fields or slopes toward the next series of defended positions. The Canadians suffered their first battering on D-Day+1, when they ran into units of the 12th SS Panzer Division (*Hitlerjugend*) under *Standartenführer* Kurt Meyer at Authie, on the way to Carpiquet airfield east of Caen. The ss later murdered many of the Canadian prisoners they took during the battle.

The check to the Canadians at Authie, combined with one to the British 7th Armoured Division at Villers-Bocage to the southwest of the Canadian positions, allowed the Germans to halt Montgomery's troops in front of Caen. Although the Allies had been able to get ashore and link up their beachheads from east to west shortly thereafter, and the Americans were able to complete their drive across the Cotentin peninsula by 18 June and capture Cherbourg on 26 June, progress southward became slow and costly. German armour could not easily move by day because of Allied control of the skies, but enough units filtered into Normandy from elsewhere to allow the enemy to hold its line across the base of the Normandy peninsula. This created an overcrowded beachhead and delayed the arrival of additional Allied reinforcements. The 2nd Canadian Infantry Division and the 4th Canadian Armoured Division did not arrive in Normandy until early July. Lieutenant-General Guy Simonds's II Canadian Corps only became operational after 2nd Division's arrival.

Unable to break through at Caen, Montgomery, his views rather clearer with hindsight in his memoirs than they seemed at the time, decided to hold German attention along his front and draw German armour to his sector, allowing the Americans to the west under General Omar Bradley to build up their strength against lighter opposition for the eventual breakout through the bocage. As a result, 3rd Canadian Infantry Division did little fighting from 11 June until, on 4 July, Keller's troops moved against Carpiquet airfield once more. Again they faced bitter resistance from soldiers of the 12th SS Panzer Division in well-sited concrete bunkers. After suffering heavy casualties, the Canadians finally took the airfield, posing a significant threat to the German positions in Caen. Despite the Canadian success, the British criticized Keller and his staff for what they judged a hesitant and ill-coordinated effort. Such criticisms have dogged Canadian officers then and since. The truth probably was that none of the Allied formations equalled the Germans in combat skill at this stage of the campaign, and that hesitation in attack and failure to follow through were all too characteristic of many US and British officers as well. These failings in leadership, combined with the sheer ferocity of the fighting, drove up casualty figures. The Canadians suffered almost 1,200 dead and wounded in the fight for Carpiquet and Caen, a city pulverized by Allied air raids before its eventual capture.

Caen taken, Montgomery ordered his formations to increase pressure on the Germans by pushing south toward Falaise, buying more time for the Americans to prepare for their breakout. II Canadian Corps played a significant role in this first effort, Operation Atlantic, an attack to clear the industrial suburbs of Caen. The Canadians then attacked the gentle slope of Verrières Ridge, its 85-metre height giving the Germans superb vantage points. The enemy had ample armour and many of the terribly accurate 88-millimetre guns, and had fortified the area's small towns and farmhouses. Operation Spring on 25 July was a disaster for the soldiers of Canada's Black Watch regiment, an attack that resulted in the sacking of a number of senior commanders. At least 450

Canadians had been killed, with 1,100 more wounded. It was the bloodiest day of the war for the army, Dieppe alone excepted.

On 25 July, at last, Bradley's American forces launched Operation Cobra, the breakout battle. It was tough going at first but, within a few days, the German lines cracked. The US First Army drove south and west into Brittany while the US Third Army turned east in a wide flanking manoeuvre. The Germans attempted a counter-stroke by attacking westward at Mortain and Avranches to choke off the American spearheads; instead, they found their own forces trapped between General George S. Patton's Third Army to the south and British, Canadian, and Polish forces to the north, pushing south from the Caen sector against what had now become the right, or northern, shoulder of a large and vulnerable German salient.

▲ The Allied victory in Normandy began the liberation of northwest Europe from the Germans. Major David Currie of the South Alberta Regiment, holding the pistol (left), won the Victoria Cross for his actions in helping to close the Falaise Gap in August 1944.

Montgomery took advantage of the German error by ordering Simonds to launch another heavy attack southwards in the direction of Falaise to catch the Germans in this giant pocket. This was a challenge for II Canadian Corps, but Simonds launched Operation Totalize on 8 August and then Tractable on 14 August. These massive operations that sent forward huge columns of tanks accompanied by infantry in armoured personnel carriers began with the aerial assault of German positions by the heavy bombers of the Royal Air Force's Bomber Command and the US Army Air Force. The bombings smashed enemy positions and demoralized the defenders, but errors in aiming also produced many casualties among Allied troops. The enemy suffered heavily from the bombing, but enough survived to provide stiff resistance. After terrible fighting, Operation Tractable brought the troops of the 2nd Canadian Infantry Division into Falaise on 17 August.

Following the break-in, the 4th Canadian and 1st Polish Armoured Divisions drove east and south of Falaise to link up with Patton's spearheads pushing north. As the gap closed, German troops, vehicles, tanks, and horse-drawn carts streamed desperately to the east to escape the pocket. At St Lambert, a company of the Argyll and Sutherland Highlanders and a squadron of the South Alberta Regiment from the 4th Canadian Armoured Division, just 200 soldiers killed, wounded, or captured 3,000 Germans while destroying seven tanks, a dozen 88-millimetre guns, and 40 vehicles. To the east on a hill they dubbed "Maczuga" (or "Mace"), the Poles took 6,000 prisoners and destroyed 70 tanks and 500 vehicles while suffering 1,400 casualties of their own. Above the struggle on the ground, fighter bombers of the 2nd Allied Tactical Air Force flew constantly to the attack, wreaking havoc. Finally, on 21 August, the Falaise Gap closed tight, and the battle of Normandy was over.

From 6 June to the closing of the Falaise Gap, the Canadian formations had suffered 18,444 casualties, of which 5,021 were fatal; overall Allied losses were 206,700. The Germans lost perhaps a half-million men. The 12th SS on D-Day had 12,000 soldiers and 159 tanks; by the end of the Normandy campaign, the division had only 100 troops and ten tanks remaining.

The Canadian role in the closing of the gap has received much criticism from commanders at the time and historians since, although more recent historiography, notably the work of Terry Copp, has been far more complimentary. Canadians had been slow and sometimes unimaginative, but critics underestimated the advantages conveyed to German forces by ground, weapons, training, and the ease of defending well-known localities scant kilometres apart. Allied victory in Normandy was one of the epic victories of the war. SEE ALSO: CRERAR; FALAISE; FIRST CANADIAN ARMY; JUNO BEACH; MEYER; II CANADIAN CORPS; SIMONDS.

READING: C.P. Stacey, *The Victory Campaign* (Ottawa, 1960); J.A. English, *The Canadian Army and the Normandy Campaign* (New York, 1991); Terry Copp, *Fields of Fire: The Canadians in Normandy* (Toronto, 2003); Brian Reid, *No Holding Back: Operation Totalize, Normandy, August 1944* (Toronto, 2005).

North, Defence of the. The Hudson's Bay Company's cession of lands to Canada in June 1870, along with Britain's cession of the Arctic islands in July 1880, expanded Canadian territory dramatically. Initially, there was no threat to Canada's new acquisitions, though Canadian sovereignty in the Arctic was maintained only by the presence of Inuit and later by a few posts of the Royal Canadian Mounted Police (RCMP). World War II forced Canada to begin consideration of its North for military purposes. The Alaska Highway reached through the Yukon, and oil development and pipeline construction began from Norman Wells. With its headquarters in Edmonton, the United States military had enough of a presence that locals joked the telephones were answered with "Army of Occupation." The British High Commissioner, Malcolm Macdonald, alerted Ottawa to the situation, and the government put an army general in place to watch Canadian interests and, at war's end, purchased every US installation at full price to ensure no claims remained that might threaten its sovereignty. Nonetheless, weather stations, operated by the

United States, had begun operation, and the Germans, seeking meteorological data of their own, had placed at least one unmanned weather station in Labrador. The equipment for weather station Kurt, recovered many years later by a historical research team, is now on display at the Canadian War Museum in Ottawa.

After World War II, the Soviet Union developed long-range bomber forces capable of delivering nuclear weapons, and the North became of genuine strategic importance. The fear was not of a Soviet invasion—in such a case, Canada's tactics, Lester Pearson said, would be "scorched ice"—but of finding sufficient warning time to let Canadian and American interceptors engage the attacking bombers. The Canadians and Americans built three radar-warning lines almost wholly on Canadian territory, the Distant Early Warning line's stations being sited some 300 kilometres north of the Arctic Circle. Its stations, constructed between 1954 and 1957, were operated by US troops until 1968; initially, there were restrictions even on Canadian official visitors, an issue that caused problems in Parliament in the mid-1950s as MPs feared for Canadian sovereignty once more. Canadian military deployments in the North scarcely existed at this time, though a few exercises to test equipment took place in the immediate post-1945 period. One military station at Alert on Ellesmere Island, initially a Royal Canadian Air Force weather station, eavesdropped on Soviet military communications from 1958 onwards. The Canadian Rangers, an Inuit, Metis, and Aboriginal force of reservists equipped with .303 rifles, red sweatshirts, and baseball caps, watched the Far North and served as guides on the occasional exercises.

The Arctic was not without military interest to other states, even if Canadians paid comparatively little attention. American, Soviet, British, and French nuclear submarines transited the Northwest Passage without seeking Ottawa's permission. In 1987, a Defence White Paper declared that Canada would build a fleet of its own nuclear-powered submarines, in part to challenge other nations' subs beneath the ice packs of the Far North. What Canadian submariners would do if they encountered American violators of Canadian sovereignty was never stated; the Cold War's end and

subsequent defence budget reductions ended the plan, its more obvious purpose—to oppose Soviet attack submarines in the North Atlantic—rendered obsolete by world events. Canada's claim to the Northwest Passage found little acceptance internationally, even—or perhaps especially—with otherwise firm allies such the United States, Britain, and the European Community, and commercial use of the Northwest Passage soon became a concern, beginning with the passage of the American tanker *Manhattan* in 1969. The Trudeau government took steps to exert environmental controls in the 1970s. Air force sovereignty patrols over the Arctic, always few in number, decreased as defence dollars became scarce. Powerful icebreakers, often promised and seldom built, were an ever-present feature of the procurement landscape, their high costs rarely justified by minimal Northern commerce, isolated communities, and—despite decades of sensationalist rhetoric—little demonstrable need.

The increased melting of Arctic ice as global warming appeared to take hold at the end of the twentieth century, however, increased nationalist concerns in Ottawa. Stephen Harper's government after 2006 pledged to increase the military and naval presence in the Arctic under its Canada First Defence Strategy. It also proposed to build new icebreakers and ice-capable naval ships at a cost of more than $5 billion. But committed funds remained scarce and construction programs became tied up in red tape. The capacity of Russian and American vessels, submarines, and scientific research teams to operate in the Far North grew steadily in technical terms, marked by public statements defending their respective right to do so, while China also moved to bolster its own Arctic capabilities. Even the Danes, with residual interests in and off Greenland (and a claim to Hans Island that competes with Canada's own claim to ownership) demonstrated an Arctic capability comparable to Canada's. Nonetheless, the Canadian Forces recently began to do small spring and summer exercises in the Arctic, showing the flag and demonstrating Canada's intent to protect its claims. Arctic melting seemed likely to create a resource scramble and to make the Northwest Passage more

▲ NORAD relied on fighter jets and missiles, such as these Nike-Hercules surface-to-air missiles, seen here in 1968, to defend North American air space against Soviet bombers.

readily navigable; whether Canada could or would act to protect its sovereignty and commercial interests under these changing circumstances remained uncertain. SEE ALSO: CANADA–UNITED STATES DEFENCE RELATIONS; CANADIAN RANGERS; DISTANT EARLY WARNING LINE.

READING: Shelagh Grant, *Sovereignty or Security: Government Policy in the Canadian North, 1936–1951* (Vancouver, 1989); Shelagh Grant, *Polar Imperative: A History of Arctic Sovereignty in North America* (Vancouver, 2010).

North American Air (later Aerospace) Defence Command (NORAD). NORAD is a bi-national military organization formally established in 1958 by Canada and the United States to monitor and defend North American airspace. It monitors and tracks man-made objects in space and detects, validates, and warns of approaching aircraft, missiles, or "space vehicles" (e.g., satellites and space debris). NORAD also provides surveillance and control of Canadian and US airspace. Much desired by the Royal Canadian Air Force and the United States Air Force at the height of the Cold War in the mid-1950s, the NORAD Agreement was put in force by an exchange of notes on 1 August 1957 and then signed by the governments of Canada and the United States on 12 May 1958. It has been renewed for varying periods since then, but the basic text of the agreement has been revised substantially only four times—1975, 1981, 1996, and 2006. The Commander of NORAD, since 1981 called the North American Aerospace Defence Command, is appointed by, and is responsible to, both the prime minister of Canada and the president of the United States. Traditionally, the commander of NORAD is American, and the deputy commander is Canadian. NORAD Headquarters is located at Peterson Air Force Base, Colorado Springs, Colorado. Its warning and control missions are exercised through the Cheyenne Mountain Operations Center, located a short distance away.

NORAD has been a focus of controversy several times. Prime Minister John Diefenbaker agreed to the air defence arrangement in the first days of his taking office and without being fully briefed. He then ran into opposition from within the Department of External Affairs and felt disingenuously criticized by the Liberal Opposition that had negotiated the arrangement and that would certainly have supported it had it been in power. Because the concurrence of the two national governments is required before formal alerts or action, difficulty also arose during the Cuban Missile Crisis of October 1962. The Americans went on standby alert as soon as the crisis was apparent, but the Diefenbaker government delayed for a period of days, angering President John F. Kennedy and, when the public learned of the delays, provoking much criticism in Canada. The matter was complicated by the fact that Bomarc surface-to-air missiles at the two Canadian Bomarc bases had no nuclear warheads, another consequence of divisions in Cabinet. The Bomarc itself was greatly resented by partisans of the CF-105 Avro Arrow aircraft, which had been cancelled by the government three years earlier in a decision that some unfairly blamed on the United States. Diefenbaker later learned that members of the media and opinion leaders had received tours of NORAD headquarters and been briefed negatively about his delays in agreeing to accept the Bomarc warheads, perhaps the major election issue when he lost power in the 1963 campaign.

After these experiences, every NORAD renewal, no matter which party was in power, became a focus for anti-American outbursts. Canadians worried when the Trudeau government agreed to let the United States test cruise missiles over Canada, and they fretted when the Mulroney government decided to upgrade the North Warning System in 1985, worrying that Canada might get involved in research for an American space-based anti-missile defence scheme known as Star Wars, after a popular series of space fantasy films. They became concerned that they might be judged complicit when the United States began in the 1990s to move its warning, detection, and surveillance systems into space. When terrorists attacked the United States on 11 September 2001, NORAD's Canadian deputy commander ran the air defence operation that monitored passenger aircraft in case of further attacks—and prepared to shoot them down if necessary. That bothered some. And when the government of Jean Chrétien in 2004 agreed to amend the NORAD agreement to make its missile warning function—a role it has been performing for the last 30 years—available to the US military commands conducting ballistic missile defence, Canadians again voiced their concerns. Nonetheless, NORAD was renewed in 2006, this time with a maritime warning mission added to its duties. The threat of seaborne attack against North America was small but genuine, and maritime domain awareness became necessary in the face of possible terrorist access to nuclear, biological, or chemical weapons. SEE ALSO: CANADA–UNITED STATES DEFENCE RELATIONS; CUBAN MISSILE CRISIS; DIEFENBAKER.

READING: Joseph Jockel, *Canada in NORAD, 1957–2007* (Montreal, 2007).

North Atlantic Treaty Organization (NATO). Canada was an original member of the North Atlantic Treaty Organization (NATO), signing the treaty in Washington, DC, on 4 April 1949. The alliance marked a definitive internationalist turn in Canadian postwar foreign policy, and would be the military focus of Canadian security efforts for most of the next six decades. NATO originally consisted of the United States, Canada, the United Kingdom, France, Iceland, Italy, Denmark, Luxembourg, Belgium, the Netherlands, Portugal, and Norway. Turkey, Greece, the Federal Republic of Germany, and Spain later joined and, after the end of the Cold War, Poland, Latvia, Lithuania, Estonia, Hungary, Bulgaria, the

Czech Republic, Slovakia, Slovenia, and Romania entered the alliance, bringing its membership to 26.

The discussions leading to NATO's creation began among the United States, Britain, and Canada in the spring of 1948. Soviet actions in Czechoslovakia were the immediate reason, but the intensifying Cold War and the demoralization of the European democracies, shaken by World War II and postwar hardships, formed the larger context. Those European countries that had signed the Brussels Treaty, an earlier European pact, were then added to the talks. The prime objective was to create a military alliance to confront the Soviet Union across what Winston Churchill had famously dubbed the Iron Curtain that divided Eastern and Western Europe.

Although the treaty came into force on 24 August 1949, NATO had little real military substance until after the outbreak of war in Korea in June 1950. NATO countries such as the United States and Britain believed that the invasion of South Korea was actually a Soviet test of NATO's resolve. On 19 December 1950, General Dwight D. Eisenhower was appointed Supreme Allied Commander Europe (SACEUR) to oversee a massive buildup of NATO military power aimed at putting at least 90 divisions in place by mid-1954, supported by a massive air force and naval power. The so-called Lisbon Force Goals were never achieved, but NATO had been permanently transformed—from a political union of security-conscious Western states designed to present a united front against possible Soviet depredations, to an increasingly proficient military organization that would fight the Russians on the battlefield, if combat were ever required.

Canada agreed to provide up to two divisions to NATO in the event of a European war. The first was to be the 1st Canadian Division that was to consist of the 27th Canadian Infantry Brigade Group, stationed in northern Germany, with two additional brigades from Canada; the second division, never formally constituted, was to come from the regular and reserve forces. The 27th Brigade had arrived from Canada in the fall of 1951. It was first stationed near Hannover, then at Soest, and finally at Lahr. The brigade later was renamed the 4th Canadian Mechanized Brigade Group.

In addition to its army contingent, Canada also agreed to provide a Royal Canadian Air Force (RCAF) air division of 12 fighter squadrons. These originally consisted of F-86 Sabres, later augmented by CF-100s. They were based first in the United Kingdom, then in France, and later in Germany. Canada also provided a substantial contribution of Royal Canadian Navy anti-submarine warfare ships for the Supreme Allied Commander Atlantic (SACLANT), surplus weapons and other equipment for the NATO mutual aid program, and monetary contributions to infrastructure costs. At its peak, the Canadian direct contribution to NATO amounted to more than 20,000 soldiers and air personnel in Europe and most of the Atlantic fleet at sea. In addition to standing forces and those immediately earmarked, in the event of war, to reinforce Europe, most of Canada's remaining military had NATO-related roles, including co-operation with American forces in NORAD, naval activity with US forces in the north Pacific, intelligence sharing, convoy planning, and training. Canada would gradually earn a well-deserved reputation for excellence in international peacekeeping, but its armed forces, through most of the postwar period, were a creature of the Cold War, and it was for Cold War operations—most of them under NATO auspices—that the Canadian military for half a century assiduously prepared.

Canada supported the NATO decision of December 1955 to equip alliance forces with tactical nuclear weapons because this was seen as the most effective form of defence and also as one way of reducing costs. Canada's NATO contingent duly took nuclear weapons after 1963, the RCAF arming its fighter bombers with tactical nuclear weapons and the army putting nuclear warheads on its Honest John surface-to-surface missiles. The army subsequently maintained two Honest John batteries, one in West Germany and the other, a training unit, in Manitoba.

The Canadian contribution to NATO remained relatively stable until 1968 when defence minister Léo Cadieux ended Canada's long-standing plan to reinforce its NATO brigade in Germany with two brigades from Canada. Instead, Canada agreed to send the Canadian Air/Sea Transportable Combat Group (CAST) by sea to Norway or Denmark in the event of war, a commitment that exercises later demonstrated to be impossible to fulfill (and that the Mulroney government finally cancelled). In 1969, following a Cabinet review of NATO policy, the Liberal government of Pierre Elliott Trudeau ordered a 50 percent force reduction in Canada's NATO force and the elimination of nuclear weapons. This cut, bitterly opposed by other NATO members, resulted in a much-reduced Canadian brigade of 2,800 troops moving south to Lahr and NATO reserve. However, the brigade's obsolete equipment was renewed with the acquisition of Leopard tanks from the Germans in the late 1970s, and the air force's role altered with new CF-18 fighters in the 1980s. In 1991, at the end of the Cold War, the Progressive Conservative government of Brian Mulroney, having earlier proposed substantial increases to Canada's European presence and NATO commitments as part of its 1987 Defence White Paper, announced that Canada's two bases in Germany would be closed by 1995 and that only a small force of approximately 1,500 troops would remain in Europe operating under NATO command. In the 1992 budget speech, the government announced that all Canadian troops would be withdrawn from Europe in 1993. At each stage in Canada's gradual retreat from NATO Europe, critics complained that Canadian troops on the continent helped keep American and British troops there as well, providing an irreplaceable link between the alliance's onshore and offshore members. Supporters, on the other hand, noted the rising prosperity of European states now capable of their own defence and the increasing anachronism of relying on conventional military forces alone for alliance unity within and security without. Canada's standing and influence within NATO measurably declined as a result of such moves; whether NATO itself was substantially—or even marginally—weakened, as doomsayers had argued it would be, is unlikely.

Canada remains a member of the alliance nonetheless and has participated in NATO operations in former Yugoslavia, Kosovo, and in Afghanistan where, alongside those few member states that have

actually fought, Canadian troops have played a major role in Kandahar and suffered serious losses. Canada also contributes personnel to NATO headquarters staffs and to the NATO Airborne Early Warning and Control System (AWACS). In addition, Canada provides low-level flying and mechanized battle group training grounds for its NATO partners at several Canadian Forces bases and provides NATO Flying Training in Canada (NFTC) at the Canadian Forces base in Moose Jaw, Saskatchewan. The alliance remains the only international organization with an integrated command structure, standardized operating procedures, and standing forces available for expeditionary deployment. Small but vocal protests marked Canadian participation in NATO missions after the Cold War, but calls for withdrawal from the alliance by the political left, peace groups, and some academics were ignored by successive governments. Canadian membership is virtually assured for the foreseeable future. SEE ALSO: MULRONEY; TRUDEAU; 27TH CANADIAN INFANTRY BRIGADE GROUP.

READING: Escott Reid, *Time of Fear and Hope* (Toronto, 1977); Sean Maloney, *War without Battles: Canada's NATO Brigade in Germany* (Toronto, 1997).

Northwest Europe Campaign (1944–1945). From D-Day, 6 June 1944, to the German capitulation on 8 May 1945, Canadian soldiers fought against the enemy in France, Belgium, the Netherlands, and Germany. The Canadians landed in Normandy on Juno Beach, one of the five Allied beaches, and struggled against strong German opposition to move inland. It took a month to capture the city of Caen, instead of the few days envisaged by Allied planners. It took more than a month longer for II Canadian Corps under Lieutenant-General Guy Simonds to batter its way up and over Verrières Ridge and then to close the Falaise Gap, trapping tens of thousands of the enemy by linking up with US forces approaching from the southwest. The cost in lives during the first ten weeks of the campaign was very high with more than 5,000 Canadians killed in battle.

After the closing of the Falaise pocket, First Canadian Army turned to the pursuit of German forces across the River Seine from 23 to 30 August 1944, and then took the long left flank of General Sir Bernard Montgomery's 21st Army Group, including the liberation of the Channel ports from Le Havre to Boulogne and Calais, the securing of the Scheldt estuary, the clearing of the Rhineland, the crossing of the Rhine River, the liberation of the Netherlands, and the destruction of German forces in northern Germany. For most of the campaign, First Canadian Army consisted of II Canadian Corps and I British Corps and included the 1st Polish Armoured Division; at various times, American divisions and Czech, Belgian, and Dutch units also served under First Canadian Army commander General H.D.G. Crerar's overall command. Late in the war, I Canadian Corps, which had been fighting in Italy since July 1943, moved to the Netherlands, and all five divisions and two armoured brigades of Canadians overseas fought under Crerar until the German surrender.

In the opening phases of the post-Normandy campaign, First Canadian Army advanced along the Channel coast, capturing Dieppe, Boulogne, and Calais and, using a brigade of Czechoslovakian troops, encircling Dunkirk, which the Germans held to the end of the war. These small ports were important as the Allies struggled to supply their ever-increasing forces, but they paled beside the huge port facilities at Antwerp and Rotterdam. Second British Army captured the former, its docks virtually intact, at the beginning of September, while the Fifteenth German Army was in full flight. Montgomery inexplicably failed to take advantage of German disarray to seize the Scheldt estuary used by merchant ships passing from the North Sea to Antwerp. The British commander had his mind focused on the bridges over the Rhine and on planning for Operation Market Garden, a combined ground and parachute assault to drive a corridor from the British lines to Arnhem, thus allowing him to get into Germany's Ruhr industrial region quickly. Market Garden failed, however, and the Germans took advantage of Montgomery's strategic error to occupy and fortify both banks of the estuary including the island of North

Beveland and the islands, joined to the mainland by narrow necks of land, of Walcheren and South Beveland.

The task of clearing the Scheldt Estuary fell to First Canadian Army, considerably augmented by the addition of British divisions. General Crerar fell ill at the opening stages of the struggle, and General Simonds took over, much to Montgomery's pleasure. The battle began in miserable weather with the clearing of the Breskens pocket on the southern bank of the estuary and continued with costly attacks on South Beveland, North Beveland, and, finally, Walcheren, which could only be liberated after the dikes were bombed and an assault force landed from the sea. By 8 November, the estuary had been cleared,

▲ The campaign in northwest Europe saw eleven months of bitter fighting. Here, Dutch civilians crowd around a halted Canadian armoured column.

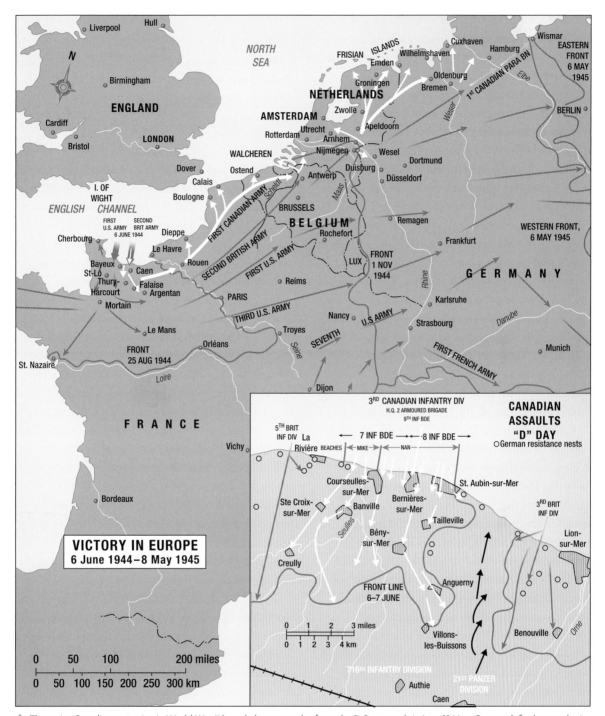

The major Canadian campaign in World War II lasted eleven months, from the D-Day assault in June 1944 to Germany's final surrender in early May 1945.

but the Canadian infantry had suffered so many losses that reinforcements could not keep up battalion strengths. This contributed to the conscription crisis of November in Canada.

Following a period of recuperation in winter quarters, First Canadian Army went into action once again in the Reichswald, the heavily forested area west of the Rhine. This was followed by the cracking of the Siegfried Line, fighting in the Hochwald, and, finally, the crossing of the Rhine River in late March. The latter operation featured an airborne assault and a massive concentration of force, the largest ever commanded in the field by a Canadian general. Fought under extremely difficult late winter conditions, with snow, mud, frozen or flooded fields, and bad roads delaying advances and causing severe discomfort to the fighting troops, these battles cost thousands of Canadian lives.

From the Rhine crossing to the end of the war, the Canadians concentrated on occupying parts of northern Germany and liberating the eastern and northern Netherlands. The 1st Canadian Parachute Battalion, serving as part of the British 6th Parachute Division, penetrated deepest into Germany, its soldiers meeting the Soviet Union's Red Army just east of the Danish peninsula. In the Netherlands, the Canadians tried desperately to minimize civilian casualties and to feed the Dutch, starved by their occupiers, at the same time as they fought the Germans. The war ended on VE Day, 8 May 1945. The Dutch still remember their liberators with extraordinary gratitude more than 65 years later. Canadian casualties in the northwest Europe campaign were 44,339, with 11,336 officers and other ranks killed in action. The Canadians had paid the full price in blood and treasure to liberate Europe from German occupation. The largest force ever commanded by a Canadian had fought continuously, and victoriously, from the English Channel to the German heartland, from Caen to Falaise, to the Scheldt, into the Rhineland, through the Netherlands, and into Germany itself. It is arguably the most remarkable chapter in all of Canadian military history. SEE ALSO: CRERAR; D-DAY; FIRST CANADIAN ARMY;

NETHERLANDS LIBERATION; SCHELDT; SIMONDS; WORLD WAR II.

READING: C.P. Stacey, *The Victory Campaign* (Ottawa, 1960); Denis and Shelagh Whitaker, *Rhineland* (Toronto, 1989); Terry Copp, *Cinderella Army: The Canadians in Northwest Europe, 1944–1945* (Toronto, 2006).

Northwest Field Force (1885). This force, raised by Canada, put down the Northwest Rebellion of 1885 launched by Louis Riel. Its 5,000 troops consisted primarily of existing militia units, augmented by volunteers and the tiny Permanent Force, led by the general officer commanding the Canadian militia, Major-General Frederick Middleton. For the campaign, the Field Force was divided into three columns: the westernmost, commanded by Major-General T.B. Strange, a retired British officer; the central, under Lieutenant-Colonel W.D. Otter, a Permanent Force officer; and the easternmost and main body, commanded by Middleton himself. Each column had its difficulties in dealing with the skilled Metis sharpshooters and Cree and Assiniboine warriors, but Middleton's column, with its overwhelming superiority in firepower and numbers, finally seized Batoche, Riel's capital, on 12 May, a victory that essentially brought the rebellion to an end. SEE ALSO: MIDDLETON; NORTHWEST REBELLION; RIEL.

READING: R.C. Macleod and Bob Beal, *Prairie Fire: The 1885 North West Rebellion* (Edmonton, 1984).

North West Mounted Police (NWMP). Founded in 1873 by the government of Prime Minister Sir John A. Macdonald, the North West Mounted Police was modelled on the Irish Constabulary and the military. Its officers ordinarily had political influence enough to secure commissions, and their task was to command a small force of red-coated mounted riflemen with both police and magistrate powers and to patrol the Prairie West. The force of 318 officers and other ranks went on the "Great March West" in the summer of 1874 and established a number of police posts along the Canada–United States boundary to establish

⌃ Members of the Northwest Field Force take their ease behind a stockade at Fish Creek, NWT, in May 1885.

a presence conducive to law and order, to counter smuggling, and to try to prevent the United States' wars with First Nations from spilling onto Canadian territory. The NWMP played an important role in the Northwest Rebellion of 1885 and in the Yukon after the discovery of gold. Many members also volunteered for service in the South African War, most serving in one of the several units of Canadian Mounted Rifles raised for the war, or with Lord Strathcona's Horse. As a token of that service, the force became the Royal North West Mounted Police (RNWMP) in 1904. The Mounties, as they remain known, provided two cavalry squadrons to the Canadian Corps in World War I. In 1920, the RNWMP joined with the Dominion Police to become the Royal Canadian Mounted Police, which remains Canada's national police force.

Northwest Rebellion (1884–1885). After the end of the Red River Rebellion in 1870, many Metis

grievances remained unresolved, to such an extent that many moved hundreds of kilometres west to the Saskatchewan country. At the same time, white settlers slowly moving into the area resented government policies; in particular, those who had settled along the Saskatchewan River were displeased that the Canadian Pacific Railway's surveyors had selected a more southerly route. As well, the First Nations in the Northwest Territories were increasingly unhappy over government failure to respect a variety of treaty provisions, grievances that Sir John A. Macdonald's government in faraway Ottawa had done little to address.

In June 1884, Metis leaders visited Louis Riel who was then in exile in Montana and asked him to lead them once more. Erratic, zealous, and obsessed with religious visions, Riel agreed and returned to Canada the following month. On 8 March 1885, he promulgated a ten-point "Revolutionary Bill of Rights"

⌃ Louis Riel's second rebellion forced Canada to send a military force to the Prairies. These gunners of the Halifax Garrison Artillery pose while crossing a stream at Swift Current, NWT, in 1885.

asserting Metis rights of possession to their farms and other demands. On 18 and 19 March, Riel formed a provisional government at Batoche, with himself as president, and an armed force. He designated Gabriel Dumont, a legendary buffalo hunter and natural tactician, as his military leader in charge of some 300 Metis. The first fighting of the rebellion occurred a week later at Duck Lake when a mixed detachment of North West Mounted Police (NWMP) and militia attempted to retake a store of supplies and ammunition. The federal troops suffered casualties and retreated to Fort Carlton, Riel persuading his Metis and Aboriginal allies not to pursue them. The Duck Lake skirmish led many Plains Cree and Assiniboine to join Riel, creating the impression in the West and elsewhere that the rebellion was spreading quickly.

When news of the rebellion reached Ottawa, the government reacted promptly. The general officer commanding the Canadian militia, Major-General Frederick Middleton, immediately went west, while

the minister of militia and defence, Adolphe Caron, supervised the raising and dispatch of a military expeditionary force, the Northwest Field Force. Since the Canadian Pacific Railway was not yet completed around Lake Superior, troops, supplies, and equipment had to be moved across gaps in the rail line by horse-drawn sleighs. In less than a month, more than 3,000 troops reached Qu'Appelle, and more followed. Most were Ontario militia, but two Quebec units and one Nova Scotia unit also marched west; some 1,700 militia and NWMP from the west also took part.

Middleton doubted the battle-readiness of his largely untrained militia and officers, his confidence resting only on the small group of regular British staff officers accompanying the force. Fearing the military and political consequences of defeat in the field, especially in light of his tenuous supply lines back to eastern Canada, Middleton was caution personified during the ensuing campaign. His three-pronged advance moved deliberately into rebel-occupied

Militia soldiers, such as these sharpshooters from the 43rd Battalion in Brockville, Ontario, made up the bulk of the force that put down Riel's 1885 rebellion.

territory. He himself led one column of troops north from Qu'Appelle toward Batoche, while Lieutenant-Colonel William Otter from the tiny Permanent Force headed a second column north from Swift Current. Further west, Major-General T.B. Strange, a retired British army officer, led the third column north to Edmonton from Calgary and then east along the North Saskatchewan River.

Movement was difficult because of the spring mud and the almost total absence of roads, and Middleton attempted to use the sternwheeler *Northcote* to bring up supplies. Though the Canadians were better equipped, bringing with them artillery and Gatling guns, and—with some 5,000 troops in total—far more numerous than their enemies, their leadership was unimaginative, even hesitant. On several occasions they escaped heavy losses only because their Metis or Aboriginal opponents failed, or refused, to press home attacks. Battles at Frog Lake, Fish Creek, Cut Knife Hill, and Frenchman's Butte were all, in some fashion, defeats for the militia. Nevertheless, though checked at Fish Creek, Middleton recognized that the Metis capital was the primary objective, and he pressed on toward Batoche. The Canadian troops

besieged the town on 9 May and, after several failed assaults, finally captured it on 12 May when two militia units disobeyed their general's orders and charged the enemy rifle pits, overrunning the Metis and killing as many as 50. Eight militia soldiers also died at Batoche, a battle that effectively brought the rebellion to an end, with Metis and natives recognizing the futility of further resistance against such superior Canadian forces in the field. Crowfoot, the Blackfoot chief, in fact had refused to allow his warriors to join in the rebellion, realizing that it had no hope of success.

Captured and tried, Louis Riel was eventually hanged for treason on 16 November 1885. That he was likely insane did not save him, though his hanging infuriated French Canada and created a lasting political divide. Gabriel Dumont, who had skilfully led his irregulars, escaped to the United States and eventually returned to Canada after an amnesty had been declared. Poundmaker, the Cree chief who had tried to restrain his men, surrendered at Battleford and received a jail term. Six Cree and two Assiniboine warriors, including Frog Lake war chief Wandering Spirit, were hanged at Battleford. Middleton received a knighthood, but was later accused

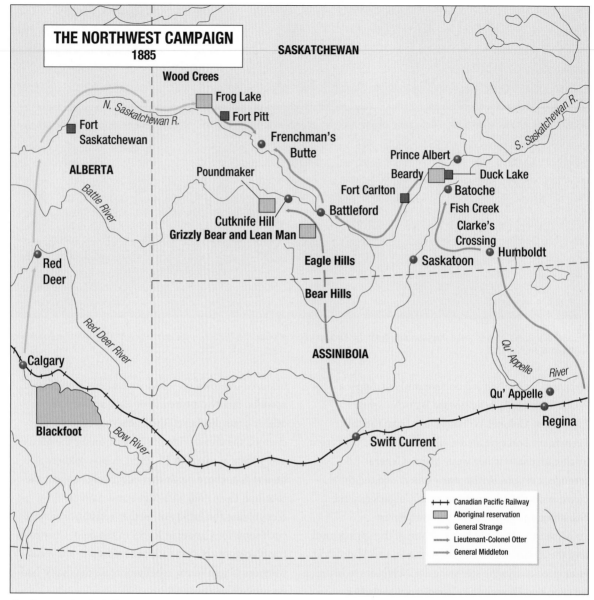

The second Riel rebellion forced Canada to mount its first real military expedition—in a little populated area of Canada.

of misappropriating a Metis trapper's furs and resigned his position in Canada. The rebellion would prove to be the last major armed conflict on Canadian soil. SEE ALSO: CARON; DUMONT; MACDONALD, JOHN ALEXANDER; MIDDLETON; OTTER; RIEL.

READING: R.C. Macleod and Bob Beal, *Prairie Fire: The 1885 North West Rebellion* (Edmonton, 1984).

Nuclear Crisis (1962–1963). John Diefenbaker's Progressive Conservative government in 1959 agreed

to build two Bomarc surface-to-air missile bases in Canada and to arm the missiles with nuclear warheads. It also agreed to acquire nuclear weapons for Canadian forces serving overseas with the North Atlantic Treaty Organization (NATO). But there were dissenters in the Department of External Affairs and in Cabinet and, by 1962, the prime minister had begun to wobble. The public learned of this during the Cuban Missile Crisis in October when Diefenbaker delayed putting the country's military forces on alert;

soon after, Canadians realized that the Bomarc bases, now almost complete, lacked the warheads that alone would make them effective because Diefenbaker had not as yet reached agreement with the United States on acquiring them. The Cabinet began to fragment on this issue, the pace of disintegration increasing when Liberal leader Lester Pearson reversed his party's position early in 1963, insisting that Canada had to fulfill its nuclear commitments. The US government less than subtly intervened, releasing a press statement that criticized the prime minister; other ministers resigned, and the government lost a confidence vote in Parliament. The Liberals narrowly won the 1963 election, and Canada acquired nuclear weapons. A defence review under Pierre Trudeau would later announce Canada's intention to retire the weapons, the last of which left Canadian soil in the early 1980s. See also: Bomarc Missile; Canada–United States Defence Relations; Cuban Missile Crisis; Diefenbaker; Pearson.

Reading: Denis Smith, *Rogue Tory: The Life and Legend of John G. Diefenbaker* (Toronto, 1995).

Nuclear Weapons. Canada decided to acquire nuclear weapons in 1959 when John Diefenbaker's government agreed to put Bomarc surface-to-air weapons on two Canadian bases and to accept Honest John surface-to-surface missiles as well as a strike/reconnaissance role for CF-104 jets in the North Atlantic Treaty Organization. The Bomarcs were armed in 1963, the other weapons systems in 1964. Canada also acquired CF-101 Voodoo jets for domestic air defence and armed them with Genie air-to-air missiles. When Lester Pearson accepted the nuclear Bomarcs in 1963, he pledged to get rid of them as soon as possible. Pierre Trudeau's government repeated the pledge and closed down the Bomarc bases in 1972 after eliminating the nuclear roles in NATO in 1970–1971. Some nuclear missiles remained in Canada until 1984. See also: Cuban Missile Crisis; Diefenbaker; Nuclear Crisis.

No. 1 Air Division, Royal Canadian Air Force. As part of its contribution to the North Atlantic Treaty

Organization (NATO), the Canadian government agreed to deploy fighter aircraft to Europe. Beginning in late 1951, 12 squadrons of F-86 Sabre jets were deployed to Europe. The first three squadrons had their bases in Britain, but eventually there were four bases on the continent, at Marville and Grostenquin, France, and at Zweibrucken and Baden-Soellingen, Germany. With 300 first-line fighter aircraft, No. 1 Air Division constituted a substantial part of NATO air defence in the tense early stages of the Cold War. In 1956, four squadrons of Sabres were replaced by CF-100 all-weather and night interceptors and, in 1962, CF-104 fighter bombers arrived as Canada undertook to play a reconnaissance and nuclear-strike role in the alliance. Reductions in aircraft strength began in 1965. The Trudeau cuts of 1969 saw the CF-100s and three CF-104 squadrons, now part of what was named No. 1 Air Group, concentrated at Baden-Soellingen in southern Germany. Three squadrons of CF-18 aircraft became the Canadian NATO contribution in 1986, and 26 aircraft saw service in the Gulf War in 1991. More than 260 members of the air force died on NATO service.

No. 6 Bomber Group (RCAF). At the outbreak of World War II, the Mackenzie King government believed that the British Commonwealth Air Training Plan (BCATP) would be its major contribution to Allied victory. Under the original terms of the agreement, Canadian graduates were supposed to be earmarked for service with Royal Canadian Air Force (RCAF) squadrons once overseas, but the Royal Air Force (RAF) did not take the stipulation especially seriously and sent large numbers of Canadians, especially those destined for service with Bomber Command, to serve with RAF squadrons. That was in keeping with the practice followed with other Commonwealth air crew. The Canadian government believed that the integration of Canadians into the RAF did not give the Canadian contribution to the war sufficient exposure and insisted that Canadians be grouped together into RCAF squadrons, a policy known as Canadianization. At first, Canada refused to pay the operating costs of these squadrons, insisting

▲ No. 1 Air Division of the RCAF, a major Canadian contribution to NATO, flew F-86 Sabre jets, the one shown here sporting a special "X" marking for a 1955 exercise.

that it had already paid its share through the BCATP. This delayed the process but, when Ottawa began to pay, Canadianization moved forward, not without RAF resistance. By the start of 1942, the RCAF had four bomber squadrons, flying with Bomber Command Nos. 405, 408, 419, and 420. These were known as Article XV squadrons, named for the clause in the BCATP agreement that gave Canada the right to so use its aircrew. Many of the officers and some of the other ranks in these squadrons were RAF or from other Commonwealth air forces.

More RCAF squadrons soon formed, and the decision was made at the May 1942 Ottawa Air Training Conference (called to decide whether or not to extend the BCATP) to form an all-Canadian bomber group to operate within Bomber Command. The RAF

accepted this decision reluctantly. No. 6 Bomber Group (RCAF) began operating with headquarters at Linton-on-Ouse on 1 January 1943. No. 6 consisted of eight squadrons on seven stations and flew its first operation—laying mines near the Frisian Islands—on the night of 3–4 January. Thereafter, additional squadrons joined No. 6 until, at its peak, it counted 15 squadrons.

No. 6 Bomber Group's first year on operations was not an easy one. Several factors combined to hold down its operational efficiency and keep its casualties high. A bomber group by definition needed to be based together but, by the time No. 6 formed, all base areas in Britain close to the continent had been allocated to RAF groups or to the United States Army Air Force. No. 6 Group was,

No. 6 Bomber Group, RCAF, was Canada's major contribution to the air war against Germany. The complement of 415 Squadron, shown here posing with one of their bombers, like their comrades, suffered heavy losses.

therefore, based in foggy north Yorkshire, requiring its aircraft to fly farther to their targets. Since it was a new and somewhat inexperienced group, Bomber Command was reluctant to allocate it new Lancaster bombers; as a result, No. 6's squadrons continued to fly older twin-engine Wellingtons or the flawed but durable four-engine Halifax bombers, beloved by many of their crews. The Canadian group also had a higher concentration of inexperienced flying crew. From March to June 1943, No. 6 lost 100 bombers.

Strategic bombing techniques evolved rapidly during the war. Navigation instruments provided increasing accuracy in pinpointing targets, even at night. The later creation of a specialist Pathfinder group, which also included Canadians, was a substantial improvement; the Pathfinders would arrive above the target area earlier than the main force waves of bombers and drop coloured flares in parachutes on the objectives for the bomb-aimers. For even greater accuracy, a "master bomber" flew on the raids, able to contact aircraft and redirect their targets when necessary and possible. Ways of improving the crews' chances included using radar to locate enemy fighters, placing machine-gun turrets in the tail and nose of bombers, and interfering with enemy radar, for example, by simulating multiple targets by

dropping chaff—long strips of aluminum foil—on the objective.

All this helped the aircrew in No. 6. On 29 February 1944, the first commander of No. 6 Group, Air Vice-Marshal G.E. Brookes, was replaced by World War I ace Air Vice-Marshal C.M. McEwen. "Black Mike" McEwen was a strict disciplinarian, and this, combined with the arrival of better aircraft, changes in operational procedures, the advances in technology, and greater experience, considerably improved the group's performance. By war's end, No. 6 Canadian Group had flown 40,822 sorties and dropped 126,000 tons of bombs at a cost of 814 aircraft; 4,272 air crew—almost all, but not entirely, Canadian—had been killed or presumed killed in action. Another 5,647 Canadian aircrew died in Bomber Command aircraft outside No. 6. Canada's contribution to the bombing campaign had been one of the country's greatest and most costly wartime efforts. SEE ALSO: BOMBER COMMAND CONTROVERSY; BRITISH COMMONWEALTH AIR TRAINING PLAN; CANADIANIZATION; MCEWEN; POWER.

READING: Brereton Greenhous et al., *The Crucible of War, 1939–1945: The Official History of the Royal Canadian Air Force,* vol. 3 (Toronto, 1994); S. Dunmore and W. Carter, *Reap the Whirlwind* (Toronto, 1991).

October Crisis (1970). Terrorist attacks by French-language separatists in Quebec led to the imposition of stringent security measures in late 1970. Known then and since as the October Crisis, the events were the culmination of a long series of terrorist incidents since the late 1960s that had been directed at federal power in Quebec. On 5 October 1970, Le Front de Libération du Québec (FLQ) kidnapped British trade commissioner James Cross from his house in Montreal. Soon after, another cell of the FLQ seized Quebec labour minister Pierre Laporte from the front lawn of his home. The FLQ's ransom demands called for the release of "political prisoners"—convicted FLQ terrorists—from jail and the broadcast of its communiqué. The communiqué was read on radio and television, and Quebec's justice minister promised safe passage to the kidnappers if they freed Cross.

With tension in Quebec near the breaking point, Prime Minister Pierre Elliott Trudeau and Quebec Premier Robert Bourassa agreed to send the army into Montreal to aid the police. On 16 October, Trudeau invoked the War Measures Act to halt "an apprehended insurrection." The act permitted the arrest and detention of people without their being charged, and security sweeps resulted in more than 450 arrests. The presence of troops on urban street corners and protecting major public buildings was a lasting image of federal power and a definitive statement of Ottawa's intention to uphold its responsibility for peace, order, and good government. In response, the FLQ strangled Laporte; his body was found 17 October near St Hubert airport. By this time, more than 90 percent of Canadians, including francophones, supported tough action against the FLQ. The terrorists released Cross unharmed on 3 December after police had determined his location; authorities allowed the cell that kidnapped him safe passage to Cuba. Laporte's murderers, caught by police in January 1971, were tried and jailed.

By 1971, public opinion had begun to turn against Trudeau's use of the War Measures Act, and Trudeau's justice minister, John Turner, had stated the act had been used to halt an "erosion of public will" in Quebec. Quebec separatism, badly wounded

▲ Schoolchildren watch Canadian soldiers guarding the headquarters of the Sûreté du Quebec during the October Crisis of 1970.

by the FLQ's viciousness, recovered, and the separatist Parti Québécois won power in 1976. There has been no return to political terrorism in Quebec since the October Crisis and the federal government's imposition of the War Measures Act. SEE ALSO: AID TO THE CIVIL POWER; TRUDEAU; WAR MEASURES ACT.

READING: John Saywell, *Quebec 70: A Documentary Narrative* (Toronto, 1972).

Ogdensburg Agreement (1940). A political agreement between Canada and the still-neutral United States during World War II, the Ogdensburg Agreement marked the start of close bilateral defence relations that have continued into the twenty-first century.

On 18 August 1940, with the war overseas going very badly for Britain and its Allies, Canadian Prime Minister Mackenzie King went to Ogdensburg, New York, to meet American President Franklin Delano Roosevelt. Then running for re-election for an unprecedented fourth term, Roosevelt was eager to safeguard North America's defences, to secure some leverage on the Royal Navy if it came to Canada in the event of a British collapse, and to acquire bases on Canadian territory by negotiating a so-called destroyers for bases agreement with Great Britain. King was uninterested in giving the United States military bases on Canadian soil, but did want a bilateral defence co-operation agreement, the first in Canadian history, that would guarantee Canadian security, regardless of the result of the war overseas, and permit Canada to exert itself to the maximum in order to assist Britain. The discussions between the two leaders created the Permanent Joint Board on Defence (PJBD) that set to work immediately coordinating continental defence planning.

Reaction in Canada to the agreement was generally positive, though Arthur Meighen, a senator and former prime minister, privately denounced it, as Conservative Party leader R.B. Hanson did publicly. In Britain, Prime Minister Winston Churchill was also unhappy, seeing only a Canada sidling up to the United States for protection and moving away from the British

Commonwealth. He was not wrong: the Ogdensburg Agreement indeed did mark a major turning point for Canada as it moved from the British to the American political and security orbit, a transition prompted more by Britain's desperate weakness in the summer of 1940 than by any inherent desire on the part of Canadian leaders for closer continental defence relations with Washington. The agreement demonstrated that King had properly assessed Canada's national interest—the first task of a leader is to secure the nation's territory and people against foreign threat; it also showed his willingness to render Britain the maximum military assistance possible, Canada's security at home now guaranteed by his pact with the Americans. SEE ALSO: CANADA–UNITED STATES DEFENCE RELATIONS; KING; WORLD WAR II.

READING: C.P. Stacey, *Canada and the Age of Conflict*, vol. 2 (Toronto, 1981).

Ogdensburg, Battle of (1813). During the War of 1812, Lieutenant-Colonel "Red George" Macdonell, commanding the defence of eastern Upper Canada from his headquarters in Prescott, disobeyed the orders he had been given only the day before by Lieutenant-General Sir George Prevost not to attack Ogdensburg, directly across the St Lawrence River, unless the garrison's numbers were reduced. Macdonnell put together a strong raiding party from the Glengarry Light Infantry Fencibles with some regulars and militia, and crossed the icy St Lawrence on 22 February 1813. The US regulars in the town resisted strongly, but the American militia melted away, and resistance collapsed when several US officers suffered wounds. Macdonnell's men looted the town—the base for past sorties against the British shore—of military stores and burned ships frozen in the ice. The raid ended any threat to British supply lines, and Ogdensburg was not garrisoned again for the rest of the war. SEE ALSO: WAR OF 1812.

Oka Crisis (1990). Between April and late September 1990, the Mohawks of the Kanesetake Reserve near Oka, Quebec, west of Montreal, staged a road blockade

The Canadian army faced off against heavily armed Mohawk warriors during the 1990 dispute at Oka, Quebec, a confrontation captured in Jean Bordeau's painting, based on an actual incident.

on Route 344. On 11 July, the Sûreté du Québec (SQ), the provincial police force, attempted to storm the barricade held by heavily armed Warrior Society members; one police officer died. The Mohawks maintained that the barricade had been built to protect their claims to land that was to be turned from a 9-hole to an 18-hole golf course. At the same time, at the Kahnawake Reserve on the south shore of the St Lawrence River near Montreal, Warrior Society members set up another barricade to support the Kanesetake action. This stopped 70,000 daily commuters from using the Mercier Bridge to reach the city and provoked sometimes-violent counter-demonstrations from outraged citizens. The SQ manifestly could no longer deal with the escalating crisis, so Quebec premier Robert Bourassa sought help from the federal government that, under Operation Salon, sent in some 3,700 soldiers. With the nation watching on television, the army besieged the barricades in both places, and then, after careful prepara-

tion, moved in at Kanesetake and succeeded in dismantling them without casualties. Those Warriors who chose not to surrender retreated to an isolated treatment centre on the reserve from which they emerged peacefully on 26 September. With the siege at Oka over, the barricades at Kahnawake were also dismantled. Some Mohawks had made their reserve "a narco para-state" to facilitate the cross-border smuggling of weapons, drugs, cigarettes, and people, but Oka nonetheless became a symbol of First Nations' demands for independence and settlement of their land claims. SEE ALSO: AID TO THE CIVIL POWER.

READING: G. York and L. Pindera, *People of the Pines: The Warriors and the Legacy of Oka* (Toronto, 1991); Timothy Winegard, *Oka: A Convergence of Cultures and the Canadian Forces* (Kingston, ON, 2008).

Oregon Crisis (1845). In 1818, the boundary between the United States and British North America from the Lake of the Woods to the Rocky Mountains was set along the 49th parallel. The area to the west of the mountains, known as the Oregon Country, was to be jointly administered, though, in fact, there were so few settlers that it was essentially the preserve of the Hudson's Bay Company. When Americans began pouring into what are now the states of Oregon and Washington in the early 1840s, some in the United States claimed the area up to latitude 54° 40 minutes; in 1845, the crisis blew up, and "54-40 or fight" became a popular slogan in the United States, 54° 40 minutes being the southern boundary of Alaska, then Russian territory. That it was America's "manifest destiny" to control all North America became widely believed. The United States under the expansionist president James Polk unilaterally ended the joint administration of the Oregon Country in December 1846 and claimed the entire region. The possibility of war between the United States and Britain seemed real, and this would likely have resulted in an invasion of Canada. But Polk also was on the verge of war with Mexico over Texas and, anxious to avoid two conflicts at once, his administration became more conciliatory. The dispute was settled by the Oregon Treaty of 1846 that extended the boundary along the 49th parallel to the Pacific Coast and thence south and west through the middle of the Straits of Georgia and Juan de Fuca to the ocean. All Vancouver Island remained British. The treaty, however, left ownership of a number of small islands unresolved. See also: San Juan Island Dispute.

Ortona, Battle of (1943). After fighting its way up the Italian boot and across the Moro River in December 1943, the 1st Canadian Division moved to capture the Adriatic city of Ortona, a key road junction with a small harbour. With its old stone buildings, high walled courtyards, and narrow roads, the town offered excellent defensive positions for the German 1st Parachute Division's tough, elite troops. On 21 December the battle began when two under-strength companies of the Loyal Edmonton Regiment and a half-squadron of Three Rivers Regiment tanks moved cautiously up Ortona's main street toward the first of three large public squares. By mid-afternoon, the

advance had slowed to a halt, and the 2nd Canadian Infantry Brigade's commander, Brigadier Bert Hoffmeister, sent a company of the Seaforth Highlanders to help. The next morning it was apparent that German resistance had stiffened, and Hoffmeister committed the balance of the Seaforths, assigning each battalion half the town. The German strategy was to use the narrow streets as prepared killing zones. After a few bad experiences, the Canadians determined that they had to avoid the streets by fighting house to connected house through holes blown in the top floor walls and then using grenades to clear the lower floors. This technique the troops called "mouseholing." The soldiers used tank gunfire and anti-tank weapons to destroy the solid houses where they could, but the basic battle was fought by infantry. The Germans retaliated against the Canadian tactics by planting booby traps and mining houses—one Canadian platoon was almost wiped out when German engineers blew up a house. Fighting continued

The narrow streets and stone buildings of Ortona, shown here, forced the infantry to fight house-to-house, digging and bombing their way from building to building.

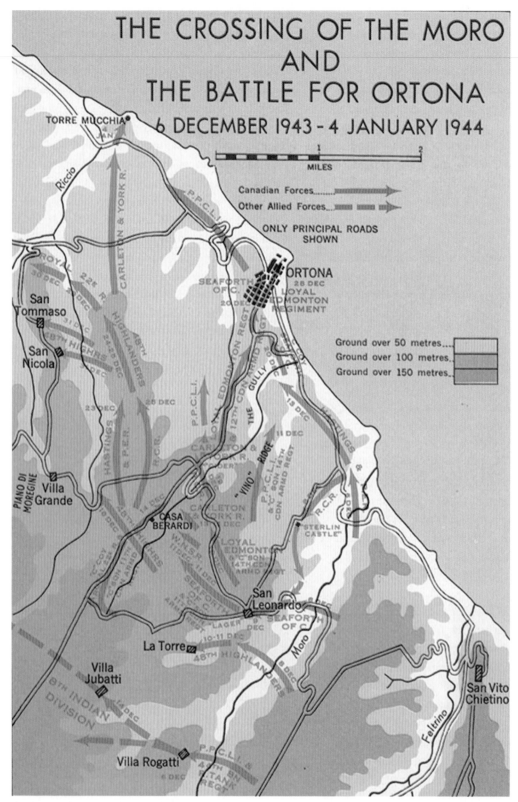

THE CROSSING OF THE MORO
AND
THE BATTLE FOR ORTONA
6 DECEMBER 1943 – 4 JANUARY 1944

MILES

Canadian Forces
Other Allied Forces

ONLY PRINCIPAL ROADS
SHOWN

Ground over 50 metres
Ground over 100 metres
Ground over 150 metres

▲ The media's description for the Ortona fighting in December 1943, "Little Stalingrad," was not much exaggerated. The Canadians closed on Ortona from the south, fighting across the Moro River and through Casa Berardi.

through Christmas Day, while companies pulled out of the line for a roast pork dinner in the ruined church of Santa Maria di Constantinopoli—one of their officers played carols on the church's organ—and then returned to the fight.

While that struggle was going on, the 1st Brigade attacked northwest of the town beginning on 23 December with a view to outflanking the German positions in the city. They succeeded in seizing the high ground and, although cut off from the rest of the division for a time, threatened German supply routes sufficiently to force the Germans to begin to withdraw. On the night of 27–28 December, the German paratroopers, just as battered and tired as the Canadians, silently pulled out.

Matthew Halton of the Canadian Broadcasting Corporation memorably reported on the battle as a little Stalingrad: "It wasn't hell. It was the courtyard of hell. It was a maelstrom of noise and hot, splitting steel … the rattling of machine guns never stops . . . wounded men refuse to leave, and the men don't want to be relieved after seven days and seven nights . . . the battlefield is still an appalling thing to see, in its mud, ruin, dead, and its blight and desolation." The Canadians suffered some 650 casualties in clearing Ortona. The dead, wounded, and ill in the hard fighting to reach and take the city had cost the 1st Canadian Division 3,956 casualties; it was effectively rendered incapable of further operations without rest and reinforcements. German casualties were high and so were civilian losses. SEE ALSO: I CANADIAN CORPS; ITALIAN CAMPAIGN; WORLD WAR II.

READING: G.W.L. Nicholson, *The Canadians in Italy* (Ottawa, 1956); Mark Zuehlke, *Ortona: Canada's Epic World War II Battle* (Vancouver, 2003).

Ottawa Treaty (1996). "The Convention on the Prohibition of the Use, Stockpiling, Production and Transfer of Anti-Personnel Mines and on Their Destruction" became open for national ratification at a meeting in Ottawa on 3–4 December 1997. Spurred by the anti-mine advocacy of Diana, Princess of Wales, and active non-governmental organizations, Lloyd Axworthy, the Canadian foreign minister, had sped the process that led to the Ottawa Treaty in October 1996 by challenging states to move from good wishes toward a binding agreement within a year. Most states eventually signed on, including Canada, but many, including Russia, the United States, China, and India, the major producers and users of anti-personnel land mines, and other states with vulnerable land borders where land mines were deemed essential to national security, did not. The treaty came into force on 1 March 1999. The so-called Ottawa Process was marked by the use of relatively new technologies, including the Internet and email, to mobilize the anti–land mines "virtual coalition," and by minor Western states, including Canada, pressing major allies on an arms control issue seen as critical to some aspects of great power security. The campaign to ban land mines was later awarded the Nobel Prize for peace.

READING: David Lenarcic, *Knight-Errant? Canada and the Crusade to Ban Anti-Personnel Mines* (Toronto, 1998).

Otter, William Dillon (1843–1929). Born near Goderich, Upper Canada, Otter received some schooling there and in Toronto, and began his working life as a clerk. He joined the Queen's Own Rifles (QOR), a Toronto militia regiment, in 1861, found that he enjoyed the order and discipline of the military, and became a lieutenant in 1864. As adjutant of his regiment, he served at Ridgeway in 1866 against the Fenians and watched in horror as the militia panicked and fled. That experience made him a lifelong believer in discipline and training, attitudes he tried to instill in the QOR when he became commanding officer in 1875; these were also the qualities he urged and wrote about in *The Guide, A Manual for the Canadian Militia*, published in 1880. When the government created a tiny Permanent Force in 1883, Otter used connections to be appointed as the commander of the Infantry School of Military Instruction in Toronto. When the Northwest Rebellion broke out in late 1885, Lieutenant-Colonel Otter went west and took command of one of the three columns created by Major-General Frederick Middleton. Otter led his column to Battleford, ravaged by the Cree and Assiniboine, and then directed his troops at Poundmaker's Plains Cree at Fish Creek. The Cree inflicted casualties on the Canadians and forced their retreat, but Otter found himself painted as a Canadian hero by the government and the press. His soldiers were less complimentary.

In 1892, the School of Infantry became the Canadian Regiment of Infantry, and Otter acted as commanding officer. Then, when the government of Sir Wilfrid Laurier succumbed to pressure to send a contingent to South Africa in 1899, Otter became the commanding officer of the 2nd (Special Service) Battalion of the Royal Canadian Regiment of Infantry (RCR). His men largely untrained, Otter did his best to instill discipline during the long voyage to Cape Town and in the ensuing two months of training and picket duty. In February 1900, finally, the RCR joined the British march to the Modder River, where 21 Canadians died in a futile charge, and on to the

siege of Boer forces at Paardeberg. In a night attack on 27 February, half of the RCR retreated in confusion, but those that held their ground found themselves perched above General Piet Cronje's Boer encampment at first light. The Boers surrendered, and the RCR were heroes, Otter first among them. He was wounded in the face at Israel's Poort in April, but returned to lead his regiment into Pretoria on 5 June.

Otter's men disliked him, and he argued with his officers far too much. Thus, when he tried to persuade his soldiers to remain in South Africa to finish the campaign, most, their terms of service expiring, refused and left for home. Otter and the remainder stayed until November 1900 and were duly hailed in London and Canada.

Now a colonel, Otter found himself in a good position when the Laurier government decided to make a Canadian the chief of the general staff in 1908. Brigadier-General Otter organized the extraordinary military review on the Plains of Abraham that marked Quebec's tercentenary and did his best to report on the condition of the militia. In 1910, he became inspector general in the rank of major-general and, in late 1911, he received his knighthood and retirement letter.

The 71-year-old Otter came back to duty when World War I began as the head of the government's internment operations, a job he held until 1919. Then he sat as chair of the committee struck to reorganize the militia, trying to adjudicate between the claims of the old and historic regiments against those of the Canadian Expeditionary Force battalions that had won the war. No one was left happy, except Otter, who received his final promotion to general in 1922, making him the second Canadian (Sir Arthur Currie being the first) to hold that rank.

Otter believed that discipline and training made efficient, capable soldiers. He was right, as the triumphs of the Canadian Corps had demonstrated in World War I. But for most of his extraordinarily lengthy military career, Otter was the proverbial voice in the wilderness. SEE ALSO: INTERNMENT; MILITIA; PERMANENT FORCE; RIDGEWAY; SOUTH AFRICAN WAR.

READING: Desmond Morton, *The Canadian General: Sir William Otter* (Toronto, 1974).

▲ Colonel William Dillon Otter in 1904.

Overseas Military Forces of Canada, Ministry of.
In October 1916, Prime Minister Sir Robert Borden created the Ministry of Overseas Military Forces of Canada (OMFC) in London to provide clear links between the Canadian Corps, the Canadian forces in Britain, and the government in Ottawa. The ministry's creation, made necessary by the mismanagement of the war effort by the minister of militia and defence, Sir Sam Hughes, established a Cabinet post in Britain with direct responsibility for the supply, maintenance, and command structure of the Canadian forces overseas. All other military matters would remain in the hands of the ministers of militia and defence and naval services in Ottawa. Outraged by the loss of his control of the forces overseas, Hughes was pushed into resigning. The first minister of the OMFC was Sir George Perley, hitherto the high commissioner in London, who served from 31 October 1916 to 11 October 1917. He was succeeded by Sir Edward Kemp who continued until 1920.

Paardeberg, Battle of (1900). Situated on the Modder River in the Orange Free State, Paardeberg was the site of the first significant action of the Canadian contingent in the South African War. The 2nd Battalion of the Royal Canadian Regiment (RCR), led by Colonel W.D. Otter, formed part of the 19th Brigade of the British 9th Division, commanded by Lieutenant-General Sir Henry Colville. The division goal was to cut off Boer general Piet Cronje's troops, besieging Kimberley. Cronje had no choice other than to retreat and, in late February 1900, he decided to make a stand at Paardeberg Drift. There he held the British off for ten days, at one point inflicting heavy casualties on the Canadians who had charged the Boer positions over open country. But in the early hours of 27 February, six companies of the RCR led a final assault that, while

▲ The Royal Canadian Regiment's share in the victory at Paardeberg brought renown to Canadian arms. This scene at the field hospital the following day indicates the heavy cost.

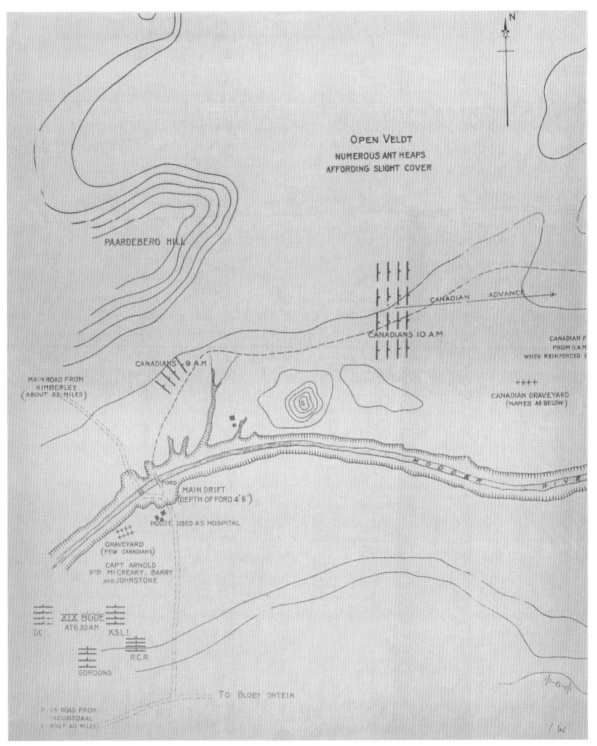

The map contains the following labels:

N

OPEN VELDT
NUMEROUS ANT HEAPS
AFFORDING SLIGHT COVER

PAARDEBERG HILL

CANADIAN ADVANCE

CANADIANS 10 A.M.

CANADIAN F
FROM 11 A.M
WHEN REINFORCED E

CANADIANS 9 A.M.

MAIN ROAD FROM
KIMBERLEY
(ABOUT 35 MILES)

++++
CANADIAN GRAVEYARD
(NAMES AS BELOW)

MODDER RIVER

FORD
MAIN DRIFT
(DEPTH OF FORD 4' 6")

HOUSE USED AS HOSPITAL

++++
GRAVEYARD
(FEW CANADIANS)

CAPT ARNOLD
PTES McCREARY, BARRY
AND JOHNSTONE.

XIX BGDE
AT 6.30 A.M.
D.C.
K.S.L.I.

R.C.R.

GORDONS

TO BLOEMFONTEIN

MAIN ROAD FROM
JACOBSDAAL
(ABOUT 40 MILES)

▲ The Royal Canadian Regiment's role in the battle at Paardeberg drew kudos from the British and spurred nationalism at home. Its position on 18 February 1900 is illustrated in this map, which served as an appendix to Colonel Otter's field report from South Africa.

largely rebuffed in substantial confusion, left some of the Canadians on high ground overlooking the Boer positions. This forced Cronje's surrender the next morning and resulted in much imperial praise for the Canadians. RCR casualties numbered more than 125, including 34 killed. SEE ALSO: OTTER; ROYAL CANADIAN REGIMENT; SOUTH AFRICAN WAR.

READING: Carman Miller, *Painting the Map Red: Canada and the South African War, 1899–1902* (Montreal, 1993).

Papineau, Louis-Joseph (1786–1871). The leader of the Rebellions of 1837 against British control in Lower Canada, Papineau was the leader of the Parti Canadien, later the Parti Patriote. Initially, he tried to get the British to liberalize the government by using the francophone majority in the Lower Canadian Assembly. When this failed, he concluded that only a rebellion could secure change. Gathering substantial numbers of Patriotes, essentially untrained and lightly armed local men, he took on British regulars and anglophone volunteers in a number of clashes, some bloody. At the battle of St Denis, the rebels forced British troops to withdraw, but at St Charles and, most notably, at St Eustache, the Patriotes suffered defeat, the rebellion collapsed, and Papineau—accused by some of his co-conspirators of cowardice—fled to the United States. He was blamed by many for the defeats in 1837 and did not take part in the renewed rebellion in 1838. Papineau returned to Canada in 1845 having been granted amnesty the previous year. He later opposed the Act of Union and advocated annexation to the United States. SEE ALSO: REBELLIONS OF 1837–1838.

Passchendaele, Battle of (1917). British planning for a major offensive in Flanders stretched back into 1916, as an effort to push German troops back from the city of Ypres, to outflank Germany's defensive lines from the north, and possibly to eliminate German submarine bases along the English Channel. In 1917, the plan came to fruition, in conjunction with a massive French offensive—ultimately unsuccessful— to the south under General Robert Nivelle. The British

attack, under Field Marshal Sir Douglas Haig, started in late July after a preparatory assault on Messines Ridge in June. Debate still rages over Haig's ultimate objectives and the importance of attrition in his plan to wear down German forces, but the Flanders offensive sought to break into the German lines, ease pressure on the French who had been all but paralyzed by mutinies and heavy losses, and reach the German U-boat bases along the Belgian coast to the north. The British offensive bogged down. Repeated assaults over appalling ground were unable to overcome German blockhouses, machine guns, and artillery. A defence-in-depth system saw attacking forces filtering through more weakly held frontal positions before being thrust back by strong counterattacks or smashed by German artillery barrages. The tactically important village of Passchendaele, situated on a low ridge, remained just out of reach. A failed attack in mid-October by British, New Zealand, and Australian troops cost 13,000 killed, wounded, and missing.

Haig's attacks persisted into the late fall, some formations, despite heavy casualties, enjoying moderate success with a bite-and-hold strategy that forced German units to concentrate farther forward where they were more vulnerable to the attackers' artillery fire. Still, it was a bloodbath, with little opportunity for any kind of breakthrough by the time Haig turned to the Canadian Corps to join the Passchendaele battle. After its successes at Vimy Ridge and Hill 70, the corps was increasingly considered an elite formation, but Passchendaele would represent one of its most difficult—if not its most difficult—tactical challenge. The Canadians were at least familiar with the terrain: the first division to arrive on the European continent had received its initiation into World War I at Ypres in April 1915; three years later, the trench lines had scarcely moved. Lieutenant-General Sir Arthur Currie, the corps' commander, inspected the battlefield and pronounced it dreadful. The battlefield approaching the ridge was a morass of mud, littered with the unburied bodies of men and horses, and dotted with all but impregnable German positions based around concrete blockhouses

▲ The mud at Passchendaele in October and November 1917 was horrendous, and the German defences were strong. The Canadian Corps suffered almost 16,000 casualties in taking the village ruins.

and pillboxes; from the low rise that dominated the area, the German lines looked over a virtual killing zone. One soldier aptly described the battlefield as "simply miles and miles of shell holes—all filled with water … " Moreover, Currie had no confidence in the Fifth British Army led by Sir Hubert Gough. He protested to Haig as strongly as he could without being sacked; he told him that taking the objective would cost 16,000 killed and wounded, and asked if it was worth the cost. Aware of the fragility of French army morale, Haig insisted it was, but he did agree that the Canadians could be switched to the Second British Army under General Sir Herbert Plumer. Currie also won more time to prepare, to move up supplies and more duckboards to permit men to move over the muddy devastation, and time to find firm

footings for his guns. His plan was to attack in a series of operations each with a limited objective until the destroyed village and a defensible position on the ridge had been occupied.

After five days of preliminary bombardment, 20,000 Canadians from the 3rd and 4th Divisions moved forward on 26 October under a heavy rolling barrage. The 3rd Division's objective was the Bellevue Spur, defended by pillboxes, and, despite the thick mud, they took it with the aid of grenades and machine guns; the 4th Division took Decline Wood, beyond their objective, but German counterattacks forced the infantry back. The next night, the Canadians retook the wood. (To call it a wood after months of bombardment was a misnomer; there was almost nothing there beyond occasional stumps.)

▲ Stretcher-bearers struggle to carry a wounded comrade from the morass of Passchendaele.

The Canadians then dug in as best they could in the mud, shelled continuously by the effective enemy guns. "I thought I had seen shell fire," Keith MacGowan, a young infantry officer, wrote home, "but I know now I never had before." He added that the Germans had also used gas against the Canadians and his men had to march wearing respirators: "You don't know what that means at night but take my word for it that next to being blinded it comes first." Casualties in some battalions reached 75 percent, and one company of the Princess Patricia's Canadian Light Infantry (PPCLI) ended the operation with a corporal commanding a company. "The 160 men we have left" in the PPCLI, its commanding officer wrote, "are cheerful and at this moment singing."

The Canadian assault resumed on 30 October, the 1st and 2nd Divisions taking the lead in co-operation with the 2nd British Corps. Under heavy artillery support and in a teeming rain, the troops moved forward to the edge of Passchendaele. There they held on for five days in mud and cold while the Germans shelled and sniped. Lieutenant Andrew Wilson from Rosetown, Saskatchewan, wrote in his diary: "Very cold and wet all day. We stood in water or mud all night. Terrific shell fire kept up continuously. Night was bitterly cold. Thought I could not hold out, as my feet and arms and legs were wet. Had a leather jerkin on which kept my body dry. Could not move all night. Had to hold up another officer who was sick all night. Night was bitterly long. Everybody down-hearted, so cold and miserable. At daylight we were sniped at again and had to keep low out of sight. Many men had to go out completely exhausted."

Meanwhile, Currie prepared for the final push. His objective was the high ground north of the village ruins and a defensible position on the eastern slope of Passchendaele Ridge. The attack jumped off on 6 November and, after some bayonet fighting, the 2nd Division seized the village. German counterattacks were driven off and, by day's end, the 1st and 2nd Divisions firmly held the ridge. Four days later, Currie launched small advances to straighten the Canadian line. On 14 November, at last, the Canadians left the area, having fired almost 1.5 million artillery shells.

For the wounded and for the stretcher-bearers who had to move them to the rear, Passchendaele had been a muddy hell. One soldier, shot in the knee, recalled that "The only way to move [my] stretcher was to push it foot-by-foot, almost inch-by-inch, over the surface. Then for each to hang on to it and drag first one leg and then the other out of the mire to replace it with more mire, perhaps a foot or so further on our way." Private John Sudbury noted that it took four hours to reach the dressing station 274 metres away. The mud in his wound led to gangrene and the amputation of his left leg.

In two weeks of savage fighting in impossible conditions, the Canadian Corps had seized Passchendaele but lost 15,654 in killed, wounded, and missing, almost precisely what Currie had estimated. This was dreadful, but it was small compared to British and Anzac losses of 310,000 and the enemy casualties that were estimated at 260,000. Haig made no further attempt to move against the U-boat bases, so exhausted were the British armies. Sadly, tragically, Passchendaele fell without a fight to the Germans when their huge March 1918 offensive rolled over the British lines. It was recaptured for good in September.

In June 1918, Prime Minister Sir Robert Borden attended the Imperial War Cabinet in London. Well briefed by General Currie, he told David Lloyd George, Britain's prime minister, that "if there is ever a repetition of Passchendaele, not a Canadian soldier will leave the shore of Canada so long as the Canadian people entrust the Government of Canada to my hands." SEE ALSO: BORDEN, ROBERT; CANADIAN CORPS; CURRIE.

READING: Dean F. Oliver, "The Canadians at Passchendaele," in Peter Liddle, ed., *Passchendaele in Perspective: The Third Battle of Ypres* (London, 1997); G.W.L. Nicholson, *Canadian Expeditionary Force, 1914–1919* (Ottawa, 1962).

Patriotes. The Patriotes of 1837–1838 in Lower Canada drew their support from a popular, democratic, liberal, and anti-colonialist movement, mainly but by no means exclusively French-speaking. The colony's governor and his largely English-speaking merchant supporters blocked the Patriotes' efforts at reform in the legislative assembly. The Patriotes' leaders, Louis-Joseph Papineau, Jean-Olivier Chenier, Thomas Brown, and Dr Wolfred Nelson, stymied in their legal efforts at reform, became increasingly ready to rise in revolt. The Rebellions of 1837–1838 featured several bloody skirmishes, but were put down with an iron hand by British troops and their colonial volunteers. The rebels faced execution, imprisonment, or exile, and the homes of many were razed. SEE ALSO: PAPINEAU; REBELLIONS OF 1837–1838.

Patriot Hunters. After the failure of the Rebellions of 1837 in Lower and Upper Canada, many of the rebels fled to the United States and continued their agitation, soon gathering American supporters who shared their desire to liberate Canada from British control. The Patriot Hunters, or Hunters' Lodges, planned a major invasion in 1838 but soon dropped this in favour of raids on Lower Canadian border towns and Prescott, Upper Canada. None of these attempts made much headway, and the British authorities dealt severely with any Patriot Hunters they captured. The Hunters' efforts continued into 1840 when several former rebels blew up the monument to British General Sir Isaac Brock at Queenston. The movement collapsed soon after when US authorities finally ordered the agitation to cease.

Peacekeeping. Peacekeeping—the interposition of observers or of an armed force either by an international organization or by a group of powers

These peacekeepers at a Middle Eastern outpost represent what most Canadians perceived as United Nations duty: watching trouble spots and keeping belligerents apart. It was often true, and often far more dangerous.

acting together to report on or separate actual or potential combatants—was first conceived by the League of Nations in 1931 with the "Convention to Improve the Means of Preventing War." The League, however, was incapable of mounting any peacekeeping operations. The United Nations (UN), created in 1945, aimed to do better.

Peacekeeping was clearly envisaged in the UN Charter that outlined a mechanism for the mobilization and command by a UN commander of the forces of member countries when deemed necessary by the Security Council for collective security. Cold War manoeuvring made the original idea impossible to achieve, but peacekeeping did develop. The UN Security Council authorized a number of military and armistice observer groups prior to 1956; examples include the UN Military Observer Group in India and Pakistan (UNMOGIP) that tried to keep peace in the disputed state of Kashmir, and the UN Truce Supervisory Organization

(UNTSO) that sought to maintain the truce between Israel and its neighbours after the formation of the Jewish state in 1948. Such forces required the consent of the states involved and depended for their effectiveness on demonstrable neutrality and the continuing support of all major parties to the conflict. But the first UN peacekeeping effort involving formed forces rather than simply observers was the UN Emergency Force (UNEF) set up in the autumn of 1956 after the Israeli-British-French attack on Egypt. UNEF involved several thousand armed soldiers from a number of nations—none of them great powers—and came to include transport and observer aircraft and armoured reconnaissance vehicles. Once again, the consent of the states involved was a requirement, and the principle that great powers not be directly involved also developed (although US logistical support frequently came to be essential).

Canada has played a continuing role in peacekeeping, both inside the United Nations and in support of other international agencies or conventions. Although there was little or no enthusiasm for the task in the Canadian military in the immediate postwar years—the soldiers viewing it as a distraction from the urgent necessity of preparing to resist the Soviet Union—Canadians nonetheless served with UNMOGIP and UNTSO and in the International Control Commissions set up in 1954 in the three states of Indochina. The secretary of state for external affairs, Lester B. Pearson, was the prime initiator of the idea of UNEF during the Suez Crisis in October–November 1956, and he won the Nobel Peace Prize for his efforts. The Security Council, paralyzed by its rivalries and vetoes, could not act, so the General Assembly stepped in to create the necessary force.

The Louis St Laurent government then suggested that an infantry battalion of the Queen's Own Rifles of Canada be sent to UNEF, but Egyptian President Gamal Abdel Nasser objected. The Canadians, Egypt claimed with some justification, dressed much like British troops, had the Union Jack on their flag, then the Red Ensign, spoke English, and were longtime allies of Britain and France. How could Egyptians be expected to distinguish between the Queen's Own and

▲ Canadian armoured personnel carriers in Cyprus, part of a 30-year peacekeeping mission.

the invaders? There was much truth in these concerns, but UNEF's commander, Canadian Major-General E.L.M. Burns, who had been leading UNTSO and was in the area, managed to persuade Egypt to accept Canadian logistics units (later expanded to include armoured reconnaissance and air units). As a result, some 1,000 Canadians served with UNEF from its inception until May 1967 when they were expelled from Egypt by President Nasser who accused Canada of siding with Israel in the period immediately preceding the Six Day War of June 1967.

Pearson's Nobel Peace Prize helped him win the Liberal leadership and become prime minister, and other politicians sometimes thought they might improve their prospects by putting Canada into more UN operations. As a result, Canadians served in a host of other UN Chapter VI peacekeeping operations (those requiring lightly armed, blue beret-wearing troops with restrictive rules of engagement), and by far the majority of those formed. Canada contributed significant

contingents to those in the Congo (1960–1964), Cyprus (1964–1993), and Egypt (UNEF II, 1973–1979). Canada also contributed to non-UN peacekeeping efforts in Vietnam with the International Commission for Control and Supervision (1973), and again in Egypt in the Multinational Force and Observers (1986–present).

Canadians, who believed that their participation in peacekeeping demonstrated that they were impartial, if not quite neutral, failed to realize that peacekeeping was part of the Cold War. In Indochina in 1954, Canada was the Western representative on a three-nation commission, alongside Communist Poland and neutral India. In 1956, the Soviet Union, playing the anti-colonialist card, had interests in stirring up Egyptian nationalism, which resulted in Nasser's nationalization of the Suez Canal, the *casus belli* for the British and French who colluded with the Israelis. UNEF let London and Paris escape from Egypt with a few (very few) shreds of dignity and, with Washington furious at them, stopped NATO from falling apart less than a decade after it had been formed. Similarly, the Congo was another Soviet anti-imperialist front, and the UN force there in 1960 can be explained as much on the basis of Congo's strategic mineral resources as on the grounds of peace and security, much less humanitarianism which was rarely a peacekeeping concern. And Cyprus, in 1964, pitted NATO members Greece and Turkey against each other; a war over Cyprus threatened to leave NATO's southern flank in ruins and the eastern Mediterranean vulnerable to Soviet influence. In other words, Canada participated in several UN operations not despite its NATO and Western democratic credentials, but because of them.

Cyprus illustrates another failing of peacekeeping: sometimes it never ends. By the time Canada finally pulled its troops out of Cyprus, 30 years of futility had passed. Some Canadian soldiers served seven or eight tours on the island, and peace was no closer when the Canadian Forces left in 1993 than when they had arrived in 1964. It may be good to freeze a crisis in place, but peacekeeping seemed sometimes to mean forever, stasis sometimes providing the excuse for erstwhile combatants never to speak seriously of peace. The same might be said of the UN missions on the Israeli-Arab borders. Peacekeeping missions sometimes led nowhere, or threatened to, in the absence of real negotiation between serious-minded adversaries.

When the Cold War ended with the collapse of the Soviet Union at the beginning of the 1990s, nationalisms that had been held in check by the superpower conflict flared anew, and peacekeeping entered a new phase. In the five years from 1996, the United Nations created 24 new peacekeeping operations, six more than in the previous 43 years. In late 2006, more than 80,000 soldiers from 82 countries were deployed on UN operations, and the UN, notoriously inefficient, scarcely seemed able to cope. Canadian Major-General Lewis MacKenzie, who served in the former Yugoslavia, has often remarked that if he called UN headquarters from Srebrenica after-hours or on the weekend no one answered the telephone. (This, at least, has now been remedied.)

These 1990s situations were different in many cases than those that occurred during the Cold War. Conflicts in Somalia and the former Yugoslavia, for example, were internal to nation states, in effect civil wars that posed new problems. UN forces monitored human rights, trained police forces (with Canadian municipal forces and the RCMP providing police officers for such duties), and tried to ensure the delivery and distribution of relief supplies. Such conflicts also frequently required UN forces that could fight to defend themselves from attack and sometimes to protect ethnic groups under attack. Not all UN forces to enter zones of conflict had been invited, and not all those that were invited received a lasting welcome. These were either UN Chapter VII peace enforcement operations with robust rules of engagement or operations conducted by NATO, an alliance increasingly treated by UN officials as the global organization's de facto peace enforcement arm. Other regional organizations, notably in Africa, seemed to assume the same status. Canada had soldiers committed to such operations, fought major battles (as in the Medak pocket in Croatia in 1993), and suffered casualties. Later, Canadian troops operated (especially after the Somalia operation revealed serious command and discipline problems in the Canadian Forces) under sometimes too restrictive interpretations of the rules of engagement that limited how the soldiers could act in dangerous circumstances in order to avoid problems for their superiors or the politicians. Canadians' early reputation in former Yugoslavia as soldiers who could not be cowed threatened to erode as politically inspired restrictions limited their effectiveness. The Canadian units were ordinarily abbreviated to "Canbat" or Canadian Battalion; after a time, some British officers in former Yugoslavia came to call them "Can't bat," a slur that stung because it seemed to be true.

Major-General Lewis MacKenzie nevertheless had become a popular hero in Canada for his willingness to use force in trying to distribute relief supplies in Srebrenica during the Yugoslav ethnic fighting in 1992. Major-General Roméo Dallaire, commanding a small, powerless UN mission in Rwanda in 1993–1994,

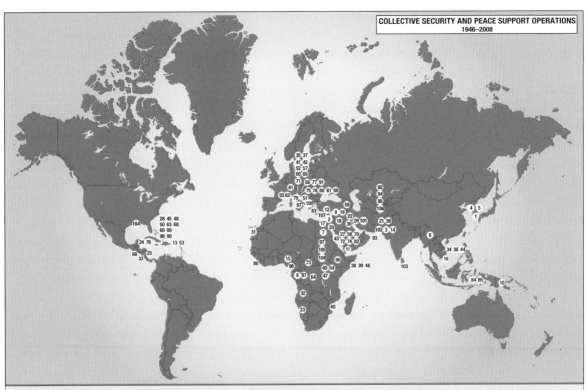

1 South Korea, 1947–1948: UNTCOK

2 Israel, 1948– : UNTSO

3 India and Pakistan, 1949–1996: UNMOGIP

4 Korean Peninsula, 1950–1953: United Nations Command Korea

5 Korea, 1953–2003: UNCMAC

6 Indochina, 1954–1974: ICSC

7 Egypt, 1956–1967: UNEF I

8 Lebanon, 1958: UNOGIL

9 Republic of the Congo, 1960–1964: ONUC

10 West New Guinea, 1962–1963: UNSF

11 Yemen, 1963–1964: UNYOM

12 Cyprus, 1964– : UNFICYP

13 Dominican Republic, 1965–1966: DOMREP

14 India and Pakistan, 1965–1966: UNIPOM

15 Nigeria, 1968–1970: OTN

16 South Vietnam, 1973: ICCS

17 Egypt and Israel, 1973–1979: UNEF II

18 Syrian Golan Heights, 1974– : UNDOF

19 Lebanon, 1978– : UNIFIL

20 Sinai, 1986– : MFO

21 Afghanistan and Pakistan, 1988–1990: UNGOMAP

22 Iran and Iraq, 1988–1991: UNIIMOG

23 Namibia, 1989–1990: UNTAG

24 Central America, 1989–1992: ONUCA

25 Nicaragua, 1989–1990: ONUVEN

26 Afghanistan and Pakistan, 1990–1993: OSGAP

27 Persian Gulf, 1990–1991: Gulf War

28 Haiti, 1990–1991: ONUVEH

29 Iraq, 1991–1999: UNSCOM

30 Kuwait, 1991–2003: UNIKOM

31 Western Sahara, 1991– : MINURSO

32 Angola, 1991–1995: UNAVEM II

33 El Salvador, 1991–1995: ONUSAL

34 Cambodia, 1991–1992: UNAMIC

35 Former Yugoslavia, 1992–1995: ECMMY

36 Cambodia, 1992–1993: UNTAC

37 Former Yugoslavia, 1992–1995: UNPROFOR I and II

38 Somalia, 1992–1993: UNOSOM I

39 Somalia, 1992–1993: UNITAF

40 Mozambique, 1992–1994: ONUMOZ

41 Former Yugoslavia, 1992–1994: UNCOE

42 Former Yugoslavia, 1992–1996: UNHCR

43 Red Sea, 1992–1997: MIF

44 Cambodia, 1992–2000: CMAC

45 Haiti, 1993– : MICIVIH

46 Somalia, 1993–1995: UNOSOM II

47 Uganda and Rwanda, 1993–1994: UNOMUR

48 Haiti, 1993–1996: UNMIH

49 Rwanda, 1993–1996: UNAMIR

50 Haiti Embargo Enforcement, 1993–1994

51 Bosnia-Herzegovina, 1993–1995: No-Fly Zone

52 Former Yugoslavia, 1993–1996: UN Naval Embargo

53 Dominican Republic, 1994: Military Observer Group

54 Rwanda, 1994: Provision of Humanitarian Aid

55 Croatia, 1995–1996: UNCRO

56 Former Yugoslav Republic of Macedonia, 1995–1999: UNPREDEP

57 Former Yugoslavia, 1995–2002: UNMIBH

58 Persian Gulf, 1995: MIF

59 Nagorno-Karabakh, 1995–1996: OSCE

60 Former Yugoslavia, 1995–1996: IFOR

61 Eastern Slavonia, Baranja, and Western Sirmium, 1996–1998: UNTAES

62 Croatia, 1996–2002: UNMOP

63 Haiti, 1996–1997: UNSMIH

64 Zaire, 1996: MNF

65 Former Yugoslavia, 1996–1997: UNMACBH

66 Guatemala, 1997: MINUGUA

67 Italy, 1997–1998: MAMDRIM

68 Haiti, 1997: UNTMIH

69 Haiti, 1997–2000: MIPONUH

70 Persian Gulf, 1997: MIF

71 Former Yugoslavia, 1997– : SFOR

72 Persian Gulf, 1998: Coalition Deployment to the Persian Gulf

73 Central African Republic, 1998–2000: MINURCA

74 Persian Gulf, 1998: MIF

75 Kosovo, 1998–1999: KDOM/KVM

76 Central America, 1998: JTFCAM

77 Former Yugoslav Republic of Macedonia, 1998–1999: NATO Extraction Force

78 Kosovo, 1999: Kosovo Verification Co-ordination Centre

79 Albania and Macedonia, 1999: Humanitarian Airlift

80 Kosovo, 1999–2002: UNMIK

81 Kosovo, 1999: UNMACC

82 Persian Gulf, 1999: MIO

83 Turkey, 1999: Disaster Assistance Response Team

84 East Timor, 1999–2000: INTERFET

85 East Timor, 1999–2001: UNTAET

86 Sierra Leone, 1999–2005: UNAMSIL

87 Democratic Republic of the Congo, 1999– : MONUC

88 Kosovo, 1999–2002: KFOR

89 Haiti, 2000: MICAH

90 Ethiopia and Eritrea, 2000– : UNMEE

91 Former Yugoslav Republic of Macedonia, 2001: NATO Operation Essential Harvest

92 Afghanistan, 2001–2002: Operation Enduring Freedom

93 Persian Gulf/Arabian Sea/Indian Ocean, 2001– : Operation Enduring Freedom

94 Afghanistan, 2002–2005: UNAMA

95 Afghanistan, 2003– : ISAF

96 Cameroon/Nigeria, 2003–2004: Advisor to SRSG

97 Sudan, 2003–2007: African Union Mission in Sudan

98 Haiti, 2004: MIF

99 Haiti, 2004– : MINUSTAH

100 Bosnia-Herzegovina, 2004–2007: EUFOR

101 Iraq, 2004–2007: UNAMI

102 Pakistan, 2005: Disaster Assistance Response Team

103 Sri Lanka, 2005: Disaster Assistance Response Team

104 United States Gulf Coast, 2005: Humanitarian Relief, Hurricane Katrina

105 Sudan, 2005– : UNMIS

106 Afghanistan, 2006: Operation Enduring Freedom

107 Cyprus/Lebanon, 2006: Evacuation of Canadian Citizens

108 Sudan, 2007– : UNAMID

▲ After the 1956 Suez Crisis, peacekeeping became the one military role Canadians liked. Dozens of missions followed.

became a hero despite his force's complete inability to prevent the tribal warfare between Hutu and Tutsi that degenerated into genocidal killings that left 800,000 Tutsi dead. Dallaire's later struggles with post-traumatic stress disorder because of what he had seen moved the public; his willingness to talk and write about his problems drew attention to those suffered by other CF members who had seen horrors in Bosnia, Croatia, Serbia, Somalia, and elsewhere.

As peacekeeping evolved into peace enforcement and peacemaking, becoming both more varied and more difficult, regional organizations such as NATO, the African Union (AU), and the European Union began to move into the field. Almost always, UN sanction was given to such operations, but some turned from peacekeeping to war, as in Kosovo in 1999, when a NATO-led force launched air attacks on Serbia without the approval of the UN Security Council in order to prevent the ethnic cleansing of ethnic Albanians inside Serbia's Kosovo province. The former Yugoslavia's conflicts spawned a plethora of UN forces, much as has the long Israeli-Arab conflict or the struggles along the Ethiopian-Eritrean border.

The new string of crises led some countries to create a rapidly deployable UN force. Canada had long had a standby battalion designated for UN service and, for example, deployed it to Cyprus in 1964 when the UN operation there was formed. But in 1996, Canada, Austria, Denmark, Norway, Sweden, the Netherlands, and Poland agreed to create the Multinational Standby High Readiness Brigade for UN Operations (SHIRBRIG). This was essentially a commander and a planning cell along with paper commitments of troops. It was used four times after its creation, most often employing its staff officers with or without some troops and, though ceasing operations in 2009, was a useful step forward for the UN.

The United Nations has grappled with the difficulties of intervening within nations that disregard the human rights of some or all of its population. Zimbabwe is one such example of a nation-state that has destroyed its peoples' lives through maladministration and corruption. No UN action to intervene has been taken because none could be agreed. Darfur in

the Sudan is another example, where one part of the population is killing another part. Although the UN discussed placing a mission in the area, Sudan has refused permission for anything meaningful, though it accepts a toothless OAU force. Especially under Liberal foreign minister Lloyd Axworthy (1995–2000), Canada tried to give meaning to the concept of the Responsibility to Protect (R2P), but the difficulties are formidable and the residual regard for state sovereignty strong.

The war in Korea (1950–1953) and the first Gulf War (1991) were not peacekeeping operations but exercises in collective security under the UN banner. Canada sent in all more than 30,000 armed forces personnel to Korea during and after hostilities, with an infantry brigade group, a number of destroyers, and an air transport squadron. A squadron of fighter jets, ground support personnel, several warships, and medical personnel were dispatched to the Gulf War. Similarly, the Afghanistan War (which began in 2001 and is ongoing), while authorized by the United Nations, is being pursued by NATO and associated states. Canada has participated in Afghanistan since the war began.

As noted above, since Lester Pearson won the Nobel Peace Prize in 1957, the Canadian public and Canadian politicians have considered peacekeeping one of the premier roles of the Canadian Forces, although its importance to the military—and sometimes to the government—has waxed and waned. The Defence White Paper of 1964, issued by the Pearson government, first mentioned peacekeeping as a Canadian defence priority and placed it high on the list. The 1971 White Paper produced by Pierre Trudeau's government that scorned the idea of Canada as "a helpful fixer," however, placed it at the bottom of the priority list. The Canadian Forces nonetheless have remained in demand for UN peacekeeping because of its special skills in communications and other logistical areas and because of Canada's continuing willingness to show the flag and to provide training for its personnel and those from other nations. As defence budgets fell in the period after 1968, peacekeeping—because it was relatively cheap in terms of soldiers' lives and because heavy equipment that Canada lacked or had only in obsolescent models was not ordinarily required—became a favoured activity that the nation's underequipped forces could do and the Canadian public, French- and English-speaking—liked. Peacekeeping was a useful contribution, but it was no panacea, no solvent for every intractable problem. Nor was it without cost. Few knew that some 116 Canadians had been killed in UN and other peace missions (to 2010), including nine when three Syrian surface-to-air missiles shot down a small Canadian aircraft painted in UN colours in 1974.

Under General Rick Hillier, the chief of the defence staff from 2005 to 2008, the Canadian Forces made a concerted effort to demonstrate that its roles went beyond peacekeeping. "We're the Canadian Forces, we kill people" was the new characterization that, however crudely put, expressed the reality. A trained military force can do peacekeeping of the most benign blue beret form, handle the many more rigorous variants of peacemaking and peace enforcement and, if necessary, fight a war. A force trained only for peacekeeping can do nothing else, and generals like Hillier believed that the national mindset had come to believe that all Canada did and should do was peacekeeping. To Hillier, that had to be changed. The long UN-sanctioned, NATO-led Afghanistan War perhaps has begun to alter such perceptions, and at no appreciable diminution in public support for the armed forces. SEE ALSO: DALLAIRE; MACKENZIE, LEWIS; MEDAK POCKET; SOMALIA AFFAIR.

READING: Sean Maloney, *Canada and UN Peacekeeping* (St Catharines, ON, 2003); Jocelyn Coulon, *Casques Bleus* (Montreal, 1994).

Pearson, Lester Bowles (1897–1972). The son of an Ontario clergyman, Lester Pearson was in university when in April 1915 he volunteered to join the University of Toronto's hospital unit in the Canadian Expeditionary Force in World War I. He served on the Salonika front for 18 months until early 1917 when he went to England for officer training. In October, Pearson decided to train as a pilot—his instructor nicknamed him Mike, which stuck—but his military career ended from a combination of being hit by a bus and neurasthenia (in effect, a nervous breakdown). Pearson returned to Canada, completed his university degree, and sought work in the United States. He won a scholarship to Oxford University where he became famous as "Herr Zigzag" on the Oxford hockey team, and then secured a post in the history department at the University of Toronto. Pearson soon took the examinations for the Department of External Affairs, and began his life as a civil service mandarin in Ottawa in 1928.

Pearson's career in the department was exceptional. He worked on tasks for O.D. Skelton, the undersecretary, and for Prime Minister R.B. Bennett. He took a posting to London where he effectively ran the High Commission for the socialite Vincent Massey, from which vantage point he watched the world drift again to war. Pearson was a nationalist and a neutralist, but once the war against Hitler began, he favoured a major Canadian effort. He returned to Ottawa in 1941 and was soon posted to Washington, where he worked to coordinate the North American

Lester "Mike" Pearson in 1944.

war effort and to create the new United Nations in 1945. After serving as ambassador to the United States, he returned to Canada in 1947 as undersecretary; the following year, he entered politics as secretary of state for external affairs in Louis St Laurent's government.

It was Pearson, a committed anti-Communist and internationalist, who directed Canada's entry into the North Atlantic Treaty Organization (NATO), its commitment to the Korean War, and the dispatch of troops to Europe. And it was Pearson in 1956, as Britain and France colluded with Israel in an attack on Egypt, who tried to rescue Canada's mother countries from political and military foolishness by proposing the creation of a UN Emergency Force to separate the combatants. In effect, Pearson was trying to save the Western alliance, as the United States bitterly opposed the British and French action, which occurred at the same time as the Soviet Union was crushing the Hungarian revolution. Pearson succeeded in getting UNEF established and won the Nobel Peace Prize, but not before Canada suffered substantial humiliation when the Egyptians tried to block Canadian participation in the UN force.

Pearson's efforts at the UN did not save the Liberals from defeat in the 1957 election, and indeed may have contributed to it. Elected Liberal leader in 1958, he sat in Opposition until 1963. What brought him back to power was, first, John Diefenbaker's ineptitude and, second, the issue of nuclear weapons. Diefenbaker had agreed to arm Bomarc missiles in Canada and Canada's NATO forces in Europe with nuclear weapons, but his Cabinet was divided and the prime minister dithered. After opposing the acquisition for years, Pearson sensed a political opportunity and reversed his position: Canada must meet its alliance commitments. The Diefenbaker government fell, an election resulted, and Pearson was in power with a minority government. He duly took the warheads and worked to restore better relations with the United States.

That would prove difficult, not least because of the Vietnam War that increased in ferocity during Pearson's five years in power. Canada could resist US calls for a military commitment to the war because it had had military observers there since 1954 at great power request. But Pearson could not resist interjecting Canada into the American debate on the war. At one point in 1965, extraordinarily, he called for the United States to stop bombing North Vietnam—in a speech in Philadelphia. President Lyndon Johnson was furious and did not forgive Pearson for "pissing on my rug." On the other hand, Johnson had been hugely grateful when Pearson's government quickly sent troops to Cyprus to form a UN force and to prevent a Greek-Turkish war over the island.

Pearson's government also launched the Canadian military on a new course by first integrating the three services, and then unifying them into a single service in 1968. A single chief of the defence staff had already replaced the three service heads, and the Canadian Forces organized themselves on a functional basis. Unification was a heated political and military issue, pitting veterans and serving soldiers, sailors, and fliers against defence minister Paul Hellyer and the Liberal government. Pearson wobbled on the issue but ultimately backed his minister. The Canadian Forces remain a unified, single-service military.

Mike Pearson's career was extraordinary. He was the first Canadian diplomat to achieve international acclaim, and his record as prime minister is now adjudged to have been almost as successful. His apparent contradictions—a peacemaker who acquired nuclear weapons, a Europeanist who sided against the mother countries in Egypt, a Cold War stalwart who piqued the United States on its own turf—are more explicable in light of broader aspects of his character. A committed realist, Pearson saw Canada's position within the Western alliance as central to its international persona and future prospects, and worked to place both national policy and international security on stable footings. He was no idealist, and tactical opportunism could sometimes be seen as inconsistency, perhaps even hypocrisy. He acquired weapons he would rather have eschewed, tweaked allies he knew were essential to Canadian interests, and drove common sense solutions where hyperbole was difficult to resist. He supported a reformed NATO, an effective UN, and a capable Canadian military. He understood the value of effective diplomacy abroad and social justice at home. He ranks regularly in public surveys as one of Canada's greatest leaders. SEE ALSO: CANADA–UNITED STATES DEFENCE RELATIONS; HELLYER; PEACEKEEPING; SUEZ CRISIS; UNIFICATION.

READING: John English, *The Life of Lester Pearson,* 2 vols. (Toronto, 1989–1992).

Pegahmagabow, Francis (1891–1952). The most decorated First Nations soldier of World War I, Corporal Pegahmagabow won the Military Medal and two bars during his service throughout the entire war with the 1st Canadian Infantry Battalion of the 1st Canadian Infantry Division. An Ojibwa from Ontario's Parry Island Band, "Peggy" enlisted in 1914, becoming a messenger, a scout, and an enormously successful sniper, reputedly with more than 300 "kills." The records are scanty, and he did his sniping alone, so there is no verification for the numbers. He is believed to have won his first Military Medal for his long service as a messenger at the front in 1915–1916, his second at Passchendaele in 1917, and his third at Amiens in 1918. Only 39 members of the Canadian Expeditionary Force won the Military Medal and two bars. Wounded in 1916 on the Somme, Pegahmagabow came back to Canada in 1919 after the war. A building at Canadian Forces Base Borden was named in his honour in 2006.

Pensions, Military. Patriotism or public pressure impels citizens into military service in time of war, but the killed, bereaved, and injured sometimes seem to be forgotten by their governments. Canada knew very little of caring for large numbers of veterans until World War I. The country's military pension rules dated back to the 1885 Northwest Rebellion and, in reality, to the War of 1812 when land grants were offered to veterans and payments were given to relatives of those killed. The spouse of one officer killed at Batoche in 1885, for example, received an annual pension of $514; that of a gunner drew only $83. In 1901, a Militia Pension Act came into effect,

although private funds and charities continued to carry a disproportionate share of relief and post-service care. The South African War resulted in only a trickle of Canadian veterans, a small portion of them disabled. How could Canada re-establish its 70,000 disabled from the Great War, or its half-million veterans? In attempting to reduce costs and minimize the "pension evil," as it was known in the United States after its Civil War experience, Ottawa would retrain the disabled and pay military pensions. The Military Hospitals Commission, launched in 1915, ran a variety of job training programs (it was absorbed in 1918 into the federal Department of Soldiers' Civil Re-establishment), and the Board of Pension Commissioners, set up in 1916, also looked to retraining to ease the pension burden. Pensions were to be based on objective assessments of medical documentation, not on personal situation or heart-rending family appeals. There were allowances for wives and children, and pensions for the completely disabled were relatively generous—but only five percent could claim them. By 1918, 25,823 veterans received pensions totalling $7.27 million a year. Others took up land under the Soldier Settlement Act; many failed as they tried to farm less-than-arable land. Grievances arose quickly, veterans' associations developed and lobbied for a bonus and enhanced pensions, and appeal tribunals and a Pension Appeal Court took shape in an effort to ease complaints. In 1930, the Mackenzie King government passed the War Veterans Allowance Act that replaced the sliding scale military pension with monthly payments ($20 for the single and $40 for the married over the age of 60 who were in need). The successor government of R.B. Bennett created the Canadian Pensions Commission. Just before the outbreak of a new war, 98,000 veterans drew annual pensions amounting to $40.4 million, some eight percent of total federal government expenditures.

World War II created a huge new class of veterans—and much more generous terms for those who had served. The Veterans Charter offered a host of programs with equal benefits to men and women, while care for the disabled and the families of the dead was much enhanced. The Pension Act amendments of 1941, the establishment in 1944 of the Department of Veterans Affairs, and the implementation of the many and varied benefits that made up the Veterans Charter combined to offer arguably the most generous programs anywhere. Pensions payable to the disabled were $900 a year for a single veteran with additional benefits for those with a spouse and children, and Canada provided hospital beds for 17,000. By 1949–1950, $50.8 million was paid annually in pensions to disabled veterans and widows. Those costs rose yearly as new programs were added. In 2007, War Veterans Allowances offered to those with low incomes amounted to $462 million. World War II veterans, all now very old, benefit from a disability pension program, the Veterans Independence Program that helps them live in their own homes (and even arranges for their walks to be cleared after snowstorms), and a residential care program that houses them when they are unable to manage on their own. There is a funeral and burial program administered by the Last Post Fund.

The New Veterans Charter of 2006, aimed at modern-day veterans of the Canadian Forces, offered retraining and rehabilitation services, disability and death payments, and family support. SEE ALSO: VETERANS; VETERANS AFFAIRS, DEPARTMENT OF; VETERANS CHARTER; VETERANS' ORGANIZATIONS.

READING: Desmond Morton and Glenn Wright, *Winning the Second Battle: Canadian Veterans and the Return to Civilian Life, 1915–1930* (Toronto, 1987); Peter Neary and J.L. Granatstein, eds., *The Veterans Charter and Post–World War II Canada* (Montreal, 1998); Serge Durflinger, *Veterans with a Vision: Canada's War Blinded in Peace and War* (Vancouver, 2010).

Permanent Force (PF). The 1904 Militia Act established a ceiling of 4,000 officers and other ranks for a Permanent Force to garrison coastal fortifications and train the militia. This was the professional army that continued the traditions first established by the creation of two batteries of garrison artillery at Kingston and Quebec in 1871 and in 1883 by the founding of the Cavalry School Corps and the Infantry School Corps. On 1 April 1914, the PF comprised 3,110 all ranks belonging to various regiments and service and administrative personnel. Many Permanent Force officers saw service with the Canadian Expeditionary Force during World War I, but the bulk of the Canadian Corps' officers came from the militia or from civilians who enlisted. After the war, the PF continued trying to train itself and the militia with neither much modern equipment nor sufficient funding. On 31 March 1939, the PF numbered 4,169 all ranks including just 446 officers, some of whom were too old or too ill for war service. The regulars nonetheless provided most of the senior officers for Canada's World War II army, including A.G.L. McNaughton, H.D.G. Crerar, Guy Simonds, Christopher Vokes, E.L.M. Burns, and Charles Foulkes, the commanders of First Canadian Army and I and II Canadian Corps.

READING: Stephen J. Harris, *Canadian Brass: The Making of a Professional Army, 1860–1939* (Toronto, 1988).

Permanent Joint Board on Defence (PJBD). The PJBD was established as a result of the Ogdensburg Agreement entered into by US President Franklin D. Roosevelt and Canadian Prime Minister William Lyon Mackenzie King on 17 August 1940 and announced on 18 August, the first military alliance between the two nations. Although the United States was then a neutral and Canada a belligerent in World War II, the board was intended to provide direct military liaison and joint defence planning between the two governments, something needed more than ever for the defence of North America in the wake of the capitulation of France and the evacuation of the British Expeditionary Force from Dunkirk two months earlier. Although its role was most important during the period before the United States entered the war when it considered the defence of the coasts, how the two countries should react if Britain fell, and the overall defence of North America, the PJBD continued as a useful body for frank intergovernmental consultation on defence matters. In the period 1945 to 1950, the board handled a number of difficult tasks including a redefinition of US rights at its leased bases in Newfoundland and the formulation of recommendations to lay the basis for postwar joint defence co-operation.

The board now ordinarily meets twice a year, its sessions jointly directed by the US and Canadian chairs. It consists of military and civilian members, the Canadian section almost always including a politically appointed chair, a senior representative from the Department of Foreign Affairs and International Trade, and a number of military representatives and officials from the Department of National Defence. In the United States, the PJBD reports to the president through the secretary of state. In Canada, the board formally reports directly to the prime minister. Decisions of the PJBD were and are issued as joint, unanimous, numbered recommendations to both governments.

The PJBD's creation in 1940 generally was hailed in Canada as it guaranteed the Dominion's security in a world that had suddenly changed following Hitler's triumphs in Europe and the Japanese threat in the Pacific. But Conservative politicians felt uneasy at what they saw as a shift in allegiance orchestrated by Mackenzie King, a leader they perceived as pro-American and anti-British. Prime Minister Winston Churchill viewed the Ogdensburg Agreement in a similar light, growling at King when he heard of the arrangement. In fact, the August 1940 agreement allowed Canada to do its utmost for the defence of a beleaguered Britain without worrying about its own security, and it formally linked a belligerent Canada with the neutral United States, a factor of some geopolitical importance. But in the long run, the creation of the PJBD might well be considered as one of the major indicators of Canada's shift out of the British orbit, a situation brought about by Britain's military, economic, and political weakness. The secrecy of the PJBD's deliberations and terms of reference have sparked periodic protests against Canadian-American defence and security integration. SEE ALSO: CANADA–UNITED STATES DEFENCE RELATIONS; KING; NATIONAL INTERESTS.

READING: C.P. Stacey, *Arms, Men and Governments: The War Policies of Canada, 1939–1945* (Ottawa, 1970).

Petawawa, Canadian Forces Base. The Department of Militia and Defence purchased some 8,903 hectares of land at Petawawa, northwest of Ottawa, in 1904, and the first military training there occurred in 1905. During World War I, Petawawa housed an internment camp for enemy aliens, mainly Germans or Ukrainians (Ukraine then was under the Austro-Hungarian Empire), and soldiers were trained there for the Canadian Expeditionary Force. In World War II, Petawawa again served as an internment camp, primarily for German and Italian men deemed a threat under the terms of the Defence of Canada Regulations, and as a major army artillery and engineer training camp. It became a regular army base in 1946, and has remained so, though it is also the location for major militia summer training exercises. Petawawa's main tenant was the Special Service Force, which included the Canadian Airborne Regiment, from 1977 to 1995. It is now home to 2 Canadian Mechanized Brigade Group.

Petite Guerre, la. "Little war" refers to the seventeenth- and eighteenth-century style of guerrilla war, raids, and punitive expeditions waged by the numerically inferior habitants of New France against the English colonists to the south. New France had faced the raiding Iroquois and learned from them how to defend and how to attack, how to use raids, ambushes, and surprise, and how to move quickly and appear with overwhelming force amidst North America's broken landscape of forests, rivers, and hills. The French colonists and their Aboriginal allies could travel in winter on snowshoes and in summer by canoe, moving soundlessly and covering substantial distances at speed. Their strikes against English villages could be brutal, sudden death and massacre visited on sleeping men, women, and children. At Schenectady, New York, in 1690, for example, the raiders slaughtered 60, took as many captive, and spared only 50 before burning the village. Unpleasant as the tactic was, it likely helped to ensure New France's survival against a more numerous foe.

Phips, Sir William (c.1650–c.1694). Phips, born near the mouth of the Kennebec in what would become Maine, made his fortune and secured his knighthood by finding a treasure ship. He received command of an expedition against Acadia in 1690 and took and looted Port Royal bloodlessly. He then moved against Quebec in October with little preparation where he had the bad luck to face Count Frontenac, who had 3,000 troops, including colonial regulars. Phips asked Frontenac to surrender and received the famous response: there would be no reply "save from the mouths of my cannon and my musketry." Phips's expedition, losing many to disease and shipwreck, sailed away in frustration on 23–24 October.

Pig War, 1859. *See* SAN JUAN ISLAND DISPUTE.

Pinetree Line. During the Cold War, North America was vulnerable to attack by the Soviet Union's long-range bombers armed with nuclear weapons. To achieve maximum warning time, Canada and the United States built radar lines, one of which—the Pinetree Line—was wholly in southern Canada and along the eastern seaboard. With 44 radar stations from Vancouver Island to Newfoundland and Labrador, the line, agreed to by the two nations in 1951, was completed in 1954 at a construction cost of $450 million, of which the United States paid 66 percent. US Air Force personnel manned many sites, Royal Canadian Air Force personnel the remainder until the 1985 North American Air Defence Modernization program led to the line's phase-out.

Plains of Abraham. Located to the south and west of the walled citadel of Quebec, the plains were named after the farmer who once owned them and were the site of the battle on 13 September 1759 that decided the fate of New France during the Seven Years' War. The battle for Quebec was the culmination of a siege mounted by the British under the command of Major-General James Wolfe and Vice-Admiral Charles Saunders that began on 26 June 1759 when a British fleet anchored between the Île d'Orléans and the south shore of the St Lawrence, just downriver

from Quebec. The French, under Lieutenant-General the Marquis de Montcalm, planned to defend Quebec by holding the escarpments along the north shore from the Montmorency Falls, below Quebec, at least as far as Ste Foy, upriver from the city. This gave the British the opportunity to bombard Quebec at will from the south shore. Outnumbered, outgunned, and with no fleet available to help him, Montcalm's task was simple: to hold out until the onset of winter when the British would be compelled to withdraw.

As summer waned, Wolfe made several failed attempts to gain a decisive victory. Then, at the urging of his brigadiers, Wolfe on 9 September decided to place 4,400 troops with supporting artillery on the Plains of Abraham, using the small cove at Anse au Foulon as a landing spot. The cove had been left unguarded by the local French commander and, under cover of darkness on the night of 12 September, Wolfe's troops gained the shore, scaled the 55-metre heights to overpower the French troops above, hauling their artillery with them, and arrayed themselves in line of battle on the plains. The British had now cut the French supply lines to Montreal; their own water-borne supply line was secure.

Montcalm ought to have stayed behind the city walls or, if he thought he had to fight, to have waited for reinforcements. Instead, he decided to attack at once with the troops available, a mixed force of some 3,400 regulars and Canadien militia. He himself led the attack. As the French line neared the British, the Canadien militia took cover while some of those Canadiens in the ranks of the regulars broke ranks to reload, leaving gaps in the line and weakening the mass of fire that the French were able to bring to bear on their opponents. Under two or more deadly volleys of British musket fire, the French broke and retreated in disorder behind the city walls, the militia and natives effectively covering the retreat of the French regulars and trying to continue the fight. Montcalm and Wolfe were both mortally wounded, but the French army made its way out of Quebec to the west before Governor Pierre Rigaud de Vaudreuil ordered the city to surrender on 18 September. In the spring of 1760, the French almost succeeded in recapturing

THE BATTLE OF THE PLAINS OF ABRAHAM, FROM A SKETCH MADE ON THE 13TH SEP., 1759, BY CAPT. HERVEY, A.D.C. TO GENERAL WOLFE.

▲ Wolfe's aide, Captain Hervey Smyth, sketched the battle on the Plains of Abraham.

Quebec after their victorious battle at Ste Foy, but the early arrival of the Royal Navy at Quebec blocked this and led to their surrender at Montreal in September 1760. SEE ALSO: MONTCALM; QUEBEC (1759); WOLFE.

READING: D. Peter MacLeod, *Northern Armageddon: The Battle of the Plains of Abraham* (Vancouver, 2008).

Pontiac's War (1763–1766). Disgruntled with the spread of white settlement, Pontiac, an Ottawa war chief who had fought alongside the French, organized the Ottawa, Potawatomi, Huron, Ojibwa, and other tribes into an alliance in 1763 shortly after the signing of the Treaty of Paris. The result of the Seven Years' War had left the British in control of the Great Lakes and Ohio River valley but, despite the peace, French influence had not been extirpated. Pontiac's braves attacked Fort Detroit in May 1763, killing 46 British soldiers and putting the fort under siege. The alliance then widened and so did the scope of the attacks: eight British garrisons fell in a short period, and some 2,500 settlers were killed and more taken prisoner. At Bloody Run on 29 July, Pontiac defeated a strong

attack launched against him from Detroit. As winter approached, however, and help promised by French traders failed to materialize, the alliance began to disintegrate, helped along by the Royal Proclamation of October 1763 that seemed to secure the natives their land. The war dragged on nonetheless until Pontiac chose to conclude treaties to end the war in the summer of 1766. The subsequent Treaty of Fort Stanwix (1768) redefined the boundaries of the Indian territory that had been laid out by the Royal Proclamation and granted the British the right to settle, under certain conditions, along the Western frontier.

READING: R. Middleton, *Pontiac's War* (Milton Park, UK, 2007).

Pope, Georgina Fane (1862–1938). Born in Charlottetown, PEI, the daughter of a Father of Confederation, Pope trained as a nurse in New York City. She returned to Canada in 1899 and went overseas as the head of the first group of four Nursing Sisters dispatched to the South African War. She served in primitive conditions at British hospitals

Nursing Sister Georgina Fane Pope at the time of the South African War.

north of Cape Town and at Kroonstadt until her return to Canada in January 1901. Pope then took another group of eight nurses to South Africa in January 1902 and led them until the end of the war. She joined the Canadian Army Medical Corps as its first Nursing Sister in 1906, achieving the rank of matron in the Canadian Army Nursing Service in 1908. At age 55, she went overseas during World War I in 1917 but had to be invalided home the next year. Pope was later memorialized as one of the Valiants, a series of statues on Confederation Square in Ottawa near the National War Memorial, installed in 2006. See also: Canadian Army Nursing Service; South African War.

Popular Music in Wartime. Popular wartime music, like much of Canadian military music in general, had rich British roots, and soldiers and civilians alike sang songs such as "We're Marching to Pretoria,"

"Tipperary," and "Mademoiselle from Armentières." From the Seven Years' War onwards, however, Canadian militia sang songs glorifying themselves and the commanders they liked and, during the Fenian Raids, Canadian militia and civilian songs, often mawkishly patriotic, had brief popularity. During World War I, such pieces as James Willing's "The Canadian Soldier," Morris Manley's "Good Luck to the Boys of the Allies," and Gordon Thompson's World War I ditty, "When Your Boy Comes Back to You," and his "When We Wind Up the Watch on the Rhine," which apparently sold more than 100,000 copies of sheet music, were hugely popular in Canada. Written by the wounded Lieutenant Gitz Rice overseas, "Keep Your Head Down Fritzie Boy" was perhaps more realistic and reflective of soldiers' feelings. Rice's "Dear Old Pal of Mine" expressed well the soldiers' longing for the girls left behind. Another morbidly (but somewhat hopeful) popular tune had the words "The bells of hell ring ting-a-ling, -a-ling, a-ling / for you but not for me." Even classically trained composers like Healey Willan and Alexis Contant produced patriotic songs.

But the soldiers overseas were far more likely to sing self-generated ditties like "We're here / Because / We're here / Because / We're here / Because we're here," the repetition conveying the boredom and tedium of much of military life and the absolute necessity to complain about everything. Very anti-war and anti-patriotic was "I Don't Want to Die," while other songs were scatological: "Bull-shit, bull-shit, it all sounds / Like bull-shit to me, to me." Other favourites included the 700 versions of "Mademoiselle from Armentières" or "Hinky-Dinky-Parlez-Vous," which, in its endless quatrains, featured the "Three German officers" who "crossed the Rhine, parlez-vous . . . To fuck the women and drink the wine, / Hinky-Dinky parlez-vous."

In World War II, Captain Robert Farnon and the Canadian Band of the Allied Expeditionary Forces, formed in Canada and dispatched overseas in 1941, established a substantial presence on the BBC where it was the Canadian counterpart to Glenn Miller's wildly popular US Army Band in Britain. For the most part,

British and American songs swept the boards as the radio popularized the big band sounds of Miller, Tommy Dorsey, Artie Shaw, and Benny Goodman, or such British and American songs as Miller's "Don't Sit Under the Apple Tree," The Mills Brothers' "Paper Doll," Vera Lynn's "The White Cliffs of Dover" and "We'll Meet Again," and Gracie Fields's "Wish Me Luck as You Wave Me Goodbye."

Everywhere they served, Canadian military personnel sang these popular songs too, and in Canada they danced to the bands of Bert Niosi and Mart Kenney. But there were also songs that only servicemen sang, often bawdy, multi-verse laments at their treatment, the foibles of their officers and sergeants, and their longings for sex and home. "The North Atlantic Squadron" was likely the most famous with its chorus: "Away, away, with fyfe and drum / Here we come, full of rum / Looking for women to pat on the bum / In the North Atlantic Squadron." But the German song "Lili Marlene" was a favourite in all armies. All have been collected in Anthony Hopkins' *Songs from the Front and Rear—Canadian Servicemen's Songs of the Second World War* (1979). Some wartime multi-verse songs are still sung by present-day servicemen and women ("There were beans / Beans as big as submarines / In the stores, / In the stores / In the quartermaster's stores"), and Vera Lynn's World War II songs can still bring tears to the eyes of all those old enough to remember the 1940s. SEE ALSO: MILITARY MUSIC.

READING: Tim Cook, "The Singing War: Canadian Soldiers' Songs of the Great War," *American Review of Canadian Studies* (September 2009).

DISCOGRAPHY: "Waiting There for Me: Songs and Poems from Canadians in World War I" (St Jacobs, ON: Red Socks Company, 2007).

Post-Traumatic Stress Disorder (PTSD). PTSD is the now widely used name for a condition that was likely first identified in the American Civil War but is probably as old as warfare itself. Soldiers who fear for their lives for long periods or who have seen almost unimaginable horrors can become depressed and irritable, suffer flashbacks and serious clinical depression, and be reduced to immobility. In World War I, such conditions were called "shell shock" and were frequently attributed to cowardice. At least 9,000 Canadians suffered from shell shock, the treatment of which included electric shock therapy and aimed to get them back into the trenches. Senior officers were not immune from PTSD, but Sir Arthur Currie, in particular, went out of his way to find safe posts in which trusted but battle-weary officers might recover.

In World War II, the preferred term was "battle exhaustion," and neuropsychiatric units operating close to the front lines attempted to treat infantrymen (who made up 90 percent of such cases) with rest and drugs. But the willingness to consider battle exhaustion as a medical condition varied depending on the commander; some thought it malingering and prescribed punishment, not treatment. In the Royal Canadian Air Force, members of bomber crews who suffered from battle exhaustion were sometimes labelled "LMF" for lack of moral fibre.

PTSD was recognized as a condition in 1980 when the American Psychiatric Association listed it as a combat-related illness. For Canadians, the first major numbers of PTSD casualties in the post–Cold War era occurred in United Nations and other missions in former Yugoslavia in the early 1990s where ethnic cleansing, slaughters, and rapes of civilians were widespread. The Canadian Forces did not seem wholly sympathetic to PTSD sufferers until Lieutenant-General Roméo Dallaire, who had commanded the abortive UN mission in Rwanda in 1994 and been traumatized by the genocide he witnessed, went public with his own major PTSD problems. Dallaire pushed and pulled the Canadian Forces into treating the condition as a serious medical one. The Afghanistan War also produced numerous PTSD cases, in part, at least, because of fear of the wholesale employment by the insurgents of suicide bombers or Improvised Explosive Devices that could be blown up at any time.

PTSD is now accepted by the Canadian Forces as a mental illness caused or aggravated by psycho-logical trauma and is treated by drugs and/or cognitive-behavioural therapy. Veterans Affairs Canada in 2008 said that some 11,000 Canadians have been affected by PTSD; in August 2008, the Department of National Defence reported that 14.1 percent of soldiers returning from Afghanistan reported symptoms of Operational Stress Injuries while 6.5 percent of that total had PTSD symptoms. The expectation is that significant numbers will subsequently develop symptoms of stress-related illness; by 2010, estimates were as high as 6,000. In June 2009, the CF launched a major mental health awareness campaign for its service personnel. SEE ALSO: CASUALTIES; DALLAIRE.

READING: Patrick Brennan, "'Completely Worn Out by Service in France': Combat Stress and Breakdown among Senior Officers in the Canadian Corps," *Canadian Military History* (Spring 2009); Terry Copp and W. McAndrew, *Battle Exhaustion: Soldiers and Psychiatrists in the Canadian Army, 1939–1945* (Montreal, 1990).

Poundmaker (1842–1886). A Plains Cree, Poundmaker (Pitikwahanapiwiyin) was the adopted son of Crowfoot, a Blackfoot chief, and the nephew of an important Cree chief. Poundmaker became a band chief in 1879, three years after he reluctantly signed Treaty No. 6 with the federal government in the hopes of government assistance. During the 1885 Northwest Rebellion, led by Louis Riel, Poundmaker tried to restrain his followers from violence. He was ignored, and members of his band plundered Battleford. They were then engaged by Lieutenant-Colonel W.D. Otter's column at Cut Knife Hill on 2 May. The Cree inflicted 23 casualties on the Canadian troops and forced Otter to retreat. Poundmaker successfully stopped his men from attacking the retreating soldiers, but with the Metis defeated at Batoche on 12 May, there was no chance of success against the Northwest Field Force. Poundmaker duly surrendered to Major-General Frederick Middleton at Battleford on 23 May and was charged with felony-treason. He served only one year of his three-year sentence and died shortly after his release. SEE ALSO: CUT KNIFE HILL; NORTHWEST REBELLION.

Poundmaker, after the 1885 Northwest Rebellion.

Power, Charles Gavan (1888–1968). Seriously wounded during World War I service with the Canadian Expeditionary Force where he won the Military Cross for gallantry, "Chubby" Power returned to Canada in the fall of 1917 a determined opponent of conscription and a candidate for the Liberals in the December 1917 federal election. He won Quebec South, a seat in his hometown that he held until appointed to the Senate in 1955. Power entered the Mackenzie King Cabinet as minister of pensions and national health in 1935. In May 1940, King appointed him minister of national defence for air, with the primary responsibility of running the British Commonwealth Air Training Plan and managing the expansion of the Royal Canadian Air Force. He also served as associate minister of national defence (1940–1944), and as acting minister of national defence for one month in 1940 following the death in an air crash of Norman Rogers. A hard drinker sometimes much the worse for wear, Power nonetheless was the driving force behind the government's Canadianization policy that eventually resulted in the establishment of No. 6 Bomber Group overseas. In November 1944, he resigned from the Cabinet in protest over the introduction of conscription. See also: British Commonwealth Air Training Plan; Canadianization; Conscription; Quebec and the Military.

Reading: C.G. Power, *A Party Politician: The Memoirs of Chubby Power* (Toronto, 1966).

Preparedness Groups. An unmilitary people, at least in the popular imagination, Canadians have usually opted for defence on the cheap and rarely advocated for a more robust military. There have been occasions when public pressure led to greater defence efforts, but governments were usually not far behind their voters. Mackenzie King, for example, abandoned a "limited liability" war as much from the war itself having changed with French defeat in 1940 as from concentrated public pressure from the disciples of a larger army; Lester Pearson likewise understood John Diefenbaker's vulnerability over the acquisition of nuclear weapons as good politics and not as the result of populist militarism. This is not to say that the preparedness lobby has been inactive or entirely without influence on public affairs.

There have been a few civilian groups calling directly and explicitly for more to be done to prepare Canada's defences, from the militia lobby of the mid-nineteenth century—with its calls for a larger military, compulsory service, and better training—to the defence industrial associations of the present day. The Navy League, formed in 1896, trained Sea Cadets, but had little influence on Canada's naval policy. The Canadian Defence League, formed in 1909, called for universal military training. Despite well-heeled Toronto and Ontario supporters, the League folded

early in World War I—which, in the event, proved its case. The only organization of major consequence thereafter was the Conference of Defence Associations, created in 1932 to lobby for the militia. It laboured without much effect until the 1990s when defence cuts after the Cold War reduced the Canadian Forces in numbers and capabilities. The organization took in naval and air groups, began to be more active, and became genuinely influential in the new century. The various branches of the Royal United Services Institutes, sometimes just gentlemen's clubs, began to advocate, and industry groupings like the Canadian Defence Industries Association and the Canadian Defence Preparedness Association became more visible. The Canadian Institute for Strategic Studies, created in the 1970s and trying to bridge the public and the academy, continued to publish conference papers and reports until it disappeared in 2008. New organizations such as the Council for Canadian Security in the 21st Century (2001–2005) had some impact on informing Canadians of the condition of the Canadian Forces. What seems clear is that, by 2004, the calls for increased defence spending had begun to be heard by Liberals and Conservatives, and new policies and greater financial resources began to be allocated to defence by the governments of Paul Martin and Stephen Harper. Even so, peace organizations dwarfed in number and in influence the handful of defence preparedness organizations.

Prevost, Sir George (1767–1816). Prevost, born in New Jersey of Swiss Protestant parents, served in the West Indies until, in 1808, he won appointment as lieutenant-governor of Nova Scotia in the local rank of lieutenant-general. A pragmatic administrator, he did well enough that he became governor-in-chief of British North America and commander of British forces in 1811. Shrewd politically, he conciliated the French Canadians as he tried to prepare for the coming war with the United States. Short of troops and supplies, his strategy, once war began, was to stay on the defensive as ordered by London; thanks to this strategy and the active campaigning of Major-General Isaac Brock, Britain kept hold of Upper Canada in

▲ "Tommy" Prince (right) with his brother at Buckingham Palace, 1945.

1812. Prevost tried to counter growing US naval strength on the Great Lakes by leading an abortive operation against Sacket's Harbor, New York, in May 1813; the next year, with 15,000 veterans of the Napoleonic Wars now added to his strength, he moved against Plattsburgh, New York, in an effort to control Lake Champlain. This offensive also fizzled out, and Prevost began to be seen as a military incompetent. His enemies forced his recall to England immediately after the Treaty of Ghent (1814) ended the War of 1812, and he died shortly after his return home of congestive heart failure. Prevost proved to be a better administrator than a commander.

Prince, Thomas George (1915–1977). Tommy Prince, born in Petersfield, Manitoba, was an Ojibwa from the Brokenhead Band. He enlisted in June 1940, served as a sapper, took parachute training, and then joined the First Special Service Force. He distinguished himself in the US–Canadian unit's battles in Italy, most notably as a scout, and received the Military Medal for his actions at Littoria on 8 February 1944. In

September, as a member of the "Devil's Brigade" now operating in southern France, Prince located an enemy encampment and provided the information that led to the capture of more than a thousand of the enemy. He won the Silver Star for this action, one of only three Canadians to have this US decoration. Prince re-enlisted in 1950 and served in Korea as a sergeant during two tours with the 2nd and 3rd Battalions of the Princess Patricia's Canadian Light Infantry, surviving the battle of Kap'yong and later "The Hook" in November 1952. Prince's medals and other artifacts are on permanent display at the Manitoba Museum.

Princess Patricia's Canadian Light Infantry (PPCLI). Hamilton Gault of Montreal donated $100,000 to organize the regiment, composed primarily of British ex-soldiers resident in Canada, in August 1914. The PPCLI fought for a year in the British 27th Division before joining the newly formed 3rd Canadian Division of the Canadian Corps in France at the end of 1915. The regiment served in many of the major battles of World War I, and three of its members earned the Victoria Cross. After the war, the PPCLI became part of the Permanent Force. In World War II, the regiment fought with the 1st Canadian Infantry Division in Sicily, Italy, and northwest Europe. It then remained an infantry unit of the regular army and expanded to three battalions as the Cold War continued. All three battalions saw action in the Korean War, and the 2nd Battalion won a US Presidential Unit Citation for its role in the battle of Kap'yong on 24–25 April 1951. PPCLI battalions subsequently served in NATO and on numerous peacekeeping and peace enforcement operations, and the regiment has fought with distinction in the Afghanistan War. The 1st and 3rd Battalions of the PPCLI are based at Canadian Forces Base Edmonton; the 2nd Battalion is located at Shilo, Manitoba.

READING: David Bercuson, *The Patricias* (Toronto, 2001).

Prisoners of War. There are 3,847 Canadians recorded as having been taken prisoner on the Western Front during World War I and approximately 9,724—in all theatres of operation—during World War II. In most cases, these POWs were treated according to international conventions on prisoners of war concluded at Geneva and The Hague in 1864, 1899, 1907, and 1929, although conditions worsened as Germany began to collapse in 1945. There was one instance during World War II, after a mass escape of 76 men from Stalag Luft III, Canadians from the Royal Canadian Air Force among them, when the Gestapo executed 50 who had been recaptured. There was also a period of several months in the fall of 1942 when the Germans manacled Canadian prisoners from the Dieppe raid (1,946 fell into German hands) in retaliation for the planned shackling of German POWs expected to be taken. Soldiers of the 12th SS Panzer Division murdered as many as 187 Canadian POWs in Normandy in 1944; the German commander, Kurt Meyer, faced trial for these murders and a court found him guilty.

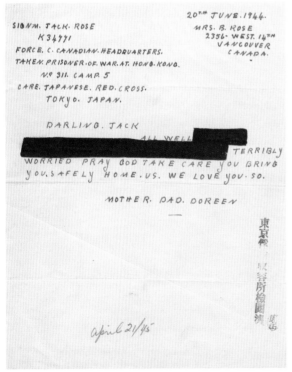

To their families, POWs were in limbo, safe from death in battle but subject to unimaginable perils. As this letter from one POW's parents, partly censored, suggests, all those at home could do was pray that prisoners of the Japanese might survive.

POWs in German hands, however, ordinarily were not maltreated, and Canadian POWs generally fared better than Russian, British, or American prisoners. Moreover, Canadian Red Cross parcels, considered the best of such belligerent supplies, had been designed by nutritional experts and made it through to the POWs, ordinarily at a rate of one a week for each prisoner. Cigarettes too were relatively plentiful, and some POWs traded parcel goods such as Lux soap or cigarettes for fresh bread with German civilians encountered on work details. By January 1945, however, Allied bombing of rail lines and Germany's worsening situation frequently stopped Red Cross deliveries. The Germans, their territory shrinking as the Soviet army advanced from the east, force-marched Allied POWs westward in January weather; hundreds of malnourished, ill-clad POWs died. The survivors were liberated in April and May 1945.

Canadian soldiers, numbering 1,689, were taken captive by the Japanese at Hong Kong on 25 December 1941 and, in general, fared far worse than those captured in Europe. They were starved for almost four years, denied medical care and Red Cross parcels except on rare occasions, and made to work long hours in vile conditions in Hong Kong and in Japan. Some were murdered. Two Nursing Sisters were among the Canadians captured in Hong Kong. They were held in a civilian camp until repatriation under Red Cross auspices in September 1943.

During the Korean War, 33 Canadians were taken prisoner and, although subject to constant efforts at political re-education, they were generally treated well when overall ration levels and the living conditions of the Chinese Communist forces themselves are taken into consideration. UN soldiers, like the Canadians captured in Korea after the spring of 1951, were held by the Chinese; Americans and others who had been held by the North Koreans in the first six to eight months of the war had been harshly treated with many being executed or starved to death.

During World War II, Canada became a favourite place for POW camps holding Axis prisoners, some of whom had been induced to surrender overseas by leaflets prepared by psychological warfare specialists.

The biggest POW camps, holding up to 25,000 men and run by the Department of National Defence with troops of the Veterans Guard providing security, were located near Lethbridge and Medicine Hat, Alberta, but other POW camps operated at Fort Henry in Kingston, and Bowmanville and Gravenhurst in Ontario. The Veterans Guard was comprised of soldiers who had served in World War I and who volunteered for service once more. The generally remote locations, it was hoped, might discourage escape attempts by the approximately 34,000 prisoners held in Canadian camps. (One German POW did manage to escape and made his way back to Germany.) A number of Axis prisoners were put to work as agricultural labourers on farms during the war and some 6,000 applied to settle in Canada at war's end; a surprising number returned to Canada as immigrants in the late 1940s and early 1950s. SEE ALSO: DIEPPE RAID; KOREAN WAR; MEYER; WAR CRIMES; WORLD WAR I; WORLD WAR II.

READING: Jonathan Vance, *Objects of Concern: Canadian Prisoners of War through the Twentieth Century* (Vancouver, 1994); M.F. Auger, *Prisoners of the Home Front: German POWs and "Enemy Aliens" in Southern Quebec, 1940–1946* (Vancouver, 2005).

Propaganda, Wartime. Like most governments at war, Canada's has attempted to persuade people to change their minds or to maintain their determination in the face of military perils. In World War I, the efforts of the Canadian-born Max Aitken, Lord Beaverbrook, produced propaganda that aimed to demonize the Hun in Britain and to enhance the image of Canadian troops among the British people. Domestic Canadian efforts focused on posters and advertisements directed at Canadians: "Buy Victory bonds," "Join the Canadian Expeditionary Force," or "Give money to the Red Cross" were among the blandishments that sought to bind Canadians to a shared purpose. Information on the war itself was surprisingly available, in the form of casualty rolls, for example, although official efforts, then as now, reduced the magnitude of defeats and enhanced the scope of victories in order to maintain favourable opinion and shield the public from the true

horrors of war. The Germans were murderers and thugs, the French beleaguered democrats, the Russians stalwart peasants. The Canadians were outsized warriors come from afar to save the Empire, reluctant soldiers of capable mien—citizen-soldiers with attitude. Propaganda targeted at English Canadians emphasized the ties of Empire, blood, crown, and race; that directed at French Canadians appealed to history, folk heroes (and heroines), tradition, and, occasionally—and not very successfully—the traditional ties to France. Private publications and advertising echoed the principal themes of a somewhat disorganized bureaucracy and inelegant arguments. Propaganda was not nearly as subtle or as scientific as it would soon become.

The broad outlines of messages remained much the same in World War II, though the effort was far better organized. Through first the Bureau of Public Information and then the Wartime Information Board and the propaganda films produced by the National

Total war demanded that everyone join in the fight—by making bombs or buying bonds—and in World War II almost all Canadians did.

Film Board, Canadian propaganda also reached a far greater audience, at home and abroad. Opinion polling pointed to public concerns, which information campaigns then duly sought to address, while posters and films addressed both general and niche markets with a growing sophistication and subtlety of message. A new addition to the mix was international and domestic radio broadcasting, and propaganda aimed at countering Vichy France's efforts at undermining Quebec's role in the war soon developed. By 1943, Ottawa had organized a Political Warfare Committee that, in co-operation with American and British agencies, had begun to reach out with daily French-language broadcasts to Europe. Questioning of German prisoners of war in Canadian camps provided propaganda lines for German language broadcasts (by 1945 proceeding from Radio Canada International), and, at much the same time, Canadian officials had begun efforts to "democratize" the POWs. This was not quite "PsyOps," as the jargon has it today, but it was a long step in this direction. Canadian Cold War propaganda shared key characteristics with that of other Western democracies, defaming enemies and deifying allies, but it was an uneven, desultory effort. Canadians needed little convincing of whose side they were on during the Cold War, but bolder calls to action were outflanked on one side by a free press and lack of government commitment to sustained efforts, and undermined on the other by the complexities of world events and the misdeeds of Canadian allies from Suez to Vietnam, from Central America to the Persian Gulf. In peacetime, propaganda has retreated to the margins of official discourse, with information control and official secrecy legislation—in effect, modulating content as much as message—replacing any formal propaganda machine. The complexity of the information spectrum in the twenty-first century makes propaganda more difficult to sustain; similar factors also make it more difficult to identify. SEE ALSO: AITKEN; PUBLIC OPINION AND THE MILITARY.

Provincial Marine. First established by the British in the Seven Years' War to provide lake transportation for troops and supplies in a largely trackless wilderness, the Provincial Marine operated under the direction of the commander of British forces in North America and was superintended by the quartermaster general. Its ships were small and had shallow draft, but they could be armed and carried marines. Early in the War of 1812, they gave Major-General Isaac Brock's forces in Upper Canada a decided advantage. As American naval strength increased and as the Royal Navy's efforts to counter this took shape, the Provincial Marine's importance as a fighting force decreased. SEE ALSO: WAR OF 1812.

Public Opinion and the Military. In peacetime, Canadians have never been enamoured of the military or its costs; in wartime, they have forgotten peacetime neglect in expecting victories without cease and courage without fail. Far from most war fronts since the late nineteenth century, Canadians have had the unusual luxury of an affordable indifference to global security and the winds of war through much of their history. The world wars were temporary affairs to be retreated from as soon as decency and transatlantic shipping would allow. Cold War or United Nations commitments were minor inconveniences, smallish and token-like for the most part, never the advance guard of larger deployments or the harbingers of greater wars. Forces posted to Europe as part of the postwar Western alliance remained broadly supported by the Canadian public for four decades and more. As numbers declined, tensions eased, and Europe recovered, however, Canadians evinced a healthy skepticism regarding the alliance's prospects and the continued wisdom of a massively militarized central Europe. There were fleeting glimpses of more martial public ardour, when to Canadians and others the Soviet Union appeared more bellicose and threatening than the Canadian Communist Party's press releases could ever allow, but moments of genuine public enthusiasm for military affairs were few and their impact limited. It was ever thus.

In pre-Confederation Canada, Canadians and Maritimers often fulminated against their American neighbours and showed some transitory interest in joining militia regiments; there was very little support for the idea of budgetary allocations for defence. It was Britain's duty to defend Canada, or so most appeared to believe, and British troops and ineffective Canadian militia turned out to fend off Fenian raiders in 1866. Confederation did not alter this laissez-faire approach, the government insisting Britain use its troops in Canada to put down the rebellion at Red River in 1869–1870. Britain's withdrawal (except from Halifax and Esquimalt) did not alter attitudes much, and it was 1883 before even the tiniest of a Permanent Force was created. In 1885, there was substantial enthusiasm for the militia dispatched to the Northwest to deal with Louis Riel's second rebellion; the weak performance of the force in action was ignored, the only criticism falling on the British commander, Major-General Frederick Middleton, and all "our boys" were hailed. It was much the same in the South African War, the hastily raised and ill-trained units getting much praise and performing well but with some ill-discipline in action.

Part of this came from the widespread attitude that hardy Canadians were natural soldiers and that professional military men were drunken layabouts, the Sam Hughes attitude, in other words. This might not have mattered if Hughes had not been militia and defence minister when World War I began, but his egomaniacal concern that his friends get the commands and contracts meant that the Canadian Expeditionary Force needed two years in action before amateurism was defeated and cronyism contained. Public opinion was hugely supportive of the war, the terrible casualty lists in the press notwithstanding. That Canadians believed that their nation was born on Vimy Ridge—and they did—was a sign of overwhelming public support, at least in English Canada. It was never true in Quebec, whose sons did not enlist in any appreciable numbers and whose attitudes to the military were and remained vastly cooler than those of their compatriots. Certainly there was no support at all for conscription, not least among the hundreds of thousands—English- and French-speaking both—who sought exemption from the draft.

Both linguistic groups, however, shared the desire to put the military behind them after the peace. Governments received support for their defence cutbacks broadly, not just in Quebec, but there was less support for rearmament in the late 1930s in French Canada than the tepid enthusiasm for it in the rest of the country. Both seemed to agree that conscription should not be imposed again; Conservative and Liberal leaders stated this in March 1939, six months before World War II began. There was little real enthusiasm for the war until the fall of France and Dunkirk. Recruitment quotas were met, but the teeming throngs in favour of war that had marked its onset in 1914 were nowhere to be seen in 1939. After France's defeat in 1940, the stakes were clearer—and almost indescribably higher—and Canada rallied. English Canada quickly turned in favour of a total commitment, though Quebec, still seeing World War II as being as imperialist as World War I, was not. This made conscription a delicate issue, and Prime Minister Mackenzie King played his hand very carefully—and very successfully— throughout the war. Polls showed that youth opposed compulsory service; older Canadians, not surprisingly, supported it. Nonetheless, English Canada's wholehearted backing of the troops and the cause remained steadfast despite severe losses.

Once again, peace brought a lack of interest in the military as the government slashed budgets yet again. The Korean War and extraordinary leadership from Louis St Laurent led to the dispatch of troops to the Far East and to NATO duty in Europe and Canada's largest peacetime military. The predictable linguistic division continued, Quebec being far less enthusiastic about rearmament and cold to the possibility of compulsory service even though the prime minister was a francophone. Peacekeeping, interest in which was spurred by Lester Pearson's Nobel Peace Prize in 1957, began to build support across all regions of Canada as a unique role that Canadian soldiers could play. Over time, this attitude hardened into the belief, still prevalent in 2010, that it was the only role Canada should play. Cuts to the unified Canadian Forces (unification was one issue that stirred public opinion in the late 1960s) were met with yawns—why did a peacekeeping force need heavy weapons?—and there was weak support for Canadian participation in the US-led coalition that fought the first Gulf War in 1990–1991. Opinion was so cool to fighting that aspects of the Canadian role in the United Nations force in former Yugoslavia, notably a pitched battle with Croatian forces, was hidden from the Canadian public for almost a decade. One additional and little-noted factor that limited the visibility of the Canadian Forces to university-educated citizens, and possibly the military's support among the country's young elite as well, was the cancellation of university reserve officer programs in the late 1960s.

The Somalia affair of the 1990s almost put paid to the Canadian Forces, so sharp was the negative and almost unanimous public response to revelations of torture, murder, and obscene hazing rituals from within the military. The government's triage operation and later disbandment of the Canadian Airborne Regiment staunched the bleeding, but barely. It took a decade and the extraordinary charismatic leadership of Chief of the Defence Staff General Rick Hillier to turn opinion around in a major and positive way.

Hillier's blunt outspokenness and his concern for his soldiers had a huge impact. This was evident when the bodies of Canadians killed in the Afghanistan War returned to Canada to be met by crowds outside the wire at Canadian Forces Base Trenton and along Highway 401, renamed the Highway of Heroes by the Ontario government, down which the hearses rolled to Toronto. Ordinary Canadians, police, and firefighters lined the bridges and overpasses to honour their dead. It was a remarkable turnaround from the dismal view of the Canadian Forces a decade before, all the more so because Canadian public opinion was far from enthusiastic about the war itself and Canada's participation in it. SEE ALSO: QUEBEC AND THE MILITARY.

Quebec (1629). British merchants interested in the fur trade and the potential of the St Lawrence River funded two expeditions to capture Acadia and Quebec in the late 1620s, using the opportunity provided by war with France to further their aims. The first attempt, led by David Kirke, seized five supply ships and took 600 prisoners in 1628; it did not attempt to capture the settlement when Samuel de Champlain rebuffed the Kirke emissary's demand to surrender. The next spring, Kirke returned, found the French settlers and Champlain starving and willing to surrender and, even though a treaty of peace had ended the war, Kirke occupied the town. Quebec and Acadia were returned to French control in 1632 by the Treaty of St Germain-en-Laye.

Quebec (1711). During Queen Anne's War (the War of the Spanish Succession), Britain aimed to drive France out of its North American possessions. Under command of Rear-Admiral Sir Hovenden Walker, a large force, numbering perhaps 12,000 all told and including five seasoned regiments pulled from the Duke of Marlborough's army fighting on the continent, sailed from England to Boston. On 30 July 1711, the expedition set sail for Quebec without up-to-date charts or competent pilots to help it deal with the currents and shoals in the St Lawrence River. This proved fatal. On 22 August, Walker's fleet, west of Anticosti Island, got caught in the currents and encountered fog; it ran into the breakers on the North Shore, losing eight ships and some 900 men, plus a number of women and children who travelled with the soldiers, as was the custom. Admiral Walker consulted his senior officers and decided to withdraw to Nova Scotia and then back to England. Quebec was spared an assault it could not have withstood, and Walker's career ended in disgrace.

Quebec (1759). Since Quebec City dominated the St Lawrence River narrows, it controlled access to virtually all of New France and was the obvious objective for British troops in the Seven Years' War. The attack on Quebec by land and naval forces was one of Britain's key strategies for the conquest of New France, the others being the reduction of the French posts in the west, primarily by the British-American militia, and an assault on Montreal from New York. The British land forces sent to take Quebec were under the command of Major-General James Wolfe; the naval forces were under Vice-Admiral Charles Saunders. The French, led by Lieutenant-General the Marquis de Montcalm, were well aware of the strategic importance of Quebec and prepared to defend it, knowing that the few French naval vessels in the area could not deny passage to Quebec by the Royal Navy. The British made their way upriver and anchored off the Île d'Orléans in late June 1759. They then proceeded to lay siege to Quebec, launching unsuccessful attacks at Montmorency and laying waste to settlements up and down the St Lawrence, as well as shelling the city unmercifully. In September, finally, Wolfe accepted his brigadiers' advice to land east of the city on 13 September and to force Montcalm into a decisive battle on the Plains of Abraham.

Montcalm did not need to come out from behind the walls—he could have waited comfortably until the coming colder weather forced the British to depart—nor did he need to attack before receiving reinforcements. But the French general marched his army out, saw them riddled by British volleys, and then led them back behind the walls, their retreat valiantly covered by the Canadien militia and native allies, only to be mortally wounded just as he re-entered the city. By then, Wolfe had already died on the battlefield. Although the French surrendered

⌃ Francis Swayne's 1763 action-filled work shows Quebec on 13 September 1759, with the British landing and ascent, and the battle itself happening at the same time.

Quebec on 18 September, they nearly recaptured it in the spring of 1760 when the Chevalier de Lévis moved his army downriver from Montreal, defeating the British at Ste Foy and laying siege to Quebec. After the spring breakup, the appearance of Royal Navy vessels instead of French ships rendered de Lévis's position untenable, and he had to withdraw back to Montreal. Facing superior British forces on all fronts, he surrendered New France in September.

The defeat of French forces during the Seven Years' War and the fall of New France to Britain remains a bone of political contention. A commemorative re-enactment set for the 250th anniversary of the battle in 2009 had to be cancelled after a separatist group threatened violence to disrupt the "celebration."

SEE ALSO: MONTCALM; PLAINS OF ABRAHAM; SEVEN YEARS' WAR; WOLFE.

READING: D. Peter MacLeod, *Northern Armageddon: The Battle of the Plains of Abraham* (Vancouver, 2008).

Quebec (1775). The American colonial rebels understood the strategic importance of Quebec City. After the first shots were fired in the American Revolution in April 1775, the Continental Congress hatched a scheme to bring a restive Quebec into the revolution and authorized military action in June 1775, more than a year before the Declaration of Independence. Having no navy that could match the power of the Royal Navy, the Continentals' assault on Quebec was to be a land affair. At the end of August 1775, an invasion force numbering approximately 2,000 commanded by Generals Philip Schuyler and Richard Montgomery left Crown Point, at the northern tip of Lake Champlain, to move against Montreal. On 4 September, they reached and besieged a mixed force of British regulars and militia at St Jean on the Richelieu River. The siege lasted until 3 November when the British capitulated, but the

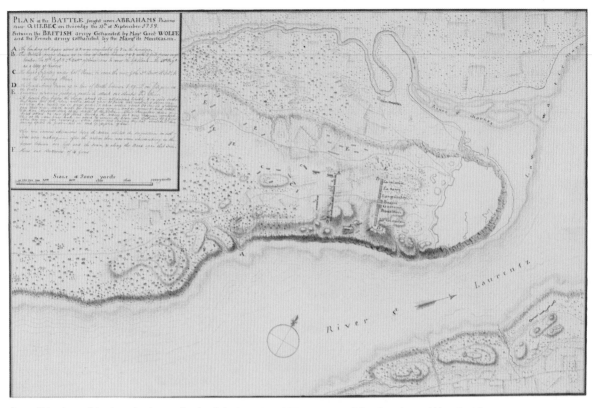

⌃ Wolfe's taking of Quebec, the decisive battle of the Seven Years' War, guaranteed that Canada would be a British possession.

two-month delay largely put paid to the American plans. Nonetheless, Governor Guy Carleton ordered Montreal evacuated and retired to Quebec where a second Continental force, under General Benedict Arnold, was approaching. Montgomery occupied Montreal and then proceeded to join Arnold at Quebec in early December. Like St Jean, Quebec City was defended by British regulars and militia. The Continental forces did not have the troops or supplies for a long winter siege and attempted to force a capture. In a snowstorm early on 31 December 1775, they launched their assault but suffered heavy losses; Montgomery himself fell. The Continentals tried to maintain pressure on the city, General George Washington sending some additional troops to Quebec and continuing the siege rather ineffectively. But in early May, British troopships appeared off Quebec, and the Continental troops withdrew to the south. SEE ALSO: CARLETON; REVOLUTIONARY WAR.

READING: G.F.G. Stanley, *Canada Invaded, 1775–1776* (Toronto, 1973).

Quebec and the Military. The differing attitudes to war held by French-speaking and English-speaking Canadians in the period from the Northwest Rebellion of 1885 through to the present and ongoing Afghanistan War have shaped the nation. Francophone opposition to war led to a widespread reluctance to enlist in World Wars I and II, for example, and to the subsequent imposition of compulsory military service by the federal government. Such measures exacerbated the incivility of communal relations in Canada and fed *nationaliste* sentiments in Quebec. English-Canadian historiography usually points to war as creating the Canadian nation. "Canada was born on Vimy Ridge" ranks as a cliché. Francophone scholars, on the other hand, point to war's divisive effects. "Conscription was the imposition of English Canada's will on Quebec" is equally a cliché. Clearly, wars can unite, but they can also divide sharply.

The earliest examples of French-English differences over military service occurred during the American invasion of 1775 and during the War of 1812, when most of the French-speaking population, though by no means all, took little active role in British North America's defence. The Continental Congress in 1775–1776 attempted to raise two battalions (the 1st and 2nd Canadian Regiments) in Quebec from the French- and English-speaking population after their troops captured Montreal and besieged Quebec City, but had scant success. British efforts to mobilize the population to defend their hold on the territory similarly had little result. The fighting in 1775–1776, in other words, was largely between British and American soldiers. The same can be said for the War of 1812 except that Canadiens in some numbers served in the Canadian Voltigeurs under a French-Canadian officer in the British regulars, Lieutenant-Colonel Charles-Michel d'Irumberry de Salaberry, and helped to defeat the American advance on Montreal in the battle of Chateauguay.

During the 1837 rebellions in Lower Canada, substantial numbers of Patriotes fought well against British regulars and English-speaking militia. The 1867 creation of the Dominion of Canada introduced a militia system that was only nominally formed, organized, or administered under the Militia Act of 1868. As a result, British troops had to be used to put down the Red River Rebellion in 1870. Fifteen years later, Louis Riel returned to Canada, this time to the North-West Territories, not yet created as the provinces of Saskatchewan and Alberta. His second rebellion was more serious, uniting Metis and Prairie Aboriginal bands against the North West Mounted Police, white settlers, the Canadian state, and, as soon as they could get to the scene, the Canadian militia and the tiny units of the Permanent Force.

The militia had some semi-efficient if ill-equipped units by this date, though fewer in numbers in French Canada than in English Canada, and, under the militia minister, Adolphe Caron, and the British general officer commanding the Canadian militia,

Major-General Frederick Middleton, militia units organized themselves with speed in Ontario and Quebec and proceeded by railway, on foot, and by river ferry to the site of the rebellion. Though there were some setbacks in the field, the Metis and Aboriginal resistance was put down thanks to superiority of numbers, cannon, and Gatling guns.

The complaints began after the fact. Quebec politicians, media, and militia leaders, "appalled by Riel's anti-Catholic apostasy," as historian Desmond Morton described it, had been prepared to join in crushing a rebellion. The subsequent execution of Riel, who was likely insane under any reasonable definition of the term, however, stirred enormous opposition in Quebec and raised fears. Some noticed that the Northwest Field Force had operated in English. Others worried that if Québécois could not stop the execution of Riel, could they ever check the untrammelled power of the English-Canadian majority? Premier Honoré Mercier, who came to power in Quebec City after the execution, broadened the attack on his Anglo compatriots by assailing their imperialism that, as early as 1888, he feared would try "to impose upon us a political regime which through conscription would scatter our sons from the icefields of the North Pole to the burning sands of the Sahara … an arbitrary tax of blood and money [to] tear our sons away from us…." Conscription was a chimera in 1888, the plaintive calls of a handful of militia enthusiasts in English Canada notwith-standing, but the 1885 rebellion nonetheless was a turning point. Quebec had been willing to join in a small expedition to put down a domestic rebellion. But could Anglo-Canadians be trusted subsequently not to support British imperial causes the world over? Would French Canadians be forced to participate in English Canada's wars on behalf of London?

The fear of imperial commitments, and domestic pressure for imperial commitments, was far from unfounded, a situation that came to pass little more than a decade later in South Africa. Britain and the Boer republics had been jousting for years over the local rights of Britons. When war erupted in 1899, in a fit of imperialistic fervour, anglophone Canada was quick to demand Canadian participation. Québécois opinion was equally adamant that South Africa was of no interest to Canada, except only insofar as the Boers were an oppressed people very similar to francophone Canadians. In brief, to be English-speaking was to be for participation in a "splendid little war"; to be a francophone was to be opposed. Prime Minister Sir Wilfrid Laurier had no desire to take Canada to war, but he could count heads. The resulting decision was for a small contingent of volunteers raised in Canada but paid by Britain once the troops, soon dubbed the Royal Canadian Regiment, arrived in South Africa. Further contingents followed, and some 7,000 participated in the South African War.

The results were clear. Quebec had learned again that its wishes could be swept away by the majority's demands. Not surprisingly, francophone enlistments for South Africa were tiny, most of the volunteers being English-speaking and Canadian born or British born. By caving in to majority demands, Laurier had blackened his reputation in the minds of *nationalistes*: he was too soft on the imperialist English Canadians, too subservient to Great Britain. When the prime minister proposed to establish a Canadian navy, Quebec opposition was very sharp. In a by-election in Drummond-Arthabaska in 1910, the anti-government candidate ran against conscription and for peace and, despite Laurier's reassuring words that his tiny navy was to be crewed by volunteers and his repeated pledges against conscription, the Liberals lost.

The Great War soon put everything to the test. In English Canada, the enthusiasm was marked, and recruits flocked to the colours to fill the ranks of the first Canadian contingent. In French Quebec, the response was much cooler, and recruits were few. Formed at Valcartier, Quebec, in a camp newly carved out of the bush, the contingent's composition was striking. Most of the officers had come from the militia, and most were Canadian born. But some two-thirds of the soldiers were British immigrants, and only 1,245, or 3.5 percent of the over 36,000 recruits, were French-speaking. There were reasons for this, the easiest to understand being the length of time French-speaking volunteers and their

families had lived in Canada. Francophones had been in Canada for 300 years and had few close ties to Europe, unlike many first-generation immigrants from the British Isles. Beyond that, as enlistment statistics during four years of war demonstrated, francophone males were less healthy, married earlier, and had larger families needing support than other potential recruitment cohorts. Most important, without a public urging them to join up, most were very reluctant to go. The military was almost entirely British, in any case, with British flags, traditions, and codes of justice; English was the working language and the barriers to success for any French-speaking recruit were, to say the least, extraordinarily high.

As a result, there were few French-speaking units. In Montreal in 1915, successful appeals were made to French Canadians to enlist in the 22nd (French-Canadian) Battalion (that its name was in English was revealing), which duly went overseas as part of the 2nd Canadian Division. Its wartime record would be outstanding. Many other efforts to raise French-speaking battalions for the front began, but none had success; all, in the end, were broken up to provide reinforcements to the 22nd, the sole French-speaking unit in a Canadian Corps of 48 infantry battalions and many other front-line units. Quebec francophone voluntary enlistment would remain terribly low throughout the war. The militia in Quebec had been neglected before 1914 and, under Sam Hughes, the minister of militia and defence in the government of Sir Robert Borden after 1911, Quebec units seemed frequently to be discriminated against. There was massive political resentment in Quebec against Ontario's Regulation 17 that tried to force Franco-Ontarians to learn English in the province's schools, and great unhappiness with the policies of the Borden government. Wartime jobs in the factories of Montreal attracted substantial numbers.

Whatever the reasons, francophones did not enlist. Quebec made up 37 percent of the population but provided only 14.2 percent of enlistments, with most of those unquestionably coming from the province's English-speaking population. The numbers overall are uncertain but, in June 1917, Parliament learned that the Canadian Expeditionary Force overseas had 14,100 francophones in its ranks, but only 8,200 from Quebec. By the end of the war, after the imposition of conscription, the best guess is that 50,000 French Canadians—including Acadians, Franco-Ontarians, French-speaking Westerners, and Québécois—were in khaki. With total enlistments running well above 619,000, French Canadians had provided at most one in twelve enlistments overall and perhaps five percent of volunteers from more than a third of the national population. When Borden introduced conscription for overseas service in May 1917 and his efforts failed to bring Laurier into the government with him to enforce it, the prime minister went to the polls in December at the head of a pro-conscription Union Government that had in it scant French-speaking representation. Only 27,557 francophones were conscripted; most did not make it overseas. The resentment over conscription was enormous, however, and remained.

Very little occurred between the wars to make Quebec more accepting of another war than it had been in 1914. The 22nd Battalion became the Royal 22e Régiment, a Permanent Force unit, but it was the sole French-speaking unit, numbering only a few hundred men, in the tiny Canadian military. Prime Minister Mackenzie King, who ruled for most of the interwar years, tried to heal the wounds of war by weakening imperial bonds and reinforcing Canada's nominal independence from Britain, a relationship bolstered by the Statute of Westminster in 1931. By the late 1930s, King had promised that if there were another war, Canada would fight it without conscription, a promise that Québécois believed had been made to them. Quebeckers trusted King because he was dependent on Quebec seats for his power. When war came in September 1939, the prime minister brought a relatively united country into the conflict, though neither French nor English Canadians evinced much enthusiasm for what King portrayed as a "limited liability" war.

Events soon changed all that, and the stunning triumphs of German arms made English Canadians press for a greater national war effort. The King

government introduced home defence conscription in the summer of 1940 and met relatively little opposition in Quebec. Voluntary enlistments were high across the country for all three services, but Quebec enlistments were low in the navy and the air force, perhaps because technical skills were lacking. Army enlistments too were well behind those in English Canada, though Army Headquarters created more French-language units in the infantry and artillery than in World War I. The language of command, however, remained English, and almost all the senior commanders were anglophones—francophone senior officers could not be created overnight from the tiny French-speaking officer cadre of the Permanent Force and militia.

As the pressure for conscription grew in English Canada, the prime minister in 1942 called a plebiscite (not a binding referendum) to ask all Canada to release him from his promises against overseas conscription. There was fury in Quebec at what was seen as King's breaking of a solemn pledge, and the plebiscite result revealed a country as divided as it had been in 1917: francophones voted massively "non" and English Canada, except for a few Ukrainian- and German-Canadian pockets, voted very heavily "yes." King escaped with his political skin intact by passing legislation (Bill 80) authorizing conscription but not implementing it—yet. The policy, he said, was "not necessarily conscription, but conscription if necessary." Quebec was unhappy, but still hoped that King could protect it from compulsory overseas service. He did—until November 1944, when casualties forced King to order 16,000 home defence conscripts overseas. Furious, Quebec could nonetheless see that King had resisted compulsory overseas service through most of the war.

Canada's war effort in the Second World War was superb. Ten percent of the population put on uniforms from a nation of 11 million. The army enlisted 750,000, the RCAF 250,000, the RCN 100,000. Although francophone enlistments were much higher than in the Great War, they were still under-represented. Estimates of French-Canadian enlistments have been put as high as 200,000; most estimates cluster around

150,000, or under 15 percent of the total national enlistment. The most credible estimate of Quebec francophones in the services is between 84,000 and 90,000, although one historian estimated that only 55,000 francophones volunteered, a number that includes Acadians, Franco-Ontarians, and others. Many francophones served with distinction, rising to high command and leading brigades in action with skill. As in World War I, the public pressure in Quebec was against enlistment; in the rest of the country, the reverse was true. The bitterness in Quebec that conscription had been imposed despite King's promises was matched by resentment in English Canada that francophones again had not joined up in the requisite numbers.

It would be comforting to believe that peace and postwar internal commitments helped bridge this divide. It did, to some extent, but the Cold War generated debates and military deployments that reopened old wounds while posing new challenges. The North Atlantic Treaty and the Korean War put Canada back into the military game after only a few years of peace, and defence spending boomed. Under Prime Minister Louis St Laurent, Canada sent troops to Korea and to Germany and France. Again, the military remained largely English-speaking, and the Royal 22e Régiment had some difficulty finding enough volunteers to keep its ranks full in Korea—in December 1950, only 12.3 percent of the army (though percentages were higher in the infantry) was francophone, while the situation in the navy and air force was no better. Nor was public opinion in Quebec supportive of the Korean War or the prospect of Cold War conscription (83 percent opposed conscription for Korean service in early 1951). Nonetheless, with St Laurent leading the nation, Ottawa made plans for conscription in the event of war with the Soviet Union, even printing the registration cards.

Over the next half-century, the Canadian military went through many changes—the acquisition of nuclear weaponry, integration and unification, falling numbers of personnel, aging equipment, and occasional periods of renaissance. To a substantial extent, the old conscription issue disappeared as no one could seriously envisage compulsory service barring the increasingly unlikely event of a major war with the Soviet-led Warsaw Pact. Francophone strength in the Canadian Forces hovered around the mandated 28 percent. Under General Jean Victor Allard, the Canadian Forces began to move to be a genuinely bilingual military, French-speaking officers regularly held every position in the military, there were French-speaking regular army and air units based in Quebec and ships at sea, and bilingualism became a prerequisite for promotion to senior rank. This was as it should be in a nation with two languages.

Quebec public opinion remained resolutely cool to military spending nevertheless, and vigorously opposed to participation in overseas conflicts. Only United Nations peacekeeping operations garnered public sympathy in French Canada, and this was true even (or especially) when francophone units went into combat. Polling during the Afghanistan War, for example, ordinarily found Quebec opinion 10–20 points less supportive of participation than English-Canadian attitudes—and sometimes 30 points less supportive than Alberta.

For better or worse, Quebec opinion constrained Canadian participation in military action, and national leaders had to watch the province carefully lest a military response abroad affect Quebec's vigorous but delicate political situation. Prime Minister Jean Chrétien stayed out of the Iraq War in 2003, some believe, because a Quebec provincial election was in full flight at the time the decision had to be made, and two-thirds of the province opposed the war even if it were to be authorized by the UN Security Council. (English-Canadian opinion at the same time was two-to-one in favour of participation.)

For more than a century, the linguistic and regional fault line in Canadian politics has remained sharp, regularly delineated by politico-military crises that pitted francophone opinions against those of anglophones. SEE ALSO: ALLARD; BORDEN, ROBERT; CONSCRIPTION; KING; LAURIER.

READING: Robert Bothwell, *Alliance and Illusion* (Vancouver, 2007); J.L. Granatstein and J.M. Hitsman,

Broken Promises: A History of Conscription in Canada (Toronto, 1977).

Queen Anne's War. Also known as the War of the Spanish Succession (1702–1713), the conflict, which started and was primarily fought in Europe, inevitably spilled over into North America. Most of the action involved *la petite guerre*, border raiding by guerrilla forces. Without the resources to conduct an assault on Boston or New York, the French and their First Nations allies carried out destructive guerrilla raids against frontier settlements such as Deerfield in Massachusetts, where they killed or captured 160 settlers in February 1704. In Newfoundland, they destroyed Bonavista in 1704 and captured St John's in 1708. The Acadians and their Aboriginal allies raided Wells, Maine, and Falmouth in New England. In counterattacks, the British took Port Royal on their third attempt in 1710 and ended French control of Acadia, soon renamed Nova Scotia. English attempts to capture Quebec in 1709 and 1711 failed utterly. The Treaty of Utrecht ended the skirmishing by settling the war in Europe.

Queenston Heights, Battle of (1812). In the early morning hours of 13 October 1812, New York State militia and some regulars crossed the Niagara River and tried to land at Queenston, Upper Canada. Sixty of the troops found a hidden path up the escarpment and seized a British 18-pounder gun position on Queenston Heights that was, with devastating effect, shelling the 500 or more Americans still coming across the river in bateaux. Major-General Isaac Brock, the British commander-in-chief and administrator of Upper Canada who had just arrived on the scene from Fort George, rallied 200 troops from the 49th Regiment to retake the position, but he fell, shot through the chest, and the British troops and militia retreated. Major-General Roger Sheaffe, arriving via a circuitous route with a thousand soldiers of the 41st Regiment, York and Lincoln militia, and Mohawk warriors led by John Norton, ascended the heights and struck the Americans from the rear. Sheaffe's forces fired a single volley and charged; the Americans broke, falling back toward the cliff. Terrified of the Mohawks, pressed back to the cliff's edge, many jumped. In the end, at least 300 Americans were killed or wounded, and almost a thousand surrendered on the orders of their commander, Lieutenant-Colonel Winfield Scott. British losses were 105 killed and wounded, but Brock's death was a major blow. The victory at Queenston Heights, coming early in the War of 1812, just after Brock's successes at Detroit and Michilimackinac, gave heart to Upper Canadians that they might be able to resist the Americans.

The British executed as traitors a dozen Americans of Irish extraction captured on the Heights, causing the US Senate to pass a bill ordering similar treatment for British prisoners. President James Madison refused to enforce the law. SEE ALSO: BROCK; NIAGARA FRONTIER; WAR OF 1812.

READING: Robert Malcolmson, *A Very Brilliant Affair: The Battle of Queenston Heights, 1812* (Montreal, 2004).

△ Charles Comfort, *The Hitler Line*, 1944
oil on canvas, 101.6 x 121.7 cm
Canadian War Museum

❰ Pegi Nicol MacLeod, Untitled (*Women's Royal Canadian Naval Service in the Dining Room*), 1944
oil on wood panel, 73.2 x 65.4 cm
Canadian War Museum

▲ Paraskeva Clark, *Parachute Riggers*, 1947
oil on canvas, 101.8 x 81.4 cm
Canadian War Museum

▲ Alex Colville, *Tragic Landscape*, 1945
oil on canvas, 61.0 x 91.0 cm
Canadian War Museum

◀ Orville Fisher
Battle for Carpiquet Airfield, 1946
oil and graphite on canvas
102.0 x 122.0 cm
Canadian War Museum

▲ Stephen Snider, *Helicopter Evac*, 1987
acrylic on hardboard, 43.8 x 66.0 cm
Canadian War Museum

▲ Allan MacKay, *Coalition Soldiers Kandahar Air Base, July 2003*, 2004
pastel, oil pastel, and wax on canvas, 81.2 x 115.0 cm
Canadian War Museum

Radarsat. Radarsat 1 (launched in November 1995) and Radarsat 2 (launched in December 2007) are commercially available Canadian-developed space satellites that can monitor environmental changes, survey Arctic ice, and do maritime surveillance. Radarsat 2 uses radar to provide high-resolution imagery of objects from one to three metres in length in light and darkness and through cloud cover. This is of major importance for the Canadian navy and for the protection of Canada's claims in the North. Developed by MacDonald Dettwiler (MDA), a Richmond, BC company, the fate of Radarsat became a public issue in 2008 when the Canadian government blocked the $1.3 billion sale of the company's Information Systems and Geospatial Services operations to a US corporation. In 2009, the Department of National Defence and MDA launched Project "Polar Epsilon" to upgrade Radarsat's

⌃ The first Canadian satellite, Radarsat 1, went into space in November 1995.

capabilities and to build two ground stations, one in Nova Scotia and one in British Columbia, to receive and process data.

Ralston, James Layton (1891–1948). After serving as a battalion commander with the Canadian Expeditionary Force in World War I, Colonel Ralston was elected to Parliament as a Liberal in 1925. He first entered the Cabinet as Prime Minister Mackenzie King's minister of national defence in 1926 and kept the post until the Liberal defeat in 1930. Although re-elected in 1930, he retired from politics in 1935 to resume his law practice. He returned to Parliament at the start of World War II and became a tight-fisted minister of finance in September 1939. He held that post until his appointment as minister of national defence in July 1940. Aided by the minister of national defence for naval services (Angus Macdonald) and the minister of national defence for air (C.G. Power), Ralston presided over the extraordinary expansion of

Canada's armed forces during the war. He was a strong supporter of conscription for overseas service and threatened to resign from the Cabinet if the measure was not introduced following the conscription plebiscite of 1942. Although he gave King his letter of resignation, it was not accepted, and he remained in office. On a tour of European battle zones in the fall of 1944, he became convinced that conscription could no longer be delayed because of the shortage of infantry reinforcements. When he made his views known to King after his return to Canada, the prime minister forced him to resign on 1 November 1944. General A.G.L. McNaughton—the former commander of First Canadian Army, sacked by Ralston in late 1943—replaced him as defence minister. Ralston was a capable minister and an honourable man who sometimes became so obsessed with detail that he overlooked the big picture.

SEE ALSO: CONSCRIPTION; KING; WORLD WAR II.

READING: C.P. Stacey, *Arms, Men and Governments: The War Policies of Canada, 1939–1945* (Ottawa, 1970).

Defence minister James Layton Ralston, 1941.

Rebellions of 1837–1838. The rebellions in Lower and Upper Canada had many causes. Economic difficulties, autocratic rule, tensions between French- and English-speakers in Lower Canada and between recent immigrants from the United States and Loyalists in Upper Canada—all these factors contributed to the uprisings.

In Lower Canada, the Patriotes, largely but not exclusively francophone, frustrated at being unable to achieve their democratic ends in the legislative assembly, began to prepare for rebellion during 1837; simultaneously, the English merchant class began to prepare to resist the Patriotes, and Britain moved troop reinforcements into the province. The Patriotes clearly underestimated British resolve. When fighting erupted in November 1837, the rebels won the first fight at St Denis. But the British troops and militia applied overwhelming force against their enemy at St Charles and St Eustache, inflicting heavy casualties and crushing the resistance. Victorious volunteers looted and burned homes across the rebel townships. The leaders fled into exile in the United States, though most were eventually offered amnesty. A second, smaller rebellion in November 1838, launched with the support of self-styled Patriot Hunters or Hunters Lodges in the United States, was again crushed, and produced harsher punishments, with 12 men executed and 58 transported to Australia.

In Upper Canada, the rebellion was a tamer affair. William Lyon Mackenzie gathered his forces at Montgomery's Tavern, just north of Toronto, in the hope that he could take advantage of the dispatch of troops east to help in Lower Canada. But the few remaining troops and loyal citizens took up arms, engaged in a brief firefight that, while not inflicting many casualties, caused many of Mackenzie's supporters to flee, and then dispersed the remainder. Mackenzie went into exile in the United States. With American supporters, he launched raids over the border that kept Upper Canada in turmoil. The Patriot Hunters tried to foment revolt from south of the border and prosecuted raids and criminal ventures with some regularity; at the one major fight in Upper Canada, the battle of the Windmill, just outside Prescott, in November 1838, they were crushed.

The rebellions led to Lord Durham's report that recommended a union of the two Canadas and the establishment of responsible government. SEE ALSO: MONTGOMERY'S TAVERN; PAPINEAU; ST CHARLES; ST DENIS; ST EUSTACHE.

READING: Gerald Craig, *Upper Canada: The Formative Years, 1784–1841* (Toronto, 1963); Fernand Ouellet, *Lower Canada, 1791–1840: Social Change and Nationalism* (Toronto, 1980).

▲ Katherine Jane Ellice, held prisoner during the rebellion in Lower Canada in 1837, painted this sketch of the Patriotes at Beauharnois.

Red River Expedition (1870). Led by British Colonel Garnet Wolseley, the expedition came from Canada to Red River in May 1870 to restore order after the rebellion launched the previous fall by Louis Riel and the Metis. The British government, in the process of withdrawing its troops from Canada, was reluctant to provide military aid for this purpose. Though it was a party to the December 1869 agreement transferring Rupert's Land from the Hudson's Bay Company to Canada, London believed the uprising was a Canadian responsibility. Nevertheless, the British agreed to send Wolseley and a contingent of 400 troops from the British army's 60th Rifles, augmented by some 800 militia soldiers from Ontario and Quebec. The expedition did not set out until May 1870, by which time a political solution to the uprising had been negotiated. Its purpose, therefore, was to take formal control of Red River for Canada and to restore law and order. The United States refused to allow the expedition to pass through the canal at Sault Ste Marie, Michigan, forcing an overland portage there; once at Thunder Bay, it had to make its way west overland and by river. Carrying its own supplies, the expedition arrived in Red River in late August 1870 to find that Riel had fled. Wolseley left the Canadian militia, renamed the Manitoba Force, and returned east with the British regulars. SEE ALSO: RIEL.

READING: Garnet Wolseley, *The Story of a Soldier's Life* (London, 1903).

Red River Rebellion (1869–1870). The rebellion of the Metis at Red River against the transfer of Rupert's Land to Canada was precipitated in October 1869 by the arrival of a survey party from Canada. The Hudson's Bay Company, Britain, and the new Dominion of Canada had arranged to transfer to Canada the company's Rupert's Land on 1 December. The Metis had not been consulted about the transfer and feared the survey presaged the loss of their lands. Under the leadership of Louis Riel, the English- and French-speaking Metis living in the area of the Red River colony united to force Canada to negotiate. Riel and his followers formed the National Committee of the Metis, seized the Hudson's Bay Company post at Upper Fort Garry, and blocked the Canadian-designated lieutenant-governor, William McDougall, from entering the area. The committee then imprisoned a number of Canadians who had been

Colonel Garnet Wolseley led the expedition to the Red River in 1870. This contemporary watercolour by William Armstrong shows Wolseley's camp near Lake Superior en route to Fort Garry.

actively agitating for annexation to Canada and declared itself a provisional government. One of the prisoners, the troublesome Orangeman, Thomas Scott from Ontario, was summarily executed by firing squad as an example to the other colonists. This blunder enraged Scott's Canadian compatriots. Prime Minister Sir John A. Macdonald stopped the transfer of Rupert's Land to Canada as soon as he heard of the uprising and insisted that a military force restore order. The British, who still maintained forces in Canada, agreed to a British-Canadian Red River Expedition. Led by British Colonel Garnet Wolseley, the force of some regulars and several hundred militia left for the Red River in May 1870; by the time it arrived in late August, the crisis had ended, and Riel had fled. Macdonald negotiated with the Metis through Donald Smith, a Hudson's Bay Company principal, who acted as intermediary. The negotiations concluded when the Metis gained many of the guarantees they sought and agreed to allow Rupert's Land to become part of Canada. The terms and conditions of the agreement were contained in the Manitoba Act, passed in May; the transfer of land took place the next month. The act created the new province of Manitoba. SEE ALSO: RED RIVER EXPEDITION; RIEL; WOLSELEY.

READING: Hartwell Bowsfield, *Louis Riel: The Rebel and the Hero* (Toronto, 1971).

Regina Trench (1916). Canadian soldiers made repeated attempts between September and November 1916 to capture this German-held trench running southwest to northeast about 1.5 kilometres north of the French town of Courcelette. The Canadian Corps made abortive efforts to capture the German line on 26 September and again on 1 and 8 October. In each of these attacks, artillery preparation to cut the barbed wire proved ineffective and, though there was limited success, many of the attackers were cut down by German machine-gunners. Finally, on 11 November, after two days of remorseless artillery bombardment of the German positions, the 4th Canadian Division, fighting its first battle in France, captured and held the rest of Regina Trench; by the 18th, they had seized

Desire Trench as well, the next objective. The battle cost the 4th Division 1,250 casualties.

Reinforcement Crisis (1944). The shortage of infantry that developed in the ranks of First Canadian Army in Italy and in northwest Europe in the late summer of 1944 was an integral part of the ongoing struggle over whether or not Canada would introduce conscription for overseas military service in World War II. The crisis stemmed from a shortage of trained infantry to replace losses suffered in line rifle companies. The fighting units of First Canadian Army had been organized on the assumption that the rate of infantry casualties (the "wastage" rate) after the invasion of Europe would be roughly that which had been suffered by the British Eighth Army in the North African desert in 1942–1943. Those assumptions were wrong. The mobile warfare of the desert produced lower infantry casualties than did the grinding battles in the towns, forests, and flooded polders of Normandy, the Scheldt, and Italy. Planners had allocated more personnel to armour, artillery, supply, and other duties than needed while providing too few for the infantry. The conscription crisis of 1944 was not caused by a general manpower shortage in the Canadian Army, but by a shortage of infantry replacements. That shortage became acute in the last stages of the Normandy battles and reached crisis proportions during the battles on the Gothic Line in Italy and during the Scheldt campaign in north-west Europe.

Before recommending to the government that conscription be applied, the army attempted to "remuster" soldiers from other duties by retraining them as infantry and posting them to forward units. The slow process involved many weeks of retraining, and still resulted in sometimes unevenly prepared infantry being fed into sustained combat operations. Since reinforcements were needed quickly, the alternative was to either convince home defence conscripts raised under the National Resources Mobilization Act (NRMA), many of whom were trained infantry, to volunteer for service overseas, or to conscript them. The first course of action failed; the second was utilized on 23 November 1944 when Ottawa ordered 16,000 NRMA men overseas as reinforcements. As it turned out, First Canadian Army saw little action for more than two months during the winter, allowing the reinforcement system to make up the infantry shortfall. Few conscripts made it to the front in time to affect matters.

The crisis had serious political ramifications. These began when defence minister J.L. Ralston returned from a visit overseas in late October 1944 to tell Prime Minister Mackenzie King that conscription now was necessary. King responded by firing Ralston and appointing General A.G.L. McNaughton, the former First Canadian Army commander sacked by Ralston in late 1943, in his place. When McNaughton failed to persuade conscripts to volunteer for overseas service and when some generals in Canada began threatening to resign, the new defence minister told King, who

Using H.J. Mowat's World War I drawing, this Remembrance Day poster from 1983 appeared during a time when remembrance seemed muted. This has changed since the 1990s with enhanced media coverage, a boom in war memoirs, and the public's support for the troops in Afghanistan.

decided to order 16,000 NRMA men overseas. The problem then became managing the Quebec reaction. Air minister C.G. Power resigned, but he was the only Quebec minister to do so; notably, Louis St Laurent, King's influential justice minister, did not follow. Though there was unhappiness in the Liberals' Quebec caucus, most understood that King had delayed conscription as long as possible. In the 1945 general election, Quebec voters kept King in power.

See also: Conscription; King; McNaughton; Quebec and the Military; Ralston.

Reading: C.P. Stacey, *Arms, Men, and Governments: The War Policies of Canada, 1939–1945* (Toronto, 1970); J.L. Granatstein and J.M. Hitsman, *Broken Promises: A History of Conscription in Canada* (Toronto, 1977).

Remembrance Day. World War I ended on 11 November 1918 at 11:00 a.m., the date and time the armistice came into effect. Ceremonies to mark the end of hostilities, at first generally known as Armistice Day for the day the fighting on the Western Front ended, have been held in many combatant nations ever since, usually on or near 11 November. In Canada, the first Armistice Day was commemorated on 11 November 1920, but the Armistice Day Act of May 1921 linked wartime commemoration with Thanksgiving Day, then a floating federal holiday. The two events were held together for the first time on 7 November 1921, the Monday of the week in which 11 November fell. The odd linkage of a holiday long weekend with sombre meditation on war and military sacrifice was never popular with veterans who suspected, accurately, the hand of business interests in emphasizing the long weekend's commercial as opposed to commemorative connotations. Gatherings continued on 11 November at 11 a.m. nevertheless, and veterans' organizations pressed strongly for the primacy of that date from at least 1925, when the Canadian Legion began a campaign to have Parliament separate Armistice Day from Thanksgiving Day and establish national commemorations on the 11th. The campaign proved successful, a parliamentary amendment to the proposed legislation also changing the event's name to Remembrance Day, reflecting the date's growing significance as a meditation on war, loss, and sacrifice instead of simply the end of World War I. On 11 November 1931, after a decade of Armistice Day/Thanksgiving weekends, Canada held its first formal Remembrance Day.

The day's events now remember the dead of all Canada's wars and peace enforcement missions with a ceremony at the National War Memorial in Ottawa and at cenotaphs across the country, accompanied by two minutes of silence, poems, fly-pasts, and widespread media coverage. Remembrance Day now occurs amidst Remembrance Week, and is marked with the wearing of red poppies, offered by The Royal Canadian Legion for voluntary donations, harking back to John McCrae's poem, "In Flanders Fields." The wearing of poppies originated in New York City in November 1918, was recognized by the American Legion two years later, spread to France soon after, to Britain in 1921, and to Canada the same year, where the Great War Veterans Association endorsed the wearing of poppies made by French women and children. In 1922, disabled Canadian veterans took over the manufacturing of poppies, a practice that continued to 1996 when the Legion arranged for a private firm to do the work.

Research and Writing. The history of Canada's wars and military excursions has been an integral part of Canadian letters from earliest times. The oral and cultural traditions of First Nations emphasized the martial aspects of tribal life and the character and choices required of notable warriors. European colonial memoirists often highlighted their own military or strategic prowess in works intended—then as now—for self-promotion, the preservation of honour, or imperial or national reputation. None of these were monographs in the modern sense, and few followed any defensible historical method, techniques that would not become common until much later, in parallel with the evolution of the historical profession itself. Still, the history of war was a feature of historical writing about Canada long before one could speak confidently about a discipline called "military history."

The eighteenth century produced biographies, memoirs, and first-hand accounts of battles and campaigns—especially Quebec in 1759—that fed public and political interest in tales of adventure, conquest, and individual heroism. British accounts extolled the success against heavy odds of Wolfe's army in the capture of New France; French accounts emphasized their own challenges against superior enemy might, noting too the failure of reinforcements from metropolitan France in sealing Canada's fate. Diaries, documents, letters, and patriotic blarney on colonial struggles, often packaged as "true accounts," appeared well into the nineteenth century, speaking as much to the motivations of old soldiers as to any emerging scholarship. They left a rich vein of contemporary opinion and observation for subsequent scholars to mine.

There was professional military writing too, much of it also of immense subsequent value in attempting to reconstruct the life and times of imperial armed forces and the local establishments they maintained. Army and navy officers produced treatises, highly technical and of practical instructional value for the most part, that were nevertheless often based on the assessment of historical or contemporary military affairs or comparisons of other military works. The more technical arms produced studies of artillery, engineering, logistics, and siegecraft, while works on infantry tactics, discipline, horsemanship, and weapons handling also appeared. The American Civil War (1861–1865) saw British officers based in or sent to Canada writing what would now be called "lessons learned" documents about the effects of fighting on everything from coastal fortifications to military morale. Narrowly circulated and selectively read, most fell on the deaf ears of an imperial establishment too inclined to view North American conflicts as the affairs of amateurs.

Some Canadians were among the sharper students of what, in retrospect, were the origins of modern war. George T. Denison III, a Canadian militia officer with service against the Fenians in 1866 and in the Northwest Rebellion of 1885, wrote a volume in 1861 on the means of defending Canada and, in 1877, an award-winning work on the history of cavalry. His studies, based in part on interviews with Civil War veterans, reflected on the transition from cavalry as *l'arme blanche* to its widespread employment as mounted infantry. An almost complete emphasis on guns-and-trumpets history or the political evolution of states, empires, and polities did not mean that such contemporary accounts lacked lasting value. Recent interpretations on the French presence in North America, the Seven Years' War, and the War of 1812 make extensive use of such work, much of it little known, seldom consulted, and infrequently cited. Its reliability remains uneven. E.A. Cruickshank's nine-volume edited account of the War of 1812 along the Niagara Frontier, published between 1896 and 1908, is a case in point: comprehensive, indispensable, and based on prodigious work in the war's extant correspondence and records, but opinionated, unreliable, and deeply misleading too.

Military involvements produced minor spasms of published work throughout the nineteenth century, most of it memoirs, letters, or personal recollections. Military history was a quasi-regular subject only at the Royal Military College (RMC) of Canada, established in 1876. Even there it was of markedly less importance than engineering, mathematics, equitation, and other supposedly essential technical pursuits. World War I witnessed the first true outpouring of military historical material, in fiction and popular culture as much as non-fiction, but its narrow nationalist focus generated as much obfuscation as genuine knowledge. An official wartime historical-propaganda effort led by Sir Max Aitken (later Lord Beaverbrook), a Canadian millionaire and British power broker, orchestrated an unprecedented and far-sighted effort to write, record, photograph, and paint the wartime experience, but no serious history emerged. A small official defence historical section, headed from 1920 by Major A. Fortescue Duguid, had managed by 1938 just a single volume of text and one book of documents on Canada's greatest conflict. War and related subjects informed at least some courses at Canadian universities in the interwar period: history in those days was far more about political and economic events

than social movements or environmental causes, while emphasis on narrative and character left greater room for kings, queens, and warring states than modern syllabi appear now to provide. A professional military journal—the *Canadian Defence Quarterly*—appeared to enhance military professional knowledge, and younger scholars, including C.P. Stacey, turned to military themes (his *Canada and the British Army* appeared in 1936 and *The Military Problems of Canada* in 1940), but more comprehensive efforts would only be sparked by a second world war.

In the half-century to come, the team of official historians assembled by the armed forces, and especially that employed by the army initially to record World War II, influenced heavily the research and writing of military history in Canada. Stacey organized a small historical section and conducted work overseas during the war, building the expertise and documentary record that later resulted in some of the finest works of historical scholarship ever produced in any combatant nation. The navy and air force were less well-served, with comprehensive treatments only emerging after decades of groundbreaking research and behind-the-scenes bureaucratic wrangling. Even so, the official history units of the Department of National Defence (DND), merged into a tri-service directorate of history in the mid-1960s, constituted the epicentre of Canadian military historical professionalism. Often threatened with organizational obliteration, and seldom free from financial threat, the directorate in its various guises maintained for more than 40 years the essential records of the armed forces' military activities, and a moderately sized cadre of skilled historians labouring full-time on their interpretation. Moreover, the unit in Ottawa became the essential port of call for all serious academic research on the Canadian military by university-based scholars, their ranks swelled in the postwar period by returning military personnel attending college on Veterans Charter benefits, and by the related explosion in the size of Canada's postwar university population. The national archives in Ottawa (now Library and Archives Canada), fully one-third of its records reflecting military subjects, was the other great focus of primary research, making the nation's capital the site of secular pilgrimage for military researchers from coast to coast.

The immediate works spun out by the defence research team—Stacey's historical summary of army activities, published in 1948, for instance, or Gilbert N. Tucker's two-volume history of the Royal Canadian Navy, which appeared in 1952—spurred additional work, both scholarly and popular. Subsequent volumes, especially those by Stacey and G.W.L. Nicholson—the latter would also write two volumes on Newfoundland's military history—would prove very nearly definitive. The official history unit also served as a training ground for historians soon to have flourishing academic careers, many of whom would, in turn, lead graduate students into the field. Other directorate graduates would write privately and, presumably, for greater profit. The list of official historian alumni is long. George Stanley would write in 1954 a seminal history of Canada's military past, mischievously subtitled "The Military History of an Unmilitary People," a description of Canadians that stuck; he would also play a leading role in the intellectual development of the Royal Military College, and shape the influential Canadian Studies program at Mount Allison University. Desmond Morton at the University of Toronto and later McGill, Jack Granatstein at York University, and Sydney Wise and Norman Hillmer at Carleton University would develop courses, publish prodigiously, and train scores of graduates. Reginald Roy, a World War II veteran, in addition to his writing and teaching at the University of Victoria, would compile one of the country's largest collections of military oral history. A.M.J. Hyatt would write a brilliant treatise on Sir Arthur Currie. In more recent years, Don Graves, Brereton Greenhous, Roger Sarty, and Marc Milner would join the directorate's fraternity of gifted researchers and writers: Graves's work on the War of 1812 is without equal in Canada; Sarty is among the finest Canadian historians of any type from any era; Milner has been instrumental in creating a successful military-research institute at the University of New Brunswick and writing his own definitive accounts of the Battle of the Atlantic.

Official history has not been the only source of federal support for military history in Canada; indeed, the overall role of federal efforts at encouraging military scholarship must be seen as preponderant in whatever current successes the genre enjoys. A Military and Strategic Studies (MSS) program of the Department of National Defence, for example, established in 1967 and now called the Security and Defence Forum (SDF), provided grants, scholarships, and institutional support to individuals and to a dozen or so post-secondary institutions. In addition to providing small centres the funds with which to leverage course development, research projects, or graduate instruction, the MSS/SDF over time created small units of military historical and related expertise that spawned publishing programs, research libraries, study trips, and professional development opportunities. Centres at the University of Calgary, Wilfrid Laurier University, and the University of New Brunswick led in the area of military and strategic studies, while Dalhousie (maritime security), Manitoba (air and space), Laval (global peace and security), and Queen's (defence management and international security) provided depth of training and analysis in related fields. Occasionally criticized, sometimes by disgruntled non-recipients of departmental aid, more often by advocates of "critical" security studies—an intellectual quagmire usually neither coherently critical nor having much to do with actual security—the MSS/SDF program proved remarkably even-handed in its largesse. It funded research on everything from Asia-Pacific security to Arctic sovereignty to ballistic missile defence, maintained a reasonable balance by region and size of institution in its centres of expertise, and compiled an enviable track record in its decisions on graduate and post-doctoral support. Military history sometimes struggled to be heard in a field thick with international relations courses and political science experts, but it nonetheless prospered in ways more or less impossible to envisage in the absence of structured funding and consistent support. Of note, MSS/SDF supported several research and teaching centres at French-speaking universities in Quebec, otherwise a virtual wasteland of military-security studies. Most of those younger scholars currently working in Canadian military history and related fields are direct beneficiaries of the program, which has also spawned publications, on-line resources, and other research tools accessible to the public. The great person theory of history was at work here too: David Bercuson played the dominant role in the rapid growth of Calgary's Centre for Military and Strategic Studies, as did Milner and David Charters at New Brunswick, and Terry Copp, Canada's leading military historian of World War II, at Wilfrid Laurier. But each centre also developed small cadres of junior staff and graduate students, using grant money to help establish courses, seminars, and public programs (for example, media speakers' bureaus or outreach initiatives) as a means of broadening their subjects' appeal to more general audiences.

Federal museums, including some of those run by the Department of National Defence, also maintained considerable research capacity in the postwar period. The Canadian War Museum, the largest military museum in the country, was not a DND institution, but instead the country's national museum of military history, a status not immediately evident for most of this period given its small facilities, few staff, and low visitor numbers. Still, it housed the country's largest collection of military material culture outside of the defence department itself, and employed a small research staff. The museum expanded considerably from the late 1990s in preparation for moving into a new facility, opened in 2005. From one professional military historian in 1998, it employed between seven and ten throughout the subsequent decade, giving it the largest concentration in Canada outside the University of Calgary, the defence department's contingent of official historians, and those teaching full-time at the country's military colleges. The Canada Aviation Museum, dating from 1960, was an additional source of research and occasional publishing on military themes, while more scholars could be found at the Department of Veterans Affairs, the national archives, the national parks service, and scattered among the small historical sections of other departments and agencies.

It took more than 20 years from the end of World War II for such scholarship to be anything more than a curiosity in most corners of Canada's academic establishment. The baby boom–driven expansion of universities created opportunities in which soldier-teachers found students interested in the wars of their parents and grandparents, and—even outside the ambit of military colleges, the defence department, or later research centres—many institutions offered courses specifically on the study of war. In an important survey published in 1995 entitled *Teaching Military History*, Ronald Haycock and Serge Bernier, themselves leading scholars and administrators at RMC and the directorate of history respectively, cited a 1968 study that found 25 percent of Canadian post-secondary educational institutions offering military history courses. Opinions varied on the quality and content of much of what such scholars produced. A growing industry of review articles, annotated bibliographies, and "state of the nation" surveys urged greater attention to battle or more to social history, deeper biographical focus or more on institutions, grander narratives or more subtle distinctions but, by the time that university campuses began to convulse in the later 1960s against social conservatism or the Vietnam War, it was no exaggeration to speak of Canadian military history as a distinct field within the broader discipline, and to hold its best practitioners as scholarly leaders. Stacey was a lonely vanguard in the mid-1940s; by the mid-1970s, he was an elder statesman amidst a large and growing crowd, many of whose careers he had played no small role in starting. By then, the Korean War had its own official history; James Eayrs was busy with a monumental, multi-volume history of Canada's external affairs; J. Mackay Hitsman had redefined scholarship on the War of 1812; and journals, regular symposia, edited collections, and bibliographical lists contributed to deeper knowledge of the distant past, and persuasive interpretations of more recent events. Private scholars added to this production, contributing a steady stream of technical works, hagiographies, and breathless hero yarns to the growing body of work based on primary sources and sober analysis, but doing as much—and perhaps more—to broaden the public market for military history beyond course texts and routine purchases by university libraries. In 1979, the first edition of Owen Cooke's indispensable bibliographical guide, *The Canadian Military Experience*, appeared, listing some 2,000 titles on Canadian military history from 1867 to 1967. A second edition, published in 1984, added hundreds more. The third edition, published in 1997, grew by an additional one-third.

J.L. Granatstein's influential jeremiad, *Who Killed Canadian History?*, published in 1998, bemoaned the weakness—and in some cases, the near-total absence—of military history from high school and university texts, but it appeared against a backdrop of research, writing, and publishing about Canada's military past that bore little comparison to past eras. By the early 1990s, just as anniversaries to mark the end of World War II roused veterans, academics, and some government departments to political action in the cause of commemoration, military history was at least tenuously established in many universities, deeply so in several that had been longer-term recipients of funding from the Department of National Defence. The subject informed a small but productive group of private scholars and publishers. Professors who had turned to military subjects found a steady supply of students, even if there were few tenured positions into which the subsequent graduates could be placed. Works of military history sold well, or at least better than most turgid academic tomes produced for adepts and seldom marketed beyond the university library circuit, and there were probably more professional Canadian military historians working in the field than at any other time. The professional development of military officers, widely criticized in the early 1990s, began to be taken seriously as well, the latent anti-intellectualism of much of the officer corps gradually eroded by degree programs, a leadership institute, formal reading lists, and distance learning.

Anniversary dates and media attention sparked further publishing, special television productions, and public events. The increasing operational tempo of the Canadian Forces after the fall of the Berlin Wall, with difficult, dangerous missions in Africa, Asia, and former Yugoslavia, and outright wars in the Persian Gulf, Kosovo, and, later, Afghanistan, brought the human dimension of armed struggle before a new generation of Canadians in ways rarely true during the Cold War. What had Canada done to support such men and women in the long, lean post-1945 decades? How had history been remembered, and heroes honoured? Major public projects emerged in response to what was widely considered a shameful record of formal neglect. An Unknown Soldier came home from World War I battlefields as a millennium project of The Royal Canadian Legion to rest beneath the National War Memorial in Ottawa. A new Canadian War Museum opened in 2005 to widespread fanfare and unprecedented visitor numbers. Stephen Harper, a prime minister perhaps more personally interested in military subjects than any of his predecessors, promoted military heritage, authorized the rewriting of an influential citizen's guide to better reflect a national narrative and a shared military past, and spent money to protect military sites, support military personnel and their families, and commemorate important milestones. The 90th anniversary of Vimy Ridge in 2007 was the very model of a modern commemoration, all the more so for being televised nationally.

From an earlier firm basis in official histories, academic monographs, and operational accounts, the field vastly expanded. Its public image did too. Jonathan Vance's 1997 award-winning work, *Death So Noble*, on the memory and meaning of World War I, in many ways reflected the discipline's maturation—a brilliant work of socio-cultural history on a military theme based on an impressive cross-section of primary and secondary research and written in an engaging, accessible style. A monograph series entitled *Studies in Canadian Military History*, launched by the Canadian War Museum in conjunction with the University of British Columbia Press in 2001 and continuing an earlier successful museum series that had published path-breaking work across the full range of military subjects, emphasized younger scholars, fresh approaches, and new subjects. It subsequently produced home front studies, military biography, bureaucratic history, and works on First Nations, conscientious objection, the militia myth, communities at war, and Cold War security. The Museum's research complement included leading scholars in several fields—Peter MacLeod on the Seven Years' War, Tim Cook on World War I, and Laura Brandon on war art. The directorate of history remains the bedrock of serious military scholarship in Canada, boasting in Stephen Harris, Michael Whitby, Jean Morin, and others, and the research projects they lead on the navy, peace support operations, and the Afghanistan war, the most capable historical team and the most ambitious endeavours since Stacey's time. They remain, regrettably, no less vulnerable than they are essential to scholarship.

In the early twenty-first century, the state of research and writing on Canadian military history still reflects the expansion of universities and public funding in the 1960s, and the hothouse atmosphere of public attention and political interest that have marked the field since 1994–1995 and the anniversary events to mark the end of World War II. It also reflects the continuing presence of federal agencies in support of military history, the vulnerability of research and writing to even minor fluctuations in public funds or political tastes, and the congenital resistance of most post-secondary institutions to military history as a teaching field. Private organizations and think tanks joined some academics and public officials in recent years to pressure provincial educational establishments to pay greater attention to military subjects, and had tremendous success in some areas, but their legacy, housed mainly in short-term grants or well-publicized teaching awards, remains uncertain and their influence debatable. A series of capable administrators at the Department of National Defence's directorate of history, including Stacey, Bernier, Hillmer, and W.A.B. Douglas, fought doggedly but not always successfully to preserve research and scholarship against financial pressures, fixations of the moment, and departmental politics. Veterans' pressure on selected files, notably the issue

of strategic bombing during World War II, the subject of a controversial documentary film, a volume of official history, private scholarship, and an exhibit in the new War Museum, damaged public institutions, threatened to politicize research, and pitted erstwhile allies—veterans and their scribes—against one another, in newspaper editorials and senate committee rooms. The selective digitization of public records, a useful complement to other research tools, including the availability of skilled archivists, has been paced by a decline in opening hours at most public institutions and general reductions in professional staff. The official history of the Canadian navy, for example, a multi-volume work of immense vision and incomparable scholarship, has been delayed as a result.

In universities and colleges, the baby-boom wave of soldier-teachers, former official historians, and specialized classes has, in substantial measure, receded. University administrators and the history departments in which most such courses have traditionally resided, never having been especially responsive to military subjects in any case, have proven consistent in their prejudices. In a handful of cases, including the University of Ottawa and the University of Western Ontario, the capacity of schools outside the old MSS/SDF network to teach or conduct serious research in military history has expanded; in most places where military history had, at least temporarily, held a precarious foothold, usually in the form of one or two dedicated professors—Memorial, Acadia, York, or the University of Toronto, to name a few—that capacity has measurably declined. Calgary, Wilfrid Laurier, and New Brunswick are the outstanding exceptions, with Calgary having quite possibly the largest group of university-based military historians anywhere. In French Canada, now as ever, the field is bereft of serious attention, excepting those who teach or write from federal precincts, notably the defence educational network, including the Royal Military College where distance learning has emerged as a powerful adjunct to in-class instruction, or the directorate of history. Efforts in the 1990s to raise military history's profile by splitting it from the broader historical field by establishing a subject-specific professional association gained little, save the enmity of colleagues; more recent attempts to reintegrate military history by working within extant associations to host panels or coordinate workshops have met much the same fate. Military scholarship is alive and well, but it continues to reside uneasily in a professional scholarly milieu that is at best disinterested, and at worst dismissive. Oversubscribed courses, long lists of graduate students, and the evident popularity of military subjects in popular culture, the press, and best-seller lists seem perennially irrelevant to university search committees or research vice-presidents.

The field in the twenty-first century is wide, rich, deep, and successful, the product of two generations' worth of serious scholarship, institutional leadership, and critical funding. It is also unevenly established, vulnerable, and rife with clever forgeries—a steady run of rehashed battle tales, thinly researched polemics, and ill-considered potboilers. In public institutions, the pressure to produce purely commemorative work as opposed to more critical analyses is considerable. Commercial publishers publish selectively but promote tolerably well; academic presses churn theses into monographs but edit poorly and market hardly at all; specialty presses eke out narrow margins, punished by big-box stores or on-line retailers demanding large discounts on one side and new media, including masses of shoddy content cobbled together from other on-line sources, on the other. A revamped *Legion Magazine* is a compelling success story—an example of practical information merged with sound content distilling serious research for a widespread readership. *Canadian Military History*, a quarterly produced by Wilfrid Laurier University with support from the War Museum, is another. Intensive research projects, including one at the University of Western Ontario on the social composition of the Canadian Expeditionary Force in World War I, or major on-line databases, like one at British Columbia's Malaspina College on soldiers' letters, make resources and interpretations available to broader audiences than ever before. Finding value in cyberspace, however, as in crowded library stacks, is

made more difficult by purely celebratory work or unreliable amateur efforts that compete for attention. It is still not too much of a good thing. SEE ALSO: AUTOBIOGRAPHY, MILITARY; BIOGRAPHY, MILITARY; COPP; MAGAZINES, MILITARY; STACEY; STANLEY.

READING: Ronald Haycock with Serge Bernier, *Teaching Military History: Clio and Mars in Canada* (Athabaska, AB, 1995); Tim Cook, *Clio's Warriors: Canadian Historians and the Writing of the World Wars* (Victoria, 2006).

Reserve Forces. The *levée en masse* was the traditional method of supplementing regular forces in the event of war or invasion, though it paralyzed the economy and produced something less than willing, effective soldiers. By the 1850s in Canada, spurred by the Crimean War, militia infantry and cavalry units had begun to be raised, and the creation of the Dominion of Canada formalized this process. The militia was not ordinarily well trained or well equipped, but it sufficed to deal with Fenians and rebels in the Northwest and to act against strikers. By the years before World War I, Canada had approximately 50,000 reservists, who provided most of the officers and senior non-commissioned officers (NCOs) for the Canadian Expeditionary Force.

After the war, the militia was reorganized, not for the first or last time. This was followed by the creation of the Royal Canadian Navy (RCN) reserve, with "ships" in most large cities, as well as a Royal Canadian Air Force (RCAF) Auxiliary. The latter two were tiny; the militia again numbered some 50,000 by the outbreak of war in 1939. A striking characteristic of Canadian reserves has been resentment of the regular forces (and vice versa). The enmity of RCN volunteer reservists helped bring down the chief of naval staff in 1943 and, early in the war, militia officers were bitterly resentful at the way they were sidelined by regulars.

The three services' reserves continued after the war. The RCN and RCAF reserves were again small. The army reserve was small too, keeping most of its traditional units across the land, but with regiments of a hundred or so all ranks overstaffed by a full cadre of officers. Tension between reservists and regulars persisted in the army, so much so that in 1995 the

Department of National Defence established a Special Commission on the Restructuring of the Reserves to rationalize structure and address resentments. The effort partially succeeded, but it was the understaffing of the regular army and the need to fill the ranks with reservists in a plethora of post–Cold War missions that largely eased problems. In former Yugoslavia and later in Afghanistan, it was the norm to have 20 to 25 percent of a Canadian contingent composed of reservists who frequently made up a much higher percentage of infantry strength. Their performance in the field went a great distance toward ending the regular-reserve squabbling. By late 2009, the Canadian Forces Reserves numbered some 27,000 (of which army reservists constituted 77 percent, the air force 10 percent, and the navy 13 percent); as many as 11,000 reservists were then on full-time service.

See also: Canadian Army (Regular); Militia.

Reading: *Special Commission on the Restructuring of the Reserves Report* (Ottawa, 1995).

Responsibility to Protect (R2P). In 2000, the Canadian government announced that it would set up an International Commission on Intervention and State Sovereignty to consider the right of humanitarian intervention. The Commission, in its report the next year, asked the fundamental question: when was it appropriate for the broader community of states to take coercive action against another state to protect its own people? The Canadian initiative had come out of events in the 1990s in former Yugoslavia, Rwanda, Somalia, and Kosovo where ethnic cleansing or genocide had been launched by nations against their own citizens. Lloyd Axworthy, the Canadian foreign minister, was a key figure in developing the concept of R2P, a useful idea that also clashed head-on with the centuries-old principal of state sovereignty. In the first decade of the twenty-first century, R2P did not seem possible in Sudan's Darfur region, or in Zimbabwe, as few nations seemed willing to intervene militarily in the face of protests from the national government, or without widespread international support. Because none would lead, few would follow. Where there was intervention, as in Afghanistan, casualties and indefinite (and expensive) military and aid commitments seemed a high price to pay for ideals and future prospects. For nations like Canada and the Nordic countries with small armed forces, the question of humanitarian intervention also was one of limited resources and competing priorities. In effect, that left the job to great powers or to "coalitions of the willing." The willing, in recent years, have not been numerous.

Reading: Lloyd Axworthy, *Navigating a New World* (Toronto, 2003).

Revolutionary War (or the American Revolution/War of Independence). The Revolutionary War began on 18 April 1775 at Lexington, Massachusetts. Both the British and the rebel colonists had been making their preparations for some time. The Quebec Act of 1774 had been designed in part to win the support of the Canadien elite and to ensure their loyalty in the event of hostilities between Britain and its British American colonies. In addition, the British "Captain-General and Governor-in-Chief" in Quebec, Guy Carleton, had been laying plans for the defence of Quebec and the raising of a colonial militia.

Well before the Continental Congress issued its Declaration of Independence on 4 July 1776, American forces invaded Quebec. Under General Richard Montgomery, they first struck north in September 1775 taking the traditional invasion route up the Hudson River and via Lake Champlain toward Montreal. Carleton tried to muster the militia to stop them, but few Canadiens rallied to the British flag despite the entreaties of the Catholic Church. The defence of the colony was thus left to a handful of British regulars supported by some militia and volunteers. Montgomery forced the surrender of Fort St-Jean on the Richelieu River and captured Montreal in mid-November. It was already winter, but the American force moved upriver to Quebec City where Montgomery joined Colonel Benedict Arnold and a force of about 700 troops. An assault on the city on 31 December was turned back by Carleton's troops, and Montgomery was one of the many Americans killed in the attack. Although the American siege continued weakly under Arnold until the spring, Montgomery's defeat effectively ended the threat to Canada. Thereafter, Britain used Canada mainly as a base of operations. In Nova Scotia, there was considerable sympathy for the American rebels, but the powerful British presence at Halifax ensured the colony's loyalty. The British defeat at Yorktown, Virginia, in 1781 brought the end of the war, which was confirmed by the Treaty of Paris of 1783. The war's outcome also led to the influx of American Loyalists into the remaining British North American colonies. See also: Carleton; Quebec (1775).

Reading: G.F.G. Stanley, *Canada Invaded, 1775–1776* (Toronto, 1973).

Rhineland, Battle of (1945). After spending November, December, and January wintering in the Nijmegen area of the Netherlands, First Canadian Army prepared itself for "Operation Veritable"—the attack on the Rhineland on 8 February 1945, an assault that had been delayed by the Germans' Ardennes offensive. The area between the Maas and Rhine Rivers was German soil, and resistance was expected to be fierce. The weather was cold and miserable, the Germans had breached the dikes and flooded the terrain, and the Siegfried Line, well fortified, ran through the area, along with the Hochwald, a great state forest.

II Canadian Corps, XXX British Corps, and Dutch, Polish, and American forces all served under command of General Harry Crerar's First Canadian Army, the largest field force ever commanded by a Canadian. Massively supported by artillery and

First Canadian Army's battle to clear the Rhineland in March 1945 was fought in cold and mud and against stiff resistance. The soldiers shown here were searching for German snipers.

airpower whenever the weather permitted—but with their progress so slowed by the condition of the ground that some units could only move in amphibious Buffalo vehicles—the Canadians and their allies fought through Moyland Wood and the Reichswald, along the Goch-Calcar road into Calcar, and then through the Hochwald Forest, beginning on 26 February, to the city of Xanten. The German defence, bolstered with elite parachute regiments, was as stubborn as expected. By 10 March, however, First Canadian Army stood on the Rhine, the Canadians having suffered 5,304 killed, wounded, and taken prisoner of the 15,634 suffered by the army as a whole. German casualties were far heavier. Two weeks later, the Canadians crossed the Rhine in the final phase of

World War II. SEE ALSO: CRERAR; FIRST CANADIAN ARMY; HOCHWALD FOREST.

READING: W.D. and S. Whitaker, *Rhineland: The Battle to End the War* (Toronto 1991).

Ridgeway, Battle of (1866). A Fenian force of some 800 crossed into Canada on the Niagara Peninsula on 1 June 1866. Led by Lieutenant-Colonel John O'Neil, the Fenians were Irish Americans, mostly veterans of the Union armies in the just-ended US Civil War. Most of the 900 Canadian militia sent to fight them were university students or almost wholly untrained citizen soldiers. The militia nonetheless fared well, at first, when they met the Fenians on 2 June at Ridgeway, but their commander, Lieutenant-Colonel

The Fenian Raids had an element of farce, but saw serious fighting nonetheless. This contemporary painting depicts (somewhat fancifully) the fighting at Ridgeway in 1866.

Alfred Booker, fearing a cavalry attack, ordered them to form square. In the resulting confusion, O'Neil's men staged a bayonet charge that left 9 Canadians killed and 37 wounded; many more fled. The Fenians had won the battle, but instead of pursuing the militia, O'Neil led them back to the Niagara River and into the United States where the Fenians and their leader were promptly arrested by the American authorities—who ought to have prevented their attempted invasion in the first place. SEE ALSO: CANADA–UNITED STATES DEFENCE RELATIONS; FENIAN RAIDS.

READING: Hereward Senior, *The Last Invasion of Canada: The Fenian Raids, 1866–1870* (Toronto, 1996).

Riel, Louis David (1844–1885). Born on the Red River and educated in St Boniface and Montreal, Riel was a Metis (one-eighth Chipewyan) with intelligence and charisma. He studied both law and the priesthood before returning to Red River in 1868. Along with many Metis, he objected to the transfer of the Hudson's Bay Company's Rupert's Land to Canada without any consultation with his people, and, as leader of the Metis' National Committee, he initiated the Red River Rebellion of 1869–1870 when he proclaimed a provisional government in the fall of that year, seized Fort Garry, imprisoned a number of Canadian settlers, and executed one of them, the troublesome and racist Thomas Scott.

Prime Minister Sir John A. Macdonald found himself forced to negotiate with Riel in order to secure the dispatch by Britain of the Red River Expedition, led by Colonel Garnet Wolseley. Although the negotiations were a success and led to the creation of Manitoba as a province, Riel fled Canada the following summer to avoid arrest by Wolseley's men for the murder of Scott.

Riel was subsequently elected twice to the House of Commons, but was expelled from Parliament and banished from the country for five years for his role in leading the rebellion. After 1870, he spent some time in a Montreal mental institution before settling in Montana where he taught school in a Metis

Louis Riel, 1865.

settlement. He also developed religious delusions, imagining himself a prophet of a new religion that was a cross between prophetic Judaism and Catholicism.

Riel returned to the Northwest in 1884 on a "divine mission" to help the Metis of the North Saskatchewan River valley after they, many Aboriginals, and some white settlers decided to invite him to help them press their various claims in Ottawa. In March 1885, he initiated the Northwest Rebellion by proclaiming a provisional government at Batoche and challenging the authority of Canada in the region. Macdonald responded by sending the Northwest Field Force of militia under the British general officer commanding the Canadian militia, Major-General Frederick Middleton. After several skirmishes, most of which the Metis, led in the field by the able Gabriel Dumont, and their First

Nations allies won, Riel and the Metis were defeated at Batoche on 9–12 May, and the rebellion petered out.

Captured and tried, found guilty of treason though he was certainly insane, Riel was hanged at Regina on 16 November 1885. See also: Batoche; Cut Knife Hill; Dumont; Fish Creek; Middleton; Northwest Rebellion; Otter; Red River Rebellion.

Reading: Thomas Flanagan, *Riel and the Rebellion: 1885 Reconsidered* (Toronto, 2000).

Ross Rifle. A military version of this Canadian-designed and Canadian-built bolt-action hunting rifle, developed by Sir Charles Ross, a British inventor, was adopted by the Canadian militia in 1901. The Ross had already been rejected as unsuitable for military service by the British War Office, the US Army, and the North West Mounted Police. Militia minister Frederick Borden, Conservative Member of Parliament Sam Hughes, and other politicians promoted the use of this .303 calibre rifle, a superior marksman's weapon manufactured in Canada. The Ross Mark I proved problematic and was recalled in 1906. The Mark II was produced in large numbers at the factory in Quebec City beginning in 1910 despite continuing British pressure on Canada to adopt the Lee-Enfield; the Ross Mark III version began mass production in 1914. In action during World War I, the long, heavy Ross jammed when fired rapidly and in muddy conditions. To the plaudits of the troops who hated it, the Ross was withdrawn over militia minister Hughes's objections and the Canadian Corps re-equipped itself with the Lee-Enfield by September 1916. See also: Borden, Frederick; Hughes.

Reading: R.G. Haycock, *Sam Hughes: The Public Career of a Controversial Canadian, 1885–1916* (Waterloo, ON, 1986).

Royal Canadian Air Force (RCAF). Some 22,000 Canadians served in the various British air services in World War I, constituting 25 percent of the Royal Air Force's (RAF) personnel by the armistice of November 1918. Several, such as W.A. Bishop and Raymond Collishaw, earned fame as top Allied aces. Shortly before Christmas 1916, the British government, with Canadian concurrence, set up the Royal Flying Corps Canada to recruit and train aircrew for the Royal Flying Corps overseas. Instructors came from Britain, and training, carried on at six camps including Borden, Armour Heights, north of Toronto, and Deseronto, Ontario, proceeded rapidly. The novice flyers trained on JN4 aircraft, built in Toronto by Canadian Aeroplanes Limited, and the successful graduates (more than 2,400 went overseas by war's end) were accepted quickly into the British air services. In many ways, the RFC Canada, as well as the short-lived Royal Canadian Naval Air Service, established in 1918 to patrol Canadian coastal waters, was the birth of the RCAF. The RCN Air Service, along with the Canadian Air Force, created in 1918 in England, disbanded at the end of the war. With the peace, the government's Air Board considered the establishment of a separate air service, and the Canadian Air Force was recreated as a branch of the militia, its name changed to the Royal Canadian Air Force on 1 April 1924.

The RCAF was not a combat force between the wars. Most of its operations were "Civil Government Air Operations"—flying supplies in the North, medical mercy missions, air photography, and air surveying, for example. The pilots thought of themselves as "bush pilots in uniform," and their aircraft were few, usually civil and not military types, and generally they flew until they no longer could. In 1926, the RCAF received the first of 12 single-engine Armstrong Whitworth Siskin biplanes and flew them for more than a decade into complete obsolescence. Not until February 1939 did the air force begin to receive modern Hurricane fighters.

As with Canada's other two services, the RCAF spent the interwar years preparing for home defence and, in the event of a major European war, to fight alongside Britain's Royal Air Force. RCAF officers received training and staff education in Britain, given that there was no such opportunity in Canada.

After the Sudetenland crisis in the autumn of 1938, the RCAF, now an independent service equal to the army and the navy, began to ready for a possible conflict. Small numbers of modern aircraft were ordered and regular squadrons expanded, as was the

Canadian aviators established an enviable record in World War I. Posed in front of a JN4 "Jennie" at Camp Borden in May 1917, these Royal Flying Corps trainees were being prepared for battle.

tiny RCAF Auxiliary. At the outbreak of war in September 1939, there were 195 mostly obsolete aircraft organized into eight squadrons in the RCAF and 12 in the RCAF Auxiliary. There were in all only 4,000 personnel, including two dozen trained staff officers and 235 pilots.

From this tiny base, the RCAF expanded rapidly during World War II and became a full-service air force. In Canada, RCAF aircraft played a significant role in providing air cover for convoys and patrolling the North Atlantic in Liberators, Catalinas, and Short Sunderlands. Fighters took part in the joint Canadian-US invasion of Kiska in 1943. Two RCAF transport squadrons of Dakotas served in Burma while a Catalina squadron flew from Ceylon. At

home, the RCAF operated the enormous British Commonwealth Air Training Plan that graduated more than 131,000 aircrew, including 72,000 Canadians. This was arguably Canada's greatest contribution to the Allied war effort. Over Europe, RCAF bomber crews flew with virtually every RAF squadron until No. 6 Group of Bomber Command—a result of the government's Canadianization policy—was formed in 1943, eventually with 15 squadrons of Halifax and Lancaster heavy bombers. Thousands of additional RCAF personnel flew in RAF fighter, transport, and anti-submarine squadrons; others were radar operators or specialists. RCAF fighter squadrons played a major role in the 2nd Allied Tactical Air

Force. In fact, the RCAF was part of the air action almost from the beginning of the war; its No. 1 Squadron (later renamed No. 401), equipped with Hurricanes, fought in the Battle of Britain.

In all, more than 250,000 men and 17,000 women served in the RCAF during the war, 94,000 of them overseas, flying aircraft or supporting operations in 47 separate squadrons overseas and 40 squadrons at home. More than 17,000 members of the RCAF died during the war, some 10,000 of them in Bomber Command. Canada's air force was the world's third largest by the end of the war, an astonishing statistic given its tiny size in 1939.

The postwar RCAF shrank to a strength of under 20,000 almost as rapidly as the wartime RCAF had expanded. But following the outbreak of war in Korea in June 1950 and the 1951 decision to send Canadian forces to Europe to serve with the North Atlantic Treaty Organization (NATO), the RCAF grew once again. A full air division of 12 fighter squadrons, equipped initially with 300 F-86 Sabre jets and later augmented by CF-100 all-weather interceptors, went to Europe, while a transport squadron played a part in the Korean campaign. The CF-104 began to replace the Sabre in 1962, and the RCAF role in NATO changed to strike/reconnaissance. The aircraft were armed with nuclear weapons.

In Canada, the RCAF worked closely with the United States Air Force to defend the continent against Soviet bombers, providing approximately 10 squadrons of CF-100 interceptors and operational training units to the overall effort. The RCAF

Recruitment shortages forced the Canadian military to enlist women in World War II, such as the member of the RCAF (Women's Division) being sworn in here.

role in continental air defence was formalized with the signing of the North American Air Defence Command (NORAD) agreement in 1957–1958, and a Canadian officer was always deputy NORAD commander. After the government's 1959 decision to halt construction and acquisition of the CF-105 Avro Arrow, Canada bought US CF-101 Voodoo fighters and Bomarc ground-to-air missiles for home defence. The fighters had nuclear air-to-air missiles available until 1984 and, after a major political controversy, the Bomarcs acquired nuclear warheads in 1963.

From its peak strength of some 50,000 in the early 1960s, the RCAF slowly declined in personnel strength and aircraft numbers as budget cuts took hold. Like the other services, the RCAF ceased to exist in 1968 when the Pearson government unified the Canadian Forces. The air force's functions thereafter were performed by Air Command, though there was substantial air representation in Maritime and Training Commands. Today, the Canadian Air Force remains an environmental command within the tri-service Canadian forces. SEE ALSO: BOMBER COMMAND CONTROVERSY; BRITISH COMMONWEALTH AIR TRAINING PLAN; CANADIANIZATION, NORTH AMERICAN AIR DEFENCE COMMAND; POWER.

READING: S.F. Wise, *Canadian Airmen and the First World War* (Toronto, 1980); W.A.B. Douglas, *The Creation of a National Air Force* (Toronto, 1986); Brereton Greenhous et al., *The Crucible of War, 1939–1945: The Official History of the Royal Canadian Air Force*, vol. 3 (Toronto, 1994).

Royal Canadian Air Force, Women's Division. The Canadian Women's Auxiliary Air Force received government authorization on 2 July 1941 and was renamed the RCAF Women's Division in February 1942. The WDs, as they were called, trained initially at Havergal College in Toronto (No. 6 Manning Depot) and later at Rockcliffe air base in Ottawa. The first group of recruits completed training in December 1941 and took up duties at British Commonwealth Air Training Plan bases in clerical/administrative roles such as telephone operators, tailors, or laundry workers. By mid-1942, the number of trades open to WDs expanded, and many served with operational squadrons in Eastern Air Command and soon overseas. The maximum strength of the Women's Division was 591 officers and 14,562 other ranks in December 1943; in all, 17,038 women served. The Women's Division closed down in December 1946. Not until 1951 were women again permitted to enlist in the RCAF.

Royal Canadian Army Cadets (RCAC). Dating back to 1861 when "drill associations" began to be formed by schools, cadet corps were prevalent enough by 1906 for the army to issue a general order regulating the kinds of cadet corps that could be established. By 1908, a Corps of School Cadet Instructors (Militia) was established, the forerunner of the present Cadet Instructor Cadre. In 1910, Lord Strathcona contributed $500,000 to a trust fund to stimulate cadet training, and this led to the creation of the Cadet Services of Canada. By 1913, there were 40,000 teenage male cadets in secondary schools in six provinces (including Quebec where cadet training was popular) and, although enrolment soared during World War I, the interwar years were fallow. During World War II, cadet enrolment again increased, and the "royal" designation was awarded in 1942. By the 1960s, high schools that had integral cadet corps began to withdraw from the program, and free-standing corps, often associated with militia units or service clubs, became more prominent. In 1975, Parliament authorized girls to join cadet corps, and approximately 20 percent of enrolment is now female. The RCAC today has 20,000 cadets on its books (Air Cadets have 24,500 and Sea Cadets 10,500), and is administered by the chief of reserves and cadets at National Defence Headquarters. International concern about child soldiers has substantially affected the kind of military training cadet corps can receive.

Royal Canadian Dragoons (RCD). Incorporating the Cavalry School Corps formed in 1883, the name of

Royal Canadian Dragoons dates to 1893. With service in the Northwest Field Force, the Yukon Field Force, and the South African War, the Permanent Force unit already had an established record when World War I began. The regiment fought alongside the 1st Canadian Division through 1915, and then reverted to its original role as part of the Canadian Cavalry Brigade from 1916 until the end of the war. Remaining a horsed Permanent Force unit during the interwar years, the RCD became an armoured car unit and served in Britain, Sicily, Italy, and northwest Europe during World War II. After the war, the tanks of the RCD deployed to Korea, Cyprus, and other peacekeeping and peacemaking operations, and to Afghanistan. The regiment is now stationed at Canadian Forces Base Petawawa.

Royal Canadian Navy (RCN). Created on 4 May 1910 by the government of Sir Wilfrid Laurier, the naval service began with two cast-off Royal Navy (RN) cruisers, *Niobe* and *Rainbow*. It could, however, build on the almost 30-year legacy of the country's

By 1945, the RCN had enlisted 100,000 men and women and had become a highly skilled navy, the world's third largest.

Fisheries Protection Service that had been established in the 1880s and eventually had eight armed vessels within its 32-ship fleet. The Royal Canadian Navy remained in ill-equipped limbo as the Borden Conservatives tried to contribute $35 million to Britain, a huge sum in that era, to build dreadnoughts rather than to build up the RCN. When World War I broke out in August 1914, the navy had only the two old training cruisers—little use at sea—and 379 officers and ratings. A small Royal Naval Canadian Volunteer Reserve (RNCVR), created just before the outbreak of war, aimed to raise reservists for the Royal Navy.

Admiral Charles Kingsmill, the director of the naval service, feared that U-boats might find easy pickings on the East Coast and in the Gulf of St Lawrence. He enlisted Fisheries Protection Service ships in the navy, bought large yachts in the United States, and took other measures to create a tiny anti-submarine patrol in 1915 that was almost completely ineffective. Three years later, the U-boats were a real threat, and Kingsmill had more than a hundred small ships at sea, 9,000 sailors in uniform, and the beginning of an RCN Air Service to carry out patrols and convoy escort duties off the East Coast. This was creditable even if the RCN had not fired a shot at the enemy; but the navy unfortunately took much of the blame for the Halifax Explosion of December 1917, its officers responsible for the traffic control that had broken down in the port. In all during the war, some 150 RCN personnel died in service, most detached to the Royal Navy or lost in the Halifax Explosion. In addition, 1,964 Newfoundlanders served in the Royal and Royal Canadian Navies; 179 lost their lives.

If the RCN had ideas of growth after the war, they were soon dashed. It had only two destroyers, a gift from Britain (a further gift of two submarines and a modern cruiser were returned to the RN), and 400 sailors: its primary purpose was to train reservists. The wartime RNCVR disbanded at the end of the war, and the new Royal Canadian Navy Volunteer Reserve and the Royal Canadian Navy Reserve came into being in 1923 with ratings being paid 25 cents a night

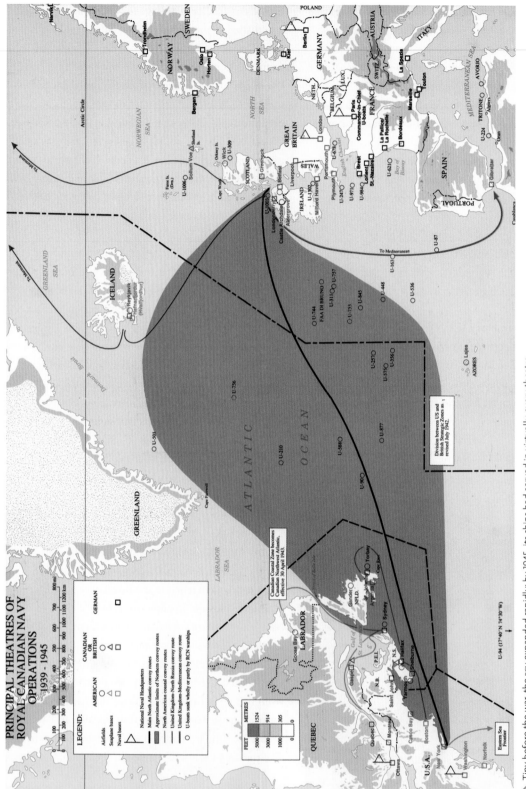

PRINCIPAL THEATRES OF ROYAL CANADIAN NAVY OPERATIONS 1939 - 1945

LEGEND:

	AMERICAN	CANADIAN OR BRITISH	GERMAN
Airfields			
Seaplane bases			
Naval bases			

National Naval Headquarters
Main North Atlantic convoy routes
Approximate limits of Northern convoy routes
North American coastal convoy routes
United Kingdom–North Russia convoy route
United Kingdom–Mediterranean convoy route
U-boats sunk wholly or partly by RCN warships

Division between US and British Strategic Zones as revised July 1942.

Canadian Coastal Zone becomes Canadian Northwest Atlantic, effective 30 April 1943.

▲ Tiny before the war, the RCN expanded rapidly; by 1945, its ships had served in virtually every theatre.

↖ The RCN had to learn its task on the job in World War II, and the North Atlantic was a tough schoolyard. This ship faced heavy seas off Halifax in January 1944.

for training and officers going unpaid. The Mackenzie King government proved unsympathetic to the RCN until, in 1929, it ordered two modern destroyers. At one point in the 1930s, the chief of the general staff, Major-General A.G.L. McNaughton, tried to swallow the RCN whole in the guise of cost-cutting, but Commodore Walter Hose, the RCN's chief, resisted with skill and determination and prevailed. In 1937–1938, as another war seemed on the horizon, the King government ordered four *River* class destroyers in Britain, giving the RCN six modern vessels. It was with this addition and some 131 regular officers, 1,850 ratings, and 1,500 reservists that the navy began World War II.

Wartime expansion, led by Admiral Percy Nelles, the chief of the naval staff, increased the RCN thirty-fold toward 100,000 personnel. In early 1940, the government ordered 92 corvettes and minesweepers with more to follow. The next year, the RCN acquired seven *Town* class destroyers from the United States Navy (USN) as part of the destroyers for bases deal between the United States and the United Kingdom, ordered big *Tribal* class destroyers in the UK and from Canadian yards, and converted three liners into armed merchant cruisers. The navy acquired frigates in 1943, two cruisers from the RN, and operated two aircraft carriers for the Royal Navy. In all, the RCN put 450 ships to sea, operated in every ocean, and, with most of its efforts devoted to fighting German U-boats, led half of all merchant convoys across the Atlantic. It was not all smooth sailing, the RCN's quickly trained wartime volunteers learning on the job on corvettes that were not always up to date while the regular officers continued their jockeying for promotion and the reserve officers believed themselves badly treated. Nonetheless, the achievement was superb. The RCN lost 2,024 dead and 24 ships during the war and participated in the sinking of 33 U-boats.

After 1945, the familiar pattern of selling or mothballing every ship seemed set to begin anew. In the immediate postwar years, the senior officers of the RCN tried to once again emulate Royal Navy style but, after several small "mutinies," the government forced better conditions for ratings and the Canadianization of the fleet on the admirals. By then, the looming Cold War, the creation of the North Atlantic Treaty Organization (NATO), and the Korean War where the Navy's *Tribals* served with distinction, made the RCN matter. The aircraft carrier HMCS *Warrior* was secured from the RN, then replaced by *Magnificent*. Tasked with anti-submarine warfare (ASW) by NATO, the RCN designed the *St Laurent* class destroyer and became the world leader in ASW, using destroyers, aircraft, and the "*Maggie*" together. During the Cuban Missile Crisis in the autumn of 1962, the RCN took over substantial responsibilities in the North Atlantic, relieving American ships required to enforce a blockade on Cuba. Unfortunately, the fleet had put to sea before the government ordered it to, so close had its ties to the USN become. Auxiliary Oiler Replenishment vessels were acquired in the 1960s, helicopter-equipped destroyers arrived the fleet, and *Magnificent*'s 1957 replacement, *Bonaventure*, arrived in 1970, it was sold off by the Trudeau government. At its postwar peak in the 1960s, the RCN had 20,000 officers and ratings and sailed 45 principal warships.

Reduced funding and the unification of the Canadian Forces in 1968 entailed a much more turbulent period in naval history. Senior naval officers led the fight against defence minister Paul Hellyer, a common uniform, and the disappearance of their service into the new Canadian Forces. They lost, and the RCN, its traditions notwithstanding, transformed into Maritime Command. SEE ALSO: AVIATION, NAVAL; CORVETTES; DESTROYERS, *TRIBAL* CLASS; HOSE; MACDONALD, ANGUS LEWIS; WORLD WAR II.

READING: Gilbert Tucker, *The Naval Service of Canada*, 2 vols. (Ottawa, 1952, 1962); W.A.B. Douglas et al., *No Higher Purpose,* vol. 2, part I, and *A Blue Water Navy,* vol. 2, part II of *The Official Operational History of the Royal Canadian Navy* (St Catharines, ON, 2002, 2007).

Royal Canadian Regiment (RCR). Formed from three companies of the Infantry School Corps, which themselves had been created in 1883, the regiment operated under a variety of names before being officially designated the Royal Canadian Regiment in 1901. Eighty men from the Infantry School served in the Northwest Field Force in 1885. Others served in the South African War in the 2nd (Special Service) Battalion, the Royal Canadian Regiment of Infantry, under Otter's command. The RCR, discriminated against by militia and defence minister Sir Sam Hughes—who dispatched it to garrison Bermuda because it was made up of the Permanent Force regulars he detested—did not get to France until November 1915. It served there as part of 3rd Canadian Division from the end of 1915 until the armistice. In the interwar period, the RCR was one of the three regular infantry regiments, and when World War II broke out in 1939, the unit formed part of 1st Canadian Division and fought with distinction in Sicily, Italy, and the Netherlands. As a postwar Active Force unit (soon comprising three battalions), the RCR served in Korea, in NATO, on peacekeeping and peacemaking operations, and in Afghanistan. Its three battalions are based at Canadian Forces Bases Gagetown, New Brunswick, and Petawawa, Ontario.

READING: Bernd Horn, *Establishing a Legacy: The History of the Royal Canadian Regiment, 1883–1953* (Toronto, 2008).

Royal Military College of Canada (RMC). Located in Kingston, Ontario, RMC opened in 1876 to train officers for the Canadian militia and frequently for

Founded in 1876, the Royal Military College at Kingston, Ontario, trained and educated junior officers. This photo, showing the cadets on parade, was shot just prior to RMC's closing during World War II.

the British army. After the establishment of the Cavalry School Corps and the Infantry School Corps in 1883, RMC also provided officers for Canada's garrison artillery and Schools of Gunnery. Originally delivered by British officers, the college's curriculum was designed to reflect military education at the Royal Military Academy, Sandhurst, and at the United States Military Academy, West Point, a mix of military and leadership subjects and field engineering. Hundreds of ex-cadets served with the Canadian Expeditionary Force in World War I, many with distinction and often in senior posts. After the war, graduates had to join either the Permanent Force or the militia as a condition of enrolment, though fees continued to be charged. During World War II, RMC had to shut its doors—a four-year program, or even a shortened two-year program to graduate a junior officer, was too slow when officer training centres could produce a 2nd lieutenant in a few

months and when the need for officers was enormous. The college's graduates nonetheless served with distinction once again, a very large number of senior officers (including H.D.G. Crerar, Guy Simonds, and Christopher Vokes) being graduates. When RMC reopened after the war, it did so as a tri-service college and soon was taking in cadets who had completed a two-year college education at Royal Roads or Collège Militaire Royal de St-Jean. Almost all entrants after 1954 enrolled under the Regular Officer Training Program (ROTP), obliging them to serve in the armed forces for three (and later for five) years; cadets were also paid during their training and education. The democratizing ROTP helped ease the perception that RMC was a snooty institution. In 1959, RMC won authority from the Ontario government to begin awarding university degrees (the first degree being awarded to Desmond Morton, later a prominent historian), and, in 1979, it began admitting women. In 1995, the government of Jean Chrétien closed the other two military colleges, and RMC remained—until 2008 when Collège Militaire Royal reopened as a two-year college—the sole Canadian military college. It is now a full-service university, offering undergraduate and graduate degrees in arts, sciences, and engineering, as well as correspondence and off-campus courses for the Canadian Forces. RMC also controls the academic curriculum at the Canadian Forces College in Toronto where staff officers and new general officers are trained.

READING: R.A. Preston, *Canada's RMC: A History of the Royal Military College* (Toronto, 1969).

Royal Newfoundland Regiment (RNR). The Royal Newfoundland Regiment today is a reserve unit of the Canadian Forces, based in St John's with smaller establishments in Grand Falls, Stephenville, and Corner Brook. A Newfoundland infantry regiment had been part of the British army since the late eighteenth century. One unit, the Royal Newfoundland Unit of Fencible Infantry, or Skinner's Fencibles, after the British major who raised it, played an important role in the defence of Canada during the War of 1812 before its disbandment in 1816. The small colony raised a volunteer infantry regiment for service in World War I, the Newfoundland Regiment, which served in Egypt (1915), the Dardanelles campaign against Turkey (1915–1916), and the Western Front in France and Belgium from early 1916. During the costly British offensive along the Somme River in mid-1916, the Newfoundland Regiment was all but annihilated in fighting at Beaumont Hamel, suffering one of the

⌃ Newfoundland's soldiers went overseas in October 1914 on the ss *Florizel*. The Newfoundland Regiment served with British forces throughout the war and suffered heavy losses.

highest percentage losses for any imperial unit in the entire war. Reconstituted in the aftermath of the Somme, the regiment saw extensive fighting later in 1916 at Gueudecourt and, in 1917, at Monchy-le-Preux during the battle of Arras, where it suffered nearly 500 killed and wounded. It also fought during the Hundred Days' campaign that ended the war, during which Private Thomas Ricketts of St John's, age 17, became the youngest combatant soldier in the British Empire to earn the Victoria Cross. King George V bestowed the title "Royal" on the Regiment in September 1917 in honour of its sacrifices and hard fighting.

Newfoundland did not raise infantry regiments for service during World War II, although two British army artillery units were recruited largely from Newfoundland communities; the Royal Newfoundland Regiment, disbanded after World War I, was reconstituted in 1949, after the dominion's union with Canada, as a militia unit. The RNR is currently part of 37 Canadian Brigade Group, a militia brigade headquartered in Moncton, New Brunswick. The regiment is deeply rooted in the local lore and popular culture of Newfoundland and Labrador, its World War I experiences having spawned best-selling novels, plays, songs, and several non-fiction histories. Hundreds of its members have, in recent years, served with Canadian Forces abroad, notably in former Yugoslavia and in Afghanistan. The regiment is one of Canada's best known and most effective reserve units. SEE ALSO: BEAUMONT HAMEL; NEWFOUNDLAND, WORLD WAR I.

READING: G.W.L. Nicholson, *The Fighting Newfoundlander: A History of the Royal Newfoundland Regiment* (2nd rev. ed., Montreal, 2006).

Royal Roads. In 1940, the federal government bought the Hatley Park Estate in Esquimalt, BC, to serve as a naval training establishment, HMCS *Royal Roads*. Two years later, the Royal Canadian Naval College, which had first operated in Halifax from 1911 until the Halifax Explosion of 1917, and then until 1922 in Esquimalt, reopened at *Royal Roads*. In 1947, the Royal Canadian Air Force and the Royal Canadian Navy began training officer cadets there. When the Royal Military College of Canada became tri-service in 1948, the Canadian Services College Royal Roads did so as well, initially with a two-year program. It fed its graduates to RMC for two additional years of training and education. In 1968, it was renamed the Royal Roads Military College. In 1975, it received degree-granting status and extended its program to four years; this continued until the cost-cutting Chrétien government closed the college in 1995, putting an end to graduates who were inevitably described as "Roadents." A private educational institution, Royal Roads University, now occupies the site.

Royal 22e Régiment. Organized in November 1914 as the "22nd (French-Canadian) Battalion" for service with the Canadian Expeditionary Force (CEF) during World War I, the 22nd arrived in Britain in March 1915 as part of the 2nd Canadian Division. Six months later—now a unit in the newly created Canadian Corps—the 22nd was in France where it fought with great distinction in all the CEF's battles through to the armistice in November 1918, the sole French-speaking unit to do so. Made a unit of the Permanent Force in 1920, renamed the Royal 22nd Regiment the following year, and given its present name *en francais* in 1928, the Van Doos, as it was informally named, formed part of the 1st Brigade of the 1st Canadian Division in World War II. The regiment served in Britain, Sicily, Italy, and northwest Europe. Continuing as a regular force unit after 1945, the Royal 22e served in Korea (and expanded to three battalions in the professional army's great expansion after 1950), with the NATO brigade in Germany, on a variety of peacekeeping and peacemaking missions, and in Afghanistan. With one battalion based at the Citadel in Quebec City, the Van Doos are the infantry component of the francophone brigade based at Canadian Forces Base Valcartier.

READING: Serge Bernier, *Royal 22e Régiment, 1914–1999* (Montreal, 1999).

Rush-Bagot Convention (1817). After the vicious naval struggles of the War of 1812, the United States and Britain agreed to place strict limits on the number of naval warships each could station on the Great Lakes and Lake Champlain: two ships each on the upper lakes and one each on Lake Champlain. The agreement took the form of notes exchanged by US Secretary of State Richard Rush and the British minister in Washington, Sir Charles Bagot. No limits on land fortifications were imposed, but the convention was a harbinger of North American harmony. The convention continues in force, though it was amended in 1946 to permit training vessels to operate on the Great Lakes. In 2004, the United States Coast Guard armed its ships on Lakes Erie and Huron to deal with smuggling and potential terrorism. The Canadian government, deciding this was for law enforcement purposes and not for military ones, did not object, though it reserved the right to act in similar fashion. SEE ALSO: CANADA–UNITED DEFENCE STATES RELATIONS.

St Albans Raid (1864). During the American Civil War, some twenty Confederate soldiers operating from Canada East raided the village of St Albans, Vermont, in full daylight on 19 October 1864 and looted three banks of $208,000. They then fled back to Canada with the hope that Union troops might pursue them, cross over the border, and violate British neutrality, thus provoking a diplomatic (and possibly military) crisis. The pursuit did not occur, however, and Canada arrested 13 of the Confederates and put them on trial. The US government sought their extradition, but when the Canadian courts inexplicably released the raiders on a technicality—and even more inexplicably gave them back the money they had stolen—tensions between London and Washington increased. The raiders gave their ill-gotten gains to the Confederacy and received a hero's welcome in the South.

St Charles, Battle of (1837). A violent skirmish between British forces and rebels loyal to Louis-Joseph Papineau during the 1837 rebellion, the clash occurred on 25 November. Defended by about one hundred villagers, St Charles on the Richelieu River had some strategic importance as the British sought to secure control of the Richelieu valley from the Patriotes. The 350 British regulars, led by Lieutenant-Colonel F.A. Wetherall, had moved north from Chambly, as one wing of a two-pronged offensive. After some brief but heavy firing and a number of casualties, the Patriotes scattered in the face of a British charge. SEE ALSO: REBELLIONS OF 1837–1838.

St Denis, Battle of (1837). The battle between 300 British regulars and some 800 Patriote supporters of Louis-Joseph Papineau on 23 November during the 1837 rebellion was a signal victory for the rebels. The British, commanded by Lieutenant-Colonel F. Gore, had advanced southwards from Sorel as part of a two-pronged effort to clear the Richelieu valley, but at St Denis they faced committed rebels led by Dr Wolfred Nelson and barricaded in two well-fortified buildings. The fight went on for five hours with 25 in all killed, and the British, short of ammunition, finally had to withdraw. The British success at St Charles two days later nonetheless secured the valley, and St Denis was burned in retaliation. SEE ALSO: REBELLIONS OF 1837–1838.

Ste Foy, Battle of (1760). After Major-General James Wolfe overcame the Marquis de Montcalm on the Plains of Abraham in September 1759, the Chevalier de Lévis assembled a 6,661-strong force of regulars, militia, and First Nations to retake Quebec in the spring of 1760. Sailing downriver from Montreal, Lévis reached the plains on 28 April and defeated Brigadier James Murray and 3,111 regulars just west of the site of Wolfe's great victory. With much hand-to-hand fighting, the casualties on both sides were heavy; Murray lost a third (1,109) of his troops and Lévis 993. The British survivors nonetheless managed to retreat inside the city walls; Lévis's army, lacking siege artillery, could not dislodge them. This victory might have reversed the tide of events had French ships arrived carrying heavy guns to batter down the walls. Instead, the Royal Navy relieved Quebec in mid-May, leaving Lévis no choice but to retreat to Montreal where he later surrendered. SEE ALSO: LÉVIS; MURRAY, JAMES; SEVEN YEARS' WAR.

St Eloi, Battle of (1916). This World War I battle pitted the 2nd Canadian Division, led by Major-General

R.E.W. Turner, VC, against a substantial body of German troops, both contesting for control of the massive craters blown in No Man's Land and under the German trenches by huge land mines in an earlier British assault. The British "Tommies" had taken the craters in hard fighting, and the Canadians came into the line on 4 April 1916 to defend them. A German assault on 6 April drove the Canadians out of all the craters but one; counterattacks then followed in a confused melee that lasted until 19 April with the 2nd Division suffering 1,373 casualties. The topography was so muddled, the maps so ambiguous that the Canadians had been defending the wrong craters, an error that left them vulnerable to enemy attack, and a mistake that was not caught and corrected by Turner's headquarters. The St Eloi battle demonstrated General Turner's weaknesses as a commander, but he had powerful political friends, and it was Lieutenant-General E.A.H. Alderson, the Canadian Corps commander, who got the sack, not Turner, who remained in command of his division until November 1916. SEE ALSO: TURNER.

St Eustache, Battle of (1837). The last and decisive battle of the 1837 rebellion in Lower Canada was fought at St Eustache, northwest of Montreal, on 14 December. Some 1,200 British troops and 200 volunteers formed into two brigades that were led by Sir John Colborne, the commander of the British army in North America. The British force clashed with a few hundred Patriotes, led by Dr Jean-Olivier Chenier and Amury Girod, who had dug into positions around the church, a convent, and houses in the town. Aided by artillery and their decisive superiority in numbers, the British smashed the rebels, killing 70 or so (including Chenier who had led the fight from inside the parish church), and capturing more. Three British soldiers died in the battle. The village of St Eustache was burned to the ground by the British after their victory. SEE ALSO: REBELLIONS OF 1837–1838.

St Jean, Battle of (1775). At the opening of the Revolutionary War, American forces under Brigadier-General Richard Montgomery moved up the Richelieu River valley with the intention of taking Montreal and then moving upriver to seize Quebec City. Sir Guy Carleton, the British commander, determined to defend Montreal by garrisoning Fort St Jean, south of the city, with 650 troops, a mix of regulars, volunteers, and militia. After their initial attack failed, the Continental troops laid siege to the fort from 19 September to 3 November 1775. At this point, short of supplies and with no prospect of relief from Carleton's shaky, unreliable forces at Montreal, the garrison surrendered. Soon after, Carleton evacuated Montreal and prepared to fight it out at Quebec; but Montgomery, his plan greatly delayed by the ponderous siege at St Jean, now faced the prospect of a winter attack. SEE ALSO: CARLETON; REVOLUTIONARY WAR; QUEBEC (1775).

St Jean-sur-Richelieu, Quebec. One of the historic military sites in Canada, St Jean lay on the invasion route north from Lake Champlain and the British American colonies. First fortified by the Carignan-Salières Régiment in 1666–1667 as one of the chain of forts defending against the Iroquois, St Jean held out against American attackers for six weeks in 1775 at the beginning of the Revolutionary War. In 1914, the 22nd (French-Canadian) Battalion formed there, and after World War I the Royal Canadian Dragoons had its home station in St Jean. The British Commonwealth Air Training Plan had a base in St Jean and, in 1952, Le Collège Militaire Royal de St Jean opened there, initially as a feeder military college for cadets proceeding to the Royal Military College in Kingston. Le Collège Militaire Royal became a degree-granting institution but was closed in the defence cutbacks of 1995. It reopened as a separate two-year institution in 2008. The Canadian Forces' major recruit training base, handling up to 6,000 recruits a year, is in St Jean as well.

St John's (1696). During the War of the League of Augsburg, Pierre Le Moyne d'Iberville captured the small fortified town of St John's, Newfoundland, from the English on 30 November 1696 after a brief siege.

Le Moyne then burned the town as part of a French assault on the English possessions; he also killed 200 and took 700 as prisoners. The French hold on St John's lasted less than a year, however, and the settlement quickly returned to England's control when Le Moyne was ordered elsewhere before he could consolidate his victories.

St Laurent, Louis Stephen (1882–1973). Born in Compton, Quebec, of French- and Irish-Canadian parents, St Laurent was a very successful corporate lawyer in Quebec City when, in late 1941, Prime Minister Mackenzie King asked him to replace the deceased Ernest Lapointe as minister of justice during World War II. St Laurent agreed, won a by-election in Quebec City in February 1942, and very quickly impressed his Cabinet colleagues with his courtesy, great intelligence, and forthrightness. He supported King during the conscription plebiscite and the struggles over Bill 80 to amend the National Resources Mobilization Act in late spring 1942 and, crucially, during the conscription crisis in November 1944. In 1946, King offered him the post of secretary of state for external affairs, the first time since 1911 it had not been held by a prime minister. After a Liberal party convention, St Laurent duly succeeded King as Liberal leader and prime minister in 1948.

Vigorously anti-Communist and committed to the defence of the West, his Liberal government took Canada into the North Atlantic Treaty Organization as well as the Korean War, making substantial troop commitments to both; had the Cold War turned hot, St Laurent was prepared to implement conscription at once, the cards for a national registration already printed and stockpiled. St Laurent's strong government also created the nation's largest peacetime military force of some 120,000, spending more than seven percent of gross domestic product in some years of the early 1950s to do so. His Cabinet included C.D. Howe, Lester Pearson, and Brooke Claxton, all ministers committed to Canada's alliances.

Under St Laurent's lead, the Liberals won large majorities in the 1949 and 1953 elections, including in Quebec, but the Suez Crisis of 1956 let his opponents paint him as being against Britain and France, Canada's mother countries, and too pro-American. To the surprise of almost everyone, St Laurent lost narrowly to John Diefenbaker's Progressive Conservatives in 1957; by then in his 75th year and tired and depressed, he stepped down as Liberal leader the next year. He deserves to rank as one of the best Canadian prime ministers. See also: Bill 80; Claxton; Conscription; King; Korean War; North Atlantic Treaty Organization; Quebec and the Military; Suez Crisis; World War II.
Reading: Dale Thomson, *Louis St Laurent, Canadian* (Toronto, 1967).

St Lawrence, Battle of (World War II). The Royal Canadian Navy (rcn) and the Royal Canadian Air Force (rcaf) played a vital role in fighting German U-boats in the Battle of the Atlantic, one of the key struggles of World War II. A subsidiary campaign within that long battle took place in Canadian waters in the St Lawrence River and Gulf of St Lawrence. The Canadian naval and air forces and government almost lost this campaign.

By 1942, the rcn was in the throes of expansion, manning corvettes just as quickly as they could come off the ways in the country's shipyards. There were too few trained, experienced captains, too few crew members who knew what they were doing, and the rcn's efforts had to be devoted to escorting vital supply convoys across the North Atlantic or to providing corvettes for the Allied assault on North Africa in November 1942. There were almost no ships based at the new naval station at Gaspé, Quebec, to protect the hundreds of ships that made their way from Montreal, Trois-Rivières, and Quebec City to join convoys at Halifax and Sydney, Nova Scotia. This was very substantial traffic: 750 ocean-going ships had departed from Montreal alone in 1941. So strapped was the rcn for ships that virtually the only defence of the St Lawrence system was provided by rcaf air patrols.

In May 1942, the U-boats entered the gulf and began picking off freighters. On the 12th, *U-553* sank

△ Beament's dramatic painting of a convoy and warships in the St Lawrence River indicates the closeness of naval battlefields to Canadian shores. The confined coastal waters complicated naval operations, while underwater conditions made the detection of enemy submarines difficult.

two freighters travelling independently between Gaspé and Anticosti Island and, although the naval authorities would have preferred to censor this news, it proved impossible as survivors and wreckage drifted ashore. That the war was not confined to Europe and Asia suddenly had been brought home to Québécois who had only recently—27 April—voted massively to oppose freeing the government from its pledges against overseas conscription.

The RCN's response to the sinkings was to institute convoys escorted by at most two *Bangor* class mine-sweepers and smaller vessels between Quebec City and Sydney. But the convoys made easy targets in narrow stretches of the waterway and, on 6 July, *U-132*

destroyed three ships in one night off Cap Chat. The minesweeper HMCS *Drummondville*, on escort duty, spotted the U-boat and attacked it with depth charges, but the enemy, though badly damaged, survived. By now there was growing concern, even panic, in some parts of the population. Some members of Parliament raised questions in the House and, in July, the government reluctantly agreed to hold a secret session to inform parliamentarians of the naval and air measures it had taken.

The Germans came back in force in August. *U-517* attacked and sank an American troopship on the 27th in the northern extremity of the gulf; at the same time, *U-165* damaged two other US ships from the same convoy, and *U-517* later finished off one of these. After an attack on a small Canadian convoy that sank one freighter, the two boats moved south into the St Lawrence River and waited for convoys to come to them. In less than two weeks, the U-boats sank two small RCN ships—HMCS *Raccoon* and *Charlottetown*—and seven cargo vessels, as well as damaging one more. The RCN, for want of ships that could not be spared from North Atlantic and North African duties, seemed helpless, and the RCAF, stepping up its patrols, had only some near-misses to its credit. Public pressure for action was intense, not least in Quebec where Ottawa continued to come under criticism for its inability to protect the province. Still, the few RCN escorts in the St Lawrence were needed elsewhere. In September 1942, responding to British Prime Minister Winston Churchill's personal appeal for any escorts the RCN could send for Operation Torch, the invasion of North Africa, the government closed the gulf to almost all oceanic shipping. That decision forced the St Lawrence cargo onto the rail system, which proved to be overloaded and a serious bottleneck. The enemy, historian Marc Milner noted, had destroyed only 1.2 percent of shipping using the St Lawrence. "And yet, by any objective measure . . . the Battle of the St Lawrence was a German victory."

The battle was not yet over. The two U-boats that had brought on the crisis returned home in late September, but five more took their place. By now, RCAF activity was intense and, although the Germans had a few successes, the area was now more effectively covered and most, but not all, of the U-boats departed. On the night of 14 October, the Sydney to Port aux Basques ferry, SS *Caribou*, came under attack by *U-69* and sank quickly; 137 of its passengers and crew members died. The ferry's escort had been a single minesweeper without radar. That dreadful blow was the last until 1944. The U-boats had sunk 21 ships and killed more than 300 men, women, and children, bringing the war home to Canadians and Newfoundlanders.

Ottawa reopened the Gulf of St Lawrence to oceanic traffic, and all went well until late 1944 when the U-boats returned. The submarines, now equipped with better torpedoes and snorkels that let them recharge their batteries while submerged, faced off against a much better-trained, better-equipped RCN and RCAF. The fight was more even this time. The enemy damaged an RCN vessel and a grain carrier in November 1944 and sank the corvette HMCS *Shawinigan* in Cabot Strait late in the month, killing the entire 91-man crew. That German success ended the battle of the St Lawrence.

Was it a German victory? To force the closing of the St Lawrence to oceanic shipping in September 1942 certainly was. But the U-boats had had only limited success in sinking cargo ships, and the fact that they abandoned Canadian internal waters for all of 1943 and most of 1944 indicated the increased danger to U-boats posed by the RCN and RCAF forces. The keys for the Canadians were training and good equipment, elements in short supply in the war's early years. SEE ALSO: ATLANTIC; QUEBEC AND THE MILITARY; ROYAL CANADIAN NAVY.

READING: Marc Milner, *Canada's Navy: The First Century* (2nd ed., Toronto, 2010); W.A.B. Douglas, et al., *No Higher Purpose: The Official Operational History of the Royal Canadian Navy in the Second World War, 1939–1943*, vol. 2, part I (St Catharines, ON, 2002).

Salaberry, Charles-Michel d'Irumberry de

(1778–1829). Born at Beauport, Quebec, de Salaberry joined the British army at 14 and was commissioned two years later. He served in several theatres during the Napoleonic Wars and received notice for his bravery. Returning to Canada in 1810, he subsequently raised, trained, and commanded the Voltigeurs Canadiens in early 1812 as a lieutenant-colonel. At the battle of Chateauguay in October 1813, de Salaberry's clever tactics enabled him to defeat a superior American force bent on attacking Montreal. He failed to receive proper recognition from his British superiors, but history has been kinder to him. SEE ALSO: CHATEAUGUAY; WAR OF 1812.

San Juan Island Dispute (1859). A pig owned by a Hudson's Bay Company (HBC) worker on San Juan Island off Vancouver Island strayed into a potato field owned by an American settler. The 1846 Oregon Treaty had specified that the boundary between the United States and British territory ran through "the middle of the channel" of the Straits of Juan de Fuca, but had not defined its terms precisely. When the settler shot the pig, a dispute erupted that almost provoked an Anglo-American war in 1859. When the HBC threatened to arrest the shooter, American settlers called for the US Army's protection. Troops were landed on the island, and this drew the Royal Navy into the fray. Fearing a "Pig War," cautious officers settled the arguments peacefully, dividing the island into zones of occupation. This state of affairs prevailed until 1872 when an international arbitration awarded San Juan Island to the United States. SEE ALSO: CANADA–UNITED STATES DEFENCE RELATIONS; OREGON CRISIS.

Saunders, Sir Charles (c.1715–1775). The commander of the Royal Navy's fleet at Quebec in 1759, Charles Saunders had joined the navy in 1727 and had gained considerable experience before being named to the Quebec command as a newly promoted vice-admiral. His instructions were to work closely with Major-General James Wolfe and to mount an effective amphibious operation; his fleet, with 49 warships and 13,500 men, was substantial. Wolfe and Saunders shared quarters on the admiral's flagship from 13 February 1759, just before the fleet sailed from England. After a difficult passage up the largely uncharted St Lawrence, the fleet arrived near Quebec at the end of June. Deciding that there was little possibility of French naval intervention, Saunders sent part of his fleet above Quebec, a tactic that made Wolfe's landing at Anse au Foulon on 13 September possible. After the battle on the Plains of Abraham and through the brief siege before the capitulation of Quebec, Saunders ensured that his sailors did everything possible to assist the army with labour, supplies, and

The battle of the Scheldt in October 1944 was among First Canadian Army's most arduous. Once it was over, Bombardier J. Koropelnicki at last had a moment to write home.

cannons; he continued this practice until he had to sail away before the onset of winter, his efforts helping the British survive French attempts to retake the city the next year. Saunders was knighted in 1761 and retired from the navy as an admiral. SEE ALSO: QUEBEC (1759); SEVEN YEARS' WAR; WOLFE.

READING: D. Peter MacLeod, *Northern Armageddon: The Battle of the Plains of Abraham* (Vancouver, 2008).

Scheldt, Battle of (1944). After First Canadian Army had cleared the Channel ports and moved into Belgium, World War II seemed to be proceeding to a satisfactory end. The British and Americans were moving eastward quickly, and Field Marshal Sir Bernard Montgomery, his troops having seized the port of Antwerp intact on 4 September, launched "Operation Market Garden," a massive effort designed to take bridges over the Rhine. The operation failed disastrously, and Montgomery and the Allies suddenly realized that their need for supplies was ever increasing while their port capacity was limited. Antwerp now was crucial, but the great port could not be used so long as the Scheldt estuary was in German hands. In September, the Germans might have folded quickly; by the beginning of October, having fortified the estuary, they would not. First Canadian Army now had the task of clearing the Scheldt and repairing Montgomery's error.

In the absence of General Crerar, recuperating from illness in England, First Canadian Army came under the acting command of Lieutenant-General Guy Simonds. He had four main operations to conduct. First, the area north of Antwerp had to be cleared to close the South Beveland isthmus; second, the Canadians had to clear the Breskens pocket on the south shore of the river behind the Leopold Canal; third, they had to take the Beveland peninsula; and, finally, Walcheren Island had to be liberated.

These tasks had to be accomplished on flat, wet terrain, only the polders rising above the water, with each metre of ground carefully pre-registered for enemy artillery fire. All three Canadian divisions struggled in the miserable conditions against determined, well-equipped German troops, all suffering heavy casualties that fell most severely on the infantry. The Leopold Canal was crossed under an umbrella of fire launched by Wasp flamethrowers, but the Canadians then had to struggle to sustain their bridgeheads; they ultimately succeeded. While Canadians hurled a succession of costly attacks over the narrow causeway connecting Walcheren to the mainland, the dikes on the island were breached by bomber attack (much to the chagrin of the Dutch who saw centuries of work at keeping the sea out destroyed in days), followed by a seaborne assault by British troops. The fighting ended on 8 November after 6,367 Canadians had been killed, wounded, and captured. After the estuary had been swept for mines, the first merchant ships arrived in Antwerp on 28 November.
See also: First Canadian Army; Simonds.

Reading: W.D. and S. Whitaker, *Tug of War* (Toronto, 2000).

II Canadian Corps. Composed of the 2nd and 3rd Canadian Infantry Divisions, the 4th Canadian Armoured Division, and the 2nd Canadian Armoured Brigade, II Canadian Corps served in England and northwest Europe in World War II. The Corps came into being as part of the First Canadian Army on 15 January 1943 under command of Lieutenant-General E.W. Sansom. He was succeeded by Lieutenant-General Guy Simonds in January 1944, and Simonds led the corps in Normandy beginning in July 1944, where it played a major role in liberating Caen and closing the Falaise pocket. It then moved east, crossing the Seine River and clearing the Channel coast before fighting in the mud of the Scheldt estuary in October and November. Casualties had been heavy, especially among the infantry, and reinforcements seemed on the verge of running out, the precipitating factor in the conscription crisis of 1944. Simonds's corps had two months' rest, however, letting the reinforcements fill the gaps in the line before it moved into more heavy fighting in the Rhineland and over the Rhine. Its final actions of the war occurred during the liberation of the Netherlands and in northern Germany. II Canadian Corps compiled a substantial reputation in the liberation of Europe from German occupation. See also: Crerar; Netherlands Liberation; Normandy; Scheldt; Simonds.

Reading: C.P. Stacey, *The Victory Campaign: The Official History of the Canadian Army* (Ottawa, 1960).

Secord, Laura (1775–1868). Born in Massachusetts, Laura Ingersoll emigrated to Upper Canada in 1795 with her father, settling in the area of what is now Ingersoll, Ontario. In the early months of the War of 1812, by now living at Queenston, Upper Canada, Secord rescued her husband, Sergeant James Secord of the 1st Lincoln militia, who had been wounded at the battle of Queenston Heights. The following year, on 21 June 1813, she overheard a number of American officers discussing an impending attack on the nearby British outpost of Beaver Dams and decided to warn the officer in charge, Lieutenant James FitzGibbon. After a hazardous journey on foot, and aided by Mohawks, she arrived at the British encampment on 22 June. Two days later, an American force of more than 400 soldiers was ambushed by the Mohawks

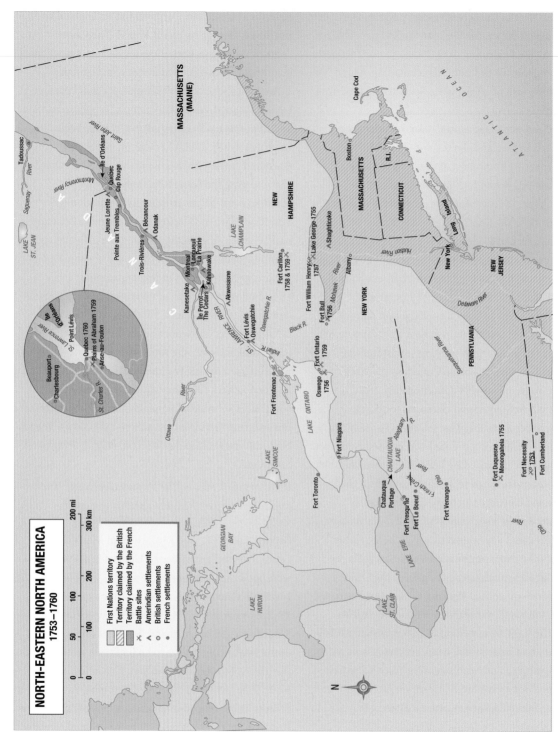

NORTH-EASTERN NORTH AMERICA
1753–1760

| First Nations territory |
| Territory claimed by the British |
| Territory claimed by the French |
✕	Battle sites
▲	Amerindian settlements
○	British settlements
•	French settlements

0   50   100   200 mi

0   100   200   300 km

LAKE ST. JEAN

Saguenay River

Tadoussac

Montmorency River

Saint John River

Île d'Orléans

Québec; Cap Rouge

Jeune Lorette

Pointe aux Trembles

Trois-Rivières

Bécancour

Odanak

Montreal

Longueuil

La Prairie

Kanesetake

Kahnawake

Île Perrot

The Cedars

Fort Lewis

Oswegatchie

Akwesasne

LAKE CHAMPLAIN

Fort Carillon, 1758 & 1759 ✕

Fort William Henry 1757 ✕ Lake George 1755 ✕

Shaghticoke ▲

Mohawk River

Albany

Fort Bull 1756 ✕

Oswegatchie R.

Black R.

Indian R.

ST. LAWRENCE RIVER

Fort Ontario 1759

Oswego 1756 ✕

Fort Frontenac

LAKE ONTARIO

Ottawa River

Fort Niagara

Fort Toronto

LAKE SIMCOE

GEORGIAN BAY

LAKE HURON

LAKE ST. CLAIR

LAKE ERIE

CHAUTAUQUA LAKE

Chatauqua Portage

Fort Presqu'île

Fort Le Boeuf •

Fort Venango •

French Creek

Allegheny R.

Ohio River

River

Fort Duquesne •

✕ Monongahela 1755

Fort Necessity ✕ 1753

Fort Cumberland ○

Susquehanna River

Delaware River

PENNSYLVANIA

NEW JERSEY

NEW YORK

NEW HAMPSHIRE

MASSACHUSETTS

CONNECTICUT

R.I.

Long Island

New York

Hudson River

Boston •

Cape Cod

MASSACHUSETTS (MAINE)

ATLANTIC OCEAN

C A N A D A

Inset:

Île d'Orléans

Point Lewis

Québec 1760

Plains of Abraham 1759

Anse-au-Foulon

St. Lawrence River

Beauport

Charlesbourg

St. Charles R.

N

∧ North America was a major theatre in the Seven Years' War, what has been called the first global conflict. France lost a continent; Britain gained an empire.

▲ The Laura Secord monument at Lundy's Lane cemetery.

while approaching the British position and forced to surrender to FitzGibbon. Secord's role did not emerge for many years because FitzGibbon failed to mention it in his report on the battle. It was not until 1860, when she was 85, that her deed finally became known. Contrary to legend, she was not accompanied on her trek by a cow. SEE ALSO: BEAVER DAMS; WAR OF 1812.

Sedentary Militia. Authorized by the Militia Act of 1777, the Sedentary Militia in effect amounted to a form of compulsory military service. Although its members typically lacked arms, uniforms, organization, and training, all able-bodied males from 18 to 60 were liable for service and obliged to attend one muster parade each year and to assist regular forces in wartime, most often as a transport or labour force. In fact, musters were infrequently held and few attended those that were. Moreover, the Sedentary Militia in many cases either evaded service or surrendered quickly when under fire, as was the case

during several, but not all, engagements in the War of 1812. The Militia Act of 1868 left the Sedentary Militia in place (with a paper strength of some 600,000), but with a new name, the Reserve Militia.

Seven Oaks "Massacre" (1816). The fierce struggle for dominance in the fur trade between the Hudson's Bay Company (HBC) and the North West Company resulted in a pitched battle on 19 June 1816. After the HBC ruined its rival's post at the strategically important forks of the Red River in the spring, a group of Metis, led by Cuthbert Grant and employed by the North West Company, retaliated in June by destroying the HBC post on the Upper Assiniboine. This led to a clash between Grant's 60 or so men and a score of HBC men under Robert Semple at Seven Oaks, a few kilometres from the HBC's Fort Douglas and Lord Selkirk's settlement on the Red River. The Metis killed 21 of their rivals, including Semple, against one casualty on their side, no massacre but a lopsided victory. The battle led to retaliatory measures including the capture of Fort William by Selkirk, and lawsuits that persisted until Selkirk died in 1820. The two trading companies united the following year.

Seven Years' War. The Seven Years' War (1756–1763) pitted Britain against France in what amounted to the first global conflict. Fighting took place in Europe, North America, India, and at sea.

In North America, the war—frequently known as the French and Indian War—actually began in 1754 as a result of the efforts of American colonists and land speculators to push France out of the Ohio River valley. Major George Washington, the future first president of the United States, led a contingent of Virginia militia into the Ohio country in the late spring of 1754, but was forced back across the Allegheny Mountains by French forces and their First Nations allies. This clash led to the reinforcement of the British army in America and a second attempt, under Major-General Edward Braddock, to expel the French in the summer of 1755. Braddock met the French near Fort Duquesne, now Pittsburgh, Pennsylvania, and suffered a catastrophic defeat, despite his superior numbers. The French, in the meantime, sent reinforcements to Louisbourg on Île Royale, present-day Cape Breton, Nova Scotia. In much of the fighting that year and in 1756, the French prevailed thanks to their shorter lines of communication, their native allies, and a better knowledge of frontier-style warfare. They did not prove successful in defending Acadia, their loss of Fort Beauséjour leading to the deportation (*le grand dérangement*) of 10,000 to 12,000 Acadians in 1755.

France dispatched the Marquis de Montcalm to New France in the spring of 1756 to take command, and he continued the string of French victories. His soldiers inflicted two major defeats on the British at Fort William Henry in 1757 and, especially, at Fort Carillon (Ticonderoga) in 1758. The tide of battle soon turned, however, with the arrival of more than 20,000 British regulars in North America. In 1758, Fort Frontenac on Lake Ontario and the fortress of Louisbourg were reduced, and the French were forced to abandon Fort Duquesne. The stage was set for 1759 when the British attacked north up the Champlain Valley, took Fort Niagara and, led by Major-General James Wolfe and Vice-Admiral Charles Saunders, attacked Quebec. That battle ended in September 1759 on the Plains of Abraham. Although Montcalm was defeated and killed and the city lost, the French were almost successful in retaking Quebec in the spring of 1760 when General François de Lévis advanced downriver from Montreal, defeated the British at Ste Foy, and laid siege to the city. The arrival of the Royal Navy at Quebec in May ended Lévis's hopes of victory and sent him back to Montreal where he surrendered on 8 September 1760. The war concluded with the Treaty of Paris of 1763, which confirmed Britain's conquest of New France, giving the Canadiens certain rights that allowed their continued existence as a people. In all of northern North America, only the tiny islands of St Pierre and Miquelon, off Newfoundland, were left under Paris's control.

In retrospect, too much can be made of Great Britain's strategic advantages in the war, including the Royal Navy, superior military numbers, and the vast population and economic weight of its North American colonies compared to the relatively tiny population of New France. In fact, France enjoyed considerable advantages as well, including a highly capable military, First Nations allies, a vast geography over which British forces could only move with difficulty and much preparation, and heavily defended strong points from the Gulf of St Lawrence to the Ohio River valley. France's commitment to defend its North American possessions was demonstrably less than Britain's in pursuing its conquest; even in 1759–1760, however, the outcome of the war in Canada remained in doubt. Quebec's defenders repulsed Wolfe's besieging army once at Montmorency; they might well have prevailed again on the Plains of Abraham had Montcalm not raced into battle, foregoing his two principal advantages—a strong defensive position, and the availability of additional reinforcements, if only he had waited for them. Even so, the later British defeat at Ste Foy offered hope, however slim, that the campaign might end in the spring of 1760 with French warships in the St Lawrence overseeing the surrender of a large, half-starved British garrison. This had been the pattern of most previous British (and colonial American) forays into Canada, and it would happen again during the American Revolution and the War of 1812. But British determination trumped French skill in the final contest for imperial pre-eminence in North America, with London also acquiring from the conflict vast possessions in other areas of the globe, notably in India, that would form the basis of one of the world's great empires for nearly 200 years to come. The Seven Years' War was a decisive global conflict, and the Plains of Abraham one of its most decisive battles. SEE ALSO: FORT FRONTENAC; LÉVIS; LOUISBOURG; MONTCALM; PLAINS OF ABRAHAM; QUEBEC (1759); STE FOY; WOLFE.

READING: William Fowler, *Empires: The Seven Years' War and the Struggle for North America, 1754–1763* (Vancouver, 2005); D. Peter MacLeod, *Northern Armageddon: The Battle of the Plains of Abraham* (Vancouver, 2008).

Sexual Discrimination. The service of women in the Canadian military, from the first nurses during the Northwest Rebellion of 1885 until the present day, has evoked forms of sexual harassment and discrimination consistent with prevailing societal norms. From low-level verbal and social affronts to rape and other forms of serious physical and psychological violence, these have no doubt been exacerbated by the political culture, behavioural codes, and social mores of the mostly male military establishment. Military service has all too often entailed for women the endurance of personal trauma and the clearing of institutional hurdles never present for most male personnel. Victorian attitudes regarding the role of women in society helped to shield nurses, members of the healing arts in a traditional nurturing role, from the worst manifestations of calculated slight and other overt forms of diminishment, but the slow expansion of women's service in the twentieth century into formerly all-male preserves opened a substantial battlefront for women's rights and gender equity.

The world wars saw widespread public reluctance over the expansion in women's wartime roles, regardless of the political and military need. A 1942 opinion poll reported that only seven percent of respondents believed that a woman's best contribution to the war was via military service. In industry, business, and agriculture, possibly even more so than in military service, women faced down centuries' worth of social stigma and legal strictures to work in factories, run small businesses, and operate farms. In some cases, their roles were not far removed from the family responsibilities of prewar days, but in others—in factories or the military, for example—their activities represented challenges to a social order that, in many cases, Canadians assumed the war would preserve. War work was often seen as temporary and military service, especially in the non-traditional areas of employment in World War II, as an anomaly soon to be expunged with the return of peace. Female enlistees in the wartime military—all three services maintained women's establishments during World War II—often faced considerable harassment before ever donning a uniform, public attitudes resulting in the common rumour that female recruits were of low moral virtue, driven to enlist by reasons other than pride, patriotism, or personal advancement. Oral histories recount verbal abuse, unwanted touching, inadequate (or non-existent) education regarding sexual intercourse and communicable diseases, and systematic mistreatment by some officers and male comrades. They were paid less, denied promotions or professional opportunities, and subject to personal scrutiny and judgment in ways never true of male personnel. Pregnant servicewomen were normally discharged; their servicemen partners—roughly 85 percent of all fathers—were not. Venereal disease was also initially grounds for dismissal of women (this was later changed), while male personnel received treatment instead. Government propaganda, a National Film Board documentary, military training, and leadership sought to erase the worst public misconceptions, but they persisted up to and well beyond 1945. Pay improved to 80 percent or so of that of men in similar jobs, female senior officers emerged, and a growing public profile changed minds and encouraged recruitment. An emphasis on femininity, deportment, and virtue remained central to the military's handling of female personnel, however, in part as a defence against public fears of immorality and in part as a morale-building component of service itself. Such discrimination was representative of the times, but was arguably a sensible precaution too as a nation pressed for recruits sought to fight a total war with the maximum of public support. Women's military roles during the war did not generally extend to combat, although many served in harm's way as medical personnel, pilots, or intelligence operatives. The return of peace threatened to erase permanently the gains achieved in wartime as official disinterest sought to disband women's military services and return women to more "appropriate" societal roles.

The clock would not be turned back so easily. Some 50,000 women had served in uniform during World War II, many of them in professions where few women had worked before. Discrimination notwithstanding, they had performed honourably and with great effectiveness, enjoying amicable relations with male colleagues for the most part, and shattering preconceptions—civilian as much as military—of women's military roles and capabilities. Precipitate campaigns to return working women, especially married women, to hearth and home—spurred by male-dominated business elites and enthusiastically supportive politicians—were a short-lived triumph for patriarchy and social conformity. For many women, surmounting wartime challenges was a formative experience, with skills, knowledge, and attitudes transferred from military service to civilian and family life. Many were delighted in the "return to normalcy" promised by official propaganda; others remained in the paid labour force, used their veterans' benefits to train for postwar opportunities, or defied categorization in the unexpected boom years that marked postwar Canada. Female veterans received essentially the same advantages as men under the groundbreaking Veterans Charter, a socio-economic advantage unprecedented in its scale and equality in mid-century Canada.

For the military too, the old order had changed. After a brief postwar hiatus when women's services had been disbanded, women returned to military service in small but noticeable numbers in the 1950s. Numbers were initially limited and their service roles circumscribed, but the later twentieth century saw women's military roles inexorably expand. Women, as well as gays, lesbians, and other historically marginalized groups, overcame institutional or public discrimination by personal determination, professional action, organized lobbying, and—increasingly—the power of legal writ and constitutional guarantees. Women slowly and not without substantial military resistance became eligible for every role in the modern-day Canadian Forces, sharing barracks with men and working with them in the field. In the era of the Canadian Charter of Rights and Freedoms, a sometimes militant feminism, and growing public intolerance of social inequality, incidents of harassment or systemic discrimination were viewed, quite properly, in a new and harsher light. Demonstrable changes were late in coming, however, and often as much a factor of the military's

humiliation or embarrassment at the public revelation of misdeeds as a result of enlightened planning or liberalizing attitudes. As late as 1965, the military's ceiling for female service members was 1,500 across all three services, or just 1.5 percent of total numbers, but numbers in the 1970s had grown to several thousand, with women serving in all theatres though not in combat roles, a barrier that would not fall completely for another 20 years. The pilot classification was not opened to women until 1980, one year after military colleges opened their doors to female candidates. Canada did not have its first female general until 1988, and its first female combat infantry soldier and first female fighter pilot until 1989. The submarine service opened to women in 2001, the last combat arm to do so.

The 1980s and early 1990s were a period of trial and assessment for the expansion of women's roles in the military, a historical phenomenon occurring in many Western countries at around the same time. Federal advisory groups and human rights panels advised, reviewed, and prodded along military organizations, sometimes dragging them beyond traditional patterns of inequality and systemic discrimination into the twenty-first century, with the courts at their back and public opinion alongside. A series of articles in the newsweekly *Maclean's* in 1998 pointed to widespread instances of rape and abuse that military authorities had allegedly covered up. The chief of the defence staff, General Maurice Baril, blamed poor discipline as the cause, created a toll-free sexual harassment line to receive complaints, and awaited the report of the Canadian Forces ombudsman. By the end of 1998, all ranks of the army underwent sensitivity training in the SHARP program, the Standard for Harassment and Racism Prevention. Incidents may not have ceased, but they appear to have lessened substantially. Defence department reports on criminal investigations, including sexual assault, began to be released publicly and made available on the Internet for curious citizens or government auditors. Regardless of added surveillance and better punitive measures, the military had irrevocably changed. By 1991, a mixed-gender Canadian warship had participated in naval exercises with allies. Always the most difficult service environment to address because of the arguments against cohabitation on long deployments in confined quarters and the risks—never entirely absent—of systematized abuse, women's access to at-sea postings was a critical waypoint on the road to equality of service and freedom from discrimination. Women in the contemporary military comprise approximately 15 percent of total enlistment, with a higher percentage in the reserves and a much lower percentage in the regular and reserve forces combat arms. Just less than ten percent of the troops in Afghanistan are women.

In October 1992, the Canadian Forces abolished any restrictions on gays and lesbians serving in the armed forces. They had always been in the military, despite barriers to their enlistment and the risks of mistreatment if found out; but the Charter made such restrictions impossible. The chief of the defence staff in 1992, General John de Chastelain, promised that "inappropriate sexual conduct by members of the forces, whether heterosexual or homosexual," would not be tolerated. The effectiveness of the edict is unknown, although the sexual orientation of military personnel has largely disappeared in recent years as an object of public debate. In 2005, Canadian Forces Base Greenwood, Nova Scotia, saw the Canadian military's first gay wedding, between two serving personnel. The Canadian military is currently viewed as an international leader in the areas of gender integration and social equality. SEE ALSO: GAYS AND LESBIANS IN THE CANADIAN FORCES.

Sheaffe, Sir Roger Hale (1763–1851). Born in Boston, Sheaffe served three tours of duty in Canada with the British army between 1787 and 1813. Sheaffe became a major-general in 1811 and, during the War of 1812, won the battle of Queenston Heights after taking control of British forces following the death of General Isaac Brock. The victory earned Sheaffe a baronetcy. He was then appointed in Brock's stead as military and civil commander in Upper Canada, but his military caution, his reputation as a martinet, and

unfounded doubts about his political loyalty made his time in command difficult. Although he likely acted soundly in retreating eastward from York to preserve his forces in the face of a superior American army in late April 1813, the Upper Canadian elite—which had been abandoned to negotiate the terms of the capitulation with US forces—was severely critical. So too were Sheaffe's superiors, and they removed him from his command in June 1813 and posted him to Montreal. He was recalled to England in November 1813. SEE ALSO: WAR OF 1812; YORK.

READING: Robert Malcolmson, *Capital in Flames* (Montreal, 2008).

Short Hills, Battle of. Discontent in Upper Canada did not end after the failure of the 1837 Rebellion. In June of the next year, a party of 26 Canadian rebels and American supporters, carrying arms for 50 more, landed on the Canadian side of the Niagara Peninsula intending to foment a revolt in the nearby and restive Short Hills area. On 20 June, some 50 rebels forced the surrender of a troop of British cavalry who had tried to defend themselves in an inn but were driven out by rebel threats to set the building on fire. Success quickly turned into panic when additional British forces arrived and took 39 rebels and their sympathizers captive. Their trials for high treason took place promptly. The invaders' leader, James Morreau, went to the gallows, 14 others suffered deportation (called "transportation" at the time) to Australia, and others were jailed. SEE ALSO: REBELLIONS OF 1837–1838.

Sicilian Campaign. On 10 July 1943, the 1st Canadian Infantry Division under the command of Major-General Guy Simonds participated in the Allied landings on the south coast of Sicily. The division, accompanied by the 1st Canadian Army Tank Brigade (soon renamed the 1st Canadian Armoured Brigade), was part of General Bernard Montgomery's British Eighth Army. Canadian participation in the Sicilian campaign came largely at Ottawa's insistence, given that the original invasion plan had not included a Canadian contingent. The

The Sicilian campaign in July–August 1943 was the army's first sustained action in World War II. Tanks of the Three Rivers Regiment move here through the ruins of Regalbuto, pummelled by Allied artillery and air bombardment prior to its capture.

Mackenzie King government worried that the lack of significant Canadian participation in the land war to that point was hurting morale both at home and in the army overseas. Initially, General A.G.L. McNaughton, the commander of First Canadian Army in Britain, objected to the splitting of his forces; he eventually relented, seeing that his troops would gain battle experience, but winning the promise from Allied commanders that the Canadians would be reunited prior to the expected invasion of the European continent. The Canadian government also had to fight—and did so successfully—to get Canada mentioned in the communiqué announcing the invasion, and McNaughton suffered the humiliation of being denied permission by Montgomery to see his division in action. Alliance warfare was complicated.

Enemy U-boats attacked the convoy carrying the Canadians to Sicily, sinking three ships, killing 58 Canadians, and depriving the division of 500 vehicles, a sizeable proportion of its transport. The Canadians, nonetheless, landed near Pachino, to the right of the Americans and the left of the British. They quickly overcame the rather limited Italian resistance in this sector and marched inland to the centre of the island where, in the dust and heat of mid-July, they first faced the Germans. Montgomery gave the 1st Division the task of turning the German right flank after the British drive toward Messina stalled in the face of heavy resistance on the east coast of the island. As the Canadians penetrated deeply into the steep mountainous countryside, the Germans used the winding mountain roads to mount an effective defence with their limited forces and relatively small numbers of tanks and artillery, repeatedly forcing Canadian columns to halt, deploy, and fight. During this portion of the campaign, the Canadians were in almost continuous action against German patrols or defensive positions, while pitched battles were fought at Grammichele, Piazza Armerina, Valguarnera, Leonforte, Assoro, Nissoria, Agira, and Regalbuto. At Agira, for example, the Germans beat off three successive attacks before a fresh brigade, with overwhelming artillery and air support, succeeded in dislodging them on 28 July after five days of hard fighting and 438 Canadian casualties.

The German tactics exacted a toll in killed and wounded as they were pushed steadily back across the island. General Simonds demonstrated that he had a flair for command, as did several of his brigade, battalion, and artillery commanders. The Canadians, with critical battle experience now behind them, went into reserve at the end of the first week in August as the Germans—who had lost some 5,000 killed and 6,600 captured in the 38-day Sicilian campaign—withdrew toward Messina and then to the Italian mainland. By then, the Canadian division and armoured brigade had suffered 2,310 casualties, including 562 killed in action. SEE ALSO: ITALIAN CAMPAIGN; MCNAUGHTON; SIMONDS; WORLD WAR II.

READING: Mark Zuehlke, *Operation Husky* (Vancouver, 2008); G.W.L. Nicholson, *The Canadians in Italy* (Ottawa, 1956).

Simonds, Guy Granville (1903–1974). Born in England, his father a British army officer, Guy Simonds came to British Columbia with his family in

1912. He attended the Royal Military College (RMC) in Kingston but, though the fees were low, he could not afford them and worked during the summers to cover the cost. But "The Count," as he was called because of his dashing good looks and manner, was a top cadet, and the RMC commandant went out of his way to assist. Simonds joined the Permanent Force's Royal Canadian Horse Artillery in 1925, served in various posts, and won a place at the British Army Staff College in 1936 where he performed brilliantly. Posted back to RMC as an instructor of tactics in 1938, Simonds made his intellectual mark by engaging in a high-level debate with Lieutenant-Colonel E.L.M. Burns on the role of mechanized warfare on the modern battlefield, documented in the pages of the *Canadian Defence Quarterly.*

The outbreak of war in 1939 started Major Simonds's extraordinary rise. He became a staff officer with the 1st Canadian Division and impressed his boss, Major-General A.G.L. McNaughton. After the fall of France in 1940, he took command of an artillery regiment, set up the Canadian Junior War Staff Course in England, and then went to the 2nd Canadian Division as the principal staff officer (GSO1). From there, he became brigadier, general staff, at Canadian Corps headquarters in August 1941 where he prepared Canadian training exercises and, the following year, drew up plans for a Canadian attack on German-occupied Norway that was never launched. In September 1942, he led a brigade and, in April 1943, at the age of 40, he took command of 2nd Canadian Division. In less than four years, he had risen from major to major-general.

⌃ Lieutenant-General Guy G. Simonds at Falaise, France, in 1966.

He soon took command of 1st Canadian Division for the Allied invasion of Sicily, serving under General Bernard Montgomery's British Eighth Army. The Canadians landed on 10 July 1943 and quickly moved inland. Simonds came under fire for the first time near Piazza Armerina. He quickly demonstrated a grasp of the best way to mount attacks on the tough Sicilian battlefield, and his combined arms operations became increasingly sophisticated. He and his division fought well, though some of his officers found him both cold and imperious.

Simonds led the 1st Division onto the Italian mainland in September and, after a serious bout with jaundice, took over the 5th Canadian Armoured Division on its arrival in Italy in November 1943. His problems were less facing the Germans than dealing with his superiors and his juniors. The commander of I Canadian Corps briefly was Lieutenant-General H.D.G. Crerar, like Simonds an artillery officer and the commandant at RMC when Simonds had been on staff there. The two had never got on well, and they engaged in an increasingly heated correspondence about Simonds's caravan—Crerar had sent an officer to measure the trailer so he could get one of his own made without asking Simonds's permission—that led Crerar to question his junior's mental state and to discuss Simonds with doctors and with General Montgomery. At the same time, Simonds fired one of his senior officers and pushed others very hard. Crerar clearly was jealous of Simonds's achievements in Sicily; Simonds, on the other hand, was highly strung, arrogant, and still worn down by jaundice. The spats did not stop Simonds's promotion to lieutenant-general or his being given command of II Canadian Corps for the Normandy invasion. He was simply too capable to ignore.

The next year-and-a-half showed Simonds at his best. He fired weak officers, installed or promoted those he trusted, and readied his corps for action in France. In July, he began his command in Normandy, directing II Corps in the great battles of July and August. In his first five weeks in France, he planned four major attacks on the Germans, Operations Spring, Atlantic, Totalize, and Tractable: these attacks played a major role in winning the Normandy struggle. Totalize and Tractable especially were innovative, using bombers to clear the way, putting infantry under cover in the armoured personnel carriers that Simonds invented, and using massive force to punch at night through the enemy's defences. The attacks were not all great successes and Canadian casualties were heavy, but Simonds had demonstrated an ability to plan, lead, and fight that few other Canadian commanders could equal.

Simonds directed II Canadian Corps across the Seine River and in the clearing of the Channel ports. When Crerar, the commander of First Canadian Army, fell ill in the autumn of 1944, Simonds became the acting army commander for the great struggle to clear the Scheldt estuary. This fighting in mud and cold was as hard as anything Canadians had done, as the troops struggled to close the Breskens pocket, cross the Leopold Canal, and then get across the causeways to South Beveland and Walcheren. Again Simonds devised innovative tactics and used seaborne strikes, bombers, and his army's first-rate artillery with great success. When Crerar recovered, Simonds went back to his corps, much to the chagrin of Montgomery, who judged Simonds a much better commander than Crerar. Simonds led II Corps through the battles in the Rhineland, across the Rhine, and into the Netherlands. Simonds had fought a brilliant war, rising further and faster than any other Canadian soldier.

But he did not become chief of the general staff with the return of peace, that post going on Crerar's recommendation to Lieutenant-General Charles Foulkes, a lesser soldier but a more skilful military politician and bureaucrat. Instead, Simonds went on course to the Imperial Defence College in Britain, became an instructor there, and then took command of the new National Defence College at Kingston. Not until 1951 did he become chief of the general staff at a time of rapid army expansion with the Korean War and the North Atlantic Treaty Organization both requiring brigades of Canadians. By every account, he did the job superbly for the next four years; when his

▲ Air Marshal C. Roy Slemon.

as deputy air officer commanding-in-chief of the RCAF Overseas in 1945. He became chief of the air staff in Ottawa from 1953 to 1957, was a strong advocate of the North American Air Defence Command (NORAD) agreement with the United States, and became NORAD's deputy commander-in-chief in 1957. As such, he opened NORAD's doors to a critical Canadian media and to Opposition politicians during the run-up to the nuclear crisis of 1962–1963 and after the Cuban Missile Crisis in the fall of 1962, both of which helped bring down the Diefenbaker government after its dithering on taking nuclear weapons and slowness in putting Canadian aircraft in NORAD on alert. Slemon retired in 1964. SEE ALSO: DIEFENBAKER; NORTH AMERICAN AIR DEFENCE COMMAND; NUCLEAR CRISIS.

READING: Joseph Jockel, *Canada in NORAD, 1957–2007* (Kingston, ON, 2007); S. Babcock, "Air Marshal Roy Slemon: The RCAF's Original," in Bernd Horn and Stephen J. Harris, eds., *Warrior Chiefs* (Toronto, 2001).

term was up, there was nowhere else for him to go but into retirement.

Tough, smart, outspoken, and abrupt, Simonds was one of the outstanding Canadian senior officers of World War II and the early Cold War. He could plan and think, and he held the high regard of Canada's allies, almost the only senior officer who did. But his restless ambition and his high-strung personality made him a marked man, a focus for jealousy and dislike. SEE ALSO: CRERAR; FALAISE; FOULKES; ITALIAN CAMPAIGN; SCHELDT; SICILIAN CAMPAIGN.

READING: J.L. Granatstein, *The Generals: The Canadian Army's Senior Commanders in the Second World War* (Toronto, 1993); Terry Copp, *Guy Simonds and the Art of Command* (Kingston, ON, 2007).

Slemon, Charles Roy (1904–1992). Born in Winnipeg, Roy Slemon joined the Royal Canadian Air Force in 1924, trained as a pilot, and flew in the north taking aerial surveys. He became senior staff officer in Western Air Command and then its commander from 1938 to 1941. He went overseas in 1942 and served as a senior staff officer in No. 6 Bomber Group and then

Smith, Donald Alexander, 1st Baron Strathcona and Mount Royal (1820–1914). Best known for his role in the Hudson's Bay Company and the building of the Canadian Pacific Railway, Strathcona funded the raising of a unit of mounted troops, Lord Strathcona's Horse, to serve in the South African War. The cost was said to be $500,000, an enormous sum in 1900. A decade later, Strathcona put another $500,000 into the Strathcona Trust to support the training of army cadets in Canada.

Somalia Affair. In late 1992, the Mulroney government dispatched the Canadian Airborne Regiment (CAR) and, a few months later, a reconnaissance squadron from the Royal Canadian Dragoons to Somalia to serve in a United States–run humanitarian peace enforcement mission. The east African nation was a failed state, with warlords fighting and people starving, and a previous United Nations (UN) operation had failed to establish control of the situation. The new Unified Task Force was authorized by the United Nations as a Chapter VII

⌃ Allan Harding MacKay's 1993 *Portrait of a Somali Woman* put Canadians in the background. At home a few years later, the Somalia mission would be the subject of enormous controversy.

intervention under the UN Charter that could use force to restore peace.

In the early 1990s, the Canadian Forces (CF) had been stretched to the breaking point by budget cuts and force reductions and a continuing string of high-profile and dangerous international security deployments. In 1992, the CAR, the Canadian Forces' quick reaction force, was the only suitable combat unit not already deployed, recovering from a deployment, or preparing for one. The regiment consisted of three commandos (equivalent in size and capability to infantry companies), one each from the three regular force infantry regiments.

Stationed in the desert at a dot on the map called Belet Huen, the CAR lived in tents in the heat and dust, ate packaged rations, and tried to restore order in the midst of chaos. Locals tried to steal what they could from the soldiers, and camp security had to be progressively tightened. There were many incidents, some shooting, and several deaths of Somalis until, on 16 March 1993, 2 Commando caught a Somali teenager red-handed and took him captive. Two soldiers then tortured and killed the boy, Shidane Arone, taking trophy photographs of the grisly beating. No one intervened, despite Arone's repeated screams and pleas for help and the proximity of his torture site to surrounding tents and other positions. Ottawa learned of the death shortly afterwards, and there were some punishments handed out by a CF board of inquiry. Little further happened until, in 1994 and 1995, videos made by CAR soldiers showed racist attitudes and vile acts during hazing rituals at

Canadian Forces Base Petawawa, the CAR's base. The resulting firestorm of public criticism all but forced the minister of national defence in the Chrétien government, David Collenette, to order the disbandment of the Canadian Airborne Regiment on 5 March 1995.

It was only the beginning. On 20 March, the government appointed a Commission of Inquiry into the Deployment of Canadian Forces to Somalia under Judge Gilles Letourneau, Judge Robert Rutherford, and journalist/academic Peter Desbarats. The commission was to examine why the CAR was chosen for the mission, the events in Somalia, and the post-deployment phase that involved an alleged cover-up at National Defence Headquarters (NDHQ) after the torture and murder of Arone had become known. The chair, Letourneau, was splenetic, aggressive, and openly dismissive of many of those called to present evidence, regularly badgering witnesses. This made sufficiently good television fodder that the commission's hearings became a public trial of the Canadian Forces itself, even though much of the coverage was devoted to the almost immaterial alteration of press releases at NDHQ. There was little public doubt that the Access to Information Act had been violated as senior officers apparently tried to protect their reputations and those of their minister. Did this represent evidence of systemic failure of command? One chief of the defence staff, General Jean Boyle, was forced to resign as a result of his disastrous testimony; other senior officers were tainted. The commission rolled along, demanding more money, an expanded mandate, and additional time.

The government had had enough. After two years, a tough and capable Liberal defence minister, Doug Young, ordered the slow-moving commission to produce its report promptly and closed it down in early 1997. The commissioners, the government's political opponents, and some members of the media cried censorship and cover-up. Most sensible observers recognized an inquiry that had become a headline-hunting fiasco, its yelps of mistreatment cloaking the steadily diminishing returns of an ever-growing mandate. The resulting five-volume report was unfortunately, if revealingly, titled *Dishonoured Legacy: The Lessons of the Somalia Affair*. It offered generally sensible recommendations on leadership, accountability, discipline, personnel selection, training, and rules of engagement. In effect, the commissioners declared that no future force should deploy without proper equipment, training, a clear chain of command, and a full understanding of its role. Had any Canadian expeditionary force ever marched or sailed with such clarity of purpose? Complex events and uncertain outcomes rarely permitted such assurances. It was not the report's only broad-brush assertion. The commission also offered critical comments on the Somalia mission, on the cover-up of the torture and murder and other incidents, and it focused on 12 officers, including seven generals, pronouncing them "failures." It made 160 recommendations in all, of which the government eventually accepted 132. It was a reasonable response to a long and gruelling investigation and painful public flogging, rendered quickly and with government thanks to still-grumbling ex-commissioners and a suspicious Canadian public.

Subsidiary research or investigative reports produced at the commission's behest, ranging from a sociological review of military "tribes" to an assessment of the mission's international security lessons, ran the gamut from forgettable navel-gazing to indispensable analysis. Every expert, it seemed, understood implicitly the deeper causes of the Somalia imbroglio, though none—for reasons that remained nameless—had proffered wisdom before or during the ill-fated mission. Pompous reports on "lessons learned" were more often than not lists of authors' favourites, uncompromised by perspective; helpful "recommendations" flowed, unbothered by hypocrisy, from the military's fiercest critics. Everyone purported to have the answer, and most overlooked the obvious, Arone's murder and the Airborne's disciplinary misdeeds notwithstanding: in truth, the Canadian Forces had performed superbly. On a difficult mission marred by international apathy and local chaos, they had disarmed the violent, fed the hungry, provided water to ease thirst, and generated security to assist daily living in areas under Canadian military control. Several individuals were decorated for acts of uncommon bravery, while the force as a whole—the airborne, mechanized units, engineers, doctors, and helicopter pilots—was lauded by the campaign's American commander (and many Somalis) as one of outstanding professionalism and competence, perhaps the best in the entire international command.

In the short term, such kudos mattered little. The Somalia mission became synonymous in public parlance with the Somalia inquiry that meant, of course, the Somalia scandal or, less judgmentally, the Somalia affair (the title used here). Its result, aside from the eventual disbandment of the Canadian Airborne Regiment, was much greater caution and much greater risk aversion among Canadian Forces personnel and a fear that Ottawa might not support independent initiatives on future missions. The military soon seemed to believe that advice from the judge advocate general was a precondition for any action. There were rules and regulations for everything, thick studies to bury all operational likelihoods in layers of bureaucratic twaddle, special training on ethics, accountability, racism, gender discrimination, and, more helpfully for impending deployments overseas, greater attention to local customs, languages, social attitudes, and living conditions. Attempts to regulate all conduct in the field bred hesitancy and mistrust, failings that showed in deployments in former Yugoslavia and elsewhere. Somalia generated disgust aplenty at the behaviour of some soldiers and their commanders, but surprising sophistication in public attitudes toward the long-suffering military. Opinion surveys found astonishing support for the men and women in uniform, and understandable distaste at how the Airborne's now well-publicized antics before and after the mission could have been permitted to flourish and to undermine proud traditions. Had emphasis on a supposedly American-style warrior ethic hijacked sound doctrine and effective discipline? Had an accumulation of defence cuts and a careerist high command ignored basic principles of management, leadership, and esprit de corps?

There was more truth in bold charges than media-shy military chiefs cared to admit. The Somalia episode over much of a decade consumed careers, directorates, forests of paper, and eons of media time. Parliamentary inquiries into the state of the military, and charismatic leadership of the kind provided by defence minister Doug Young and General Rick Hillier (chief of the defence staff from 2005) gradually restored public confidence, military prospects, and operational efficiency. The CF culture, unhealthily subsumed in management, public affairs, defensiveness, and accountancy, morphed back toward its warrior roots, operational competence, and national service. Its connections to Canadian values had been far less generically threatened than the sordid actions of the few in Somalia had appeared to indicate, but they had nevertheless been threatened. The turn of the century found such essential bonds emotionally reinforced and broadly respected. At the same time, studies of the Canadian Forces produced for defence minister Young in 1997 had focused sharply on the ill education of CF officers, half of whom (47 percent) had no university degree and almost none of whom (only 6.8 percent) had graduate degrees. This too soon began to be remedied, with better education and leadership, public and political support, and the evident competence of Canadian units in the field, at home, and abroad.

The Somalia affair led to increased scrutiny of the Canadian Forces. Muckraking books and articles, denounced regularly by senior officials, revealed fiddled expense accounts, the evasion of responsibility, the cover-up of misdeeds, and, at times, a moral climate unsuitable for the CF (or any public organization) and unworthy of the country it served. The Arone murder and the inquiry-affair that followed represented, in many ways, the nadir of Canada's modern military. Recovery, born of media scrutiny, public interest, and political attention, was slow in coming but gradually decisive. Enlightened leadership and the overall quality of the rank and file were instrumental in seeing the Canadian Forces

⌃ The Somme in 1916 was a charnel house, a battle of attrition in which both sides suffered huge losses for little gain. The Canadian Corps, some of its soldiers pictured here, saw heavy action near the battle's end; the Newfoundland Regiment had been all but annihilated on the first day.

through and beyond the pyrotechnics of scandal to the force that would perform with near-unflagging competence on missions from Kosovo to Afghanistan. See also: Chrétien; Mulroney; Peacekeeping.

Reading: Grant Dawson, *"Here is Hell": Canada's Engagement in Somalia* (Vancouver, 2007); David Bercuson, *Significant Incident: Canada's Army, the Airborne, and the Murder in Somalia* (Toronto, 1996).

Somme, Battle of the (1916). One of the most horrific battles of the Great War, the struggles around the river Somme in northern France (along with the battle the following year at Passchendaele) typified the failure and futility of World War I generalship. Lives were thrown away in the hundreds of thousands for small territorial gains, and attrition was the preferred strategic aim.

Launched in February 1916 and continuing into the summer, the German attempt to take the French fortress of Verdun was devouring the French armies wholesale. General Douglas Haig's British Expeditionary Force, which included the Canadian and Newfoundland forces in France and Belgium, decided to strike at the enemy along the Somme to relieve pressure on the Verdun front, to break through the German lines, and to turn loose British cavalry on the enemy's rear. The great British assault went over the top on 1 July, a battle that became the worst military disaster the Empire had ever suffered. British casualties on the first day numbered 57,470 killed, wounded, and missing, and the Newfoundland

Regiment, serving with the British 29th Division, lost 710 men killed and wounded of the 801 or so engaged in its attack at Beaumont Hamel. Had objectives been achieved anywhere on the Somme front, the casualties might conceivably have been deemed worth it, but the Germans' machine guns and barbed wire fended off the attackers almost everywhere (except for a French army involved in the assault that took its initial objectives).

The Canadian Corps, commanded by British Lieutenant-General Julian Byng, fortuitously had not been tapped to participate in the Dominion Day bloodbath, and it was not committed to the Somme until September. The first Canadian effort on 15 September, the troops advancing on a 2,000-metre front behind a creeping artillery barrage that had great effect, pitted General R.E.W. Turner's 2nd Division against defences around the village of Courcelette. Aided by a half-dozen tanks in their first ever use on the battlefield, the division took its initial objectives, and the follow-on brigades moved into Courcelette in broad daylight. The struggle there was vicious, including hand-to-hand fighting in the cellars of destroyed houses, and German counterattack followed counterattack. Struggling to hold its positions in front of the town, the 22nd Battalion drove off seven such attacks on the night of the 15th, and fourteen in all by 17 September. "If hell is as horrible as what I saw there," the Van Doos' commanding officer, Lieutenant-Colonel Thomas Tremblay, wrote later, "I wouldn't wish it on my worst enemy." Tremblay was widely known for his courage, one soldier recalled: "We would see Tremblay in the front line, every time … He was cool, he was calm, he never was frightened." That helped the 22nd, which suffered 207 casualties at Courcelette.

The 3rd Division, meanwhile, attacked the Fabeck Graben, an elaborate enemy trench system. After more vicious fighting, the Canadians cleared the trenches, only to come under heavy fire from the Zollern Graben, yet another adjacent and heavily fortified position. The Canadians took it, then lost it to a German counterattack on 20 September. Nonetheless, the British high command deemed the Canadian operations before Courcelette a success—for 7,320 casualties, the corps had made an advance of almost 3,000 metres.

The next objective was the German line a thousand metres beyond Courcelette dubbed Regina Trench. The initial attack on 26 September by the 1st and 2nd Canadian Divisions failed; a second attack on 1 October by the 2nd and 3rd Divisions was a partial success; and the third, one week later, to take what remained of Regina Trench, still in German hands, failed again. The three divisions of the Canadian Corps then left the Somme, but the 4th Canadian Division, just arrived at the front and knee-deep in mud, finally took Desire Trench, the next enemy line beyond Regina, by 18 November. The 4th had gained a kilometre but lost 1,250 killed and wounded in its first battle, a rude introduction to the Western Front.

Overall, the Canadian Corps earned a reputation on the Somme as "shock troops," but in its seven weeks on the front, suffered 24,029 casualties. The British and French had gained up to eight kilometres but lost more than 623,000 killed and wounded in the epic and stalemated five-month struggle; the Germans (their numbers are uncertain) apparently lost some 670,000. Summing up the balance sheet of gains and losses, the Canadian Expeditionary Force's official historian, Colonel G.W.L. Nicholson, judiciously pronounced the struggle a draw; he then noted, with uncommon bluntness, "We cannot close our eyes to the horror of the mass butchery to which [Haig's] tactics had condemned the troops under his command." See also: Byng; Canadian Corps; World War I.

Reading: G.W.L. Nicholson, *Canadian Expeditionary Force, 1914–1919* (Ottawa, 1962); Thomas L. Tremblay, *Journal de Guerre, 1915–1918* (Montreal, 2006); Bill Rawling, *Surviving Trench Warfare: Technology and the Canadian Corps, 1914–1918* (Toronto, 1992).

South African War. The South African War (or Boer War) began on 11 October 1899 and ended on 31 May 1902. Although it was presented publicly as a war fought to ensure the rights of British subjects in the

Private James Montgomery Thomas (seated, with bugle) and other Canadian soldiers pose in South Africa, around 1900.

Boer-governed South African republics, it was also a war for the advancement of British imperial and commercial interests in southern Africa. The growth in power and prestige of the two Boer republics, the Transvaal and the Orange Free State, had resulted from the discovery and exploitation of large gold deposits in the Transvaal.

When fighting began, Canadian opinion was divided with imperialists, led by big city newspapers such as the *Montreal Star*, pushing for Canada to participate, and most Québécois strongly opposed. The British general officer commanding the Canadian militia, Major-General Sir Edward Hutton, had already drawn up a contingency plan for the dispatch of Canadian troops. The Colonial Office in London, anxious for representation from the self-governing dominions, pressured Canadian Prime Minister Sir Wilfrid Laurier to support the effort. Pressed by the English-language media and from within his Cabinet and facing an election in the near future, Laurier capitulated and authorized the

raising of a 1,000-strong contingent—all to be volunteers, provided that the British would pay the costs once the unit reached South Africa. It was not a precedent, Laurier said, but a young Liberal Member of Parliament named Henri Bourassa denounced the prime minister. A precedent was a precedent, Bourassa maintained, and he would be proven right.

The contingent, commanded by Lieutenant-Colonel William D. Otter, an officer in the small Permanent Force, was designated the 2nd (Special Service) Battalion, Royal Canadian Regiment of Infantry (RCR). Signing on for one year, the men came from many regiments, both regular and militia, and off the street. Over time, Laurier agreed to additional contingents, amounting in all to another 6,000 volunteers. One new regiment, Strathcona's Horse, was funded entirely by Lord Strathcona, the Canadian High Commissioner in London. Eventually, Canada would pay almost $3,000,000 for raising, transporting, and maintaining its troops.

The RCR arrived in South Africa at the end of November 1899, just at the time Boer fortunes were at their zenith. They had their introduction to battle on 31 December when one company of the Royal Canadian Regiment took part in an action at Sunnyside Kopje alongside British and Australian troops. The Boer position there was quickly captured with no losses suffered by the Canadians. Then in late February 1900, the British regrouped and mounted a major counteroffensive. After a long, hard march through dry and dusty country, the RCR participated in an attack against a large force of Boers entrenched at Paardeberg commanded by General Piet Cronje. There was much confusion but also much courage, and the RCR, perched on a hill above the Boer camp as daylight broke, was widely credited as the unit that forced the Boer surrender. The marching, the heat, the filth and disease, as well as the casualties sustained in action, had taken a heavy toll on the Canadians.

The RCR participated in the hot, dusty advance to Bloemfontein, the capital of the Orange Free State, which followed at once. The town fell without a fight, the Boers' tactics beginning to shift from confronting the British and imperial troops in set-piece battles to

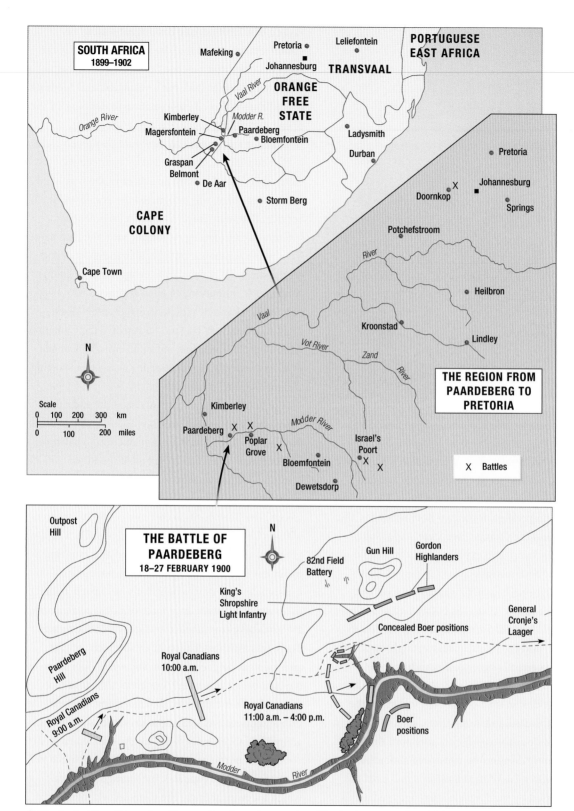

SOUTH AFRICA
1899–1902

Mafeking

Pretoria

Leliefontein

PORTUGUESE EAST AFRICA

Johannesburg

TRANSVAAL

Vaal River

ORANGE FREE STATE

Orange River

Kimberley

Modder R.

Magersfontein

Paardeberg

Bloemfontein

Ladysmith

Durban

Graspan

Belmont

De Aar

Storm Berg

CAPE COLONY

Cape Town

N

Scale

0   100   200   300   km

0   100   200   miles

Pretoria

Doornkop   X

Johannesburg

Springs

Potchefstroom

River

Heilbron

Kroonstad

Lindley

Vaal

Vot River

Zand

River

THE REGION FROM PAARDEBERG TO PRETORIA

Kimberley

Paardeberg   X   X

Poplar Grove

Modder River

X

Bloemfontein

Israel's Poort

X

X

X   Battles

Dewetsdorp

Outpost Hill

THE BATTLE OF PAARDEBERG
18–27 FEBRUARY 1900

N

82nd Field Battery

Gun Hill

Gordon Highlanders

King's Shropshire Light Infantry

Concealed Boer positions

General Cronje's Laager

Paardeberg Hill

Royal Canadians 10:00 a.m.

Royal Canadians 11:00 a.m. – 4:00 p.m.

Boer positions

Royal Canadians 9:00 a.m.

Modder   River

▲ The South African War, or Boer War, saw Canada send troops abroad for the first time; political debate over the wisdom and conduct of the mission was immediate and fierce.

classic guerilla warfare using groups of fast-mounted riflemen they called "commandos." Still, small but savage battles remained to be fought, as at Israel's Poort on 25 April when the RCR attacked a Boer position. Other engagements followed at Doornkop, Johannesburg, and Pretoria, the Transvaal capital, taken on 5 June 1900.

By the time Pretoria fell, the RCR had been reduced to 437 men, only 38 percent of those who had left Canada. The soldiers, fed up with the conditions, the killing, and their commanding officer, wanted to go home. Although Colonel Otter tried to persuade his men to sign on for another year, only 39 percent agreed, most of them members of the Permanent Force or reinforcements whose year of service had not expired. The rest returned to Canada to be feted as heroes; they were followed in November by the remainder of the first contingent who, after stopping first in London, received another royal welcome when they arrived back home.

But the war dragged on, and new Canadian units arrived—the 1st Canadian Mounted Rifles, the Royal Canadian Dragoons, and batteries from the Royal Canadian Field Artillery. Canadians, notably Strathcona's Horse, participated in some harsh anti-guerilla operations as the British high command created concentration camps for women and children and ruthlessly ordered the burning of farms and homes to deny food, water, and shelter to the Boer fighters. At one very sharp clash at Liliefontein in November 1900, three members of the Royal Canadian Dragoons—part of the regiment acting as a rearguard for the larger force that was retiring—won the Victoria Cross for their part in saving two Canadian field guns from a large attacking force of mounted Boers. As late as 31 March 1902, the 2nd Canadian Mounted Rifles, having arrived in South Africa only in January, suffered 13 killed and 40 wounded at Harts River in the western Transvaal when a large Boer force defeated a British one. The enemy horsemen cut off the Canadians and, though they fought until their ammunition was gone, overran them. Paardeberg aside, this was the most costly Canadian engagement of the war.

In all, Canada sent 7,368 men to the war (and 12 nurses, the first women to be posted overseas), more than 2,000 of whom arrived after the Boer surrender. Eighty-seven Canadians were killed in action, 135 died of disease, and 252 were wounded. Imperial wars could be costly as well as divisive. SEE ALSO: LAURIER; OTTER; PAARDEBERG; ROYAL CANADIAN REGIMENT.

READING: Carman Miller, *Painting the Map Red: Canada and the South African War, 1899–1902* (Montreal, 1993).

Spartan Exercise. In March 1943, First Canadian Army participated in Spartan, the largest exercise in which Canadians based in Britain took part during World War II. Lieutenant-General Andrew McNaughton was in overall command of both the I and II Canadian Corps in this exercise; II Corps was newly formed, and his own army headquarters was also functioning in the field for the first time. The result was much confusion and tactical clumsiness, and senior British generals soon concluded that McNaughton was incapable of commanding large forces on operations, while General Harry Crerar's command of I Canadian Corps drew some praise. Others of McNaughton's commanders were deemed to have performed badly and were soon replaced. McNaughton's relief as general officer commanding-in-chief of First Canadian Army, though it did not occur until December 1943, was inevitable after Spartan. Crerar duly succeeded him as army commander.

READING: John Rickard, *The Politics of Command: Lieutenant-General A.G.L. McNaughton and the Canadian Army, 1939–1943* (Toronto, 2010).

Special Forces. Canada has experimented with a variety of Special Forces since the beginning of World War II when it provided soldiers to the First Special Service Force (FSSF) formed jointly with the United States. The FSSF served in the Aleutian Islands, and in intensive combat in Italy and southern France. Other Canadians served as commandos, primarily in British-directed units. At the same time, the army organized the 1st Canadian Parachute Battalion that, serving with the British 6th Airborne Division, jumped into Normandy and later across the Rhine.

After World War II, the army organized a Special Air Services company in 1946 and a Mobile Striking Force brigade with parachute capability in 1948. The Canadian Airborne Regiment was created in 1968, then made part of a brigade-sized Special Service Force in 1977. The Airborne Regiment served in Cyprus and Somalia, and was disbanded in 1995. A Special Forces capability was on hand at its dissolution, however; JTF2 (Joint Task Force 2) began operations as an elite commando unit in 1993, its role initially for hostage rescue and counterterrorism operations. Over time, JTF2 transformed into a force similar to Britain's SAS or the US Special Forces, and its members served in Haiti, apparently in Peru against Shining Path guerillas, and, most notably, in Afghanistan from 2001 where they earned accolades for their (still secret) work. Since 2006, JTF2 has formed part of Canadian Special Operations Forces Command, along with the Griffon helicopters of

427 Special Operations Aviation Squadron, the Canadian Joint Incident Response Unit that deals with nuclear, biological, and chemical threats, and the Canadian Special Operations Regiment (CSOR). The CSOR is tasked with supporting JTF2 but also conducting highly covert missions that require heavy firepower, including the hunt for Taliban leaders and bomb-makers in Afghanistan.

Stacey, Charles Perry (1906–1989). The founder of modern Canadian military history, Charles Stacey arguably was Canada's finest historian. He wrote easily and with style, he taught at the University of Toronto from 1959 to 1975 with a mordant wit, and he continues to inspire those who follow in his footsteps. Born in Toronto, Stacey was educated at Toronto, Oxford, and Princeton where he did his doctoral work and taught until the outbreak of World War II. He then went overseas as the Canadian army's historian, amassing the records he used to write the official histories as a colonel and army historian in Ottawa until his retirement from the army in 1959. He returned to Ottawa to head the unified Directorate of History at National Defence Headquarters in 1965–1966. Stacey followed his magisterial, prize-winning official volumes with studies of the fall of Quebec in 1759, the "very double life" of Mackenzie King, a two-volume history of Canadian foreign policy, and his own memoir, *A Date with History* (1982).

READING: Tim Cook, *Clio's Warriors: Canadian Historians and the Writing of the World Wars* (Vancouver, 2006).

Stanley, George Francis Gilman (1907–2002). An Alberta Rhodes Scholar, George Stanley earned a D. Phil. at Oxford and taught at Mount Allison University until he joined the army in 1940. He served in Charles Stacey's historical section at Canadian Military Headquarters in London, ending the war as a lieutenant-colonel. He then joined the Royal Military College's history department in 1949 where he wrote *Canada's Soldiers* (1954), his best-known work of military history. Stanley left RMC in 1969 to go to

∧ Colonel Charles P. Stacey, army official historian, 1950.

Mount Allison for the next six years. He became lieutenant-governor of New Brunswick but continued to write and publish on land operations in the War of 1812 and to edit the collected works of Louis Riel.

Steele, Sir Samuel Benfield (1848–1919). Sam Steele, born in Purbrook, Upper Canada, served in the Red River Expedition in 1870, enlisted in the new Canadian artillery school the next year, and joined the North West Mounted Police (NWMP) in 1873. Steele served with great distinction in the Mounties, both on the Prairies and in the Yukon during the gold rush days. Offered command of Lord Strathcona's Horse in January 1900, he led the new unit (formed in large part from the NWMP) to South Africa where he and his troops performed well in action; however, Steele drew criticism for his unit's summary treatment of Boer prisoners. After five years' service in the South African Constabulary, Steele returned to Canada and to peacetime military service. In December 1914, World War I now underway, militia minister Sam Hughes offered Steele command of the 2nd Canadian Division, an appointment vetoed by the War Office on grounds of age. Hughes insisted on the appointment and secured a compromise—Steele could command the division until it proceeded to France. An imperial patriot, a zealous soldier, and a capable administrator, Steele commanded training camps in England until the end of the war, and then died in the influenza epidemic of 1918–1919. SEE ALSO: LORD STRATHCONA'S HORSE; SOUTH AFRICAN WAR.

READING: Samuel B. Steele, *Forty Years in Canada: Reminiscences of The Great North-west with some Account of His Service in South Africa* (Toronto, 1915, 1972).

Stephenson, Sir William Samuel (1897–1989). Born in Winnipeg, Stephenson joined the army in 1916 then became a highly decorated pilot in the Royal Flying Corps before he was shot down and taken prisoner. Between the wars, he made a fortune and became friendly with Winston Churchill who, soon after the outbreak of World War II, sent him to New York to run British Security Coordination, in effect, British intelligence operations in and liaison with the United States. Stephenson's efforts were important, not least in setting up Camp X to train agents in Ontario, but his postwar publicity machine, playing on his code name "Intrepid," embellished his work into a war-winning mythology à la James Bond. He was knighted in 1945 and later made a Companion of the Order of Canada.

READING: David Stafford, "'Intrepid': Myth and Reality," *Journal of Contemporary History*, vol. 22, no. 2 (1987).

Stoney Creek, Battle of (1813). On 27 May 1813 during the War of 1812, nearly 6,000 American soldiers staged a successful amphibious landing at the mouth of the Niagara River, routed the British garrison, and quickly seized Fort George. Short of supplies and low on ammunition, British troops under Brigadier-General John Vincent retreated westward toward Burlington Heights, placing the entire Niagara Peninsula in jeopardy. Ten days later, on the night of 5–6 June, some 700 British regulars, supported by Canadian militia and small numbers of native fighters under the command of Colonel John Harvey, struck at the 3,000 US soldiers encamped at Stoney Creek, near present-day Hamilton. In a night action that was first bungled by the British and then won by a bayonet charge led by Major Charles Plenderleath, they battered the invaders' army and forced its pell-mell withdrawal to Fort George. The total American losses remain in dispute, but 205 men became prisoners, two brigadier-generals among them, and at least 150 more were killed or wounded. A contemporary described one of those captured brigadier-generals, William Winder, as knowing "no more of military affairs than his horse," and the way the Americans conducted themselves suggested that the phrase may have some truth to it. British losses numbered 110 killed, wounded, and captured. The battle and the subsequent British victory at Beaver Dams later in June ensured that the Niagara Peninsula remained under British control. SEE ALSO: BEAVER DAMS; WAR OF 1812.

READING: James Elliott, *Strange Fatality: The Battle of Stoney Creek, 1813* (Montreal, 2009).

Strathcona, Lord. *See* SMITH, DONALD A.

Submarines. Canada acquired its first two submarines, CC1 and CC2, in the early days of World War I when British Columbia Premier Sir Richard McBride purchased two US-built submersibles, originally destined for Chile, for use as offshore patrol vessels. Shortly after they arrived at Esquimalt, they were transferred to the Canadian navy. In 1917, they sailed to Halifax where the navy used them as training craft until they were scrapped in 1920. At the end of World War II, the Royal Canadian Navy briefly acquired and used two surrendered German U-boats, *U-190* and *U-889*. In the 1960s, Canada acquired five submarines: HMCS *Grilse* in 1961, secured from the United States Navy (USN); *Rainbow,* also from the USN, in 1968; *Ojibwa* in 1965; *Onondaga* in 1967; and *Okanagan* in 1968. The latter three, purchased in Britain, were all *Oberon* class, top-of-the-line conventional submarines that became the foundation stones for the navy's submarine service.

In the 1987 Defence White Paper, the Progressive Conservative government of Brian Mulroney declared that it would buy up to a dozen nuclear-powered submarines to protect Canada's sovereignty and face off with the Soviet Union's fleet in the event of World War III. The pledge attracted much criticism outside the navy, not least from the United States, unhappy that French nuclear technology might have been used. The idea died when the Berlin Wall came down in 1989 and the Cold War ended. Meanwhile, the aging *O* class boats remained in operation to the end of the century. They were replaced by four second-hand conventionally powered *Upholder* class subs: HMCS *Windsor, Corner Brook, Chicoutimi,* and *Victoria,* secured from Britain in 1998 in a preferential deal. The submarines, very useful for surveillance and for training, ran into an unfortunate succession of engineering and structural difficulties, the most serious of which was a fire at sea that disabled *Chicoutimi* and killed one officer in 2004.

Suez Crisis (1956). Tensions remained on the Israeli-Egyptian border after the creation of the Jewish state in 1948 and the Israeli victory in stopping Arab invasions. Tensions increased after a nationalist colonel, Gamal Abdel Nasser, seized power in Cairo, and they increased even further following his nationalization of the Suez Canal on 26 July 1956. This angered Britain and France, the owners of the canal, and began to draw Egypt close to the Soviet Union, greatly upsetting Washington. Diplomatic efforts to resolve the canal crisis failed and, in secret meetings, Israel, France, and Britain decided to attack Egypt. Israel was to invade and, in the guise of protecting the canal, France and Britain would also attack; the aim was to drive Nasser from power and cripple Egypt's military strength. Britain advised none of its major allies of the impending assault, including the United States, Canada, partners in the North Atlantic Treaty Organization, or key states in the British Commonwealth.

The attack began on 29 October 1956, Israeli troops moving rapidly into the Sinai desert. Britain and France, both of which had been gathering troops on Cyprus, issued ultimatums but, although they began bombing Egyptian targets on 31 October, were unable to land troops until 5 November. This not only gave Nasser time to recover, but it also gave the furious Americans, in the final days of a presidential election and with the USSR crushing the Hungarian revolution at precisely this point, incentive to halt their allies' disastrous gamble.

For Canada, this was a first-rank crisis with the nation's mother countries engaging in an act of aggression. Prime Minister Louis St Laurent was outraged at the "supermen" of Europe and furious that British Prime Minister Anthony Eden had, he believed, lied to him. Foreign minister Lester "Mike" Pearson set off for the United Nations (UN) to try to find a way out for the Western alliance. His first instinct was to obtain for the Anglo-French invaders the status of a UN force; given global rage, however, this was a complete non-starter. He then hit on the idea of a UN emergency force—a good-sized, armed, impartial force from non-involved nations—to be interposed between the combatants. In a late-night address on 4 November, Pearson proposed this, said

A Canadian soldier of UNEF I surveys the Suez Canal. For many Canadians, peacekeeping at Suez in 1956 was a noble precedent; for others, it was sheer perfidy, abandoning Britain in a time of need.

Canada was willing to participate, and watched as his resolution carried in the General Assembly. London and Paris declared a ceasefire on 7 November and, in effect, accepted the UN force.

Difficulties quickly arose for Ottawa. The Canadian unit proposed was the Queen's Own Rifles of Canada (QOR), a light infantry unit that spoke English, wore British-style Canadian uniforms, had the Union Jack in the corner of its Red Ensign, and carried an unfortunately British-sounding name. The Egyptians promptly refused to let the QOR be part of the UN force, saying their people could not distinguish them from the attackers. Fortunately for Canada and Pearson, the UN had a Truce Supervisory Organization that had been trying to monitor the Arab-Israeli borders, and the commander at this point was Canadian Major-General E.L.M. Burns who was acting as the designated commander of the yet-to-be-created United Nations Emergency Force (UNEF). Burns

persuaded the Egyptians to accept Canadian logistical personnel, understanding that no force could function without supplies and transport, and recognizing that many other nations could provide infantry. The Egyptians agreed, and Burns, in fact, later persuaded Cairo to agree to an armoured reconnaissance and air contribution from Canada. The first UN troops arrived in Egypt on 15 November.

The Suez Crisis did not lead to a resolution of the Egypt-Israel dispute; indeed UNEF, including its Canadian contingent, was tossed out of Egypt in 1967 just before another war erupted. It did win Mike Pearson a Nobel Peace Prize and the leadership of the Liberal Party, though it likely helped the Liberals to lose the 1957 election as Canadian public opinion sharply split on the merits of Canada's actions at the UN. It demonstrated the military weakness of Britain and France and, as the pound sterling began to collapse during the crisis, London's economic weakness too. Pearson's role, nonetheless, froze the crisis and prevented an irreparable split between the United States and its senior allies.

In the longer term, Pearson's Nobel Prize made peacekeeping *the* Canadian role. Progressive Conservative leader John Diefenbaker had capitalized on what he saw as the Liberals' disregard for Britain and France in the 1957 election, but he also claimed that he had invented the idea of UN forces, and he sent Canadian troops to every UN force thereafter. So too did Prime Minister Pearson after 1963, and his foreign minister, Paul Martin, tried hard to get a Peace Prize for his role in the Cyprus crisis of 1964. Peacekeeping was the Canadian thing after 1956, and the Egyptian response to the Queen's Own may well have contributed to the Pearson government's adoption of a distinctive Canadian flag and to the unification of the Canadian forces with distinctive uniforms. SEE ALSO: BURNS; PEACEKEEPING; PEARSON.

READING: John English, *The Life of Lester Pearson: The Worldly Years 1949–1972*, vol. 2 (Toronto, 1992); Michael Carroll, *Pearson's Peacekeepers: Canada and the United Nations Emergency Force, 1956–67* (Vancouver, 2009).

Tecumseh (c.1768–1813). A powerful Shawnee war chief who aligned with other First Nations leaders alongside British regulars and Canadian militia during the War of 1812, Tecumseh had long been fighting against American expansion into Aboriginal territory in what is now Ohio. He took part in several major battles of the war, including the capture of Detroit by General Isaac Brock in August 1812. In May 1813, fighting alongside the forces of General Henry Proctor, he helped defeat a force of Americans that sought to relieve a siege at Fort Meigs. In September of that year, British naval forces on Lake Erie challenged the Americans under Commodore Perry and were defeated at Put-in-Bay. As a result, Proctor decided to retreat eastward from Fort Malden, and a reluctant Tecumseh accompanied him. With US

⌃ In this stylized early twentieth-century image, Tecumseh meets Major-General Isaac Brock during the War of 1812. First Nations and British forces fought together against the United States, but often with different objectives.

General William Henry Harrison hard on his heels, Proctor was forced to stand and fight at Moraviantown. The British were soundly defeated, Proctor and his troops fled, and Tecumseh, leading some 500 First Nations warriors, mainly Shawnee, against 3,000 American troops, was killed on 5 October 1813. Despite the mythology, Tecumseh was not fighting for the British or for Canada, but to keep native lands free of American settlers. SEE ALSO: MORAVIANTOWN; WAR OF 1812.

READING: Jim Poling, Sr, *Tecumseh: Shooting Star, Crouching Panther* (Toronto, 2009).

Terrace Mutiny. On 23 November 1944, at the climax of the conscription crisis of 1944, the Mackenzie King government announced that 16,000 home defence conscripts would be dispatched overseas to solve the infantry reinforcement shortage in northwest Europe and Italy. Almost immediately, there was a series of violent reactions in some of the British Columbia army camps where large numbers of these NRMA (National Resources Mobilization Act) men were based. The most serious incident occurred at Terrace, home of the 3,000-strong 15th Infantry Brigade, beginning on 24 November. Close to 2,000 mutineers, both English- and French-speaking and led by soldiers from the Fusiliers du St-Laurent, seized weapons and ammunition and trained 6-pounder guns on the approaches to Terrace from a spot overlooking the town. The francophone conscripts, in particular, had difficult relations with the Skeena River town's 400 residents, and this may have played a part in the situation. At the time of the mutiny, most senior officers from the camp were in Vancouver attending an inquiry. When they returned, the situation, arguably one of the most serious breaches of discipline in Canada's military history, was gradually brought under control and discipline was restored by 29 November. A few of the movement's ringleaders were punished, but, because there had been no property damage, no harsh measures were imposed. The government rigidly censored news of the mutiny from being published. SEE ALSO: CONSCRIPTION; NATIONAL RESOURCES MOBILIZATION ACT.

READING: R.H. Roy, *For Most Conspicuous Bravery: A Biography of Major-General George R. Pearkes, VC, through Two World Wars* (Vancouver, 1977).

Thames, Battle of the. *See* MORAVIANTOWN.

Tiger Force. Canada's contribution to the war against Japan, in what was called "Stage II" of World War II, took time to work out. The Royal Canadian Air Force's (RCAF) contribution to the British Commonwealth's Tiger Force initially was expected to be very large, perhaps as many as 60 squadrons of bombers, fighters, and transports. But Prime Minister Mackenzie King was cool to participation in the Pacific, certainly in the southwest where he did not want Canadians to appear to be supporting imperialism by liberating British colonies from the Japanese. Instead, Canada was to participate in the north Pacific, supporting the planned invasion of the Japanese home islands. The RCAF contribution—later scaled down to twelve bomber squadrons flying Lancaster or Lincoln bombers and six day-fighter squadrons, or 23,000 Canadians in all—was reduced yet again as the Americans began to question the need for any Commonwealth air participation at all. By the summer of 1945, Ottawa planned to provide only two Lancaster squadrons for the Tiger Force advance element (with two more to be available by 1 January 1946) and to provide a group headquarters. All was in preparation by the late summer of 1945 and, as only volunteers could go to the Pacific in accordance with government policy, men and women in the RCAF had been canvassed to serve in the Pacific theatre. The atomic bombings of Hiroshima and Nagasaki and the Japanese capitulation on 14 August 1945 put an end to the planning and to Tiger Force.

Tomb of the Unknown Soldier. At the instigation of The Royal Canadian Legion, the Canadian government created the Tomb of the Unknown Soldier and placed it in front of the National War Memorial on 28 May 2000. The remains of an unknown Canadian soldier from World War I—hitherto buried in a cemetery maintained

^ This gravestone, now in the Canadian War Museum, marked the resting place in Cabaret Rouge Military Cemetery near Souchez, France, of a World War I Canadian soldier. In 2000, his remains were chosen as Canada's Unknown Soldier, returned to Canada, and re-interred at the south side of the National War Memorial in Ottawa.

by the Commonwealth War Graves Commission near Vimy Ridge, France—were flown to Canada on 25 May and laid in state in the Hall of Honour in the Parliament buildings for three days. The remains were then laid to rest in a splendid but simple sarcophagus at the south base of the National War Memorial. The Unknown Soldier has since become a focal point of Remembrance Day ceremonies when spectators and participants on 11 November honour Canada's war dead by leaving poppies on the Tomb.

Townshend, George, 1st Marquess (1724–1807). Educated at Cambridge and with service in Germany and at the battle of Culloden, political preferment made Townshend one of General James Wolfe's three brigadiers at Quebec. He and his two colleagues suggested that Wolfe land to the west of Quebec to force Montcalm to come out from behind the walls to defend his line of communications. Townshend commanded the left wing of the British line on the Plains of Abraham and, as commander of the British forces after Wolfe's death, he accepted the city's surrender from the French on 18 September 1759, having offered lenient terms. A talented caricaturist, he circulated sketches in England after his return that ridiculed Wolfe. This led to much criticism, but it did not stop him from holding important politico-military administrative posts or from becoming a field marshal near the end of his career.

Treaty of Ghent (1814). The War of 1812 had been bitterly fought to a draw although, from the Canadian perspective, mere survival in the face of the superior numbers of the United States was a victory. Peace negotiations had been mooted since 1813; they began in earnest only in July 1814. By September, both Britain and the United States began to compromise and the treaty, negotiated in Ghent, Belgium, was signed on 24 December. In effect, the conflict ended with a return to the status quo antebellum, with all captured land returned. The battle of New Orleans, a decisive American victory, took place two weeks after the treaty's signature, thanks to the slow seaborne communications of the era. SEE ALSO: WAR OF 1812.

Treaty of Paris (1763). The Seven Years' War ended with the signature of the Treaty of Paris on 10 February 1763 by Britain, France, and Spain. The British received Canada, the Great Lakes basin, and Île Royale (Cape Breton Island) from France, and Florida from Spain. Louisiana remained in French hands, and France retained the right to fish in the Gulf of St Lawrence and secured St Pierre and Miquelon as unfortified shelters for its fishing vessels. The treaty guaranteed the Canadiens the liberty of the Catholic religion. SEE ALSO: SEVEN YEARS' WAR.

Treaty of St Germain-en-Laye (1632). England and France had gone to war in 1627, and the adventurer David Kirke and his brothers, acting on behalf of English merchants, seized Acadia and Quebec in 1628–1629. The treaty of St Germain-en-Laye of 1632 gave back France's North American possessions while, in return, Charles I received the unpaid dowry of his wife, Henrietta Maria, the daughter of Henri IV of France.

Treaty of Utrecht (1713). The treaty, signed in 1713 in the Dutch city of Utrecht, ended the War of the Spanish Succession or, in North America, Queen Anne's War. Its North American terms saw France cede its claims to Hudson Bay, Newfoundland, and Acadia. But France retained its important fishing rights in Newfoundland, Île Saint Jean (Prince Edward Island), and Île Royale (Cape Breton) where it soon began construction of the fortress of Louisbourg. The treaty, in other words, marked a truce, not a true peace.

Treaty of Versailles (1919). The treaty, signed in the Hall of Mirrors at Versailles, France, on 28 June 1919, ended World War I between Germany and the Allies. The most controversial clause was that requiring Germany to accept responsibility for the war. For Canada, the treaty was especially significant because Prime Minister Sir Robert Borden won the right for Canada to be part of the British Empire delegation (with two representatives at the Peace Conference) and to sign the treaty—though Canada and the other dominions signed as part of the British Empire with their signatures indented. Canada sought no reparations and, unlike other dominions, no territorial gains. What Canada did secure was the right to be a member of the new League of Nations and the right of election to the League Council. All these legalistic points were steps on the road to Canadian autonomy and independence, and they were directly attributable to the nation's war effort. SEE ALSO: BORDEN, ROBERT; WORLD WAR I.

READING: Margaret MacMillan, *Paris 1919* (London, 2001).

Treaty of Washington (1871). Signed on 8 May 1871 in Washington, DC, the treaty settled disputes between Britain and the United States that largely arose out of the American Civil War and its aftermath.

Prime Minister Sir John A. Macdonald was one of five British commissioners given that several issues concerned the Dominion. The major issue, which did not concern Canada, was compensation for the damage caused by the Confederate cruiser *Alabama*, which had been built in Britain. The Canadian issues were as follows: the American claim for free navigation of the St Lawrence; the rights of US fishing vessels to fish in Canadian waters; the possession of San Juan Island on the West Coast; and the indemnity to be paid to Canada for damages done by Fenian raiders. Canada received nothing on the last point, the United States refusing to consider it (though Britain later gave Canada a loan guarantee as compensation). The San Juan dispute went to international arbitration and was soon awarded to the United States. The United States won the right to free navigation of the St Lawrence, and Canada received equivalent access to Lake Michigan and the Yukon River. The Canadian fisheries were opened to the Americans for 12 years, and a commission later awarded Canada $5.5 million for this concession, as well as free access for Canadian fish to the US market. The treaty, nonetheless, was widely seen as disastrous for Canada, and Macdonald complained bitterly that the British had sacrificed Canadian interests to win American favour. But the prime minister signed the treaty and supported it in Parliament, believing that he had no other option. SEE ALSO: CANADA–UNITED STATES DEFENCE RELATIONS; FENIAN RAIDS; MACDONALD, JOHN ALEXANDER.

Trent Affair. The Royal Mail Ship *Trent* was a British mail packet intercepted and boarded by the USS *San Jacinto* in the Caribbean on 8 November 1861 during the American Civil War. Two diplomats from the Confederacy, James Mason and John Slidell, were removed from the *Trent*, an event that provoked a diplomatic crisis between Britain and the United States that threatened to erupt into war. Britain promptly sent reinforcements to its British North American colonies, began efforts to train the colonies' militia, and began to assemble the Royal Navy, but President Lincoln's administration rethought its position and disavowed the actions of Captain Charles Wilkes of the *San Jacinto*. On 27 December, Washington released the two diplomats into British custody.

Troupes de la marine. Raised by France's naval ministry to help garrison the colonies, the first *troupes de la marine* arrived in New France in late 1683. The men were soldiers, not shipboard marines, and they shortly acquired the designation of *Compagnie franches de la marine*. The units were organized in 28 or so companies, ordinarily of less than a hundred soldiers each, scattered across New France. By the eighteenth century, these companies had developed skills in bush warfare and conducted raids against English possessions, often in company with militia and native warriors. Canadians soon filled most of the officer positions; the soldiers were almost all French.

Troupes de terre. In 1755 and 1757, France dispatched 12 battalions from the regular army, known as the *troupes de terre*, to Canada and Louisbourg. Well trained and disciplined, they reinforced the Louisbourg garrison and played a key role in the French victories in Canada prior to 1759. Montcalm's decision to incorporate untrained militia into regular battalions contributed significantly to his defeat at the Plains of Abraham.

Trudeau, Pierre Elliott (1919–2000). Born in Montreal to French- and English-speaking parents, Pierre Trudeau grew up in comfortable circumstances. During World War II while he was at university and law school, he vigorously opposed conscription, campaigned for anti-conscription candidates, and urged revolution. He was, nonetheless, obliged to join the Canadian Officers Training Corps but did not serve in the military; indeed, he did not see the importance of the war until he attended Harvard University in 1944 and, seeing few men in his classes, realized that the struggle was more than a British imperialist war. Trudeau travelled extensively after 1945, taught law, and edited the journal *Cité Libre*, calling for change in Quebec society. As the Quiet Revolution gathered force in the 1960s, he became

alarmed at the growing calls for Quebec independence and, in 1965, ran for the Liberal Party in Montreal. He became Lester Pearson's parliamentary secretary, even though in 1963 he had denounced Pearson in remarkably bitter terms for accepting nuclear weapons.

Trudeau's charisma and intelligence soon captivated the nation and, in 1968, he succeeded Pearson as Liberal leader and prime minister and promptly won a majority mandate. He immediately launched a review of defence policy, clearly wishing to remove all Canadian troops from service in Europe with the North Atlantic Treaty Organization (NATO). A struggle in Cabinet prevented this but, in the spring of 1969, the commitment was cut by 50 percent, nuclear weapons in Europe were relinquished, and defence spending was frozen at $1.8 billion for the next three years. Personnel strength was cut by 20 percent to 80,000, and historic units in the army disappeared—the Canadian Guards, the Black Watch, the Queen's Own Rifles, and the Fort Garry Horse vanished from the regular force. A subsequent review of foreign policy clarified Trudeau's preference for a more non-aligned role for Canada as well as his antipathy to United States foreign policy, a view sharpened by the Vietnam War.

Trudeau's views were not static. On October 1970, cells of the separatist Front de Libération du Québec kidnapped James Cross, the British trade commissioner in Montreal, and Quebec labour minister Pierre Laporte, murdering the latter. Trudeau put the army onto the streets of Ottawa and Montreal and proclaimed the War Measures Act to control an "apprehended insurrection." He had all but unanimous support in all parts of Canada for his action. After the crisis ended with the trade commissioner's recovery, however, opinion turned quickly against him, and Trudeau won only a minority mandate in 1972. He got his majority back in 1974. Trudeau narrowly lost the 1979 election to Joe Clark's Conservatives, but won the country again in 1980, just in time to handily defeat the Parti Québécois government of René Lévesque's referendum on Quebec sovereignty.

Trudeau's government pushed the military to watch more closely over Canada, necessary enough after October 1970, and also pressed for more bilingualism in the Canadian Forces. In the late 1970s, it gave the Canadian Forces new equipment—Leopard tanks, ordering CF-18 fighters and new frigates—in part, at least, to bolster the prime minister's campaign for a special economic arrangement with the European Union. Trudeau also agreed in 1978 to go along with a NATO buildup by increasing defence spending by 3 percent a year (after inflation), a major change that, by the end of his time in power in 1984, had raised the defence budget to $8 billion. But Trudeau, nonetheless, was never a firm or reliable ally of the Americans and NATO, fighting with President Ronald Reagan and British Prime Minister Margaret Thatcher over their hard line toward the USSR during the Soviet war in Afghanistan and the shooting down of a Korean airliner by Soviet fighter aircraft. His "peace initiative" of 1983–1984 saw him travel to Europe and Asia in an effort to mobilize support for détente, but it was fruitless in its results and made Canada's allies uncomfortable.

After a brief Liberal successor government under John Turner, Progressive Conservative Brian Mulroney won consecutive majority governments. Pierre Trudeau departed office in 1984, having patriated the constitution and secured the Canadian Charter of Rights and Freedoms. He left the Canadian Forces in markedly worse shape than he found them 16 years before, despite the programs spawned in the late 1970s by the Defence Structure Review. Canada's alliance partnerships were damaged, its key relationships with London, Washington, and other NATO allies seriously weakened. SEE ALSO: ALLARD; ALLIANCES, CANADIAN; CANADA–UNITED STATES DEFENCE RELATIONS; DEXTRAZE; OCTOBER CRISIS.

READING: John English, *Citizen of the World: The Life of Pierre Elliott Trudeau, 1919–1968*, vol. 1 (Toronto, 2006) and *Just Watch Me: The Life of Pierre Elliott Trudeau, 1968–2000*, vol. 2 (Toronto, 2009).

Turner, Richard Ernest William (1871–1961).
A native of Quebec City, Lieutenant Turner won the Victoria Cross during the South African War in an engagement at Liliefontein. Although wounded twice in the action, Turner (an officer in the Royal Canadian Dragoons) dismounted, deployed his men, and drove off a party of Boers, saving a battery of British guns from capture. In August 1914, militia minister Sam Hughes named him one of the brigade commanders in the First Canadian Contingent, and he led his troops—not wholly successfully—during the struggle at Ypres in April 1915. Promoted to major-general and given command of the 2nd Division in July 1915, he ran into difficulty directing his division in the melee among the craters at St Eloi the next year. Senior commanders wanted him removed, but Canadian politics instead resulted in the replacement of Lieutenant-General E.A. Alderson as Canadian Corps commander. Turner too was soon gone, sent in November 1916 to become chief of the general staff over Canadian troops in England. He also vied with Sir Arthur Currie for command of the Canadian Corps in the summer of 1917 but lost, and remained in his post in Britain, becoming a lieutenant-general and receiving a knighthood. He played an important postwar role in the Great War Veterans Association. SEE ALSO: SOUTH AFRICAN WAR; WORLD WAR I.

25th Canadian Infantry Brigade Group (25 CIBG).
On 7 August 1950, Prime Minister Louis St Laurent announced that Canada would raise the Canadian Army Special Force for Korean War service. Soldiers were to serve for 18 months, and 12 of these months were to be in Korea. Soon named the 25 CIBG, it did its advance training at Fort Lewis, Washington. One infantry battalion, the 2nd Battalion, Princess Patricia's Canadian Light Infantry (2 PPCLI), left for Korea on 25 November at a time when the United Nations forces had the initiative. It seemed then that 25 CIBG might be used in North Atlantic Treaty Organization (NATO) service and Canada's Korean commitment satisfied with one battalion. But the Chinese intervention in Korea in December and the

△ General Sir R.E.W. Turner, VC, inspecting officer cadets, 1918.

major setbacks to the United Nations (UN) position that followed led to the brigade group's dispatch. It went into the line in May 1951 under the command of Brigadier J.M. Rockingham. The brigade group consisted of three infantry battalions, each one bearing the name of one of the army's Regular Force units; armour from Lord Strathcona's Horse; and the requisite artillery, engineers, and support units. The 2 PPCLI, meanwhile, saw action at Kap'yong in April 1951. The 25 CIBG became part of the 1st Commonwealth Division in July 1951. The brigade's constituent units were twice replaced by fresh rotations from Canada later in the war. SEE ALSO: KOREAN WAR.

READING: H.F. Wood, *Strange Battleground: Official History of the Canadian Army in Korea* (Ottawa, 1966).

27th Canadian Infantry Brigade Group (27 CIBG). Announced on 4 May 1951 by Minister of National Defence Brooke Claxton, the 27 CIBG became Canada's army commitment to the North Atlantic Treaty Organization's forces in West Germany. The government tasked the militia to raise three composite battalions: the 1st Canadian Rifle Battalion, the 1st Canadian Highland Battalion, and the 1st Canadian Infantry Battalion. The government selected five militia units to provide troops for each battalion, much as the Loyal Edmonton Regiment did for the 1st Canadian Infantry Regiment. The brigade included an armoured squadron equipped with British-made Centurion tanks. The 5,800-strong formation went to Germany in late autumn 1951, initially to Hannover, and then to its permanent post at Soest. It was attached to the I British Corps of the British Army of the Rhine. Regular Force troops of 1 Canadian Infantry Brigade Group replaced 27 CIBG in 1953, and brigade rotations followed every two years until 1958; from 1959, unit rotation became the norm. Renamed the 4th Canadian Mechanized Brigade Group in 1968, the force remained in NATO until the Canadian withdrawal from Europe in 1993, though its strength had been reduced by a series of defence cuts beginning in 1968 and amounting to 50 percent of strength in 1970–1971. Its role changed in consequence from front-line to reserve. SEE ALSO: NORTH ATLANTIC TREATY ORGANIZATION.

READING: Sean Maloney, *War without Battles: Canada's NATO Brigade in Germany, 1951–1993* (Toronto, 1997).

Uganda, HMCS. The Royal Navy (RN) transferred this 8,940-tonne light cruiser to the Royal Canadian Navy (RCN) in October 1944 after the ship had been refitted at Charleston, South Carolina. The RN name of the ship inexplicably was retained in a demonstration of abject naval colonialism. The cruiser had a top speed of 30 knots, carried approximately 700 officers and ratings, and was armed with nine 6-inch and eight 4-inch guns, as well as torpedoes and numerous 20mm and 40mm anti-aircraft guns. In April 1945, it joined a Royal Navy task force in the western Pacific, serving principally as an anti-aircraft screening vessel during carrier strikes against Japanese targets in the Ryukyu Archipelago and the island fortress of Truk. In July 1945, late in the war against Japan, a vote of its crew saw some 80 percent—576 ratings and 29 officers—refuse to volunteer to remain in theatre. *Uganda* then sailed ignominiously to Esquimalt in compliance with government policy that Canadian units in the Pacific war be crewed only by those who had specifically volunteered to serve there. The policy also called for 30 days' leave for those so volunteering. In the circumstances and to the fury of the Royal Navy with which it was serving, the RCN had no option except to withdraw *Uganda*, "the ship that voted itself out of the war." Used as a training ship after World War II and refitted for service during the Korean War, it was belatedly renamed *Quebec* in 1952 and paid off in 1956.

UKUSA Agreement. In 1946, Britain and the United States agreed to continue wartime communications intelligence co-operation. This BRUSA agreement was followed by the United Kingdom–United States Security Agreement (UKUSA), signed June 1948, the Cold War successor to World War II intelligence and cryptographic co-operation. Canada, Australia, and New Zealand—the old white Dominions—also continue to work under the agreement, which outlined spheres of signals intelligence and cryptographic influence, divided responsibility among the participants, and laid down standardization regulations. Initially using the Communications Branch, National Research Council, and later the Communications Security Establishment, Canada had the task of covering the northern Soviet Union (and now Russia) and part of Europe and the Far East. Information has been and is collected from all forms of electronic communication, ranging from email to microwaves to radio. The rules for the exchange of Canadian information with the United States were codified in the CANUSA agreement of 1950.

READING: Kurt Jensen, *Cautious Beginnings: Canadian Foreign Intelligence, 1939–1951* (Vancouver, 2008).

Undefended Border. One of the great clichés of Canadian-American relations, the term "undefended border" describes a state that scarcely ever existed. The border was crossed by attackers repeatedly: the Continental Congress invaded Canada in 1775 before the Americans' Declaration of Independence; the Americans attacked Upper Canada in 1812, after Major-General Brock struck at Detroit and Michilimackinac; there were attacks by Patriot Hunters from 1837 to 1838; and raids by Fenians from 1866 to 1871. Notwithstanding such agreements as the Rush-Bagot Convention that regulated warships on the Great Lakes after the War of 1812, there were border disputes that almost led to conflict, such as that over the Alaska boundary at the opening of the twentieth century. During World War I, Canada kept 50,000 troops at home, in part from fear of invasion by German-Americans, and the general staffs in both countries prepared war plans for use against each other in the 1920s. After the Permanent Joint Board on Defence came into being in 1940 and Canada and the United States became military allies, the border was genuinely undefended. The defensive perimeter in World War II and the Cold War was around North America, not around Canada or the United States. After the terrorist attacks on New York and Washington on 11 September 2001, however, the border, while still nominally undefended, did become "toughened up" to provide heightened security. By 2009, the United States had begun to increase its border patrols and to fly Unmanned Aerial Vehicles along the dividing line. SEE ALSO: CANADA–UNITED STATES DEFENCE RELATIONS.

Unemployment Relief Camps. Sponsored by the Department of National Defence and the Department of Labour, the R.B. Bennett government's unemployment relief camps operated between October 1932 and 1936 and were the brainchild of the chief of the general staff, Major-General A.G.L. McNaughton. Located across the country, they housed a combined total of 170,248 single, unemployed men. The Department of National Defence operated the camps with military-like discipline, although they were nominally run by civilians. The men, who entered voluntarily and could leave at any time, were paid 20 cents a day—roughly the equivalent of $3 in 2010—for 44 hours of work a week on a variety of public projects, including the construction of airstrips, bush clearing, and the repair of public buildings. In addition, camp residents received their accommodation, meals, work clothing, and medical care. The government feared that the camps had become a favourite target for Communist agitators who succeeded in organizing the On-to-Ottawa trek in the late spring and early summer of 1935. At Regina, Saskatchewan, the Royal Canadian Mounted Police stopped hundreds of camp-dwellers trying to reach Ottawa on freight cars. The ensuing riot on 1 July 1935 left one Regina police officer dead.

The Mackenzie King government shut the camps in 1936. SEE ALSO: MCNAUGHTON.

Unification. Repeated efforts to rationalize administrative personnel and functions in the Canadian armed forces date back to 1923 when a single ministry was put in place to direct all three services, a situation replicated after World War II in 1946. Additional steps toward integration were the establishment of the position of chairman of the chiefs of staff committee in 1951 to coordinate the training and operations of the services; making the Royal Military College a tri-service training college for junior officers; and establishing common legal, medical, and chaplain services, along with food procurement, dental, and postal services provided by the army to all three services.

Until Paul Hellyer became minister of national defence in Lester Pearson's Liberal government in 1963, however, no one had seriously considered melding Canada's three services into one. Hellyer had been in the Royal Canadian Air Force in World War II and been released when the British Commonwealth Air Training Plan shut down. Taken into the army, he underwent inoculations and basic training once more, an experience he considered wasteful and unnecessary. His party leader, Lester Pearson, the foreign minister during the Suez Crisis, had seen the Egyptians object to Canadian troops serving in the United Nations Emergency Force because the Canadians' regimental names and uniforms were indistinguishable from those of the British soldiers who had invaded their country. That too made an impression, as did the Royal Commission on Government Organization's report of 1962. Charged with examining waste and duplication in the public service, the commission stated that the forces cost too much to administer and pointed to duplicated and triplicated functions as evidence.

Hellyer's Defence White Paper of 1964 reflected the minister's views about the desirability of eliminating waste and triplication in the services and pointed to military integration. The first step, on 13 April 1964, saw Hellyer introduce a bill, "Integration of the

Headquarters Staff," to create a chief of the defence staff to replace the three service chiefs. This bill received royal assent in July, and Air Chief Marshal Frank Miller became chief of the defence staff at the same time as the heads of new functional branches at Canadian Forces Headquarters (CFHQ) took over. The former services were no longer independent entities with their own administrations. Attention then turned to the command and control of integrated units. In January 1966, the minister decided to establish six functional commands to replace the eleven service commands, and every Regular establishment in Canada was to be reallocated to the appropriate command by 1 April 1966.

Mobile Command was formed to maintain combat-ready land and tactical air forces capable of rapid deployment in circumstances ranging from North Atlantic Treaty Organization (NATO) service in Europe to peacekeeping operations. Its Tactical Air Group would consist of CF-5 tactical ground support fighter aircraft, Buffalo transport aircraft, and heavy and light helicopters. Maritime Command, embodying all sea and air maritime forces on both the Atlantic and Pacific Coasts, was primarily responsible for anti-submarine defence, but was intended to become increasingly capable of such other tasks as patrolling the Arctic region. Air Transport Command would provide the forces with strategic airlift capability, the emphasis being on troop-carrying operations. Air Defence Command was to contribute squadrons of CF-101 Voodoo interceptors and surveillance and control radar to the North American Air Defence Command. Training Command was responsible for all individual training, including flying and trades training. And Materiel Command would provide the necessary supply and maintenance support to the other functional commands. Canadian Forces Europe, consisting of the 4th Canadian Infantry Brigade Group and No. 1 Canadian Air Group, was maintained as an independent organization reporting directly to CFHQ.

On 4 November 1966, Hellyer introduced the Canadian Forces Reorganization Act in Parliament to amend the National Defence Act (1922). The Canadian Army, the Royal Canadian Navy, and the Royal Canadian Air Force—previously separate and independent services—would become one. A common rank terminology was to come into effect, and a committee began to design a common uniform. The names army, navy, and air force were to disappear, replaced by the designations land, sea, and air environments. Following extensive and bitter debate in the House of Commons and in the country, the bill received third and final reading in April 1967, clearing the way for unification. The Canadian Forces Reorganization Act came into effect on 1 February 1968.

A number of senior officers resigned in protest over the loss of the distinctiveness of their service, the opposition being most vigorous among senior naval officers. Hellyer had argued that Canada was setting the pace for other nations; none followed Canada's lead. He had clearly hoped that his strong leadership in pushing unification ahead over the opposition to it might propel him into the Prime Minister's Office. Instead, it was the impression of his rigidity that stuck, and he lost the Liberal leadership to Pierre Trudeau in the 1968 convention. SEE ALSO: ALLARD; HELLYER; PEARSON.

READING: Paul Hellyer, *Damn the Torpedoes!* (Toronto, 1990).

University Naval Training Divisions (UNTD). Created in 1942 as a pilot project at the Ontario Agricultural College in Guelph, Ontario, the UNTD, or the "Untidies," as it quickly became universally known, spread to all Canadian universities. The Untidies program trained reserve officers for the Royal Canadian Navy. To 1968, when it disappeared as part of defence minister Paul Hellyer's unification project, the UNTD had put some 6,000 university students through naval officer training, giving as many as a thousand a year summer sea experience on frigates. After its shutdown, the UNTD was followed by the Naval Reserve Officer Training Program and the Naval Reserve Officer Cadet scheme, neither of which had direct connection to the nation's universities.

Valcartier, Canadian Forces Base. In 1914, the minister of militia and defence, Sam Hughes, scrapped the mobilization plan that had been prepared in Ottawa and telegraphed militia units across Canada to raise troops and send them to Valcartier, Quebec, 35 kilometres north of Quebec City. The site had no training facility, but, in little over a month, a huge camp able to hold more than 30,000 recruits had been constructed, complete with water supply, roads, rifle ranges, railway sidings, and training areas. The camp operated during World War I, but afterwards remained largely unused except for occasional summer training. From 1932 to 1935, Valcartier was an unemployment relief camp. The training camp went into full operation again during World War II and continued after the war. Canadian Forces Base Valcartier is now home to the Canadian Forces' Ve Groupe-brigade mécanisé du Canada, a French-speaking brigade that includes the Royal 22e Régiment's three battalions and the 12e Régiment Blindé.

▲ Georges Vanier during World War I.

The Valiants Memorial. Under the leadership of former soldier and diplomat Hamilton Southam, the Valiants Foundation raised funds and persuaded the federal government to allow the installation of 13 busts and one full-size statue around the Sappers' Stairway on Confederation Square, close to the National War Memorial in Ottawa. Dedicated on 5 November 2006, the statues commemorate 14 individuals deemed by the Foundation to have played major roles in Canada's wars from the era of New France to World War II: Count Frontenac, Pierre Le Moyne d'Iberville, Joseph Brant, John Butler, Isaac Brock, Charles-Michel de Salaberry, Laura Secord, Georgina Pope, Arthur Currie (the one full-size representation), Joseph Kaeble, John Thomas, Paul

Triquet, Andrew Mynarski, and Hampton Gray. Created by John McEwen and Marlene Hilton Moore, the sculptures drew praise for the respect they rendered to Canadian military heroes and heroines, and criticism for their artistic merit and odd placement, so close to the National War Memorial and the Tomb of the Unknown Soldier, both of which stand for all Canadian service personnel.

Vanier, Georges-Philias (1888–1967). Educated at Université Laval and trained as a lawyer, Georges Vanier joined the 22nd Battalion in early 1915 and served with it in the 2nd Canadian Division in the Canadian Corps during World War I. He won the

Military Cross and the Distinguished Service Order and, in the great battles of the Hundred Days' campaign in late 1918, suffered grievous wounds in the chest and legs. Although his right leg had to be amputated, Vanier continued to serve with the "Van Doos" in the tiny postwar Permanent Force, taking command of the regiment in 1925. He left the army to join the Department of External Affairs, serving in the 1930s in Geneva, London, and Paris. After returning to Canada and the army in 1941 as a major-general and district officer commanding in Quebec City, he worked at the difficult, sometimes thankless, task of recruiting. In 1942, Vanier returned to London as Canada's minister to the Allied governments-in-exile, where he developed a close relationship with General Charles de Gaulle, the Free French leader. In 1944, in newly liberated Paris, he became ambassador to de Gaulle's France where he served until 1953 and retirement. Prime Minister John Diefenbaker named him governor general in 1959 when he was 71, the first Canadien in that post, and for almost eight years he was, as a 1998 profile in *Maclean's* put it, "the exemplar of service and duty and courage—the great military virtues that he embodied and honoured." When President de Gaulle meddled in Canada-Quebec relations during the late 1960s, Vanier, near death, was appalled at such interference after Canada's sacrifices in liberating France. SEE ALSO: QUEBEC AND THE MILITARY; ROYAL 22E RÉGIMENT.

READING: Robert Speaight, *Vanier: Soldier, Diplomat and Governor-General: A Biography* (Toronto, 1970).

Vaudreuil, Philippe de Rigaud de Vaudreuil, Marquis de (c.1643–1725).

A Musketeer, Vaudreuil served with the French army in Flanders before coming to Canada in 1687 as commander of the small garrison of French troops. He trained his soldiers to fight the Iroquois and was notably successful, twice defeating war parties. Appointed governor of New France in 1703, for the next 22 years his primary concern was the military security of the approaches to New France from the south and the assertion of French control over the western fur trade. In 1709,

▲ Pierre de Rigaud de Vaudreuil de Cavagnial, Marquis de Vaudreuil, as painted in the early 1750s.

British and colonial forces led by Sir Hovenden Walker tried to mount an attack on Quebec that foundered in confusion; Vaudreuil, nevertheless, reaped the credit in Paris and consolidated his power.

Vaudreuil, Pierre de Rigaud de Vaudreuil de Cavagnial, Marquis de (1698–1778).

Born in New France, the fourth son of the soon-to-be governor, Vaudreuil served as a soldier and with distinction as the governor of France's colony of Louisiana. Appointed governor general of New France in 1755, his task was to preserve the colony through the Seven Years' War in the face of Britain's military and demographic superiority, a task he tackled with vigour by taking advantage of the colony's interior lines of communication and the ability of his First Nations allies at *la petite guerre*. He had difficulty with his military commanders, Baron Dieskau and the Marquis de Montcalm. Montcalm, in fact, rejected his strategy and connived against Vaudreuil, a task made easier when Montcalm became a lieutenant-general in

⌃ Two World War II veterans, one wearing his campaign ribbons over his heart and his Royal Canadian Legion ribbons on his right, at a Remembrance Day Ceremony in Trenton, Ontario.

1758 and outranked the governor. After the defeat on the Plains of Abraham on 13 September 1759, Vaudreuil favoured attacking the weakened British the next day but was overruled by his surviving military commanders. He continued New France's resistance into 1760 but, in the face of superior force, he surrendered the colony and was returned to France on a British ship. SEE ALSO: MONTCALM; PLAINS OF ABRAHAM; QUEBEC (1759).

READING: D. Peter MacLeod, *Northern Armageddon: The Battle of the Plains of Abraham* (Vancouver, 2008).

Veterans. Canada has had veterans as long as it has had wars but, aside from charitable handouts, meagre pensions, or postwar land settlement grants—the latter a tactic as old as the Roman legions—the status often conferred little save personal pride. The South African War (1899–1902) saw parades, celebrations, and a patriotic fund to ease the heroes' lot, with greater

attention to soldiers' families and post-service care than any previous conflict. Public monuments and memorials, a prominent feature of civil life since the War of 1812, received a boost as well, but the veteran as a demographic cohort remained insignificant until 1914. The massive mobilization that marked World War I spawned a steady trickle of veterans of wartime service from the first training accidents and honourable discharges; in 1918, it became an unprecedented flood. The term for those who served in World War I was generally "returned men," whose reintegration and postwar care was a social challenge for policy-makers and pension actuaries that defied historic comparisons. Interwar organizations of former service personnel and charitable groups sought greater benefits, extra cash, and a more grateful society, but social conservatism and a shattered economy combined to defer better treatment until the full coffers and stronger economy sparked by a later war.

World War II saw earlier planning for veterans' welfare and wider possibilities for enlightened policy, the Great Depression having convinced many Canadians that social welfare was a public good and not a temporary evil. The term "veteran" came to designate those men and 50,000 women who had completed military service and who were eligible for the benefits of the Veterans Charter, the name given to the omnibus package of benefits crafted by Mackenzie King's ministers and mandarins to rehabilitate and compensate those who had served. The package had weaknesses and inconsistencies (First Nations and merchant sailors were among those treated unequally), but it was farsighted too and, internationally, second to none. It served most veterans well and many splendidly, helping to ensure a smooth transition from war to peace in which upheaval had been feared and unrest expected.

Veterans guarded jealously their status and prerogatives. Their organizations, now swelled in membership and impact by two world wars' worth of former combatants, objected to the definition of "veteran" being applied to members of the merchant marine on the grounds that they had not been under military discipline and had received higher pay than sailors or soldiers. Decades passed, objections eased (or appeared increasingly unreasonable), and definitions changed. Merchant sailors, their wartime losses catastrophic, gradually became eligible for benefits they ought probably to have always received; and inequalities between First Nations veterans and non-Aboriginals largely disappeared. Policy-makers now wrestled with the particular challenges posed by the non-wars and violent peaces that marked the modern age. Did the Cold War generate veterans and, if so, what had they been veterans of, surely not a World War III that had never happened? Peacekeeping could be boredom personified, or danger incarnate: were blue berets veterans, or just blue helmets? Korean War veterans agitated for more than remembrance, but for basic benefits too; the extension of the Veterans Charter to them was a key precedent in handling modern conflicts that often carried no start or end date, no declarations of war,

and muddied the distinctions between active service and pensionable time. Administrative hair-splitting—Special Duty Areas, for example, to distinguish conflict zones from ordinary service—were eventually supplanted, in 2006, by a New Veterans Charter that updated the range and type of benefits and assistance programs available to former Canadian Forces members and their families.

The last of Canada's World War I veterans, John Babcock, aged 109, died in February 2010, but 163,000 World War II veterans (average age 86) remained, along with 12,500 Korean War veterans (average age 78), and some 591,000 veterans (average age 55) with post-1953 Canadian military service.

Veterans Affairs, Department of (DVA). Canada created the Department of Soldiers' Civil Re-establishment in 1918 to manage the reintegration and care of veterans returning from World War I. At its peak in 1920, the federal department had 9,000 employees administering medical, dental, and psychiatric care, pensions, training for the disabled, an artificial limb factory, loans, and employment place-ment services. It co-operated (usually) with charitable agencies, provincial government departments, and veterans' groups in delivering one of the most compre-hensive veterans' programs in any country. The short-term nature of much of the department's work saw its budgets and staffing levels decline in the postwar period, but it remained a huge operation, in the pensions area especially, and was merged with the Department of Health in 1928 to create the new Department of Pensions and National Health.

A Cabinet reorganization in 1944 recreated a separate federal department to manage the affairs of former military personnel. Its first minister was the volatile but capable Ian Mackenzie who, as minister of national defence from 1935 to 1939, had been implicated in a procurement scandal and moved to head the Department of Pensions and National Health as a result. Mackenzie's department oversaw a wide array of benefit programs designed to rehabilitate and re-establish Canada's World War II veterans, a package consolidated into the Veterans Charter in 1945. The department's mandate once included the provision of medical care to veterans; but it has since dropped that task and, until recently, was largely concerned with ensuring the smooth operation of Canada's remaining World War II and Korean War veterans' financial assistance programs. Under the name Veterans Affairs Canada, the current portfolio includes the Department of Veterans Affairs, the Veterans Review and Appeal Board, and the Office of the Veterans Ombudsman (created in 2007); the department reports to the minister, while the appeal board and the ombudsman report to Parliament through the minister. DVA has responsibility for pensions, benefits, and services to all veterans, including those from Canada's peace support operations. The terms of the Canadian Forces Members and Veterans Re-establishment and Compensation Act, usually called the New Veterans Charter, adopted in 2006, updated veterans' benefits for the complex wars and emergencies of the post–Cold War era. DVA also maintains substantial responsibilities in the areas of commemoration and remembrance under the Canada Remembers program. SEE ALSO: VETERANS CHARTER.

Veterans Charter. Drafted during World War II by Ian Mackenzie, the minister of pensions and national health, and his staff, the Charter promised "opportunity with security" for Canadian veterans. Its generous provisions included paid access to education and training, grants to start businesses, the right to return to former jobs with full seniority and pension rights, land grants, and rehabilitation credits for the purchase of household items. It was rightly hailed both as the most generous such program anywhere and as a building block of the Canadian welfare state. The Charter fell under the Department of Veterans Affairs with Mackenzie as its first minister.

In 2006, the government passed the Canadian Forces Members and Veterans Re-Establishment and Compensation Act, usually called the New Veterans Charter. The act gave serving members and veterans access to rehabilitation services, financial and health insurance benefits, assistance with job placement, disability and death payments, and family support.

The act is administered by Veterans Affairs Canada. By 2009, veterans' organizations and an advisory group established in 2007 to review the implementation of the new charter were already pressing for changes in the areas of family support, financial security, rehabilitation, promotion of programs, and performance measurement. SEE ALSO: VETERANS; VETERANS AFFAIRS.

READING: Peter Neary and J.L. Granatstein, eds., *The Veterans Charter and Post–World War II Canada* (Montreal, 1998).

Veterans' Organizations. Veterans appear to have begun organizing in Canada as early as the 1840s to press governments for pensions and benefits. Such benefits frequently included land grants but little else, cash benefits largely being left to voluntary benefactors. The political influence of American Civil War veterans in the United States, a huge lobby for pensions, served as both an incentive to Canadian veterans and a warning to governments, the phrase "pension evil" coming to mean the long-term, constantly expanding bill for the post-service remuneration of former service personnel. The relatives of those killed during the Northwest Rebellion (1885) became eligible for small government pensions; those disabled could similarly receive support. This policy also covered South African War veterans.

After World War I, the federal government had little choice other than to provide better pensions, training, and rehabilitation to veterans but, during the war and after, heated complaints arose. The Great War Veterans Association, created during the conflict, lobbied hard for more government support, but there were many veterans' organizations, all sorely divided. It took British Field Marshal Earl Haig to urge unification of the fractious groups. With the creation in 1925 of the Canadian Legion of the British Empire Service League (later the Royal Canadian Legion), most groups came under the same tent, and lobbying for better pensions and other forms of care became more coordinated, and measurably more effective. In 1918, there had been 25,823 pensions paying

$7,274,000 in force; in 1939, there were 98,000 pensions paying $40,413,000.

World War II provided more than a million more potential members for veterans' organizations and for lobbying. Lessons from the interwar period, in everything from administration to social welfare, gave rise to greater efficiency and more open-mindedness in the second war, but veterans' effective lobbying efforts also pressed against an open door. Federal officials began in fall 1939 to create the web of benefits, programs, and agencies that would be consolidated into the Veterans Charter of 1945. It was a regime far more generous than anything that had followed the 1914–1918 war and one that was in a class of its own for the 1940s as well. The political necessity and the moral obligation to provide for those who had served were far clearer, and more widely shared, in 1945 than they had been in 1918.

The Royal Canadian Legion remained the main veterans' organization in Canada after 1945, with some 350,000 members, including 94,000 women, in 2010, its advocacy efforts ranging from services on behalf of veterans to commemorative campaigns and historical awareness. Its financial operations, including the sale of commemorative memorabilia, and its membership dues combined to support hundreds of projects, many of them related to children's education or community work. The Legion initiated the project to repatriate a Canadian Unknown Soldier from the World War I battlefield of Vimy Ridge for interment at the National War Memorial in 2000, and continues to coordinate national Remembrance Day services at the latter site each 11 November. The Legion's annual poppy campaign is the country's largest benevolent campaign of its kind, raising millions of dollars annually to be held in trust for the support of veterans and their dependants. The Army, Navy, and Air Force Veterans in Canada, or ANAVETS, the National Council of Veterans Associations, and a host of other old and new organizations combine socializing and civic responsibility with advocacy for their members or other closely related groups. Jewish war veterans, Aboriginal veterans, peacekeeping veterans, Korean

War veterans, merchant sailors, and others maintain their own associations and collective objectives, often in conjunction with the larger organizations, and occasionally in conflict with them. Since World War II, veterans' efforts have evolved from simple pension advocacy and individual redress to encompass challenges as diverse as popular awareness of military history and public support for the disabled. Most are financially engaged in providing educational assistance by way of scholarships or by funding learning opportunities for students across the country. Veterans' organizations have also played a critical role in the preservation of historical memory, with noted involvement in oral history projects, support to federal and other museums and memorials, commemorative sites overseas, and video and multimedia productions.

Social conservatism and the inherent narrowness of veterans' interests have sometimes led to public controversy. Veterans' political influence has sometimes been affected, positively or negatively, as a result. After the bruising fight during World War II over the imposition of conscription, some postwar veterans' organizations continued to support compulsory military service for the nation's youth, a peacetime non-starter. During the early 1990s, the Legion sought to ban Sikh members from wearing turbans inside Legion halls, an affair that made international headlines, few of them complimentary to veterans. In a country changing demographically and socially due to immigration, an official policy of multicultural accommodation, and the legal implications of the Charter of Rights and Freedoms (adopted in 1982), the positions of veterans' organizations on contemporary social issues could sometimes appear calcified and irrelevant to non-members. The pointed concerns expressed by veterans' groups, including the Legion, with the announcement of Michaëlle Jean as governor general in 2005 were a case in point. Doubting publicly her loyalty to the Queen due to her French (and Canadian) citizenship and her past relationships with pro-sovereignty Québécois and some former members of the Front de Libération du

Québec, veterans expressed the doubts of many Canadians at the appointment while also courting perceptions of their own intolerance—Jean is a French-speaking Quebec resident of Haitian descent. Senior representatives of veterans' groups backed away from calls for a public protest of Jean's appointment (some veterans had suggested turning their backs on her at Remembrance Day events in November), later expressing publicly their belated support for the Queen's representative after Buckingham Palace accepted her as governor general designate.

The political relevance of veterans' organizations remains considerable, although membership is in general decline. The broadening of membership criteria in some organizations—and links to youth, public service associations, or other likely allies—has attempted to relieve the demographic pressure caused by the aging of Canada's World War II population. Veterans' organizations continue to provide vital services and advocacy support to members and the veteran population more broadly, and to support civic causes from education to health care. Their work since the early twentieth century in many of these areas has been uniquely effective; in recent decades, their work in the areas of historical awareness and public remembrance has been equally valuable. SEE ALSO: VETERANS.

READING: Desmond Morton and Glenn Wright, *Winning the Second Battle: Canadian Veterans and the Return to Civilian Life, 1915–1930* (Toronto, 1987).

Vimy Memorial. Designed by Canadian sculptor Walter Seymour Allward, the huge Canadian National Vimy Memorial stands atop Vimy Ridge to commemorate the 11,285 Canadians killed in France during World War I who have no known graves. The monument was built over eleven years at a cost of $1.5 million. The land, 36 hectares in all, was donated in perpetuity to Canada by the French government in 1922. Some 10,000 Canadian veterans and family members attended the unveiling of the monument by King Edward VIII on 26 July 1936. Maquettes (models) of many of Allward's gigantic figures on the Memorial are displayed in the Canadian War Museum in Ottawa. In April 2007, no Vimy veterans were left to return to France on the occasion of the 90th anniversary of the battle from 9 to 12 April 1917, but thousands of Canadians turned out for the re-dedication of the memorial, refurbished over a three-year period after it had shamefully been allowed to decay.

Vimy Pilgrimages (1936, 2007). The great memorial erected on Vimy Ridge in France to honour Canada's World War I dead was unveiled and dedicated by Edward VIII on 26 July 1936. Five passenger liners carried some 6,000 veterans and family members from Canada to France, each travelling on special passports issued free of charge. At the ceremony at Vimy, there were an estimated 8,000 Canadian veterans and upwards of a hundred thousand French, British, and others present, including perhaps 50,000 veterans in total from all nations. Each Canadian

Designed by Walter Allward and built on land deeded to Canada in perpetuity by France, the Vimy Memorial commemorates Canadians killed in France with no known grave.

↑ The dedication of the Vimy Memorial in 1936 drew a huge crowd, including thousands of Canadian veterans who crossed the Atlantic for the occasion.

participant received a special medal to commemorate the occasion, as did those who participated in the 90th anniversary ceremony at the completely refurbished Vimy Memorial in April 2007. Queen Elizabeth II and Prime Minister Stephen Harper presided at the latter before an audience that included, among others, almost 10,000 Canadian high school students.

Vimy Ridge, Battle of (1917). In the years since World War I, the battle of Vimy Ridge, a stunning but costly Canadian victory, has assumed almost mythic proportions in Canadian reflections on the war. Most Canadians see the 1917 battle as a nation-building event, a key marker in the development of Canadian nationalism. Many participants reflected such views, even at the time, cognizant of the national implications of Canadian success where other Allied attacks had failed. For those at home, after years of horrific casualty rolls with few victories to celebrate, Vimy was a unique and overdue achievement, a good news story—despite the casualties—in a grim struggle

that seemed no closer to conclusion in 1917 than it had three years before.

For some, the battle's impact came from its military achievement alone—scaling an enemy-held ridge against long odds and fierce resistance; for others, it was a Cinderella story—citizen-soldiers, volunteers all, showing professionals their business in a war short on creativity and long on dumbness; and for others still it was a political morality tale, a fledgling dominion earning its just desserts within the old Empire by dint of hard labour and the blood of its sons. There was truth and much fiction in all of this, and rather more of the latter in the postwar legend, bred of potboiler histories and back-slapping memoirs, that Vimy had somehow been a decisive battle that helped end the war or secure some lasting Allied advantage. The omnipresent view, expressed still in each year's television coverage of the battle's anniversary or 11 November Remembrance Day events, that Vimy was an all-Canadian triumph as much over Allied (especially British) incompetence as enemy competence is a delightful conceit, grounded

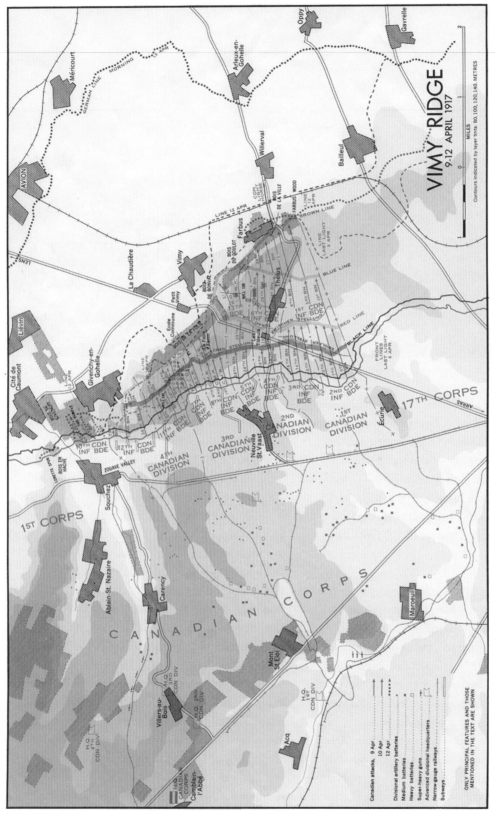

VIMY RIDGE
9–12 APRIL 1917

MILES

Contours indicated by layer tints. 80, 100, 120, 140. METRES

▲ Fighting together for the first time, the four divisions of the Canadian Corps took Vimy Ridge in a legendary feat of arms. Patriotic fervour attributed the success to Canadian uniqueness, but a British general, Sir Julian Byng, had commanded the Corps at Vimy.

Canadian attacks, 9 Apr. ....
                    10 Apr. ....
                    12 Apr. ....
Divisional artillery batteries ....
Medium batteries ....
Heavy batteries ....
Super-heavy guns ....
Advanced divisional headquarters ....
Narrow-gauge railways ....
Subways ....

ONLY PRINCIPAL FEATURES AND THOSE
MENTIONED IN THE TEXT ARE SHOWN

too much in sloppy heritage and too little in awkward history. It was a great and unprecedented victory to be sure, and a key turning point in the development of Canada's almost preternaturally effective army corps during the war. But it was smaller, less costly, and less impressive than battles yet to come; it had been fought under British command with British staff work laying victory's essential foundations; and it had little impact on the outcome of the war. And, for most Canadians, it is rightly legendary just the same—the supreme moment, of many such that a ghastly war provided, when Canada became Canada, and the mythology of nationhood unalterably changed.

In April 1917, the Great War was not going well for the Allies. The Russian Empire, dissolving in revolution, teetered on the brink of leaving the war, and the French armies, battered beyond endurance in a succession of battles, verged on mutiny. Britain and the dominions alone seemed resolute, but casualties greatly outpaced new recruits to the colours. Many in Canada had begun to call for conscription, though the government of Sir Robert Borden had yet to move. The only bright spot for the Allies came on 6 April when United States President Woodrow Wilson brought his nation into the war. The United States was not prepared, however, and it would be more than a year before large numbers of "doughboys" began to reach the trenches. Allied victories were scarce and the Germans' weapons, tactics, and leadership seemed to dominate the battlefields of Europe. In mid-March, the Germans shortened their defensive lines, withdrawing on a 150-kilometre stretch of the Western Front to the heavily fortified Hindenburg Line that ran south from Arras to St-Quentin. There, defence in depth—the enemy's new doctrine—would be put into practice.

Allied plans for offensives in the West had to be altered in light of the new situation on the ground, and the British Expeditionary Force (BEF) now took on the task of outflanking the enemy's new defence line as a subsidiary portion of a major attack by the French, the great (and, as it turned out, unsuccessful) attack planned by General Robert Nivelle. The battle of Arras, as it came to be called, involved two British armies, the

1st and the 3rd, and the goal, while never explicitly stated, was attrition, the wearing down of the enemy forces by inflicting losses in killed and wounded that the outnumbered German defenders could not indefinitely sustain. The Canadian Corps' attack at Vimy Ridge was one part of this larger British drive.

The high ground, of which Vimy Ridge was the major feature, dominated the Douai Plain of northern France and looked out over Lens to the east and Arras to the south. The ridge itself, except for Hill 145 and The Pimple at its northern end, rose gradually from west to east. The sharp drop was at the eastern edge, behind the main German positions, and the ridge was important primarily because its possession gave—or denied—a view of a great swathe of German-held territory. Vimy Ridge had been seized by the Germans in October 1914 and then assaulted without success by the French in 1915 and the British in 1916. Fought over so viciously, the ground had been torn up by shellfire, by sappers sinking mine shafts to plant explosives (more than a hundred British mines had been exploded in 1916), and by ever-deeper trenches and dugouts. When the Canadians arrived at Vimy, efforts to seize the ridge had already cost 300,000 casualties. As one soldier later remarked, Vimy "was the central point of an immense graveyard."

The German Sixth Army had had ample time to perfect its defences atop the ridge. There were three main defensive lines with trenches and deep dugouts, all protected by belts of barbed wire and concrete machine-gun posts. The chalky soil of the ridge had been carved up with tunnels and communication trenches, and the enemy's second line, situated as much as three kilometres east of the ridge, featured vast bunkers, some of which could hold a battalion in safety. The third line, eight kilometres to the rear, relied on heavily fortified positions. And there was a fourth defensive belt under construction further back, the Drocourt-Quéant Line that Canadians would encounter during what would become known as the Hundred Days in 1918. The fatal flaw in German planning was that counterattack divisions were 12 to 24 hours march to the rear. If the Canadians could crack the enemy defence lines on Vimy Ridge, they could not soon be driven off by German counterattacks.

By the winter of 1917, the Canadian Corps, led by British Lieutenant-General Sir Julian Byng, was an experienced formation. It had fought well in the costly battles on the Somme in the autumn of 1916, and its divisions, brigades, and battalions were well led. A majority of its men had been born in Britain, not Canada, but its spirit and sensibility increasingly was Canadian. Its four divisions had learned their trade over two years of fighting, mastering trench warfare, learning how to make the best use of infantry, and studying how to employ aerial reconnaissance, gas, and the war-winning weapon, artillery, most effectively. The Canadian Corps was a learning institution, an organization that sought answers to the question that plagued strategists: how could the advantages that favoured the defence on the Western Front be overcome?

Every commander wrestled with that question, but some of the answers came from the 1st Canadian Division's practical, analytical, and open-minded commander, Major-General Arthur Currie. Sent by Byng to study how the French had fought at Verdun in December 1916, Currie's report pointed to good reconnaissance as the key, along with efforts put into familiarizing every soldier with the objectives sought and then practising each one's role prior to the battle. For the first time, maps and photographs went down to platoon level, and each of the *poilus* (French infantry) had been trained to operate every infantry weapon—and those belonging to the Germans as well. The French relied on fire and movement, with infantry consolidating on captured positions, and fresh troops, moving in rushes and leading the assault forward, employing machine-gun fire and grenades to keep the enemies' heads down.

Many British officers had drawn similar conclusions from their ally's tactics, but it is fair to say that Byng implemented them with greater vigour than most. As did British units, his Canadian Corps reorganized, its companies now made up of four platoons, each of four sections, and each employing fire and movement in the attack. Officers stressed

individual initiative, and platoons became more self-reliant, a policy that brought specialists, like Lewis machine gunners, bombers and rifle grenadiers, back into the platoon and made it capable of integrated action. But throughout the British Expeditionary Force, of which the Canadian Corps formed part, the rifle and bayonet remained the key. Johnny Canuck temperamentally might have had more innate flexibility than the Tommy, a dubious contention but one popularly believed in Canada, but the template for attack that each used was very similar. What was different, as Brigadier-General William Griesbach of the 1st Brigade was wont to say, was that the Canadian Corps was well trained, well led, and driven by a commitment to learning.

Byng and his staff, the key ones imperial officers trained at the British army's staff colleges, had a plan for the assault on Vimy ready by the beginning of March 1917. The intention was to jump off on Easter Monday, 9 April, in a four-stage attack, designed to employ the Canadian Corps' four divisions arranged in order, from the 4th on the left to the 1st on the right of the Canadian line. Each division would attack at 5:30 a.m. with two brigades in the lead. The first objective, the Black Line, encompassed the Germans' front-line trenches, to be seized within 35 minutes. Then, the troops were to pause for 40 minutes to consolidate and regroup. Within a further 20 minutes, the Red Line, the final objectives for the 3rd and 4th Divisions, were to be in the Canadians' grasp. The reserve brigades of the 1st and 2nd Divisions, plus a British brigade, were then to assault toward the Blue Line, taking the Germans' second-line defences that centred on the village of Thélus. Finally, after a halt for precisely 96 minutes, the same brigades would advance to the Brown Line, the final objective, some 3,700 metres beyond the start line.

If everything went to plan, the Canadian Corps' action would be concluded by 1:18 p.m. Byng's orders took into account the need to prepare for German counterattacks. Machine guns in profusion had to be brought forward quickly and defensive lines readied hastily on the newly won ground. Much depended on the artillery. Indeed, artillery preparation was the key to victory. The enemy trenches were blasted by a bombardment that began on 20 March and intensified on 2 April, one week before the assault. Special attention was paid to the German barbed wire defences, these to be destroyed by shells fitted with the new No. 106 fuse that exploded on contact with the wire. So effective were they that only a few units reported difficulty moving forward on 9 April. Enemy guns were located by aerial-spotting, sound-ranging, and flash-spotting, and put out of action by counter-battery fire, this whole process managed by Lieutenant-Colonel Andrew McNaughton. By the hour of attack, 83 percent of the 212 German guns defending Vimy had been neutralized.

A plethora of guns had been made available for the Canadian Corps' needs: eleven heavy artillery groups, comprising 245 guns, and 15 field artillery brigades with 618 guns. Vickers machine guns, 150 of them, fired indirectly on enemy strongpoints. Even more firepower was available on call. Most of the guns, like most of the logistical effort backing up the front-line battalions, came from British army resources. The guns had another vital role. A creeping barrage would move forward in 90-metre steps, all carefully timed. The advancing infantry had to be careful to remain behind the barrage or risk destruction from friendly fire.

A huge quantity of shells had to be amassed, stored, and moved forward at the appropriate time. So too

▲ Vimy Ridge was an artillery triumph. Canadian and British guns fired hundreds of thousands of shells, using scientific techniques to find and suppress enemy batteries.

did food, 2,730,000 litres of water each day, engineer stores, ammunition, medical supplies, forage, and everything else the 100,000 troops of the Canadian Corps and their 50,000 animals required. A system of tramways carried light supply trains forward into tunnels dug by the corps' five tunnelling companies. Equipped with lighting, telephones, and water, these tunnels sheltered many of the troops during the buildup for the attack.

While the preparations gathered speed, the attacking battalions practised their roles again and again. Rehearsals took place on roughly similar patches of ground to the rear, with taped lines showing objectives. The aim was to have every soldier know where to go and what to do, and to understand his unit's overall objective. Surprisingly,

this worked. One Lewis gunner in the 2nd Canadian Mounted Rifles said later that "when we finally reached the top of the hill, we not only landed in exactly the right place, but we knew we were in the right section of those trenches we were supposed to be in."

The Germans knew an attack was coming, but Byng hoped to achieve tactical surprise and to mislead the enemy. The rate of gunfire could be altered, for example, and the guns eased off after midnight on Easter Monday. There was no traditional final bombardment that heralded Allied attacks. Officers only learned the hour of the attack on Easter Sunday and briefed their men soon after. At 5:30 a.m., first light, with a northwest wind fortuitously driving snow into the faces of the German sentries, everything was

⌃ Huge naval guns were included in the massed artillery supporting the Canadian Corps' attack on Vimy Ridge.

in place. The attack began with a huge artillery barrage, as each gun fired four rounds a minute. The 15,000 infantry in the first wave of 21 battalions left their start lines on a 6,400-metre frontage. Each carried a rifle and bayonet, gas mask, 120 rounds of ammunition, grenades, a water bottle, possibly a haversack with iron rations, and a pick or a shovel, and the infantry had to lug some 50 to 75 pounds on their backs. The mud, churned up by continuous shelling, slowed the advance, but the infantry pushed ahead. The artillery pounded the enemy batteries and main defensive positions, and the effective creeping barrage let the infantry stay close to the wall of shrapnel.

When they reached the first enemy trenches, most battalions right on schedule, they found the Germans still in their dugouts. Enemy troops surrendered or were hit by grenades and small arms fire. The brief pause on the Black Line let the attackers consolidate. Then the advance began again, progressing well on the right of the line. The Germans had now begun to react, and snipers, machine-gun fire, and artillery caused Canadian casualties, but this scarcely slowed the advance. The Blue Line fell easily to the reserve brigades of the 1st and 2nd Divisions, "in precisely the same manner as it had been worked out on the practice fields," or so said the British official historians. The final objective, the Brown Line, reached after a downhill bayonet charge by men of the 6th Brigade, was quickly in Canadian hands.

The Canadian Corps' major difficulties came in the 4th Division's sector on the left. At Hill 145 and The Pimple, dug-in German troops, who had the advantage of the highest points on the ridge, offered fierce resistance. The enemy had bunkers on a reverse slope that made them safe from artillery bombardment, and the 11th and 12th Brigades battered against machine-gun strongpoints without much success. Indeed, German counterattacks at times threatened their efforts.

As night fell, the Germans still held Hill 145. It was not until the 4th Division sent in two companies of Nova Scotia's 85th Battalion, new to the front and intended only for use as a labour battalion at Vimy, that the Germans there gave up. The remainder of the Red Line positions facing the 4th Division, except for The Pimple, fell on the morning of 10 April after a bayonet charge by two battalions. The Pimple had been designated for capture by British troops. Instead, on 12 April, three battalions of the 4th Division's 10th Brigade launched a night attack in a howling gale and seized the position in a hand-to-hand struggle with a German Guards regiment. "I am King of the Pimple," said Brigadier-General Edward Hilliam. Vimy Ridge, including the site of the eventual Canadian memorial on Hill 145, was in Canadian hands.

The Canadians now began to move their guns and all kinds of materiel, food, and water forward. Every man knew that taking the ridge was a significant victory. Percy McClare of the 24th Battalion wrote his mother that he "was in the whole of that battle and it was Hell." But, he added, "I am glad to say that I was through it, as it will be one of the biggest things in Canadian history." It was, but the cost was heavy. The Canadian Corps suffered 10,602 casualties in the Vimy fighting, including 3,598 dead, its highest losses of the war in a single action. The 4th Division, not surprisingly, had the most casualties with 4,401 of its infantry—or one in three—killed or wounded.

The carefully planned and brilliantly fought set-piece battle was a triumph of combined arms that produced an advance of almost five kilometres, the greatest by the Allies to that point. The victory demonstrated how much the Canadians had learned in action, and it proved that the corps was without peer as a fighting formation. Unfortunately, the battle did not alter the course of the war. There was no attempt to exploit the breakthrough achieved by "Byng's boys", no effort to send the cavalry streaming through the German lines. The enemy retreated a few kilometres to new positions and the struggle continued. The battle of Arras, of which Vimy formed part, was only a limited success; the French attacks that had been intended to be the main Allied effort failed, and mutinies quickly spread across the French army.

Vimy's transcendental importance was for Canada. It was a great victory achieved by the army of a nation that was only then becoming aware of its nationality. That a majority of the soldiers and the key staff officers were British-born made no difference. The battle was then and has remained since quintessentially Canadian—in deed, in death, in national memory. That the battle occurred at Easter gave it additional contemporary resonance, a Christian significance that added to the meaning of sacrifice and the nationalism it fostered. In planning postwar memorials and the location of Canada's principal place of remembrance, Passchendaele and Hill 70 would later have their advocates, while historians would linger admiringly on the hammer blows rained from the Canadian Corps during the decisive victories of the Hundred Days. But none of those were Vimy, none were first or greatest or most poignant in the collective imagination, and none would ultimately have Allward's breathtaking monument to draw pilgrims, artists, veterans, and the reflections of a nation on the horrors and the triumphs of war. SEE ALSO: BYNG; CANADIAN CORPS; CURRIE; WORLD WAR I.

READING: Geoffrey Hayes et al., eds., *Vimy Ridge: A Canadian Reassessment* (Waterloo, ON, 2007); Bill Rawling, *Surviving Trench Warfare: Technology and the Canadian Corps, 1914–1918* (Toronto, 1992).

Volunteer Militia Act (1855). The Province of Canada passed this act at a time of patriotic fervour created by the Crimean War. Unwilling to create a standing army, the government agreed to establish an Active Militia that was to be supplied with arms and ammunition, paid for its training days, and compensated for the costs of uniforms. Authorized companies recruited quickly, and such was the demand that unpaid but equipped Class B companies had to be created. The volunteer units used 1853 Enfield rifles, the cavalry used Colt six-shooters, and the artillery used modern British guns. There were 35,000 militia volunteers by 1863 when the government agreed to purchase and supply uniforms. The colonies in the Maritimes, not yet part of Canada, had roughly similar militia acts and success.

Wainwright, Canadian Forces Base. Acquired in 1940 by the Department of National Defence, Camp Wainwright was used as a World War II training camp and in 1945–1946 to house German prisoners of war (of whom two escaped). Korea-bound army units also trained there in the early 1950s. Canadian Forces Base (CFB) Wainwright now has a small airfield and is the main Reserve force training base for Land Forces Western Area. It also trains Regular force recruits when CFB St Jean cannot. It houses the high-tech Canadian Manoeuvre Training Centre that provides two-week Weapons Effects Simulation programs to all soldiers before deployment, putting battle group sub-units through an Afghanistan-like exercise where an "enemy" offers opposition.

Walker, Sir Hovenden (c.1656–c.1725). The naval commander of the abortive British attack on Quebec in 1711, Walker was born in Ireland and served in Europe and the West Indies. Early in 1711, appointed a rear-admiral and given a knighthood, he had a large force of 12,000, including five regiments pulled from the Duke of Marlborough's armies in Europe. But the preparations for the venture were less than complete, and Walker lacked competent pilots and charts to lead him up the treacherous St Lawrence when he set out from Boston on 30 July. He lost eight ships in fog and command confusion west of Anticosti Island on 22 August, and the timorous admiral abandoned the expedition and returned to England to answer for the debacle. His government eventually sacked him and destroyed his naval career.

War Art. There was Canadian war art before World War I, though much of it was of such "Canadian" subjects as the famous painting of the death of

The Canadian war art programs produced wonderful work in both wars. Here, Captain Lawren P. Harris, the son of the Group of Seven painter, sketches at Ortona in December 1943.

General James Wolfe by Benjamin West, an Anglo-American painter, who was not at the battle on the Plains of Abraham in 1759. Painters did portraits of senior officers, while sketch artists and illustrators accompanied Wolseley's Red River Expedition in 1870, the troops fighting against Riel in 1885, and the Canadians in South Africa. Military engineers produced art of a sort as well, drawing rivers, canals, fortifications, or strategic points as part of their survey work and defence planning; many of these illustrations still exist in museums or galleries across the country. Period artists worked forts, soldiers, naval themes, or military regalia into occasional depictions of urban life or frontier exploration, but of war art there was little and of dedication to military subjects none at all. The vast, lengthier, and far more terrible experience of World War I changed ideas of war art, resulting in far more of it, and official war artists for the first time recorded the experience of the nation in arms.

The government of Sir Robert Borden put Max Aitken, soon to be Lord Beaverbrook, in charge of Canadian propaganda overseas through the Canadian War Records Office (CWRO). In November 1916, Beaverbrook spun off the Canadian War Memorials Fund from the CWRO and began to commission British artists to paint the Canadian effort overseas. Over time and under pressure from the National Gallery of Canada, Canadian artists joined the program, their selection handled by a Canadian War Artists Advisory Committee. The result was an extraordinary collection, both traditional and modernist, by some of the best painters of the era, ranging from Britons such as Augustus John to Alfred Munnings to C.R.W. Nevinson and Eric Kennington, to Canadians such as David Milne, Maurice Cullen, A.Y. Jackson, and Frederick Varley. At home in Canada, artists received commissions to paint the domestic war effort. Painters such as Arthur Lismer created superb works from and of Halifax during the war; equally talented were Mabel May, a Montreal artist, and Dorothy Stevens, a Toronto graphic artist, showing women's roles in war industry. The art produced was of very high quality and, if the War Memorial gallery that Beaverbrook and others envisaged in Ottawa did not get built, the art itself— some 1,000 pieces by more than a hundred artists— nonetheless, did survive. The Senate Chamber in the Parliament buildings hung several large paintings but, after a few exhibitions, most of the war art went into storage at the National Gallery, almost as if the subject of war was too painful for its art ever to be displayed.

When World War II began, there seemed little interest in replicating Beaverbrook's program, and efforts to employ artists to record the war were sporadic until January 1943 when Prime Minister Mackenzie King, responding to requests from Vincent Massey, the high commissioner in London, agreed to an official war art program. The criteria for selecting artists—eventually 31 in all—were military experience and talent. The army was quickest off the mark. The official historian in Britain, Major Charles Stacey, was supportive of the project and had already employed E.J. Hughes, Orville Fisher, and W.A. Ogilvie. The Royal Canadian Navy (RCN) was slowest. But once unleashed, the war artists followed the Canadian divisions through Sicily and Italy and into northwest Europe right up to the uncovering of Hitler's concentration camps. Painters such as Charles Comfort, Alex Colville, Bruno Bobak, and Orville Fisher did superb work with the army, while the artists of the Royal Canadian Air Force (RCAF) included Albert Cloutier, Jack Humphrey, Carl Schaefer, and Miller Brittain, whose *Night Target, Germany,* is one of the great paintings of the war. The RCN's notable artists included Tony Law, a serving officer on motor torpedo boats, and Jack Nichols. Only one woman, Molly Lamb, earlier a private in the Canadian Women's Army Corps, became an official war artist, and she was not permitted to go overseas until after VE Day. In Canada, however, artists like Pegi Nicol MacLeod and Paraskeva Clark received commissions to paint the women's services. Overall, the style of World War II art was arguably more traditional than that produced in World War I, a reflection more on the difference in quality between the earlier artists as a group and those—many of them enthusiastic amateurs or part-time artists—who painted the second war. The national significance of both programs is difficult to overestimate, however, the vast body of work offering unique perspectives of lasting value on both conflicts, in a variety of media with a broad range of emotional, documentary, and artistic messages.

After a few postwar exhibitions, the 5,000 or so pieces of official World War II art also went into storage at the National Gallery. Some of it found its way into officer's messes or Department of National Defence offices in Ottawa, and much was damaged or disappeared. In 1971, the National Gallery picked out the pieces it wanted—much of the best British work and the paintings by David Milne—and gave the rest of the war art from the two world wars to the Canadian War Museum, then a museum with completely inadequate exhibition space and poor storage facilities. Some of the larger World War I paintings, rolled up in 1920 or so, remained unseen until their restoration began in 1999. The construction of a new Canadian War Museum, completed in early 2005, finally allowed Canada's war artists to receive their due with ample storage space for the 13,000 pieces in the collection, covering all periods, and including official and unofficial war art and thousands of wartime posters. The new museum's permanent and temporary galleries had the requisite environmental conditions for the safe exhibition and public enjoyment of what was now called the Beaverbrook Collection of War Art. Many pieces were immediately placed on public display in the new building, while hundreds of others have been used in temporary or travelling exhibitions, or loaned to other institutions.

The range, brilliance, and quantity of output from the two wartime programs have never been repeated. No postwar official war art program appeared until 1968, when the Canadian Armed Forces Civilian Artist Program began to send civilian artists on peacekeeping missions ranging from Cyprus to Somalia. Others painted military operations on bases in Canada or in Germany, offering a peacetime home front dimension to a program that was little known and infrequently exhibited. The program died in budget cuts in 1995. A new program, the Canadian Forces Artists Program (CFAP), replaced it in 2001, in time for artists to go to the war in Afghanistan. Painters such as Allan Harding MacKay and Karen Bailey, civilian volunteers like all other members of CFAP, began to produce a substantial body of work, much of it based on front-line observation and experience. In many ways, the newer works as a group departed stylistically from the more ritualized forms and modes of expression of the earlier official programs. The current program also accepts artists who work in other media—poetry, prose, acting, and audiovisual, a broadening of the artistic mandate that will, over time, greatly expand the range and complexity of Canada's military artistic record. Membership in the program is determined by competitive application, the vetting committee including representatives from the defence department, the National Gallery, the Canadian War Museum, the Canada Council for the Arts, and the artistic community.

War art has never been confined to official programs or membership initiatives. Commemorative or documentary art, though usually of middling to poor artistic quality, has been widely popular, especially among military personnel and their families. Protest or political art has been produced in some profusion as well, normally in response to international events or crises of the moment. The latter is also marked by uneven quality and limited range, and few institutions have followed or collected such works with any rigour. Other artistic forms, notably literature, film, and the performing arts, have explored war as subject matter in far greater detail and with far greater artistic impact. SEE ALSO: AITKEN; CANADIAN WAR MUSEUM; STACEY.

READING: Dean F. Oliver and Laura Brandon, *Canvas of War: Painting the Canadian Experience, 1914–1945* (Vancouver, 2000).

War Brides. Soldiers fighting a war away from home have always sought comfort with local women, and many Canadians married overseas. In World War I, this was relatively uncommon for members of the Canadian Expeditionary Force, though Major Maurice Pope, to cite one example, married a Belgian countess he met after the armistice. (Pope ended World War II as a lieutenant-general.) In World War II, however, Canadians arrived in Britain in late 1939, and some were still there in 1946. Virtually every Canadian who went overseas passed through the United Kingdom, and tens of thousands spent long periods in Belgium and the Netherlands. Inevitably, there were countless liaisons and some 52,000 marriages, some producing children before the Canadians were repatriated at war's end. In all, the government of Canada moved 69,733 war brides and children to Canada, a process that began in August 1944 and continued to the end of 1946. The women travelled to Canada by ship and then went by train to their husband's home town; all seem to have been impressed by the amount of food available and the size of Canada, but not all seem to have been impressed by the urban or rural Canada they discovered when they disembarked. Sadly, thousands of illegitimate children remained in Britain and continental Europe after the Canadians had left. To this day in the Netherlands, an organization searches for their fathers among the declining numbers of veterans who return on pilgrimages to the battlefields.

READING: M. Jarrett, *War Brides: The Stories of Women Who Left Everything Behind to Follow the Men They Loved* (Toronto, 2009).

▲ Ross Munro of the Canadian Press reported in 1943 from Sicily to the folks at home.

War Correspondents. Press reports from the battlefield are as old as newspapers, and the first Canadian examples appear to come from the Northwest Rebellion of 1885 when the telegraph made reporting events relatively prompt, if sketchy. *The Canadian Illustrated War News*, a broadsheet magazine, reported on the war and provided illustrations. By the time of the South African War in 1899, four authorized correspondents accompanied the Royal Canadian Regiment, all of whom had a difficult relationship with Lieutenant-Colonel W.D. Otter—the commanding officer—who called one "obnoxious and dirty" and another "a sneak." The correspondents, for their part, or at least C.F. Hamilton of the Toronto *Globe,* reciprocated the dislike, and Hamilton's private letters to his editors in Toronto were full of gossip about Otter and his stern incompetence. The published reportage, however, tended to be straightforward and to stress the heroism of the soldiers.

In World War I, Canadian journalists' access to the front was strictly controlled by the Canadian War Records Office (CWRO) in London and by official military censorship. The Canadian Press had only one representative in France—and that only after March 1917. Lord Beaverbrook's CWRO produced a substantial number of books, however, by authors such as Beckles Willson, Theodore Goodridge Roberts, and Sir Charles G.D. Roberts; patriotic periodicals like *Canada in Khaki*; and Beaverbrook's own best-selling "history," *Canada in Flanders: The Official Story of the Canadian Expeditionary Force*. What was lacking was hard reportage, and all that most Canadians saw were the lengthy casualty lists and bowdlerized accounts of battles.

Matters were substantially better in World War II, the army aiming to achieve a positive image in the media though censorship remained fierce on operational matters and, as in the reportage on the November 1944 mutiny at Terrace, BC, on politically sensitive matters as well. Newspaper and magazine reporters such as Greg Clark, Ross Munro, Charles Lynch, Ralph Allen, and Lionel Shapiro reported vividly from the battlefield and almost all journalists closely identified themselves with the war's aims and the soldiers fighting for them. Radio was now the most immediate medium, and the Canadian Broadcasting Corporation was among the first in the field with Matthew Halton and Peter Stursberg as lead reporters, and Marcel Ouimet reporting for Radio-Canada. The result was reportage that was sanitized and shaped by the military but coverage, nonetheless, that did not slavishly follow the official line. In Korea, journalists such as Pierre Berton of *Maclean's*, Bill Boss of the Canadian Press, and René Lévesque of the International Service covered the war with substantial freedom.

By the time of the Afghanistan War, embedded media were free from censorship and had controlled access to everything so long as they observed a list of reasonable restrictions, notably not to reveal operational details. Journalists who chose not to be embedded, and hence remained free of the military's impediments, had a much more difficult—and dangerous—time. Press reporters such as Stephen Thorne of the Canadian Press, Chris Wattie of the *National Post,* Rosie DiManno of the *Toronto Star*, and Christie Blatchford of *The Globe and Mail* enhanced their reputations in Kandahar. The availability of satellites to provide almost instantaneous television coverage of events dramatically altered the way war could be covered, and the management of the media, a lesson first learned by the United States military in Vietnam and perfected in the two wars with Iraq, became a critical factor in maintaining—or losing—public support for a conflict. SEE ALSO: AITKEN; CENSORSHIP; PROPAGANDA.

READING: Timothy Balzer, *The Information Front: The Canadian Army and News Management during the Second World War* (Vancouver, 2010); A.-J. Bizimana, *De Marcel Ouimet à René Lévesque: Les Correspondents de Guerre Canadiens-Français durant la Deuxième Guerre Mondiale* (Montréal, 2007).

War Crimes. In June 1944, soldiers of the 12th SS Panzer Division murdered as many as 187 Canadian prisoners of war (POWs) in Normandy. The Canadian government and the armed forces eventually created an independent war crimes unit and set out to find those responsible and to prosecute them for war crimes. The Unit's German Commander, Kurt Meyer, captured in Belgium, went on trial for the murders before an army court martial in December 1945; he was found guilty and sentenced to death by firing squad. His sentence was commuted to life imprisonment, and Meyer served nine years in Dorchester prison in New Brunswick until his release. Canadian war crimes investigators also tracked down Nazi officials who had encouraged the lynchings of airmen who had escaped their shot-down bombers over Germany. After the defeat of Japan, Canada prosecuted one Japanese Canadian who had tortured and murdered Canadian POWs captured at the fall of Hong Kong in December 1941. Inouye Kanao, the "Kamloops Kid," was executed for his crimes. In the former Yugoslavia almost a half-century after the end of World War II, ethnic cleansing was the norm, and Canadian soldiers provided evidence used in the trials of perpetrators.

During the Afghanistan War, controversy arose in Canada over the handling of suspected Taliban captured by Canadian troops. The Canadian Forces did not have its own prison there, and Canadian officials were loathe to turn prisoners over to American forces after controversies arising from the treatment of detainees at US prisons in Abu Ghraib, Iraq, and Guantanamo Bay, Cuba. The result was that prisoners taken by Canadian forces were handed by agreement to Afghan authorities. The Afghans apparently tortured many of their prisoners routinely and, when word of specific cases dating to 2006 filtered back to Canada and became public in 2009–2010, a political furor ensued. Whether such cases constituted war crimes by Canadian Forces' members or the political and bureaucratic officials who had made the agreement with Kabul was largely moot, as legal arguments took a backseat to a searing political debate, one made more dangerous for the Conservative government of Stephen Harper by virtue of its tenuous minority status in the House of Commons. After a controversial prorogation of Parliament in early 2010, the government refused to release documents pertaining to the detainee question pending their review by a senior judge appointed by the Harper government. Opposition critics complained of stalling, censorship, and contempt of Parliament; the government claimed due diligence and operational security. As of May 2010, the debate continued, the government working to a mid-month deadline imposed by the Speaker of the House for it to accede to Parliament's demands to see documents relevant to the file, or else be found in contempt of Parliament. SEE ALSO: MEYER; PRISONERS OF WAR.

READING: P.W. Lackenbauer and C. Madsen, *Kurt Meyer on Trial* (Kingston, ON, 2007); Howard Margolian, *Conduct Unbecoming: The Story of the Murder of Canadian Prisoners of War in Normandy* (Toronto, 1998).

War Diaries. When the Canadian Division proceeded to the front in March 1915, its units began to keep war diaries, daily records of their actions in the field. The war diary contained the details of each unit's operations, activities, and administration, and good diarists—usually a unit adjutant—made it a point to include as appendices operations orders, intelligence reports, maps, lists of casualties, and administrative orders; others were less careful and scrupulous. The war diary was intended to be complete and accurate, but in action events moved quickly; in defeats, a unit might be overrun; and if a commander made errors, there might be incentive to distort what was recorded. Even so, the unit war diary, sent monthly to headquarters and then to safekeeping, remains the best available record of what happened. Such diaries were also kept at brigade, division, and corps headquarters. The practice continued during World War II, Korea, and in other operations, and continues still. World War I unit war diaries are available on-line at Library and Archives Canada (www.collectionscanada.gc.ca).

War Films. There is a dearth of Canadian-made war feature films. Lord Beaverbrook's Canadian War Records Office produced a film in 1916, *The Battle of Courcelette*, that was a great success, and much footage of the Canadians in action was shot—and

↖ Late in World War I, a Canadian Corps cinematographer and his assistant, shooting for Lord Beaverbrook's Canadian War Records Office, film a gas attack east of Arras, France.

subsequently lost. When found in the early 1930s, the Department of National Defence created a committee that produced a compilation *Lest We Forget*, in 1935, that received mixed reviews. Of fictional feature films, *Carry on, Sergeant* shot in Trenton, Ontario, in an Ontario government film studio in 1927 seems to have been the first. Produced by British filmmakers, it tried to tap the Canadian market and satisfy the demand for something other than US features showing American heroism. The movie failed.

In World War II, there were no Canadian dramatic features, though the British 1941 film *Forty-Ninth Parallel* traced the attempted escape of a U-boat crew from Hudson Bay southwards. (This film was most notable for casting Laurence Olivier as

a French-Canadian trapper!) Another film, released in 1942, was *Captains of the Clouds* that had James Cagney as a troublesome bush pilot training in the British Commonwealth Air Training Plan. Air Marshal Billy Bishop had a cameo appearance. *Corvette: K-255* (1943), starring Randolph Scott, depicted a Canadian warship during the Battle of the Atlantic, its performance serving as the stage for a somewhat contrived love story. Timothy Findley's *The Wars*, a hugely successful World War I novel, became a moderately successful film in 1981 (and then a play in 2007); the 2006 feature *Eighteen* treated a veteran's memories sympathetically; and Paul Gross's *Passchendaele,* released in 2008 as the featured film at the Toronto International Film Festival, received mixed reviews. *War Brides* (1980), *Dieppe* (1993), with Victor Garber as Lord Mountbatten, and *Above and Beyond* (2006) were decent productions that found small markets. *Nouvelle France* (2004), titled *New France* for its Anglo-Canadian release but *Battle of the Brave* in the United States, expensively—and dreadfully—recreated the imperial struggle for North America. Canadians have sometimes done better as sidelines in large-budget Hollywood pictures, including *The Devil's Brigade* (1968) about the joint Canadian-American First Special Service Force, and *Legends of the Fall* (1994), in which Brad Pitt's character leaves the United States for Canada where he enlists in a Canadian unit and fights in World War I. *Submarine X-1* (1968), *The English Patient* (1997), and *Shake Hands with the Devil* (2007) also featured Canadian stories as part of larger international narratives.

The Canadian forte was the documentary. There are bits of newsreel footage of the first contingent departing for South Africa, and there is much more on World War I (all collected on the National Film Board's website [www3.nfb.ca] under the heading "Images of a Forgotten War"). The National Film Board (NFB), created in 1939 and put under the charge of British filmmaker John Grierson, produced hundreds of documentaries during World War II. Many of these, including animated films by Norman McLaren, can also be accessed on the NFB website under "On All Fronts: World War II and the NFB." Some are crude propaganda directed against the Axis powers, but many are first-rate analyses of geopolitics, of those who served, and of all who waited. After the war and continuing into the twenty-first century, Canadian filmmakers produced countless documentaries, touching on every aspect of the conflict from war brides to specific campaigns or battles or compilations of Canada's World War II history. *Canada: A People's History* (2000–2001) was a 32-hour Canadian Broadcasting Corporation effort that included some of the most elaborate battle recreations ever filmed in Canada, notably the Plains of Abraham. The emergence of television's History and Military Channels, as well as the production of

small-budget CDs, videos, and on-line compilations, has resulted in a booming industry for small-market history products. SEE ALSO: AITKEN; PROPAGANDA.

War Finance, World Wars I and II. When Canada went to war in August 1914, it did not know it faced a long war, and it had no idea how to finance such a conflict. No one anywhere did. The federal government was small, its budget was only $184 million, revenues were tiny, and taxation scarcely existed (most state revenues came from tariffs). Initially, Ottawa expected Britain to pay the war's costs and, moreover, British investors to continue putting the money into Canada that would finance corporate expansion and development. These ideas were dashed within months. Britain's costs of financing a total war were huge and soon beyond its resources. Before long, the British were seeking loans in the United States, and Canadian finance minister, Sir Thomas White, was scouting for ideas. One of the anti-reciprocity Liberals who had joined with Robert Borden to defeat the Laurier government in 1911, White did not want Canada to borrow in the United States. By the summer of 1915, however, Ottawa—for the first time—turned to New York for a loan of $40 million in one- and two-year notes at 5 and 5.25 percent. This was a historic event. At the same time, Britain was pressing Ottawa to carry more of the war's costs, and, in 1916, Canada agreed to cover the Canadian costs of the Imperial Munitions Board (IMB), Britain's production and purchasing agent for armaments.

White had not wanted to raise funds through taxation, and he had doubts about Canada's ability to raise much through domestic war loans. But necessity made its demands. The federal government introduced a business profits tax in 1916, a federal income tax in 1917, and, much to White's surprise, the government found the bulk of its war finance from domestic borrowing. In fact, White used the oversubscription to the first war loan of November 1915 to cover the IMB's costs in Canada. The government also inflated the currency and stood by while prices increased. Wartime inflation fed public unrest as wages could not keep up. The near-revolutionary unrest across Canada in 1919 had much to do with the government's failure to manage inflation.

But the main problem for Ottawa was to find the American dollars it needed to finance wartime imports from the United States to keep war factories in operation. This became critical in the late spring of 1917 when London said it could no longer afford to pay for goods from Canada. The choice for Ottawa was clear: give the British the goods free of charge or close factories and hurt farmers. The British blackmail worked, and Canada agreed to put up $25 million a month to cover the exports, provided that London could provide $15 million (US) to Canada each month. The more Canada did to help Britain, the greater the Canadian trade deficit with the United States became; only regular infusions of American dollars could keep the deficit down. The British agreed, squeezed more money out of the United States

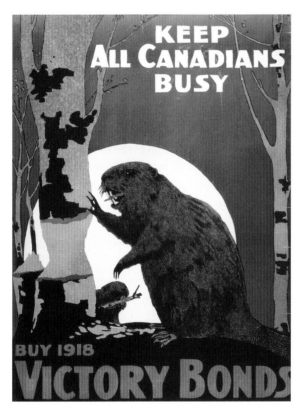

In 1914 no one believed either that it was necessary to raise funds to fight the war or that Canadians would contribute. By 1918, however, Canadians bought Victory Bonds in large amounts to finance Canada's contribution to the Allied war effort.

to which they were hugely indebted already, and helped secure Canada the right to place a private loan in New York. In effect, World War I had begun the process of switching Canada from London to New York as the engine of its financial system.

In 1900, US foreign investment in Canada was 14 percent of the total, while British investment in the Dominion amounted to 85 percent. In 1914, the figures were 23 and 72 percent, and, in 1918, 36 and 60 percent. By 1922, US investment exceeded British for the first time. Imports showed a similar pattern. In 1901, UK imports were $42 million and US imports $110 million. By 1918, however, imports from the south were ten times those from the UK. World War I had begun to change everything; World War II would complete the transition from one financial empire to the other.

The Department of Finance that fought World War II was still a tiny department with Clifford Clark (the deputy minister), W.A. Mackintosh (brought in from Queen's University), and Robert Bryce the stars. Around them were a second group of generalists like Mitchell Sharp and A.F.W. Plumptre, a number of academic and private sector experts brought in from outside the civil service, as well as departmental specialists in tax and trade policy. Small as it was, the economic constellation of wartime Ottawa was broader than merely the Department of Finance, which had learned much from the experience of the earlier war. The Economic Advisory Committee sat at the top of the food chain, an irregular gathering place for the key officials from the Departments of Finance, External Affairs, Trade and Commerce, the Cabinet secretariat, and from agencies such as the Bank of Canada and the Wartime Prices and Trade Board (WPTB). This was where policy was smoothed and aligned by the most senior officials. The Bank of Canada and its key officials such as Graham Towers, Donald Gordon, Louis Rasminsky, and Robert Beattie played critical wartime roles, and the bank worked closely on foreign and domestic financial matters with Clark's department. The Foreign Exchange Control Board, under the bank's control, similarly co-operated. The War Finance Committee, charged with managing the Victory Bond campaigns, again was under the bank. The WPTB, controlling wages and prices and rationing, initially came under the Department of Labour and only went to the Department of Finance in August 1941. Donald Gordon, its chair when it became the critical player in late 1941, had come from the bank, and the WPTB fit very much into the ambit of the Department of Finance. No such institutions had existed in World War I.

If the bureaucrats formed a harmonious whole, the Liberal politicians under whom they laboured were only slightly less in agreement. Prime Minister William Lyon Mackenzie King could lead on critical issues, but was also strong and confident enough to give his key ministers their heads. Colonel J.L. Ralston and J.L. Ilsley, the two finance ministers during World War II, were able men with a firm grasp on policy and practice. C.D. Howe, the minister of munitions and supply, then minister of reconstruction, and later the "minister of everything"—was a hugely powerful figure with matchless ties to the industrial powers in the land. The key issues were complex: raising the moneys necessary to fight the war, fighting inflation through wage and price controls, and planning for the postwar world. This was a heavy agenda, made harder still because it had to be handled while fighting and financing a vast overseas war. By and large, it was brilliantly managed.

The base from which the King government began was narrow. Canada was a small, weak nation in 1939. The population was only 11.2 million, the gross domestic product only $5.6 billion, and the total of all federal expenditures in 1939 only $680 million. The Dominion-Provincial Taxation Agreement Act, 1942, gave the federal government the taxation room it needed to fight the war, and Ottawa began to levy taxes. Excise, sales, and retail purchase taxes were increased or imposed. A War Exchange Tax, ordinarily 10 percent, raised revenue and deterred unnecessary imports, thus preserving scarce US dollars. The rates of corporation and personal income taxes were increased dramatically. At the beginning of the war, a married man with two children paid no income tax at all unless he was in the upper brackets;

if he earned $3,000, his income tax was $10. Four years later, after tax increases that squeezed hard, the $3,000-a-year man was paying $334 in income tax and an additional amount of $1,200 in "compulsory savings," a surcharge in the form of a loan to be repaid at the end of the war. Corporation taxes also increased from 18 to 40 percent, generating $636 million—or nearly half of all corporate profits—in 1943. Excess profits taxes produced more revenue. All profits in excess of 116 2/3 percent of standard profits (the average of profit from the not-so-buoyant years from 1936 to 1939) were taxed at 100 percent. Corporations, however, were to receive a 20 percent rebate after the war.

But taxation could not finance all war costs, though vastly more was secured from taxpayers than had been the case in World War I. Then, the printing presses had pumped out currency, and at least some of the war's cost had been carried by deliberate inflation. This time, a different tack would be tried, and borrowing was stepped up to cover the huge increases in spending and thus in the federal deficit. In 1939, the deficit was a mere $2 million; in 1944 and 1945, it was $1.9 billion, and the government raised almost $16 billion from the sale of securities, while seeing net debt rise to just under $18 billion. Almost all this debt was held in Canada by Canadians— Ottawa did not borrow abroad in World War II as it had done during World War I. Banks and insurance companies bought some $3.5 billion in government securities, the public taking the rest. In a succession of brilliantly managed War Loan and Victory Bond campaigns, the government raised approximately $12.5 billion, in the process borrowing from its citizens at costs ranging from 1.5 to 3 percent—again these figures were much lower than the 5 percent interest cost of the 1914 war. Purchasing Victory Bonds was made as easy as possible with payroll deductions readily available, while citizens could also buy War Savings Certificates and schoolchildren could purchase War Savings Stamps at 25 cents each. It was a total war.

There was still too much money chasing too few goods. Canadians had jobs and all the overtime they wanted; for the first time since the 1920s, people had money in their pockets and wanted to spend it. Ottawa had created the Wartime Prices and Trade Board at the beginning of the war to oversee the inflationary pressures that were sure to come. In World War I, huge price increases had wracked the economy and fuelled postwar unrest. No one wanted that to recur, but inflation took hold. In 1940, the cost of living increased by just 4 percent but, in the first nine months of 1941, it rose by 7 percent. Support for tighter controls began to increase, and the Cabinet made its first gesture in this direction by moving the WPTB to the Department of Finance from the Department of Labour. Finance minister Ilsley and, gradually, his most senior officials came to the conclusion that half-measures could not work. Only a total freeze on wages and prices could check the coming inflationary spiral. No one believed this would be easy to manage and, with the WPTB given a new chair in the person of Donald Gordon, the Bank of Canada's deputy governor, the policy was announced on 18 October 1941. After 1 December, the prime minister stated in his national broadcast announcing the freeze, "No person may sell any goods or supply any services at a price or rate higher than that charged by him for such goods or services during the four weeks from 15 September to 11 October [1941].… " Prices could fall below the ceiling but could not rise above it. Wages too were frozen: "It is obvious that the prices of finished goods cannot be controlled successfully unless the cost of production is also controlled," King said. No employer could increase his present basic wage rates without permission but, to ensure that wages kept pace with prices, a cost of living bonus, determined by the WPTB, would come into force. The cost of living, which had increased by 17.8 percent between 1 August 1939 and 1 October 1941, rose only 2.8 percent between that latter date and 1 April 1945. The cost of fuel and light actually dropped, the cost of clothing was stable, and the cost of food—much of which was rationed—was the sole major sector to increase.

Canadians worried about what would happen when the war ended. Would the Depression return with high unemployment? Would inflation take off when the controls were removed? Would there be jobs for the boys who had won the war? All these concerns were subsumed into a broad, all-encompassing phrase: "reconstruction." The first building block in reconstruction came in 1940 when the federal government secured provincial consent to amend the constitution to permit Ottawa to operate an unemployment insurance (UI) scheme. This was an insurance plan, one that required the employed to pay into it so that in the event they lost their jobs, they could draw on the accumulated funds. UI, in other words, could only be started in good times, and the war years were a time of full employment. The UI fund was in good shape to meet any postwar downturn.

But the key to planning was to have an array of programs that would put money into the hands of those who would spend it and those who would create jobs. Planning for the reintegration of veterans, for example, was in the hands of a Cabinet Committee, and the Veterans Charter that eventually emerged was hugely important in providing an array of services for veterans that were second-to-none in their generosity and comprehensiveness. Officials in the Department of Finance knew that the money would be spent on new houses, furniture and appliances, clothing, and foodstuffs. That would help cushion the transition to peace.

This alone was not enough. Originally devised as a measure to put some extra money in the hands of those families who were hurt by the wage freeze, the idea of family allowances quickly became a massive effort to put spendable cash in the hands of young mothers. Would the national interest not be served by having this money spent to create jobs? In the Depression years, governments had slashed spending to the bone as their way to deal with hard times. Now, the wartime government was preparing plans to spend large sums in order to head off the possible return of economic troubles. That children might be better fed and housed as a result of the "baby bonus" was an equal, if coincidental, benefit. Family allowances passed through Parliament in

1944, encountering some tough opposition. The scale of the measure was huge; its cost approximated $256 million for the first year of operation—almost half of the total federal prewar budget—and it was to be spent for a single program. The days of $600 million federal budgets were gone—and why not, when the government's spending in 1945 was $5.14 billion and the GDP had more than doubled during the war to $11.8 billion? The elaborate plans for postwar reconstruction, along with Canada's extraordinary war effort, won the 1945 federal election for the Liberals. The provinces, however, refused to agree to any major restructuring of fiscal federalism, the only failure in World War II domestic war finance.

Internationally, Ottawa's first task was to secure sufficient US dollars to cover the cost of the increased imports needed to run vastly expanded war industries. Various control measures were put in place, but it was not until the Hyde Park Agreement of April 1941 that Prime Minister King and President Roosevelt found the way to fix the problem. The Americans would buy more in Canada, thus providing more US dollars in an increasingly integrated continental economy. The second problem to be managed was Britain's inability to pay in hard currency for the goods and munitions Canada provided. Canada built up large sterling balances in London; but when the United States offered the Lend-Lease program to Britain, the British took a tough line in bargaining with Ottawa for a Canadian equivalent. The answer was a billion-dollar gift in 1942 followed by the creation of Mutual Aid that gave away Canadian munitions to the Allies—to keep Canadian factories working at full blast and to help win the war. In effect, Canada went from an impecunious nation in 1939 to one that was on a per capita basis more generous with its aid than the United States during the war. SEE ALSO: WAR INDUSTRY; WORLD WAR I; WORLD WAR II.

READING: J.L. Granatstein, *How Britain's Weakness Forced Canada into the Arms of the United States* (Toronto, 1989); R.B. Bryce, *Canada and the Cost of World War II: The International Operations of*

Canada's Department of Finance, 1939–1947 (Montreal, 2005).

War Industry, World Wars I and II. Canadian industry was ill-suited for munitions production at the outset of World War I. The Dominion Arsenal factories in Quebec City and Lindsay, Ontario, were small, and the nation's general industrial plant was not large. Orders for artillery shells began to be placed in 1914 by the Shell Committee, created by Sam Hughes, the minister of militia and defence, to supply the British Ministry of Munitions. Hughes allowed these orders to go to his cronies, and the $170 million in orders remained largely unfilled well into 1915. There were, nonetheless, by 1915 some 250 factories employed in war production with approximately 60,000 workers. Disorganization was everywhere, and, in November 1915, Sir Robert Borden, in consultation with the British government, replaced the Shell Committee with the Imperial Munitions Board (IMB), run by Toronto businessman Joseph Flavelle. War production soon grew in volume and scope. Flavelle established national factories owned by the IMB to make what private industry could not; by war's end, Canada had produced more than $2 million a day of war materiel and manufactured everything from one-third of Britain's requirements of shells to 2,600 training aircraft and flying boats to 103 ships. More than 289,000 workers laboured for the IMB in war manufacturing. The expansion of war production brought some 30,000 women into the workforce while union membership doubled across the country. War manufacturing also increased Canadian managerial expertise and improved manufacturing techniques. The lessons learned would be applied in the 1939–1945 war.

In the course of the Second World War, Canada's factories, mines, and fields produced billions and billions of dollars' worth of goods and foods to support the war effort. The nation created and produced more than Canada's million men and women in uniform needed to fight and win. Arms, equipment, food, minerals, and metals were sold or—if allies did not have the money to pay—given away in billion-dollar gifts to

Britain and billions more in Mutual Aid for the cause of victory. This was an impressive feat of production and organization, a massive effort by every sector of the Canadian economy and by Canadian workers and business leaders. Canadians won the economic war and ensured that the postwar years would be very different than the bleak decade that had preceded it.

Canada was a small and weak country in 1939. The gross domestic product, the sum total of all the goods and services created by the population of 11.2 million Canadians, was only $5.6 billion. (For comparison, the GDP in 2008 was more than $1.2 trillion.) The federal government's expenditures in 1939 were only $680 million, and Canadian corporations paid only $115 million in taxes, while income taxes generated only an additional $112 million. Unemployment remained very high, though it had declined from the worst years of the Great Depression. There was almost no armaments production, save for a small federally owned arsenal in Quebec City (that primarily made limited quantities of small arms ammunition) and a subsidiary plant in Lindsay, Ontario, reopened in 1937. Just before the war started, the British government had placed a small contract with Marine Industries Limited of Sorel, Quebec, to make one hundred 25-pounder field guns. There were a few tiny aircraft manufacturers that produced airplanes on an almost piecework basis. In Toronto, the John Inglis Company in March 1938 had won a contract to build 7,000 Bren light machine guns for the Canadian military and 5,000 for Britain—through a contracting process that produced cries of scandal and resulted in a Royal Commission to investigate.

Partly as a result of the Bren Gun affair, in June 1939 the Liberal government of Mackenzie King had passed the Defence Purchasing, Profits Control, and Financial Act that aimed to control profits and the costs of defence contracts. Profits could not exceed 5 percent, a stipulation that meant that soon after the war began, C.D. Howe, the minister of transport, told the House of Commons that Canada had not managed to place a single contract. The act had also created the Defence Purchasing Board to coordinate purchases, and, in its short life—from 14 July to 31 October 1939—the board managed to buy only $43.7 million worth of goods, with three-quarters of the orders placed after Nazi Germany had invaded Poland in September 1939. One of the first casualties of World War II was this system of profit controls, quickly repealed so that war orders could be placed. A second casualty was the Defence Purchasing Board itself, replaced on 1 November 1939 by the War Supply Board, led by Wallace Campbell, the president of the Ford Motor Company of Canada. Initially, the new board fell under the control of the finance minister but, in mid-November, in a fateful and fortunate move, Mackenzie King placed the War Supply Board under his then–minister of transport, Clarence Decatur Howe, who he had also just named the minister of munitions and supply. Howe at first had no department to go along with the additional title but, when the War Supply Board was swallowed by the new Department of Munitions and Supply on 9 April 1940, just days after the King Liberals' re-election, Canadian war production had found its czar.

Howe was American-born, a graduate of the Massachusetts Institute of Technology, a former engineering professor at Dalhousie University, and a man who had made himself rich by constructing grain elevators throughout the West. In 1935, he had won election to Parliament from Port Arthur (now Thunder Bay), Ontario, and he instantly went into Cabinet. Tough, blunt, familiar with business and the men who ran it, Howe proved to be the right minister to lead the nation's wartime industrial mobilization.

But even Howe could do little until the urgency of war began to drive matters. The British-French defeat of May–June 1940 removed the financial concerns that had crimped British armaments orders in Canada and restrained Ottawa's own purchases. Both London and Ottawa now wanted and needed everything at once. The dollar no longer reigned, and the idea that Canada would fight a "limited liability" war had disappeared, a casualty of the blitzkrieg.

Commissioned by the Canadian War Memorials Fund to do a series of etchings on home front munitions-makers, Toronto artist Dorothy Stevens beautifully presented men and women workers making artillery shells.

Howe set out to seize the initiative. He began to look to Canadian business for executives who could step in to organize and galvanize war production and allocate scarce commodities. He expected their employers to pay their salaries, and he offered nothing beyond a dollar a year, except expenses, and many of those he brought to Ottawa declined to take their expenses at all. These "dollar-a-year men" were the cream of Canadian business, men like R.C. Berkinshaw from Goodyear Tire and Rubber; Henry Borden, a powerful corporate lawyer from Toronto; E.P. Taylor, entrepreneur and brewery owner; and H.R. MacMillan, the British Columbia lumber giant. There were many more—a parliamentary return in late February 1941 noted that 107 dollar-a-year men were employed across the government. Howe's department with its array of executives, accountants, and lawyers had by far the most, but there would be many more as the war went on.

Howe and his lieutenants did everything in a hurry. As his biographer, Robert Bothwell, noted, "There was no time to consider production programs in detail. No one could hope to know when production would actually come on stream—merely that a commitment to production must be made, often orally, and ratified with government dollars." The Department of Munitions and Supply offered loans and grants, it purchased licenses to permit Canadian production of foreign-owned weapons and equipment, and it helped secure the British and

Munitions industries flourished in small-town Ontario during World War I. In Woodstock, Canadian Linderman's prewar crosscut saw factory worked flat out to fill war orders.

American experts to let Canadian firms get up and running. This was usually sufficient to get detailed planning underway; getting the actual armaments produced was more difficult.

Canadian industry was small and slow, the plants were often obsolete, machine tools were scarce, and skilled workers were in short supply. Howe's production chief, Harry Carmichael, who had come to Ottawa from his post as vice-president of General Motors, had the answer—subcontracting. The lead firm could likely produce a few artillery pieces a month, for example, if it worked on its own. But if it could get carefully machined parts from other smaller plants across the country that could be screwed into place at the main shops, production

could be stepped up. That was how the big automobile plants worked, Carmichael said, so why couldn't the same methods be employed in building artillery or ships or aircraft? It required planning and control, a careful allocation of scarce materials, and a high level of inspection to ensure that the requisite quality was maintained, but it could be done. It was a "bits and pieces" program, as Howe called it, but it worked, and, moreover, it spread wartime jobs across the country, not just in central Canada. That was a political necessity if complaints from the Maritimes and the West that Ontario and Quebec received all the jobs were to be dealt with. "Will Saskatoon get its share [of jobs]?" election campaigners asked in a 1939 by-election.

In fact, Saskatoon and virtually every city and province did.

There were inevitable bottlenecks and failures, of course, but one way around them was to create Crown corporations, 28 of which came into being during the war, some manufacturing, some purchasing and distributing, others supervising and controlling. The establishment of Crown companies, operating with great flexibility outside the usual bureaucratic restraints, allowed for efficiencies. Even so, Howe and his advisers believed that private enterprise was inherently more efficient than government-run operations. World War II made the government—or at least Howe's part of it—operate much like a corporation. The state helped with plant expansion and retooling, and corporate Canada itself put its money into wartime growth. It had to—more than half of Canadian war production came from plants that had not existed in 1939. In 1939, some $3.65 billion had been invested in the country's factories. Four years later, capital invested was $6.3 billion, a

huge jump. Much of that was government money, but because Howe and his controllers ran what the press called "a graftless war," one almost wholly without patronage and preferment, there were relatively few complaints.

Certainly, Canadian business was paying its full share of the war's costs. Business contributed billions of dollars to Victory Loans, helping the government finance the war. Corporation taxes increased from a rate of 18 to 40 percent. Excess profits taxes produced even more revenue. Profit on government contracts was limited to 10 percent, and all profits in excess of 116 2/3 percent of standard profits (the average of an individual corporation's profits for the lean years from 1936 to 1939) were taxed at 100 percent by 1942. Corporations, however, could claim double depreciation against taxes for plant renovations, machinery acquisition, and other expenses, and they were to receive a 20 percent rebate on their excess profits taxes after the war, a conscious attempt to help in the eventual reconversion to peacetime production.

For most Canadians working in war industry, there were great gains. Average wages increased dramatically, rising from $956 in 1938 to $1,525 in 1943. There was as much overtime as people wanted, and many worked 50 or even 60 hours a week. Families that had struggled to keep one breadwinner employed in the Depression years now had a son in the army and two or more family members bringing home good paycheques each week from factory work. The government's National Selective Service system controlled where people could work in an economy struggling to find enough workers for factories and recruits for the army, navy, and air force; the flood from small-town and rural Canada into the urban factories was enormous, not least the huge numbers of women who went to work for the first time. By 1943, 254,000 women were employed in war factories and making almost equivalent wages to the male workers who numbered 896,000. The growth in wages across the country, moreover, outstripped inflation, thanks to the federal government's wage and price control system. And wartime Canadians ate better

Some 300,000 women, including these munitions workers packing primers, took jobs in Canada's World War II war plants.

and spent more, despite rationing and controls, than they had in the 1930s.

And Canada delivered the goods, producing 40 percent of Allied aluminum and 95 percent of the nickel. It mined 75 percent of the asbestos, 20 percent of the zinc, 12 percent of the copper, and 15 percent of the lead. Canada's raw materials, $5.8 billion in all produced from 1939 to 1945, made an extraordinary contribution to victory. Without the aluminum Canada provided, for example, Britain's Royal Air Force could not have secured the aircraft with which it fought the war.

At the same time, Canada produced an extraordinary array of military equipment, its war production overall ranking fourth among the Allies, behind only the US, the UK, and the Soviet Union. For a nation of just 11.2 million people, this was little short of amazing, and it required a massive mobilization of workers for war plants; by mid-1943, some quarter-million of them were women. Orders went out for Anson aircraft, for example, so that training under the British Commonwealth Air Training Plan could speed up, with $58.4 million provided for this in December 1940. Canadian firms could build the airframes but none could manufacture the engines that had to be imported. In 1941, only 88 Ansons came off the lines; in 1942, total production had risen to 1,432; and, by the end of 1943, to 2,269. The story was much the same for other aircraft types, more than 16,400 aircraft in all being produced in Canada by 116,000 workers, including 30,000 women. It was a massive, hugely successful effort.

Howe and his mandarins sometimes overreached Canada's productive capacity. The minister had agreed in September 1941 that Canada would build 15 Lancaster heavy bombers a month beginning in 1943 at the Malton, Ontario, plant of what became Victory Aircraft, a Crown corporation. The Lancs would go to the Royal Canadian Air Force's (RCAF) No. 6 Bomber Group in England. But the huge aircraft were complex, and a succession of problems slowed production. The first Canadian-made Lancaster, the *Ruhr Express*, took part in a raid in November 1943, but no others saw service until

March and April 1944. By VE Day, only three RCAF squadrons had the Canadian-made bombers. Even so, Victory Aircraft produced 450 Lancs all told, exceeding Howe's promised production rate.

The story was very similar for naval and merchant ship construction. At the beginning of the war, the Canadian shipbuilding industry was tiny—there were only some 2,000 skilled workers and four shipyards with nine berths capable of handling a 10,000-tonne vessel. The first such cargo ship was delivered in December 1941. Two years later, there were 38 berths and 70 yards (and by the war's end 90 yards), turning out three 10,000-tonne merchant ships a week. One cargo ship, the ss *Fort Romaine*, was built from scratch in just 58 days in the summer of 1943. In all, Canada's 100,000 male and female shipyard workers produced 410 merchant ships, as well as other marine equipment.

The growth was as rapid in naval construction, which eventually employed some 30,000 workers. The first orders for corvettes, the Royal Canadian Navy's main escort vessel, were placed in February 1940, and the first ten keels were laid that month. By the end of the year, 44 corvettes had been launched and an even dozen manned. In all, 206 corvettes were built in Canada, most on the East and West Coasts but many in Great Lakes ports and on the St Lawrence. At the same time, Canadian yards built frigates and minesweepers, tugs and landing craft, motor torpedo boats, patrol boats, and *Tribal* class destroyers. Constructing the last class of ships, though greatly desired by the navy, was a monumental task for Canada's shipbuilding industry, as difficult in its sphere as building Lancaster bombers had been for the fledgling aviation sector.

For army equipment, the equivalent was the Ram tank. The German blitzkrieg had demonstrated the superiority of the German panzers (tanks), and the Allies scrambled to find something better than the weak, slow, under-armed vehicles with which they had begun the war. The Canadian army planned two armoured divisions and two armoured brigades, and needed tanks; the Montreal Locomotive Works received Howe's authorization to set up a tank factory to manufacture the American-designed M-3 Grant. But the Grant had a fixed gun, and Canadian armoured specialists recognized this as a flaw. Instead, Canada would manufacture a modified Grant with its gun on a revolving turret, thus giving it a 360° range of fire and a lower silhouette. The prototype of the Ram, with its engines imported from the United States, was ready in the summer of 1941. The story is long and complicated but, while almost 2,000 Rams eventually came off the lines, their relatively high costs guaranteed that the Ram was superseded by the American-made Sherman, soon the Allies' main battle tank. The Sherman was much superior to the Ram (though very much inferior to German Tiger and Panther tanks), and US productive capacity simply swamped the potential of the Montreal factory. The Rams, nonetheless, equipped Canada's armoured divisions until they acquired Shermans, and the Canadian-made tanks ended the war converted into Kangaroos, the first armoured personnel carriers.

The Canadian and Allied armies were huge beneficiaries of the production of the nation's factories. The major contribution—indeed, arguably Canada's biggest industrial contribution to victory—was in the form of trucks, particularly Canadian Military Pattern vehicles. These vehicles, produced in huge numbers by Ford and General Motors (along with some 180,000 military versions of Chrysler's D60 truck model), came in a bewildering variety of ambulances, field workshop vehicles, and army troop carriers, in all 815,729 military vehicles that equipped the Canadian and Commonwealth armies.

Large as it was, Canadian war production amounted in all to only ten percent of the total of Commonwealth production. On the other hand, only 34 percent of Canadian war production was used by the Canadian services, while the rest went to the Allies. In all, Canadian wartime industrial production was valued at more than $9.5 billion, and another $1.5 billion was spent on defence construction and the expansion of war plants, all paid for by the government. For a nation that had begun the war with a gross national product (GNP) of just $5.6 billion, this was incredible. That Canada's GNP in 1945 was $11.8 billion, more than double the total six years before, is accounted for, in large part, by the extraordinary production of the nation's war factories, farms, and mines. SEE ALSO: FLAVELLE; HOWE; IMPERIAL MUNITIONS BOARD; KING.

READING: Robert Bothwell and William Kilbourn, *C.D. Howe: A Biography* (Toronto, 1979).

War Measures Act. This legislation, put on the statute books in August 1914 at the beginning of World War I, gave the federal government sweeping emergency powers for use during war, invasion, or apprehended insurrection. The act also let the federal government intrude on provincial areas of jurisdiction during the emergency period. Under the War Measures Act, German and Austrian immigrant aliens (the latter including Ukrainians then under the Austro-Hungarian Empire) were interned during the 1914–1918 war; in World War II, the Royal Canadian Mounted Police rounded up Germans, Italians, and Communists suspected of disloyalty. The government also employed the powers of the act (laid out in the Defence of Canada Regulations) to forcibly evacuate Japanese Canadians from the Pacific Coast in early 1942. In October 1970, the Trudeau government invoked the act's powers to deal with "the apprehended insurrection" sparked by the Front de libération du Québec. The act was repealed in 1988 and replaced by the (milder) Emergencies Act, though the Chrétien government adopted anti-terrorist legislation after the attacks of 11 September 2001 that gave the state powers previously available only under the War Measures Act. SEE ALSO: EMERGENCIES ACT; INTERNMENT; JAPANESE CANADIAN EVACUATION; OCTOBER CRISIS.

War Memorials. Canadians have erected memorials to their war dead since at least the War of 1812. There is the National War Memorial in Ottawa, the Vimy Memorial in France, and countless others overseas and at home. In Calgary, for example, there is a memorial in the Canadian Pacific Railway's

Ogden stockyards to honour those company employees who died in World Wars I and II. At Glenmore Park, the surviving veterans of the 137th Battalion of the Canadian Expeditionary Force erected a memorial to their dead comrades. The Naval Museum of Alberta put up a monument to mark Calgary's naval dead in Korea and those who served; along the city's Memorial Boulevard, trees planted in 1922 to commemorate the city's residents who died in World War I were augmented in 1990 to honour those killed in World War II, Korea, and on peace support missions. World War I monuments mark most municipal downtowns, their purviews later expanded as other wars and conflicts followed; most now serve as the centrepiece for local Remembrance Day or anniversary events, including Vimy Day, Battle of the Atlantic Sunday, and D-Day. Some monuments have proven easier to erect than others, with structures to mark Korean War service, peacekeeping, and merchant navy participation sometimes running afoul of veterans' politics, bureaucratic infighting, and fiscal conservatism by successive governments. The Department of National Defence and the Organization of Military Museums of Canada, in co-operation with the Royal Canadian Legion and other organizations, are creating a National Inventory of Canadian Military Memorials and, by 2009, had 6,068 listed.

READING: Jonathan Vance, *Death So Noble: Memory, Meaning, and the First World War* (Vancouver, 1997).

War of the Austrian Succession (King George's War). Britain and France were already at war over trade when a general European war broke out in 1740 over rival claims to the Austrian throne. The two empires took opposite sides in the dispute and the war soon spread to their North American colonies. A 4,200-strong force organized by the governor of Massachusetts with men provided by several colonies seized the fortress at Louisbourg in June 1745 after a siege of six weeks. For their part, French and Aboriginal war parties raided British settlements on the frontier from Massachusetts to New York,

destroying Saratoga in late 1745 with much carnage. The Treaty of Aix-la-Chapelle, signed in 1748, brought a temporary peace and returned Louisbourg to France. SEE ALSO: LOUISBOURG.

War of 1812. The War of 1812 arose out of growing tension between Britain and the United States during the Napoleonic Wars. In enforcing an embargo on all trade to the European continent, Royal Navy warships routinely stopped American vessels to search for contraband; where crew members aboard those ships were found to have deserted the Royal Navy, they were immediately seized. The Americans deeply resented such actions, which helped fuel the demands of "warhawks" from Midwestern and Southern states who sought to annex Canada and drive the British from North America. Over the bitter opposition of New England representatives who feared the power of the Royal Navy, Congress voted on 18 June 1812 to declare war on Britain. The US military prepared to attack Canada, and the British commander-in-chief and administrator of Upper Canada, Major-General Isaac Brock, laid plans for the colony's defence.

Although badly outnumbered, the British regulars and colonial militia succeeded in their defence of the Canadas. Their tactic of constantly striking at American weak points and keeping the enemy off balance in his own territory worked well. Brock began the war by seizing Detroit and Fort Michilimackinac, instantly upsetting American plans. The Americans, moreover, were not well prepared, and their militias seemed even more hesitant than the Canadian militia; this gave the British regulars, far better trained than the US Army in 1812, the edge. Then there was the invaluable aid given Britain by its First Nations allies such as the Shawnee chief Tecumseh, and the fact that for most of the war, the United States was deeply divided with New England, in particular, against the war.

In Canada, the war had five fronts: at Michilimackinac; along the western shores of Lake Erie; on the Niagara frontier; along the St Lawrence River between Kingston and Cornwall; and the Lake Champlain-Richelieu River line south of Montreal.

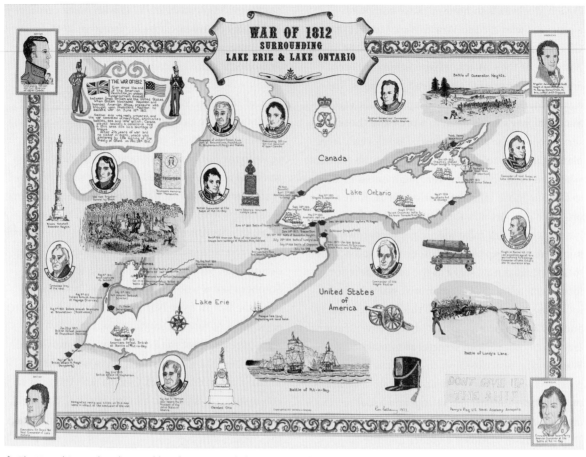

The United States thought it could easily seize Canada, but British regulars, First Nations warriors, and Canadian militia fended off successive waves of invaders.

Brock's soldiers took Michilimackinac in mid-July 1812 to prevent US passage through the strategic straits there and held it for the duration of the war. At the western end of Lake Erie, repeated battles for control of the water passage from Lake Huron to Lake Erie took place at Detroit, Fort Amherstburg, Put-in-Bay, Fort Meigs, Frenchtown, and Moraviantown. Through skilful aggressive action and with the help of Tecumseh, the British seized the advantage in 1812, capturing and holding Detroit, but they lost their hold the following year after a naval battle on Lake Erie at Put-in-Bay where the US Navy took effective control of the lake, forcing the British to withdraw from Detroit. During that withdrawal, the Americans killed Tecumseh at the battle of Moraviantown on 5 October; it was an American victory, but one not followed up.

On the Niagara frontier, General Brock defeated the US invaders at Queenston Heights on 13 October 1812, a battle in which Brock was killed. In 1813, however, the Americans fared better. After capturing and burning York in May, they took Fort George at the mouth of the Niagara River. Only a surprise British attack at Stoney Creek in June checked American expansion. In 1814, the US Army tried again, only to be repulsed on 25 July at the bloody battle at Lundy's Lane.

The battles along the St Lawrence and south of Montreal in the fall of 1813 resulted from an American effort to mount a two-pronged operation aimed at Montreal to be followed by an eventual assault on Quebec City. The first prong was a combined land and naval attack down the St Lawrence, mounted from Sackets Harbor,

New York, which ended with American defeat at Crysler's Farm on 11 November by a small force of regulars, militia, and First Nations. The other used the traditional invasion route toward Montreal from the south. It was choked off by the British victory at Chateauguay, and General Sir George Prevost then prepared a substantial force to strike at northern New York. His hopes collapsed when the US Navy won a victory in Plattsburgh Bay, and Prevost timidly withdrew.

The war was fought on other fronts as well. British forces occupied much of Maine, captured and burned Washington, and disastrously attacked New Orleans, while important naval engagements took place on the Atlantic Coast (where the Royal Navy mounted an effective blockade), the Great Lakes, and on Lake Champlain. When the war ended with the signing of the Treaty of Ghent on 24 December 1814, no boundaries were altered, and the status quo before the war was effectively restored. At the least, this was a moral victory for the British whose leadership, aggressiveness, and military professionalism had denied the United States its expected victory. The Canadian militia had played a relatively minor part in the fighting, but the experience of holding a numerically superior foe at bay became a major part of Upper Canadian mythology in the decades that followed. SEE ALSO: BROCK; CRYSLER'S FARM; LAKE ERIE; LUNDY'S LANE; PREVOST; QUEENSTON HEIGHTS; TECUMSEH.

READING: J.M. Hitsman, *The Incredible War of 1812* (rev. ed., Montreal, 1999).

War of the League of Augsburg (King William's War). In 1689, Britain, France, and other European states began a decade-long conflict, the North American portion of which was known as King William's War. As was customary, the French and their native allies launched raids against English settlements, sacking and burning Schenectady, New York, in 1690, and a succession of villages in subsequent years. Britain fought to retain its control of Hudson's Bay Company posts and the Newfoundland fishery, but Pierre Le Moyne captured Moose Factory and other posts at the southern end of the Bay in 1686

and defended them against a succession of unsuccessful counterattacks. York Factory changed hands several times with Le Moyne wintering there in 1694. He also raided St John's and neighbouring fishing villages in Newfoundland in 1696 but abandoned them within the year. The English, for their part, captured Port Royal and then attacked Quebec in 1690, but they were repulsed by Count Frontenac. The Treaty of Ryswick, concluded in 1697, returned Hudson Bay to the British while the French retained Acadia. The peace was short-lived, however, and combat resumed in 1702 as Queen Anne's War. SEE ALSO: FRONTENAC; LE MOYNE.

War on Terror. The phrase "War on Terror" (or "War on Terrorism") refers to the undeclared conflict between the international community of states and, especially, the principal democratic Western states, and the international terrorist network al Qaeda or related transnational terrorist organizations. It is usually dated from the 11 September 2001 bombings of several targets in the United States, including the World Trade Center complex in New York City and the Pentagon in Washington, DC, by agents of al Qaeda, a fundamentalist Islamic organization dedicated to the ouster of American forces from the Middle East.

Canadian involvement in the War on Terror commenced with 9/11, although terrorist activity in Canada had a history that included separatist violence in the province of Quebec against federal authority, Sikh nationalist attacks on Indian targets, and Arab militants using Canadian soil to plot actions against the United States. In a celebrated December 1999 incident, Ahmed Ressam, an Algerian Muslim living illegally in Canada and wanted by authorities, was arrested attempting to enter the United States from British Columbia and later convicted of attempting to bomb Los Angeles International Airport. But the September 2001 attacks saw immediate responses by all Canadian police, military, and security agencies, and continuing activities in the form of domestic agencies and legislation crafted specifically to combat terrorism, military and security deployments at home and abroad, and heightened political and intelligence

▲ Soldiers of 3 PPCLI are caught in a helicopter downdraft at Tora Bora, May 2002. In Afghanistan, the War on Terror entailed real war against an elusive, dangerous foe. Canadian forces were among the coalition's most consistently effective and reliable troops.

co-operation with major allies around the globe. An Anti-terrorism Act (2001) made the assembly of evidence and the surveillance and prosecution of terrorism suspects at home easier, but the major initial effort in the War on Terror was the deployment of sea, air, and land formations to Afghanistan, where they joined a United States–led, United Nations–sanctioned war, first to depose the pro–al Qaeda government of the Taliban, and later to support that country's nascent democratic regime. Since early 2002, nearly 30,000 Canadians have served in the conflict, in a variety of roles, including special operations forces, while thousands of others have been involved in related support functions at home. The Canadian Forces' overseas missions during the War on Terror have been its highest tempo of

operations, and experienced its highest rate of casualties, since the Korean War in the early 1950s. In March 2010, Prime Minister Stephen Harper reaffirmed an earlier promise to bring Canadian combat troops home from Afghanistan in 2011, while continuing other forms of assistance, including diplomatic and development aid.

At home, anti-terrorism legislation, extra resources for border security, new cross-border arrangements with the United States, and a demonstrable willingness to test existing rights and freedoms in the interests of enhanced police powers marked the greatest securitization of Canadian domestic affairs since the early Cold War. Added—and sometimes ridiculously invasive—airport security measures were the most obvious elements of a revamped domestic regime that saw billions spent on emergency preparedness, transportation safeguards, anti-terrorism training at the federal, provincial, and municipal levels, and a swath of critical infrastructure and cyber-terrorist safeguards. Public Safety Canada, a federal department created in 2003 to coordinate the work of several agencies in responding to crises ranging from natural disasters to terrorist attacks, drew few plaudits for its efforts, least of all from the auditor general of Canada, who reported in late 2009 on the department's failure, after six years, to exercise "the leadership necessary to coordinate emergency management activities, including protection of critical infrastructure in Canada." The federal government's National Security Strategy (2004) had articulated an "all hazards" approach to emergency preparedness that was to have

been coordinated by the new department, an organization that, by fiscal year 2008–2009, had more than 400 employees and a $60 million budget, but the auditor general was critical of the department's work in this role. While noting that the Government Operations Centre, created by the department in 2004 to gather, analyze, and disseminate information to decision-makers, had performed useful work in some instances, the audit also concluded that no lessons from past events or exercises had been formally integrated into the emergency response architecture to improve future performance. Coordination processes remained unclear for nuclear, chemical, biological, and other potential emergencies.

Domestic criticism of Canada's role in the War on Terror mounted steadily in the months after 9/11,

⌃ In Afghanistan, mines and IEDs—Improvised Explosive Devices—caused most Canadian casualties. Two soldiers from the 5ième Régiment d'Artillerie Légère du Canada mark and clear mines in May 2004.

even as Canadian military and diplomatic personnel drew widespread praise for their work, and public support for Canadian Forces personnel in particular solidified in the face of a slow but steady stream of combat casualties. Even in the attacks' immediate aftermath, many Canadians had voiced concerns that American foreign policy had precipitated in some way the terrorists' actions, while the government of Prime Minister Jean Chrétien seemed initially somewhat reluctant to join the international community's more robust response. American speculation, unfounded but not entirely unreasonable, in light of the earlier Ressam case, that the 9/11 bombers might have entered the United States from Canada, tainted Canadian reactions to the American crisis and to subsequent events. Canadians welcomed stranded American and international travellers by the thousands when continental air traffic temporarily ceased after the 9/11 attacks, and were broadly united over sending troops to Afghanistan, but many showed no appetite for involvement in the subsequent Iraq war (though English-speaking opinion was mostly supportive of participation), despite the urgings of Opposition Leader Stephen Harper, later to become prime minister. Ottawa refused to participate in Iraq, opting instead to commit troops to Afghanistan, fighting transnational terrorism where it clearly did exist instead of floundering in search of it where, as increasingly became evident, it did not.

The decision to stay out of Iraq as a possible battlefield in the War on Terror was controversial at the time and brilliant in retrospect. American influence and credibility—deployed in earnest at a famous February 2003 United Nations Security Council session in which US Secretary of State Colin Powell sought to prove Iraq's defiance of UN sanctions and plead for international military support—eroded by leaps and bounds in the subsequent war. Evidence mounted as well that the War on Terror had bred terror of its own, in the form of unethical, illegal, and often simply sadistic state-sponsored practices by the anti-terrorist coalition, most notably by the United States in facilities from Iraq to Guantanamo Bay, Cuba, but practices in which many other states,

including Canada, may to various degrees have been complicit. The case of Mahar Arar, a Syrian-born Canadian citizen seized in September 2002 by American officials in New York on suspicion of terrorist connections and rendered to Syria by way of Jordan for interrogation, appeared to exemplify the extent to which the War on Terror had weakened civil protections internationally, privileging security allegations over basic human rights. Arar, his innocence avowed vigorously by a Canadian commission of inquiry in 2006, was released from Syria in 2003 after a long and brutal incarceration, and later received an official apology and a financial settlement of more than $10 million from the Canadian government. His attempts at legal restitution in the United States proved unsuccessful.

The Arar case led to greater efforts between Canada and the United States to coordinate issues of rendition, meaning the handing over or extrajudicial transfer of a person from one state's jurisdiction to that of another, and to a running skirmish between the two countries over how Arar had been remanded into Syrian custody—with or without Canadian complicity or assistance. The commissioner of the Royal Canadian Mounted Police, Giuliano Zaccardelli, resigned in December 2006 over issues related to his testimony to a parliamentary committee on the Arar file. More importantly, the domestic debate over Arar and the ongoing War on Terror undermined Canadian confidence in security institutions and weakened public faith in the persistence and danger of actual terrorist threats. The growing capacity of domestic security institutions, including the Canadian Security Intelligence Service, was a noted feature of Canada's post-9/11 security environment, as was a more determined effort by successive governments to act legislatively against funding efforts by civil organizations with known connections to international terrorist groups. The Harper government listed the World Tamil Movement, better known as the Tamil Tigers, as a terrorist organization in September 2008, for example, and added Al Shabaab, a Somali group, to its terrorist list in March 2010.

The ongoing threat to Canadians and to Canadian interests was evident in the June 2006 arrest of 18 terrorist suspects in the Toronto area, the so-called Toronto 18. The result of successful international intelligence sharing, a widespread and effective counterterrorism operation, and the infiltration of the group by a police informant, the security coup was notable more for subsequent calls to guarantee minority rights and the protection of Muslim Canadians from other Canadians than for expressions of public gratitude or relief at the threat potentially removed from Canadian streets. Several members of the group later pled guilty to terrorism-related charges, and the ringleader, Zakaria Amara, received a sentence of life imprisonment for a wide-ranging plot that included a terrorist training camp and a triple-event attack on the city of Toronto. Each of the proposed bombs had the same destructive force as that used in the October 1995 Oklahoma City bombing in the United States, an incident that killed 198 people. While charges against seven of the accused were later dropped, successful prosecutions proceeded against the others; the first to be convicted in September 2008, a youth, became the first conviction under Canada's anti-terrorism legislation passed in 2001.

Canadian efforts in the War on Terror continued at home and abroad into 2010, with large-scale military, aid, and diplomatic efforts in Afghanistan, extensive security co-operation with allies, especially the United States, on transnational threats ranging from illegal immigration to weapons trafficking, and enhanced funding for public safety efforts and the coordination of key agencies. The overall thrust of the campaign, however, has, in recent years, been denied precision and, to a great extent, public legitimacy, despite the obvious persistence of terrorist threats (Canada has long been named a target of al Qaeda activity) and the less obvious but equally real enhancement of Canadian capabilities in the areas of security, intelligence, and military affairs. Since the Taliban's speedy defeat and subsequent tenacity in Afghanistan and the concurrent corruption of that country's elected government, the War on Terror as a term, a technique, and a cost centre has tended to diffuse into normal governmental operations. Its specificity and, importantly, its financial implications, are correspondingly difficult to discern, even to close students of the campaign's history. Several detailed estimates of the military costs of the war in Afghanistan, including one by the parliamentary budget officer in September 2008, ranged from $14 billion to more than $22 billion through 2011, numbers far in excess of official estimates. None of the heightened estimates included diplomatic or domestic security efforts, foreign aid, or the activities of related departments such as the RCMP, CSIS, or the Canada Border Services Agency, created in late 2003, in part, from the former border control agency, Canada Customs. The financial cost of the war has joined the broad issues of the Afghanistan war and the proper balance between civil liberty and national security as a key flashpoint for political debate and public concern. Parliamentary testimony in early 2010 opened another front in this affair—the extent to which Canadian officials in Afghanistan may have been complicit in handing over captured Taliban suspects to Afghan authorities, in whose custody torture was a distinct, even likely, possibility.

The War on Terror is increasingly a misnomer, applied imprecisely to a range of government activities that includes everything from basic border security to high-intensity combat operations in Afghanistan. Its historic focus, fighting specific forms of transnational terrorism in response to the 9/11 attacks and similar incidents, continues in more limited form, but will diminish considerably after the planned withdrawal of Canadian combat troops from Afghanistan in 2011. Its more lasting impacts will take longer to assess. The growth and complexity of domestic security agencies, the challenge to civil liberties and basic governance posed by the securitization of domestic affairs, the impact of Afghanistan on the Canadian Forces and its members, and the nature of those relationships— foreign and domestic—forged or eschewed by virtue of Canada's post-9/11 War on Terror, will be among them. SEE ALSO: AFGHANISTAN WAR; CHRÉTIEN; HARPER.

War Photography. The development of photography in the 1830s inspired some to photograph the American war with Mexico in the 1840s, and James Brady's great photos from the Civil War resonate still. The first Canadian war photographs of some of those who fought, though limited by the bulky cameras and cumbersome plates that could not be developed except in the studio of the 1860s, appear to have been taken during the Fenian raids of 1866. In 1885, Captain James Peters, an artillery officer, took his camera and 120 plates with him during the Northwest Rebellion, where he took some 63 successful photographs of the rebellion. His photos included one of Louis Riel as a captive, a number of soldiers alive and dead, and even some action shots of the battle of Fish Creek. By the time of the South African War, the technology had advanced dramatically, cameras were smaller, and roll film had been widely distributed. F.C. Cantrill, a Canadian serving in the South African Constabulary from 1901, carried his Kodak with him and produced at least 26 photographs that have survived.

Photography reached its battlefield zenith in World Wars I and II. Soldiers could use their cameras at home and in training, but commanders tried to stop their use at the front. Official photographers, however, produced tens of thousands of images in both wars, and these were widely published in newspapers, put on postcards and sold to raise funds for war charities, and exhibited. Only rarely in World War I were the photographers credited by name; in World War II, the Department of National Defence frequently named the photographer, and Gilbert Milne and Ken Bell—to name only two of many—became very well-known for work that told the Canadian military story to newspaper readers. The Korean War and Canadian peacekeeping operations were also extensively covered by official photographers and, increasingly, by civilian journalists.

By the 1990s and even more by the time of the Afghanistan War, the widespread availability of digital cameras with huge capacity—not to mention cellular telephones that can take photos and the laptop computers that can deliver them almost instantly around the world—made battlefield censorship very difficult. The huge (and deserved) embarrassment suffered by the US Army in Iraq when photographs showed the torture and humiliation of prisoners at Abu Ghraib mirrored that of soldiers of the Canadian Airborne Regiment who photographed the torture and murder of a Somali youth at Belet Huen in 1993. SEE ALSO: CENSORSHIP; PROPAGANDA; WAR ART.

Warships. The Royal Canadian Navy (RCN; in early years called the Naval Service) began its life in 1910 with two old cruisers, HMCS *Niobe* and *Rainbow*; these two were all Canada had when it went to war in August 1914. British Columbia's government bought two submarines from an American shipyard and turned them over to the navy, and, in the next year, fearing U-boat attacks, naval headquarters created a St Lawrence patrol by purchasing yachts and chartering civilian craft. The submarine threat increased over the next two years, and Ottawa ordered 12 steel trawlers, while Britain's Royal Navy (RN) placed orders for 160 anti-submarine trawlers, many of which eventually passed to Canadian control. In 1918, the navy had 130 vessels in all.

Between the wars, the RCN fell and rose. The cruiser *Aurora* was acquired and paid off at the beginning of the 1920s, but, in 1929, two modern destroyers were ordered with four more purchased from the RN in 1937–1938. Canada thus began World War II with six relatively modern destroyers.

In the first months of the war, the RCN placed orders for 92 corvettes and *Bangor* class minesweepers; the RCN eventually had 122 Canadian-built corvettes, 12 *Castle* class corvettes from the RN, and 66 *Bangor* class and 12 *Algerine* class minesweepers. Orders for four *Tribal* class destroyers were placed in Britain and delivered in 1943–1944, and four were built in Canada, but completed after the end of the war. The RCN acquired seven *Town* class destroyers in 1941 from the United States (as part of the destroyers-for-bases deal), converted liners into three *Prince* class armed merchant cruisers, acquired 70 frigates beginning in mid-1943 and two cruisers the next year, and crewed two RN aircraft carriers. The navy also operated 80 *Fairmile* sub-chasers, used as coastal convoy escorts. In all, the wartime RCN had some 450 vessels.

Almost everything disappeared with the peace after 1945 as ships were paid off at a frantic pace. The aircraft carrier *Warrior* came into RCN service, however, and soon was replaced by HMCS *Magnificent*. Construction of the *St Laurent* class destroyers and the follow-on destroyer designs began in Canada in the 1950s, making the RCN the world leader in anti-submarine warfare ships. At its Cold War peak, the RCN could deploy 40 major warships.

But there were no Auxiliary Oiler Replenishment (AOR) ships until 1963, and the RCN entered its period of postwar decline and rust-out. *Magnificent* was paid off and replaced by *Bonaventure*, and the Trudeau government scrapped the "*Bonnie*" in 1970. Still, the helicopter-equipped destroyer (*DDH 280*, as the class was called) program began, and a ship replacement program received authorization in 1977. The life of the navy's aging destroyers was extended by major refits, and the government placed orders for a dozen Canadian-built patrol frigates that came into service in the second half of the 1990s. Twelve Maritime Coastal Defence Vessels (MCDVs) and three *Oberon* class submarines also were acquired, the latter replaced at the end of the 1990s by four *Upholder* class submarines. The navy thus entered the twenty-first century with 33 warships: twelve frigates; four submarines; two oilers; three destroyers; and twelve MCDVs. Only the frigates were top-of-the-line warships, however, and the remainder had become either obsolete or strictly limited in their capabilities. See also: Corvettes; Destroyer Escorts; Royal Canadian Navy; Submarines.

Reading: Marc Milner, *Canada's Navy: The First Century* (2nd ed., Toronto, 2010).

War Time Elections Act (1917). Passed in the summer of 1917 to assist the election prospects of Prime Minister Sir Robert Borden's government in the forthcoming federal election, the act disenfranchised voters who were conscientious objectors and those from "enemy alien" countries who had immigrated to Canada after 31 March 1902 and who did not have immediate family serving with the Canadian Expeditionary Force. At the same time,

the legislation gave the vote to all women with husbands, brothers, and sons serving in the Canadian military. The effect was to remove a large number of potential anti-conscription voters from the electorate, while adding a substantial number of voters who might be expected to support a pro-conscription government. See also: Borden, Robert; Conscription; Military Voters Act.

Reading: Roger Graham, *Arthur Meighen: The Door of Opportunity*, vol. 1 (Toronto, 1960).

War Trophies. As long as there have been wars, nations have displayed the trophies captured from their enemies. In World War I, the Canadian Corps captured thousands of weapons from the Germans and, at the end of the war, the Dominion archivist, Sir Arthur Doughty, was named the controller of war trophies. Doughty gathered a huge collection, much of which went to the Imperial War Museum in London, England. The remainder—including 516 artillery pieces, 304 trench mortars, 3,500 machine guns, and 44 aircraft—came back to Canada intended for a great museum that would display the booty, the war art, and the records of the corps. This idea died, and much of the collection was dispersed to communities across the country for display. Much was lost over time. But the surviving pieces went to the Canadian War Museum when it reopened in 1942; these artifacts now form the basis of its World War I collection. More came to the Canadian War Museum after World War II, the Korean War, peacekeeping operations, and the Afghanistan War. See also: Canadian War Museum; War Art.

Webster-Ashburton Treaty. Signed on 9 August 1842 by US Secretary of State Daniel Webster and British envoy Alexander Baring, 1st Baron Ashburton, the treaty resolved the dispute over the location of the border between New Brunswick and Maine that had produced the skirmishes known as the Aroostook War of 1839. It also definitively settled the border between Lake Superior and Lake of the Woods, and reaffirmed the 49th parallel as the border west to the Rocky Mountains. See also: Aroostook War.

⌃ Soldiers inspect German military trophies in 1917, two of them wearing distinctive German *pickelhaube* spiked helmets. Military authorities in both world wars shipped home thousands of trophies, from uniforms to artillery to aircraft.

White Papers, Defence. A White Paper is a government policy statement intended to chart the direction to be followed in the coming years. Canadian governments have issued five defence policy statements that might be characterized as White Papers: "Defence 1947," produced by defence minister Brooke Claxton after World War II and before the Cold War became contested; "The White Paper on Defence," issued in 1964 by Paul Hellyer, the defence minister who pushed Canada toward a unified armed forces; "Defence in the 70s," released by Donald S. Macdonald just months after the October Crisis made domestic security a critical matter; "Challenge and Commitment," defence minister Perrin Beatty's tough anti-Soviet paper that called for the acquisition of nuclear submarines; and "Defence 1994," prepared for David Collenette as Canada was on the verge of major defence cutbacks after the Cold War. White Papers are infrequent and do not necessarily forecast the future with any accuracy: nuclear submarines may have made sense in 1987, for example, but after the Berlin Wall came down and the Cold War ended, they were widely seen as costly anachronisms.

READING: Douglas Bland, *Canada's National Defence: White Papers*, vol. 1 (Kingston, ON, 1997).

Windmill, Battle of (1838). Members of the Hunters' Lodges—Americans who sympathized with the Canadian rebels who had attempted to overthrow British rule in the rebellions of 1837—raided Prescott,

Upper Canada, in November 1838 intending to capture Fort Wellington. Had they succeeded, the raiders could have cut British communications along the St Lawrence River. Some 300 Patriot Hunters had set out, but one ship with a hundred men aboard was unable to make it to the Canadian shore and hastened back to the United States. The other raiders established themselves in a nearby 25-metre-high gristmill and several stone houses. Up to 2,000 British regulars and Canadian militia rushed to the scene with artillery, while three naval vessels patrolled the river, cutting off any possibility of a retreat. A five-day battle ensued from 11 November with casualties on both sides. In all, 80 Hunters were killed and 159 more were taken prisoner. The British and the militia suffered some 20 casualties. After courts-martial at Fort Henry in Kingston, the Canadian authorities later executed eleven of the Hunters and transported sixty to Australia. (John A. Macdonald, later Canada's first prime minister, unsuccessfully defended Nils Von Schoultz, the Hunters' leader, who was hanged on 8 December.) See also: Patriot Hunters; Rebellions of 1837–1838.

Wolfe, James (1727–1759). The son of a soldier, James Wolfe received his commission in 1741 and saw substantial action on the European continent and at Culloden. He earned a reputation as a good trainer of troops. Named a temporary brigadier, Wolfe came to North America with Major-General Jeffery Amherst in 1758 and played an important role in the capture of Louisbourg. Commanding Amherst's elite troops, Wolfe put them ashore with small loss and led the northern wing of the besiegers that was instrumental in forcing the surrender of the fortress. Wolfe favoured moving at once on Quebec, but the naval commanders decided it was too late in the season, and he instead led forces that laid waste to French settlements in the Gaspé, ordering that everything be burnt. Amherst had been impressed with this young officer, and Wolfe, returning to England, lobbied politely to get command of the attack on Quebec in 1759. His appointment came through on 12 January 1759, along with a promotion to major-general.

James Wolfe, the victor of Quebec.

His command was to consist of ten regular battalions in a force numbering some 8,500 troops in all. He had a hand in selecting his brigadiers, James Murray, Robert Monckton, and George Townshend, although the last was not his choice. The naval commander was Vice-Admiral Charles Saunders. Wolfe himself was in poor health, irritable, and difficult.

Wolfe's army arrived off the Île d'Orléans on 27 June 1759, already late in the campaign season. His opponent, Lieutenant-General the Marquis de Montcalm, had a larger force than Wolfe, but most of its members were untrained Canadien militia. The British commander's aim was to force Montcalm to stand and fight. As he wrote to his mother two months later, "My antagonist has wisely shut himself up in inaccessible entrenchments, so that I cant get at him without spilling a torrent of blood, and that perhaps to little purpose. The Marquiss de Montcalm is at the head of a great number of bad soldiers, and I am at the head of a small number of good ones, that wish for nothing so much as to fight him—but the wary old fellow avoids an action doubtful of the behaviour of his army. People must be of the profession to understand the disadvantages and difficulties we labour under arising from the uncommon natural strength of the country."

Wolfe's leadership was not impressive during the long siege. He was completely indecisive, and his relations with his three brigadiers grew very testy. His assault against the entrenched French positions just to the west of the Montmorency River at the end of July was a total and costly failure. His gunners, based at Pointe-Lévy across the St Lawrence, rained devastating fire on Quebec City, and his troops laid waste to every settlement they could reach. But Wolfe could not decide what to do to bring Montcalm to battle as the siege dragged on and the summer drew close to an end. Ill in his bed, Wolfe asked his brigadiers their advice, and they offered it: "to direct the Operations above the Town: When we establish ourselves on the North Shore, the French General must fight us on our own Terms; We shall be betwixt him and his provisions … " Wolfe sensibly accepted this and himself chose the little cove of Anse au Foulon to the west of the city as the best place to land his troops who then climbed up a steep cliff to the Plains of Abraham, hauling their cannon with them, early on 13 September. When he saw the British soldiers drawn up in formation, the Marquis de Montcalm rushed to offer battle. If he had waited for reinforcements to reach him, he could have fought with greater weight of numbers, or he might have refused to fight at all, waiting behind Quebec's walls for the British to depart with the onset of cold fall weather. Montcalm's decision to fight was a fatal mistake for France as the British regiments' volleys blasted the French line to pieces and forced a pell-mell retreat. Wolfe, however, like Montcalm, was mortally wounded in the fighting.

The victory of 1759 fixed Wolfe's reputation as a great hero and general. He was not, no more than Montcalm. He had a streak of ruthlessness, demonstrated by the devastation he wreaked on the civilians of New France. He was a ditherer and no great tactician. But he had the good sense to accept the suggestion of his brigadiers, and on the Plains of Abraham he commanded his line well. Competent

▲ The very model of a modern commander, Garnet Wolseley, 1884.

rather than brilliant, Wolfe deserves to be remembered for the results of the battle at Quebec, and rather less for the way in which he won it. SEE ALSO: AMHERST; LOUISBOURG; MONTCALM; PLAINS OF ABRAHAM; QUEBEC (1759).

READING: Stephen Brumwell, *Paths of Glory: The Life and Death of General James Wolfe* (Montreal, 2007).

Wolseley, Garnet Joseph (1833–1913). Born in Ireland, Wolseley served with the British army in India, the Crimea, and China prior to his being posted to Canada in 1861, where he earned a reputation as a proficient trainer of militia both before and after the Fenian raids and, at age 34, became a colonel and deputy quartermaster general. He actively sought command of the Red River Expedition in 1870, and he again drew praise and a knighthood for his skilful supply and transport arrangements that took the small force of British regulars, militia, and civilian voyageurs across the 900 kilometres of wilderness

As World War II expanded and the armed forces grew larger, women assumed ever more important roles. The explicit message in this CWAC recruiting poster was one of equality.

north of Lake Superior to the Red River. Returning to Britain in September 1870 when London withdrew its regulars from Canada, he continued his inexorable rise with service in the Ashanti wars, Egypt, and the Sudan in 1884–1885 where he planned to use Canadian voyageurs to get his army around the cataracts on the Nile. Although the Sudanese expedition failed in its efforts to rescue General Charles George Gordon at Khartoum, Wolseley became 1st Viscount Wolseley for his efforts and, in 1894, a field marshal. From 1895 to 1900, he was commander-in-chief of the British army. SEE ALSO: NILE EXPEDITION; RED RIVER EXPEDITION.

READING: Halik Kochanski, *Sir Garnet Wolseley: Victorian Hero* (London, 1999).

Women in the Military. Other than nursing sisters who performed vital services in war and peace from the Northwest Rebellion of 1885 onward, no women served in the Canadian military until World War II. Each of the services then created women's divisions that trained them for a variety of non-combat but essential roles ranging from typing to cooking to flying aircraft and intercepting enemy signals. In all, 49,963 served. Gradually, other military occupations were opened but, in 1971, women made up no more than 1.8 percent of Canadian Forces personnel. By 1974, 18 of 27 officer classifications were open to women, and 64 of 97 trades. But still combat was excluded and, in 1979, the military ran trials to see if women could be integrated into combat support units. The tests were not wholly successful, but political pressure to act continued to increase. In 1980, women became eligible to become "lady cadets" at the Royal Military College and did well in every respect, and the Charter of Rights and Freedoms of 1982 ratcheted up the pressure even more. By 1989, a Human Rights tribunal ordered that women be integrated into all military occupations

The Wrens made their mark in World War II. Nancy Pyper posed proudly for Yousuf Karsh in her winter uniform.

^ The Wrens, as they were universally known, did virtually every shore-based task in the RCN during World War II.

within ten years. The military then opened the doors, but the army found that women had difficulty meeting the physical standards required in the combat arms; the result inevitably was that physical tests were "gendered," or lowered, for women. Further difficulties arose with sexual harassment and a "non-supportive environment," and all ranks began to receive sensitivity training. Notwithstanding these problems and recruitment challenges for both genders, the military has accepted women into all roles and in all of the service environments with increasing enthusiasm as time has passed. Indeed, in the twenty-first century, Canada is considered an international leader in the integration of women in the armed forces. The current military target is for 28 percent of the Canadian Forces

to be women, but this has not yet been reached. The first Canadian woman in the combat arms to be killed on active service was Captain Nichola Goddard, an artillery officer serving in Afghanistan; she died in 2006.

SEE ALSO: CANADIAN WOMEN'S ARMY CORPS; ROYAL CANADIAN AIR FORCE, WOMEN'S DIVISION; SEXUAL DISCRIMINATION; WOMEN'S ROYAL CANADIAN NAVAL SERVICE.

Women's Royal Canadian Naval Service (WRCNS). Established on 31 July 1942, after six months of planning at Naval Service Headquarters, and patterned after the British Women's Royal Naval Service from whom six officers were borrowed to create the

503 _ Attaque aux gaz _
Somme _

⌃ This stunning aerial photograph, taken over the Somme battlefield, shows a gas attack in progress, the fumes drifting westward on the wind. For soldiers in the trenches, gas masks provided protection but the claustrophobia they induced could be terrifying.

Canadian service, the WRCNS had a total wartime strength of 6,783; of these, 11 died, none from enemy action. The first Canadian director was Commander Adelaide Sinclair who took command in September 1943. Wrens, as they were universally known, served throughout Canada and at Royal Canadian Navy establishments in Newfoundland, the United States, and Britain, and were initially paid 66 percent of the wages going to males in similar rank; this was later raised to 80 percent. Wrens participated in a wide variety of support trades, including driving vehicles and food preparation, but were especially important in clerical, telegraphy, and signals work. In this last capacity, they staffed the shore-based radio intercept stations that were a key means of detecting U-boats, and worked on the West Coast collecting signals intelligence. On demobilization, Wrens received all benefits owing under the Veterans Charter to those who had served.

World War I. The war that began in Europe in August 1914 found Canada unprepared in every respect. The country's population was only some eight million, and the professional military was tiny and ill trained, the militia even more so. The navy consisted of two obsolete ships, and there was no air force. Industry was small, geared primarily to the domestic market, and agriculture, though it produced vast quantities of wheat for export, was as yet almost completely unmechanized.

But unprepared or not, Canada was at war. As a colony of Great Britain, the Dominion did not control its foreign policy, and Britain's declaration of war committed Canada to the fight. Not that there was any doubt that most Canadians wanted the Dominion to participate. German ambitions had been watched with concern for years, and the Conservative government of Sir Robert Borden had tried—and

▲ The first contingent that arrived in England in 1914 included Raymond Brutinel's machine-gun-carrying armoured cars, an innovation in warfare.

▲ This famous photograph from 1916 showed Canadians going "over the top." It was staged behind the lines.

After taking an enemy trench in July 1916, these soldiers from the 13th Battalion in the 1st Canadian Infantry Division had to consolidate the position, preparing to face the inevitable German counterattack.

Battlefield communications were always difficult on the Western Front, and pigeons, here being carried forward on the back of a dispatch rider, were frequently used to send tactical messages.

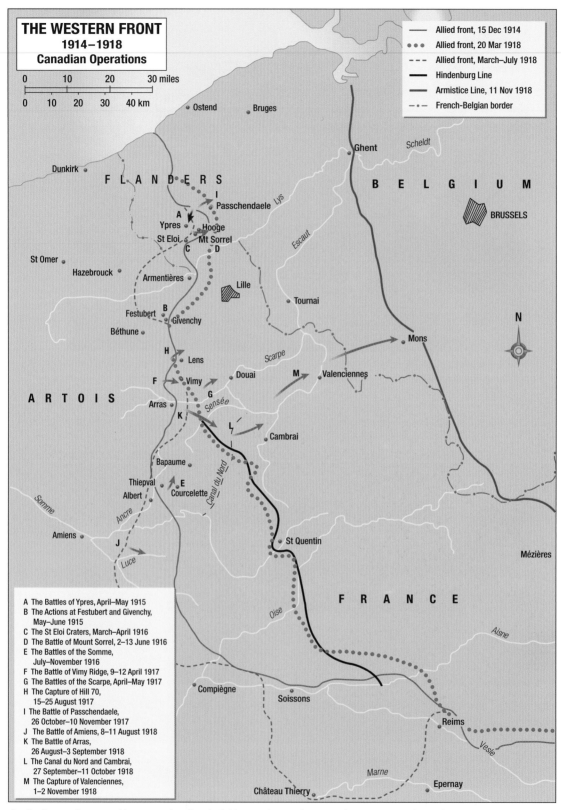

THE WESTERN FRONT
1914–1918
Canadian Operations

0	10	20	30 miles
0	10 20	30	40 km

Allied front, 15 Dec 1914
Allied front, 20 Mar 1918
Allied front, March–July 1918
Hindenburg Line
Armistice Line, 11 Nov 1918
French-Belgian border

Ostend
Bruges
Ghent
Scheldt
BELGIUM
BRUSSELS
N
Dunkirk
FLANDERS
Passchendaele I
Lys
A Ypres Hooge
St Eloi Mt Sorrel
C D
Escaut
St Omer
Hazebrouck
Armentières
Lille
Tournai
B
Festubert
Givenchy
Béthune
Mons
H
Lens
Scarpe
Valenciennes
F Vimy Douai M
ARTOIS
Arras G
K Sensée
L Cambrai
Bapaume
Canal du Nord
Thiepval E
Albert Courcelette
Somme
Ancre
Amiens
J
Luce
St Quentin
Mézières
FRANCE
Oise
Aisne
Compiègne
Soissons
Reims
Vesle
Marne
Château Thierry
Epernay

A The Battles of Ypres, April–May 1915
B The Actions at Festubert and Givenchy,
  May–June 1915
C The St Eloi Craters, March–April 1916
D The Battle of Mount Sorrel, 2–13 June 1916
E The Battles of the Somme,
  July–November 1916
F The Battle of Vimy Ridge, 9–12 April 1917
G The Battles of the Scarpe, April–May 1917
H The Capture of Hill 70,
  15–25 August 1917
I The Battle of Passchendaele,
  26 October–10 November 1917
J The Battle of Amiens, 8–11 August 1918
K The Battle of Arras,
  26 August–3 September 1918
L The Canal du Nord and Cambrai,
  27 September–11 October 1918
M The Capture of Valenciennes,
  1–2 November 1918

⌃ The first total war, World War I produced unthinkable casualties and yawning divisions in Canadian politics.

failed, thanks to defeat in the Liberal-dominated Senate—to make a gift of $35 million to Britain to build three dreadnoughts for the Royal Navy. Now with war screaming from the headlines, Canadians' major concern was that their soldiers might not make it overseas before the victorious British and French troops staged their victory parade down Berlin's Unter den Linden, likely at Christmastime. With great speed and amidst much confusion, Canada raised a division of mostly untrained and ill-equipped soldiers and dispatched it overseas early in the autumn. By April 1915, the Canadian Division had experienced its first battle at Ypres where it sustained some 6,000 casualties, including more than 2,000 killed, in holding off German troops who employed chlorine gas for the first time on the Western Front. Such losses were almost inconceivable. In 1885, Canadian troops had only a handful of casualties— only eight killed at Batoche, for example; in South Africa, fewer than 300 had been killed by enemy action, illness, or disease over almost three years. The long lists of killed, wounded, and captured at Ypres represented the harsh reality of twentieth-century total war.

Propaganda struggled to assure Canadians that the right side was winning, but, from 1915, the war—for all belligerents—assumed a grim, determined quality far different from the boisterous enthusiasms of 1914. The statistics for money, soldiers, production, and materiel needed for eventual victory were unthinkable in 1914, and mundane four years later. The scale of conflict altered the role of government in society, at least temporarily, on a massive scale; the scale of loss blighted a generation and wreaked havoc on an international system that had remained in stasis, more or less, since the defeat of Napoleon Bonaparte a century before. Governments everywhere rejigged their ministries and financial agencies to raise money for the carnage. Canada's, under Borden's Conservatives, tiny and inefficient enough for prewar purposes, started with a federal budget well under $200 million and most of its meagre revenues coming from tariffs. Ottawa had expected Britain to pay most of the war's costs but, within months of the onset of

fighting, it was clear that Canada must finance its own effort. Money was borrowed in New York for the first time, the first of a succession of domestic war loans was raised in November 1915, and taxes of various kinds began to be introduced in 1916. Inflation raced ahead and wages could not keep up, fuelling domestic discontent.

But there was work for almost everyone who wanted it. Orders for artillery shells came in late 1914 from the Shell Committee created by militia minister Sam Hughes. Canadian industry could not yet produce such technically sophisticated armaments, and few orders were met. By November 1915, confusion in the country's 250 war plants was such that Borden replaced Hughes's committee with the Imperial Munitions Board (IMB) and secured Joseph Flavelle, a Toronto industrialist, to direct the operation. The efficient Flavelle built national factories, negotiated with the labour unions that were growing in strength, and produced $2 million a day in war goods by late 1918. By then, Canada was manufacturing a third of Britain's shells and had built 2,600 training aircraft and 103 ships. Some 30,000 women worked in the munitions factories, while others moved into virtually every kind of work as men went into uniform, including driving streetcars in Kingston, Ontario. The war began the industrialization of Canada and the emancipation of women.

Although the conflict had initially been cheered all across the country, there soon were obvious strains. French-speaking Canadians, while happy enough to work in war factories, did not enlist in large numbers in the Canadian Expeditionary Force (CEF). Nor did many native-born English Canadians, at least not at first. The initial rush to the colours was made up very heavily of British-born immigrants, such men comprising 23,000 of the 36,000 in the first contingent. Only 10,880 in that draft were Canadian born, a number that included only 1,245 francophones. By November 1918, Canada had enlisted 620,000, and British-born men, who had numbered 804,000 in the 1911 Census, produced 228,000 of the recruits. The Canadian-born made up 77 percent of the population, but produced only 319,000 recruits, a number swollen by conscripts after January 1918. With 27 percent of the population, moreover, Quebec generated only 14 percent of CEF enlistments, many (probably most) from the province's anglophones. At best, 25,000 to 50,000 French speakers, many of those from outside Quebec, served in the CEF, again a number that included conscripts.

Why? The reasons lie in history, in errors in mobilization, in gross insensitivity by politicians and the media. Ultimately, the bulk of social and political pressure in Quebec was not to enlist; in the other provinces, public pressure was precisely the opposite. When the Borden government decided upon conscription in May 1917 and won a decisive and divisive election on that issue in December, it left an angry nation in its wake. Conscription did produce almost 100,000 soldiers, those who reached France before the armistice providing reinforcements that made up for the heavy losses of the Hundred Days. Had the war continued into 1919, as almost all had expected, the conscripts would likely have been sufficient to keep Canada's four divisions up to strength.

The nation that emerged from the war had been shattered by its almost quarter million killed and wounded. The human, material, and financial costs of the war had been staggering. The cost of living had soared, "aliens" and "slackers" were scorned, and farmers were unhappy enough to have begun political mobilization. Against these discontents, however, could be set the public's unbounded pride in the matchless fighting record of the CEF. The efforts of the soldiers, moreover, had allowed Borden to press for increased autonomy for Canada within the British Empire. Canada signed the Treaty of Versailles in 1919 and took up a seat in the new League of Nations. The colony of 1914 was gone, in its place a new nation that, however bruised by war, had emerged changed, victorious, and divided. SEE ALSO: BORDEN, ROBERT; CONSCRIPTION; HOME FRONT; WAR FINANCE; WAR INDUSTRY.

READING: R.C. Brown, *Robert Laird Borden: A Biography*, 2 vols. (Toronto, 1975, 1980); Canadian War Museum, "Canada and the First World War," www.warmuseum.ca/cwm/exhibitions/guerre/home-e.aspx.

World War II. The Canada that went to war on 10 September 1939 was tired and dispirited. Ten years of grinding economic depression had ravaged Canadians, and the gross domestic product (GDP) stood at $5.6 billion, well below its level in 1929. Unemployment was still high, people needed work, and wages were low. Moreover, there was little enthusiasm for war. Canadians increasingly saw Hitler as a menace, but memories of the terrible casualties of the "Great War," World War I, remained strong and Europe was far away. Prime Minister Mackenzie King took Canada into war one week after Britain and France, but he did so on the premise that this would be a war of "limited liability," and a guarantee directed, primarily but not exclusively, at Quebec that there would be no conscription for overseas service.

Based in Halifax during the war, Arthur Lismer painted and sketched the return of Canada's armies. This drawing shows a beaming soldier, his liberated German *pickelhaube* (spiked helmet) just visible behind his rifle, on his journey home.

▲ The Battle of the Atlantic was gruelling enough in good weather, but the North Atlantic could be dreadful in winter. The British destroyer HMS *Leamington* in 1943 had to contend with the ice that, if left on the deck and rigging, could overturn a vessel. Already worn-out crewmen could spend hours chopping—and falling further behind as spray froze.

When the war ended six years later, Canada was flush. Its war effort had been huge, its armies stood on German soil, its navy ruled the North Atlantic's waves, and its air force was the world's third largest. The nation's GDP extraordinarily had more than doubled, and Canadians had jobs, money in the bank, and plans for the future. Social security legislation was on the books to protect workers against unemployment and to give family allowances directly to mothers of young children. The Veterans Charter, an impressive package of rehabilitation and training measures, guaranteed that those who had fought the war would receive everything they deserved.

It is too easy to read the war's outcome from the security of hindsight. A hair's breadth separated victory from disaster. The German blitzkrieg had rolled over western Europe, crushed France, and driven Britain back across the English Channel in May and June 1940. The possible defeat of Britain forced

Mackenzie King and US President Franklin Roosevelt to agree to the Permanent Joint Board on Defence in August 1940, Canada's first military alliance with the Americans. For a year, until Hitler attacked the Soviet Union, Canada, with only 11 million people, was Britain's ranking ally in a desperate struggle. The army had expanded from nearly nothing in 1939 until, by late 1940, Canada had two divisions in England and more training at home. The Royal Canadian Air Force was implementing the British Commonwealth Air Training Plan at airfields across the land, graduating the first of what would become a steady stream of tens of thousands of Allied aircrew. The Royal Canadian Navy, like the army beginning from scratch, was soon to acquire corvettes and to learn how to use them to fight the deadly U-boats.

Canada mattered, but the USSR, attacked by Hitler in June 1941, and the United States, brought into war by the Japanese attack on 7 December 1941 and Hitler's foolish subsequent declaration of war, gradually tipped the scales against Germany, Italy, and Japan. It was hardly the war of raw numbers that some historians have assumed, taking almost four more years and nearly incalculable losses in order to achieve victory. The limited liability war Mackenzie King had promised Canadians turned into a massive mobilization—1,081,865 Canadians or ten percent of the population wore uniforms—and conscription, eventually, became the law. This was initially for home defence until, in November 1944, the government ordered 16,000 infantry conscripts overseas to reinforce battalions in northwest Europe and Italy. The First Canadian Army fielded five divisions and two armoured brigades by 1943 and fought in Sicily, Italy, France, Belgium, the Netherlands, and Germany; the Royal Canadian Air Force commanded No. 6 Bomber Group and dozens of fighter, coastal patrol, and transport squadrons; and the Royal Canadian Navy by the end of the war had escorted half of all convoys across the North Atlantic, operated aircraft carriers and cruisers, and served everywhere.

The nation's industrial capacity also underwent full-scale mobilization after a slow start. The Hyde

^ Camouflaged tanks from the 1st Canadian Armoured Brigade, here preparing for action near Cassino in Italy, fought from Sicily up the Italian boot.

Park Agreement of April 1941 linked the two North American economies and solved Canada's shortage of American dollars, and it was full speed ahead thereafter. By late 1942, Canada's factories, many operated by government-owned Crown corporations, produced billions of dollars worth of military vehicles (816,000 in all), aircraft, guns, and ships, while billions more in foods and minerals (for example, almost all of the Allies' nickel) came from Canadian farms and mines. When the Allies could not pay, Canadians gave them the goods, billions of dollars worth. The economy boomed, and hundreds of thousands of women joined the labour force in a social and industrial revolution that changed

⌃ Total war involved everyone, even these Canadian children knitting socks and gloves in 1942 for soldiers overseas.

Canada forever. Another aspect of that revolution was the creation of the foundations of a Canadian social welfare state. Canadians demanded guarantees that economic depression not return with the peace, and the government listened. Unemployment insurance came into law in 1940 and the first "baby bonus" cheques reached mothers in the summer of 1945. This was a start, the beginnings of a more humane nation. Hospital insurance and medicare still lay in the future, but the ideas had begun to germinate.

At the same time, emboldened by its war effort, a newly nationalist Canada toughly bargained its way into Allied councils. Canada claimed the right to be treated as a great power in some areas, although not in the planning of the Allies' grand strategy. Large as

it was, Canada's contribution in this area paled compared to those of the great powers. In the areas of food and mineral production, however, or for relief aid to ravaged Europe or for air transport, Canada actually was a great power. Ottawa's diplomats pushed the case with vigour and made gains. By 1945, Canada had achieved general recognition as the first among the "middle powers" with responsibilities, most of them self-assumed, that would become the hallmarks of Canadian diplomacy in the half-century to come.

The war cost Canada 47,200 killed and 54,414 wounded in the army, navy, air force, and merchant marine. Almost 8,300 were taken prisoner, some spending close to four years in Japanese prison camps after their capture at Hong Kong on Christmas

△ A sergeant leads a patrol from the 1st Canadian Parachute Battalion through a Belgian barnyard in typical winter weather in early 1945.

Day 1941; others became prisoners of the Germans after the slaughter at Dieppe on 19 August 1942. Many of the survivors had the rest of their lives blighted by pain and stress. Canada emerged from World War II altered in almost every respect—in government, in social policies, in military capabilities, in public attitudes. It was more urbanized, more industrial, and more governed; it was richer and more employed, most of its citizens enjoying the highest living standards in Canadian history to that point; it was capably led and, more or less, politically united.

The stains of war were not limited to casualties on the battlefield. They included the treatment accorded

Japanese Canadians, forcibly removed from homes and businesses by a government ostensibly fighting for liberty; the unequal treatment accorded First Nations veterans by the otherwise excellent Veterans Charter; and tawdry efforts—explicable in their context, regrettable in their effects, and ultimately unsuccessful from a statistical perspective—to push women back into the domestic sphere at war's end to make room for returning men. Later textbook writers, appropriately enamoured of such causes, would highlight them—and spectacular defeats such as Hong Kong and Dieppe—to the near exclusion of all else. Had Canada actually won the war, and contributed materially to defeating naked aggression? It was sometimes difficult to tell. High school and university students learned of assaults on civil liberties, for example, but little of the context—a total war—that had generated such debates. Veterans would struggle to have their histories told in a country seemingly embarrassed by its wars and shamed by past indications of martial prowess. Historiography and political support for remembrance and related causes gradually came to terms with what most participants already had long known: World War II had been the century's epic struggle against unprecedented despotism and unmitigated evil, a struggle in which there had been no end save victory, a war to the finish in which no one side had acted beyond reproach, but from which only one could be permitted to emerge victorious. SEE ALSO: CONSCRIPTION; HOME FRONT; KING; QUEBEC AND THE MILITARY; WAR FINANCE; WAR INDUSTRY.

READING: C.P. Stacey, *Arms, Men, and Governments: The War Policies of Canada, 1939–1945* (Ottawa, 1970); David Bercuson, *Maple Leaf against the Axis* (Toronto, 1998).

Yeo, Sir James Lucas (1782–1818). Yeo was born in England and joined the Royal Navy in 1793. He earned a reputation as a daring and unconventional sailor and won his knighthood in 1810 for driving Napoleon's forces out of French Guiana. Appointed commodore and commander-in-chief on the lakes of Canada in 1813, Yeo's task was to keep control of Lake Ontario and to maintain communications between Kingston and the Niagara Peninsula. This was no easy task, the United States Navy vigorously fighting Yeo for control as the balance of naval power swung back and forth, each side trying to build bigger warships. Yeo managed to hold control of Lake Ontario until the early fall of 1813 when he barely survived the "Burlington Races" against a superior American force that pinned him down at Lake Ontario's western end in late September. After a winter of improving his fleet, he recorded a naval success at Oswego in the spring of 1814 and controlled the lake thereafter, thanks to the construction in Kingston's shipyard of the 2,305-tonne HMS *St Lawrence,* with its extraordinary 112 cannon. British North America survived the War of 1812, something Yeo, in his reports to London, attributed to the "stupidity" of the enemy. The failures in the war he blamed on the British army's commanders, notably General Sir George Prevost. Yeo died at sea in 1818. SEE ALSO: PREVOST; WAR OF 1812.

York, Battle of (1813). On 27 April 1813, American forces (nominally under General Henry Dearborn, but in practice led by Commodore Isaac Chauncey and Brigadier-General Zebulon Pike) landed near the Upper Canadian capital of York in the first combined army-navy assault in American history. Using naval gunfire to support them on the beach, the 1,700 US soldiers quickly overwhelmed the outnumbered defending force of British regulars and colonial militia at the shoreline and pushed them back to the fort. Major-General Roger Sheaffe promptly ordered a retreat of the survivors among his force of 600, but not before he prepared the explosion of York's powder magazine. The blast killed Pike and 38 of his men and wounded another 224 (about a fifth of the attackers), and the angry Americans then sacked much of the very small town and looted and burned important public buildings such as the provincial Parliament (perhaps aided by American sympathizers among the population). After pillaging what they could from York's 650 citizens (and General Sheaffe's own belongings, which he had left behind in his haste), the Americans then abandoned the town. Further American incendiary attacks at Newark and Port Dover followed, and the British burned Washington in retaliation in August 1814.

The mace looted from the Parliament buildings turned up later in a military museum in Annapolis, Maryland. President Franklin Roosevelt returned it on the occasion of Toronto's centennial in 1934. SEE ALSO: SHEAFFE; WAR OF 1812.

READING: Robert Malcolmson, *Capital in Flames: The American Attack on York, 1813* (Montreal, 2008).

Ypres, Battle of (1915). The first major engagement fought by Canadians in World War I, the second battle at Ypres began on 22 April 1915. The Canadian Division, with a French colonial division to its left and a British division to its right, held a hitherto quiet salient in front of the city of Ypres, Belgium. The German attack began in late afternoon with the first gas attack on the Western Front. Using 160 tonnes of yellowish-green chlorine that drifted on the breeze toward the Allied lines, the Germans advanced, their

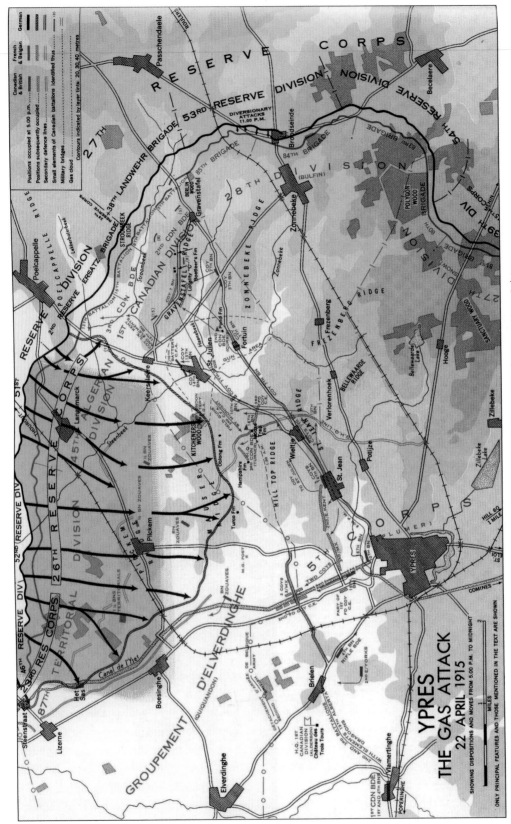

YPRES
THE GAS ATTACK
22 APRIL 1915

SHOWING DISPOSITIONS AND MOVES FROM 5.00 P.M. TO MIDNIGHT
ONLY PRINCIPAL FEATURES AND THOSE MENTIONED IN THE TEXT ARE SHOWN

| | MILES | |
| 1 | | 2 |

Canadian & British	French	Belgian	German
Positions occupied at 5.00 p.m.			
Positions subsequently occupied			
Secondary defence lines			
Small elements of Canadian battalions identified thus			
Military bridges			
Gas cloud			
Contours indicated by layer tints: 20, 30, 40 metres			

DIVERSIONARY ATTACKS 11.00 P.M.

◄ The Canadian Division, as shown graphically in this map, faced a German gas attack in its first sustained action at Ypres, Belgium.

⌃ The Ypres Salient was the scene of vicious fighting on repeated occasions in World War I. The town was left in ruins, as this 1916 photograph of St Martin's Cathedral made clear.

troops wearing primitive respirators. The French colonial troops and British gunners fled the choking gas, leaving a six-kilometre gap in the line, but the Canadians, some less heavily exposed, held their positions, though their left flank was now open. Men urinated on their handkerchiefs or puttees, trying to negate the effect of the chlorine, a partial solution at best. That night, Brigadier-General R.E.W. Turner of 3rd Canadian Brigade ordered his troops into St Julien on the left flank. An attack on Kitcheners' Wood failed with heavy losses as did two additional counterattacks, and the fighting continued into the next day, both sides rushing reinforcements to the front. On 24 April, the Germans again used gas against the two Canadian brigades still in the line. Hampered by the jamming of their Ross rifles and by the confusion of their commanders, the Canadians nonetheless clung to their lines, and the Germans, despite heavy artillery support, were unable to secure a breakthrough. By 4 May when the Canadian Division finally was relieved, its casualties numbered more than 6,000, with some 2,000 killed, out of an effective front-line strength of perhaps 12,000, staggering losses compared to earlier Canadian conflicts. A British War Office communiqué observed that though the Canadians "had many casualties … their gallantry and determination undoubtedly saved the situation." SEE ALSO: GAS WARFARE; WORLD WAR I.

READING: G.W.L. Nicholson, *Canadian Expeditionary Force, 1914–1919* (Ottawa, 1962); Andrew Iarocci, *Shoestring Soldiers: The 1st Canadian Division at War, 1914–1915* (Toronto, 2008).

Yukon Field Force. The federal government sent a 203-strong contingent from the artillery, cavalry, and

infantry units of the Permanent Force to assert Canada's sovereignty and help the North West Mounted Police maintain law and order in the Yukon in 1898 during the height of the Klondike Gold Rush. The miners, mostly American, tended to be obstreperous, and the government feared that the United States might try to seize the territory in the guise of restoring order. The tiny Field Force, under command of Colonel T.D.B. Evans and soon including four nurses from the Victorian Order of Nurses, a female reporter from the Toronto *Globe*, and the wife of an NWMP officer, set out for the Yukon from Ottawa on 6 May 1898. The group then proceeded from Vancouver by water and then by overland trail up the very difficult Stikine River route to Dawson and Fort Selkirk. Half the force was withdrawn in 1899 when the South African War broke out. The situation in the Yukon, now stabilized, allowed Ottawa to order the remaining troops to leave in 1900.

Zombies. A derogatory term used in Canada during World War II, Zombies describes men conscripted into the army for home defence under the terms of the National Resources Mobilization Act of 1940. In Hollywood films of the era, zombies were the soulless, mindless living dead; in the eyes of army volunteers and many English-speaking Canadian civilians, the conscripts were their equivalent for refusing to volunteer for active service and to go overseas.

SEE ALSO: CONSCRIPTION.

Zouaves. Raised between 1868 and 1870 by Bishop Ignace Bourget and the Roman Catholic Church in Quebec to help defend the Papal States in Rome against the republican army led by Giuseppe Garibaldi and then the Italian army of King Victor Emmanuel II, the Pontifical Zouaves wore the Moorish-inspired uniform that gave them their name. Some 507 well-educated and anti-liberal young ultramontane francophones enlisted, though not all made it to Rome before the end of the struggle in 1870. Eight of the Zouaves died.

Appendix: Ministers and Military Chiefs

Ministers

Full Name	Period in Office	Remarks
Ministers of Militia and Defence		
Sir George Étienne Cartier	1 July 1867 – 20 May 1873	Red River Rebellion
Hector-Louis Langevin	21 May 1873 – 30 June 1873	Acting
Hugh McDonald	1 July 1873 – 4 Nov 1873	
William Ross	7 Nov 1873 – 29 Sept 1874	
William Berrian Vail	30 Sept 1874 – 20 Jan 1878	
Alfred Gilpin Jones	21 Jan 1878 – 8 Aug 1878	
Louis-François-Rodrigue Masson	19 Oct 1878 – 15 Jan 1880	
Sir Alexander Campbell	16 Jan 1880 – 7 Nov 1880	
Sir Joseph-Philippe-René-Adolphe Caron	8 Nov 1880 – 6 June 1891	Northwest Rebellion
Sir Joseph-Philippe-René-Adolphe Caron	16 June 1891 – 24 Jan 1892	
Sir Mackenzie Bowell	25 Jan 1892 – 24 Nov 1892	
James Colebrooke Patterson	5 Dec 1892 – 12 Dec 1894	
James Colebrooke Patterson	21 Dec 1894 – 25 Mar 1895	
Arthur Rupert Dickey	26 Mar 1895 – 5 Jan 1896	
Sir Mackenzie Bowell	6 Jan 1896 – 14 Jan 1896	Acting
Alphonse Desjardins	15 Jan 1896 – 27 Apr 1896	
David Tisdale	1 May 1896 – 8 July 1896	
Sir Frederick William Borden	13 July 1896 – 6 Oct 1911	South African War
Sir Samuel Hughes	10 Oct 1911 – 12 Oct 1916	World War I
Sir Albert Edward Kemp	23 Nov 1916 – 11 Oct 1917	World War I
Sydney Chilton Mewburn	12 Oct 1917 – 15 Jan 1920	World War I
James Alexander Calder	16 – 23 Jan 1920	Acting
Hugh Guthrie	24 Jan 1920 – 28 Dec 1921	
George Perry Graham	29 Dec 1921 – 31 Dec 1922	
Ministers of National Defence		
George Perry Graham	1 Jan 1923 – 27 Apr 1923	
Edward Mortimer Macdonald	28 Apr 1923 – 16 Aug 1923	Acting
Edward Mortimer Macdonald	17 Aug 1923 – 28 June 1926	
Hugh Guthrie	29 June 1926 – 12 July 1926	Acting
Hugh Guthrie	13 July 1926 – 24 Sept 1926	
James Alexander Robb	1 – 7 Oct 1926	Acting
James Layton Ralston	8 Oct 1926 – 6 Oct 1930	
Donald Matheson Sutherland	7 Aug 1930 – 16 Nov 1934	
Grote Stirling	17 Nov 1934 – 22 Oct 1935	
Ian Alistair Mackenzie	23 Oct 1935 – 18 Sept 1939	Outbreak of World War II
Norman McLeod Rogers	19 Sept 1939 – 10 June 1940	World War II
Charles Gavan Power	11 June 1940 – 4 July 1940	Acting / World War II
James Layton Ralston	5 July 1940 – 1 Nov 1944	World War II
Andrew George Latta McNaughton	2 Nov 1944 – 20 Aug 1945	World War II
Douglas Charles Abbott	21 Aug 1945 – 11 Dec 1946	
Brooke Claxton	12 Dec 1946 – 30 June 1954	Korean War, Cold War
Ralph Osborne Campney	1 July 1954 – 20 June 1957	Cold War, Suez Crisis
George Randolph Pearkes	21 June 1957 – 10 Oct 1960	Cold War

Full Name	Period in Office	Remarks
Ministers of National Defence		
Douglas Scott Harkness	11 Oct 1960 – 3 Feb 1963	Cold War
Gordon Churchill	12 Feb 1963 – 21 Apr 1963	Cold War
Paul Theodore Hellyer	22 Apr 1963 – 18 Sept 1967	Cold War, Unification
Léo-Alphonse-Joseph Cadieux	19 Sept 1967 – 16 Sept 1970	Cold War
Charles Mills Drury	17 – 23 Sept 1970	Acting / Cold War
Donald Stovel Macdonald	24 Sept 1970 – 27 Jan 1972	Cold War, October Crisis
Edgar John Benson	28 Jan 1972 – 31 Aug 1972	Cold War
Jean-Eudes Dubé	1 – 6 Sept 1972	Acting / Cold War
Charles Mills Drury	7 Sept 1972 – 26 Nov 1972	Acting / Cold War
James Armstrong Richardson	27 Nov 1972 – 12 Oct 1976	Cold War
Barnett Danson	13 Oct 1976 – 2 Nov 1976	Acting / Cold War
Barnett Danson	3 Nov 1976 – 3 June 1979	Cold War
Allan McKinnon	4 June 1979 – 2 Feb 1980	Cold War
Gilles Lamontagne	3 Mar 1980 – 11 Aug 1983	Cold War
Jean-Jacques Blais	12 Aug 1983 – 16 Sept 1984	Cold War
Robert Carman Coates	17 Sept 1984 – 12 Feb 1985	Cold War
Charles Joseph Clark	13 – 26 Feb 1985	Acting / Cold War
Erik H. Nielsen	27 Feb 1985 – 29 June 1986	Cold War
Henry Perrin Beatty	30 June 1986 – 29 Jan 1989	Cold War
William Hunter McKnight	30 Jan 1989 – 20 Apr 1991	Cold War, Gulf War
Marcel Masse	21 Apr 1991 – 3 Jan 1993	Somalia Crisis
A. Kim Campbell	4 Jan 1993 – 24 June 1993	Somalia Crisis
Thomas Edward Siddon	25 June 1993 – 3 Nov 1993	
David Michael Collenette	4 Nov 1993 – 3 Oct 1996	
Douglas Young	4 Oct 1996 – 10 June 1997	
Art C. Eggleton	11 June 1997 – 25 May 2002	Kosovo, 9/11, Afghanistan
John McCallum	26 May 2002 – 11 Dec 2003	Afghanistan
David Pratt	12 Dec 2003 – 19 July 2004	Afghanistan
William Carvel Graham	20 July 2004 – 5 Feb 2006	Afghanistan
Gordon O'Connor	6 Feb 2006 – 13 Aug 2007	Afghanistan
Peter Gordon MacKay	14 Aug 2001 – present	Afghanistan
Ministers of Veterans Affairs		
Ian Alistair Mackenzie	18 Oct 1944 – 18 Jan 1948	World War II, Cold War
Milton Fowler Gregg	19 Jan 1948 – 6 Aug 1950	Cold War
Hugues Lapointe	7 Aug 1950 – 20 June 1957	Cold War, Korean War
Alfred Johnson Brooks	21 June 1957 – 10 Oct 1960	Cold War
Gordon Churchill	11 Oct 1960 – 11 Feb 1963	Cold War
Marcel Lambert	12 Feb 1963 – 21 Apr 1963	Cold War
Roger-Joseph Teillet	22 Apr 1963 – 5 July 1968	Cold War
Jean-Eudes Dubé	6 July 1968 – 27 Jan 1972	Cold War
Arthur Laing	28 Jan 1972 – 26 Nov 1972	Cold War
Daniel Joseph MacDonald	27 Nov 1972 – 3 June 1979	Cold War
Allan Bruce McKinnon	4 June 1979 – 2 Mar 1980	Cold War
Daniel Joseph MacDonald	3 Mar 1980 – 30 Sept 1980	Cold War
Joseph-Georges-Gilles-Claude Lamontagne	1 Oct 1980 – 21 Sept 1981	Acting / Cold War
William Bennett Campbell	22 Sept 1981 – 16 Sept 1984	Cold War
George Harris Hees	17 Sept 1984 – 14 Sept 1988	Cold War
Gerald Stairs Merrithew	18 Sept 1988 – 3 Jan 1993	Cold War
A. Kim Campbell	4 Jan 1993 – 24 June 1993	
Peter L. McCreath	25 June 1993 – 3 Nov 1993	
David Michael Collenette	4 Nov 1993 – 4 Oct 1996	
Douglas Young	5 Oct 1996 – 10 June 1997	
Fred J. Mifflin	11 June 1997 – 2 Aug 1999	
George S. Baker	3 Aug 1999 – 17 Oct 2000	
Ronald J. Duhamel	18 Oct 2000 – 14 Jan 2002	

Full Name	Period in Office	Remarks
Ministers of Veterans Affairs		
Rey D. Pagtakhan	15 Jan 2002 – 11 Dec 2003	Afghanistan
John McCallum	12 Dec 2003 – 19 July 2004	Afghanistan
Albina Guarnieri	20 July 2004 – 5 Feb 2006	Afghanistan
Greg Thompson	6 Feb 2006 – 16 Jan 2010	Afghanistan
Jean-Pierre Blackburn	19 Jan 2010 – present	Afghanistan
Assoc. Ministers of National Defence		
Charles Gavan Power	12 July 1940 – 26 Nov 1944	World War II / Position created
Ralph Osborne Campney	12 Feb 1953 – 30 June 1954	Cold War
Paul Theodore Hellyer	27 Apr 1957 – 20 June 1957	Cold War
Pierre Sévigny	20 Aug 1959 – 8 Feb 1963	Cold War
Louis Joseph Lucien Cardin	22 Apr 1963 – 14 Feb 1965	Cold War
Léo Alphonse Joseph Cadieux	15 Feb 1965 – 18 Sept 1967	Cold War
Harvie Andre	20 Aug 1985 – 29 June 1986	
Paul Dick	30 June 1986 – 29 June 1989	
Mary Collins	30 June 1989 – 3 Jan 1993	
Albina Guarnieri	12 Dec 2003 – 20 July 2004	Afghanistan
Mauril Bélanger	20 July 2004 – 6 Feb 2006	Afghanistan
Ministers of National Defence for Air (1940 – 1946)		
Charles Gavan Power	23 May 1940 – 26 Nov 1944	World War II
Angus Lewis Macdonald	30 Nov 1944 – 10 Jan 1945	Acting
Colin William George Gibson	11 Jan 1945 – 7 Mar 1945	Acting
Colin William George Gibson	8 Mar 1945 – 11 Dec 1946	World War II
Ministers of National Defence for Naval Services (1940 – 1946)		
Angus Lewis Macdonald	12 July 1940 – 17 Apr 1945	World War II
Douglas Charles Abbott	18 Apr 1945 – 11 Dec 1946	World War II
Ministers of Defence Production (1951 – 1969)		
Clarence Decatur Howe	1 Apr 1951 – 20 June 1957	Korean War
Howard Charles Green	21 June 1957 – 11 May 1958	Acting
Raymond Joseph Michael O'Hurley	12 May 1958 – 21 Apr 1963	
Charles Mills Drury	22 Apr 1963 – 5 July 1968	Cold War
Donald Campbell Jamieson	6 July 1968 – 31 Mar 1969	

Military Chiefs

Ranks are those at time the post was held.

Full Name	Dates of Appointment
General Officers Commanding the Canadian Militia	
Major-General Edward Selby Smyth	1875 – 1880
Major-General Richard George Amherst Luard	1880 – 1884
Major-General Sir Frederick Dobson Middleton	1884 – 1890
Major-General the Rt Hon. Ivor John Caradoc Herbert, 1st Baron Treowen	1890 – 1895
Major-General William Julius Gascoigne	1895 – 1898
Major-General Edward Thomas Henry Hutton	1898 – 1900
Major-General Richard Hebden O'Grady-Haly	1900 – 1902
Major-General the Rt Hon. Douglas Mackinnon Baillie Hamilton Cochrane, 12th Earl of Dundonald	1902 – 1904
Brigadier-General the Rt Hon. Matthew Lord Aylmer (Acting)	1904
Chairmen, Chiefs of Staff Committee	
General Charles Foulkes	1951 – 1960
Air Chief Marshal Frank Robert Miller	1960 – 1964

Chiefs of the Defence Staff

Air Chief Marshal Frank Robert Miller	1964 – 1966
General Jean Victor Allard	1966 – 1969
General Frederick Ralph Sharp	1969 – 1972
General Jacques Alfred Dextraze	1972 – 1977
Admiral Robert Hilborn Falls	1977 – 1980
General Ramsey Muir Withers	1980 – 1983
General Gérard Charles Édouard Thériault	1983 – 1986
General Paul David Manson	1986 – 1989
General A. John G.D. de Chastelain	1989 – 1993
Admiral John Rogers Anderson	1993
General A. John G.D. de Chastelain	1994 – 1995
General Joseph Édouard Jean Boyle	1996
Vice-Admiral Larry Murray	1996 – 1997 (Acting)
General Maurice Baril	1997 – 2001
General Raymond Henault	2001 – 2005
General Rick Hillier	2005 – 2008
General Walter Natynczyk	2008 – present

Chiefs of the General Staff

Major-General Sir Percy Henry Noel Lake	1904 – 1908
Major-General William Dillon Otter	1908 – 1910
Major-General Colin John Mackenzie	1910 – 1913
Major-General Willoughby Garnons Gwatkin	1913 – 1920
Major-General James Howden MacBrien	1920 – 1927
Major-General Herbert Cyril Thacker	1927 – 1929
Major-General Andrew George Latta McNaughton	1929 – 1935
Major-General Ernest Charles Ashton	1935 – 1938
Major-General Thomas Victor Anderson	1938 – 1940
Major-General Henry Duncan Graham Crerar	1940 – 1941
Lieutenant-General Kenneth Stuart	1941 – 1943
Lieutenant-General John Carl Murchie	1943 – 1944 (Acting)
	1944 – 1945
Lieutenant-General Charles Foulkes	1945 – 1951
Lieutenant-General Guy Granville Simonds	1951 – 1955
Lieutenant-General Howard Douglas Graham	1955 – 1958
Lieutenant-General Samuel Findlay Clark	1958 – 1961
Lieutenant-General Geoffrey Walsh	1961 – 1964

Directors, Naval Service

Admiral Sir Charles Kingsmill	1910 – 1920
Commodore Walter Hose	1921 – 1928

Chiefs of the Naval Staff

Rear-Admiral Walter Hose	1928 – 1934
Vice-Admiral Percy W. Nelles	1934 – 1944
Vice-Admiral George C. Jones	1944 – 1946
Vice-Admiral Howard E. Reid	1946 – 1947
Vice-Admiral Harold T.W. Grant	1947 – 1951
Vice-Admiral E. Rollo Mainguy	1951 – 1956
Vice-Admiral Harry G. DeWolf	1956 – 1960
Vice-Admiral Herbert S. Rayner	1960 – 1964

Commanders, Maritime Command

Vice-Admiral K.L. Dyer (Principal Naval Advisor)	1964 – 1966
Rear-Admiral William M. Landymore	1966
Vice-Admiral Ralph L. Hennessy (Principal Naval Advisor)	1966 – 1968

Full Name	Dates of Appointment
Commanders, Maritime Command	
Vice-Admiral J.C. O'Brien	1966 – 1970
Vice-Admiral Henry A. Porter	1970 – 1971
Rear- Admiral Robert W. Timbrell	1971 – 1973
Vice-Admiral D.S. Boyle	1973 – 1977
Vice-Admiral A.L Collier	1977 – 1979
Vice-Admiral J. Allan	1979 – 1980
Vice-Admiral J.A. Fulton	1980 – 1983
Vice-Admiral James C. Wood	1983 – 1987
Vice-Admiral Charles M. Thomas	1987 – 1989
Vice-Admiral Robert E. George	1989 – 1991
Vice-Admiral John Rogers Anderson	1991 – 1992
Vice-Admiral Peter W. Cairns	1992 – 1994
Vice-Admiral Larry Murray	1994 – 1995
Vice-Admiral Lynn Mason	1995 – 1996
Chiefs of the Maritime Staff	
Vice-Admiral Gary Garnett	1996 – 1997
Vice-Admiral Greg R. Maddison	1997 – 2001
Vice-Admiral Ron D. Buck	2001 – 2004
Vice-Admiral M. Bruce McLean	2004 – 2006
Vice-Admiral Drew W. Robertson	2006 – 2009
Vice-Admiral P. Dean McFadden	2009 – present
Commanders, Mobile Command	
Lieutenant-General Jean Victor Allard	1965 – 1966
Lieutenant-General William Alexander Beaumont Anderson	1966 – 1969
Lieutenant-General G.A. Turcot	1969 – 1972
Lieutenant-General Stanley Charles Waters	1973 – 1975
Lieutenant-General Jacques Chouinard	1975 – 1977
Lieutenant-General J.J. Paradis	1977 – 1981
Lieutenant-General Charles H. Belzile	1981 – 1986
Lieutenant-General James A. Fox	1986 – 1989
Lieutenant-General Kent Richard Foster	1989 – 1991
Lieutenant-General J.C. Gervais	1992
Lieutenant-General G.M. Reay	1992 – 1995
Chiefs of Land Staff	
Lieutenant-General Maurice Baril	1995 – 1997
Lieutenant-General William Leach	1997 – 2000
Lieutenant-General Mike Jeffrey	2000 – 2003
Lieutenant-General Rick Hillier	2003 – 2005
Lieutenant-General Marc Caron	2005 – 2006
Lieutenant-General Andrew Leslie	2006 – 2010
Lieutenant-General Peter Devlin	2010 – present
Officers Commanding, Canadian Air Force	
Lieutenant-Colonel William Avery Bishop (Officer Commanding-designate of the Canadian Air Force Section of the General Staff, Headquarters Overseas Military Forces of Canada)	1918
Air Commodore A.K. Tylee (Air Officer Commanding)	1920 – 1921
Wing Commander R.F. Redpath	1921
Wing Commander J.S. Scott	1921 – 1922

Full Name	Dates of Appointment
Directors, Royal Canadian Air Force	
Wing Commander J.L. Gordon	1922 – 1924 (Acting)
Wing Commander William G. Barker	1924
Group Captain J.S. Scott	1924 – 1928
Wing Commander Lloyd S. Breadner	1928 – 1932 (Acting)
Squadron Leader A.A.L. Cuffe	1932 (Acting)
Senior Air Officers	
Group Captain J.L. Gordon	1932 – 1933 (Acting)
Wing Commander G.O. Johnson	1933 (Acting)
Air Vice-Marshal G.M. Croil	1934 – 1938
Chiefs of the Air Staff	
Air Vice-Marshal G.M. Croil	1938 – 1940
Air Marshal Lloyd S. Breadner	1940 – 1943
Air Marshal Robert Leckie	1944 – 1947
Air Marshal W.A. Curtis	1947 – 1953
Air Marshal C. Roy Slemon	1953 – 1957
Air Marshal Hugh Campbell	1957 – 1962
Air Marshal C.R. Dunlap	1962 – 1964
Commanders, Air Command	
Lieutenant-General Bill Carr	1975 – 1978
Lieutenant-General George Allan MacKenzie	1978 – 1980
Lieutenant-General Kenneth Lewis	1980 – 1983
Lieutenant-General Paul David Manson	1983 – 1985
Lieutenant-General Donald Malcolm McNaughton	1985 – 1986
Lieutenant-General L.A. Ashley	1986 – 1989
Lieutenant-General F.R. Sutherland	1989 – 1991
Lieutenant-General D. Huddleston	1991 – 1993
Lieutenant-General G. Scott Clements	1993 – 1995
Chiefs of the Air Staff	
Lieutenant-General Allan Marvin DeQuetteville	1995 – 1998
Lieutenant-General David N. Kinsman	1998 – 2000
Lieutenant-General Lloyd C. Campbell	2000 – 2003
Lieutenant-General Ken R. Pennie	2003 – 2005
Lieutenant-General J. Steve Lucas	2005 – 2007
Lieutenant-General W. Angus Watt	2007 – 2009
Lieutenant-General J.P André Deschamps	2009 – present

Illustration Credits

The publisher is grateful to the following for their permission to reproduce the illustrations contained in this book. Every possible effort has been made to trace the original source of visual material. Where the attempt has been unsuccessful, the publisher would be pleased to hear from copyright holders to rectify any errors or omissions.

investiture at Buckingham Palace / Christopher
J. Woods / Canada. Dept. of National Defence /
Library and Archives Canada / PA-142289

Letter from home   343
CWM 19990063-001
George Metcalf Archival Collection
Canadian War Museum

I'm Making Bombs And Buying Bonds!   344
    Buy Victory Bonds
CWM 19920196-077
Canadian War Museum

Francis D. Swayne / *A View of the Launching*   349
Place Above the Town of Quebec, Describing the
Assault of the Enemy, 13 September, 1759 /
Library and Archives Canada, Acc. No. 1997-220-1

Plan of the battle fought upon Abrahams   350
    Plains near Quebec
CWM 19680153-004
George Metcalf Archival Collection
Canadian War Museum

Charles Comfort   356
The Hitler Line
CWM 19710261-2203
Beaverbrook Collection of War Art
Canadian War Museum

Pegi Nicol MacLeod   356
Untitled (*Women's Royal Canadian*
    Naval Service in the Dining Room)
CWM 19710261-5822
Beaverbrook Collection of War Art
Canadian War Museum

Paraskeva Clark   357
Parachute Riggers
CWM 19710261-5679
Beaverbrook Collection of War Art
Canadian War Museum

Alex Colville   358
Tragic Landscape
CWM 19710261-2126
Beaverbrook Collection of War Art
Canadian War Museum

Orville Fisher   358
Battle for Carpiquet Airfield
CWM 19710261-6183
Beaverbrook Collection of War Art
Canadian War Museum

Stephen Snider   359
Helicopter Evac
CWM 19880005-004
Beaverbrook Collection of War Art
Canadian War Museum

Allan MacKay   359
Coalition Soldiers Kandahar Air Base, July 2003
CWM 20040060-001
Beaverbrook Collection of War Art
Canadian War Museum

RADARSAT-1 Canada's first Earth observation   360
satellite / Canadian Space Agency

Hon J.L. Ralston, Canadian Minister of   361
    National Defence, in a tank
CWM 19860237-012
George Metcalf Archival Collection
Canadian War Museum

Katherine Jane Ellice / *The Insurgents, at*   362
Beauharnois, Lower Canada / Library and
Archives Canada / Acc.
No. 1990-215-24R

William Armstrong / *Red River Expedition,*   363
Colonel Wolseley's Camp, Prince Arthur
Landing on Lake Superior / Library and
Archives Canada / Acc. No. 1969-3-1

Harold James Mowat   365
Remember; N'oublions pas
Veterans Affairs Canada poster
CWM 19810922-004
Canadian War Museum

Canadian Army looking for German snipers   374
    behind Allied advance
CWM 19780736-017, #3
George Metcalf Archival Collection
Canadian War Museum

South African War
1899–1902

Northwest Rebellion
1884–1885

Treaty of
Ghent
ends War
of 1812
1814

1900	1880	1860	1840	1820

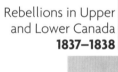

Red River Rebellion
1869–1870

Rebellions in Upper
and Lower Canada
1837–1838